2015

中国·阿勒泰国际古老滑雪文化论坛报告

Altay·China International Ancient Skiing Cultural Forum Report

单兆鉴 Shan Zhaojian
阿依肯·加山 Ayiken·Jiashan
主编 Chief Editors

U0952729

光明日報出版社

图书在版编目（CIP）数据

中国·阿勒泰国际古老滑雪文化论坛报告 / 单兆鉴，阿依肯·加山编.
—北京：光明日报出版社，2016.5

ISBN 978-7-5194-0978-4

Ⅰ.①中… Ⅱ.①单… ②阿… Ⅲ.①雪上运动—传统体育项目—
阿勒泰地区—文集 Ⅳ.①G863.1-53

中国版本图书馆 CIP 数据核字（2016）第 121529 号

中国·阿勒泰国际古老滑雪文化论坛报告

编　　者：单兆鉴　阿依肯·加山

责任编辑：曹　杨　　　　策　　划：北京卡宾滑雪集团
封面设计：刘孟孟　　　　责任校对：程　刚
责任印制：曹　净

出版发行：光明日报出版社
地　　址：北京市东城区珠市口东大街 5 号，100062
电　　话：010-67078258（咨询），67078870（发行），67019571（邮购）
传　　真：010-67078227，67078255
网　　址：http：//book.gmw.cn
E - mail：gmcbs@gmw.cn caoyang@gmw.cn
法律顾问：北京德恒律师事务所龚柳方律师

印　　刷：三河信达兴印刷包装有限公司
装　　订：三河信达兴印刷包装有限公司

本书如有破损、缺页、装订错误，请与本社联系调换
开　　本：710×1000mm　1/16
字　　数：745 千字　　　　印　　张：38
版　　次：2016 年 6 月第 1 版　　　　印　　次：2016 年 6 月第 1 次印刷
书　　号：ISBN 978-7-5194-0978-4

定　　价：116.00 元

2015中国阿勒泰国际古老滑雪文化交流研讨会
阿勒泰—人类最古老的滑雪地域
Altai– the oldest ski tracks in the world
组委会
Organizing Committee
The International Ancient Skiing Cultural Exchange and Seminar in Altay City, China 2015

历史将记载和叙说:
History will Record and Speak:

- “阿勒泰—人类最古老的滑雪地域
2015 中国阿勒泰国际古老滑雪文化交流研讨会”
Altai-the Oldest Ski Tracks in the World
The International Ancient Skiing Cultural Exchange
Seminar in Altay City, China 2015

- 《2015 中国 · 阿勒泰国际古老滑雪文化论坛报告》
The International Ancient Skiing Cultural Forum
Report in Altay, Xinjiang 2015

- 阿勒泰—人类滑雪的摇篮 世界滑雪文化的起点
The Cradle of Human Skiing
The Origin of World Skiing Culture

与会者合照 Group photo

签名墙签字留念 Signature wall

ational Ancient

老滑雪文化交流研讨
Skiing Culture Seminar In 2015

讨会
In 2015

Seminar In 2015

ture Seminar

man Skiing
ing Culture Seminar

2015

China Altay

n Skiing
Culture Seminar

Altay International

national Ancient

Altay—Cradle of
nternational Ancient

签
名
墙

颁发参会证书 Issuing certificates

共同欣赏　Appreciation

阿尔泰山的滑雪人　Skiers in Altay

冬季乌梁海人

古老滑雪狩猎作品 Ancient skiing hunting painting

观看阿勒泰农牧民古老毛皮滑雪板比赛

Watching Altay traditional fur ski race by farmers and herdsmen

汗德尕特乡万年滑雪狩猎岩绘画

Skiing hunting rock paintings in Handegate

在古老滑雪雕塑前合照

A group photo in front of ancient skiing sculptures Handegate

在汗德尕特乡与当地农牧民合照

A photo taken with local farmers and herdsmen in

专家在乌鲁木齐合照 **Group photo of experts in Urumq**

启动仪式　Opening ceremony

中国•新疆•阿勒泰地理位置

Geographical location of Altay • Xinjiang • China

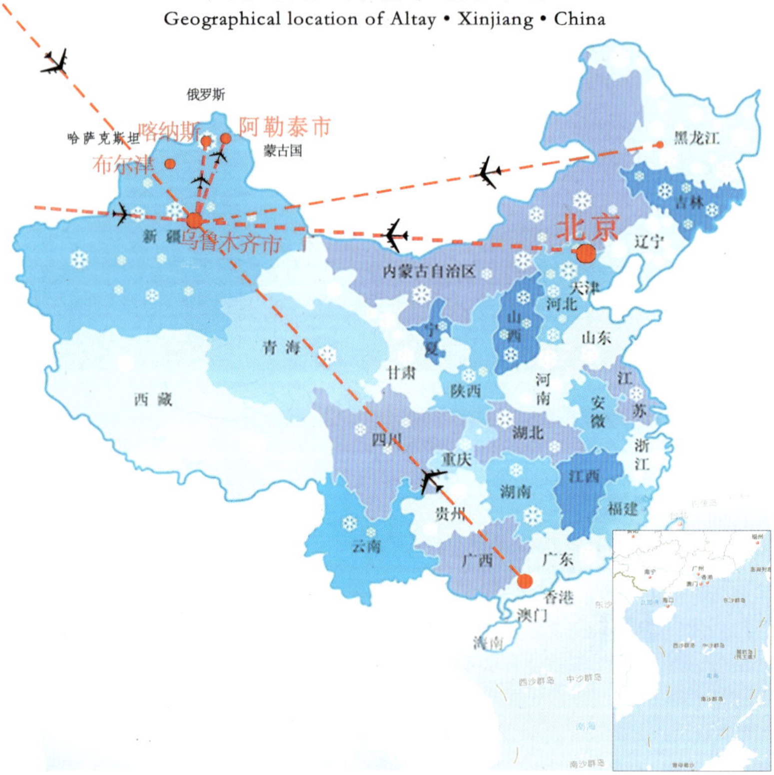

审议和宣读《2015阿勒泰宣言》
Deliberation and announcement of *Altay Declaration 2015*

古老毛皮滑雪板比赛及与当地首长会晤

Ancient skis race and a meeting with local senior officer

研讨会会场 **In the seminar**

中挪双方交流制作古老滑雪板

Communication about making ancient skis between China and Norway

欢聚“大巴扎” A happy party in “Grand Bazaar”

体验中国饮食文化 To experience Chinese culinary culture

参观新疆博物馆 **Visiting Xinjiang Museum**

考察新疆丝绸之路滑雪场

Investigating the Silk Road International Ski Resort in Xinjiang

阿勒泰市长接受“上海基尼斯之最”认证牌

Mayor of Altay city receives *Shanghai Guinness* authentication certificate

单兆鉴获国际组织颁发的嘉奖牌

Presenting a medal to Shan Zhaojian by the International Skiing Organization

与新疆旅游局首长会晤

A meeting with senior officer of Xinjiang Tourism Bureau

2006年北京人民大会堂新闻发布会

Press conference in the Great Hall of the People in 2006

编委会

EditorialCommittee

序

2015年初，在新疆阿勒泰市举行了“阿勒泰人类最古老的滑雪地域—2015中国阿勒泰国际古老滑雪文化交流研讨会”。中国专家与世界各国专家共聚阿勒泰市，经过充分地实地考察与认真研讨，达成共识，发布了《2015阿勒泰国际古老滑雪文化交流研讨会专家宣言》，对中国专家的研究成果—“中国阿勒泰地区是人类滑雪起源地”给予肯定和支持，认为这是人类滑雪的宝贵遗产，是对世界滑雪文化的重大贡献。

会后，历时一年之久，对各国专家、学者的发言及论文进行系统地梳理、翻译和编辑，汇总了这本《2015中国·阿勒泰国际古老滑雪文化论坛报告》。全面汇集了本次研讨会议的信息资料，体现出“弘扬阿勒泰古老滑雪传统，繁荣世界滑雪文化”的宗旨，使该书不但具有文化学术性，还具有滑雪文化的历史性、权威性和国际性。必将对推动中国及世界滑雪文化的交流和发展方面起到积极作用，具有重大的现实历史意义。

作为中国专家，应发扬以往的研究精神，广泛吸收各国专家的研究成果，为发展中国体育文化事业做出更大的贡献。

最后，对出版该书做出贡献的北京卡宾滑雪集团以及所有策划、翻译及编辑人员表示感谢！

国家体育总局中国体育文化管理中心

2015年11月

Preface

At the beginning of 2015, *Altai– the oldest ski tracks in the world*, *The International Ancient Skiing Cultural Exchange Seminar in Altay City*, *China* 2015 was held in Altay city. Chinese and foreign experts gather together in Altay city, and make a consensus and deliver the *Altay Declaration —The International Ancient Skiing Cultural Exchange Seminar in Altay City*, *China* 2015 after fully on–the–spot investigation and serious discussion. The seminar has spoken highly of the research fruits— "T*he Original Place of Skiing –Altay Prefecture*" by Chinese experts, regarding it as precious heritage of human skiing and great contribution to the world skiing culture.

During a year after the seminar, we have been sorting, translating and compiling the speeches and papers by experts at home and abroad, summarizing *The International Ancient Skiing Cultural Forum Report in Altay*, *Xinjiang* 2015. All the document information of this seminar reflects the aim of "promoting ancient skiing tradition and flourishing world skiing culture", making the book have cultural, academic and historic meaning and exerting positive effect on world skiing culture development and exchange.

As Chinese experts, we should carry forward the spirit of previous studies and widely absorb the research achievements of international experts to make greater contribution to the development of Chinese sports culture.

Finally, we would like to express gratitude to Beijing Carving Ski Group and all the planners, designers, translators and editors!

The Chinese Sports and Culture Management Center

November 2015

编者的话

2006年12月15日在北京人民大会堂举行的“中国·新疆·阿勒泰是人类滑雪最早起源地”的新闻发布会，与会中国专家从不同角度学科严谨地论述了中国新疆阿勒泰地区是人类滑雪最早起源地的证据。会中中国专家代表单兆鉴宣读了《阿勒泰宣言》。

2015年时隔9载，“阿勒泰人类最古老的滑雪地域—2015中国阿勒泰国际古老滑雪文化交流研讨会”于1月14日–18日在阿勒泰市举行，并获得了巨大的成功！1月18日参会的中、外专家学者通过了《2015阿勒泰国际古老滑雪文化交流研讨会专家宣言》，并签字，中国专家单兆鉴先生、挪威专家卡琳·博格女士、美国专家尼尔·拉尔森先生分别代表亚洲、欧洲、美洲三大区域共同宣读了具有重大历史意义的《2015宣言》。表达了与会者共同的心声。

《2015宣言》中指出：

“此次研讨会很好地结合了会议交流和实地考察两大环节，主题突出，内容丰富，必将在中国及世界领域产生积极而深远的影响”。

“中国新疆阿勒泰是世界上最重要的古老滑雪地域。这不仅是人类滑雪历史上宝贵的遗产，亦是对世界滑雪文化的重大贡献。我们对阿勒泰市政府和中国专家的专业成果给予充分的肯定及支持”。

专家们还衷心倡议：“中国阿勒泰要不断弘扬古老滑雪传统，并将它世代传承”。

为了举办这次国际研讨会，阿勒泰市与研讨会组委会做了精心的安排。这些远道而至的客人，在阿勒泰市“度过了终身难忘”的几日，他们首先参观了几个博物馆，实地考察万年滑雪狩猎岩画，这些来自世界多地域的贵客，始终与当地的土著民族在阿尔泰山雪的世界中相识交流、亲融，共享欢乐，观看了“姑娘追”“赛马”，乘坐马拉爬犁、共饮自酿酒，接领“哈达”，并兴致勃勃地观看了具有民族情结的精彩文娱演出。更使客人们难忘的是观看了当地农牧民古老毛皮滑雪板的制作和比赛，这种场景，将古老的滑雪狩猎文化展现在他们面前，使他们惊讶，使他们兴奋，充实了他们学术研究的内涵、使他们“身临其境地感受和掌握了很多东西”。

在将军山滑雪场，阿勒泰地区的首长与部分专家进行了热情地交谈。接着在2天的研讨中，专家们畅所欲言，他们指出“阿勒泰人类滑雪起源的文化是属于世界滑雪文化共同的遗产”，有的专家道“真是舍不得离开阿勒泰”，对于滑雪最早起源阿勒泰这个问题，有些专家说到：来阿勒泰之前，还有些“半信半疑”，通过研讨会，离开阿勒泰时却是“坚信不疑”。由于古老滑雪文化源远流长，跨越万年时空，各国专家在其研讨会发言中，论文中及今后的研究过程中，对某些领域产生分歧意见是自然的。学术研究是一项艰苦的工作，不同的见解恰是一种推动的力量，分歧会在争论和研讨中逐渐求得共识。

阿勒泰 2015 年 1 月是一个沸腾的冬天！各国权威专家的到来为新疆·阿勒泰增添了无限光彩。

来自挪威、瑞典、芬兰、丹麦、斯洛文尼亚、奥地利、瑞士、美国、捷克、蒙古国、韩国、英国、中国等近百名专家、学者参加会议（其中国外专家 30 余名），国际雪联官员也参加了会议。另有哈萨克斯坦、蒙古、芬兰、波兰、俄罗斯等国专家有的已报名，但因天气或工作时间冲突没能亲自到会，他们送交了论文和发言提纲。

阿勒泰研讨会议结束后，各国专家学者又应新疆旅游局的邀请，于 20 日－21 日参加了乌鲁木齐市的活动，首先参加了“第二届中国新疆国际丝绸之路旅游发展大会——丝绸旅游暨冰雪旅游高峰论坛”，对新疆冬季旅游的发展，对新疆滑雪旅游的国际化联手助推，受到新疆旅游界的同声喝彩！

之后，客人们还考察了丝绸之路国际滑雪场，并进行了交流活动，参观了新疆博物馆。

新疆旅游局首长与国外专家面对面进行了交流互动。

有关此次阿勒泰与乌鲁木齐市两地会议的全部信息资料经翻译、编辑完整地汇总成《2015 中国·阿勒泰国际古老滑雪文化论坛报告》，将分赠给参会各国专家及滑雪文化领域的研究机构、研究人员参阅。

该书与 2011 年出版的《人类滑雪起源地—中国·新疆·阿勒泰》书籍形成姊妹篇，将会对世界古老滑雪文化的研究提供素材，起到引领、推动、深入、提升的作用。具有重要的历史意义。由于参会专家来自不同国家，使用多种语言，翻译工作十分困难，难免有些不足和错误之处，敬请谅解并指正。

编委会

2016. 04. 10

Editor's Note

At the Press Conference for Altay, Xinjiang, *China is the Original Place for Human Skiing* held in the Great Hall of the People in Beijing on 15th December 2006, experts and scholars elaborated the proof of Altay being the original place for human skiing. And Mr. Shan Zhaojian, the representative of the experts, announced the *Altay Declaration*.

Nine years after the Press Conference, Altay — the oldest ski tracks in the world, 2015 Altay International Ancient Skiing Cultural Conference was held successfully in Altay City from January 14 to 18. On the last day of the Conference, participants from home and abroad have signed their names on the *Declaration of* 2015 *Altay International Ancient Skiing Cultural Conference*. Chinese ski expert Shan Zhaojian, Norwegian expert Karin, American expert Nils Larsen have jointly read the *Declaration* of great significance, which has well voiced the common wish from all the participants.

The declaration says: *"The Conference has been rich in content, with a good agenda of presentations and field trips. We are confident this conference will have a strong and positive impact nationally and internationally."*

"Altay of Xinjiang, China, is the world's most important ancient skiing region. This is not only a precious heritage in the history of skiing culture, but also a great contribution to the skiing culture of the world. We give great credit and support to the government of Altay and Chinese experts for their professional work."

The experts also cordiallyadvocated *Altay, China to promote the ancient skiing traditions and pass them onto future generations.*

To ensure a successful conference, Altay City and the committee have made full preparation with years of elaboration and wide connection. These guests coming far away from their countries have spent unforgettable days here in Altay. They firstly visited museums and skiing hunting rock paintings of ten thousand years. They acquainted themselves and enjoyed themselves with the local Altai residents, watching girls chasing racing horses, taking horse-pulling sleds, drinking home-made wines, accepting Hada and watching wonderful local entertainment performances. What most special to these experts was that they saw the local peasants and herdmen making ancient fur skis and the competitions, which has well presented the ancient skiing hunting culture to them. They were shocked, excited, enriched and have gained so many things to learn.

In Jiangjunshan Ski Resort, the leaders of Altay, and some experts had intense conversation.

In the following two-day conference, the experts expressed their mind freely and some even gave impromptu speech. They indicated that the culture of Altay being the original place for human skiing is the common heritage of the world skiing culture. Some of them expressed their unwillingness to leave Altay. Before the conference, some of them were doubtful about Altay as the original place for skiing, while after the conference, they all became convinced.

January, 2015 in Altay was absolutely an exciting winter, as participants from the world have brought so much honor to the event!

Near a hundred ski experts and researchers from home and abroad including Norway, Sweden, Finland, Denmark, Slovenia, Austria, Switzerland, the US, Czech Republic, Mongolia, South Korea and the UK participated in the conference. Experts of Kazakhstan, Mongolia, Finland, Poland, Russia and China also registered but failed to attend the Conference because of the bad weather or the wrong time, however, they still gave the papers or presentations to the Organizing Committee.

After the conference, the experts were invited by Xinjiang Tourism Administration to events in Urumqi from 20 to 21. They attended The Second Xinjiang, China Silk Road Tourism Development Conference-Silk Tourism and Snow Tourism. After that, the guests went to Silk Road International Ski Resort, where they share thoughts and experiences and visited Xinjiang Museum. The secretary of Xinjiang Tourism Administration made face-to-face exchanges with the visitors.

All the information relating to the Conferences in Altay and Urumqi will be edited into a book *The International Ancient Skiing Cultural Forum Report in Altay, Xinjiang 2015.* It takes over a year to collect and translate the information. It will be given to experts and institutes in the field of skiing to read, study and treasure.

This book is the companion volume of the*The first origin of the human skiing --China · Xinjiang · Altay* which was published in 2011. It provides materials for the world ancient skiing culture research as well as guide, promote and deepen the research. It has important historical meaning. As it involves many languages, the translation work was quite hard. Please understand if any translations are inadequate.

Editorial Committee

October 4, 2016

目　录

Contents

第一章　研讨会形成的《2015 阿勒泰宣言》

Chapter One The Formation of *Altay Declaration* 2015

经过 2 天的实际考察和 2 天的大会研讨，在会议结束之前，根据专家们共识意见，单兆鉴先生主笔起草，与卡琳·博格女士、尼尔·拉尔森先生、阿依肯·加山先生的合议审改，最后形成《2015 阿勒泰宣言》，单兆鉴先生、卡琳·博格女士、尼尔·拉尔森先生三人用中、英文共同宣读。与会专家用掌声通过，并签字。会后，《2015 阿勒泰宣言》又译成哈萨克、俄罗斯、蒙古文文字。（各种文字宣言的前后顺序以开头汉字笔画排列。）

After two days' investigation and discussion, experts make a consensus before the end of the meeting. MrShan ZhaoJian takes a lead to draft, with lady Karin Berg, Mr Nils Larsen and Ayken Jiashan, and finally the 2015 Altay Declaration formed according to their agreement. Mr Shan ZhaoJian, lady Karin Berg, and Mr Nils Larsen, read out the Declaration in Chinese and English. Attending experts reach an agreement on it with applause and sign it with confirmation. After the conference, *2015 Altay Declaration* is translated into Kazakh, Russian, Mongolian language. （The following declarations are arranged in order of strokes of initial Chinese character.）

1.1　中外专家共同宣读《2015 阿勒泰宣言》　Reading out *Altay Declaration* 2015 by Chinese & foreign experts

讨论审议宣言　**Discuss and review the Declaration**

1.2 中文宣言 Declaration in Chinese

2015阿勒泰国际古老滑雪文化交流研讨会专家宣言

我们是从事滑雪历史及相关领域的研究者。2015年1月14日-18日，我们相聚中国新疆阿勒泰市参加了“阿勒泰—人类最古老的滑雪地域—2015中国阿勒泰国际古老滑雪文化交流研讨会”。

经过此次研讨会的讨论和协商，我们达成了以下共识：

1. 此次研讨会很好地结合了会议交流和实地考察两大环节，主题突出，内容丰富。我们确信此次会议必将在中国及世界领域产生积极而深远的影响。我们衷心感谢此次会议的组委会对活动的精心安排，尊重中国阿勒泰地区古老滑雪历史和文化的科学研究及记载。

2. 中国新疆阿勒泰是世界上最重要的古老滑雪地域。这不仅是人类滑雪历史上宝贵的遗产，亦是对世界滑雪文化的重大贡献。我们对阿勒泰市政府和中国专家的专业成果给予充分的肯定及支持。

3. 我们倡议中国阿勒泰要不断弘扬古老滑雪传统，并将它世代传承。

4. 我们希望能与阿尔泰山脉周边国家建立牢固的合作关系，及时分享知识、信息与成果。

最后，我们有决心弘扬阿勒泰古老滑雪传统，繁荣世界滑雪文化。

2015年1月18日 于中国·新疆·阿勒泰

单兆鉴（中国）、卡琳·博格（挪威）、尼尔·拉尔森（美国）共同宣读《2015阿勒泰宣言》 Shan Zhaojian（CHN），Karin·Berg（NOR）and Nils·Larsen（USA）jointly read *Altay Declaration* 2015

1.3　英文宣言　Declaration in English

The Declaration of 2015 Altay International Ancient Skiing Culture Conference

In Altay City, Xinjiang, China Jan. 18, 2015

We are the researchers of ski history and other related fields. We have gathered together in Altay, Xinjiang, China from *14* to *18* January *2015* for the celebration of the ancient skiing culture of the Altay area, and the conference "Altay — the oldest ski tracks in the world — *2015* Altay International Ancient Skiing Culture Conference".

After discussion and consultation during the conference, we have reached the following agreements:

1. TheConference has been rich in content, with a good agenda of presentations and field trips. We are confident this conference will have a strong and positive impact nationally and internationally. We would like to express our thanks and respect to the organization of the conference, and to the research and documentation of the ancient ski history and culture of the Chinese Altay region.

2. Altay of Xinjiang, China, is the world's most important ancient skiing region. This is not only a precious heritage in the history of skiing culture, but also a great contribution to the skiing culture of the world. We give great credit and support to the government of Altay and Chinese experts for their professional work.

3. We advocate Altay, China to promote the ancient skiing traditions and pass them on for future generations.

4. We would like to build up a solid and strong cooperation with countries around the Altay Mountains, sharing knowledge, information, and achievements over time.

In conclusion, we wish to promote Altay ancient skiing traditions and flourishskiing culture all over the world.

1.4 哈萨克文宣言 Declaration in Kazakh

2015 التاي حالىقارالىق بايىرعى قارشاڭعى مادەنيەتى تالقى جيىنداعى ماماندار مالىمدەمەسى

(بۇل حۇجات جيىندى ۇيىمداستىرۋ القاسى جاريالاعان ناقتى مالىمدەمە)

ٴبىز قار شاڭعى تاريحى جانە قاتىستى سالالاردى زەرتتەۋشىلەرمىز. 2015-جىلى 14-قاڭتاردان 18-قاڭتار دەيىن، ٴبىز جۇڭگو شينجياڭ التاي قالاسىندا باس قوسىپ، «التاي-ادامزاتتىڭ بايىرعى قار شاڭعى مەكەنى-2015 جۇڭگو التاي حالىقارالىق بايىرعى قار شاڭعى مادەنيەتى تالقى جيىنىنا» قاتىناستىق.

بۇل رەتكى تالقى جيىنىندا تالقىلاۋ جانە اقىلداسۋ ارقىلى، ٴبىز تومەندەگىدەي ورتاق تانىمعا كەلدىك:

ٴبىرىنشى، بۇل رەتكى تالقى جيىنىندا، ٴوزارا پىكىر الماستىرۋ مەن ناقتىلى كوزدەن كەشىرۋ سىندى ەكى تۇيىن تاماشا بىرلەستىرىلىپ، تاقىرىبى ايقىن، مازمۇنى كەڭ بولدى. ٴبىز بۇل رەتكى جيىننىڭ جۇڭگو جانە دۇنيە جۇزىندە تەرەڭ ىقپال تۋدىراتىندىعىنا كامىل سەنەمىز. بۇل رەتكى جيىننىڭ ۇيىمداستىرۋ القاسىنىڭ قيمىلدى مۇقياتتىلىقپەن ورنالاستىرعاندىعىنا راحمەت ايتامىز، جۇڭگو التاي ايماعىنداعى بايىرعى قارشاڭعى تاريحى مەن مادەنيەتىنىڭ عىلىمي زەرتتەۋلەرى مەن جازبالارىنا قۇرمەت بىلدىرەمىز.

ەكىنشى، جۇڭگو شينجياڭ التاي-دۇنيەدەگى ەڭ ماڭىزدى بايىرعى قار شاڭعى مەكەنى. بۇل تەك ادامزات قارشاڭعى تاريحىنداعى اسىل مۇرا بولىپ قانا قويماي، دۇنيە قارشاڭعى مادەنيەتىنە دە ەلەۋلى ۇلەس قوستى. ٴبىز التاي قالالىق ۇكىمەت پەن جۇڭگو ماماندارىنىڭ كاسىپتىك تابىسىن تولىق تۇراقتاندىرامىز جانە قولدايمىز.

ٴۇشىنشى، ٴبىز جۇڭگو التايدىڭ بايىرعى قارشاڭعى ٴداستۇرىن ۇزدىكسىز ساۋلەلەندىرۋىن ٴارى ۇرپاقتان-ۇرپاققا جالعاستىرۋعا ۇندەيمىز.

ٴتورتىنشى، ٴبىز التاي تاۋ سىلەمى ايناسىنداعى مەملەكەتتەردىڭ بەرىك سەلبەستىك ورناتىپ، ٴبىلىم، ينفورماتسيا جانە تابىستان ورتاق يگىلىكتەنۋىن ۇمىت ەتەمىز.

سوڭىندا، ٴبىز التاي بايىرعى قارشاڭعى ٴداستۇرىنىڭ ونان ارى ساۋلەلەنىپ، دۇنيە قارشاڭعى مادەنيەتىنىڭ ونان ارى گۇلدەنەتىنىنە كامىل سەنەمىز.

2015-جىلى 18-قاڭتار جۇڭگو . شينجياڭ . التاي قالاسى

1.5　俄罗斯文宣言　Declaration in Russian

декларации эксперта　семинара
Международных лыжных древних культурных обменов
Алтай–2015

Мы исследователи истории на лыжах и в соответствующих областях. Мы собрались в городе Алтая СУАР КНР и приняли участие семинар международных лыжных древних культурных обменов Алтай КНР 2015 – "Алтай–самый старый район на лыжах человечества" с 14 января 2015 года по 18 января 2015 года.

После обсуждения и консультации Предстоящего семинара, достигли следующих консенсус:

1. Предстоящий семинар есть два больших звено и конференция по обмену и экспедиция, Тема особо, Богатые по содержанию. Мы убеждены, что предстоящий семинар непременно окажет позитивное и глубокое влияние в китае в области мира. Мы искренне поблагодарим оргкомитетоми предстоящего семинара, что тщательно распределять мероприятия. Уважение исследования и документально древние истории на лыжах и древние культуры на лыжах округа Алтая КНР.

2. Алтай СУАР КНР–это самое важное в мире старый район на лыжах. Это не только в истории человечества на лыжах ценное наследие, но и для мировой культуры на лыжах важный вклад. Мы в полной мере уверен и поддержку правительства города Алтая и результатов специалистов Китая.

3. Мы инициативы, что Алтай КНР будут непрерывно развивать древние традиции на лыжах и передачи из поколения в поколение.

4. Мы надеемся, что могу сотрудничествовать прочные отношения соседние страны Алтайского гора, своевремено обменять знаниями и информацией.

Наконец, у нас есть решимость развивать древние традиции на лыжах Алтая, процветание мировой культуры на лыжах.

Город Алтай СУАР КНР

18–01–2015

1.6　蒙古文宣言　Declaration in Mongolian

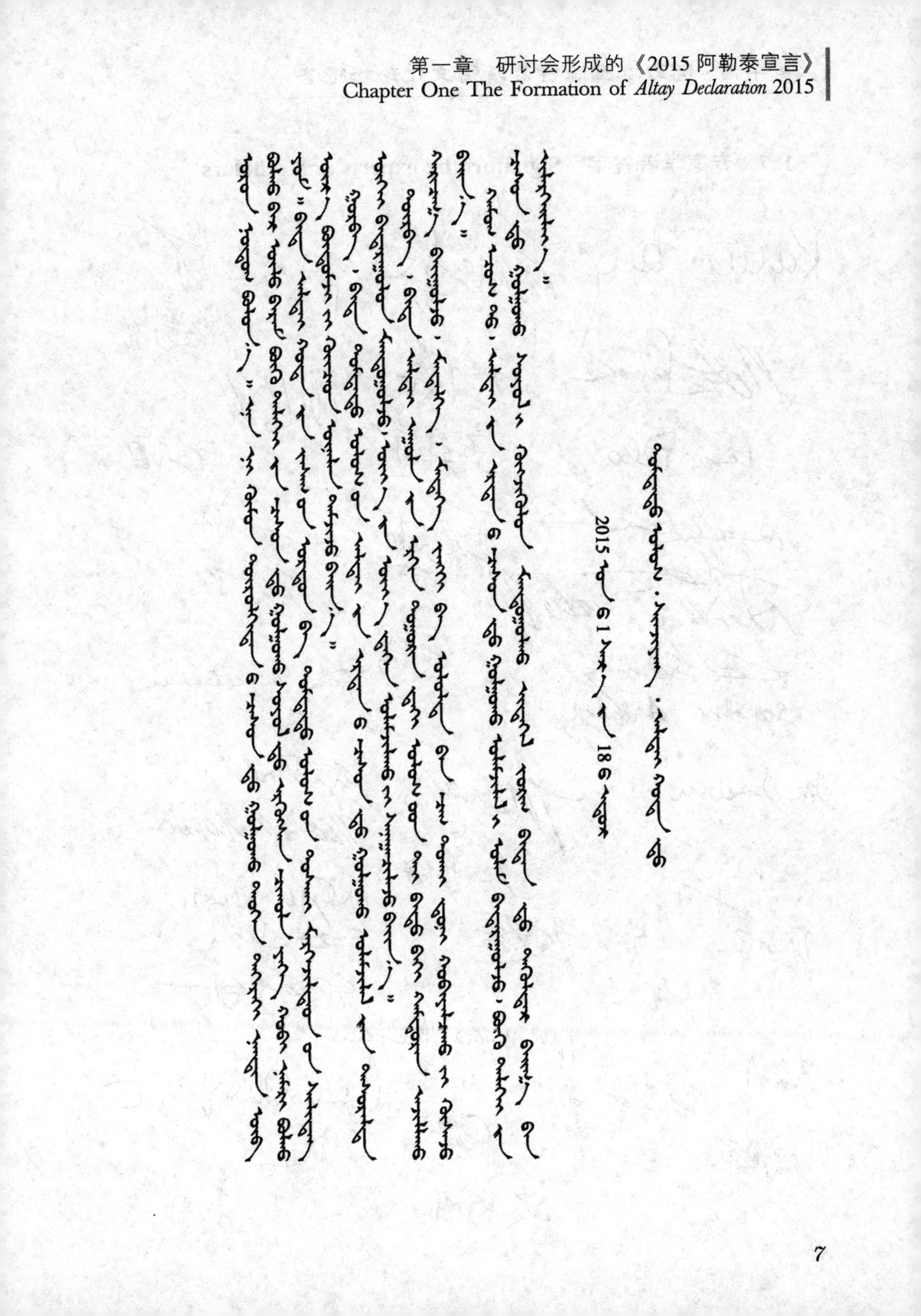

1.7 专家学者签字 Signature by experts and scholars

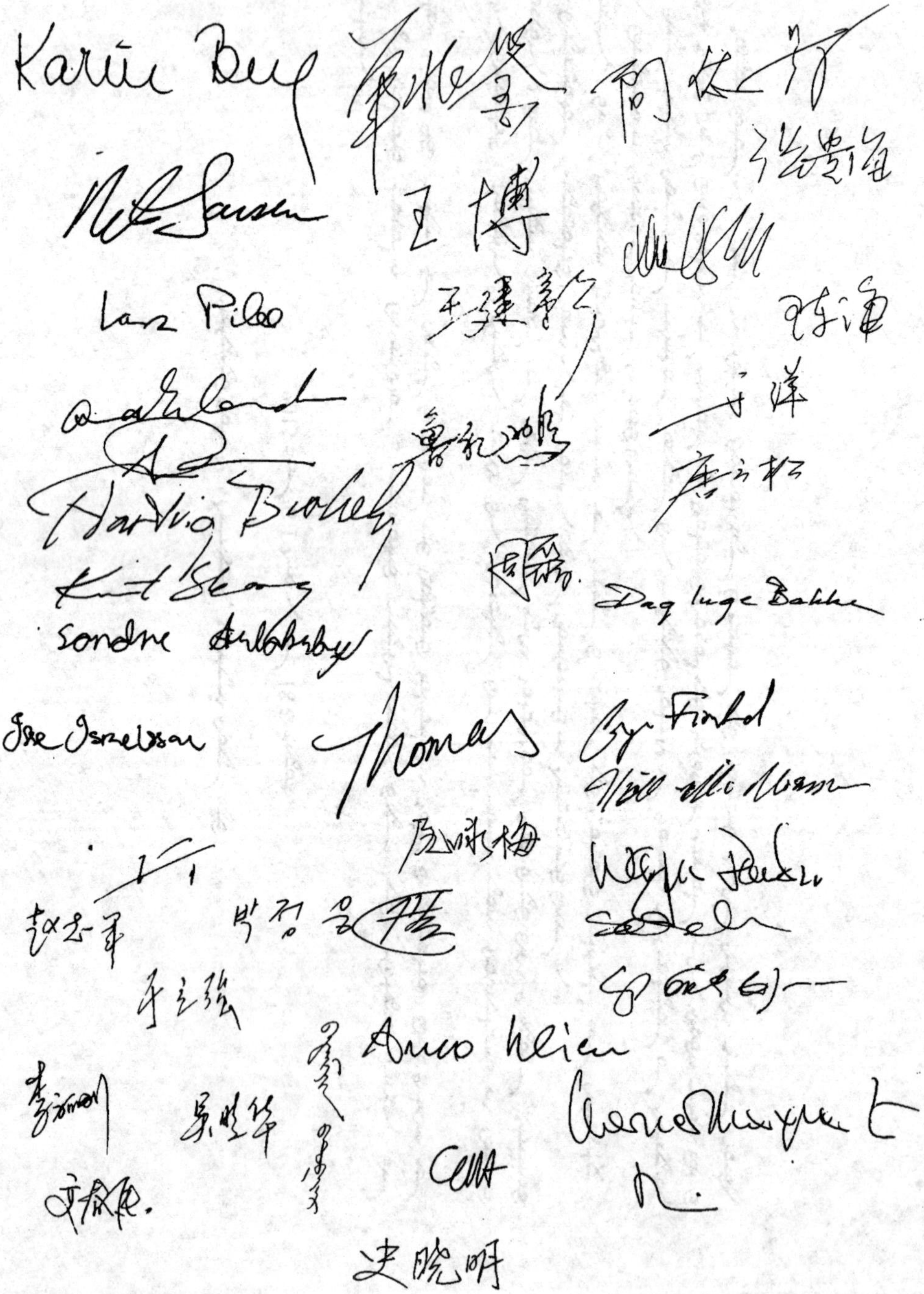

第二章　研讨会实地考察活动
Chapter Two Field Trips during Seminar

2.1　参观多处博物馆　Visit to museums

在阿勒泰市期间，先后参观了“阿勒泰市摄影展览”“阿勒泰市博物馆”“阿勒泰地区博物馆”“汗德尕特乡博物馆”，部分人还参观了“布尔津县博物馆”。

During the period of visiting the Altay city, we looked over “Altay City Photography Exhibition”, “Altay City Museum”, “Altay Region Museum” and “Handegate Township Museum”, some people also visited “Burqin County Museum”.

2.2　参观拉斯特乡哈萨克族民俗活动　Visit to Kazakh folk activity in Rast township

拉斯特乡是哈萨克民族聚居地，在阿勒泰市东12公里，交通便捷。该乡农牧民仍在传承和弘扬着古老滑雪文化。与会专家们在这里体验和参观了哈萨克民族的骑马、马拉爬犁、“叼羊”、“姑娘追”等民俗表演。

Rast township is the habitation of Kazakh nationality, in the east of Altay city about 12 kilometers, and the traffic is convenient. The farmers and herdsmen still pass and promote the ancient culture down. Experts attending the conference here experience the horse riding, horse-drawn sleigh and “holding sheep in the mouth”, “girl chasing” and other folk performances.

2.3 考察汗德尕特乡万年滑雪狩猎岩绘画 Investigation to skiing hunting rock paintings in Handegate

阿勒泰市汗德尕特乡位于阿勒泰市东部，距市内32公里。住在该乡的居民多为蒙古族乌梁海部落人。该乡是世界最古老的滑雪狩猎岩画（距今1-3万年）发现地；至今仍被传唱的民间口传“滑雪狩猎”歌谣的挖掘地；古老毛皮滑雪板在该乡分布面广；人类滑雪起源的痕迹突出，是人类滑雪起源考察研究的重要区域。

Introduction of Handegate township in Altay City. Handegate township, locatedin the East of Alay city, 32 kilometers distance from the city, is a Mongolian township. Most of the inhabitants here are Mongolian Tuvas Uriankhai tribe. The township is the discovery site of the oldest ski hunting rock painting (1-30000 years ago) in the world, up to now the folk song "ski hunting " still sang is found here. The old fur skis are widely spread in this township. The traces of the origin of human skiing is centralized and obvious, thus it is a main area for studying the origin of human skiing.

2.4 观看阿勒泰农牧民古老毛皮滑雪板比赛 Watching Altay traditional fur ski race by farmers and herdsmen

古老毛皮滑雪板在阿尔泰山脉已流行几千年，自2006年开始，每年1月16日都在阿勒泰市举行农牧民古老毛皮滑雪板的比赛，有个人项目和拖拉兽皮雪橇的接力项目，至2015年已举行了十届。

Ancient fur skis in theAltai Mountains have been popular for thousands of years. From the beginning in 2006, every year on January 16, the Old Fur Skis Race is held in Altay city, having individual events and animal-drawn sleigh relay events. And it has been held 10 times to 2015.

2.5　在将军山滑雪场与阿勒泰地区首长对话——参观夜间冰灯大世界　Viewing the Ice Lantern World at night in the Jiangjunshan Ski Resort—a talk with a senior officer from Altay Prefecture

将军山滑雪场是融在阿勒泰市域中的滑雪场，山势独特，天然雪丰沛。多条滑雪道蜿蜒起伏，汇集在滑雪服务大厅之前。雪场功能齐全，是中国西北部最具特色，最具古老滑雪内涵的滑雪场。

冰灯大世界是阿勒泰市冬季旅游的特色项目，位于将军山滑雪场的东侧。

GeneralMountain Ski Resort lies in the Altay city, with unique mountain form and abundant natural snow. Multiple ski trails wind ups and downs, coming together before the ski service hall. Ski resort's function is rather comprehensive and the resort is the most distinctive one with ancient connotation in northwest of China.

The Ice Lanterns World is characteristic of Altay city's winter tourism projects, on the east side of the General Mountain Ski Resort, built in accordance with the ups and downs of the terrain, with magic and peculiar shape.

第三章　研讨会活动及文书信息

Chapter Three Activities and Document Information of Seminar

3.1　研讨会徽标及其含义　The meaning of seminar logo

1. 地球显示具有国际性；

2. 雪、山、林代表阿勒泰丰富的雪资源和自然资源，蕴含着滑雪起源的基本条件；

3. 雪板、弓箭和单杆滑雪杖是当前古老滑雪的组成器件，并组成一个英文“ski”的图形，显示阿勒泰至今仍在沿袭的古老滑雪文化；

4. 一个“S”曲线和六个岩画人，表示不同阶段的滑雪痕迹，标志着阿勒泰古老滑雪文化源远流长，跨越万年时空；

5. “S”曲线与6个滑雪岩画人布局方向，表示滑雪从东方起源滑向西方。

2014. 11. 14

1. The earth represents internationalization.

2. Snow, mountains and forest show Altay’s rich snow and natural resources, which are the basic conditions for origin of skiing.

3. Skis, bow and single ski pole are the oldest components of skiing, and they form a graphic of “Ski”, which indicates the survivals of ancient ski culture in Altay.

4. The “S” curve and six rock people, showing different stages of ski trails, indicate that Altay’s ancient skiing culture has a long history and spanned million years.

5. The layout direction of "S" curve and six skiing rock people represents that skiing began in the east and spreads to the west.

11. 14. 2014

3.2 研讨会邀请函和参会证书 Invitation and Certificate of Seminar

邀请函

先生/女士：

"阿勒泰人类最古老的滑雪地域-2015中国阿勒泰国际古老滑雪文化交流研讨会"，将于2015年1月14日—20日在中国·新疆·阿勒泰市和乌鲁木齐市举行，热诚邀请您届时光临。

（附：报名表和会议正式通知）

2014年11月12日

INVITATIONS

Nov. 12, 2014

Mr. / Mrs.

We sincerely invite you to visit Altai the oldest ski tracks in the world - The International Ancient Skiing Cultural Exchange and Seminar in Altay City, China which will be held in Altay City and Urumqi City, Xinjiang, China from January 14 to 20, 2015.

(Registration Form and the Conference Notice attached)

Yours sincerely

阿勒泰市人民政府

People Government of Altay

参加会议证书

先生/女士，于2015年1月14日—20日参加了在中国·新疆·阿勒泰市举行的“阿勒泰人类最古老的滑雪地域-2015中国阿勒泰国际古老滑雪文化交流研讨会”,特颁此证。

2015年1月20日

Certificate

January 20, 2015

Mr. / Mrs. has attended Altai the oldest ski tracks in the world - The International Ancient Skiing Cultural Exchange and Seminar in Altay City, China held in Altay City and Urumqi City, Xinjiang, China from January 14 to 20, 2015, and hereby is given this certificate.

阿勒泰市委书记　会议组委会主任　　会议组委会秘书长　顾问

Secretary of Altay Municipal Party and Director of Organizing Committee of the Seminar

Representative of Chinese Experts and Secretary of Organizing and counselor Committee of the Seminar

3.3 研讨会通知书

一、会议举办单位与组委会

1. 研讨会由阿勒泰市政府、新疆旅游局、阿勒泰地区行署、新疆博物馆等联合举办。

2. 研讨会由阿勒泰市政府、新疆旅游局主办。

3. 研讨会协办单位：新疆丝绸之路滑雪场、北京卡宾滑雪集团。

4. 组委会主要成员：

特邀中国滑雪协会原主席王揖涛先生（曾在人民大会堂新闻发布会代表中国滑雪协会发言）为组委会荣誉主任。

特邀挪威资深滑雪文化研究专家，奥斯陆滑雪博物馆馆长卡琳·伯格女士为组委会荣誉主任。

特邀为阿勒泰古老滑雪文化考察研究作出贡献的美国专家尼尔·拉尔森先生为组委会荣誉主任。

主任：由阿勒泰市领导担任

常务副主任：木拉提·卡开（阿勒泰市委副书记、市长）

秘书长：赛力克·阿布德合力（阿勒泰市委常委、宣传部部长）

副主任：俞光普（阿勒泰市副市长）

顾问·秘书长：单兆鉴（中国滑雪专家）

副秘书长：

阿依肯·加山（中国滑雪历史研究专家）

杨建英（阿勒泰市委宣传部副部长）

史志强（阿勒泰市旅游局局长）

二、会议主题与宗旨

弘扬阿勒泰古老滑雪传统，繁荣世界滑雪文化。

1. 促进国际间滑雪文化交流。

2. 向世界各国专家学者提供机会，亲临考察中国阿勒泰古老滑雪文化与资源，并对阿勒泰地区的最古老滑雪文化进行考察和研究。

三、会议时间、地点

1. 会议时间：2015 年 1 月 14 日–20 日

2. 会议地点：先后在中国新疆阿勒泰市和乌鲁木齐市两地举行。

四、会议内容

1. 参观

（1）参观阿勒泰 4 个展览馆。

（2）参观阿勒泰滑雪岩画。

（3）参观阿勒泰毛皮滑雪板比赛。

（4）参观阿勒泰毛皮滑雪板制作过程。

（5）观看当地具有传统文化特色的表演活动。

2. 研讨发言

（1）部分“论文摘要”将有机会在研讨大会上宣读（每人限 20 分钟内）。

（2）摘要及发言不拘形式，畅所欲言。

3. 倡导各国专家之间进行会外广泛的成果信息交流。

五、参加者资格

资格：滑雪文化和旅游研究人员，包括滑雪研究部门人士、学校研究人士、滑雪博物馆人士、新闻媒体研究宣传人士、个体研究人士等。

六、费用

1. 参加者至阿勒泰市往返的差旅费用自付。

2. 会议期间的住宿、餐饮、交通、参观、资料费用由组委会支付。

3. 参加者各自办理自身此次旅行的各种保险。

七、论文要求

1. 论文及发言主题范围

（1）人类滑雪起源的基本条件及起源的依据研究。

（2）滑雪与人类生产、生活间关系的研究。

（3）人类滑雪发展不同阶段的文化研究。

（4）滑雪发展与当代旅游业的研究。（此议题移到乌鲁木齐市进行，参加中国新疆国际高端旅游论坛会议）滑雪文化与旅游文化的融合；新疆·阿勒泰冬季滑雪旅游的国际化。

2. 论文利用英文规范格式书写。

中文字号要求：宋体字，大标题用小二号，分标题为四号加黑，正文为四号，注释为小四号。

3. 论文及其摘要体裁不限，也不受是否发表过的限制，可充分利用音频视频。

4. 中、英文“论文摘要”即“宣读稿”交送截止日期：2014 年 12 月 20 日，用信箱发至相关联络人。中、英文“论文全稿”送交截止日期：2015 年 1 月 14 日，直接送交组委会。

5. 因故没有参加会议的人士，可以将宣读稿发给相关联络人，组委会可以在会中代发言。论文也将编入《会议论文全集》。

6. 会议利用中国语言和英语。

7. 论文及摘要均要粘贴上本人的照片。

8. 全部论文将收集到《会议论文全集》中，由于翻译的原因，待会后分寄给每位参加者。

八、最后报名日期

最后报名日期2014年12月15日。

填好报名表，通过电子版报名。

报名时提供本人工作照片和证件照片的电子版，还要提供本人简介（不超过150字）。

请务必于2015年1月14日晚到达阿勒泰市。

九、联络人

1. 斯堪的纳维亚各国及欧洲方面：

卡琳·伯格女士　邮箱：karin. berg@ skiforeningen. no；

阿依肯·加山　邮箱：ayhen35@ gmail. com。

2. 美国·加拿大方面：

尼尔·拉尔森　邮箱：freeheels@ wildblue. net。

3. 亚洲及中国方面：

马元常　邮箱：mayuanchang@ snowfeeling. com. cn；

刘孟孟　邮箱：849247603@ qq. com。

4. 新疆方面：

王博先生　邮箱：1019903728@ qq. com；

周磊女士　邮箱：383622143@ qq. com。

5. 阿勒泰市：

史志强　邮箱：326734565@ qq. com；

邵长立　邮箱：359320238@ qq. com；

佐兰（英语联络人）邮箱：1536865759@ qq. com。

6. 总联络人：

单兆鉴　邮箱：shanzhaojian@ 163. com。

十、其他

1. 关于阿勒泰古老滑雪文化及人类滑雪起源地的信息资料，可从《人类滑雪起源地—中国·新疆阿勒泰》书中和相关网站信箱中获取。

中国滑雪协会网　网址：www. skiing. org. cn；

中国滑雪设备网　网址：www. skiequipment. com. cn；

中国滑雪产业网（滑雪起源）网址：www. xuechangsheji. com；

美国阿勒泰滑雪公司网址：www. altaiskis. com。

2. 航班信息：乌鲁木齐有国际机场，有多条航线供选乘；乌鲁木齐至阿勒泰市每天有两个航班，航程 45 分钟。

3. 附地图，阿勒泰市位于北纬 47°13′00″~48°39′00″，东经 86°53′00″~88°53′00″。阿勒泰市正常情况下 1 月份气温白天一般在-10℃~-15℃，夜间更低些，请自备好冬装、雪地鞋。

4. 阿勒泰市入住酒店：金桥大酒店

电话：0906-2127588；传真：0906-2127584；乌鲁木齐入住酒店：环球大酒店　0991-3330999；崑仑饭店　0991-5191113。

5. 2015 年 1 月 14 日在乌鲁木齐转机时，将设接待站。

联系人：吴永敏　电话：18951799987。

6. 提前到达者及延期返回者，当地旅游部门将提供协助，费用自理。

7. 1 月 18 日晚从阿勒泰飞往乌鲁木齐的航班由组委会统一订购（包机），2014 年 12 月 15 日前每人须提供本人的姓名、性别、国籍、护照号（身份证号）、手机号。

研讨会组委会秘书长　　研讨会组委会顾问

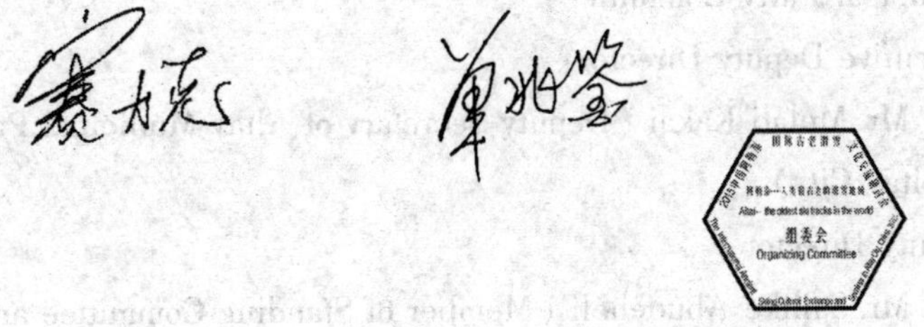

2014 年 11 月 12 日

Altai-the Oldest Ski Tracks in the World

The International Ancient Skiing Cultural Exchange and Seminar in Altay City, China 2015

NOTICE

（Finally revised on November 11, 2014）

3.3 Seminar notices

I. Organizing units and organizing committee of the seminar

1. The seminar will be jointlyorganized by the Altay City Government, the Tourism Administration of Xinjiang Uyghur Autonomous Region, the Altai Prefecture Government and Xinjiang Museum.

2. The seminar will b jointly hosted by the Altay City Government and the Tourism Administration of Xinjiang Uyghur Autonomous Region.

3. The co-organizer of Seminar will be the Xinjiang Silk Road Resort and the Beijing Carving Ski Group.

4. Key Members of the Organizing Committee:

Honorary Director: Mr. Wang Yitao (specially invited, the former President of Chinese Ski Association who presented a speech at the Press Conference in the Great Hall of the People on behalf Chinese Ski Association)

Honorary Director: Mrs. Karin Berg (specially invited, Norway senior ski culture research expert and Curator of Oslo Ski Museum)

Honorary Director: Mr. Nils Larsen (specially invited, American Ski Expert who has contributed to Altai ancient ski culture research)

Director:

Mr. Wang Shibin (Member of AltaiPrefecture Government and Secretary of Altay Municipal Party Committee)

Executive Deputy Director:

Mr. Mulati Kakai (Deputy Secretary of Altay Municipal Party Committee and Mayor of Altay City)

Deputy Director:

Mr. Sailike Abudeheli (Member of Standing Committee and Minister of Propaganda Department of Altay City)

Mr. Yu Guangpu (Deputy Mayor of Altay City)

Secretary General:

Mr. Shan Zhaojian (Chinese ski expert)

Deputy Secretary General:

Mr. Ayiken Jiashan (Chinese Ski History Researcher, Tourism Reasearcher of Norwegian Arctic University)

Yangjianying（Deputy Secretary of Altay Municipal Party Committee and Mayor of Altay City）

Shizhiqiang（director general of the Tourist Administration）

II. The aim and theme of the seminar

Develop Altai Ancient Ski Culture and create a Thriving World Ski Culture

1. To promote international skiing and cultural exchanges.

2. To provide an opportunity for world experts and scholars to come and exchange information on ancient ski cultures and resources, and to observe and study the traditional ski culture found in and around the Altai Prefecture.

III. Time and place of the seminar

1. Time：January 14th to 20th，2015

2. Place：Altay City and Urumqi City，Xinjiang Uyghur Autonomous Region，China

IV. Topics of the seminar

1. Sites to visit include：

（1）Four exhibition halls in Altay City.

（2）Altai cave paintings with skiers.

（3）Altai ski race by traditional skiers using fur covered skis

（4）A demonstration of the Altai traditional ski construction process.

（5）Local traditional cultural performances in Altay City

2. Presentations：

（1）Some of the paper abstracts can be presented at the seminar.（20 minutes are given to each presentation）

（2）Paper abstracts and presentations are informal and express your opinion freely.

3. Participants are encouraged to exchange fruitful and relevant information out of their presentations.

V. Qualifications for participants

Researchers of skiing culture and tourism，including researchers of skiing research departments，institute research departments，ski museums，media researchers，and individual researchers.

Please offer your electronic version of ID photo with your registration.

VI. Expenses

1. Participants are responsible for their ownround－transportation to Altay City. If you are in for the whole seminar, including the ending segment in Urumqi, the flight from Altay City back to Urumqi will be covered by the conference.

2. Food and lodging, transportation, visiting tickets and material costs are paid by the Organizing Committee for the participants during the seminar.

3. Insurance is the responsibility of the participants.

VII. Requirements of papers

1. The Themes and Scope of Papers and Presentations

(1) The study of the basic conditions and reasons that led to the origin and development of skiing.

(2) The study of the relationship between skiing and human production and life.

(3) Cultural research into the development of skiing at its different stages.

(4) The study of recreational skiing development and tourism to the present level of skiing and winter tourism. (This topic will be discussed in Urumchi)

2. Papers are written in the standard format in English

3. The type of the papers or paper abstracts is free and theycan be presented at the seminar even they were published in the past. Audio or video of the papers can be also used at the same time.

Thedeadline for providing your paper is December 1, 2014.

4. The deadline for submitting Chinese and English" paper abstract" or "the presenting one": December 20, 2014. Send them to your Contact person by e－mail please.

Thedeadline for submitting Chinese and English "whole paper is: January 14, 2015. Hand them over directly to the Organizing Committee please.

5. Those who could not attend the seminar can send their presenting paper to the contact person by e－mail and the Organizing Committee will arrange somebody to read the paper at the seminar. All papers will be collected in *Seminar Paper Collected Works*.

6. Chinese and English languages will be used at the seminar.

7. Your ID photo should be put on your papers or paper abstracts.

8. The *Seminar Paper Collected Works* will be sent to you afterwards.

VIII. Deadline of the final registration

1. Final registration date: December 15, 2014.

2. Fill in the registration form and register through electronic vision

Please offer your electronic version of ID photo and personal resume with your registration. (less than 150 words)

3. Please arrive in Altay city on in the late afternoon of January 14. 2015.

IX. Temporary contact

1. Scandinavian countries & Europe: Mrs. Karin Berg, Mr. Ayiken Jiashan

E-mail: karin. berg@ skiforeningen. no, ayhen35@ gmail. com

2. United States and Canada: Mr. Nils Larsen

E-mail: freeheels@ wildblue. net

3. Asia & China:

Mr. Ma Yuanchang, E-mail: mayuanchang@ snowfeeling. com. cn

Liu Mengmeng, E-mail: 849247603@ qq. com

4. Xinjiang:

Mr. Wang Bo, E-mail: 1019903728@ qq. com

Miss Zhou Lei, E-mail: 383622143@ qq. com

5. Altai:

Mr. Shao Zhangli, E-mail: 359320238@ qq. com

Mr. Shi Zhiqiang, E-mail: 326734565@ qq. com

Zuolan (English contact person), E-mail: 1536865759@ qq. com

6. Head:

Shan Zhaojian, E-mail: shanzhaojian@ 163. com

X. Additional information

1. Information of the Altai Ancient Skiing Culture and the ski origin can be found in the book *The Original Place Of Skiing-Altai Prefecture Of Xinjiang, China* and the following websites:

China Ski Association, website: www. SKiing. org. cn

Altai skis company in US website: www. altaiskis. com

Chinese Ski Equipment, website: www. skiequipment. com. cn

China's Ski Industry (skiing origin) website: www. xuechangsheji. com

2. Flight information: There is international airport in Urumqi with many airlines available. There are two flights from Urumqi to Altay every day. The flight time is 45 minutes.

3. A map is attached. Altay City is located in 47°13 ′00″– 48°39′00″N and 86°53′00″– 88°53′00″E. The temperature in Altay City is normally–10 ℃ ––15 ℃ by day and lower during the night in January. Please bring your own good winter clothing, snow-shoes or skis!

The Location of Altay City

4. The hotel in Altay:

Jinqiao Hotel

Telephone: 0906–2127588; Fax 0906–2127584

The hotel in Urumqi:

Huanqiu hotel

Telephone: 0991–3330999

Kunlun hotel

Telephone: 0991–5191113

5. On January 14th 2015, there will be service station in Urumqi, when your flight transfers. The contact person:

Mr. / Miss_ Wuyongmin_ Mobile–phone: 18951799987

6. The local tourismdepartment will offer assistance to those who arrive earlier and leave later. They would take their own expense.

7. On the 18th January, we will fly to Urumqi from Altay. the flight will be ordered by the organizing committee uniformly (chartered airplane), Before December 15th 2014 every one's name, gender, passport, number (ID number) and telephone number, should be provided.

Seminar Committee Secretary–General & Seminar Committee Counselor

Nov. 12, 2014

3.4 研讨会计划日程

1月14日 在新疆阿勒泰市会议报到，领取会议资料。晚：举行欢迎晚宴。

1月15日 参观敦德布拉克滑雪狩猎岩画、布尔津县博物馆、阿勒泰市博物馆、阿勒泰地区博物馆。

1月16日 参加新疆滑雪节开幕仪式，参观阿勒泰农牧民古老滑雪比赛，体验古老滑雪板及古老射箭等，访问当地古老滑雪者。晚：观看歌舞剧《相约美丽阿勒泰——冰雪颂》。

1月17日 上、下午研讨发言。休息期间：观看制作阿勒泰本地古老毛皮滑雪板和挪威古老滑雪板制作过程，及其所用的工具（挪威方面将派工匠参加演示）。中外专家合影。

1月18日 上、下午研讨发言。晚：乘飞机去乌鲁木齐市。

1月19日 上午：全体会议代表应邀参加中国国家旅游局与新疆维吾尔自治区人民政府联合举办的“2015丝绸之路旅游年启动仪式”。领导人会见，中外专家及会议代表合影。下午：参加中国新疆国际高端滑雪旅游论坛会议。中外专家发言共议：滑雪文化与旅游文化的融合；新疆—阿勒泰冬季滑雪旅游国际化。晚：观看大巴扎歌舞晚会。

1月20日 上午：研讨会总结大会，交流、互动。下午：考察丝绸之路滑雪场、参观新疆博物馆。晚：参加欢送晚会。

1月21日 会议结束。

研讨会组委会秘书长　　研讨会组委会顾问

2014.11.12

3.4 SCHEDULE

January 14th Welcome, Registration (includes materials), food served throughout the evening.

January 15th Cave Painting Tripto Kandegate, Museumes visit in Altay City, in Burqin, and in Altai Prefecture, visit with indigenous skiers.

January 16th Traditional Ski Festival. Traditional Ski Race, Ski-Sled Race, and other sightseeing activities.

Evening: Watch amusical drama "Meet in beautiful Altay—Ice and Snow Song"

January 17th All day conference with presentations.

During Break: 'Making a ski' demonstration (local and Norwegian style).

Take a group photo for Chinese and foreign experts

January 18th All day conference with presentations.

Evening: Go to Urumqi by air

January 19th Take part instarting ceremony of Silk Road Tourist Year

Afternoon: Presentations to be given by both Chinese and foreign experts at the Xinjiang international ice-snow tourism forum presentation The fusion of ski culture and tourism culture, Xinjiang-Altay is an international resort for skiing in winter.

Evening: Enjoy Bazaar Singing and Dancing Party

January 20th Morning: Conference Summary

Afternoon: visit the Silk Road ski resort and Xinjiang Museum

Evening: Farewell Party

January 21th Conference-End of conference

Seminar CommitteeSecretary-General & Seminar Committee Counselor

Nov. 12, 2014

3.5 研讨会前致国内参会专家的信件—单兆鉴

各位同仁：

"阿勒泰人类最古老的滑雪地域—2015 中国·阿勒泰国际古老滑雪文化交流研讨会"将于 2015. 01. 14—20 日分别在阿勒泰市、乌鲁木齐市举行。会议的信息通知书及日程已发去，想你已阅知。这是我国滑雪界一件大事儿，保证此次会议举办成功，是每位参加这次会议的专家、学者、老师、研究者的共同责任。为达到此目的，作为中国一位老滑雪工作者，阿勒泰市荣誉市民，"阿勒泰—人类滑雪起源地"研究的专家组组长，特向大家敬致此信。

一、这次会议的主题不只局限在"人类滑雪起源地"的方面，应广泛对人类滑雪历史文化、当代滑雪旅游产业发展等多领域，从不同的角度进行思考与研究。(详见 2014. 11. 13 日《会议最后通知书》)。

二、根据多年的研究经验，研讨中应注意的环节：

1. 阿勒泰完全具备滑雪起源必须具备的基本条件

（1）滑雪起源一定是在天气寒冷的地域（阿勒泰至今气候寒冷，冬季漫长）

（2）滑雪起源一定是在降雪量大，且存雪时间长的地域（阿勒泰地区至今雪量丰沛，山区雪期可达半年之久）

（3）滑雪起源一定是在能提供制造“滑雪器材”所需的木材来源方便（森林多）的地域（阿勒泰地区至今林木茂盛，森林覆盖面积大）

（4）滑雪起源一定是在能体现出滑雪速度与实用功能的多山丘地域（阿勒泰地区到处是山峰与丘地、山前地广阔。每到冬天是林海雪原景象）

（5）滑雪起源一定是在人类早期生活、生产的地域，滑雪能成为当时人类冬季狩猎的重要工具（阿勒泰地区旧石器时期人类生活的遗址多处，古迹繁多；至今仍有三大河系，56 条河流，野兽种类 34 种，野生禽类 100 多种）

2. 人类滑雪起源及发展与人类的进化密不可分

人类滑雪起源的年代是石器时代，人类在寒冷大雪面前，根据当时人类的智慧和种种条件所限，用石头工具不可能制造出滑雪板。他们能做的首先是扩大脚下的支撑面积，踩着树枝、木头，或者把树枝、木头类捆在脚下在雪地中走动，不使双脚陷雪太深，逐渐经过千百年的进化，人类变得聪明，在中国阿尔泰山出现了能用“马蹄善走”，到用山羊角在“雪中奔跑”，这是一个了不起的进步！之后滑雪器材不断演化，在中国北方出现称为“木马”的滑雪板，后来又演化到今天的滑雪板。

阿拉泰地区由于地处边远腹地，交通闭塞，“与世隔绝”，社会发展很慢，至今仍使用毛皮滑雪板，这种毛皮滑雪板虽历史悠久，但也只能有几千年的历史。所以我们不能用后续发展的滑雪板去与原始的“滑雪器具”相提并论。

3. 岩画的作用十分重要

（1）古代滑雪板是用木材制作的，时间长久便会腐烂，滑雪起源又早于文字的形成，距今万年之久，目前研究滑雪起源的考古材料极其有限，主要依赖下列两点，结合其他要素综合判定：

口传的诗歌、故事、叙述。

岩画，岩画已成为当今考古研究十分重要的途径。

（2）判定岩画是不是与滑雪有关，判定岩画中的人物是否是滑雪人物，须根据以下条件综合判定：

① 身体基本呈站立姿态；

② 脚下有延长物；

③ 体态有动感；

④ 人物周围的岩画是否与弓箭、狩猎有关；

⑤ 岩画产生的大约年代及当时的人类生活、生产状况。

4. 分清滑雪"起源"与"发展阶段"间的关系。

滑雪起源的研究应集中在石器时代人类与雪的关系，当时人类在茫茫的大雪面前，如何为了自身的生存去适应雪、征服雪、利用雪的尝试，如何扩大脚下支撑面积，如何从迈腿走动开始，向滑动演变。这是一个必然的漫长的发展历程。

如果研究追溯的是哪个国家地区，哪个民族首先穿起了滑雪板，这不是对滑雪起源的研究，是对滑雪起源之后发展的某一阶段的研究，两者不是同一时空的概念。

三、滑雪起源的研究跨越的时空很大，由于不同的国域，不同历史文化背景等原因产生分歧意见是正常的，只能通过学术研讨的方式解决。会议期间各自发表意见，如有不同的意见，原则上我们也不要进行正面的争论。我们是东道主，应抱着一种包容的精神。经与国外权威人士反复商定的这次会议的名称"阿勒泰人类最古老的滑雪地域—2015 中国·阿勒泰国际古老滑雪文化交流研讨会"，就已经说明了问题。

四、你撰写的论文不要太长，应力求精简，另有一份"摘要"，用于宣读。论文也不受过去是否发表的限制。

五、现由阿勒泰市人民政府和研讨会组委会向你发出电子版正式邀请函，请你届时光临。

六、请你能认真阅读研讨会《最后通知书》。

七、现将研讨会的有关信息一并发你参阅。

单兆鉴

2014. 11. 13

A Letter to Participating Experts by Mr. Shan Zhaojian Before the Seminar

Dear colleagues,

"Altay–the oldest skiareas in the world, the International Ancient Skiing Cultural Exchange and Seminar in Altay City, China 2015" will be held separately in Altay and Urumchi from January 14th to 20th, 2015. The notice and schedule of this seminar have been sent to you. As a significant event in Chinese skiing, experts, researchers, scholars and teachers in this area should bear responsibility to ensure the smooth development of this conference. Considering my plentiful professional experience and my positions as an honorary Altay citizen and the team leader of "Altay, the origin of human skiing" research, I write this letter with my good hope and full respect for your reference.

1. The theme of this seminar should not be limited to the origin of human skiing, but also concerns about the culture and history of human skiing, the development of modern skiing tourism, etc.

2. According to the research, there are some critical factors:

A. Altay owns the basic conditions that are necessary for the origin of skiing:

a. Cold climate. The weather in Altay is cold, and the winter lasts long.

b. Large amount and long-lasting snowfall. Altay has heavy snowfall, and the period of snowfall in mountain area can be half a year.

c. Dense forest. Altay has dense forest, which can offer wood to make the skiing equipment.

d. Mountainous region. The terrain of Altay is hills and vast mountain fronts, which is ideal for skiing sport.

e. Primitive society. In primitive era, human hunted animals to live and reproduce, and it is efficient to hunt in winter with the help of skiing. Altay still remains some Paleolithic aged sites, and there are three river systems, 56 rivers, 34 species of wild animals and more than 100 bird species.

The close connection between the origin and development of human skiing and human evolution.

The origin of human skiing is the stone age, according to the limits of wisdom of mankind and various conditions at that time, human beings could not make skis with stone instruments in the face of cold snow. The first work they could do was to expand the supporting area, stepping on branches, woods or binding branches and woods together, putting them under the feet in order that the feet would not be deep in the snow, gradually after thousands of years' evolution, humankind became smarter and smarter, in the mountain area of Altay in China, the "horseshoe good" appeared, and then the goat horns are used for people to run on the snow, which is really a great progress! After the continuous evolution of ski equipment, in the north of China a ski board called "Trojan horse" appeared, and later it was evolved to today's skis.

Because Altay area is located in the remote hinterland with blocked traffic, isolated situation with other societies, the development of society is very slow, up to now, the fur skis is still used, even though this kind of skis has a long history, but just only several thousands of years. Therefore the follow-up development of skis could not be mentioned in the same breath with original "ski equipment".

The effect of rock painting is very important

(1) The ancient skis are made of wood, which arecorroded with the time. The origin of skiing is earlier than the formation of text, which has already ten thousand years' history. Because of the extremely limited archaeological documents about origin of skiing. Now we make a comprehensive decision mainly dependent on the following two points, combined with other elements:

Poetry, story, narrative oral;

Rock painting, rock painting has become a very important way of archaeological research.

(2) determining if the rock painting is related to skiing, determining whether the figure in the rock paintings is a skier, we should make judgment comprehensively according to the following conditions:

① The body shows basically a standing posture

② There is an extension under feet

③ The body is dynamic

④ If the surrounding of figure is concerned with the bow and hunting

⑤ About the time, when the rock painting appeared and the life of human beings and production conditions at that time.

The study of the origin of skiing should focus on the relationship between the human and the snow in the stone age, at that time in the face of vast cold snow, how the human beings adapted to the snow, conquered the snow and took advantage of snow, how to expand the supporting area under feet, how to move from the one step then evolved in sliding. It must be a long development process.

If the study goes back to which country, which nation first puts on a ski board, that is not a study of the origin of skiing, but research on a certain development phase after origin of skiing. The two are not the same concept of time and space.

The study of the origin of skiing spans across a great range of time and space, because of different countries, different historical and cultural backgrounds and other reasons, it is very normal for people to hold different opinions, which can only be solved by academic research. During the conference, we should express our opinions, but if there are some differences, in principle we should not make a face to face argument. Because we are the host and should show the spirit of opening and tolerance. The name of this conference, which is discussed many times with foreign authorities, is " The oldest Ski Area in Altay-2015 China Altay International Ski Culture Exchange Seminar "

Four, you should not write the paper too long, try to be brief and should also provide a "summary" for reading. The paper is not limited if it was published in the past.

Five, now the Altay Municipal People's government and the OrganizingCommittee of the seminar send you an electronic version of the official invitation, welcome your arrival.

Six, please read the seminar "final notice" seriously.

Seven, now the relevant information of the seminar will be sent to you as references.

Shan Zhaojian

13rd November 2014

3.6 欢迎词—阿勒泰市市长木拉提·卡开 Welcoming speech by Altay city's mayor Mutila·Kakai

各位专家学者、中外来宾，女士们、先生们：

大家上午好！在这个银妆素裹的季节，我们相聚在"人类滑雪起源地"—美丽的阿勒泰，隆重举行2015年中国阿勒泰国际古老滑雪文化交流研讨会。首先，我代表阿勒泰市委、市人民政府对本次会议的召开表示热烈的祝贺，对出席会议的各位嘉宾、朋友表示衷心的感谢！

阿勒泰自然风光独特，哈萨克民族文化底蕴深厚，夏季气候宜人，风景优美；冬季千里冰封、万里雪飘，具有天然雪期长、雪质好等得天独厚的条件，2007年获"人类滑雪起源地"认证。依托"人类滑雪最早起源地"优势，阿勒泰市把培育壮大冬季冰雪旅游作为旅游业大发展的突破口，着力在培育特色、挖掘文化内涵、塑造品牌等方面狠下功夫，不断丰富冬季旅游文化内涵，人类滑雪最早起源地品牌影响力不断扩大。

女士们、先生们，冬季的阿勒泰，冰雪风光雄奇壮美，冰雪艺术如梦如幻，冰雪运动丰富多彩。我们衷心希望通过此次研讨会，加深国内外专家学者对阿勒泰古老滑雪文化与资源的认同，促进国际间滑雪文化深入交流。我们将认真听取国内外专家学者的意见、建议，进一步弘扬古老滑雪传统，为繁荣世界滑雪文化做出应有的贡献。

最后，祝本次研讨会取得圆满成功！祝各位来宾、各位朋友们身体健康、万事如意！

谢谢大家！

Respected Specialists and Scholars, Ladies and Gentlemen:

In this white charming season, we are so glad to meet here, Altay, the original place of human skiing, to attend China Altay International Ancient Skiing Culture Seminar in 2015, On behalf of Party committee, and government of Altay City, I would like to extend our warmest welcome to all the guests here from all over the world.

With unique natural scenery and profoundKazakhstan culture, Altay, is an ideal summer resort for its cool climate and beautiful scenery. Altay is also rich in snow and ice resources, with frequent snow fall, which is in high quality and has long snow period.

In 2007, Altay city got the certificate of "Cradle of human skiing ", taking advantage of the fame, the Party Committee and government of Altay City have attach great importance to developing snow and ice tourism, and striving to bring up snow and ice tourism. Especially, much attention has been paid to promoting features, exploring cultural connotation, and building trademark. Therefore, winter tourism has been improved a great deal, and the fame of cradle of human skiing has influenced in all aspects.

Ladies and gentlemen, Altay in winter, has magnificent scenery of snow, mysterious snow art like a dream, colorful snow sports and simple but elegant custom. We hope sincerely that all of the experts both at home and abroad can reach a consensus and deepen understanding to foster cultural exchange in international skiing. We would like to listen to the opinions and suggestions from the experts to promote ancient skiing tradition, and do our greatest contribution to flourish the world skiing!

Finally, I wish a full success to the seminar!

And best wishes to you all !

Thank you !

研讨会现场 Live seminar

3.7 贺词—中国专家代表单兆鉴 Greeting speech by Chinese expert Shan Zhanjian

各位国内外专家学者，各位与会领导、嘉宾，各媒体单位的朋友们：

大家上午好！

经过两天的实地考察之后，“阿勒泰——人类最古老滑雪地域——2015 中国阿勒泰国际古老滑雪文化交流研讨会”的会议发言阶段于今天拉开了序幕。

此时此刻，我非常荣幸代表中国专家向这次研讨会致贺词。

这次国际研讨会将是一次盛大的世界滑雪会议，对阿勒泰古老滑雪文化而言，是继 2006 年发布《阿勒泰宣言》并开始举办古老毛皮滑雪板比赛；2010 年出版《人类滑雪起源地—中国新疆阿勒泰》综合研究成果书籍，同年国际滑雪组织向中国专家组组长授予《单兆鉴—对世界滑雪运动做出贡献》的荣誉之后，又一件非常重要，非常有历史意义的事件。

为了筹备这次会议，中国专家在国内外进行了多年的精心策划，广泛联络，多领域充分的准备，最终得到了阿勒泰市委、市政府的支持，搭建平台，亲自组织，使研讨会得以进行。在这里，我们还要感谢关心支持研讨会的新疆旅游局、阿勒泰地区行政公署，尤其感谢阿勒泰市委、市政府在人力、财力、活动等各方面实际的支持。另外，北京卡宾滑雪集团、新疆丝绸之路滑雪场、喀纳斯景区管委会作为协办单位，给予了力所能及的协助，在这里，我们一并致以衷心的感谢！

2015 年初，是中国从事滑雪历史研究人员兴奋的时刻，我们所敬仰的世界级专家从四面八方，不远万里，费时费力，长途跋涉来到了阿勒泰与我们会聚，不少专家因为天气原因，旅途中遇到了很多麻烦，但到了阿勒泰后却是精神抖擞的投入到考察之中，使我们受到了很大的鼓舞！

世界著名滑雪学术界专家，来自挪威的卡琳女士，对阿勒泰古老滑雪研究作出贡献的美国专家尼尔．拉尔森先生，来自相关国家几十位资深权威专家，还有国际雪联官员、高级顾问等人士前来参加会议，我们向这些朋友们表示热烈欢迎！向你们致敬！

我们在阿勒泰相聚的日子，定能很好完成“弘扬阿勒泰人类最古老滑雪地域的传统文化，繁荣世界滑雪文化”的研究使命！让我们共享古阿勒泰人留给我们共同的滑雪遗产！我们将携手走向更广阔的未来！

2015. 01. 17

Respected scholars from home and abroad, noted leaders, guests and media:

Good afternoon!

After two days of on-site study, "Altay-the oldest ski tracks in the world-2015 Altay International Ancient Skiing Culture Conference has come to the stage of speech giving today.

Now, it is my huge honor to make a congratulation speech on behalf of experts from China. This will be a big international skiing conference. The Altai ancient skiing culture has become another significant and historical event after the release of *Altay Declaration* and ancient fur ski competitions in 2006, the publication of *The Original Place of Human Skiing-Altay, Xinjiang, China* in 2010 and Mr. Shan Zhaojian being honored as The Great Contributor to the World Ski Sports by FIS.

To ensure a successful conference, Chinese experts have made full preparation with years of elaboration and wide connection. With the great support of Altay government to provide this great platform and organize the conference, the success was well guaranteed. Here, I would also like to give thanks to Xinjiang Bureau of Tourism, Altay Region Administration Office for their firm support, and especially thanks to Altay government's support in terms of human resource, finance and activity. Moreover, Beijing Carving Ski Group, Xijiang Silk Road Ski Resort and Kanas Scenic Spot Administration Committee have also given the best possible assistance. I would like to give my sincere gratitude to all of you.

This early 2015 is an exciting moment for Chinese skiing history researchers. Experts from all over the world gathered together in Altay, regardless of the long distance and bad weather. Their spirit really inspired us!

Karin Berg, world famous skiing expert from Norway, Nils Larsen, American expert who has made great contribution to Altay ancient skiing research and some other authoritative experts from abroad, as well as FIS officials and senior consultants are all here at the conference. We welcome you all!

The effort we have made in Altay will surely contribute to accomplishing the mission of Carrying Forward the Traditional Culture of Altay-the oldest ski tracks in the world, and will also prosper the world skiing culture. So, let us share and enjoy our skiing heritage that Altai people have left us! Holding hands, we will step forward into a brighter future.

Shan Zhaojian
2015. 01. 17

3.8 主持词—阿勒泰市委张华勇副书记 **Host speech by Altay city's municipal party Deputy Secretary Zhang Huayong**

各位来宾、女士们、先生们:

大家上午好!

今天，我们非常荣幸得邀请到诸多中外专家、学者参加“阿勒泰—人类最古老的滑雪地域”2015年中国阿勒泰国际古老滑雪文化交流研讨会开幕式。

首先，我代表阿勒泰市委、市人民政府，对各位来宾的到来表示热烈的欢迎!

下面我介绍参加研讨会开幕式的专家、学者及来宾:

中国滑雪历史文化研究专家、中国第一位滑雪冠军、《阿勒泰宣言》主起草者及发布者、古老毛皮滑雪板比赛倡导者、本次研讨会组委会秘书长单兆鉴先生;

世界最 大最悠久的滑雪博物馆——挪威奥斯陆滑雪博物馆馆长、北欧古老滑雪文化研究者和传承人、挪威著名滑雪专家南森先生的继承人、本次研讨会组委会名誉顾问 Karin Berg 卡琳·博格女士；美国古老滑雪文化研究专家、西方第一位来阿勒泰研究挖掘古老滑雪文化学者、中国专家合作者 Nils Larsen，尼尔·拉尔森先生；新疆博物馆研究员、《阿勒泰宣言》专家组副组长王博先生;

中国滑雪历史研究员、中国第一位赴国外学习研究古老滑雪文化的学者、本次研讨会组委会副秘书长阿依肯·加山先生；参加今天研讨会的还有挪威、瑞典、芬兰、丹麦、奥地利、美国、韩国、斯洛文尼亚、中国等19个国家100余名专家、学者，以及媒体朋友们。

参加研讨会开幕式的阿勒泰市领导有：阿勒泰市委副书记、市长木拉提·卡(qia)开先生；阿勒泰市政协党组书记柳运森先生;

下面，请木拉提·卡(qia)开先生致欢迎辞;

下面，请单兆鉴先生讲话;

感谢单兆鉴先生的精彩讲话。

下面，请卡琳·博格女士讲话；

感谢卡琳伯格女士的精彩讲话，可见卡琳·博格女士对古老滑雪有着深入研究。

下面，请阿勒泰市学者哈德尔讲话；

下面，观看阿勒泰古老滑雪板与挪威古老滑雪板制作过程。

首先，有请挪威滑雪板制作人上场展示；

下面，有请阿勒泰古老滑雪析板制作人上场展示；

各位专家、学者研讨会开幕式到此结束，下面，先有请各位领导和国内外专家、学者到会场门口，为此次活动签名后到楼外合影留念，休息十分钟之后进行研讨会。衷心预祝本次研讨会圆满成功，谢谢！

2016. 01. 17

Distinguished Guests, Ladies and Gentlemen:

Good morning !

It's our great honor to have invited so many experts, scholars to attend the opening ceremony of Altay-cradle of human skiing, China Altay international ancient skiing culture Seminar in 2015.

First of all, on behalf of Altay Party Committee and government, I'd like to extend our warmest welcome to all the guests here from all over the world!

Now, please allow me to introduce the experts, the scholars and the guests.

China skiing history culture research expert, the first ski champion, editor and declarer of Altay Declaration, advocator of skiing competition of ancient leather skis, general secretary of organizing committee for the seminar, Shan Zhaojian.

The director of Norway Oslo Ski Museum, the largest ski museum with the longest history, researcher and disseminator of Northern European ancient skiing culture, inheritor of Nanson, Norwegian skiing expert, honorary advisor of organizing committee for the seminar, Mrs Karin Berg, America skiing history culture research expert, the first scholar to China to study Altay ancient skiing culture, China expert partner, Mr Nils Larsen! Researcher of Xinjiang Museum, deputy leader of Altay Declararion. Mr Wangbo! China skiing history researcher, the first scholar travelled abroad to study ancient skiing culture, deputy general secretary of organizing committee for the seminar, Mr Ayiken. Jiashan.

Today, we also have greathonor to exchange ideas with more than 100 experts, scholars and media friends from 19 countries, which are Norway, Sweden, Finland, Danmark, Austria, America, Korea, Slovenija, China. etc

The municipal officials are as follows:

The Deputy general secretary of Altay Party Committee, mayor of Altay city, Mr Mulati. Qia kai

Thegeneral of Altay People's Political Consultative Conference, Mr Liu Yunsen.

Now, Let's invite Mr Mulati. Qia kai to issue a welcome speech!

Well, It's time to invite Mr Shan Zhaojian to give us a short speech.

Thanks for Mr Shan's excellant speech

Now, ladies and gentlemen, please welcome MrsKarin Berg.

Thank you, MrsKarin, we can tell clearly that Mrs Karin has done so much study about ancient skiing.

Ok, now, please give your hands to Mr Harder, scholar from Altay.

Well, Ladies and Gentlemen, now, please enjoythe process f making Altay ancient skis and Norwegian ancient skis.

Repected Experts and Scholars, The opening ceremony is over, The following matters are related to the seminar.

Sincerely wish a success to the seminar! Thank you !

1. 17. 2016

3.9 研讨会期间古老滑雪板制作演示（中国—挪威） Demonstration of making ancient skis during the seminar（China—Norway）

在会议期间，来自挪威的古老滑雪板研究制作专家托马斯先生与阿勒泰当地古老毛皮滑雪板制作工匠斯兰别克·沙合仕先生共同向与会者展示了他们的技艺并进行了广泛交流。

During the conference, Norwaygian ancient ski researching and making expert, Mr. Thomas and Mr. Bieke · duheshi who is the Altay local craftsman in ancient fur ski showed the attendees their sills and achieved an extensive exchange.

现场演示 Live presentation

古老滑雪板展示 Ancient skis presentation

3.10 欢送词—阿勒泰市政府俞光谱副市长总结发言 Farewell speech by Deputy Mayor Yu Guangpu from Altay City

各位专家、各位朋友，女士们、先生们：

近年来，阿勒泰市在冰雪旅游方面下大力气做足文章，利用“人类滑雪最古老的地域”等滑雪文化遗产条件，发掘“人类滑雪起源地”的历史文化底蕴。结合阿勒泰市雪期长、雪量大、山形饱满、各种高度差齐全等自然条件优势，紧紧围绕“生态园林、山水宜居、民俗文化、休闲度假”的城市发展定位，通过培育特色、挖掘文化、塑造品牌，大力开发冰雪、生态、民俗等特色旅游项目，我市冬季旅游发展势头良好，冬季旅游文化内涵不断丰富。

在这种形势下，“阿勒泰人类最古老的滑雪地域——2015 中国阿勒泰国际古老滑雪文化交流研讨会”在这里举行，各国各地专家汇聚在此对古老滑雪领域进行深入研究，丰富了世界滑雪文化，对各国专家的光临阿勒泰感到万分荣幸！通过考察、研讨，在这次会议中，形成了《2015 阿勒泰宣言》，这一巨大的研究成果，是各位专家、学者共同努力的结果。具有国际的权威性质。相信此次研讨会的成功举办，将进一步拓展国际间古老滑雪文化交流的广度与深度，同时也将带动我市冬季旅游事业的发展和提升我市在海内外的旅游知名度。谢谢大家，谢谢来自世界多国的朋友们！

让我们共同祝贺此次研讨会圆满成功！祝各位嘉宾、朋友返程平安，身体健康，万事如意！

2015.01.18

Ladies and gentlemen,

In recent years, Altay makes great efforts to thetourisms of ice and snow, e. g. taking advantage of Skiing culture heritage (the most ancient human skiing area) to explore the historical cultural values of the origin of human skiing. Based on the natural strengths e. g. long period and large amount of snow, full contour of mountain, various height differences, and closely around the city's orientation of "Ecological garden, livable landscape, folk-custom culture, leisure resort ", the development trend of the winter tourism is good, and cultural connotation is continuously enriched through fostering characteristic, mining culture, shaping brand, and vigorously developing the characteristic tourism projects of snow and ice, ecology, folklore etc.

In this situation, the conference "Altay, the most ancient human skiing area, 2015 international conference of Altay's ancient skiing culture" is held here, experts from all over the world gather in Altay to conduct further research and enrich the world's skiing culture; we are much honored for the presence of experts. Through researches and discussions, we have formed a great research result "2015 Altay Statement" in the meeting, which is the joint effort of experts and scholars, and has international authority. We believe, the success of conference will not only expand the width and depth of international exchange of ancient ski culture, but also promote the development of the city's winter tourism and enhance the world visibility of the city. Thank you, thank you for all the friends from many countries of the world!

Let's congratulate the complete success of the conference! I wish all the guests and friends a safe journey home, good health, good luck in everything!

Jan. 18, 2015

3.11 阿勒泰当地媒体对研讨会的综合报道选编 Some reports by local media in Altay

2015 年国际古老滑雪文化交流研讨会在阿勒泰市圆满结束
国内外专家学者进一步论证“阿勒泰是人类滑雪最早起源地”

《阿勒泰日报》专讯(记者杜鹏飞)

2015 年中国阿勒泰国际古老滑雪文化交流研讨会在阿勒泰市正式拉开帷幕，来自挪威、瑞典、芬兰、美国、奥地利、斯洛文尼亚等 18 个国家和地区的专家、学者与会。本次研讨会从1月14日至18日为期5天，期间包括对阿勒泰古老滑雪岩画及文化传统进行了实地考察研究；观看毛皮滑雪板制作、民族表演等活动；最后进入会议研讨阶段。

1月15日上午，专家学者们在阿勒泰市参观了地、市博物馆，并在阿勒泰市拉斯特乡观看了民族表演及毛皮滑雪板制作。

1月15日下午，因路面积雪厚车辆难以行使，专家学者们从阿勒泰市汗德尕特乡徒步来到该乡敦德布拉克滑雪狩猎岩画处进行实地考察。受到当地民众热烈欢迎。

据专家介绍，该处岩画画面所表现的是一组脚踏滑雪板、手持单杆滑雪狩猎人的形象，其年代可以上溯到距今1至3万年的旧石器时代晚期，比以往其他国家发现的人类滑雪岩画以及滑雪板残片所反应的年代至少提前几千年以上。滑雪狩猎者形象的岩画所产生的年代，论证了阿勒泰是迄今为止人类滑雪最早起源地。

中国滑雪协会技术顾问单兆鉴说："感谢阿勒泰市对于敦德布拉克滑雪狩猎岩画的细心保护，这是世界滑雪文化的宝贵遗产，希望通过本次研讨会让世界更多的人了解人类滑雪起源地"。使阿勒泰成为世界滑雪朝圣的"麦加"。

1月6日，2015年"北京卡宾杯"中国·新疆·阿勒泰第十届古老滑雪比赛在阿勒泰市将军山滑雪场举行，参加2015年中国阿勒泰国际古老滑雪文化交流研讨会的各国专家学者观看了本次比赛。

来自阿勒泰地区的16支代表队的177名运动员参加了个人项目与团体接力项目的比赛，选手们脚穿自制传统的毛皮滑雪板，使用独木滑雪杖，拖拉着兽皮雪橇在皑皑白雪上激烈角逐。

在现场，观众们的欢呼呐喊声此起彼伏，选手们在比赛中你争我赶全力以赴，各国专家学者们看的津津有味，并纷纷拿出相机进行抢拍，他们对选手们的古老毛皮滑雪板表现出浓厚的兴趣。

瑞典学者安娜·埃兰德松对记者说："我来自瑞典的北部，第一次看到这样的古老滑雪比赛，我觉得选手们的滑雪技术非常高，这与现代的滑雪比赛完全不一样，古老毛皮滑雪板更具有挑战性。"

比赛间隙，阿勒泰地区和阿勒泰市首长举行了与各国专家面对面的洽谈会，听取了专家们建设性意见。

1月16日晚，阿勒泰"冰雪大世界"正式开园迎客，当晚这里人潮涌动，丰富多彩的冰雕、惟妙惟肖的雪塑，吸引了前来参加"2015年中国国际古老滑雪文化交流研讨会"的世界专家学者的目光。

斯洛文尼亚与会学者布鲁特·巴塔利对记者说："白天，我们观看了滑雪比赛，晚上又到这里欣赏冰、雪雕塑，这些作品精美、不可思议，我非常感兴趣。”

1月17日-18日，2015年中国国际古老滑雪文化交流研讨会进入大会的研讨阶段，会议以：“弘扬古老滑雪传统繁荣世界滑雪文化”为主题。专家们在研讨会期间交流世界滑雪文化、宣读他们的研究成果。

挪威奥斯陆滑雪博物馆馆长卡琳·博格在研讨会上进行了发言。卡琳·伯格在勒泰地区多地进行了考察，她表示，阿勒泰拥有非常丰富的冰雪资源和古老传统文化，是当之无愧的人类滑雪的摇篮，当地对古老滑雪文化进行了很好的保护和挖掘，值得称赞。古老滑雪文化和毛皮滑雪板得到了越来越多的认识和认可。

美国古老滑雪文化研究专家、中国专家合作者尼尔·拉尔森表示，将会把阿勒泰收集拍摄到的有关古老滑雪起源地论证资料视频播放给各国专家学者们，让更多的人了解阿勒泰古老滑雪的历史文化，呼吁对其进行更好地保护和挖掘。尼尔·拉尔森说：“世界其他地方也会有山有雪，但是没有一个地方像阿勒泰这样有历史渊源运用古老滑雪起源地这一品牌促进现代滑雪，将古老滑雪和现代管理方式相结合，这在世界上是独一无二的。”

本次会议由自治区旅游局、阿勒泰地区行署、阿勒泰市政府联合主办，自治区旅游局和阿勒泰市政府承办，自治区博物馆、新疆丝绸之路滑雪场、北京卡宾滑雪集团、喀纳斯管委会协办。此次研讨会是到目前为止国内举办的最大规模、最高档次的国际性滑雪历史研讨会，是人类滑雪起源研究及古老滑雪文化多领域研讨的国际盛会，本次会议进一步夯实了中国新疆阿勒泰是人类滑雪最早起源地，形成《2015阿勒泰宣言》，这将对国际滑雪文化与产业的发展产生重大而深远的影响。

1月19-20日，专家们乘坐大巴专车赴乌鲁木齐参加“第二届中国新疆丝绸之路旅游发展大会—丝路旅游暨冰雪旅游高峰论坛”会议。

Further Studies on *Altay—the First Origin of Skiing in the World* Successful Conclusion ofThe International Ancient Skiing Cultural Exchange and Seminar in Altay City, China 2015

Pengfei Du

Altay Daily - In 2015, The International Ancient Skiing Cultural Exchange and Seminar in Altay City, China officially kicks off in Altay city. Experts and scholars from Norway, Sweden, Finland, the United States, Austria, Slovenia and other 18 countries and regions have attended this conference. This seminar lasts from January 14th to 18th, 2015. Topics of the seminar includes field study on Altai cave paintings and traditional cultures, appreciation about a demonstration of the Altai traditional ski construction process and local cultural performance. And the final stage is free discussion.

The morning of January 15th, experts and scholars visited municipal museums in Altay city and watched the national performance and the construction process of fur covered skis.

The afternoon of January 15th, because of snowy weather, experts and scholars went from Dundebulake, a Mongolian countryside, in Altay city to a petroglyphic site with ski hunting paintings for field trips. The local people presented a warm welcome.

According to an expert, the petroglyphic scenes reflect an image of a hunter, standing on skis and holding a pole. The scenes can date back to the late Stone Age, 10, 000 to 30, 000 years before. These petroglyphies are earlier than ever found pieces of paintings and fragmental skis by at least several thousand years in advance. The image of a hunter demonstrates that Altay is by far the oldest ski tracks in the world.

The technical consultant of Chinese Skiing Association Shan Zhaojian says: " We are grateful for the careful preservation of rock paintings with hunters, which are precious heritage of skiing culture. We hope more people will have a better understanding of skiing origin after this seminar" . And Altay may become the "Mecca of skiing" across the world.

On January 6th, 2015, the "Beijing CARBIN CUP" Altay, Xinjiang, the 10th oldest skiing race was held in the Altay city, All the experts and scholars have participated this race.

Coming from Altay city, 16 teams with 177 athletes have participated the individual and relay events. The players, wearing the homemade traditional uniforms, using the wooden ski poles, dragged sleigh covered with fur in the snow for fierce competition. During the games, the audience cheer up loudly and the players try their best to perform well. The experts and scholars take out their cameras to record the exciting moment and show great interest.

The Swedish scholar Anna LanDeSong tells the reporter: " I come from the north of Sweden. It is the first time I watch the oldest ski race. I players have superb skills, and this skiing is completely different from the modern skiing race. The ancient skiing is more challenging. "

At the interval of competition, the leaders of Altai region have a meeting with the experts and listened to their constructive opinions.

At the evening of 16th January, Altai "Snow World" officially opens its door to welcome guests. People are crowded and attracted by colorful ice sculptures and snow statues. The experts and scholars are also attracted by these fabulous sights.

An Slovenian expert Beirur-Betail tells the reporter: "in the daytime, we have enjoyed the ski race; in the evening, I came to here and enjoy the ice and snow sculptures. They are so beautiful and incredible, and I am very interested in that."

In January 17th - 18th, the International Ancient Skiing Cultural Exchange and Seminar entered into the phase of research and discussion with the topic of "the promotion of the ancient skiing tradition and prosperity of the world skiing culture". During the seminar, experts exchange the skiing culture and read out their research results.

Karin Berg, curator of the Ski Museum in Oslo, Norway, delivers a speech at the seminar. Karin Berg has made many investigations in the Altai region. She says that Altay has rich resources of ice and snow and the ancient traditional culture. They are preserved by local people. And Altay fully deserved the honor of the cradle of human skiing. The ancient skiing culture and fur skis have become recognized by more and more people.

Neil Larsen, an expert of the oldest skiing culture research and collaborator of China experts says that he will show the videos about the origin of skiing shot in Altai region to the experts and scholars of various countries. So that more people will understand the Altai ancient skiing history and culture and call people to protect them. Neil Larsen says: "There are also mountains and snow in the rest of the world, but no a place like Altay having such a history with traditional excellence of skiing to use the brand to promote modern skiing, to combine ancient skiing and modern management together. That is unique in the world.

The conference is jointly organized by a great many authoritative institutes and NGO, such as Tourism Administration of the Autonomous Region, Prefecture Administrative Office, Altay City Government, Museum in Autonomous RegionMuseum, Xinjiang Silk Road Ski Resort, Beijing Carving Ski Group, etc. The seminar so far is the largest, highest level international meeting. The conference further demonstrates the fact that Altay Xinjiang China is the first origin of skiing and *The Declaration of 2015 Altay* is based on that, which will exert far-reaching influence on international skiing culture and industry.

第四章　研讨会专家学者发言及论文汇编
Chapter Four Speeches and papers by experts and scholars

经过 2 天的实践考察后，1 月 17 日-18 日两天在阿勒泰地区宾馆内进行了研讨活动。到会专家逐一踊跃发言，部分未到会者也送交了论文。期间，专家们在会场内观看了阿勒泰古老毛皮滑雪板和挪威古老滑雪板制作工艺。

After two days of practice investigation, a two-day discussion is held during January 17-18 in a Altay hotel. The experts speak enthusiastically, and the absent ones also send papers. In the period of meeting, the experts have watched hand-made artistry of fur skis performed by inheritors of Altay fur skis and Norwegian old skis, signing on the signature wall.

4.1　中国新疆阿勒泰—世界最古老滑雪地域的研究历程　The Research Course of China's "Altai—the Oldest Ski Tracks in the World"

单兆鉴（中国）　Shan Zhaojian（CHN）

个人简介　Brief Introduction

单兆鉴，男，中国籍，1938 年出生于吉林省，1961 年毕业于吉林体育学院。是中国第一位全国滑雪冠军，从事滑雪运动 60 余年。曾任国家体委滑雪处处长、中国滑雪协会秘书长、亚洲冬季两项滑雪联盟技术部主任等职。著有多部滑雪专著及几十篇滑雪论文。1993 年首先提出"滑雪的发源地可能在中国阿勒泰地区"，并就这一课题从事了长达 13 年的艰难考察、研究，是"阿勒泰地区是人类滑雪起源地研究"的发起人和组织者，阿勒泰古老毛皮滑雪板比赛的倡导者，也是《阿勒泰宣言》的主起草人和发布者。2010 年 3 月荣获国际滑雪组织授予的"单兆鉴——对世界滑雪运动做出贡献"的特制奖牌。2011 年与王博先生主编《人类滑雪起源地——中国·新疆·阿勒泰》，全面阐述了人类滑雪起源的研究理论、根据及时间历程。

Shan Zhaojian, male, Chinese, born in Jilin Province on May, 1938, graduated form Jilin Sports Collage in 1961. He is the first national skiing champion and has engaged in the sport for over 60 years, during which he served as the director of the skiing department of National Sports Committee, Secretary General of Chinese Skiing Association, and technical director of Asian Winter Biathlon Union Skiing Department, etc. He has written many monographs and dozens of papers for skiing. In1993, He first raised the idea that "The Altay Prefecture of China may be the Original Place of Skiing" for which he had investigated for up to 13 years. He is also the initiator and organizer of the research on the place of origin of skiing. the advocate of ancient ski match and the main drafter and issuer of the Altay Declaration. On March 3rd, 2010, he was rewarded by International Skiing Organization the medal and certificate for his contributions to the world skiing. In 2011, as chief editor, he together with Mr. Wang Bo edited the book *The origin of Chinese skiing-Altay in Sinkiang* , China, fully demonstrated the research theory, reason and time span of the origin of human skiing.

一、中国新疆阿勒泰地区可能是人类滑雪起源地学说的提出

"中国新疆阿勒泰地区可能是人类滑雪起源地学说"，首先由单兆鉴根据当时已获悉的信息于 1993 年所著《怎样练习滑雪》中提出（第 3 页，人民体育出版社出版），此后，他默默地开始了十余年的研究考察历程。

1994 年由中国滑雪协会、国家体委体育文史工作委员会审编的《中国滑雪运动史》中再次提出这一学说（第 1 页，刘永年、单兆鉴、张德山编著，武汉出版社出版）。

1994 年单兆鉴与已退休的中国滑雪协会首任主席刘永年先生共商决定，以刘永年名义撰写了题名为《新疆阿勒泰地域是人类滑雪发祥地之一》的文章，发表在国家体委《体育文史》1994 年第四期上。

2004 年单兆鉴编著的《滑雪运动指南》中多次提到阿勒泰地区可能是人类滑雪发源地或发源地之一（第 14 页、244 页、250 页，人民体育出版社出版）。

2005 年 8 月出版的由王揖涛、任洪国为主、副审，单兆鉴、王石安为主编，中国滑雪协会审定的中国第一本《高山滑雪初级教程》中阐述"中国新疆的阿勒泰地域是人类滑雪的发源地或发源地之一"（第 1 页，人民体育出版社）。

I. The Theory that "Altay, Xinjiang, China May Be the Place of Origin of Skiing" Was Put Forward

The theory that "Altay, Xinjiang, China may be the place of origin of skiing" was first put forward by Shan Zhaojian according to the already-known information (on Page 3 of How to Practice Skiing, 1993, People's Sports Publishing House) . Since then, he has started quietly to have his more than ten years of research and investigation.

In 1994, the theory was brought up again in The History of Skiing in China, compiled by the Sports Literature and History Commission of Physical Culture and Sports Commission of the PRC（on Page 1, written and compiled by Mr. Liu Yongnian, Mr. Shan Zhaojian and Mr. Zhang Deshan, printed by Wuhan Publishing House）.

In 1994, Mr. Shan Zhaojian discussed with Mr. Liu Yongnian, the retired first President of the Chinese Ski Association, and agreed to write the article "Altay, Xinjiang, China is one of the origins of skiing" in the name of Mr. Liu Yongnian, which was published in the 4th issue of Journal of Sport History and Culture by Physical Culture and Sports Commission of the PRC.

In 2004, the idea that Altay, Xinjiang, China may be the place of origin or one of the places of origin of skiing was mentioned many times in Guide to Skiing compiled by Mr. Shan Zhaojian（on Page 14, 244 and 250, People's Sports Publishing House）.

In August 2005, it was stated that Altay, Xinjiang, China may be the place of origin or one of the places of origin of skiing in Primary Course of Alpine Skiing, thefirst version of China, authorized by the Chinese Ski Association, with Mr. Wang Yitao and Mr. Ren Hongguo as the chief and deputy examiners respectively and Mr. Shan Zhaojian and Mr. Wang Shian as the chief editors,（on Page 1, printed by People's Sports Publishing House）.

二、确立科学的研究思维与理论导向

1. 首先研究人员认为，人类滑雪的起源须具备特定的基本条件，这是研究某一区域滑雪起源的首要前提。

单兆鉴根据古老滑雪的功能、特点和本人对滑雪领域的经验与感悟，于2004年完成了“人类滑雪起源应具备的基本条件”的研究，然后以这些基本条件与阿勒泰地区所具备的各种条件与长期实地考察的结果进行参照对接，撰写了《中国新疆阿勒泰地区具备了人类滑雪起源的一切基本条件》的文章，为“中国新疆阿勒泰地区是人类滑雪起源地学说”的最后确立奠定了理论基础。

在研究中发现，人类滑雪起源的基本条件与阿勒泰在人类滑雪起源所具备的条件完全一致。(见图 1-4)

图 1　阿勒泰的连绵山脉

Fig. 1　Continuous and rolling Mountains and Irtysh River

图 2　阿勒泰的林海雪原

Fig. 2　Snowy Forest in Altay

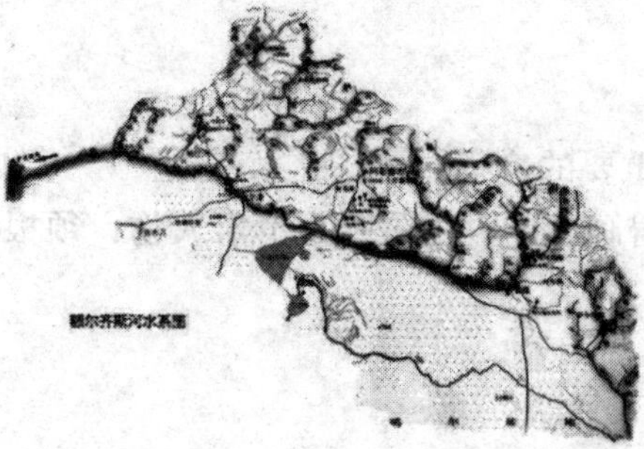

图 3　阿尔泰山和额尔齐斯河区域水系图

Fig. 3　Snowy Forest in Altay

图 4　古老阿勒泰人滑雪狩猎

Fig. 4　Ancient Skiers in Altay are Skiing and Hunting

（1）滑雪起源一定是在天气寒冷的地域（阿勒泰至今气候寒冷，冬季漫长）

（2）滑雪起源一定是在降雪量大，且存雪时间长的地域（阿勒泰地区至今雪量丰沛，山区雪期可达半年之久）

（3）滑雪起源一定是在能提供制造“滑雪器材”所需的木材来源方便（森林多）的地域（阿勒泰地区至今林木茂盛，森林覆盖面积大）

（4）滑雪起源一定是在能体现出滑雪速度的多山丘地域

（阿勒泰地区到处是山峰与丘地，山前地广阔。每到冬天是林海雪原景象）

（5）滑雪起源一定是在人类早期生活、生产的地域，滑雪能成为当时人类冬季狩猎的重要工具（阿勒泰地区旧石器时期人类生活的遗址多处，古迹繁多；至今仍有三大河系，56 条河流，野兽种类 34 种，野生禽类 100 多种）

2. 人类滑雪起源及发展与人类的进化密不可分

人类滑雪起源的年代是石器时代，人类在寒冷大雪面前，根据当时人类的智慧和种种条件所限，用石头工具不可能制造出滑雪板。他们能做的首先是扩大脚下的支撑面积，踩着树枝、木头，或者把树枝、木头类捆在脚下在雪地中走动，不使双脚陷进雪里过深，经过千百年的进化，人类逐渐变得聪明，在中国阿尔泰山出现了能用“马蹄善走”，到用山羊角在“雪中奔跑”，这是一个了不起的进步！之后，滑雪器材不断演化，在中国北方出现称为“木马”的滑雪板，后来又演化到今天的滑雪板。

阿勒泰地区由于地处边远腹地，交通闭塞，“与世隔绝”，社会发展很慢，至今仍使用毛皮滑雪板，这种毛皮滑雪板虽历史悠久，但也只有几千年的历史。所以我们不能用后续发展的滑雪板去与原始的“滑雪器具”相提并论。

3. 岩画的作用十分重要

（1）古代滑雪板是用木材制作的，时间长久便会腐烂，滑雪起源又早于文字的形成，距今万年之久，目前研究滑雪起源的考古材料极其有限，主要依赖下列两点，结合其他要素综合判定。

① 口传的诗歌、故事、叙述；

② 岩画，岩画已成为当今考古研究十分重要的途径。

（2）判定岩画是不是与滑雪有关，判定岩画中的人物是否是滑雪人物，须根据以下条件综合判定：

① 身体基本呈站立姿态

② 脚下有延长物

③ 体态有动感

④ 其周围的岩画是否与弓箭、狩猎有关

⑤ 岩画产生的大约年代及当时的人类生活、生产状况。

4. 分清滑雪“起源”与“发展阶段”之间的关系。

滑雪起源的研究应集中在石器时代人类与雪的关系，当时人类在茫茫的大雪面前，如何为了自身的生存去适应雪、征服雪、利用雪的尝试，如何扩大脚下支撑面积，如何从迈腿走动开始，向滑动演变。这是一个必然的漫长的发展历程。

如果研究追溯的是哪个国家地区，哪个民族首先穿起了滑雪板，这不是对滑雪起源的研究，是对滑雪起源之后发展的某一阶段的研究，两者不是同一时空的概念。

II. Establishment of the Scientific Research Thinking and Theory Guide

1. First of all, the researchers think that the place of origin of skiing must meet special basic conditions, which are the primary prerequisite for the study of the origin of skiing in an area.

Based on the functions and characteristics of ancient skiing and his personal experience and his understanding of skiing, Mr. Shan Zhaojian had completed the study on "the basic conditions that an area should meet as the origin of skiing" in 2004. Then he compared and combined these basic conditions with all conditions existing in Altay and the results of a long-term investigation of the area. From this he wrote the paper, *Altay, Xinjiang, China has met all the basic conditions for the origin of skiing* , laying the theoretical foundation for the final establishment of the theory that "Altay, Xinjiang, China is the place of origin of skiing" .

The study found that he basic conditions that existed in the origin of human skiing are fully consistent with those that exist in the origin of human skiing in Altay. (see Fig. 1-4)

1) The origin of skiing must be in the cold region (Altay has a cold climate and long winter time) .

2) The origin of skiing must be in the region where existed a big snowfall and a long period of snow (Altay area has plentiful snow and its mountain area has a long period of snow up to six months per year) .

3) The origin of skiing must be in the region where there is rich source of wood in the forest needed for making "ski tools" (Altay area has lush trees and a large area of forest cover) .

4) The origin of skiing must be in the region with plenty of mountains and hills where people could have speed ski (Altay area is full of mountains and hills normally with vast flat foot space, where a snowy forest scene appears in the winter) .

5) The origin of skiing must be in the region where the earliest human lived and skiing was very important in their winter hunting (In Altay area there are several Sites of human life in Paleolithic period and many Historic Sites. There are still three large river systems, 56 rivers, 34 kinds of wild animals and over 100 kinds of wild birds today) .

2. Human Origin of Skiing and development are inseparable from the human evolution.

The human origin of skiing started in the Stone Age when, facing to the cold snow, people could not make skis by using the stone tools due to the limitations of the human wisdom and all kinds of the conditions. What they could do was first to enlarge their feet support on snow by stepping on the branches and wood on snow, or binding branches or wood under feet to walk on snow to avoid their feet falling into snow so deep. After thousands of years of evolution, people became clever. In Altai mountain of China, they started to ski with a tool like a "hoof style ", and afterwards they could run fast in the power with "goat horns style" skis, which was a great progress. After continuous evolution, in the north of China it appeared skis called as the "Wooden Horse" and later on the skis became the modern ones using today.

Altay area, which is located in the hinterland, has the traffic block, cuts off from the outside world and develops slow, people still use fur skis today, which has a few thousands of years of history only. Therefore the evolutionary skis afterwards should not be placed in the same category with the original "ski tool".

3. Rock painting is very important

1) Since the original skis was made of wood and would be decay over the years, furthermore the origin of skiing was earlier than the formation of the characters and thousands of years ago, so now there is little archaeological materials to use for the study of the origin of skiing. But it mainly depends on the following two points to make the comprehensive judgment combining the other elements:

(1) Oral poetry, stories and narratives

(2) Rock paintings, which is very important for the archaeological research today.

2) The following points to be used to judge whether the rock paintings relate to the skiand painting figures are ski figures:

(1) Body is basically in a standing posture.

(2) There are long objects under feet.

(3) The figure is dynamic.

(4) To see if the other painting around involves any bows and hunting.

(5) To check the around age of the rock paintings and the people's life and production around the period.

4. Recognizing the relation between the "origin" and "developing period" of skiing

For the research of the origin of skiing, it should focus the relation between the people and the snow. It has been a very long period of development that facing the heavy snow by then, in order to get used to, conquer and utilize the snow for life, how people try to enlarge their feet support and move their first step, and finally they ski on the deep power. It is not the right research of the origin of skiing if you trace back to which county or region and nationality rode the skis first, which is just a research of one period of ski development after the origin of ski.

三、口传诗歌"滑雪狩猎民谣"自古就在阿勒泰大地传承

从新疆阿勒泰市汗德尕特乡乌梁海蒙古族中挖掘整理出来的口传诗歌"滑雪狩猎民谣"，自古就在阿勒泰大地上传承，其源头可追溯到古人打猎生存的岁月，呈现出阿勒泰古老滑雪狩猎文化的源远流长。该诗歌在开始部分唱道：

在那高高的阿尔泰杭盖山中，
身上背着柳木制作的弓箭，
双手斜推着滑雪棒的，
脚踩着红松、白松木制作的滑雪板，
身后拖着山羊皮囊的，
很快地滑着奔跑在松树林中的，
是那勇敢而又灵活、聪明的猎人。
看那个猎人啊……

（详见尼咏梅女士提供的《阿勒泰民间口传诗歌“滑雪狩猎民谣”源远流长》）

《滑雪狩猎民谣》把古人滑雪狩猎的环境、场景言传得十分形象，将古阿勒泰人滑雪狩猎的情景展现在我们的眼前。研究人员认定，这首口传诗歌也势必成为阿勒泰地区是人类滑雪起源地的史证。（图5）

图5　男女老幼齐唱口传诗歌

Fig. 5　Men and Women, old and young singing the oral poetry

另外，阿勒泰人从自己祖先那里一代接一代传承下来的，至今仍广泛保留着的古老的滑雪器具、古老的滑雪传统活动以及蕴涵在当地农牧民中滑雪的“传说故事”等，也都可作为辅助佐证。80余岁的老人木巴拉克，年轻时就是阿勒泰滑雪狩猎的勇士，现在身穿的狼皮大衣，头顶的狐狸皮帽子就是他当年的“猎获”（图6、图7）。

图6　穆巴拉克老人在野雪中滑行（2005年）

Fig. 6　Mr. Mubarak skiing in the field

图7　阿勒泰的少儿也会古老滑雪

Fig. 7　Altay's kid can also ski with old skis (2005)

III. "Hunters' Ditty", a Traditional Ballad, Has Been Handed Down in the Altay since Ancient Times

Recently, "Hunters' Ditty", a traditional Mongolian ballad from Wulianghai of Altay, has been found and recorded. This song has been handed down in the Altay since ancient times, and can be traced back to the hunting age of the ancient people of the area. It indicates the long and ancient culture of hunting and skiing in the Altay. The ballad begins with:

Among the high Altay Hanggai Mountains,
Willow-made bow and arrows on his back,
Inclined skiing stick is pushed with both hands,
Standing on the ski made of red pine or white pine,
Skiing quickly and smoothly in the pine forest,
Brave, agile and smart, the hunter is.
Lo, the hunter……

(It is recorded in detail in "Hunters' Ditty" —a traditional Mongolian ballad in Wulianghai of Altay organized and provided by Ms. Ni Yongmei.)

The use of skis for hunting by the ancient inhabitants has been described in "Hunters' Ditty" graphically and correctly, and gives us a vivid image of hunting with skis by the ancient Altay people. The researchers firmly thought that this traditional ballad would be a piece of historical evidence for this area of the Altay being the Original Place of Skiing. (See Fig. 5)

Moreover, the widely-shared ancient skiing implements, the age-old traditional skiing practices and the legends or stories spread among the local skiing famers and herdsmen, passed down by their ancestors from one generation to the next, can also be used as the auxiliary evidence. More than 80 years old Mubarak was a brave skiing hunter when he was young in the Altay. The wolf-fur overcoat and the fox-fur hat he wears are both gained from hunting in those days (See Fig. 6 and 7).

四、阿勒泰诸多的滑雪狩猎岩画

1. 新疆阿勒泰市敦德布拉克古老滑雪岩绘画的发现与定性

多年来，在阿勒泰地区是人类滑雪起源地的研究、考察过程中，期盼寻找到历史实证。每次去阿勒泰等地考察都想在山洞、岩石上找到滑雪形象的岩画，在沼泽地、古坟墓中找到雪具残片或重要文物…

2005 年 3 月下旬，单兆鉴持中国滑雪协会介绍信再次前往新疆阿勒泰市考察，在新疆阿勒泰市市委、市政府支持与协同下，实地考察工作获得重大突破。

新疆阿勒泰市旅游局长徐培兰对单兆鉴说：在新疆阿勒泰市汗德尕特蒙古族乡的敦德布拉克1号岩画棚内，其中有的岩画人物像似在滑雪，单兆鉴听到此消息，立即到市委宣传部，史志强提供了几张岩画照片，经仔细鉴别，初步认定是滑雪岩绘画，单兆鉴与大家心情十分兴奋（图8）

图8 一万年前的新疆阿勒泰市敦德布拉克古滑雪岩绘画

Fig. 8 Rock drawings of ancient skiing in Dundebulake in Altay City 10000 years ago.

关于阿勒泰市汗德尕特乡敦德布拉克岩棚的岩画，据称是20世纪中叶由欧吉省等三位少年偶尔发现，当时岩棚口被爬山松封闭的很隐蔽。直到21世纪初由乡政府主抓考古文化的副乡长尼咏梅正式向上报到文物部门，之后，由新疆维吾尔自治区博物馆考古专家王博、阿勒泰地区文物局专家郑颉率领人员对实地进行了考察与备案，结论如下：敦德布拉克岩棚画，在绘画的艺术风格上有些变化，显示了时代有早晚之分。从内容上看，基本上反映的都是狩猎的场面，并以围猎为主。从阿尔泰山地草原文化发展及岩棚画的情况看，它应属于旧石器时代晚期的岩棚画，距今约1-2万年，（详见《吐鲁番学研究》2005年第1期，第120-121页，王博、郑颉所撰《阿尔泰山敦德布拉克的旧石器时代晚期岩棚画》）。

单兆鉴将岩绘画照片带回到北京，向中国滑雪协会主席王揖涛、常务副主席任洪国作了汇报，聘请多名滑雪专家对敦德布拉克岩绘画中第三组人物的动作进行了鉴定分析，认为岩绘画中的人物姿势基本呈站立式，脚下有延长物，上体前倾，膝部前屈，而且动感明显，符合滑雪人的姿态要求。岩画中几个脚踏雪板，有的还手持单杆滑雪人的动作形态图像栩栩如生，属于滑雪狩猎岩绘画。岩绘画中滑雪人的姿态与阿勒泰地区至今农牧民穿用古老滑雪器具的滑雪姿态，有着惊人的相似之处。该组人物可能是多人（约10人）呈一列滑雪，也可能是一个人流线形从眼前滑向远方。

关于岩绘画的产生年代，经多位权威考古专家、历史民族学专家根据阿勒泰地区几万年前的旧石器时代中晚期就是古人类活动的区域；赞同王博先生此前对岩棚内岩画年代的划定意见；又根据和参照世界考古界对印度、欧洲同类岩绘画年代确认的常规，专家们将新疆阿勒泰市敦德布拉克滑雪岩绘画的年代确定为距今至少一万年。

这些专家们的意见详见王博先生所撰《阿勒泰是人类滑雪最早起源地探索》、王建新先生所撰《对新疆阿勒泰敦德布拉克岩画的几点认识》、刘国防先生所撰《阿勒泰地区人类早期活动的相关证据》、刘永年先生所撰《新疆阿尔泰山地域是人类滑雪起源地之一》等文稿。

敦德布拉克古滑雪岩绘画这一辉煌的考古成果，使研究工作获得了关键的史证。据现在掌握的资料，阿勒泰地区的古老滑雪岩画远不只是这一组，详见《中国·新疆·阿勒泰地区滑雪岩画的分布及旅游、考察路线图》。

2. 阿勒泰地区布尔津县滑雪狩猎岩画

布尔津滑雪狩猎岩画发现于布尔津县冲乎尔乡塔合尔吐别克，现收藏于布尔津县博物馆内。(见图 9)

3. 采自博物馆与《阿勒泰山岩画图录》的滑雪狩猎岩画（作者：鲍幸君）(见图 10–12)

图 9　布尔津县滑雪狩猎岩画

Fig. 9　Pictographs Catalog in Buerjin

图 10　滑雪狩猎岩画

Fig. 10　Pictographs Catalog of Altay Mountain

图 11　滑雪狩猎岩画

Fig. 11　Pictographs Catalog of Altay Mountain

图 12　滑雪狩猎岩画

Fig. 12　Pictographs Catalog of Altay Mountain

IV. Numerous skiing hunting rock painting in Altay

1. The Discovery and Qualitative of the Rock Drawings of Ancient Skiing in Dundebulake in Altay City.

Over the years, the researchers have been looking forward to finding some historical evidence in the process of the study and investigation of the idea that the Altay is the place of origin of skiing. Every time they went to the Altay area they wanted to find some rock drawings with ski figures in the caves as well as some ski tool debris or important cultural relics in the swamp and the ancient tombs.

In late March 2005, Mr. Shan Zhaojian went to Altay City again for his investigation with a letter of introduction issued by the Chinese Ski Association. With the assistance and support of the CPC Altay Committee and the People's Government of Altay City, the investigation made a great breakthrough. Mrs. Xu Peilan, director of the Altay Tourism Administration of Xinjiang Uygur Autonomous Region told Shan that some of the drawing figures look like skiing in Rock Cave No. 1 in Dundebulake of the autonomous Mongolian town of Handegate in Altay City. Hearing this news, Shan immediately went to the municipal Party CommitteePropaganda Department and Mr. Shi Zhiqiang offered him several rock paintings. After careful identification, they were preliminary identified as skiing rock paintings, so Shan and everyone felt excited (See Fig. 8).

About the rock paintings in the cave, which its entrance was hidden by the heavy mountain pines by then, in Dundebulake, Hadegate Town, Altay City, it is said that they were occasionally discovered by Ou Jisheng and the other two young kids in the mid twentieth Century. Until the beginning of twenty first Century, after Mrs. Ni Yongmei, the Deputy Director of the Township Government in charge of the archaeological culture, reported this formally reported to the higher department of culture relics. Mr. Wang Bo archaeological expert of Museum of the Xinjiang Uygur Autonomous Region and Mr. Zheng Jie, specialist of the Altay Administration of Cultural Relics of the Xinjiang Autonomous Region led a group to make the investigation and record on the spot. They reached the following conclusion: the rock paintings are changed somewhat in the art of painting style, showing the age earlier or later, from the content, basically reflects the hunting scene and mainly the surrounding hutting, and from the Altai upland meadow culture development and the cave painting situation, it should be the rock paintings belong to the late Paleolithic, approximately 1-2 millions of years ago. (See TURFANOLOGICAL RESEARCH, No 1. 2005, Page 120-121 and Drawings in the Rock Shelter of Late Paleolithic Age in Dundebulake of the Altay Mountains by Wang Bo and Zheng Jie.)

Mr. Shan Zhaojian brought the photos of the rock drawings to Beijing and reported to Mr. Wang Yitao, President of Chinese Ski Association and Ren Hongguo, the standing Vice President of CSA. He invited several ski experts to make analysis and identification for the position of the third group of the rock drawing figures found in Dundebulake, and they thought that the drawing figures are in the basic standing posture, wear extended object on their feet, lean forward their upper body, bent their knees and are obviously dynamic, fully complying with the attitude of skier. In the rock drawings the moving shape of several skiers is lifelike, who ride skis under their feet and some of them have single pole in their hands. They belong to the skiing and hunting painting. The postures of the figures in the rock drawings are extremely similar to those of today's farmers and herdsmen in Altay area who use the ancient style of skis. This group of characters might be many people (about 10 people) skiing in a column, or might be one person skiing from the front to the distance in a streamline shape.

As for the age of the rock drawings, a number of authoritative archeological experts and historical ethnology experts have identified the age of the rock drawings in Dundebulake of Altay City to be at least 10000 years, based on the fact that the Altay was a place where ancient human activities had occurred in the middle to late Paleolithic age tens of thousands of years ago, . the opinions of the delineation of the age of the cave rock paintings by Mr. Wang Bo, and referred to the general rules for determining the age of this kind of rock drawings used in India and Europe.

The specialists' comments on these drawings are described in detail in the articles as The Exploration of Altay as the Place of Origin of Skiing by Mr. Mr. Wang Bo, Some Understanding of the Rock Drawings in Dundebulake of Altay City by Mr. Wang Jianxin, The Relevant Evidences about the Ancient Human Activities in the Area of Altay by Mr. Liu Guofang, and Altay, Xinjiang, China Is One of the Origins of Skiing by Mr. Liu Yongnian.

This excellent archeological discovery, the rock drawings of skiing in Dundebulake of Altay City, has been presented as a key piece of historical evidence for this research work. According to the information now available, the ancient rockdrawings of skiing in the area of the Altay are much more than this group, see Tourism and Exploration Route Map of the Skiing Rock Paintings in Altay · Xinjiang · China.

2. Rock Paintings of Skiing Hunters in Buerjin County of Altay

Found in Taheertubieke of Chonghuer Township of Buerjin County and Preserved in the Museum of Buerjin County. (Fig. 9)

3. Below Photos Are Selected from Pictographs Catalog of Altay Mountain authored by Bao Xingjun（Fig. 10-12）

五、密切关注与研究国外相关信息

在研究过程中，研究人员充分注意到了国外对人类滑雪起源研究的成果与趋向。

1. 日本札幌市冬季运动博物馆内有一幅挂图，箭头表示人类滑雪从阿勒泰地方起源及向外传播的路线。此图将人类滑雪的起源地锁定在阿勒泰地方（图13）。

2. 公元前450至前400年间，希腊史学家希罗多德曾长途跋涉向东考察，其到达的终点可能是阿尔泰山系的西缘，他所描述的当时“看守黄金”和“有山羊脚”人的活动区域，应该在阿尔泰山系以南，自古就是黄金产地的今日的新疆阿勒泰地区。希罗多德在世界史第四卷中对滑雪有这样一段记载：“住在阿勒泰地区的人们，拥有山羊脚（编者注：指当时的山羊脚式滑雪板或雪踏），冬季在雪中奔跑”，此文乃是世界上至今为止有关滑雪最早的文字记载。与中国史书《山海经》对古阿勒泰丁零族滑雪的描述基本吻合。

图13　日本札幌市冬季运动博物馆滑雪起源及传播路线挂图

Fig. 13　The wall map about the origin area and spreading outward routes of skiing in the Winter Sports Museum of Sapporo, Japan.

3. 欧洲是近代、现代滑雪的发达地区。北欧与中欧对近代、现代滑雪的发展作出了卓越的贡献，多项世界滑雪运动发展过程中的“之最”，都产生于这里，挪威被誉为“滑雪运动的故乡”，奥地利则被颂为“滑雪王国”。

在关于人类滑雪起源研究方面，《大不列颠百科全书》滑雪运动条目称：在瑞典和芬兰的沼泽地带所发现的古代滑雪板，考证的年代为距今4000至5000年。挪威北部也发现了距今4500年左右的滑雪岩刻画（图14）。

上述滑雪史实发现的年代较久（如瑞典沼泽地带的古代雪板是1921年发现的），流传的范围很广，在国际滑雪界几乎是“家喻户晓”，故以往欧美等地区关于人类滑雪起源研究的盛行观点是起源于北欧。

4. 20世纪60年代，俄罗斯考古界自称其在乌尼尔山脉维斯的泥炭沼泽中，发现了距今 8000 年前制作的滑雪板残片，而且有制动器。这一考古信息虽已经历半个世纪，但人们仍很陌生，尚没有得到普遍传播与公认。

图 14　挪威北部山洞内的滑雪岩刻画

Fig. 14　A skiing petroglyph in a mountain cave in northern Norway

苏联 1980 年《滑雪运动教科书》第一章滑雪运动史中称，“滑雪是人类为了生存，在雪中作为代步工具逐渐发展起来的。最早的滑雪板是在哪个区域先出现，准确地讲，还没有定论。但普遍公认的最早采用滑雪板作为代步工具的是生活在西伯利亚地区从贝加尔湖到阿勒泰地区的人们，随着人类的迁移，扩展到阿拉斯加东部、日本和斯堪的纳维亚半岛西部与西北部，直到欧洲中部”。（2004 年 12 月 17 日 张玉绮供稿）

5. 美藉老华人李臻吾先生曾致信单兆鉴先生，信中概要地介绍了美国滑雪界对人类滑雪起源的普遍观点，认为滑雪的历史超过 5000 年，并介绍了北欧早期滑雪的信息。

6. 美国滑雪文化与历史研究学者尼尔·拉尔森（NILS LARSEN）先生，对中国新疆阿勒泰的古老滑雪文化及滑雪起源很感兴趣。他的团队曾连续多年来到阿勒泰喀纳斯、禾木地域进行了广泛而深入的访问和考察，对古老毛皮滑雪板的历史、制作程序、功能进行了认真研究，对当地居民古老滑雪文化进行了录制，并刻成光盘《永远的阿勒泰滑雪人》，在其国内宣传。

尼尔森先生介绍说：在 1890 年，挪威著名的滑雪爱好者和探险家弗里德约夫·南森（FRIDTJOT NANSEN）撰文说滑雪运动很可能起源于东方。他绘制了一幅图，图上显示所有滑雪的根词都来自中亚中心地区。

尼尔森先生认为“目前有很多证据证明滑雪可能起源于一万年以前”“阿勒泰地区可能是许多古老语言和文化发展的中心”，尼尔森认为“通过对旧石器中石器时代文化、古代语言、旧石器时代考证和考古学的认真研究，可以形成一个清晰的有关滑雪起源的线索。滑雪事实上是人类一项非常古老的技术，它使得远古时期的猎人得以在冬季恶劣的气候条件下扩大自己的活动范围”。尼尔森先生撰写的《永远的阿勒泰滑雪人》对喀纳斯、禾木地区的古老滑雪文化做了深刻而有趣的描述。

对新疆阿勒泰市敦德布拉克岩绘画，尼尔森先生是这样描述的：“位于山丘下的小山洞岩顶上画的人物应该是滑雪者。”

尼尔森先生讲道“单兆鉴是中国优秀的滑雪历史学家，我在 2006 年夏天来北京时与他见了面。那时，他邀请我于 2007 年 1 月前往新疆阿勒泰市参加了滑雪节。单先生致力于研究推广中国的滑雪历史，并认为人类滑雪起源于中国的阿勒泰山区。世界上很多国家都声称是人类滑雪起源地，中国也是其中之一。滑雪起源于中国的说法可能是正确的”。

7. 研究伊始就注意到蒙古国、俄罗斯、哈萨克斯坦也有称呼近似“阿勒泰”的地方，与中国新疆的阿勒泰地区同属一个大地域概念，据了解，那些区域也有同中国阿勒泰地区相似的古老毛皮滑雪板，滑雪的历史也很久远。

但随着人类滑雪起源研究工作的深入，阿尔泰山脉南麓富饶的中国广大阿勒泰地区，逐渐彰显出人类滑雪最早起源地的多项不可撼动的论据和史证，确立了中国新疆阿勒泰地区是至今为止人类滑雪最早起源地的稳定地位。（参见本文“结束语”部分）

V. Close Attention to and Study on the Relevant Information Abroad.

In the investigative process, the researchers have paid close attention to the research results and trends on the study of origin of skiing abroad.

1. There is a wall map in the Winter Sports Museum of Sapporo, Japan, in which the arrows indicate the routes of the human ski spreading outward from the origin in Altay area. This map will lock the origin of human skiing in Altay area (See Fig. 13) .

2. 450 B. C. to 400 B. C. Herodotus, a Greek historian, traveled a long distance eastward on an exploratory journey and might have reached the terminus of the western edge of the Altai Mountains. What activities he described as “the men who guarded gold and worn goat horns” at that time should be the gold producing area to the south of Altai Mountains, which is now located in the area of Altay, Xinjiang. In the 4th volume of The Histories by Herodotus, there is a paragraph describing skiing as: “the people in the area of Altay have goat-like feet (the editors’ notes: it meansskiing shoes or skis) and run in snow in winter” . These words are the earliest literal report about skiing in the world, and basically identical to the description that the ancient Dingling people skied in A Chinese Bestiary, a history book in China.

3. Europe is the most flourishing area of skiing in the modern and contemporary ages. Northern Europe and Middle Europe have made great contributions to the development of skiing in the modern and contemporary ages. Many “Bests” in the development of skiing were created here. Norway is praised as “The Homeland of Skiing” while Austria is lauded as “The Kingdom of Skiing”.

In the aspect of the study on the origin of skiing, the article on skiing in *Encyclopedia of Britannica* reads as: the ancient skis found in the boglands in Sweden and Finland was traced back to 4000-5000 years ago through the textual research. In northern

Norway, petroglyphs of skiing, which were engraved in rock around 4500 years ago, were also found (See Fig. 14).

The above historical facts of skiing found a long time ago (e. g. the ancient ski was found in the swampland in Sweden in 1921), were spread widely and well known in the world of international skiing, so the popular view is that skiing originated in northern Europe.

4. In 1960s, the archeological community of Russia declared that they had found some remains of skis made 8000 years ago, including brake in the peat swampland in Vesh near the Urals. This archeological information has been published for half a century but it is still unknown to people and has not been widely spread or generally accepted as yet.

In 1980, in Chapter 1 (History of Skiing) of the Textbook for Skiing printed by the previous SU, it reads "skis gradually developed as a substitute from a walking tool on snow when human beings struggled for survival. Precisely speaking, where the earliest ski comes from has not been decided. However, it is generally accepted that the earliest ski used as a tool for walking was made by people who lived in the area from Lake Baikal to the Altay in Siberia, and spread to eastern Alaska, to Japan, to the west and northwest of the Scandinavian Peninsula, and to the Central Europe, with the migration of people". (Provided by Mr. Zhang Yuqi on December 17, 2004).

5. Mr. Li Zhenwu, an American citizen of Chinese descent, had written to Mr. Shan Zhaojian to summarily introduce the view about the origin of skiing widely accepted by American ski circle that skiing has a history of more than 5000 years and presented some information about skiing in the early period of North Europe.

6. Mr. Nils Larsen, American researcher of ski culture and history, is very interested in the ancient skiing culture of Altay, Xinjiang of China and the origin of skiing. His group has visited Kanas and Heben in Altay for many years to carry out a deep investigation, and conducted some research on the history, the construction and the functions of the ancient fur skis, and also has made a DVD on the ancient skiing culture of the local residents, named The Timeless Skiers of Altay for popularization in USA.

He stated: in 1890, a famous Norway skier and adventurer named is Fridtjof Nansen once wrote that the skiing possibly originates the East. He illustrated a picture, showing that all the original root words for 'skiing' come from Central Asia.

Mr. Larsen believes that "so far, lots of evidence indicates that skiing might originate at least 10000 years ago and the Altay area might be the center of the development of various ancient languages and cultures. He believes that " based on the careful study of Paleolithic-Mesolithic cultures and Mesolithic culture, ancient languages, Paleolithic textual research and archaeology, a clear clues about the origin of ski can be formed. As a matter of fact, ski is a very old technology which allowed the remote ancient hunters to enlarge their scope of activities under the bad climate conditions in winter" . Mr. Larsen's The Timeless Skiers of Altay has made deep and interesting description to the ancient ski cultural of the Kanas and Hemu area.

"The painting figures on the rocks in the cave located in the hills could be skiers", Mr. Larsen says about the rock drawings in Dundebulake in Altay.

7. Ever since the beginning of the research, it has been noted that some places in Mongolia, Russia and Kazakhstan are similarly called "Altay" and belong to the same area of the greater region as that of Altay, Xinjiang. It is said that there are ancient fur skis found in these areas that are similar to those found in the area of Altay, Xinjiang, showing that skiing in this region has a very long history.

However, with the deepening study on the origin of skiing, the wide and richly-endowed Altay area at the southern foot of the Altai Mountains has been clearly seen as the earliest area for the origin of skiing due to the amount of irrefutable evidence and reasons given, so far it has established the stable status that Altay region, Xinjiang, China is the earliest human skiing origin. (See "conclusion" part of this paper).

六、《阿勒泰宣言》的形成

"中国新疆阿勒泰地区是人类滑雪起源地学说"于1993年提出后，并没有引起有关方面的注意，研究工作只是在局部阶段性地进行着。进入21世纪之后，随着研究、考察步伐节奏加快，情况有所好转。世纪之初，中国滑雪协会秘书长田有年等人员前往新疆阿勒泰市考察，将滑雪起源地研究的信息带去，引起新疆阿勒泰市市委、市政府的重视，新疆阿勒泰市市委宣传部的史志强先生撰写了当地第一篇有关滑雪起源研究的新闻报导稿，刊于2002年1月份《阿勒泰日报》上。

时任新疆阿勒泰市市委主管副书记巴合提·布兰拜积极组织和配合考察活动，亲自参与古老滑雪文化的考察工作。

单兆鉴根据研究工作的进展，于2005年底，在主、客观条件日趋成熟的情况下，抓住时机，完成了中国新疆阿勒泰地域是人类滑雪最早起源地的《阿勒泰宣言》的起草工作。与此同时，考古专家王博先生率先进入角色，推动了研究工作的进程。

2006年1月中旬，滑雪、考古等多领域学科研究专家聚集新疆阿勒泰市金桥饭店，组成专家组，组长是单兆鉴（来自中国滑雪协会，滑雪专家），成员有王博（来自新疆维吾尔自治区博物馆，考古专家）、王建新（来自中国西北大学，考古专家）、吕恩国（来自新疆维吾尔自治区考古研究所，考古专家）、刘国防（来自新疆社会科学院，民族历史学家）、鲁礼鹏（来自新疆维吾尔自治区博物馆，考古专家）、郑颉（来自阿勒泰地区文物局，文物研究专家）及因病缺席的刘永年（来自吉林省体委，滑雪历史研究学者）。

专家研讨会于1月15日至1月16日两天内，先后采取封闭式与大会开放式两种方式进行。始终围绕《阿勒泰宣言》草案的核心内容：1）阿勒泰地区是否具有人类早期滑雪起源的基本条件；2）国外对人类滑雪起源的研究动向及成果；3）敦德布拉克岩绘画中人物的动作形象是不是滑雪及其产生年代认定的根据；4）对当代阿勒泰地区古老滑雪传统的印记等进行了科学的逐条逐字的讨论、审议、论证。

1月16日，正式举行公开研讨大会，除专家外，新疆阿勒泰市领导及相关部门、媒体单位等参加。会议由市委副书记刘新利与单兆鉴先后主持。与会专家发言踊跃，会场气氛严肃而热烈，多数专家提前准备了文字发言稿或幻灯片，进行宣讲与演示，最终通过了《阿勒泰宣言》，专家们当场在修改后的《阿勒泰宣言》稿上签字（刘永年因病缺席，由单兆鉴代签）（图15、图16）。单兆鉴在研讨大会的最后代表专家组宣读了“中国新疆阿勒泰地区是世界滑雪最早起源地”的《阿勒泰宣言》。见《阿勒泰宣言》和《阿勒泰宣言专家组成员简介》。

图15　专家们在《阿勒泰宣言》上签字

Fig. 15　Experts sign the *Altay Declaration*

图 16 《阿勒泰宣言》专家组成员签名

Fig. 16 Brief Introduction to the Members of Expert Group of Altay Declaration Shan Zaojian, Wang Bo, Lv Enguo, Wang Jianxin, Liu Yongnian, Lu Lipeng, Liu Guofang & Zheng Jie

《阿勒泰宣言》

中国新疆阿勒泰地区是世界滑雪最早的起源地

(2006 年 1 月 16 日于新疆阿勒泰市)

(2006 年 12 月 15 日于北京人民大会堂)

我们是相关学科的研究人员，经过认真的考察和研究，今天我们聚集在新疆阿勒泰市向世人郑重宣布：中国新疆阿勒泰地区是世界滑雪最早的起源地。其根据如下：

一、阿勒泰地区具备了滑雪起源的一切自然与人类活动的基本条件。

二、国内外已有学者指出，阿勒泰地区最先开始了人类滑雪活动，并逐渐向斯堪的纳维亚、阿拉斯加等地传播。

三、经过对阿勒泰地区实地考察发现，古人在洞穴中彩绘的人物滑雪图像，证实古阿勒泰人早在距今一万年左右就已开始了滑雪活动。

四、虽经漫长的时代变迁，现阿勒泰居民仍广泛沿袭脚踏自制的“毛皮滑雪板”、手持单只木杆在雪地里滑行的古老传统。

我们将在更广泛的领域中进行深入的考察和研究，使“中国新疆阿勒泰地区是世界滑雪最早的起源地”学说，得到国内外普遍认同并广泛传播。

……

当晚在新疆阿勒泰市举行了隆重的庆贺酒会，专家们被授予“新疆阿勒泰市荣誉市民”。

《阿勒泰宣言》宣布后，在阿勒泰及新疆引起强烈反响，主要媒体纷纷报导、评论，掀起了一个宣传的高潮。

中国滑雪协会秘书长田有年先生以书法方式抄写了《阿勒泰宣言》全稿。

目前《阿勒泰宣言》已译成英文、俄文、蒙古国家文，并配上附图，为境外朋友们阅读、研究提供方便。

VI. Formation of Altay Declaration

After the theory that “Altay, Xinjiang, China is the place of origin of skiing” was first put forward in 1993, it had not been noted by relevant authorities and the research work was done partially and periodically only. After entering the 21st century, the situation has improved with the accelerating pace of the study and investigation. At the beginning of the 21st century, Mr. Tian Younian, the Secretary General of the Chinese Ski Association and others went to Altay City for investigation and brought some information about the study on original place of skiing, which got the attention of the CPC Altay Committee and People’s Government of Altay City. Mr. Shi Zhiqiang from the CPC Department of Altay City wrote the first news report of the origin of skiing, which was published on Altay Daily issued in January 2002.

Mr. Baheti Bulanbai, the Deputy Secretary of the CPC Altay Committee at that time, actively organize and cooperate with the research activities, attending the research of ancient skiing culture personally.

According to the progress of the research work, Mr. Shan Zhaojian took the opportunity that the subjective and objective conditions were gradually fledged to complete the draft of the Altay Declaration, stating that “Altay, Xinjiang, China is the place of origin of skiing” at the end of 2005. At the same time, Mr. Wang Bo, an archeologist, first got involved in the project and pushed the development of the research work.

In the middle January 2006, specialists from ski, archaeology and other scientific fields gathered in Jinqiao Hotel in Altay City and formed an expert group. Mr. Shan Zhaojian, the group leader (expert from the Chinese Ski Association), Mr. Wang Bo, the member (archaeologist from Museum of the Xinjiang Uygur Autonomous Region), Mr. Wang Jianxin, the member (archaeologist from China Northwest University), Mr. Lü Enguo, the member (archaeologist from the Institute of Archaeology of Xinjiang Uygur

Autonomous Region), Mr. Liu Guofang, the member (national historian form Xinjiang Academy of Social Sciences), Mr. Lu Lipeng, the member (archaeologist the Museum of the Xinjiang Uygur Autonomous Region), Mr. Zheng Jie, the member (s cultural relics research expert from the Altay Administration of Cultural Relics of the Xinjiang Autonomous Region), and Mr. LiuYongnian (skiing history scholar from the Physical and Culture Sports Commission of Jilin Province) who was absent due to illness.

On January 15 and 16, 2006, the charrette was held in both closed and open way, its core content focusing on the draft of Altay Declaration, such as:

1. Whether basic conditions needed for the origin of ancient skiing exist in Altay.

2. The research trends and achievements of the origin of skiing had been made abroad.

3. If the motion or posture of the rock painting figures in Dundebulake are skiing style and the foundation is taken for identifying its age.

4. The marks of the ancient skiing tradition in today's Altay were discussed, examined and argued word by word in details.

The open symposium was held on January 16, 2006, which besides the specialists, the leaders of Altay City, departments concerned and media etc. attended. The meeting was in a serious and warm atmosphere, presided over by Mr. Liu Xinli, the Deputy Secretary of Altay City, and Mr. Shan Zhaojian successively, during which, the specialists spoke enthusiastically and most of them wrote their speeches and prepared their slides beforehand to present, and finally Altay Declaration was adopted and signed by all the specialists on the spot (Mr. Shan Zhaojian signed on behalf of Mr. Liu Yongnian because of his absence due to illness) (See Fig. 15、16) At the end of the meeting, on behalf of the Expert Group Mr. Shan Zhaojian read the Altay Declaration stating that "Altay, Xinjiang, China is the place of origin of skiing" . See Altay Declaration and Brief Introduction to the Members of the Expert Group of the Altay Declaration.

Altay Declaration

Altay Prefecture in Xinjiang Uyghur Autonomous
Region of China is the World's Original Place of Skiing

(Issued on Jan. 16th, 2006 in Altay)

(Dec. 15th, 2006 at the Great Hall of the People in Beijing)

We, the undersigned are researchers in relevant disciplines. With careful investigation and research, we solemnly announce here in Altay City that Altay Prefecture in

Xinjiang Uyghur Autonomous Region of China is the world's Original Place of Skiing, based on the following facts:

1. Altay Prefecture satisfies the basic natural conditions needed for the human activities and the origination of skiing.

2. Some scholars both at home and abroad have pointed out that it is in Altay Prefecture that skiing originated and that skiing later spread to Scandinavia, Greater Europe and North America.

3. In the field surveys conducted in Altay Prefecture we have discovered colorful pictures of people skiing painted on the cave walls, proving that the ancient people in this region started skiing as early as about ten thousand years ago.

4. Over this long period of time, native residents in Altay Prefecture still carry on the old traditions of skiing with a pair of hand-made skis attached to their boots and a single wooden pole in hand.

On that evening, a grand celebration reception was held in Aletai City, Xinjiang, and the experts have been awarded the "Honorary Citizen of Altay".

After Altay Declaration was announced, strong response was caused in Altay and Xinjiang, and a publicity climax was launched with the reports and comments given by the major media.

Mr. Tian Younian, the Secretary General of China Ski Association has transcribed the whole Altay Declartion in calligraphy.

At present, Altay Declaration has been translated into English, Russian and Mongolian and attached with photographs for the convenience to the foreign people and the research work.

七、"新疆阿勒泰是人类滑雪最早的起源地"得到"上海大世界基尼斯总部"的认证

2007年1月，新疆阿勒泰是人类最早的滑雪起源地得到"上海大世界基尼斯总部"的认证，认证的起源时间为距今1万年至2万年前，并向新疆阿勒泰市颁发了《最早的滑雪起源地——新疆阿勒泰》的纪录证书，新疆阿勒泰市市长哈德穆·热合木拜接领"大世界基尼斯总部的认证书"（图17、图18）。2008年1月此认证项目又荣获"第十届大世界基尼斯最佳项目奖"。见本书"大世界基尼斯总部"认证书。

图 17 新疆阿勒泰市市长哈德穆·热哈木拜接领“大世界基尼斯总部认证书”

Fig. 17 Hademu Rehemubai, the Mayor of Altay City, accepting “the Best Prize” certificate issued by Big-World Guinness Record of Shanghai.

图 18 大世界基尼斯之最认证书

Fig. 18 Shanghai Great World Guinness Record Certificate

VII. “Altay, Xinjiang, China Is the Place of Origin of Skiing” Certificated by “The World Guinness Record of Shanghai”.

In January 2007, “Altay, Xinjiang, China is the place of origin of skiing” was certificated by “The World Guinness Record of Shanghai”. The certificated time is 10000 to 20000 years ago, and the certificate was issued to Altay City. Hademu Rehemubai, the Mayor of Altay City, accepted the certificate (see Fig. 17 and 18) In January 2008, the certificate was awarded “The Best Item of the 10th World Guinness Record” (See The Certificate for World Guinness Awarded by Shanghai World Guinness).

八、保护、弘扬阿勒泰古老滑雪传统文化成效显著

在阿勒泰地区是人类滑雪起源地的考察研究过程中，同时也推进了该地区古老滑雪文化的保护、弘扬与传承工作。

1. 阿勒泰人古老的毛皮滑雪板及其配套的滑雪器具经过世世代代的传承，一直保留到今日，已成为阿勒泰人滑雪的宝贵历史文化遗产。

为了使这一滑雪历史遗产能长久原貌般地保存下去，研究人员在广泛调查与测量的前提下，应时地制定了《当今阿勒泰古老毛皮滑雪板及其他配套器具的规范》。

2. 使用自制的古老滑雪器具在高山峻岭、林海雪原中滑雪行走和打猎是阿勒泰古老滑雪文化的核心，为了使这一实用滑雪的传统不至于由于现代生活对其实用需求价值的减低而“消亡”，专家们在《阿勒泰宣言》中倡议，并得到新疆阿勒泰市政府的支持，决定每年在人类滑雪起源地纪念日的1月16日在新疆阿勒泰市举办古老滑雪比赛（图19）。2006年1月15日举行了由北京冰雪游体育器材公司赞助奖品的 首届阿勒泰古老滑雪比赛，近百名农牧民踊跃参加，至今已进行了多届。该公司董事长马元常先生表示“我们企业界能够为这个重要历史活动贡献力量，深感荣幸”。

图19　阿勒泰市市委副书记巴合提·布兰拜在中国新疆阿勒泰首届古老滑雪开赛仪式上致词

Fig. 19　Baheti Bulanbai, Deputy Secretary of Altay Municipal Committee of Communist Party, delivers a speech in the opening ceremony of the first ancient skiing game.

每届比赛，阿勒泰的农牧民就像参加自己的吉庆节日，带着长长的古老毛皮滑雪板投入到古老的比赛当中，参加的人数逐届增长，参加的范围逐渐扩大，住在喀纳斯、禾木的蒙古族图瓦人也从2008年开始参加比赛，体现出比赛已经逐渐被普及。所穿用的毛皮滑雪板都是自己手工制作的。(图20-23)

图20　工匠和全家人动手自制毛皮滑雪板

Fig. 20　The family is making their hand-made fur skis for the games.

图 21 古老滑雪比赛中的奋力拼搏

Fig. 21 Competing in the traditional skiing race

图 22 阿勒泰古老弓箭

Fig. 22 Ancient bow and arrow of Altay Prefecture

图 23 比赛中拖拉的阿勒泰山羊毛皮囊

Fig. 23 The participants in race are hauling their Altay-type goat fur sleds

3. 新疆阿勒泰市政府适时组成“阿勒泰古老滑雪队”走出阿勒泰，先后到乌鲁木齐、北京、吉林市举办表演、赠送古老滑雪板等活动，扩大了影响空间。在首都北京雪场的表演引起了不小的轰动（图 24）。

2006 年第 20 届冬季奥运会与 2007 年第 6 届亚洲冬季运动会期间，中央电视台对境内外进行了广泛的宣传，引起全国滑雪界与境外同行们的关注。

图 24　新疆阿勒泰市古老滑雪队在北京表演

Fig. 24　The traditional skiing group of Altay performing in Beijing

通过这些古老的滑雪比赛和表演活动，不但保护了阿勒泰人得以自豪的古老滑雪传统文化，而且激励起阿勒泰人沿袭、传承滑雪文化遗产的自觉精神，呼唤起他们对祖先滑雪狩猎的追溯与敬仰。在弘扬古老滑雪传统的同时，自身也获得了健康的体魄，陶冶了情操，丰富了生活。

新疆乌鲁木齐市晚报旅游专业记者周磊所撰写的新闻稿汇集《一幅阿勒泰古老毛皮滑雪板的诞生及其与现代滑雪板的对比》，对制作古老毛皮滑雪板的程序以及古老滑雪比赛、活动从媒体的视角做了生动的描述，收到很好的宣传效果。

VIII. Remarkable Achievements Made in the Protection and Promotion of the Ancient Traditional Skiing Culture in Altay.

In the process of study on "Altay, Xinjiang is the place of origin of skiing", the protection, development and inheritance of the traditional skiing culture have been promoted in this area at the same time.

1. The ancient fur skis and its matching tools are passed down by the Altay people from generation to generation, having been kept until now, and have become a valuable part of the historical and cultural heritage of skiing for the Altay people.

In order to pass down the historical legacy of this skiing culture forever, researchers have established Current Standards for Altay Ancient Fur Skis and the Accessories in time, based on their extensive investigation and measurements.

2. It is the core of the ancient skiing culture of Altay that people took their self-made classical skiing tools to ride and hunt in the high mountains and on the deep snow. In order to avoid the disappearance of this practical skiing tradition due to the decrease in its application in modern life, in the Altay Declaration, the specialists proposed to hold the Oldest Ski Race on each January 16 the Memorial Day of the Origin of Skiing, which was supported by Altay Municipal Government. (Fig. 19) On January 15, 2006, the first Oldest Ski Race was held in Altay, with the prizes sponsored by Beijing Bingxueyou Sports Ltd. and nearly 100 farmers or herdsmen actively participated in the race. Until now, the Race has been held

many times. Mr. Ma Yuanchang, the board chairman of the company, said: "we are deeply honored to make a contribution to this important historical activity".

For each traditional ski race, the farmers and herdsmen in Altay take it as their happy festival and participate the race with their long old fur skis. The number of the participants increases every year and th range of the participates expands gradually. Since 2008, the Mongolia tribe Tuwa people in Kanas and Hemu have taken part in the Race, reflecting the game gradually popular. All of the fur skis are hand made. (See Fig. 20, 21, 22 and 23)

3. The Government of Altay City organized "Altay Traditional Skiing Team" at the right moment, who walked out of Altay to make the demonstrations and presented old skis in Urumqi, Beijing and Jilin, expanding its impact. The demonstrations the team made in Beijing ski resorts caused not a small sensation (See Fig. 24).

During the 20th Winter Olympic Games in 2006 and the 6th Asian Winter Games in 2007, CCTV carried out a wide promotion of Altay ancient skiing both at home and aboard, attracted the attention of both the whole national skiing circles and abroad.

Through the traditional skiing races and performances, it has not only protected the ancient skiing culture with the pride of Altay people, but also encouraged the Altay people's conscious spirit to maintain and pass down the skiing culture heritage and aroused their traceability and admiration to the their ancestors' hunting and skiing. People have gained their healthy bodies, cultivated their temperaments and enriched their life while they have carried forward the traditional skiing culture.

The new release collection-*Birth of a Pair of Altay Ancient Skis and Its Comparison with the Modern Skis* written by Miss Zhou Lei, tourism professional journalist of Urumqi Evening News, Xinjiang, with her view of journalist, have vividly described the process of making the ancient fur skis, oldest ski race and relevant skiing activities, which has got a very effective propaganda.

九、北京人民大会堂新闻发布会

经过新疆阿勒泰市积极主动地工作和中国滑雪协会大力支持，“中国·新疆·阿勒泰是人类滑雪最早起源地新闻发布会”于2006年12月15日在北京人民大会堂隆重举行。发布会由新疆维吾尔自治区博物馆、西北大学两个单位联合发布，新疆阿勒泰市人民政府、中国滑雪协会为主办单位。

图 25　中国·新疆·阿勒泰是人类滑雪最早起源地新闻发布会图片

Fig. 25　the Press Conference of " Human Skiing Originated in Altay, Xinjiang, China"

来自国家体育总局冬季运动管理中心、中国滑雪协会、国家旅游局、中国体育博物馆、新疆维吾尔自治区旅游局、体育局、新疆维吾尔自治区博物馆、中国西北大学等单位的领导或代表以及首都近百家媒体和40多家旅行社、旅游企业参加了这场新闻发布会。新疆阿勒泰市市委副书记刘新利主持会议，新疆阿勒泰市市委书记李新民在会上致辞，中国滑雪协会主席王揖涛等多部门领导在发布会上讲话。

单兆鉴、王博、王建新、刘国防四位专家从不同角度先后在发布会上作了专题发言，从不同学科严谨地论述了中国新疆阿勒泰地区是人类滑雪最早起源地的证据。

单兆鉴在发言中首先介绍了阿勒泰是人类滑雪起源地研究、考察的历程。着重阐述了阿勒泰地区的自然条件、历史人文条件都符合了人类滑雪起源的基本条件，解答了新疆阿勒泰市敦德布拉克滑雪岩绘画被鉴定为是滑雪人形态的依据，还谈到阿勒泰所具备的滑雪起源的基本条件与古滑雪岩绘画的发现，显示出人类滑雪最早起源于阿勒泰地区有其必然性。

王博先生发言中结合人类滑雪起源应具备的五项基本条件进行了深入的多视角分析，认为阿勒泰是人类滑雪最早起源地是有其内在因素的。敦德布拉克滑雪岩绘画是距今1-2万年前阿勒泰旧石器时代晚期居民的作品，是滑雪狩猎图。滑雪狩猎表现了当时人类的生产方式。

王博先生还指出，敦德布拉克滑雪岩绘画也是目前我们所知世界上最早的滑雪狩猎场面的考古资料，这为滑雪起源于阿勒泰地区提供了可靠的理论根据与考古证据。

王建新先生发言中分析阿勒泰敦德布拉克岩绘画从岩绘的形式、内容和绘制场所等情况看，与欧洲和印度旧时器时代晚期的岩绘基本相同，而岩绘较岩刻产生的年代要久远，故敦德布拉克岩绘的年代应属距今1万年以前。在阿尔泰山南北两侧都发现了不少旧时期时代晚期的遗存，这也为我们提供了重要的旁证资料。

王建新进一步分析到滑雪开始于阿尔泰山南麓的可能性更大，因为到了寒冷的冬季，人们主要选择避风向阳的阿尔泰山南麓生活，这是适应环境的一种非常自然的选择。

刘国防先生发言中指出：境外多国科学家的研究结论是“古中亚群体是欧亚大陆上最古老的人类群体”“阿尔泰山地区是地球上人类向亚洲大陆北部和东部移动的远古中心之一”。所以，我们有理由认为，阿勒泰地区至少从旧石器时代中晚期，就有人类活动了。

刘国防先生还谈到语言学家的研究，表明欧亚大陆的许多地方的人群的语言同属于阿勒泰语系，该语系横跨欧亚……这种现象是人类迁徙和语言借代的结果，这与欧亚大陆人类迁徙的学说大略一致。

刘永年先生在1994年所撰的文章结论中指出：“可以有理、有据地说，中国新疆阿尔泰山脉一带的丁零族是中国开展滑雪活动最早的民族，也是人类滑雪活动的最早的地区之一”。

发布会上单兆鉴代表专家组庄重宣读了《阿勒泰宣言》。

图26 发布会中重点发言者

Fig. 26 Main Speakers at the Conference

发布会期间，专家与领导回答了记者的重要提问。新疆阿勒泰市政府向中国滑雪协会、中国奥林匹克博物馆等部门赠送了阿勒泰古老毛皮滑雪板及古老单木竿滑雪杖（图27）。

图 27　向中国奥林匹克博物馆赠送古老滑雪板

Fig. 27　Presenting old skis to the China Olympic Museum.

参加新闻发布会的领导、专家及工作人员会后仍沉醉在喜悦之中，高兴地聚在一起合影留念（图 28），中国滑雪历史又开启了令全国滑雪界的朋友们骄傲的新篇章！

图 28　参加发布会的领导、专家及工作人员的合照

Fig. 28　Team picture for all leaders, experts and workers for the conference.

VI. Press Conference at the Great Hall of the People in Beijing

With the active and effective work of Altay City and the great support of Chinese Skiing Association, the Press Conference of " Human Skiing Originated in Altay, Xinjiang, China" was held ceremoniously in the Great Hall of the People in Beijing on December 16, 2006. It was sponsored by Altay People's Government, Xinjiang and the Chinese Skiing Association and jointly released by Xinjiang Uygur Autonomous Region Museum and Northwest University

Leaders and representatives from the Winter Sport Management Center of China General Sport Administration, Chinese Skiing Association, China National Tourism Administration, China Sports Museum, Tourism Bureau and Sports Bureauof Xinjiang Uygur Autonomous Region, Xinjiang Uygur Autonomous Region Museum and Northwest University as well as a hundred capital media units, over 40 travel services and enterprises attended the conference. Mr. Liu Xinli, Deputy Secretary of Altay City Party Committee presided at the conference, Mr. Li Xinmin, Secretary of Altay City Party Committee addressed the conference and Mr. Wang Yitao, Chairman of the Chinese Skiing Association and some others made their speeches at the conference.

Mr. Shan Zhaojian, Mr. Wang Bo, Mr. Wang Jianxin and Mr. Liu Guofang, four experts made their presentations on different specific topics respectively, critically discoursing the evidence of that Altay of Xinjiang, China is the origin of human skiing from different disciplines.

Mr. Shan Zhaojian first introduced his research process of thatAltay is the origin of human skiing in his presentation, stressing that the natural conditions and historical and humanistic conditions are all in line with the basic conditions for the origin of human skiing. He explained the evidence for identifying the rock paintings in Dundebulak in Altay as the skiing postures and mentioned that the basic conditions for the origin of skiing existing in Altay and the founding of the old skiing rock paintings shows it has the inevitability for Altay to be the origin of human skiing.

Mr. Wang Bo gave a deep and multi view analysis of the five basic conditions needed for the origin of human skiing in his presentation, believing that it has the inherent factors that Altay is the birthplace of skiing. The rock paintings in Dundebulak were made by inhabitants of Altay area in the late stage of the Paleolithic Age, ten thousand to twenty thousand years ago. They belong to the paintings of skiing and hunting and depicted the people's way of life at that time.

Mr. Wang Bo also pointed out that the rock paintings in Dundebulak are the earliest archeological materials of skiing and hunting in the world we know so far, giving us reliable theoretical basis and archeological evidence for that the birth of skiing is in Altay of Xinjiang.

Mr. Wang Jianxin analyzed in his speech that the rock paintings in Dundebulak are basically the same as the Paleolithic rock paintings in Europe and India in their form, content and drawing places, but the rock paintings would be much earlier than the rock carvings, so the rock paintings in Dundebulak should be ten thousand years ago. A lot of relics from the late stage ofthe Old Stone Age found on the southern and northern sides of the Altai Mountains also provide us with important evidences.

Wang Jianxin gave a further analysis that skiing had a strong probability to originate in the southern slopes of the Altai Mountains. It was natural for the dwellers to choose such wind sheltered and sun exposed location to live in the frigid winters.

Mr. Liu Guofang pointed out in his speech that many foreign scientists' research conclusion is "ancient Central Asia Group is the oldest human group on the Eurasian Continent ", and " the Altai Mountains was one of the ancient centers for humans to migrate to the north and east of the Asian continent on the earth. Hence, we had grounds to believe at least as far as the middle and late stage of the Old Stone Age, that humans have lived in Altay of Xinjiang.

By referring to the research of linguists, he also said many languages in the Eurasian continent belonged to the Altaic language family and noted that this language family had crossed the continent, the language transfer the result of human migration. This aligns with the theory of human migration on the Eurasian continent.

By referring to the research of linguists, he also said many languages in the Eurasian continent belonged to the Altaic language family and noted that this language family had crossed the continent, the language transfer the result of human migration. This aligns with the theory of human migration on the Eurasian continent.

At the conference, Mr. Shan Zhaojian, as a representative of the expert's team, solemnly announced the *Altay Declaration.*

Mr. Liu Guofang pointed out in his speech that many foreign scientists' research conclusion is "ancient Central Asia Group is the oldest human group on the Eurasian Continent ", and " the Altai Mountains was one of the ancient centers for humans to migrate to the north and east of the Asian continent on the earth. Hence, we had grounds to believe at least as far as the middle and late stage of the Old Stone Age, that humans have lived in Altay of Xinjiang. (Fig. 27)

Full of joy, the leaders, experts and staff of the conference got together for a group photo (See Fig. 28), and China's ski history started a new chapter, making China's skiers both excited and proud.

十、得到国际滑雪指导员联合会的认同和表彰

2010 年 3 月 5 日，在《人类滑雪起源地——中国 · 新疆 · 阿勒泰》即将出版之前，国际滑雪指导员联合会主席克里斯蒂安 · 阿姆特曼先生及国际雪联高级顾问艾尔文 · 施特勒克先生在北京共同亲自向该书主编、《阿勒泰宣言》的主起草人单兆鉴颁发了特制奖牌（图 29、图 30），表彰 “单兆鉴对世界滑雪运动作出贡献”，这既是对单兆鉴 60 余年在中国滑雪运动的不同时期、诸多领域努力工作的鼓励，更是对 “人类滑雪起源于中国新疆阿勒泰地区” 研究的赞许和认同。

图 29　单兆鉴接领国际滑雪组织颁发的特制奖牌

Fig. 29　Mr. Shan Zhaojian (middle) receiving the Award given by international skiing organization

图 30　单兆鉴荣获的奖牌

Fig. 30　Medal won by Mr. Shan Zhaojian

主席克里斯蒂安 · 阿姆特曼先生和艾尔文 · 施特勒克先生代表联合会颁发了这一具有重大历史意义的奖牌。表彰单兆鉴为中国滑雪事业所做的出色工作及对中国新疆阿勒泰地区是人类滑雪最早起源地的研究成果。现场上百名中国滑雪产业各领域的精英人士报以热烈的掌声。

X. Identification and Recognition by the International Ski Instructors Association

At the eve of the publication of this book, Mr. C. Amtmann, Chairmen of the International Ski Instructors Association, and Mr. Ervin Stricker, Senior Adviser of FIS personally issued the special medal and certificate to Mr. Shan Zhaojian (Figs. 29 and 30), the Editor of the book and the Main Drafter of the *Altay Declaration* , for his contributions to world skiing on March 5th, 2010. This shows the encouragement to Mr. Shan Zhaojian for his good work in China's skiing about 60 years, but more approval and recognition to the research of the human skiing origin in Altay, Xinjiang, China.

Mr. C. Amtmann, Chairmen of the International Ski Instructors Association, and Mr. Ervin Stricker, Senior Adviser of FIS personally issued the medal and certificate of important historical significance to Mr. Shan Zhaojian to commend his excellent work in China's skiing industry and research result of human origin of skiing in Altay, Xinjiang, China. Hundreds of elites of all fields in China's ski industry on the spot responded with warm applause.

十一、《人类滑雪起源地——中国·新疆·阿勒泰》一书的出版

《阿勒泰宣言》诞生以来，相关领域的专家并未停止深入研究的步伐，期间还得到国外专家学者的参与和支持。又经过五年策划运作，对收集的资料进行了筛选与梳理，经过严谨的编审、选图、翻译等多项工作，于 2001 年初，由（北京）人民体育出版社、新疆人民出版社共同出版了《人类滑雪起源地——中国·新疆·阿勒泰》书籍。

图 31　《人类滑雪起源地——中国·新疆·阿勒泰》封面和封底

Fig. 31　Cover and back cover of *The Original Place of Skiing—Altay Prefecture of Xinjiang, China*

该书由 23 位中外人士撰稿，主编：单兆鉴、王博。全书分为前序篇（中、英文并列）、中文篇、英文篇（其中《阿勒泰宣言》还译成俄文、蒙古国文）三个部分。该书系统、全面、科学地论述了人类滑雪起源地重大理论问题，客观介绍了境外这一领域的研究趋势与成果，并以多方面翔实史料认证了中国新疆阿勒泰地区是至今为止人类滑雪最早的起源地。

XI. *The Original Place of Skiing—Altay Prefecture of Xinjiang, China* Published

Since the birth of *Altay Declaration* , the relevant experts have never stopped the investigation and have gained the participation and support from the foreign experts in the meantime. After the researchers had made more strict editing work, *The Original Place of Skiing—Altay Prefecture of Xinjiang*, *China* was published by Beijing People's Sports Press and People's Press 5 years later at the beginning of 2001.

The book is divided in three parts, the Preface Part both in Chinese and English, Chinese Version and English Version (Altay Declaration inside is also in Russian and Khalkha Mongolian) . It discusses some major theories of the origin of skiing in a systematic, comprehensive and scientific way, objectively introduces the research trends and results in this field abroad, and supported by a variety of evidence, it certificated that Altay of Xinjiang is the original place of skiing.

十二、结束语

专家们认为，研究滑雪的起源，应紧紧依据滑雪起源的综合基本条件和丰富翔实的历史资料。基本条件体现在自然条件、当时古人的生存、生活条件及原始滑雪的特征与功能等方面。历史资料包含历史文献、流传的史诗、考古文物、岩画等。

研究人员反复地、综合地梳理、研究、分析了古阿勒泰地区的基本条件与已掌握的丰富历史资料，确认人类滑雪最早起源于该地区有其充分的依据。（详见各专家、学者的相关论文）

1. 既然古阿勒泰地区具备了滑雪起源的一切自然条件，又由于旧石器时代中晚期古人类就在这里生息繁衍，古人类出于当时的生存、生产需求，出于对雪的感悟和利用，势必会孕育和催生古滑雪的产生与起源。

2. 我国多部史书中，对北方丁零等民族不同历史时期的滑雪从不同视角做过描述和记载，国内外多位学者对这些描述和记载进行过注释与研究，其著作发表在多种学术刊物上。公元前五世纪希腊史学家希罗多德对古阿勒泰人冬季滑雪的记载是至今为止记述人类滑雪最早的文献资料。

3. 阿勒泰乌梁海蒙古族和蒙古族图瓦人中世代口传下来的民间诗歌“滑雪狩猎民谣”，生动地追述着古老滑雪狩猎的情景。

4. 至今阿勒泰广大地区仍然处于较封闭的状态，可见古阿勒泰更为封闭，因此可以认定，阿勒泰人世代传承下来的古老滑雪器具与古老滑雪方式是本地区固有的传统滑雪文化，而非外来和引进。可视为该地区滑雪文物的“活化石”。

5. 国际上关于人类滑雪起源的年代普遍约定在距今 5000 年左右。俄罗期发出了在其境内发现距今 8000 年前的滑雪板残片的信息。而中国新疆阿勒泰市敦德布拉克滑雪岩绘画的产生年代却要久远得多，被考证为距今至少 10000 年。

十余年人类滑雪起源的考察研究是一个非常漫长艰苦的过程，曾几次陷于困境，但研究人员在中国滑雪协会及新疆阿勒泰市市委、市政府的支持鼓励下，克服多方面困难，坚韧不拔，不断地纠正自身的主观片面意识，不断冲破周围各种迷信意识及以往国外研究趋向的条框束缚，科学地把研究工作坚持到最后的成功。

我们可以自豪地说："中国新疆阿勒泰地区是至今为止人类滑雪最早起源地"的论证是科学的，是经得住时间与空间的检验的！

中国滑雪协会王揖涛主席在北京新闻发布会的发言中指出："中国新疆阿勒泰是至今为止人类滑雪最早起源地这一宣言是面向世界、面向人类的……！"（详见《国家体育总局冬季运动管理中心主任、中国滑雪协会主席王揖涛在"中国·新疆·阿勒泰是人类滑雪最早起源地"新闻发布会上的讲话》）。

编者注：

① 本文的照片来自作者本人及新疆阿勒泰市市委宣传部、史志强、张亮、高扬、秋林等先生。

② 本文中提到的所有文稿将全部收集在《人类滑雪起源地—中国·新疆·阿勒泰》一书中。

XII. Conclusion

Experts think that research for skiing origin should be based upon comprehensive basic conditions and plentiful and accurate historical materials. The basic conditions are reflected in the natural conditions, the survival and living conditions of ancient peoples at that time as well as the features and functions of the original skiing. The historical materials include historical books, traditional epics and stories, archeological and cultural relics, and rock paintings.

Researchers gave a repeated and comprehensive review, research, and analysis for the basic conditions in Altay and the rich historical materials already found, and confirmed that this region was the birthplace of human skiing with a plenary basis. (Relevant papers of experts and scholars could be consulted)

1. The ancient Altay Prefecture possessed all the natural conditions for the origin of skiing and ancient humans had lived here through the middle and late stage of the Old Stone Age. The ancient humans, inspired and motivated by the abundance of snow, were bound to invent and develop the origin of skiing for their survival and livelihood.

2. Stories and records of skiing from a variety of views and datescan be found in many historical books of our country for some nationalities like the Dingling and other northern areas. Relevant stories and records had been noted and researched by a number of scholars at home and abroad. Many works has been published in a variety of scholarly issues. The description of the ancient Altay Skiing in the winter by Herodotus, a histori-

an of Greece in the fifth century B. C. , is the oldest document with a description of skiing known to date.

3. An ancient song named "Skiers and Hunters' Ditty" passed down from a middle Ages song by Wuliang Tuwa Mongolian and Wulianghai Mongolian in Altay vividly gives us a picture of the ancient scenes of skiing and hunting.

4. Until today, the wide Altay Prefecture still is a remote and isolated area. Hence, the ancient Altay could have been more remote. So, it is concluded that the ancient skiing equipment and modes are the inherent and traditional skiing culture and not foreign introductions, and can be considered a "living fossil" of the area.

5. For human's skiing, a historical age of about 5, 000 years has generally been accepted in international academic circles. And information on the discovery of some skiing relics dating back 8000 years has come out of Russia. But the rock paintings in Altay have a longer history, being at least 10, 000 years, through textual research.

The research for origin of skiing in the past ten years was a long and hard process and got into hobble several times. But researchers, with the encouragement and support from the Chinese Skiing Association and Altay City Party Committee and Altay People's Government, overcame difficulties in many aspects; constantly correcting their subjective and one-sided consciousness with courage; they continuously broke through various false beliefs and subservience to overseas research trends, and carried out their research work scientifically until their final success.

We can say with pride "Altay, Xinjiang of China is the birthplace of skiing" is scientifically verified, and will stands up to the inspection of time and space!

Mr. Wang Yitao, Chairman of Chinese Skiing Association indicated that in the speech at the conference in Beijing "the declaration that Altay, Xinjiang of China is the birthplace of skiing now faces humans all over the world…"! (See *A Speech Delivered on the Press Confrence of "Altay of Xinjiang, China is the Original Place of Skiing" by Wang Yitao–Director of the Winter Sports Management Center, China General Adiministration of Sports and Chairman of Chinesc Skiing Association on Dec. 15, 2006*)

Notes by the Editor:

① The pictures of the article are from the writer and the propaganda Department, Altay City Party Committee, Mr. Shi Zhiqiang, Mr. Zhang Liang, Mr. Qiu Ling and Mr. Gao Yang etc.

② The manuscripts mentioned in the article are all collected in the historical book " *Altay, Xinjiang of China is the original place of skiing*" .

十三、附录

美国专家尼尔·拉尔森先生参加了阿勒泰古老滑雪文化的考察和研究，撰写了考察论文报告，并自拍自编了《永远的阿勒泰滑雪人》的DVD，十分生动和有趣。(图32、图33、图34)

图32　DVD拍摄编辑者尼尔·拉尔

Fig. 32　DVD photography and edit Kanas mountains by Mr. Nils Larsen

图33　乘用马拉爬犁在哈纳斯的群山中考察拍摄

Fig. 33　Investigating and shooting in Altay by Horse Pulling Sledges

图34　尼尔·拉尔森先生（左二）与单兆鉴（左三）、阿依肯·加山（左一）、周磊在一起讨论问题

Fig. 34　Mr. Nils Larsen and Mr. Shan Zhaojian、Ayiken Jiashan、Leizhou are having a discussion

XII. Appendices

Mr Nils Larsen, an Americn expert, attended the exploration and research ofAltay ancient skiing culture and accomplished the research report. *The Timeless Skiers of the Altay* , which is filmed and compiled by himself, is very vivid and interesting. (Fig. 32、33 and 34)

4.2　挪威奥斯陆霍尔门科伦滑雪跳台与世界上最古老的滑雪博物馆——挪威最具游客吸引力的景点　Holmenkollen and the World's oldest Ski Museum——Norway's most visited tourist attraction

卡琳·博格（挪威）　Karin·Berg（NOR）

个人简介　Brief Introduction

Karin Berg has been director of the Holmenkollen Ski Museum for over 30 years. After finishing her philosophy degree, majoring in history, she worked as a research assistant at the Historical Museum/Norwegian Coin Cabinet and participated as a numismatic at archeological expeditions under stave churches. Karin has been the Ministry of Culture's representative for the project of the restoration of polarship FRAM, and has also been a part of many other committees. She has published several books about skiing and skiing history, as well as Fridtj of Nansen.

卡琳·博格，挪威，她已经在霍尔门科伦滑雪博物馆担任了超过三十年的主任一职。她在完成了历史学位后，在一家历史博物馆/挪威硬币博物馆担任研究助理，并在考古考察队中做钱币研究。在对极地船 FRAM 的修复项目中，卡琳是文化部的代表，同时她也是其他许多委员会的成员，是资深的滑雪历史文化的研究学者，知名度高，影响力大。她还和南森先生（南森先生是世界著名的滑雪家，极地探险家）一起出版过一些关于滑雪以及滑雪历史的书。

English paper：

Oslo is called the winter capital of the world. Whether you arrive by plane, boat, car or train the profile of the Holmenkollen Ski Jump is the first landmark you see. The hill as it is today was built for the 2011 World Championships. The first competition was in Holmenkollen took place in 1892, and it is the oldest ski jump in the world that is still in the same place and is still used in competitions. The hill has been rebuilt 19 times.

Holmenkollen is the 3rd most famous sports arena in the world, next to Webley and Wimbledon. The national arena hosts annual international official competitions in Nordic skiing and biathlon, which draws thousands of spectators every year. It is also an arena where many different teams and athletes come to practice every day, all year.

Almost one million people a year visit the tourist attraction, and the Ski Jump is a national symbol, in the same way as the Eiffel Tower in Paris.

Built into the mountain next to the ski jump is the world's oldest ski museum. The first building was raised in 1923. The museum has been expanded many times, and it is owned and operated by the Association for the Promotion of Skiing.

Before going further into the museum there is a few terms and expressions that need to be explained.

The word Ski means split piece of wood. It has become an international word, used about activities and disciplines related to snow. Slalåm also comes from Norway, from Telemark county. Sla means steep hill and låm is the track down the hill.

A common expression is "Norwegians are born with skis on", meaning that at an early age children are taught to have fun on skis. Without poles to practice their balance.

It is also said that ski is Norway's gift to the world. To understand this expression we have to go back to the 1890s. During this decade, many young Norwegian students travelled to Germany, Austria, Switzerland etc to study economy and medicine. It was natural for them to bring their skis and show off their skills in the parks around the city. Moreover, it was contagious. Many Europeans also wanted to fly across the air. It resulted in a great demand for Norwegian skis, which was shipped around Europe. The same happened when Norwegians immigrated to other parts of the world.

Let us enter the world's oldest–and largest–ski museum. It is a museum specialized in skis and we have around 3000 pair of skis in our collections. Most of them are kept in our special storage. We document, research and communicate about our national cultural treasure, skis.

Like other museums, we have permanent exhibitions as well as areas for temporary exhibitions. As an engaged part in the society it is important to create different, thematic exhibitions. That way we reach more people, different target groups, start a debate and get media attention. The last exhibition was about disabled and skiing. The current exhibition is about snowboard and modern skiing, and young people are heading to the ski museum. In our auditorium, we have lectures, concerts and other activities. Right now the spectacular film *The Northern Lights–a lifetime experience* is showing, a film specially made for the museum.

The first thing you see when entering the museum is a polar bear. The question is why does it have such a central location? The answer is connected to Fridtjof Nansen, Norway's greatest polar hero. Nansen was also a scientist, diplomat and humanist, and received the Nobel Peace Price in 1922. What few people know is that we was very skilled artist.

One of his drawings shows a polar bear sniffing the ski tracks. This is the situation we wanted to recreate, and let our bear sniff a track that takes us 6000 years back in our ski history. The oldest rock carving that has been found in Norway is 6000 years old.

Fridtjof Nansen's expedition to Greenland in 1888, his expedition to the North Pole in in 1893-96, as well as Roald Amundsen's race to the South Pole, against British naval officer Robert Falcon Scott, together makes one the most important exhibitions in the museum. All the artifacts are original, there are no copies.

I would like to focus a moment on Nansen's expedition to Greenland. The book Nansen wrote was published in 1890, and it was quickly translated to English and German. In one of the chapters Nansen writes about skiing, its history and development. In that regard, he asks an important question, where is the cradle of skiing? This question has been asked by ski historians for many years. Nansen used comparative language to get answers. One of his conclusions is thatfinnish-ugric and tungusic tribes, both from the Altai area, used the same word for ski (suks). Nansen then concludes: "Altai is the cradle of skiing".

It is an historic event that China now has taken the initiative to host the first international ski conference in Asia. It is an honor and a privilege to be a part of this.

The Ski Museum in Holmenkollen hosted the first international ski research conference in 1998. Several similar conferences has been organized later on, sadly without Chinese participants.

These conferences bring ski historians together, academically and socially, and create a network. At the same time, they also bring about an interest and awareness within the public. The media contributes to generate further attention. As we saw in 1998 more people became familiar with the Ski Museum and the number of visitors increased significantly.

So, I hope this conference will contribute to added attention towards Altai an other cities with interesting cultural history museums, and make these destinations even more attractive for tourism.

With these words, I welcome you to Holmenkollen and the world's oldest and biggest Ski Museum to see the rest of our exhibitions.

Finally, I have the honor of decorating Mr. Shan with a very special ski, The Holmenkollen Ski.

中文论文：

奥斯陆被称为世界冬季之都。无论您乘坐飞机、船、汽车还是火车到达奥斯陆，最先看到地标性建筑的必定是霍尔门科伦滑雪跳台。它的最近一次重建是为了举办2011年的世界锦标赛。该赛事于1892年在霍尔门科伦举办，它是至今仍用于举办赛事的世界上最古老的滑雪跳台。该跳台已进行了19次重建。

霍尔门科伦是仅次于卫斯理和温布尔登的世界最著名运动胜地。国家竞技场每年都会举办国际北欧滑雪及冬季两项比赛，每年都会吸引成千上万的人前来观赛。另外，全年都会有运动团队和运动员来此练习。

紧挨着滑雪跳台的山间有着世界上最古老的滑雪博物馆。该馆首建是在1923年，并已历经多次扩建。另外，滑雪博物馆的所有权和经营权归滑雪促进协会。

在介绍该博物馆之前，我们需要先了解几个专业术语。

"Ski" 本来意思为"被切割开的木板"，现在已成为一个国际词汇，经常用于与雪有关的活动和学科。"Slalåm" 意为"转弯"，也源自于挪威语，来自于挪威的泰勒马克郡，"Sla" 指"陡峭的山"，"låm" 指"下山的小道"。

人们常说："挪威人生在滑雪板上。"这句话意思是，挪威人在孩子很小时便开始让孩子玩滑雪板，并且为练习孩子的平衡而不使用雪杖。

人们又常说："滑雪是挪威人送给全世界的礼物。"要理解这种说法，我们必须回到19世纪80年代。在这十年间，很多年轻的挪威人外出到德国、奥地利、瑞士等地学习经济和医学。他们自然也带上了滑雪板，并在城市周边的公园里展示他们的滑雪技术。这一运动传播很快。很多欧洲人也想要飞在空中。这就导致了成千上万的挪威滑雪板被运到了欧洲。当挪威人移民到世界的其他地方时，相同的情形也发生了。

接下来，让我们来了解一下世界上最古老、最大的滑雪博物馆。这是一个专门收藏滑雪板的博物馆，馆藏3000多副滑雪板，大多数馆藏被特殊保管收藏。我们对这些国家文化瑰宝——滑雪板进行记载、研究并与他人交流相关信息。

如同其他的博物馆一样，我们有永久展区和临时展区。对于一个致力于社会活动的公共团体来说，举办与众不同的主题展览十分重要。通过这种方式，我们可以接触到更多的人和不同的目标团体，还可以开展辩论和得到媒体的关注。最近一期的展览是关于残疾人与滑雪板的。当前的展览是关于单板和现代滑雪，吸引了很多年轻人前来滑雪博物馆。在我们的展博厅里，我们也举办演讲、音乐会和其他活动。目前正在上映的恢弘巨作"北极光——一次终身难忘的经历"是一部专为博物馆制作的电影。

进入博物馆后，首先你会看到一只北极熊。将它放在这样一个中心位置的原因与挪威最伟大的极地英雄，弗里德约夫·南森有关。南森还是一位科学家、外交家和人道主义者，并于 1922 年获得诺贝尔和平奖。鲜为人知的是，他还是一位技艺精湛的画家。

他的一幅画展示的正是一只北极熊正在嗅滑雪道。我们想要重现这一场景，让一只熊嗅着带我们回顾六千年历史的轨道。在挪威发现的最古老的岩石雕刻已有六千年的历史。

弗里德约夫·南森 1888 年的格陵兰岛探险、1893-1896 年的北极探险，以及罗阿尔德·阿蒙森的南极探险和英国海军军官罗伯特·福尔肯·斯科特的极地探险，共同组成了我们博物馆最重要的展览之一。所有展品都为真品，无复制品。

我将集中介绍一下弗里德约夫·南森的格陵兰岛探险之旅。南森所撰写的书于 1900 年出版，不久后被译为德语和英语。在该书的一章中，南森介绍了滑雪的历史和发展。在这方面，他提出了一个重要的问题：滑雪的摇篮在哪？这个问题也困扰了滑雪历史学家很多年。在该书中南森用比较语言的方法得到了答案。他的结论之一是芬兰-乌戈尔部落和通古斯部落都来自于阿勒泰地区，并且过去用同一个词“suks”来表示滑雪。因此，南森得出结论：“阿勒泰是人类滑雪的摇篮。

中国能够主动举办此次亚洲首届国际古老滑雪研讨会，具有重大历史意义。我们为能够参加此次会议感到无比荣耀。

这些会议在学术方面和社交方面将滑雪历史学家聚集到了一起，并创建了一个人际社交平台。会议还引起了公众的兴趣。同时，媒体的介入也引起了更广泛的关注。正如 1998 年会议的影响，越来越多的人增进了对滑雪博物馆的了解，参观者的数量明显增加。

所以我希望，此次会议能够有助于增加对阿勒泰和其他有特色历史文化博物馆城市的关注，并使之更具旅游吸引力。

我欢迎大家到霍尔门科伦世界最古老的滑雪博物馆来参观丰富的展品。

最后，我有幸能够赠送单兆鉴先生一副十分特别的滑雪板——霍尔门科伦滑雪板。

Photos in her speech 演讲稿展示的照片如下：

FORENINGEN TIL
SKI-IDRETTENS FREMME
滑雪促进协会

Holmenkollen 霍门尔科伦

The Ski Museum
滑雪博物馆

Holmenkollen 霍门尔科伦

Holmenkollen 霍门尔科伦

Holmenkollen 霍门尔科伦

The Ski Museum 滑雪博物馆

The Ski Museum 滑雪博物馆

The Ski Museum 滑雪博物馆

The Ski Museum 滑雪博物馆

The Ski Museum 滑雪博物馆

The Ski Museum 滑雪博物馆

The Ski Museum 滑雪博物馆

The Ski Museum 滑雪博物馆

The Ski Museum 滑雪博物馆

The Ski Museum 滑雪博物馆

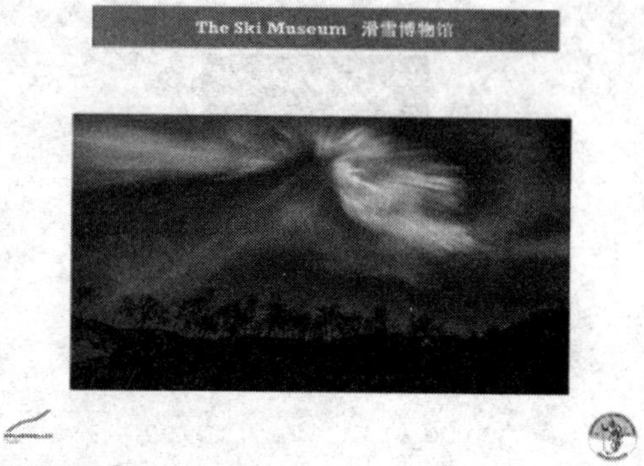

4.3　古代滑雪器具演变初探　A preliminary study on evolution of ski tools

王博（中国）Wang Bo（CHN）

个人简介　Brief Introduction

王博：男，中国籍 1949 年出生于甘肃省，1975 年毕业于中国西北大学历史系考古专业。现为新疆维吾尔自治区博物馆考古部研究员，擅长欧亚草原青铜时代考古和种族人类学的研究。在考古工作中独自或与他人合作出版了《中国阿尔泰山草原文物》、《丝绸之路·新疆古代文化》等近 20 部考古专著，论文 10 余篇，与古老滑雪文化研究有直接关联的论文有数篇，主要的是《阿勒泰是人类滑雪最早起源地探索》等，也是《人类滑雪起源地——中国新疆阿勒泰》主编之一。在中国新疆阿勒泰地区是人类滑雪最早起源地之《阿勒泰宣言》形成过程中起到重要作用。

Wang Bo, male, Chinese, born in Gansu Province in 1949, graduated from the History Department of Northwest University in 1975 an archeology major. He is working an archeology researcher in Xinjiang Museum and likes the archeology of the Bronze Age of Eurasian grassland and the research for ethnicity & anthropology. In his archeology work, he published more than 20 books by himself or with others, such as *Research for Grassland Golemon*, *the Silk Road* and *Cultural Relics in Altay Grassland of China* , released over ten theses and several papers directly related to ancient research on ski culture, by himself or with others, such as *Research on Altay is one of the earliest origin place of human skiing* he is also one of the chief editors of *The origin of Chinese skiing-Altay in Sinkiang China*. He played an important role in the forming of Altay Declaration of the "Altay-the place of origin for skiing" .

论文 Paper

2005年，敦德布拉克滑雪狩猎岩棚画的发现，在阿勒泰市政府的支持下，于2006年1月16日，通过体育方面的滑雪起源研究学者单兆鉴、刘永祥，新疆历史学者刘国防和考古方面的王建新、吕恩国、郑颉、鲁礼鹏和王博等专家的研究，认为：中国阿勒泰是人类滑雪最早起源地。同时，发表了阿勒泰宣言。有点振奋人心，这是体育人主导历史考古研究的作风。2006年12月15日在北京召开了“中国·新疆·阿勒泰是人类滑雪最早起源地”的新闻发布会。后来出版了中英文的《人类滑雪起源地—中国新疆阿勒泰》论文集，应该来说，研究取得了可喜的效果。在后来的日子里，单兆鉴先生经常念叨说，如果能开一个国际性的学术会就好了，以平常人的心理来说这也算是一个功德圆满。这个愿望看来是实现了，这不仅仅是单兆鉴先生不懈努力的结果，也是地方政府大力支持的结果，这里也包含着诸位滑雪爱好者的美好愿望以及世界滑雪起源探索者的辛勤劳动。对世界滑雪起源的认识，也从“阿勒泰是人类滑雪最早起源地”到了“阿勒泰是人类最古老的滑雪地域”的变化，这不仅仅是中文文字的拼对游戏，这是人们对研究世界滑雪起源地的涵义有了更进一步的认识，有了更广阔的探索空间。

在单兆鉴先生探索精神的鼓舞下，我也想作一点工作，做一点探索。对自己来说，滑雪起源的研究也仅仅是一个开始，参加以上的这些活动感觉为滑雪起源的研究开了一个很好的头，其实很多的问题都值得深思、值得进一步推敲、分析。我们需要一个国际性的相关滑雪起源的研讨会，去了解国外人对滑雪起源的研究状况，我们更多的是等待或者说是期盼着欧亚山地滑雪遗迹考古的新发现，为滑雪起源的探索不断地铺垫坚实的基石。

在后来的阿尔泰山地草原考古的调查中[①]，又发现了新的滑雪狩猎岩画，此外，也收集到除新疆之处的一些欧亚草原其他地域的岩画和民族民俗学方面的滑雪材料，感觉滑雪器具即滑雪板形状和滑雪杖数量的变化，就是一个值得我们注意的问题。[②] 新疆阿尔泰山地岩画，除在敦德布拉克滑雪狩猎岩棚画上发现绘画有滑雪器具外，塔合尔吐别克滑雪狩猎岩刻画上也雕刻了滑雪器具。[③] 查找国外的古代滑雪资料时，不仅找到了欧亚草原的俄罗斯境内发现过的滑雪岩画，而且还找到了滑雪器具的实物资料。挪威滑雪岩刻画中的脚踩巨大滑雪板的人物，给我的印象非常深刻，这也是一个值得探讨的问题。此外，也找到了一些民族民俗学方面的滑雪材料，将这些古代滑雪器具资料与现代民族民俗滑雪材料结合起来，进行一些分析，对我们认识欧亚山地古代居民的滑雪历史，会有一定的帮助。

In 2005, rock shack paintings of skiing and hunting in Dundebulake were discovered. On January 16 2006, in the support of Altai government, through the research of Shan Zhaojian and Liu Yongxiang－the sports scholars of ski origin, Liu Guofang－the Xinjiang historian, as well as Wang Jianxing, Lu Enguo, Zhen Jie, Lu Lipeng and Wang Bo－experts on archaeology, thought that Altay was the place of origin for human skiing. And they issued " Altay Declaration " . It was some inspiring, that sport man dominated historical and archaeological research. The press conference on "Skiing of humankind originated in Altay, Xinjiang, China" was held in Beijing on December 16, 2006. Later the collection of the *Original Place of Skiing－Altay Prefecture of Xinjiang, China* , was printed. It should be achieve gratifying effect. After that, Mr. Shan Zhaojian made an effort to organize an international academic conference. Nowadays, it came true. It was not only unremitting effort by Mr. Shan Zhaojian, but also the support of the local government. And it also contained good wishes from many ski enthusiasts and hard work from researchers on skis origin. The recognition of the ski origin also changed from "Skiing of humankind originated in Altay" to "Altay was the most ancient ski place of humankind " . This wasn't only a Chinese spelling game. It was that researching on the meaning of ski origin in world got further understanding and broad exploring space.

Inspired by Mr. Shan Zhaojian, I want to do some research. To myself, it is just a beginning of study on the birth place of skiing, and need more thinking. We need an international conference about the skis origin to understand the research status from abroad and expect new archaeological discoveries of ski relics in Eurasian mountains, which

① 这里指布尔津塔合尔吐别克滑雪狩猎岩画。

② 这个问题的提及是单老师的一次问话，他说：这个滑雪板的发展演化好象有点问题？

③ 此外，去年夏在额敏县又听到在县境内的岩画上也发现了滑雪的人物，资料待发表。

benefit ski origin exploring.

Later, in the archaeological investigation of Altai mountain and steppe①, people found some new skiing-for-hunting rock paintings, and assembled some rock paintings from other Eurasian glass regions beyond Xinjiang and skiing material in ethnology. According to that, we felt that it was worthwhile to note the changes of skiing tools about the shape and pole's number②. Except skiing tools on rock shack paintings of skiing and hunting in Dundebulake, we found the same in Taher. ③Referring to foreign ancient ski materials, we not only found ski rock painting in Eurasian glass in Russian, but also found ski tool entities. The ski rock painting with people standing on large skis in Norway impressed me deeply and it was a worth discussion. Besides, we found some ski materials in folklore, and both of them will help us to know the ski history of ancient inhabitants in Eurasia mountains.

一、岩画的滑雪器具

我们收集到的岩画资料中，敦德布拉克滑雪狩猎岩棚画、塔合尔吐别克滑雪狩猎岩刻画、俄罗斯白海岩画和挪威北部小岛勒德滑雪岩画上都表现了滑雪器具。

1. 敦德布拉克滑雪狩猎岩棚画的滑雪器具

敦德布拉克岩棚画，位于阿勒泰市汗德尕特蒙古自治乡东南约4公里的敦德布拉克河上游沟谷中，共发现四座岩棚里有岩画，反映滑雪场面的岩画在1号岩棚。1号岩棚的岩画，有早晚之分。其中表现滑雪人物的一组画面，绘画比较简朴，红色偏深赭红色者应属于早期作品，年代推测在公元前1万年前（图1）。

图1　敦德布拉克1号岩棚滑雪人物图

Fig. 1　Skiers on No. 1 rock shack in Dundebulake

滑雪人物图，处于岩棚的东壁，大概是10个人，其中有7个人的图像比较

① It meant Tubek's skiing-for-hunting rock painting.

② This question was from Mr. Shan. He said that there were some questions on the evolution of the skis.

③ Besides, last summer I heard skier was discovered on rock painting in Emin county. The material hadn't published.

明显，一字形排开。人物的头，分圆头和非圆头两种，非圆头有点象某种动物的头像，或为带角的鹿头。此外，后 4 人的形象非常地相似，人身体的上体较宽大，似背负着东西；细腿，皆弓身屈腿，作谨慎、慢步前行状。

单兆鉴先生称：滑雪人的形象线条图形，几个脚踏雪板，手持单杆滑雪人的图像栩栩如生。作为我不懂得滑雪的人来说，感觉单兆鉴先生的分析是很有道理的。虽然非滑雪专业人看起来“手持单杆（杖）”、“脚踏雪板”初看不明显，需要仔细辨别，但是曲腿滑雪慢行的动作相当地形像。同时在后两人的脚下发现了比较短的滑雪板，这一点单兆鉴先生及其研究滑雪的专家都认识统一，觉得非常明显。这是阿尔泰山地发现的年代最早的滑雪岩画，有比较长的单杆和比较短的滑雪板。①

2. 塔合尔吐别克滑雪狩猎岩壁刻画的滑雪器具

塔合尔吐别克岩刻画，位于布尔津县冲乎儿乡的塔合尔吐别克岩画地点。现收藏在布尔津县博物馆。

2009 年 1 月 15 日，我随单兆鉴先生、吕恩国、乌东军、阿力等专家，在布尔津县冲乎尔乡政府领导的指引下，调查了这幅岩壁刻画。乌鲁木齐晚报记者周磊也参加了这次活动。岩壁刻画是冲乎尔乡牧民努尔别克·祖科发现的，发现时岩画的岩块已从山岩壁体上脱落了下来，搬回了自家，放在小院子里。塔合尔吐别克滑雪狩猎岩画是岩壁刻画，当时起名，称：“滑雪者与狼羊图”（图 2）。

图 2　塔合尔吐别克滑雪狩猎岩刻画

Fig. 2　Skiing-for-hunting rock paintings in Tubek, Taher

岩壁刻画的岩石呈三角形，色发黑，很明显是一块山石。其中的一面保存着岩石光滑的自然面，其余两面是不很平整的剥离面，并且保存有已经变干了的黄

① 行文中，以岩画讲滑雪板的长短，主要根据滑雪板与人身体高的比例关系来判断：其长不及膝的是短滑雪板，长过膝至腰胸的是中长滑雪板，高于胸的就是长滑雪板。

色石花①，覆盖着岩画的局部，这也说明了岩画的雕刻已有了相当长一段时间。由剥离面保存迹象看，剥离的时间不会太短，有长时间暴露于外的陈旧感觉。石头不大，长 87 厘米，高 32 厘米。滑雪者处于画面的左侧，高和宽皆为 13 厘米：圆头、躬身、双腿呈叉状分开，两脚各踩一滑雪板，两滑雪板大小相近，大体呈平行状布置。滑雪者双臂前伸，两手各持一滑雪杖。滑雪者的背上有一长出臀部的方木形的东西，怀疑是一狩猎工具。

在滑雪者的前方，即画面的右侧雕刻着羊和狼。羊、狼各两只，皆上下布局，相互呈对视状，非常有意思。从羊角的形状看，两只羊应该是北山羊：上面的一只羊个体较大，作急停状；下面的一只羊个体较小，似作立状，感觉非常的惊慌。狼的形状由于被石花所压不是很明显，不过大体上可以看出：上面的一只狼作立状，体形较瘦，尾曲而长，耳相对较短，吻部向前伸出且接近到了羊角；下面的一只狼也作立状，体形较大，曲状长尾，耳长且尖，吻部突出。

岩画的颜色有些相近，经岩画研究方面的专家的现场分析，岩刻画中的滑雪者和狼、羊为同一时期的雕刻，并与阿尔泰山地其他岩刻画进行了雕刻技术及艺术风格的比较，认为属于公元前 900~前 800 年的岩刻画。

在后来一段时间里，我自已又作了些比较分析、考虑，认为当时的分析是有道理的，岩画的时间可以推测在青铜时代晚期，② 也可以作为新疆阿尔泰山地青铜时代晚期岩画考古的标型岩画来考虑，这也比较符合我们对新疆阿尔泰山地岩画的分期研究。③

岩画中的滑雪板与敦德布拉克滑雪狩猎岩棚画的相比，明显的要长且宽。而且使用的是双杖，杖的下端好像有保护尖的装置。看起来已非常地先进了。

3. 俄罗斯白海岩画的滑雪器具

在收集的俄罗斯白海岩画中有两幅岩画，发现者及研究者都认为是滑雪的场面。其中白海三个滑雪者图，很明显是滑雪岩画，而扎拉夫鲁加追猎图，从发表的线图资料中我没有找到滑雪人的场面。

第一幅，白海三个滑雪者图的滑雪器具

岩画发现于俄罗斯的卡累利阿白海地区（图 3），介绍者称：В. И. 拉夫多尼·卡斯将最古老的岩画（发现于白海地区）与狩猎法术和图腾崇拜信仰相联属，而较为晚期者（发现于奥涅加湖地区），则视之为日、月神话的反映。据他看来，

---

① 即鲜苔一类的植物。当地有的居民称石花，听起来比较顺耳。

② 会议期间与王建新老师谈及塔合尔吐别克滑雪狩猎岩壁刻画，他说经过近几年在中亚的岩画调查，它属于青铜时代是没有任何的问题。

③ 对新疆早期铁器时代的时间，学者间存在一些不同的观点，如有的学者认为公元前 1000 年新疆进入了早期铁器时代。一般都认为在公元前 800 年进入了早期铁器时代。

那些神秘的图形——绘有光束的圆和半圆，是日、月的象征，而其他图形，则为种种宇宙表记。显而易见，在卡累利阿岩画中，带有繁衍因素的渔猎崇拜确有反映，其中有些又可能与太阳崇拜有某些关联①。但也有一些研究者认为，新石器时代即有太阳崇拜之说，论据尚嫌不足。“三个滑雪者”岩画反映的是：三个滑雪者脚踏滑雪板，手执滑雪杆，正在奋力滑行。

此外，在白海附近，用点状手法凿刻的最抽象化的构图中，有鹿的足迹、滑雪板的辙迹，以及滑雪杖的戳痕。尼夫赫人用雕刻来装饰木勺时，总要在从洞中爬出的狗熊旁边加上它们的足印，而在滑雪者身后刻上两道雪上的辙迹和滑雪杖的戳痕。这些抽象化图形，对于现代画家是无关重要的，然而对古代岩画创造者却是很重要的。由词根“足迹”派生出的词很多，从这一点足以说明寻觅足迹在过去的作用。无须解释寻觅足迹对于猎人的意义，因为那是显而易见的。他们的双眼无时无刻不在注视着野兽、飞禽和人类留在地上的错综复杂的足迹，而且毫不费力地读懂这本大自然的书。②

图 3　白海三个滑雪者岩画

Fig. 3　The three skiers rock painting in White sea

三个滑雪者岩画，是单色彩绘，即将红色、淡黄色或褐色的赭石捣成粉末，与水或油脂搅拌，用毛刷乃至手指涂于洞壁或岩壁之上的。三人脚下的滑雪板长度相近，与塔合尔吐别克岩刻画的相比，感觉长度相近且也比较宽，使用的是单杆，这与敦德布拉克岩棚画的相同。这幅岩画的年代，推测是旧石器时代晚期或新石器时代。

第二幅，白海附近扎拉夫鲁加追猎图

乘滑雪板岩画，发现于白海附近扎拉夫鲁加。画面中有许多的动物，主要是驼鹿（图 4）。研究者称：白海之滨和奥涅加湖畔的岩画，不是一般的描写动物及狩猎的有巫术意义的岩画，而是复杂得多的综合体。俄国学者，如 B. И. 拉夫多尼卡斯、C. H. 扎米亚特宁、A. M. 里涅夫斯基等许多学者都曾试图对它进行解释。K. Д. 拉乌什金写的一篇文章，他将奥涅加湖的构图与卡累利阿的民族史

① K. д. 拉乌什金《奥涅加的圣所》载《斯堪的纳维亚论集》第Ⅳ、Ⅴ卷塔林 1959、1962 年版。转引自（前苏联）谢．亚．托卡列夫著魏庆征译《世界各民族历史上的宗教》中国社会科学出版社 1985、1988 年版。

② 盖山林著《世界岩画的文化阐释·第五节俄国卡累利阿白海之滨和奥涅加湖畔岩画》北京图书馆出版社 2001 年 6 月出版，第 34~35 页。

诗《卡列瓦拉》和萨阿米人①的口头创作进行了比较。驼鹿的形象频繁出现于奥涅加湖的右岸上和濒临白海的扎拉夫鲁加花岗岩峭壁上。奥涅加湖的鹿岛墓地、立陶宛的什维扬托伊，伏尔加河上游的萨克蒂什，均发现杖头为驼鹿头像的骨杖。当野牛在南方灭绝后，人们开始在岩石上刻画鹿与山羊的简略图案。在奥涅加湖和乌拉尔地区的新石器时代岩画中，鱼的形象依然极少。

这幅岩画是岩刻画，学者推测是新石器时代的，有人称“俄罗斯白海附近扎拉夫鲁加岩画中凿刻的驼鹿、小船和乘滑雪板的追猎者的形象。”我们在这幅岩画中很难找到文字中提到的乘滑雪板的人物，如果说有，那么有可能就最下部靠中右一侧鹿和人物了，在倒数第二只大鹿的后面有一人物，脚上似踩着滑雪板，手持一个长长的可能是雪杖一类的东西。

图4 俄罗斯白海附近扎拉夫鲁加岩画中的乘滑雪板的追猎者的形象

Fig. 4 Hunter by skis in Zalafulujia's rock painting near the white sea

4. 俄罗斯其他滑雪岩画的滑雪器具

我们找到至少是三幅与滑雪相关的材料，即滑雪射猎鹿图、滑雪套猎图和伪装滑雪图。皆发现于俄罗斯境内。

第一幅，滑雪射猎鹿图

滑雪射猎鹿图是岩刻画，画面中表现了一滑雪者，左臂偏向后、直曲，右臂向前下伸（雕刻的现象不是很好理解），手持一带箭的弓。弓上没雕刻弦。猎人面对着一只鹿，鹿雕刻了四腿，两只角，角上有小的分枝。鹿头较大，身体也比较宽。形体上与扎拉夫鲁加岩画的鹿图案有些像，可能也是驼鹿（图5-1）。

第二幅，滑雪套猎图

滑雪套猎图的滑雪者，头呈勾状，上身短、宽肩。双腿较长，作前曲状，脚上似穿短腰靴，靴尖踩在前部翘起的滑雪板上，后跟离开了滑雪板。可能表现的是，前部固定，后跟可以分离的一种滑雪板（图5-2）。滑雪板的大小，发于中等长，与A滑雪射猎鹿图的相比较，略显得要长一些、前宽后窄，。滑雪者，左手持单滑雪杆，右臂前伸，似手作投套兽绳状。

第三幅，伪装滑雪图

伪装滑雪图的滑雪者，很明显是一个伪装成动物的滑雪猎人（图5-3）。猎

① 萨阿米人为居住在挪威、瑞典、芬兰及俄国的民族。

人的头虽有些夸张或有些变形，但可以认为是一个张着大嘴的兽头，有点像童话中狼头，上部还有一个小的、尖状突起。左臂向前、向上曲伸，右臂向后作下曲状，双腿前屈，腹部雕刻生殖器。双脚踩短滑雪板，右脚的滑雪板比较明显，前长后短。滑雪者整个动作表现出是快速的滑雪状。

图 5-1　滑雪射猎鹿图
Fig. 5-1　hunting-for-deer by skiing

图 5-2　滑雪套猎图
Fig. 5-2　set of hunting by skiing

图 5-3　伪装滑雪图
Fig. 5-3　Camouflage hunting

图 5　俄罗斯其他滑雪岩画
Fig. 5　Other ski rock paintings in Russia

5. 挪威北部小岛勒德滑雪岩画的滑雪器具

我查找到一个资料称：在挪威北部边远的小岛勒德于发现过一幅公元前2500年左右的岩刻画（图6），① 刘国防先生的论文中称：目前，世界大多数人认为人类滑雪起源于斯堪底那维亚半岛上的挪威，其主要根据是考古学家在挪威的一个名叫罗带（Rodoy）的地方，发现了一幅绘有一名手持木棍的滑雪猎人的岩画，据称已有4500至5000年的历史。

图 6　挪威岩刻画滑着巨大滑雪板的人
Fig. 6　The rock painting in Norway with people standing on large skis

① 彼得·詹姆斯、尼克·索著《世纪古代发明·滑雪板与冰鞋》世界知识出版社，第77~79页。

刘国防先生论文中的“罗带（Rodoy）”与我查找的“勒德”的发音似比较相近，同时推测的年代也差不多，不知指的是不是同一个地方的同一幅岩画。①

岩画上雕刻着一个穿着巨大滑雪板滑雪的人，整个画面都是用粗线条来表现。滑雪者，看似身体前倾，上身直且短，下身的腿较长，膝关节处呈钝角、有些曲。两臂呈叉状前伸，双手持一件前伸的倒“7”字形的器具。也可能表现的是单杖滑雪的姿势。头上戴着兔耳帽，可能是一种伪装。滑雪的姿势相当标准，一眼就能看出来是一个滑雪者（图6）。

滑雪器具的特点是：长长的滑雪板，板体宽窄相近，相对比较窄，前部不仅向上、向前曲翘，而且有短的直平小头。滑雪板的尾部也有些向上弧曲。在新疆阿尔泰山地至今没有发现这样长的滑雪板，可能反映了滑雪板区域发展的一种现象。

以上的8幅岩画画面中，其中7幅画面上都能看到比较明显的滑雪板的图画，5幅画面上能看到滑雪杖的图画。这些岩画的年代，学者们推测是旧石器时代晚期至早期铁器时代。首先，可以推测滑起源于旧石器时代晚期即公元前5~1万年，或认为在距今1.2万年前。其次是，旧石器时代晚期至新石器时代的滑雪板，可能存在一个由短变中长的一个过程，而在青铜时代出现了挪威北部小岛勒德岩画中的巨大滑雪板，滑雪板的制作达到了一个非常自由的状态。在旧石器时代晚期至青铜时代的岩画里，反映出的滑雪者都使用的是单滑雪杖，而在早期铁器时代的岩画里出现非常先进的双滑雪杖，这是一个突变，但也滑雪狩猎发展的必然。

Ⅰ. Ski tools on rock paintings

In ourassembled rock paintings materials, skiing-for-hunting rock paintings in Dundebulake, Tubek, White sea and Lud show ski tools.

1. Ski tools onskiing-for-hunting rock shack paintings in Dundebulake

The rock shack painting in Dundebulake is located in the upstream valley of Dundebulake river, about 4 kilometers southeast of Handegat Mongolian autonomous county in Altai city. Four of them had rock paintings, and No. 1 rock painting reflects ski scene. No. 1 rock paintings belongs to different times. One group of them with skiers painted simple with dark red ochre color, which should belong to earlier time, dating to 10000 B. C. (Fig. 1).

Ski figure picture has 10 people in the east shelf. 7 of them are obvious and in

① 刘国防《阿勒泰地区人类早期活动的相关证据》单兆鉴主编《人类滑雪起源地——中国新疆阿勒泰》人民体育出版社、新疆人民出版社2011年1月第1版。

line. People's heads divide into round and non-round. The non-round heads look like some animals or deer with antlers. Besides, after four figures look alike, with broad upper bodies, carrying something and thin legs. They bow and curve legs, walking carefully and slowly.

Mr. Shan Zhaojian said that the picture with skiers standing on skis and holding a single pole was vivid. I felt his analysis was reasonable, although I didn't understand ski. To non-experts, holding single pole and standing on skis were not clear and needed carefully distinctions, but slowly skiing with curved legs was considerable image. And we found two behind people wore the shorter skis. On this point, we all came to an agreement and thought they were obviously. It is the earliest skiing rock painting in Altai mountain with longer single pole and shorter skis. ①

2. Skiing tools on rock paintings of skiing and hunting in Tubek, Taher

Rock paintings in Tubek, Taher, are located in Chunkor, Buerjing county. Nowadays, they are collected in Buerjing county Museum.

On Jan 15th 2009, under the direction of Chunkor government leadership, Mr. Shan Zhaojian, Lu Enguo, Wu Dongjun, A-li and I investigated the rock paintings, as well as Zhou Lei the journalist from Urumqi evening paper. This rock painting was found by Chonghur herdsman named Nuebike · Zuke, when it had fallen from rock. He took it back home and laid in yard. The skiing-for-hunting rock painting was named hunter with wolf and goat (Fig. 2).

The rock is triangle, black and obviously mountain rock. One side reserves smooth original surface. Others are roughly peeling surfaces with dry yellow rock flowers②, which means the rock paintings had been a long time. According to peeling surface, it was being a long time after peeling, and looked like old. The rock is not big, 87cm long and 32cm high. Skier is in the left side of the painting, and 13cm high and wide. His head is round. He bows, and two legs separate like fork and stand on a pair of skis with similar sizes and paralleling to each other. Skier's arms stretch forward and hold ski poles. A square wooden thing is on skier's back, may be hunting tool.

In front of skier cave goats and wolves. They were in the right side of the painting. Each two sheep and wolves were in upper and lower layout and faced each other. It

① Judging the length of skis on rock painting, mainly accord proportions between skis and people's height. The length of skis below knees is short skis, above knees to waist is middle one. And above chest is long skis.

② That is a kind of moss, called rock flower by local people.

is very interesting. Judging from the shape of horns, the two goats should be Capra ibex. The upper one is big and looks like quick stop. And the lower one is smaller, and stand in alarm. Because of stone flowers covering, wolves are not obviously. But we can see that the upper one stand and is thin, with long curly tail, short ears and mouth stretches to goat's horn. The lower one also stand and is bigger, with long curly tail, long point ears, and mouth protrusion.

The rock paintings' color are similar. Through spot analysis by experts on rock painting, they think skiers, wolves and goats were caved in the same time, and comparison with other rock paintings' caving skill and artistic style in Altay, they are between 900B. C. and 800B. C.

Later, I made some comparative analysis and thought it was reasonable at that time. Rock paintings' date may be in late Bronze age. [Talking with Wang Jianxing on skiing-for-hunting rock painting in Tubek, he said that it belonged to Bronze age undoubtedly, through rock painting investigation in Central Asia.] Considered as archaeological standard rock painting in late Bronze age at Altai mountain area was also in conformity with our study by stages on Altai mountain rock paintings [Researchers had different opinions on the date of early Iron age in Xing Jiang. Some people thought before 1000B. C., Xinjiang was early Iron age, and most people thought before 800B. C.

Skis on rock painting is long and wide compared to skiing-for-hunting rock shack painting in Dundebulake. Skiers use double poles, and the bottom of the them maybe have protection device, which looks like very advanced.

3. Skiing tools on rock painting in White sea, Russia

On rock paintings in White sea, two of them are considered as skiing by founder and researcher. The three skiers paintings in White sea are obviously skiing rock paintings. But in Zalafulujia's hunting painting, I didn't found skier.

No. 1 picture, is ski tools on three skiers painting in White sea

The rock paintings were found in Karelia white sea area, Russia (Fig. 3). B. H. Lafudonika related the most ancient paintings (in white sea) to hunting and totem worship, while thought the later (in Onega Lake) as the reflection of sun and moon. In his opinion, the mystical patterns as circle and semi-circle with beams were the symbol of sun and moon. Others were kinds of universe signs. Obviously, on Karelia's rock paintings, some reflected propagation with hunting-for-fishing totem motif, and others maybe relate with sun totem①. But some researchers thought that sun totem in Neolithic period was doubtful. The rock painting ofthree skiers described that three skiers stood skis, holding poles and gliding hardly.

Otherwise, near the white sea, in the most abstract pattern by dotting, there are deer's footprints, skis track, and pole's prod mark. When Nivkh dedicated wooden spoon, they always caved footprints near the bear, skis track and pole's prod marks behind skiers. This abstract patterns are unimportant to modern painters, but ancient rock painting creators. Many words were derived from the root of "track" which illustrated the useful of looking for track in past time. The mean of looking for track is obviously to hunter. His eyes always paid attention to the complicate footprints of beasts, birds and human and knew about the natural book easily.②

The rock painting with three skiers is single color painting. That is pounding red, light yellow, and brown ochre to power mixing with water and grease painted the wall of cave and rock by brush or fingers. The length of the three skiers' skis are similar. Compared with Tubek's rock paintings, they are similar in length and also broad. They skied by single pole. So did Dundebulake's. The date of this rock painting is in the late Paleolithic period or Neolithic period.

No. 2 picture, is Zalafulujia's hunting near the White sea

The rock painting of skiing by skis was discovered in Zalafulujia near the white sea. There are many animals in the painting, and most of them are moose (Fig. 4). The researcher said the rock painting didn't just described normal animals and hunting, but more complicated complex. Many Russia researchers such as B. H. Lafudunikasi, C. H. Zamiyatenin, A. M. Liniefusiji, tied to explain it. In к. д. Lawushenkim's article, he compared Onega Lake's composition with Karelia's national epic *Kaliewala* and Sami's oral creation③. Moose figures appeared frequently on the right bank of Onega Lake and granite cliff of Zalafulujia near the white sea. And the head of the bone sticks with moose were discovered all in deer island graveyard in Onega Lake, Shenweiyangtuoyi in Lithuania, and Sakedishen in the upper reaches of Volga. After bison dying out in south, people begun to cave simple patterns of deer and goat on rock. In Neolithic period, Onega

① к. д. Lawushenkim, Orogen's Holy Place, Scandinavian Collection, Vol. Ⅳ, Ⅴ, 1959, 1962. From Xie · Yar · Tokarev, Trans. Wei Qingzheng, China Social Sciences Press, 1985, 1988.

② Gai Shanlin *Cultural explanation on world rock painting · Section five: rock paintings of Karelia White sea beach in Russia and Onega Lakeside*, Beijing Library Press, in June, 2001, P. 34-35.

③ Sami lived in Norway, Sweden, Finland and Russia.

Lake and Wular area, fish motif was till less on rock paintings.

The rock painting was presumably in Neolithic period. People said that in white sea near Zalafulujia, rock paintings caved moose, boat and hunter by skis. It was difficult to find skiers referring in word in this rock painting. If had, they were deer and figures in the lower part and center-right. After the penultimate big deer, there was a human standing on skis and holding long poles.

4. Skiing tools on other skiing rock paintings in Russia

We at least found three pictures with skiing, which was hunting-for-deer by skiing, set of hunting by skiing, and camouflage skiing. All of them were found in Russia.

No. 1 picture, is hunting-for-deer by skiing

The rock painting describes a skier, whose left arm is back and curve, right arm stretches front and down (It was hard to know the caving phenomenon.) holding a bow without string. Hunter faces a deer with four legs, two horns with small branch. The deer has big head and broad body, similar to Zalafulujia's in body, which may be the moose (Fig. 5-1).

No. 2 picture, isset of hunting by skiing.

The skier's head likes hook, and upper body is short, shoulder was broad. His double long legs bending forward, maybe wear bootees. The boot toes treads on the top of skis and heels away from them. Maybe this kind of skis is fixing in head and away from heels (Fig. 5-2). The skis are middle size and longer than No. 1 picture's, becoming narrow from head to end. Skiers hold single pole in left hand and stretch right arm liking rope beast.

The ski hunter in the picture obviously disguises as animal (Fig. 5-3). The hunter's head may be exaggerated or deformed. However, it is considered as animal head with big mouth liking wolf's head. The upper part of head has a small and pointed protuberance. The left arm is forward and flexes extension upward. And the right arm is opposite. The hunter was caved reproductive organ, and stood on short skis. The right skis is obviously, long in head and short in end. Skier's acts looks like skiing fast

5. Skiing tools on rock paintings of skiing in Lud, a small island in the north of Norway

Material show that in Lud, a small island in the north of Norway, there is a rock painting dating about 2500 B. C. (Fig. 6). In[①]Mr. Liu Guofang's thesis says that at

① Peter · James and Nic · So, Century Ancient Civilization · Skis and Skates, World Knowledge Press, P. 77-70.

present most people think ski originated on Norway in Scandinavian Peninsula. Because archaeologist finds a rock painting of skiing hunter holding a stick in Rodoy Norway 4500-5000 years old.

Rodoy is similar to Lud in pronunciation in Mr. Liu Guofang's thesis, and the date is near, whether they are the same one. ①

The rock painting caves a skier standing on large skis with broad strokes. Skier leans forward. His upper body is straight and short, and legs are long and bend in knee. His arms cross stretched forward and hold a tool like inverse figure "7" which maybe hold single pole. He wears a rabbit ears hat for camouflage. Skiing position is standard, and knows as a skier immediately (Fig. 6).

Skiing tools features are long skis with similar width, warping forward and cropped in head, curved in end. Such long skis weren't find in Altay mountain area yet, that maybe reflect skis area development phenomenon.

Above eight pictures, 7 of them have skis and 5 pictures with poles. It is a guess that the date of the rock paintings is from late Paleolithic period to early Iron age. Firstly, skiing originates in late Paleolithic period (50000B. C. to 10000B. C.) or 12000 years ago. Secondly, skis became short to medium from the late Paleolithic period to Neolithic period. In Bronze age, a pair of large skis was discovered on rock paintings in Lud, a small island in the north of Norway. The manufacturing methods of skis was up to a freely condition. From the late Paleolithic period to Bronze age, people all skied with single pole. But on early Iron age rock paintings, people skied with advanced double poles. It was a mutation, and an inevitable trend of development of skiing hunting.

二、古代滑雪器具实物

要在考古调查或发掘中，发现滑雪器具，有很大的难处。因为滑雪器具大都是用木、动物皮来制作，不易保存。有趣的是，20 世纪 60 年代在俄罗斯东北部乌拉尔山脉维斯一地的泥炭沼中，发现了一件认为是滑雪板的器具（图 7-1）。称：呈弯曲状，雕刻有驼鹿头状的“制动器”。年代推测在（距今）8000 年前的新石器时代。②

---

① Liu Guofang, Relative Evidence on Human early life in Altai area, Chief editor Mr. Shan Zhaojian, the Original place of skiing-Altay Prefecture of Xinjiang, China, People Sport Press, Xinjiang People Press, first edition, in January, 2011.

② 王博《阿勒泰是人类滑雪最早起源地探索》单兆鉴主编《人类滑雪起源地——中国新疆阿勒泰》人民体育出版社、新疆人民出版社 2011 年 1 月第 1 版，第 46~63 页（新疆社会科学院历史研究所编《新疆历史与文化》新疆人民出版社 2010 年 6 月出版，第 69~82 页）。

图 7-1　俄罗斯东北部乌拉尔山维斯发现的滑雪板

Fig7-1　Skis discovered in Wiess, Ural Mountain in the north of Russia

图 7-2　单滑木式猎人雪橇残片

Fig7-2　Sled piece made by single wood

图 7　俄罗斯境内发现的滑雪板

Fig. 7　Skis discovered in Russia

乌拉尔山维斯滑雪板，从我掌握的叙述文字及线图，很难看清楚它的全貌。有待进一步的考古发现来认识它。

有资料称：在极北地区的晚亚石器时代（旧石器时代末期）的骨器文化中，发现过单滑木式猎人雪橇残片。从发表的线图来看，确实象是雪橇的一个局部，不过制作的相当精质。这个材料非常重要，它虽然讲的不是滑雪板而是雪橇，但在旧石器时代末期能制作出这样精质的木雪橇，可以看出来，当时居民加工木器的能力，这样复杂的雪橇都能制作出来，那么，制作木滑雪板就是相当简单的一件事情了。

Ⅱ. Ancient skiing tool entities

It was difficult to find skiing tools in archaeological investigation or excavations. Because most skiing tools were made from wood and animal fur damaged easily. Interestingly, in 1960s, a tool considered as skis was found in Wiess mud swamp, Ural Mountain in the north of Russia (Fig. 7-1). It is bent and has "brake" liking moose's head. It was in Neolithic period 8000 years ago. ①

① Wang Bo, Research on Altay is the earliest birth place of human skiing, Chief editor Mr. Shan Zhaojian, the Original place of skiing-Altay Prefecture of Xinjiang, China, People Sport Press, Xinjiang People Press, first edition, in January, 2011, P. 46-63 (edited by Xinjiang academy of social sciences history research institute, Xinjiang History and Cultural, Xinjiang People Press, June 2006, P. 69-82).

According to word records and graphs, it is difficult to know about the full view of it. We need more archaeological discoveries.

Some material show that sled piece made by a single wood was discovered in the end of Paleolithic period. According to published graph, it really likes a part of sled, and is quite delicate. This material are very important. Although it is sled not skis, it reflects the inhabitant's capability of wood process at that time, who could made delicate wood sled. So making wood skis became an easy thing.

三、史料的滑雪器具

有一条资料称：640 年来，自贝加尔湖地区的游牧民族派使臣前往中国朝廷："该国的宫廷档案在谈到他们时写道：他们的国家总被霜雪迅速覆盖，因此他们脚踏宽逾五寸，长逾七尺的木板，滑行于冰雪之上，猎取麋鹿和其他动物。"① 唐尺一尺合今约 30 厘米，长七尺即约合今 210 厘米，应该是长滑雪板。宽五寸即约合今 15 厘米，相对比较窄。

此外，有两条关于达斡尔人的滑雪板的记载。其一，称：达斡尔人自制的肯骨楞（达斡尔语滑雪板），用公野猪皮贴包肯骨楞宽约 12 厘米，厚约 3 厘米，长 1.35 米；② 其一，称：长约七尺，宽六寸，厚五分，铺鹿皮。③ 前者滑雪板长度属中等，后者则比较长，同时蒙皮也不一样，有鹿皮和猪皮之分。

如是，虽然不好判断滑雪板的形状，但能了解到它的长度。唐代贝加湖居民使用的是长滑雪板，而达斡尔人的滑雪板有中等偏长的，也有长滑雪板。

Ⅲ. Skiing tools in historical materials

One material show that in the past 640 years, nomad in Lake Baikal sent ambassadors to Chinese state. In their records said that their country always covered by snow and they stood on wooden boards gliding on the ice and snow, hunting elk and other animals. ④ The board was 30cm in length and 15cm in width. Maybe it is long skis.

---

① 日本正仓院所藏唐尺 26 支，长度从 29.4 到 31.7 厘米，平均 29.75 厘米。1976 年西安郭家滩 78 号唐墓出土唐尺，尺长 30.09 厘米。

② 张碧波、董国尧主编《中国古代北方民族文化史》（专题文化卷）黑龙江人民出版社 1995 年哈尔滨，第 592~593 页

③ 秋浦《鄂伦春社会的发展》上海人民出版社 1978 年出版，第 22 页。

④ Zheng Cang Yuan in Japan collected 26 Tang Chi, from 29.4cm to 31.7cm in length, average 29.75cm. In 1976, Guo Jia Tan No. 78 Tang graveyard unearthed Tang Chi was 30.09cm long in Xi'an.

Otherwise, two records are about Dawer's skis. One records that Dawer made Kenwaleng (skis in Dawer's language) by themselves. It is covered with the wild boar's fur and 12cm wide, 3cm thick, 1.35m long. ①The other is covered with deer's fur and 210cm long, 18cm wide and 1.5cm thick. ② The former is medium and the latter is long and skinned different.

It is hard to judge the shape of skis, but we can know its length. Habitant in Lake Baikal used long skis in Tang dynasty, medium and long skis by Dawer.

四、民族民俗资料的滑雪器具

在一个清代生活的皇清职贡图上，看到一个称作“七姓人乘木马射猎图”的绘画。③ 很明显，“木马”就是滑雪板。滑雪中等长，大体上是尾部弧圆、前部尖呈三角形的滑雪板，因为人物正在持弓射猎，没有表现出滑雪杖（图 8-1）。

2006 年 10 月，俄罗斯在北京举办的《俄罗斯民俗艺术展》陈列上，见到了三幅反映滑雪的图画和一付滑雪板实物。第一幅，反映了基尔亚克人及其生活的场面，画面资料介绍称：基尔亚克是北方部落，生活在黑龙江下游和鞑靼海滨地区。画面的前部有两个较明显的人物，其中右侧的一人手上拿着一付滑雪板，左侧一人手上拿着单滑雪杖。滑雪板的高度到了人的颈、下颌部，应该是长滑雪板，形状是两头尖，中部平行宽（图 8-2）。第二幅，反映了通古斯人的狩猎，画面资料称：通古斯人—猎人。画面中有三人，其中靠前的两人是年青的一男一女，脚下踩着滑雪板。将滑雪板与人体高度比较，也应该是长滑雪板，形状是中部宽、两头尖的滑雪板（图 8-3）。第三幅，反映楚左奇人的生活画面，有钻木取火者、看守小婴孩的，楚左奇人。画面中有一站着人物，手持弓，脚踩滑雪板。滑雪板与通古斯人的相似，即中部宽、两头尖的滑雪板（图 8-4）。

---

① Chief editors Zhang Bibo and Dong Guoyao, Cultural History on North Nationalities in Ancient China (special culture volume), Hei Longjiang People Press, 1995, Harbin, P592-593.

② Qiu Pu, The Social Development of Orogen, Shanghai People Press, 1978, P.22.

③ 张碧波、董国尧主编《中国古代北方民族文化史》（专题文化卷）黑龙江人民出版社 1995 年哈尔滨，第 594 页。

图8-1

图8-2

图8-3

图8-4

图8-5

图8-6

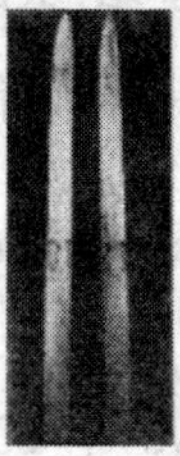
图8-7

图8-8

图 8-1　七姓人乘木马射猎图《皇清职贡图》

Fig. 8-1　Duty Tribute picture of Qing dynasty with people hunting by wooden horse

图 8-2　基尔亚克人及其生活图

Fig. 8-2　Jieryak and their life scenes

图 8-3　通古斯猎人图

Fig. 8-3　Turgus' hunter

图 8-4　楚左奇人生活图

Fig. 8-4　Chu Zuoqi's life scenes

图 8-5　俄罗斯鄂温克人 20 世纪初有滑雪

Fig. 8-5　Ewenki in Russia

图 8-6　内蒙古鄂温克人滑雪和滑雪板图

Fig. 8-6　Ewenki's skiing and skis in Mongolia

图 8-7　黑龙江鄂伦人的滑雪板

Fig. 8-7　Orogen' skis in Hei Longjiang

图 8-8　2005 年阿勒泰民俗滑雪板

Fig. 8-8　Altai folklore skis in 2005.

在北京《俄罗斯民俗艺术展》有陈列上，展出了生活在东西伯利亚鄂温克人 20 世纪的滑雪板（图 8-5）。滑雪板中等长，是形状是两头呈角状尖、中部平行宽的滑雪板。这与画面中的基尔亚克人的相似。此外，在内蒙古博物馆的民族民陈列上我们也见到了鄂温克人的滑雪板（图 8-6），其中展柜里的滑雪板没的拍完整，而猎人脚上的滑雪板也不很清楚。不过，秋浦《鄂伦春社会的发展》对其有较为详细的记录，称："每逢进入冬季，气温降至摄氏零下四十多度，大雪覆盖着山野，道路为之阻塞的时候，鄂伦春人就戴上马尾眼镜，缚上滑雪板，往来于树丛之中去寻觅兽踪。马尾眼睛系用马尾编织而成，戴上它，可以避免强烈光线的刺激，有助于视线的清晰。滑雪板是用煮过的桦木或松木制成，长约七尺，宽六寸，厚五分，前端肖成尖形而向上翘，铺鹿皮，令毛尖向下，以钉固之。滑雪板的中段有毛圈，用以系足。用时，把它用绳子缚在脚底下，两手各撑一竿，就行走如飞了"①。同时附有照片即部分生产工具（二）滑雪板图（图 8-7），是 1955 年黑龙江鄂伦春人的调查资料，非常的珍贵。滑雪板的形状呈：尾部宽、渐窄、头尖的形式。

今天的阿尔泰山地的阿勒泰市、布尔津县禾木喀纳斯蒙古族乡的居民，冬季滑雪的季节仍然在制作滑雪板。两地的滑雪板形状大体相似，属长滑雪板，尾部平且宽，呈渐窄的三角形曲翘尖头滑雪板。滑雪杖是单圆木杆，直径 4~6 厘米，长 1.7 米左右（图 8-8）。

这样以来，我们对民俗资料进行类型分析时，很难考虑滑雪板的长度，主要是根据器形的变化，可以看出滑雪板的四种类型：

A 型，圆弧状尾，逐渐变成尖头的滑雪板（图 9-1）；

B 型，两头呈尖角状、中部平行宽的滑雪板（图 9-2）；

C 型，中部宽，向两头逐渐变窄、变尖的滑雪板（图 9-3）；

D 型，尾部宽、向前渐窄、头尖的滑雪板（图 9-4）。

图9-1

图9-2

图9-3

图9-4

图 9-1　A 型　Fig. 9-1　Type A；图 9-2　B 型　Fig. 9-2　Type B

图 9-3　C 型　Fig. 9-3　Type C；图 9-4　D 型　Fig. 9-4　Type D

图 9　民族民俗资料中滑雪板的类型

Fig. 9　Skis' types in folklore material

---

① 秋浦《鄂伦春社会的发展》上海人民出版社 1978 年出版，第 22 页。

Ⅳ. Skiing tools in folklore material

The Duty Tribute picture of Qing dynasty draws people hunting by wooden horse. Obviously,[①] the wooden horse is skis, medium long, arch end and triangle head. Because people are hunting with bow, there aren't pole (Fig. 8-1).

In October 2006, three skiing pictures and a pair of skis entity were on Russian folklore art exhibition held in Beijing. The first reflected Jieryak and their life scenes. According to picture data, Jieryak was north tribe and lived in the lower reaches of Heilongjiang River and Tatar beach. In the front of the picture there were two people. The right one held a pair of skis, and the left one maybe hold single pole. The height of skis was up to people' head and jaw. They were long skis, tipped in ends and balance in middle (Fig. 8-2). The second reflected Turgus' hunt. Turgus is hunter. There were three people in the picture. The front were young man and woman standing on skis. Compared the height of skis with human body, they should be long skis, wide in middle and tipped in ends (Fig. 8-3). The third reflected Chu Zuoqi's life scenes, such as drilling wood to make fire and looking after children. In the picture, there were people holding bow and standing on skis. It was similar to Turgus', which was abroad in middle and tipped in ends (Fig. 8-4).

Skis used in 20 century by Ewenki living in eastern Siberia were on Russian folklore art exhibition (Fig. 8-5). The skis were medium long, wide in middle and tipped in ends, which was similar to Jieryak's. Otherwise, in Mongolia museum, we found Ewenki's skis in folk exhibition (Fig. 8-6). Skis didn't take a full photo in cabinets, and hunter's skis were not clear. But the development of Orogen society written by Qiu Pu recorded that every winter, the temperature fell to-40 degrees. When snow covered mountain and blocked road, the Orogen took ponytail glasses and put on skis to look for animals in forest come-and-go. Ponytail glasses waved by horse tail, with them, people can keep out of strong light and had a clear sight. Skiswere made from boiled birch and pine, about 210cm long, 18cm wide and 1.5cm thick. The front end was sharpened into point and forward. They were covered by deer's fur and fasten by nails. In the middle of skis there were woolen loops for tying feet. Wearing them people could walk fast[②]. Meanwhile attaching skis pictures (Fig. 8-7) were investigation material by Orogen in 1955. They were very precious. The skis were wide in ends and becoming tipped.

---

① Chief editors Zhang Bibo and Dong Guoyao, Cultural History on North Nationalities in Ancient China (special culture volume), Hei Longjiang People Press, 1995, Harbin, P594.

② Qiu Pu, the Social Development of Orogen, Shanghai People Press, 1978, P. 22.

Today, in Altay and Kazas Mongolia county, habitant still make skis in winter. They are similar in shape and both long, wide in back, and become narrow to triangle front end. The pole is single round wooden stick, 4 to 6cm in diameter and about 1.7m long (Fig. 8-8).

So when we made category analysis to folk material, it was difficult to consider the length of skis, but the changes of form, which shown four kinds:

Type A was arch back and became to point (Fig. 9-1);

Type B was balance in middle and tipped in ends (Fig. 9-2);

Type C was wide to narrow from middle to ends (Fig. 9-3);

Type D was wide back and became narrow and point in front end (Fig. 9-4).

五、结语

在考古调查和发掘资料中，我们还是找到一些与古代滑雪相关的器具材料，这对我们认识滑雪器具的时代、地域变化是有宜的。

1. 通过滑雪板材料以及工艺的调查，滑雪板的主要用材是：木和动物皮(包括筋)。这两样东西很容易找到。其次是工艺技艺，从旧石器时代晚期居民已经掌握了娄勒瓦娄哇（Levallois）打制石器技术，能够设计性的打制出非常精致的石器。这一时期的木器加工技术，推测也会比较成熟。从极北地区旧石器时代晚期制作的单滑木式猎人雪橇残片看，旧石器时代晚期的北方居民已经可以制作较为复杂的滑雪器具了，何况是相对简易的滑雪板，而且可以制作的比较的理想。

2. 滑雪起源于旧石器时代晚期即公元前5~1万年，或认为在距今1.2万年前。旧石器时代晚期至新石器时代的滑雪板，可能存在一个由短变中长的过程，至青铜时代出现了挪威北部小岛勒德岩画中的巨大滑雪板，滑雪板的制作达到了一个非常自由自在的状态。

旧石器时代晚期至青铜时代早期，滑雪使用的都是单滑雪杖，至青铜时代晚期出现了非常先进的双滑雪杖，这是一个突变，具有偶然性，但也是滑雪狩猎发展的必然。

3. 虽然我们从史料中很难了解到滑雪板的形状，但能反映出唐代贝加尔人的滑雪板，相当地长，而清代达斡尔人的滑雪板则为中等长的形式。

此外，民俗学资料还显示，滑雪板分四种类型：一是，圆弧状尾，逐渐变成尖头的滑雪板；二是，两头呈尖角状、中部平行宽的滑雪板；三是，中部宽、渐窄、两头逐渐变尖的滑雪板；四是，尾部宽、渐窄、头尖的滑雪板。反映的滑雪器具在发展中，存在区域性的变化。

4. 通过上面一些现象看，在滑雪技术和滑雪器具传播的过程中，地域的发展是不平衡的，有着区域性创造及创新。

5. 通过新疆阿尔泰山地岩画和民俗滑雪器具的变化分析，反映出阿尔泰山地居民创造了滑雪狩猎，而且在器具上发展的很快，在青铜时代晚期就使用了当时最先进的双滑雪杖。在游牧业迅速发展的过程中，随着拓疆、扩张、争夺草场战的频繁，同时，骑马狩猎逐渐地在完全代替滑雪狩猎，居民渐渐地在遗忘滑雪器具制作的技艺，或者说滑雪狩猎退出了狩猎经济的主导地位。这样以来，阿尔泰山地居民的滑雪器具自然地又恢复到其原始的状态。不管怎么说，滑雪狩猎是阿尔泰山地居民的最爱，才使得它能长久地保存了下来。同时，也可以看出来，山地草原居民的某些文化现象的发展是波浪形的，在历史的经历中有高有低的变化，目前保留下来的一些看似比较原始的文化现象，不是历史上发展的最高水平，而是历史的一些原因使它走入低谷的结果。这或许也是山地草原一些历史文化现象发展的一般规律。

2005 年，在单兆鉴先生的启发下开始研究滑雪起源，至今已有 10 年了。10 年的时间里，一直在想着碰碰运气查找到一点好的滑雪考古、滑雪历史的资料，也一直在想着作点滑雪起源方面的研究，先生也一直在鼓励我学会滑雪去感受滑雪的力量。滑雪起源研究，对我来说不仅仅是科学研究，而且是考古人生活的一种享受。

V. Conclusion

In archaeological investigation and excavation material, we found some tool materials about ancient skiing, which were benefit for recognizing the date of skiing tools and regional variation.

1. Throught the investigation of skis' material and craft, skis was mainly made from wooden and animal fur (including vein), which were found easily. The second was technology. Since the late Paleolithic period, people had mastered Levallois, and could make delicate stone tools creatively. It was a guess that wood processing technique was mature. According to hunter's sled piece with a single pole in the Paleolithic period in the polar regions, residents in the north had made more complex skiing tools.

2. Skiing originated in the late Paleolithic period (50000B. C. to 10000B. C.), or about 12000 years ago. It is possible that the skis changed from short to long in the late Paleolithic to Neolithic period. Until Bronze age, a pair of large skis wasdiscovered on rock painting in Lud, a small island in the north of Norway. Making process of skis came to a very freely state.

From the late Paleolithic to the early Bronze age, people all skied with a single pole. In the late Bronze age, they skied with very advanced double poles. It was a mutation, may be accidental, but an inevitable trend of development of skiing hunting.

3. It is hard to know the shape of skis in historical material, but it reflects that Baikal's skis was rather long in Tang Dynasty, and Dawer's was middle in Qing Dynasty.

Besides, in folklore materials, skis was separated into four kinds: the first kind was arch back and becoming tipped in front end; the second kind was balance in middle and tipped in the ends; the third kind was wide to narrow from middle to ends, and tipped in ends; the fourth kind was wide in back and becoming tipped from back to front end. These reflected that in the development of skiing tools existed regional variations.

4. It was unbalanced on regional development in the spread of skiing techniques and tools, having regional innovations and creations.

5. In Altay, the changes of rock paintings and folklore skiing tools reflected that Altai mountain inhabitants created skiing hunting and the tools developed fast. In the late Bronze Age, people had used the most advanced double poles. Along with frequent development and scrambling for steppe, while horse hunting was instead of skiing hunting completely, or skiing hunting economy withdrew leadership inpeople's life, people forgot the advanced skill of making skiing tools gradually. So skis in Altai mountain naturally came back to original state. However, skiing hunting was favorite to Altai inhabitants, which made it reserved for a long time. At the same time, some culture phenomenon in mountain glass dwellers developed in waves, through the changes of high and low in history. it seems that the primitive culture phenomenon wasn't the highest level in historical development, but because of historical reasons it fallen down. This may be general rules on development of historical culture phenomenon in mountain grassland.

In 2005, I begun to research the skis origin inspired by Mr. Shan Zhaojian. It has been ten years already. In ten years, I always wanted to found better material about skiing archaeology and history and study the skiing origin. And he also encouraged me to learn skiing and feel its strength. Researching on the skiing origin was not only scientific study, but also a kind of enjoyment to archaeologist's life.

【注释】

行文中，以岩画讲滑雪板的长短，主要根据滑雪板与人身体高的比例关系来判断：其长不及膝的是短滑雪板，长过膝至腰胸的是中长滑雪板，高于胸的就是长滑雪板。

会议期间与王建新老师谈及塔合尔吐别克滑雪狩猎岩壁刻画，他说经过近几年在中亚的岩画调查，它属于青铜时代是没有任何的问题。

对新疆早期铁器时代的时间，学者间存在一些不同的观点，如有的学者认为公元前1000年新疆进入了早期铁器时代。一般都认为在公元前800年进入了早期铁器时代。

【参考文献】

1. К.д. 拉乌什金《奥涅加的圣所》载《斯堪的纳维亚论集》第Ⅳ、Ⅴ卷塔林1959、1962年版。转引自（前苏联）谢．亚．托卡列夫著魏庆征译《世界各民族历史上的宗教》中国社会科学出版社1985、1988年版。

2. 盖山林著《世界岩画的文化阐释·第五节俄国卡累利阿白海之滨和奥涅加湖畔岩画》北京图书馆出版社2001年6月出版，第34~35页。

萨阿米人为居住在挪威、瑞典、芬兰及俄国的民族。

3. 彼得·詹姆斯、尼克·索著《世纪古代发明·滑雪板与冰鞋》世界知识出版社，第77~79页。

4. 刘国防《阿勒泰地区人类早期活动的相关证据》单兆鉴主编《人类滑雪起源地——中国新疆阿勒泰》人民体育出版社、新疆人民出版社2011年1月第1版。

5. 王博《阿勒泰是人类滑雪最早起源地探索》单兆鉴主编《人类滑雪起源地——中国新疆阿勒泰》人民体育出版社、新疆人民出版社2011年1月第1版，第46~63页（新疆社会科学院历史研究所编《新疆历史与文化》新疆人民出版社2010年6月出版，第69~82页）。

6. 日本正仓院所藏唐尺26支，长度从29.4到31.7厘米，平均29.75厘米。1976年西安郭家滩78号唐墓出土唐尺，尺长30.09厘米。

7. 张碧波、董国尧主编《中国古代北方民族文化史》（专题文化卷）黑龙江人民出版社1995年哈尔滨，第592~593页

8. 秋浦《鄂伦春社会的发展》上海人民出版社1978年出版，第22页。

9. 张碧波、董国尧主编《中国古代北方民族文化史》（专题文化卷）黑龙江人民出版社1995年哈尔滨，第594页。

4.4　在阿勒泰的十年　Ten Years in Altay

尼尔·拉尔森　Nils Larsen (USA)

个人简介　Brief Introduction of Nils Larsen

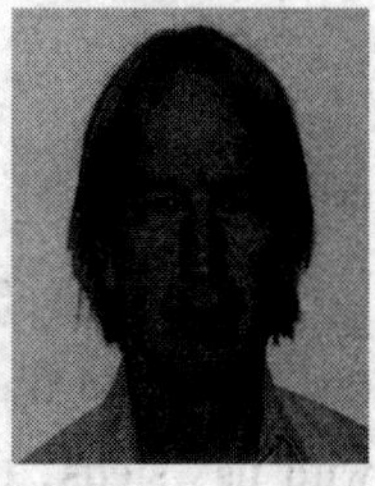

Nils Larsen was born in Hawaii and spent his childhood there. He has been an avid backcountry skier since moving to the west coast of the United States in the early 1970's. In the early 1980s he started teaching skiing and working in the ski industry as a rep, instructor, Cross Country Ski store owner, designer and consultant. Nils has also produced a number of films on backcountry and free heel skiing.

Since 2005 Nils has been traveling to the Altai Mountains in NW China to research and document the traditional skiing culture still practiced in the mountains there. He has shot and produced one video on the subject and in 2013 led a National Geographic team there to do a story (in the December issue 2013) on the skiing traditions there. He has been researching ancient ski history since 2005 as well as studying the ski techniques and construction of traditional skis found in the Altai Mountains.

In 2011 Nils and Francois Sylvain started Altai Skis, a small ski company that designs and builds specialized backcountry skis based on the traditional utilitarian concepts found in the Altai Mountains.

He now lives in NE Washington State and runs his business from there. He continues to ski whenever possible and teaches locally and at special events.

尼尔·拉尔森出生于夏威夷，并在此度过了童年。自从在20世纪70年代早期移居到美国的西海岸，他就是一位野外滑雪爱好者。在20世纪80年代早期，他开始教别人滑雪，并在滑雪企业里当滑雪代表、滑雪教练、越野滑雪店主、设计师和顾问。尼尔斯也导演过许多关于偏远地区和自由式滑雪的电影。

自从2005年，尼尔斯便经常到中国的阿尔泰山去调查研究，记录该地传承下来的古老滑雪文化。他拍摄过关于滑雪文化题材的录像，并在2013年带领一支国家地理队演绎了一个关于滑雪传统的故事（在2013年12月发行）。他自从2015年就一直在研究古代滑雪史，探究在阿尔泰山区发现的滑雪技艺和传统滑雪板的构造。

在2011年，尼尔·拉尔森和弗朗索瓦·迪斯丁开办了一家小的阿勒泰滑雪板公司。该公司基于在阿尔泰山区发现的实用古老滑雪板的概念而设计和构造出专业野外滑雪板。

他现在居住在华盛顿州，经营自己的公司。无论何时何地，他将一如既往地坚持滑雪，教本地人滑雪及参加特殊的滑雪赛事。

English Paper：

Ten Years in Altay

Nils Larsen

In March of 2005 I traveled into the Chinese Altai Mountains with two friends to document the traditional skiing still being practiced there. We took way to much baggage with us：sleds，camping gear，food，cameras …. I also carried excess baggage of another kind：my western view of skiing. I have been active in Alpine and Nordic skiing as an instructor，skier，and designer，working on developing skis and bindings mostly for the backcountry skiing world. This abundance of experience has proved a blessing and a curse，giving me a good understanding of ski mechanics and skiing but also an excess of hubris in all things skiing. I was quite certain on how skis worked and how and what made up good skiing.

This "ull cup" led to a lot of preconceived ideas on the nature and workings of skis and skiing. Some of the more glaring of these are as follows.

—I was quite sure that due to the rudimentary nature of their skis，the Altai peoples' use of skis would be closer to snowshoeing then actual skiing.

—Due to the length，stiffness，and design of their skis as well as their rudimentary bindings，their skis would not be turnable while skiing.

—We would of course be faster and more skilled，and our equipment would give us a big overall advantage in both the up and the down while skiing in the Altai region.

This is not to say I was not entranced by the idea that skiers were still using equipment that dated back to the dawn of skiing. I was. I was simply stuck in the western linear view of progress running in a straight line from ancient to modern.

So here I sit，ten years and nine trips to the Altai wiser. My views have changed on skiing in general，and in particular about skiing and the skiers I met in the Altai Mountains. In large part this is because I did not really understand the many differences between recreational skiing and the utilitarian skiing still practiced in the Altai Modern skiing runs in two fairly distinct tracks，Alpine Skiing and Nordic（Crosscountry）skiing. Both are almost exclusively recreation based and both in their own way focus on glide and speed. I think it is safe to say that racing and competition has in large part driven the changes and development of both styles of skiing, even though not all skiers compete. Both disciplines, Alpine and Nordic, have become evermore specialized to achieve better performance in their respective areas.

What follows is a brief overview of skiing in the Chinese Altai Mountains. This skiing style was practiced throughout the Altai region and beyond with some variations based on conditions and specialized uses.

Traditional skiing is driven by a number of factors, most of them absent in modern skiing today. Here is short list that I have come up with-Specific to the Altai Mountains -probably incomplete, but covering the major points.

Conditions:

Skis and skiing develop organically to suite the conditions and needs of the particular group. In the Altai the climate is severely continental, meaning there is no ocean influence to moderate the climate and it is very cold for the whole winter season. Seasonal snowfall totals are less then more maritime locations. My experience and in talking with long time residents in the mountains is as follows.

Snowpack varies by location but generally below alpine (where skiing takes place) can run from a low of 50 cm to a high of 2 meters. Individual storms can be quite large with several storms during my visits dropping close to a meter of snow over a few days. It does not rain in the winter.

Winter temperatures never get above freezing during the main months of winter. This would be mid November through March, with the exception of solar radiation on sun exposed slopes towards spring. Temperatures from November through February can run between-15c and-45c.

The net result of this as it relates to skiing is the snowpack is often too shallow to avoid deep faceting of the snow due to cold temperatures. This creates a snowpack that has no base or structural support: a bottomless snow that makes for very difficult travel.

Six out of eight midwinter trips featured a faceted snowpack in most areas. Below tree line the snow was almost never wind affected. Virtually every winter trip featured nearly uniform deep and cold soft snow conditions, the exception being late March/April on sun affected slopes which were at times crusty but general deep isothermic snow.

Finally, avalanches are very common, even expected, after any large snowfall. The faceted snowpack makes for extremely unstable snow that remains that waythrough out the winter. This is a constant concern while skiing and terrain based avoidance is the common practice of local skiers.

Terrain:

The Altai Mountains are a large range pretty much dead center in the Eurasian continent. The area I inhabited on my visits was exclusively in the Chinese Altai, so in the southwestern part of the range. Just a few days ski north of this area is the Altai Knot-a junction of Kazakhstan, Russia, Mongolia, and China. In my descriptions I will be describing the area I was in.

The mountains in this area are quite rugged and the majority of the mountains are alpine terrain, that is: above tree line and unused in the winter. Tree line trends around 2000-2100 meters. A number of deep valleys cut into the Altai carrying rivers flowing out to the south and into the Irtysh River. These valleys and surrounding countryside can be heavily forested, predominately with Birch, Larch, Spruce and various poplars.

The mountains themselves are often very steep and rocky and other then river bottoms, ancient lake terraces, and some larger lakes much of the terrain is either up or down. The terrain often used for herding and hunting is steep hillsides and ridges that have dense forest on the north aspects and broken forest on the south sides. Due to the terrain and conditions Avalanches are common and expected in avalanche terrain after any large snow event or during the spring transition period.

Ski Usage:

Skis in the Altai Mountains were used for a wide variety of tasks in the winter months. The most common day-to-day uses-particularly during large snow years-were as follows.

—1154847964-Finding and feeding live stock.

—1154847963-Collecting water for household use.

—1154847962-Collecting and hauling firewood.

—1154847961-Visiting or traveling to neighbors or extended family.

Perhaps the most common and important use for skis was hunting and trapping. This could range from a partial day on skis to check local trap lines to a two weeklong expedition into the mountains. Trapping was a source of barter and currency for locals, and hunting was an important supplement to their diet during the winter months.

In the Altai area, single horse drawn sleds (*chanas*) are commonly used in the winter for travel and hauling, particularly hay and firewood. Until 2008 the road into the Altai was left to the snows and remained closed all winter to motor vehicles. *Chanas* were used to travel in and out of the Altai to get supplies, visit families, or pick up children away at boarding schools. *Chanas* worked well for the two-day trip as long as the trails were packed from use. During and after large snowfalls groups would set out to open the trails, with the first group breaking a trail on skis, followed by horses; mounted or led, then *chanas* to fully open the route. This was does on the major trails in and out of the mountains to the main villages and continues on trails to remote settlements away from the main roads.

Finally, skis were used for recreation as well. I have recorded many stories of people skiing for fun (both men and women), races held, and young boys allowed to ski for no particular purpose but to have fun. From a practical perspective, skiing-particularly skiing on the traditional skis used in the Altai-is a difficult skill to master and takes years to become accomplished at it. Like other essential skills, introducing skiing as play to young boys is the most effective way to insure that they are comfortable on skis by the time they take their places with the other men hunting and traveling on extended trips into the mountains. Perhaps the best analogy to this would be archery, also reported to have started at an early age with young boys for pleasure and play.

Combining Conditions and Ski Usage:

When we look at the intersection of the conditions and terrain found in the Altai Mountains with the usage of skis we can begin to understand the design challenges and needs both in ski construction as well as technique. Add to this the need for skis to be durable, reliable (in the given conditions), reparable, and sourced from local materials.

Ski Design:

Altai skis vary in length and a committed skier often has a least two pairs (and a spare kept back in the cabin). A shorter pair will be used for local skiing around the winter home, and a longer pair is often used for longer multiday trips. Multiday trips mean many hours of breaking trail and the longer skis will support the skiers weight with less snow penetration-a fair trade for a little extra weight and less maneuverability. Ski width averages 10-12 cm. under the foot and skis generally are widest from under and back to the tail. There is some variation in the amount but most skis taper from in front of the foot to the tip of the ski-the reverse of modern alpine skis. Skis often have a center ridge for stiffness and a raised and flattened platform for the foot. The skis have very little flex to them, much stiffer then any modern skis. Ski length generally is 200cm to as much as 240cm.

Some skis will have small holes in the tips for leather strings; these can be used for pulling the skis behind a horse or man.

Binding Design:

Bindings are made of rawhide, generally cow. The leather is often oiled and worked before or after being used. Various oils are preferred; one that seem especially well regarded is made from Birch. Four holes are drilled vertically through the skis, a common design throughout Siberia. The rawhide is laced through the four holes to form an X that the boot can slide into. A single strap of leather runs around the heel from one side of the X to the other to keep the boot in the binding. Holes for the bindings are generally drilled so the ball of the foot is on the balance point of the ski.

Fur Base Covering:

The ski base is covered from tip to tail (or close to the tail) with animal skin with the hair aligned to the rear, allowing the skier to climb with excellent traction as the hair stands up, and descends with minimal resistance as the hair lays down going forward. The skin of choice is called *Puspak*, the leg skin of a horse. The keg skin is tough and the fur is very straight from the forelock often up into the rump. There is also a strong preference for the winter coat, which is much denser then the summer coat. Other skins are used as well, notably elk (*Boghu*) . Hunting these is now illegal so use of this is uncommon. One old hunter claimed that the best fur was that of an otter, and it would take six otters to make a good pair of skis. These skis would be so special as to be used for a wedding gift or for ceremonial purposes.

Skins are attached wet, overlapping from tip to tail. Nowadays skins are mostly attached with small iron tacks into the edge and often the top of the ski where the skin can be stretched over. As the skin dries it shrinks and tightens on the ski.

The Pole:

The single pole used by all skiers is called a *Tiak* , which literally means "stick" . Preferred wood is a young and straight larch sapling. Most skiers will cut either a wedge or a point on the end of their *tiak* and often put a leather thong through the top end of it. Length varies (longer poles are better in deeper snow) but generally *tiaks* are a head taller then the user.

Ski Design-the Point:

Above is a basic summation of the design of traditional ski, binding, and pole used in the Altai. Again, there are some variations but there is also a definite uniformity in design that one can argue has stood the test of time for thousands of years. Quality of manufacture varies quite a bit, especially since many mountain dwellers no longer ski or ski very rarely. Well made skis take time as they are made completely by hand using primarily an axe, a block plane, a knife, and a hand auger. One can often judge the quality of a skier by looking at the care he put into his skis. Looking at the construction with the needs I laid out earlier: first and foremost they needed to be matched to the conditions and terrain found in this region of the Altai.

Skiing Conditions, Comparisons:

On all but one trip I primarily used western (modern) skis, designed for backcountry use. They were fairly wide by our standards, lightweight, and some had a fishscale type base (for limited traction) that I used in conjunction with removable climbing skins. I use a Nordic 3pin binding and on all but one trip a stout leather boot. This was a mix of very modern and some older equipment that I assembled and tinkered with on all my trips.

The first year in the Altai we were a constant source of curiosity for the locals, as most of them had not seen modern ski equipment. They were constantly telling us our skis were too short (170-180 cm), too soft, and were basically not good for skiing around there. We would politely laugh, thinking that they did not know what they were talking about. As it turned out, on many counts they were right.

Local conditions-particularly the deep faceted snow, made our (by comparison) short soft skis sink in the deep snow-even when following several of the local skiers. Their skis-stiff and straight-stayed much higher in the snow and traveled easily while I often struggled out of holes I had made in the deep faceted snow. The modern skins did not climb as well as their fur skins, and the glide was much better on the fur skins as well, particularly in the cold dry snows common to the Altai. On top of that our skins, with glue designed to stick on and peel off when not in use, failed constantly in the cold weather, icing up and then falling off.

The single pole they used, a seemingly outdated anachronism, proved ideal for the Altai. Using it to form a sort of tripod, they were in balance and always a bit on their heels, keeping their tips up and their bodies balanced through the deep and often obstacle laced route down the hill. By the third trip I had started using the single pole, and found it a very intuitive way to ski.

Terrain Comparisons:

As to the terrain, our seemingly big advantage in having skis that glided better on the downhills rarely proved to be true. Their ski trails, whether hunting, trapping or just skiing, tended to take them on a very up and down track, way to steep for fishscales and so varied between up and down that the time needed to take skins on and off put me way behind. Hunting in particular meant chasing an animal until you caught up to it. Elk in particular were traditionally hunted this way with great success. Following an elk meant going where they did, often up and down repeatedly for a day or more. Stopping to put skins on and off just did not work.

In addition, the perceived slowness of their skis–slow skis being always a negative in the modern ski world–prove a positive for them as they negotiated their way down through forest and cliffs with a variety of turns and techniques to slow orstop as needed. The single pole in this environment was very effective as well.

Other Comparisons:

As to the other points I spoke of earlier: "skis need to be durable, reliable (in the given conditions), reparable, and sourced from local materials" .

Durability, Reliability, and Reparability:

Altai skiers use their skis very hard, skiing through rocks and over woody debris without regard.

The skis are quite durable though definitely breakable. I have seen several skis break while out skiing. This is a trade off between lightness and strength. Though not as strong as Birch or Larch, Spruce is a very light wood with a good weight to strength ratio. Many skiers keep a spare ski blank at home for this eventuality.

The horse skin used on the base of their skis is exceptionally durable and withstands a lot of abuse. When needed, worn or damaged skins can easily be replaced.

Bindings break but are generally field reparable with only a knife. Hunting skis generally have a much better quality of leather used on the bindings so as to be more reliable. Poles break but they simply grab a new one out in the forest and ski on. Materials are all available locally with the exception if the iron tacks, which they buy at a local store in one of the villages. Prior to iron tacks, skins were laced on with rawhide or attached with a combination of wood tacks and lacing out of rawhide or a certain type of reed or grass.

The Skiing:

The skiers of the Altai are slowly fading away. The main reason for skiing–hunting–is now illegal, and the main road into the Altai is plowed in the winter, making access in and out easier and skis less necessary. The main towns accessible by road have fewer and fewer skiers as there is no compelling reason to ski and lots of modern attractions to lure young men away from their traditions.

Out of town there are still skiers, and some of them are very good. Many of them started skiing between 5 and 7 years old and still ski on a regular basis every winter. These skiers have shown me what is possible on what at first seemed like completely unskiable skis.

The basics of their skiing style are as follows:

The Pole/ *Tiak*:

Skiers in the Altai could not begin to ski what they do without a *Tiak*. The central point of using a single pole is a tripod. The pole does not work as a rudder or a brake. The tripod is a wonderful system of balance, working in uneven terrain and constantly adjustable as needed. As well, the *tiak* puts the skier in a slightly rearward position (completely anathema to modern ski technique), an excellent place to be if one is unsure about what's ahead or what the snow conditions might be.

The *tiak* also lets one get into positions that would normally be out of balance, but with a *tiak* are quite doable. This is especially useful for skiing in tight trees.

The tripod created with the *tiak* lets one add a lot of leverage to the skis by adjusting body position to one side or the other. This makes the very floppy boot binding system-arguably the hardest aspect of learning to use these skis-functional.

The *tiak* is also used in climbing, somewhat like a kayak paddle, but merely to keep the skiers center up over his feet.

The *tiak* is has also been used as a weapon, sometimes to strike down game as the skier approaches.

The Skis:

The skis, long and stiff, are excellent for breaking trail and traveling in deep-snow. The javelin tip design and tall tip do not bog down and penetrate through the new snow evenly and smoothly. The horsehide skin is quiet (unlike modern skins which buzz a bit) and is very smooth and fast in comparison to our skins. Skiers tour much like we do, slinging a ski forward in a pendulum motion and stepping down on the ski to compress the new snow. They can climb easily as steep as we do and with one hand freed, they have no reserve about using the other to pull themselves through an awkward spot using a branch or small tree.

The steeper they climb the more likely they will use the *tiak* to assist in keeping their weight up over their feet.

Ski Maneuvers:

Turning, which at first glance seemed impossible on these skis is quite possible with practice. The technique uses what appears to be a huge disadvantage to the skis;

the lack of any latterly stiffness to the binding. The bindings are so soft one can move ones heels to almost right angles to the skis with little effect.

Swiveling ones heels off the skis starts the turn. This allows the skier to tilt the skis, both tilted in one direction. Once tilted the skier can then push and drive the skis into a turn. Once again this works only with the aid of a *tiak* . The *tiak* is allowed to drift behind the skier to where support is needed to get the proper leverage on the skis. The inside turn is the easy side as the pole drifts out wide of its normal position to support the skier. The outside turn is the harder of the two, as the pole must drift behind the skier a bit to support the lean in the opposite direction.

A good skier can make medium radius turns and can turn sharply to stop or avoid an obstacle. As a rule, skiers in the Altai do not turn unless needed, skiing straight (often at high speeds) is the norm and in their view, more fun.

Since I, as a western skier, do turn a lot, local skiers will often follow making turns as well.

Slowing and Stopping:

Stopping can be done by a single sharp turn to the inside. Slowing is often done using a similar technique to turning. Both heel are swiveled off the skis but rather then being done to the same side the heels are both moved to the inside of the skis, tilting the skis up on inside edges like in a snowplow maneuver. Rather then putting the skis in a wedge position (difficult with these skis) . The heels are dropped down and pushed into the snow, acting as breaks. This is quite effective and I have seen it used for descending in difficult snow or tight spaces.

Conclusion:

This is a brief summary of the skis and skiing style found in the Altai Mountains of NW China. There are a lot of aspects I did not touch on, snow camping, their use of skin sleds, and many small nuances that make their skiing effective and a pleasure to watch.

I included my perspective as I think it is generally reflective of a modern skier in all my biases and point of view. The ski instructor in me had a very hard time overcoming some really basic functional aspects to their skiing: particularly the backseat position used by virtually all the skiers on traditional gear.

Their skiing would not work as well in many of the places I ski. Their skins would ice up in the warmer snows. The often hard and frozen snow we get would be difficult to impossible on their skis that completely lack any sort of edge grip. But that's the point. Their skis are perfectly suited to their environment. In the Altai their skis are equal to or superior to my modern gear-for their intended use.

Utilitarian skiing is quite different from our modern recreation centered skiing. For their purposes, the skiers in the Altai region have made some tradeoffs, glide mayseparate skis from snowshoes, but it is not the end all from a utilitarian perspective; their skis need to climb and descent, often steeply, without interruption; they need to be able to be made with what is at hand and they need to be durable and functional in a very cold and unconsolidated snowpack.

In all these elements their skis have succeeded beautifully, formed over thousands of years of trial and error. Along with their skis they style of skiing, their ski techniques have also developed in tandem with their skis. I expect this style is quite similar to many of the ski cultures that have existed for millennia, each with their own nuances and adjustments in technique and build to perfectly suit their environment and utilitarian needs. Sadly, most of these cultures are gone or have lost this skill. Fortunately the skiers in the Altai can still give us a window into the ski traditions of the past and perhaps broaden our view about skiing and its truly ancient history.

中文论文：

在阿勒泰的十年

尼尔·拉尔森

2005 年 3 月，我和两个朋友到中国新疆阿尔泰山区（主要集中在喀纳斯-禾木乡）考察现在还在传承着的古老滑雪。我们带了很多的行李：雪橇，野营装备，食物，相机……。我还携带了另一种超重的包袱：以西方角度看待滑雪。我一直活跃于高山和北欧滑雪，并且是作为一个教练、滑雪者、设计师，致力于开发滑雪板和专注于野外滑雪的世界。这些丰富的经验已经表明这既是一个福音也是一个讽刺，它给了我一个很好的了解滑雪力学和滑雪的机会。我很确定滑雪板如何运行，如何和怎样滑好雪。

这种“满杯”的想法引发了很多关于雪板的属性、运行和滑雪的先入为主的观点。其中一些明显的观点如下：

——我十分明白，由于阿勒泰毛皮滑雪板的基本性质，阿勒泰居民使用的滑雪板相较于实用性的滑雪更接近于以往雪鞋。

——由于阿勒泰毛皮滑雪板的长度、硬度和雪板的设计以及基本的固定器，在滑雪时雪板不能随意转动。

——我们在阿勒泰地区滑雪可以更快和更熟练，我们的滑雪设备会给形成一个完全的优势。

这并不代表我被阿勒泰人仍在使用滑雪黎明时期的滑雪设备的做法所迷住。我只是被西方从古代到现代的线性滑雪发展的观点所困顿。

所以我在阿勒泰呆了十年，并且九次前去采访该地的智者。我对滑雪的观点整体上改变了，特别是对于在阿尔泰山遇到的滑雪活动和滑雪者的认识。在很大程度上，这是因为我没有真正理解休闲滑雪和阿勒泰地区实用性滑雪之间的许多差异。

现代滑雪发展成两种相当不同的路径，即高山滑雪和北欧滑雪（越野滑雪）。它们几乎都完全以娱乐为基础，以不同的方式注重滑行和速度。我认为比赛和竞争在很大程度上驱动着这两种滑雪形式的发展变化，虽然并不是所有的滑雪者都有竞争的动机。高山和越野滑雪在各自的领域内更专业化，已实现更好的展现形式。

下面的内容是中国阿尔泰山区滑雪的概况。这种风格的滑雪盛行于整个阿勒泰地区，并且基于不同地区的条件和专业用途有一些变化。

传统滑雪受多种因素的影响，而许多因素在现代滑雪中是没有的。在这里我整理出一个简短的列表，主要针对于阿尔泰山区，虽然不全面，但覆盖了主要的要点。

气象条件：

滑雪板和滑雪的开发要与当地的条件和群体的特殊需求有机结合。阿勒泰地区是典型的大陆性气候，这意味着没有海洋调和气候的影响，这里整个冬天是非常寒冷的。季节性降雪总量少于受海洋影响的地区。

在与当地山民长期交谈中我了解到：

积雪因位置不同而各不相同，低处达 50 厘米，高处可达 2 米。在我考察期间遇到过几次大风暴，期间的积雪达 1 米深。在这里冬天不下雨。

冬季主要的几个月里，气温一般都在零度以下。主要在 11 月中旬到次年 3 月，除了快到春天时太阳照射到的斜坡上。温度从 11 月到 2 月可以在-15 度和-45 度之间。

最终结果，因为涉及到滑雪的积雪往往太浅，又要避免低温雪的深层影响。这可能造成一个积雪场没有基础性的支撑：深不见底的积雪使行走异常困难。

3/4 的冬季旅行都会碰到积雪。林木线以下雪几乎是没有风的影响，几乎每个冬天的旅行都会碰到同样深度及寒冷软雪的条件。

最后，雪崩是非常普遍的，甚至在每场大雪降后都会发生。有多刻面的积雪场使雪层极其不稳定，还会使道路不通行。当滑雪时，这是滑雪者比较担心的一种情况。

地形条件：

阿尔泰山区几乎大范围位于欧亚大陆的中心。我在考察期间主要居住在中国阿勒泰喀纳斯-禾木地区，这个地区处于西北部。有些天居住在这个地区更北部，是这个地区的枢纽处—连接着哈萨克斯坦、俄罗斯、蒙古和中国。

下面我将描述一下我所在的这个地方。

这个地区的山脉崎岖不平，大部分山脉是高山地形。上面是：冬天林木线和未开发的。林木线总体在 2000-2100 米间。许多深谷切入在阿尔泰山南部，河流后注入额尔齐斯河。这些山谷和周边农村地区森林茂密，主要有桦木、落叶松、云杉和各种各样的杨树。这些山脉本身通常很陡峭且多岩石，古老的河流穿梭其间。这种地形通常用于放牧和狩猎，主要是陡峭的山坡和山脊，其间有茂密的森林。由于地形条件和雪崩的缘故，在大雪过后或冬春过渡期雪崩的发生是常见的也是不可预测的。

滑雪板的用法：

滑雪板在阿尔泰山脉主要被用于各种各样的冬季活动中。最常见的日常使用，特别是在下大雪年用途如下：

——发现和饲养家畜。

——收集水供家庭使用。

——收集和搬运柴火。

——拜访或前往邻居或亲戚家。

最常见和重要的滑雪板用途可能是狩猎和诱捕。包括过些日子就穿着滑雪板检查本地的诱捕或到山地为期一周巡查。捕获猎物是当地人物物交换和货币来源的主要渠道，狩猎是他们冬季食物的重要补充。

在阿勒泰地区，单匹马拉察纳爬犁（Chanas）在冬天常用于旅行和运输，特别是运输干草和柴火。直到 2008 年，阿勒泰地区到了冬季道路仍然不通。察纳爬犁用于获取供应，访问亲戚，或接孩子于寄宿学校。只要路径能够通行，察纳爬犁用于为期两天的旅行，运行起来是很好的。在大雪过后，小组分队会前往打开路径，然后马匹跟随其后，之后察纳爬犁就可以完全打开道路了。

最后，滑雪板也被用于娱乐。我记录了很多人滑雪趣事（主人公有男性和女性），有的是在比赛中。年少的小男孩可以滑雪，但不是为特别的目的而是玩乐。从实用的角度来看，滑雪，尤其是使用的传统的滑雪板滑雪在阿勒泰地区是一种困难的事情，需要好几年的时间才能娴熟掌握其技巧。也许最好的类比是射箭，这项技能始于年少时期，而早期的动机只是为了快乐和好玩。

结合条件和滑雪板用法：

当我们看到阿尔泰山区使用滑雪板的综合条件和地形时，我们可能开始了解到滑雪板设计技能的挑战性和需求性。现实需求使滑雪板要有耐磨性、可靠性和可修复性，并且要就地取材。

滑雪板设计：

阿勒泰滑雪板长度各不相同，一位技巧娴熟的滑雪者至少有两副雪板（一副备用的放到小屋）。那副短的用于近距离旅行，那副长的用于远游。多天的旅程意味着许多小时的摩擦，而长的滑雪板能够支撑滑雪者的重量，减少雪的摩擦渗透——一点额外的重量和更少的可操作性。滑雪板宽度平均10–12厘米。在脚下的滑雪板部分是最宽的。雪板的参数有变化但大多数滑雪板的顶部是尖的—与现代高山滑雪板相反。滑雪板通常有一个中心脊和一个脚踩的突起的平台。滑雪板很少有弯曲，比现代滑雪板坚硬。滑雪板的长度通常是200厘米到240厘米。

固定器设计：

固定器一般由生牛皮制成。皮革通常在使用之前或之后都要用油润滑。所用的油是各种各样的，一种被认为是最好的油是由桦树提炼出来的。四个孔钻垂直穿过滑雪板，这种设计形式在西伯利亚地区是常见的。生牛皮条穿过四个孔形成X形，使雪鞋可以滑入。皮革带子绕着脚跟从一侧的X形穿过，以保证雪鞋在固定器中。

底部毛皮覆盖：

滑雪板底部从板头到板尾都由动物的毛皮覆盖，皮毛接近尾部，当毛皮上的毛竖起来滑雪者也能运动自如。当向下滑行时，毛皮又有一定的抵挡作用。选择的这种动物的毛皮叫做Puspak，通常是马腿部的毛皮。这种毛皮是十分坚硬的。人们制作冬衣时也偏爱用这种毛皮，这种冬衣比夏衣更密实。有时也会用其他的毛皮，特别是麋鹿的（Boghu）。现在非法狩猎麋鹿是很少见的。一个老猎人声称，最好的皮毛是水獭皮，六个水獭的毛皮才能做副好滑雪板。这些特别的雪板将作为结婚礼物或用于礼仪的目的。

雪杖：

滑雪者所用的单只雪杖被称为Tiak，字面意思就是“棍子”。首选的木材是竖直年轻的落叶松小树。大多数滑雪者还将木杆的末端削成楔状或在tiak的末端镶嵌上一个锐器等，常常把一条皮带束在顶部。雪杖的长度不同（长点的雪杖在深雪中滑行更好些），但通常比滑雪者要高些。

滑雪板设计——关键点：

以上是设计一副传统滑雪板的基础元以及固定器和雪杖。虽然有一些变化的元素，但有一些设计元素是明确统一的，所以千年以来人们才能在雪板上自如滑行。近来雪板制作质量变化显著，尤其是当山民不再滑雪或很少滑雪。好的雪板几乎全部由手工制成，工具有斧头、一块木板、一把刀、一只手钻。通过一位滑雪者对其雪板的爱护程度，我们可以判断这位滑雪者的品德。

回顾一下我们前面的文章构思形式：首先最重要的是阿勒泰地区相匹配的气象条件和地形条件。

滑雪条件的比较：

一般我主要使用为野外滑雪而设计的西方（现代）滑雪板，这样的滑雪板相当宽、质量轻，有一些雪板底面呈鱼鳞形式（有限的运转），我可以和可拆卸的用于攀爬的仿制毛皮一起使用。使用北欧 3 层定制的固定器和一双结实的皮革靴。这是一个非常现代的而又有些老旧的设备，在所有的旅行中，我不断组装和修补它们。

第一年在阿勒泰时，我们对当地人怀有很强的好奇心，他们中的大多数没有看到过现代滑雪设备。他们不断告诉我们的滑雪板太短（170–180 厘米），太软，基本上不适合滑雪。我们会礼貌地笑笑，以为他们不知道他们在谈论什么。当后来的事实证明，在许多方面证明他们是对的。

当地条件，特别是在深雪中，我们（相比之下）短而软的滑雪板会轻易陷在雪中，即使跟随在几个当地的滑雪者的后面也会这样。他们的滑雪板坚硬而挺直，与雪保持一定的距离，并且容易在雪地上滑行。现代仿制的动物的毛皮不及他们所采用的毛皮，阿勒泰毛皮雪板上的毛皮能使雪板在干冷的雪地中稳健滑行。

他们使用的单只雪仗，看起来仿佛是过时的历史错误，而事实证明在阿勒泰地区是正确而理想的。用它和两条腿来形成一个三脚架，借以帮助维持向下滑的平衡，重心总是在脚后跟后，有效保持身体平衡，躲避开途径的障碍。

地形比较：

至于地形，雪板向下滑行的巨大优势在下山滑时很少证明是正确的。我们看似巨大的优势在雪橇滑行更好在下坡很少被证明是正确的。他们的滑雪路径，无论是狩猎、诱捕或滑雪，都倾向会上下颤动。狩猎尤其意味着追逐一只动物，直到你捕捉到为止。特别是麋鹿，用这种传统狩猎方式通常会取得巨大成功。追逐一只麋鹿意味着要如影随形的跟着它们，经常反复上下一天或更多。用现代滑雪板停下来再装卸毛皮是不行的。

此外，阿勒泰毛皮滑雪板在滑行时有种缓慢的感觉，滑雪板的缓慢在现代滑雪世界里总是负面的一个因素。当地人穿着滑雪板穿过森林和悬崖或转弯、减缓或停止时，单只雪杖在这种环境中是非常有效的。

其他的比较：

就如我前面提到过的有人谈过："阿勒泰古老毛皮滑雪板需要有耐用性、可靠性（在给定的条件下）、可修复性，并且取材于当地"。

耐久性、可靠性和可修复性：这些特性在滑雪的过程中都可以体现出来，具体主要体现在雪板、雪杖的取材和制作，滑雪动作的展现（转弯、减缓和停止）。

结论：

这是我在中国西北部的阿尔泰山区发现关于爬犁和雪板的一个简洁的总结。其实还有很多方面我还没有涉及到，比如雪地露营、毛皮雪板的使用、有效滑雪的小细节和观看滑雪的乐趣等。

我总结的我的观点，从我的偏见和观点来看，这通常是一位现代滑雪者的反思。这反映了现代滑雪者的我所有的偏见和观点。作为一名滑雪教练，我很难克服关于滑雪的一些非常基本的功能方面：传统的滑雪者几乎全都是采用后坐的姿态。

在我滑雪的许多地方，对他们的滑雪方式并不适合。雪板上的毛皮在温暖的冬季会结冰。我们的雪板在坚硬和冷冻雪地里很难滑行，而他们的雪板能够很好地滑行。这正是问题的关键。他们的滑雪板是完全适合他们的环境。在阿勒泰地区他们的滑雪板等于或优于我的现代滑雪板。

实用性质的滑雪是完全不同于我们现代以娱乐为中心的滑雪。为了他们的实用目的，阿勒泰地区的滑雪者做了一些权衡，滑行可能使雪板和雪鞋分离，但从实用的角度看，这并不是全部，他们的滑雪板需要无障碍地攀爬和下坡，他们的制作需要能够就地取材。它们在异常寒冷和松散的积雪中能够有持久性和有效性。

他们的雪板能兼顾所有这些元素而顺利滑行，经受了数千年的实践检验。他们的滑雪技术，连同他们的滑雪风格与雪板一起不断发展。我希望这种风格与滑雪文化一样，历经千年而愈加璀璨。每种风格都有自己的细微差别和调整的技巧，能适应当地的环境和实际需要。令人遗憾的是，大多数的这样文化正在消失或已失去了这种技能。幸运的是阿勒泰地区的滑雪者能够给我们一扇了解古老滑雪传统的窗口，拓宽我们对于滑雪和古老滑雪历史的世界视野。

4.5　关于墩德布拉克滑雪岩画的年代问题　Discussions about Age of Dundebulak Rock Paintings

王建新　Wang Jianxin（CHN）

个人简介　Brief Introduction

王建新，男，中国籍，西北大学文化遗产学院教师，教授，博士生导师。文化遗产研究与保护技术教育部重点实验室主任、西北大学丝绸之路文化遗产保护与考古学研究中心主任、西北大学丝绸之路研究院首席考古学家、西北大学学术委员会委员。

兼任：国内外多家考古、学术、研究机构职务。

主要研究领域：中国新石器时代考古、秦汉考古、东北亚地区考古、中亚地区考古、游牧考古、佛教考古、文化遗产管理与保护规划。

主要研究成果：出版学术专著2部，主持编制完成并通过国家文物局审查和地方政府颁布实施大遗址保护规划2项，发表学术论文50余篇。

Jianxin Wang, male, Chinese, is a teacher, professor, doctoral supervisor in the School of Cultural Heritage, Northwest University. He is also the director of the key laboratory of Ministry of education, the research and protection technology of cultural heritage, the director of research center of Northwest University Silk Road cultural heritage protection and archaeology, the chief archaeologist of the Silk Road research institute in Northwest University and the member of Northwest University Academic Committee.

Concurrent posts: many positions in archaeological, academic and research institutions at home and abroad.

Research results: publishing 2 monographs, presiding over and compiled two big relics protection examined by the State Administration of Cultural Heritage reviewand the local government enactment, publishing more than 50 papers.

中文论文：

墩德布拉克彩绘岩画最早是由中国考古学者发现的。在岩画发现之初，考古学者就根据岩画所处的环境和岩画的形式、内容，认为其应属旧石器时代晚期。

墩德布拉克岩画及其周围环境　Rock paintings in Dundebulake and surrounding environment

墩德布拉克岩画属于在岩棚上用颜料彩绘的岩画。洞穴和岩棚是旧石器时代晚期欧亚大陆早期人类居住的主要场所。在欧亚大陆西部的法国和西班牙旧石器时代晚期的岩洞中，发现了一些在洞穴中彩绘的岩画，其中有野牛、野马、野猪、鹿和人的形象，其年代最早可达距今3万年前。在岩棚上彩绘的岩画，也有许多发现。印度中央邦皮摩波特卡（Bhimbhetka）发现的岩棚彩绘岩画，用红色和赭色的颜料绘有大量人物和动物的形象，与墩德布拉克岩棚彩绘岩画的存在形式、所用颜料和岩画形式都十分相似，其年代为距今35000年。

法国拉斯科洞穴岩画

西班牙阿尔塔米拉洞穴岩画

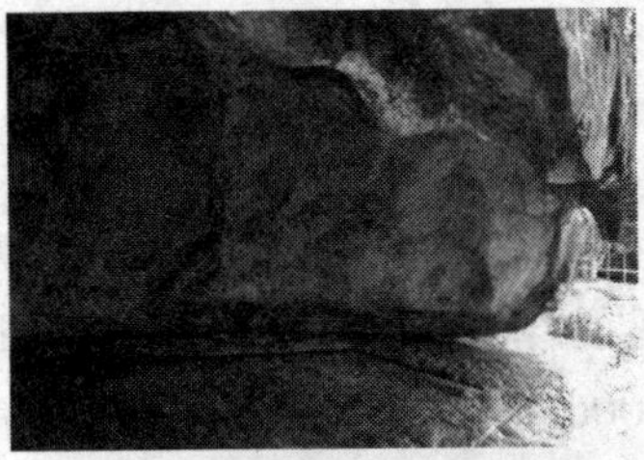
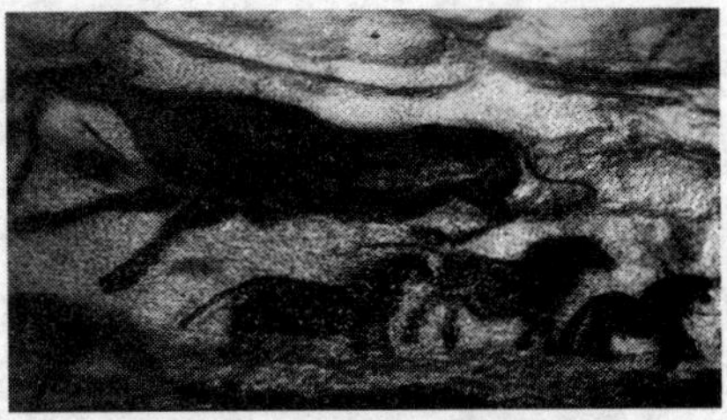

印度中央邦皮摩波特卡（Bhimbhetka）岩画（距今 35000 年）

墩德布拉克岩画

印度中央邦皮摩波特卡（Bhimbhetka）岩画

2014 年 9 月，我们现场考察了乌兹别克斯坦卡什卡达里亚州古利克萨伊（Gaukhana）发现的岩棚彩绘岩画。从现场观察的情况看，该处岩画也是用红色和赭色的颜料绘制在岩棚上，有人物、动物和手印等形象，其存在形式和所用颜料也与墩德布拉克岩画相似。与我们一起考察的乌兹别克斯坦考古学家认为该处岩画属旧石器时代晚期，距今约 3 万年左右。

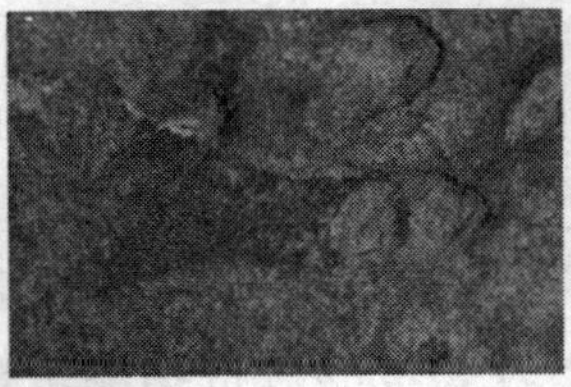

乌兹别克斯坦卡什卡达里亚古利克萨伊（Gaukhana）岩棚彩绘岩画
Colored rock paintings in Gaukhana Qashqadaryo Province Uzbekistan

因此，中国考古学家在发现墩德布拉克岩画之初，就认为其应属旧石器时代晚期是有根据的。

墩德布拉克岩画发现之后，单兆鉴先生作为一位滑雪运动的专家，在参观墩德布拉克岩画的过程中，以敏锐的职业眼光，发现了岩画中有滑雪的形象，这使得墩德布拉克岩画的价值内涵有了更高的发现。2006 年 1 月，经过由滑雪专家、考古学家、历史学家共同组成的专家组认真而激烈的讨论，最后大家达成一致意见，发表了《阿勒泰宣言》，认为墩德布拉克岩画的年代应在距今一万年左右。即使如此，根据已知的考古资料，墩德布拉克岩画的发现也证明了阿勒泰山区是世界上最古老的滑雪地域。

阿勒泰山区的滑雪传统源远流长。继墩德布拉克岩画的发现之后，近年来考古工作者又在布尔津县和额敏县的相继发现了在岩石上刻画的滑雪形象，其年代推测在距今 4000~3000 年左右。阿尔泰山南麓中国境内流传至今的用马腿皮包裹滑雪板和单撬滑雪的独特传统，在阿尔泰山北麓的俄罗斯境内也同样存在。这些都证明，阿尔泰山区在世界上是一个具有古老传统的滑雪区域。

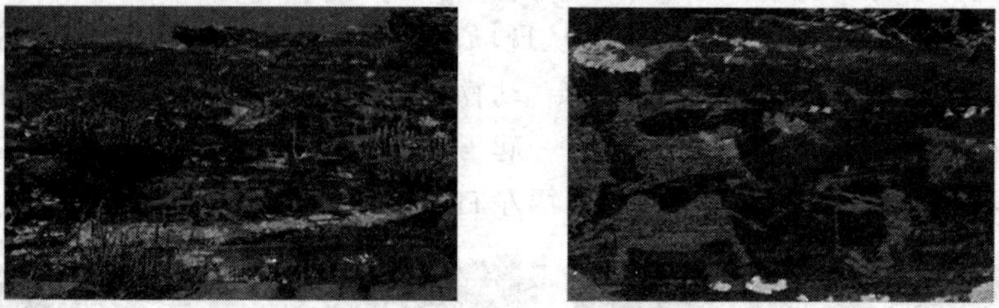

新疆塔城地区额敏县喀拉也木勒滑雪岩画

墩德布拉克岩画的具体年代，还需要采用科学测年的方法进行测定。作为一个考古工作者，从参与《阿勒泰宣言》的起草之后，我又多次前往墩德布拉克岩画现场考察，试图解决岩画科学测年问题。

目前，国际上对彩绘岩画测年的技术主要有和质谱加速器碳 14 测年法。铀系法主要用于石灰岩，但墩德布拉克岩画的石质，可能不是石灰岩。因此，提取岩画颜料中含有机质的胶料，运用碳 14 测年法进行分析测试是目前唯一可选的测年技术。传统的碳 14 测年法需要较大量的有机物测试标本，而墩德布拉克岩画的彩绘颜料在岩石上的附着层很薄，不可能采取大量的颜料，而且这还将对岩画本身造成破坏。采用最新的质谱加速器碳 14 测年法，只需要微量的有机质测试标本就可分析。目前，我国在广西花山彩绘岩画已开展了这样的测年研究。

English paper：

Dundebulak Rock Paintings were discovered by Chinese archeologists. They defined that those paintings belong to Palaeolithic Age (Old Stone Age) according to the surroundings, content, and styles.

Dundebulak Rock Paintings were coloured paintings on the roof of caves. , where early Eurasia humans lived in the late Palaeolithic Age. Some Rock Paintings in caves were discovered in France and Spain, which could be traced back to 30, 000 years ago, bison, wild horse, wild boar, deer, and human's image are in the paintings.

The coloured rock paintings in Bhimbhetka, India, dating back to 35, 000 years ago, have many similarities with those in Dundebulak in style. The images of human and animals in the paintings were coloured by red and ochre.

In Septemper of 2014, we surveyed the coloured rock paintings in Gaukhana, Qashqadaryo Province, Uzbekistan. Its style and the pigment is also similar to those of Dundebulak paintings, an archeologist from Uzbekistan believed that the paintings could be traced back to late Palaeolithic Age, about 30,000 years ago.

Therefore, Chinese archeologists had enough confidence to tell that Dundebulak Rock Paintings belong to late Palaeolithic Age when they first discovered the paintings.

After discovering Dundebulak Rock Paintings, Shan Zhaojian, an expert of skiing, found that there were images in the paintings about posture skiing when visiting the site, which enhanced the value of paintings. In January, 2006, a conclusion was drew by skiing by skiing experts, archaeologists and historians after serious and heated discussion, so Declaration of Altay was issued, which states that Dundebulak Rock Paintings can be traced back to 10, 000 years ago. Even so, the discovered of Dundebulak Rock Paintings, according to the historical records, proved that Altay mountains is the original place of ancient skiing in the world.

The tradition of skiing in Altay Mountains has a long history. After the discovering of Dundebulak Rock Paintings, the archeologists discovered the paintings one after another in Buerjing County and Eming County depicting images of skiing, and it is speculated that those paintings were 3000 to 4000 years ago. At southern foot of Altay Mountains in China, the tradition of wrapping skis with horse fur from legs and using single ski is passed down to nowadays, and it is the same with Russia. All of above prove that Altay mountains is the area of ancient traditional skiing.

Scientific method is needed to adopt for determination of dating. As an Archeologist, having got involved in editing Declaration of Altay, I inspected Dundebulak Rock Paintings many times, trying to solve the problem of scientific method.

At present, the international paintings dating techniques mainly include uranium series method and mass spectrometry accelerator carbon 14 dating method. Limestone is suitable for uranium series method, however, Dundebulak rocks may not be limestones. Therefore, the only way to date is to extract organic matter in the rubber from pigment on the paintings and date paintings by mass spectrometry accelerator carbon 14 dating method, whose traditional way needs lots of sample, however, layer of pigment on the paintings so thin that we can't take away much of it, concerning about protecting the relics. The new way of carbon 14 dating method can analyze only by little amount of sample. At present, HuaShan coloured rock paintings in Guangxi is under the study of dating by this way.

4.6 将中国阿勒泰地区的传统滑雪文化作为一个特殊的事件来庆祝
Festivalizing the Traditional Ski Culture in Altay as a Special Event

阿依肯·加山（中国） Ayiken Jiashan（CHN）

个人简介 Brief Introduction

阿依肯·加山，男，中国籍，生于1977年11月7日。新疆乌鲁木齐人。2005年参加阿勒泰古老滑雪探险团工作，专职美国考察团翻译。从2007年加入单兆鉴老师团队成为阿勒泰古老滑雪研究组成员。多年和国外专家合作，推广阿勒泰古老滑雪文化，积极策划古老滑雪国际研讨会项目。阿依肯·加山曾协助美国专家Nils Larsen完成阿勒泰古老滑雪历史纪录片的拍摄制作工作，为该纪录片做出了贡献。

2013年协助组织了美国国家地理杂志专题团考察阿勒泰，首次把阿勒泰古老滑雪文化内容纳入在世界顶级杂志上刊出。

阿依肯·加山目前正在挪威北极大学攻读冬季旅游发展研究班，他的研究课题正好是阿勒泰古老滑雪和阿勒泰冬季旅游发展。

Ayiken Jiashan, male, Chinese, was born on July November, 1977. He is from Urumqi, Xinjiang. In 2005, he worked for Altay ancient skiing exploring group as the translator for American investigation group. In 2007, he joined Mr. Shan Zhaojian's team and became a member of Altay ancient skiing research group. Ayiken Jiashan has worked with foreign experts, promoted Altay ancient skiing culture and actively planned for the international workshop on ancient skiing for many years. He once assisted American expert Nils Larsen with the filming of historical documentary of Altay ancient skiing and made a great contribution to this historical documentary.

In 2013, he helped to organize the investigation of the project team of National Geographic Magazine to Altay which was the first time that Altay ancient skiing culture was published in the world's top magazine.

Ayiken Jiashan now is studying in a winter tourism development research class in Norway Arctic University. His research subject is precisely about Altay ancient skiing and winter tourism development.

中文论文:

将中国阿勒泰地区的传统滑雪文化作为一个特殊的事件来庆祝

阿依肯·加山（中国）

1. 介绍

关于滑雪起源的讨论诸多。一些学者提及了斯堪的纳维亚半岛（在挪威，第一个 myrfunn 于 1906 年在阿尔夫达尔制作，我们的最古老的滑雪板来自努尔兰的韦夫斯恩的 Drevja，时间具体到公元前 3343-2939 年 Øvrebø-雪板），而有一些学者认为起源地应为俄罗斯，因为考古学家发现部分雪板是在位于白海附近的俄罗斯北部，可追溯到大约公元前 6000 年。考古学家还在中国阿勒泰市附近的阿尔泰山里发现了一个石雕，其可追溯到大约 1.2-1.5 万年前（单兆鉴，2011：22）。不管怎样，在现代社会有少数人仍保留着他们的传统滑雪文化，他们就是位于中国阿尔泰山脉的半游牧民族。在这些深山里，土著人滑雪存活至今，这些人们在漫长寒冷的冬季仍将他们的滑板用作旅行和狩猎的工具。随着现代的发展，一些如上山的石板路和简易的车辆等替代了木马（由古中国谚语命名的传统滑雪板）。气候的变化，如降雪量少，以及受“禁止打猎”的法律影响的野生动物都是使滑雪传统濒临灭绝的原因。

本篇论文将采用事件管理和节日的理论去分析可被保存下来中国阿勒泰地区的传统滑雪的现状。

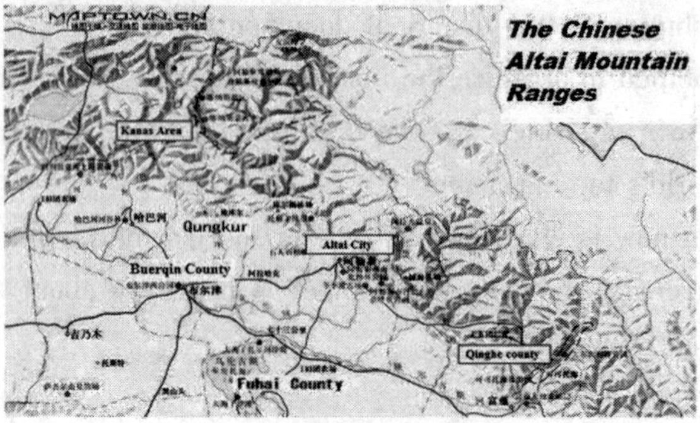

中国阿尔泰山脉

为了继承和发扬阿勒泰古老滑雪文化，同时纪念建立“阿勒泰是人类滑雪起源地”的理念，阿勒泰当地政府将1月16日定为阿勒泰传统滑雪日或阿勒泰传统滑雪节（ATSF）。每年的1月16日，将会在阿勒泰市外的将军山滑雪场举行一场传统滑雪竞赛（单兆鉴，2011）。这一天，来自阿勒泰山脉不同地区不同民族的数以百计的当地滑雪者，如哈萨克族人，图瓦人，蒙古族人相聚在一起。节日为期三天，由不同的赛事组成，如12千米单人滑雪竞技、10千米接力赛、拉雪橇滑雪竞赛、射箭滑雪。另外，还有一些包含其他节目的附加节目，阿勒泰市冰雕，音乐会，雪板制作艺术展，滑雪历史博物馆等。

2. 理论

（1）事件

事件的定义是指公众仅在限定的时间内被邀请去参加的某一主题的庆祝或展示的形式，是年度性的或发生的次数很少（Getz1997）。事件：发生在某一确切的时间和地点；发生在特定的环境下；一个重要的事件（Getz2012）。从定义上来说，事件具有开始和结尾。事件是具有时间性的规划项目或事项，十分具体并事先做好宣传工作。

① 特殊事件是指常规项目之外的一次性或发生次数很少的活动，或是由赞助主体或组织主体发起的活动。

② 对于顾客或客户来说，特殊事件是正常选择范围之外或日常活动之外的一个休闲、社交或文化体验的机会（Getz，2012：15）。

这意味着事件是“某些事物”的产物和创新，这些事物就是一些唯一、特殊的时刻或经历。

（2）传统滑雪节作为一个特殊策划的事件

Getz引用Goldblatt和Nelson对于特殊事件的定义，即用典礼和仪式来庆祝一段特有的时间，以满足具体需求（Getz，1997）。根据这个定义，阿勒泰传统滑雪节（ATSF）就是一个在保护传统免遭绝迹基础上建立起来的文化节日（仪式)。Getz 给出了两种定义：一.）特殊事件是指常规项目之外的一次性或发生次数很少的事件，或是由赞助主体或组织主体发起的事件；二.）对于顾客或客户来说，特殊事件是正常选择范围之外或日常活动之外的一个休闲、社交或文化体验的机会（Getz，2012：15）。根据 Getz 给出的定义，阿勒泰传统滑雪节并不是一直发生的事件，同时它是当地普通老百姓之间的竞赛，与世界上其他任何滑雪竞赛不同。该节日还是一个规划性事件，而规划性事件是具有预定开始和结尾的时空现象。传统滑雪节日因其互动发生在背景、人物和类似此项目的管理体系之间而具有其独特性。

(3) 传统滑雪节作为一种文化庆典

正如 Getz 所说，“庆典”是带有社交聚会或娱乐活动的事件，并且文化涵盖可识别的人类社会和团体如何生活、整理事物并和他人区分开来的多种多样的方式（Getz，2005）。具有公共性质的事件种类繁多。文化庆典可包含如传统纪念活动、嘉年华、节日、宗教活动、游行示威、文娱、艺术展（Getz2005）。传统滑雪的设计和使用与现代滑雪大相径庭。在过去，传统滑雪并不用于娱乐或现实竞赛中，而是用于运输、打猎等，主要用于生存。在该节日期间，不仅仅滑雪比赛，连民间音乐会、射箭、雪板制作展览还在延续。

① 纪念仪式

节日是一种被纪念的历史事件（Getz，2005）。根据牛津词典的解释，纪念仪式是一种纪念某个人或某个事件的仪式或典礼（牛津词典，2014）。2006 年 1 月 16 日，中国当地政府通过阿勒泰宣言命名阿勒泰为世界滑雪起源地，并把这一天定为一个滑雪节日。阿勒泰传统滑雪节今年 1 月庆祝了她的第十个生日。

阿尔泰山古老滑雪者

Aneient Skiers

② 节日

据 Getz 所说，节日是一个公共的、具有主题的庆典，它展示文化碎片，这些文化碎片能够指引顾客理解主流文化和社区。节日是一种文化庆典，或具有世俗性或具有宗教性，由公众所创并为公众所创，独立排期或与其他事件衔接（Getz，1997）。这就意味着节日体现于嘉年华、宗教活动或遗产纪念仪式中。节日是市民荣誉、凝聚力、娱乐和休闲的重要组成部分。节日所带来的机遇可提升教育价值观、展示工艺品，同时去展现在音乐、美术、戏剧和文化方面的新思想（ibid，1997）。我们前面提到过，该滑雪节包含各种各样的活动，吸引来自中国乃至世界其他国家的数以百计的游客。

③ 游行

公众游行，特指庆祝一个特殊的日子或事件，并包含游行乐队和彩车（牛津词典，2014）。游行可以是许多其他类型事件的一部分，或者作为一种文化庆典形式来体现其自身价值。在阿勒泰传统滑雪节的开幕式上，许多游行由一些少数民族进行，他们在大街上穿着传统服饰，演奏他们的民间音乐。

④ 文艺

Getz 从多方面定义了“文艺”事件。一．）视觉事件，如雕塑、手工艺品；二．）表演事件，如音乐、舞蹈、讲故事等；三．）参与性事件，意思是指观众或游客融入到当地表演者中（Getz，2005）。阿勒泰传统滑雪节展现了许多艺术作品，如滑板制作比赛、弓箭制作等，还展现了民间音乐会，如蒙古族滑雪音乐、哈萨克斯坦族滑雪者舞蹈、古图瓦族滑雪者讲述的民间滑雪故事。

⑤ 艺术展

艺术展是给观众提供欣赏（有形的和无形的）艺术品的一个空间，或是博物馆和不同的画廊（Getz，2005）。位于阿勒泰市附近的 Handigate 的传统滑雪博物馆是在该节日中主要景点之一。该博物馆收藏、保存和展示滑雪历史元素，用于研究、教育和启发灵感。

（4）事件旅游

① 事件旅游的背景

在文化发展的长河里，人们相聚在一起来庆祝很多场合，这些事件几千年来已经成为了人类社会重要的一部分。（道格拉斯，道格拉斯和格瑞特，2001）尽管事件数千年来已是人类本性的重要组成部分，但它发展成一种真实商业的时间并不长。事件作为特殊利益旅游的一个重要组成元素已成为了旅游业的一部分，并且在全世界范围内，针对事件旅游的单位正在旅游组织范围内快速建立起来。当这种现象已发展成为谋取商业利益的可能性时，就出现了无数的专业方面的机遇，事件组织公司风生水起。结果，在许多教育机构里事件旅游正日益被当作是一个独立研究领域。（Getz 1997 和道格拉斯等 2001）。由于事件旅游既是一个迅速发展的行业，也是一个研究的领域，关于此话题的文学也正在日益发展壮大。在文学领域，你能找到 Donald Getz，他从两方面定义了事件旅游。一方面，经过策划、开发和营销的事件，本身就是旅游景点；另一方面，他争辩道，事件旅游是市场的一部分，人们在这个市场内旅游参加事件，并能受到激发去这样做。（Getz 1997）

由于旅游业的未来并不取决于大众旅游，所以利基营销显得更为重要。例如，气候变化和不同的危机正不断影响当代旅游业的发展。结果，旅游业和旅游景点越来越注重旅游者的需求。因此，正逢大众旅游受限之时，事件旅游将会变得更加重要。除此之外，事件旅游在文学研究领域和目的地管理领域都是次领域。

② 事件旅游的定义

Getz 从三方面对事件旅游进行了定义。前两种定义总结起来为供应端，第三种属于需求端。

事件旅游在城市或旅游景点层面上来讲是策划事件，作为旅游景点、催化剂、动画师、广告策划工作者和地方营销人员的开发与营销。这个过程包含竞标、促进和制作事件、把事件的档案当做目标资产进行管理。

对于个人事件来说，事件旅游意味着采取市场取向来吸引游客，有时作为附加部分，有时作为核心业务。当游客是核心业务时，我们称之为“目的地事件”。

事件旅游是在旅游中参加事件，既有专门的事件游客，他们专门为某些事件而旅游，也有其他离开家去参加事件的游客。（Getz，2013：5）

（5）事件旅游的影响

事件旅游是一个经济利益导向型的旅游领域。尽管如此，我们也在个人层面和社会层面上对其影响进行研究，还可以研究它对文化改变和环境改变的影响（Getz，2008）。

① 经济和环境方面的影响

根据下表所示，事件旅游的经济方面，对通过外汇收入、就业等的当地社区的影响。来自旅游、住宿、物品和服务的税收巨大。其中一个重要的经济影响是事件创造就业就会，它包含提供工作以促进当地业务和加速当地社区就业率。事件旅游的环境影响是就当地景区、环保基础设施发展如建筑、道路和交通而言。下面的表格总结出事件对东道社区的影响，标出了正面和负面影响。

事件对旅游的影响（Allen et al. 2011，61）

旅游的影响	正面影响	负面影响
经济	促进经济目标和增加游客访问量	社区对旅游业的反感
	延长停留时间	失去其真实性
	增加就业	损害声誉
	增加财政收入	开采
	商业机遇	机会成本
环境	展示环境	环境破坏
	提供最好的练习模型	污染

旅游的影响	正面影响	负面影响
	环保意识增强	破坏文化遗产
	基础设施遗产	噪音干扰
	交通及通讯设施改善	交通堵塞
	城市改造和更新	
社会和文化	共同经历	社区异化
	复兴传统	操控社区
	建立社区骄傲	消极的社会形象
	对社区组织的验证	不良行为
	增加社会参与	滥用物资
	引进有挑战性的新思想	社会失调
	文化视角扩张	丧失安乐生活

② 社会文化方面的影响

事件旅游的主要方面之一是社会-文化部分。本文表中所列可以看出在增强传统和价值观的同时展示了许多正面和负面的影响；更多的参加体育、文艺或其他和事件主题有关的活动。通过参加事件适应新的社会形态和文化形态。其他长期的好处可能是以增加志愿服务和社区团体活动、跨文化交际和合作的形式体现。

根据里奇所说，事件的五点正面效益表现为：社区荣誉或成就；社会互动和社区发展；凝聚力或信息共享；社区认同、自我形象或地方意识；还有社区健康。主要的负面效益为：志愿者倦怠；系统资源负担过度；交通和噪音干扰；机械破坏；设备的限制、过度使用；社区的常规消耗（里奇，1984）。

里奇还争辩到，事件的社会-文化方面的影响可能包含跟事件（文艺、体育）相关的活动增加方面的效益，并加强地域价值观或地域传统。但是事件和事件旅游项目可能会给东道社区带来社会和文化成本。尽管主客互动有望通过节日和事件中的共同参与得到改善，但一般也会因其承受巨大压力（ibid，1984）。

许多遗产专家十分担心旅游与遗产型景区之间的联系。Herbert 指出遗产观光能带来金钱效益、社区参与、引进当地支持并创造就业机会。但另一方面，它可在支持娱乐中失掉历史真实性，掩盖历史有争议或不愉快的方面，把居民当做景点，破坏自然背景（Herbert，1995）。

3. 讨论

现在我们来讨论一下事件旅游对文化遗产的一些影响。人们在某些方面认为旅游对文化遗产是有害的，如文化变迁和文化修改。“这包含传统价值观的退化，仪式和礼仪的修改，对人类祖先和土著历史的重视减弱”（Timothy. D. J，2003：153），正如美国滑雪历史研究学者尼尔．拉尔森表明，阿勒泰的历史滑雪文化背后拥有阿勒泰深远的传统。古代人们将那些雪板用于生存的工具，如猎食、运输等，而非比赛或娱乐（作者）。根据拉尔森所说，阿勒泰的滑雪节主要针对比赛或滑雪比赛，它导致了阿勒泰滑雪传统使用风格的改变。然而，有许多旅游因素在某些文化阶段的劣势或衰退上扮演了重要的角色。旅游，尤其是事件旅游，在创建对有形和无形资源保护的公共意识和支持方面是一个核心因素，这些资源将会转变为更大的政治上和资金上的进一步保护活动（Mckercher&Cros，2002：10）。旅游能对阿勒泰的传统滑雪文化的保护和复兴作出宝贵的贡献；它可以助其复兴失去的传统、艺术和文化习俗。

每年有数以百计的滑雪者参加滑雪赛事，并且越来越多的新生滑雪者加入到滑雪团队来。旅游还能为当地社区的多数人提供新的谋生机会。如对比赛的前20名的冠军、为游客赶马拉雪橇和当地寄宿等提供奖金。遗憾的是这些积极影响常常与旅游负面影响相矛盾，如拥挤、文化变迁和商品化、文化盗窃和通过不当开发和基础建设更改旅游景点的物理特性（联合国教科文组织，曼谷，2004）。结果，成千上万的游客每年都集中在这三天的滑雪比赛；空间、环境、交通设施、住宿设施和当地社区居民都不够。大众旅游减弱了当地文化并摧毁当地社区传统的生活方式。中国滑雪历史研究协会主席单兆鉴先生争辩道当地滑雪者把他们的雪板做得比以前的更短、更薄或更轻，改变了传统雪板的物理特性。

文化节是一个复杂的研究领域，在同一个标题下展现出许多不同的文化元素（不仅仅是传统滑雪比赛），但是其他的文化遗产在不同背景的游客之间包含并具有一系列可能的释义和标识，如滑雪狩猎、滑雪博物馆、民间音乐会、雪板制作比赛等（Mathisen. S，2009）。

4. 结论

本篇论文调研了中国阿勒泰地区的传统滑雪。根据调研问题和讨论，本人总结了如下主要发现：

中国阿勒泰的传统滑雪具有几千年的历史，它是世界上最古老的滑雪发源地，阿尔泰山脉的当地居民仍然世代保留着这种滑雪文化。而现今，该文化将要在中国阿勒泰地区消失。其原因是野生动物和降雪的减少，还有便利的交通和道路，使人们不再使用雪板狩猎。

传统滑雪在过去是一种传统艺术，也将继往开来。它具有当地阿勒泰人的精神价值、思维方式和想象力。因此它正向文化遗产靠拢。旅游是当今世界上一种新兴和有潜力的领域，尤其大事件旅游受到国家和民族文化的关注，特别针对阿勒泰地区人民的生活方式。一方面，它具有积极的经济和社会影响，能有助于保护其文化遗产。另一方面，它也具有导致一些传统元素衰退的负面影响。有一些讨论围绕把传统滑雪滑作为一种事件旅游的层面来发展。我把自己的论文标题定为庆祝传统滑雪形式，如节日、博物馆、传统狩猎方式等。在文章中我加入了一些理论用以和读者共同讨论积极和消极的方面。作者仍在与世界不同国家的研究学者研究阿勒泰项目的滑雪传统，试图寻找更多的关联性，并将其与旅游联系起来，以更好的对其进行保护。

【参考文献】

Allen, J., O'Toole, W., Harris, R. & McDonnell, I. 2011。节日和特殊事件管理。澳大利亚约翰．威立出版社；

Douglas, Norman, Douglas, Ngaire and Derrett, Ros. 2001。特殊旅游业。澳大利亚约翰．威立出版社；

Getz, Donald 1997，第二章：趋势和力量，事件管理和事件旅游，22-40 页；

Getz, Donald 2005，第一章：事件研究介绍，事件管理和事件旅游。摘自：事件管理和事件旅游（第二版）。Cognizant Communication Corporation（出版社），1-31 页；

Getz, Donald 2008，事件旅游：定义、演变和研究。摘自：旅游管理 29（2008）403-428 页；

Getz, Donald 2012, 1. 事件研究介绍和概述。摘自：事件研究。策划事件的理论、研究和政策。Routledge（出版社），1-35 页；

Getz, Donald 2012，第二章：充满策划事件的世界。摘自：事件研究。策划事件的理论、研究和政策。Routledge（出版社），36-70 页；

Getz, Donald 2013，第一章：事件旅游介绍。摘自：事件旅游。概念、国际案例研究和调研。Cognizant Communication Corporation（出版社）1-42 页；

Herbert, D. 1995 遗产地，休闲和旅游。摘自：遗产、旅游和社会，Herbert 版，1-20 页．New York：Mansell（出版社）；

Mathisen, Stein R.（2009）。边界的节日文化遗产：在芬兰森林共和国统治下由民族史和文化遗产构成。民族学和民俗学杂志 3（2）：13-31 页；

Mckercher&Cros, 2002：10，第一章：文化旅游介绍 1-10 页；

牛津词典，www.oxforddictionaries.com［网络访问 2014 年 5 月］；

Ritchie, J. R. B., 1984. 评价贺曼公司事件的影响：概念问题和研究问题。旅行研究杂志，22（1），2-11 页；

单兆鉴、王博 2011。中国．新疆．阿勒泰-人类滑雪起源地；

Timothy. D. J，2003 第四章：保留过去，文化遗产观光，Timothy. D. J pp. 87-132 页，联合国教科文组织，曼谷，2004，影响：旅游对亚太地区文化和环境的影响：老挝拉勃拉邦的旅游和文化遗产管理。

English paper:

Festivalizing the Traditional Ski Culture in Altay as a Special Event

Ayiken Jiashan

1. Introduction

There are many discussions about the birth place of skiing. Some researcherstold Scandinavia (In Norway, the first myrfunn made in Alvdal in 1906, our oldest ski is from Drevja in Vefsn in Nordland, age specific to 3343-2939 BC Øvrebø-ski), and the others told birthplace should be Russia, because of archeologists uncovered the part of skies in northern Russia, near white sea and dated it around 6000BC. Then Archaeologists found one stone carving in Chinese Altai mountain, near Altai city, dated back to 12000-15000 years ago (Shan Zhaojian, 2011: 22). Anyway, there are a few people still keep their traditional ski culture in the modern world, whom are the semi-nomadic people in Altai mountain ranges in China.

Deep in these mountains, indigenous skiing survives to today, still using their skies as a tool for travel and hunting during the long and brutally cold winters. Following the modern development, such as paved roads to mountains and easy vehicles replaced those wooden horses (traditional skies named by old Chinese saying). Climate changes such as less snow and few wild animals affected "forbidden hunting" laws are also caused the ski tradition is facing to extinction (Author).

This paper is going to use theories from event management and festival to analyses the present conditions of traditional skiing in Chinese Altai can be preserved.

To inherit and develop Altai ski culture and to commemorate the establishment of the concept that "the Altai area is the place of origin of skiing", Altai local government fixed 16 th of January is the day of Altai traditional ski day or Altai traditional ski festival (ATSF). On January 16 th of every year, a traditional ski race was hold at Jiangjun Shan ski resort just out of Altai city (Shan Zhaojian, 2011). On that day, hundreds of local skiers gather from different ethnic groups such as, Kazakhs, Twvas, Mongols, and from different areas of Altai mountain range. The ferstival lasts for three days and consists of different events put together in a festival program such as, individual ski race for

12 kilometers, 10 kilometer relay race, sled-pulling ski race, archery skiing. More than that, there are some additional programs containing among others; Ice statues in the city of Altai, music concerts, ski making art exhibitions, ski history museum etc (Author).

2. Theory

(1) Events

An Event is defined as a — celebration or display of some theme to which the public is invited for a limited time only, annually or less frequently ‖ (Getz1997) . Event: a happening at a exact place and time; a special set of circumstances; a significantoccurrence (Getz 2012) . Events, by definition, have a beginning and an end. Events are temporal planned programmes or schedules with detail and well publicized in advance.

① A special event is a one time or infrequently occurring event outside normal programmes or activities of the sponsoring or organizing body.

② To the customer or guest, a special event is an opportunity for a leisure, social or cultural experience outside the normal range of choices or beyond everyday experience. (Getz, 2012: 15)

It means an event is the production and creation of ‘something’, that something being the unique special moment or experience.

(2) Traditional ski festival as a special and planned event

Getz cited from Goldblatt and Nelson's definitions about special event, a unique part of time celebrated with ceremony and ritual to satisfy specific needs (Getz, 1997) . According to this, ATSF is a cultural festival (ceremony) which is based on preserve the tradition from extinct.

There are two definitions given by Getz: 1) A special event is a one-time, or infrequently occurring event outside the normal program or activities of the sponsoring or organizing body.

To the customer or guest, a special event is an opportunity for an experience outside the normal range of choices or beyond everyday experiences (Getz, 2005) . According to Getz's definition, ATSF is not occurring all time and it is a competition of local ordinary people which different than any other ski races in the world. The festival is also planned festival and planned events are spatial-temporal phenomenon with prearranged beginning and end. Traditional ski festival is a unique because of the interactions taking place between the setting, people, and management systems such as the program.

(3) Traditional ski festival as a cultural celebrations

As Getz said "celebration" is an event with a social gathering or enjoyable activity and culture contains the many and diverse ways that identifiable human societies and groups live their lifestyle, organize their stuffs, and differentiate themselves from others (Getz, 2005) . The different types of events that are of public nature are plenty. Cultural celebrations can include events such as heritage commemorations, carnivals, festivals, religious events, parades and processions, art and entertainments, and art exhibits (Getz 2005) . Design and utilize of traditional skiing is much different than modern skiing. It is not used for recreation or real competition, but for transportation, hunting etc, mainly for surviving in old days. During the festival not only ski competition, but also folk concerts, archery, ski making exhibitions going on.

① Commemorations

Festival is an historic event that is to be remembered (Getz, 2005) . According to oxford dictionary, commemoration is A ceremony or celebration in which a person or event is remembered (oxford, 2014) . On 16 th of January 2006, Altai named the origin places of skiing in the world through the Altai Declaration by Chinese local authorities and this day was fixed as a ski festival day. Altai Traditional Ski Festival had it is 10 th birthday this January.

② Festival

According to Getz, festival — is a public, themed celebration ……. in which cultural segmentsare displayed which can lead the guests to understanding about the host culture and community. Festival is a cultural celebration, either secular or religious, created by and for the public, scheduled alone or in conjunction with other events (Getz 1997) . Which means it is displayed in carnivals, religious events, or heritage memorials. Festivals are important components of community pride, cohesion, fun and relaxation. Opportunities exist for festivals to advance educational values, for arts and crafts to be demonstrated, to showcase new ideas in music, art, drama, sports and culture (ibid, 1997) . As we mentioned previous part, the ski festival contains various activities and attracts hundreds of visitors from China and some other countries as well.

③ Parades

A public procession, especially one celebrating a special day or event and including marching bands and floats (Oxford, 2014) . Parades can be a part of many other types of event, or stand on their own as a form of cultural celebration. On the opening ceremony of ATSF, many parades perform by several ethnic groups who wear their traditional clothes accompanied by their folk music in the street.

④ Art and Entertainment

Getz defind " Art and Entertainment" events from many segments. 1) Visual events, such as, sculptures, handicrafts; 2) Performing events, such as, music, dancing, storytelling, etc; 3) Participatory, which mains audience or tourists integrated to local performers (Getz, 2005) . ATSF embodies some art works Suchas, ski making competition, archery making etc, and folk concert suchas, skier song of Mongols, Skier dance by Kazakhs and folk ski story telling by Twa old skiers.

⑤ Art exhibits

Art exhibit is the space in which a work of art (tangible and intangible) meet an audience or is museums and different galleries (Getz, 2005) . Traditional Ski Museum in Handigate near Altai city is one of main attraction during the festival. The museum collects, conserves, and exhibits elements of ski history for research, education and inspiration.

(4) Event tourism

① Background of event tourism

Along the history of cultural development, people have gathered to celebrate for plenty occasions and such events have always been the important segment of human society for thousands of years. (Douglas, Douglas &Derrett, 2001) Even though events have been an integral part of human nature for thousands of years, it has only recently developed into real business. It has become a part of the tourism industry as a key element of special interest tourism, and around the world, units for event tourism are increasingly being established within tourist organisations. As the phenomenon has grown into becoming a possibility of making business, numerous opportunities for professionalism have come to exist and event organising firms are popping up everywhere. Consequently, event tourism is increasingly being recognised as a fieldof study on its own in a number of educational institutions. (Getz 1997& Douglas et al. 2001) As event tourism is a rapidly growing business, as well as a field of study, there is an increasing amount of literature available on the topic. In literature one can find Donald Getz, who defines event tourism from two perspectives. On the one hand, events are tourist attractions if planned, developed, and marketed as such. On the other hand, he argues, event tourism is a segment of the market where people travel to attend events and can be motivated to do so. (Getz 1997)

The future of tourism is not depending on mass tourism, therefore, niche marketing is more important. For example, climate changes and diverse crisis are continuously influencing the development of modern tourism. As a result, travel industry and tourist destinations are focusing more on the demands of tourists. For that reason, event tourism will become more important even as constraints on mass tourism take hold. More than that, Event tourism is both sub-field in academic research and destination management.

Getz defined the event tourism in three aspects. First two definitions summed up to supplyside, and the last one belongs to demand-side.

Event tourism at the city or destination level is the development and marketing of planned events as tourist attractions, catalysts, animators, image makers and the place marketers. This process includes bidding on, facilitating and creating events, and the management of portfolios of events as destination assets.

For individual events, Event tourism means taking a marketing orientation to attract tourists, sometimes as an additional segment and sometimes as the core business. When tourists are the core business we can refer to "destination events".

Event tourism is travel to attend events, both on the part of dedicated event tourists who are motivated to travel for specific events, and other tourists who attend events while away from home. (Getz, 2013: 5).

(5) Impacts of the event tourism

Event tourism is an Economic profit oriented tourism field. Even so, we can study impacts at the personal and societal levels, and also in terms of cultural and environmental change (Getz 2008).

① Economical and environmental impacts:

According to the figure 1.1, economic aspects of event tourism, impacts on local community through foreign exchange income, employment etc. There are a large amount of total revenue from travel, accommodation, goods and services… One of the important economic impacts an event is create job opportunity which includes create jobs to promote local businesses and stimulate the local communities employment rate. Environmental impacts of Event tourism is pointing out the local destinations, environmental friendly infrastructure development such as, constructions, roads and transportations. Underneath is a table summarizing the impacts of events on host communities highlighting both the positive and negative outcomes.

Impacts of events（Allen et al. 2011，61）

Impacts of eventtourism	Positive impacts	Negative impacts
Economic	Destination promotion and increased touristsvisits	Community resistance totourism
	Extended length of stay	Loss of authenticity
	Job creation	Damage to reputation
	Increased tax revenue	Exploitation
	Business opportunities	Opportunity costs
Environmental	Showcasing the environment	Environmental damage
	Provision of models for best practice	Pollution
	Increased environmental awareness	Destruction of heritage
	Infrastructural legacy	Noise disturbance
	Improved transport and communications	Traffic congestion
	Urban transformation and renewal	
Social andcultural	Shared experience	Community alienation
	Revitalisation of traditions	Manipulation of community
	Building of community pride	Negative community image
	Validation of community groups	Bad behaviour
	Increased community participation	Substance abuse
	Introduction of new and challenging Ideas	Social dislocation
	Expansion of cultural perspective	Loss of amenity

② Socio-cultural Impacts：

One of the main aspects of event tourism is socio-cultural part. There are many positive and negative outcomes suggested in Figure 1. 1as strengthening of traditions and values；greater participation in sports，arts，or other activities related to the event theme；adaptation of new social patterns or cultural forms through exposure at the event. Other long-term benefits might take the form of increased volunteerism and community group activities，interculturalinteraction，and cooperation. According to Ritchie，five positive benefits of events suggested：community pride or achievement；social interaction and community development; togetherness, or sharing of ideas; community identity, self-images, or a sense of place; and community wellness. The major negative benefits were: volunteer burnout; overtaxing the system's recources; intrusion by traffic and noise; physical disturbance or reduced access to and overuse of facilities; and a general drain on the community (Ritchie, 1984).

He also argued that socio-cultural impacts of events could include the benefits of an increase in activities associated with the event (arts, sports) and strengthening of regional values or traditions. But events and event tourism programs also have potential to introduce social and cultural costs to the host community. Host-guest interactions, although hopefully improved through joint participation in festivals and events, can also be strained by events and tourism in general (ibid, 1984).

Many heritage experts are worrying about the link between tourism and heritage sites. Herbert pointed that heritage tourism can produce money, engage in the community, generate local support, and create jobs. But, on the other hand, it can compromise historical authenticity in favor of entertainment, cover up controversial or unpleasant aspects of history, turn residents into attractions, and harm the physical setting (Herbert, 1995).

3. Discussion

Now we are going to discuss about the impacts of event tourism on cultural heritage. Tourism is treated as a bad character to cultural heritage in some aspects, such as cultural change and modifications. " *This includes the deterioration of traditional values, a modification of ceremonies and rituals and a decreased appreciation for one's ancestors and indigenous past* " (Timothy. D. J, 2003: 153). As Nils Larsen, US ski history researcher suggested that historical ski culture in Altai has Altai's deep tradition behind. Those skies used for struggle for surviving such as hunting for food, transportations etc, rather than for racing or recreational activities in old age (author). According to Larsen, ski festival in Altai mainly oriented in race or ski competition, it causes change of using style of the ski tradition in Altai. But there are several tourism impacts play important role in weakness or declining of some culture phases. *Tourism, especially event tourism, is a central factor in creating public awareness of and support for preservation of tangible and intangible resources that will translate into greaterpolitical and finding support for further conservation activities* (Mckercher&Cros, 2002: 10). Tourism can make a valuable contribution to the preservation and revitalization oftraditional ski culture in Altai. It can help to revive lost traditions, arts and cultural practices.

There are hundreds of skiers participate in ski race event and More and more new born skiers joining to the skiing group in each year. Tourism can also provide new livelihood opportunities for large numbers of people in local communities. Such as incentive payment for the champions in first 20 of the race, horse sledging for tourists, local home stay etc. Unfortunately these positive impacts are often contradicted by the worse impacts of tourism such as, crowdedness, cultural change and commodification, cultural theft, and change the physical character of a tourism destination through inappropriate development and infrastructure (UNESCO, Bangkok, 2004). As a result, hundreds of thousands of tourists each year are concentrated in these three days ski race; There is no enough space, environment, transport facilities, accommodation facilities, as well as local community residents. Mass tourism decreases the local culture and destroys the local community traditional lifestyle. Mr Shan zhaojian, the leader of Chinese Ski History Research Association, argued that local skiers make their ski shorter and thinner or lighter than previous race, which changes the physical characteristic of traditional skies (author).

The cultural festivals constitute a complicated area of research, with many different cultural elements being presented under one heading (not only traditional ski race), but other cultural heritages include and with a variety of possible interpretations and identifications among visitors of different background, such as, ski hunting, ski museum, folk concert, ski making competition etc (Mathisen. S, 2009).

4. Conclusion

This paper investigated the traditional skiing in Chinese Altai area. According to the research questions and discussions, I summarized the main findings like following:

History of traditional skiing in Chinese Altai traces back to many thousand years and which is one of the oldest skiing origin in the world and the locals in Altai Mountains still keep this ski culture alive from generation to generation. Recently, this culture is going to slip away from Chinese Altai area. The reason is no more people use skies for hunting because of not only less wilds and snow, but also paved roads and convenient vehicles.

The traditional skiing is a traditional art from the past and going to show to present. It has spiritual value, thinking method and imaginations of local Altai people. So it is belonging to cultural heritage. Tourism is the new and potential industry in the world, especially event tourism is concerned with a nation or ethnic culture, specifically the lifestyle of the people inAltai area. One hand it has a positive economic and social impact, which helps preserve the cultural heritage. The other hand, it has negative impacts, which cause declining of some of the heritage elements. There are some discussions about developing the traditional ski activity as an event tourism level. I developed my topic about fesivalising the traditional skiing form, suchas a festival, a museum, a tradition way of hunting etc. I used some theories in to the chapter to discussed with readers both positive and negative ways. The author is still working on ski tradition of Altai project with other researchers from differentcountries and trying to find more link and relate it to tourism for better preserving.

Reference

Allen, J., O'Toole, W., Harris, R. & McDonnell, I. 2011. Festival & Special Event

Management. Australia: John Wiley & Sons

Douglas, Norman, Douglas, Ngaire and Derrett, Ros. 2001. Special Tourism. John Wiley &Sons Australia, Ltd.

Getz, Donald 1997, Chapter Two: Trends and Forces, *Event management & Event Tourism*, pp22-40

Getz, Donald 2005, Chapter 1 Introduction to Event Studies, Event Management, and Event Tourism. In: Event Management and Event Tourism. 2nd ed. Cognizant

Communication Corporation, pp 1-31

Getz, Donald 2008, Event tourism: Definition, evolution, and research. In: Tourism

Management 29 (2008) pp. 403-428

Getz, Donald 2012, 1. Introduction and Overview of Event Studies. In: *Event Studies. Theory, Research and Policy for Planned Events*. Routledge, pp 1-35

Getz, Donald 2012, Chapter 2 The World of Planned Events. In: *Event Studies. Theory, Research and Policy for Planned Events*. Routledge, pp 36-70

Getz, Donald 2013, Chapter 1 Introduction to Event Tourism. In: Event Tourism. Concepts, International Case Studies, and Research. Cognizant Communication Corporation, pp1-42

Herbert, D. 1995 Heritage Places, Leisure and Tourism. In Heritage, Tourism and Society, D. Herbert, ed., pp. 1-20. New York: Mansell.

Mathisen, Stein R. (2009). Festivaling Heritage in the Boarderlands: Constituting Ethnic History and Heritages under the Rule of the Finn Forest Republic. Journal of

Ethnology and Folkloristic 3 (2): 13-31

Mckercher&Cros, 2002: 10, Chapter 1 Introduction, Cultural Tourism Pp. 1-10

Oxford Dictionary, www. oxforddictionaries. com [internet access May 2014]

Ritchie, J. R. B., 1984. Assessing the impact of Hallmark events: Conceptual and research issues. Journal of Travel Research, 22 (1), 2-11

Shan Zhaojian, Wang Bo 2011. The original Place of Skiing-Altay Prefecture of Xinjiang China

Timothy. D. J, 2003 Chapter 4 conserving the past, Heritage tourism, Timothy. D. J pp. 87-132

UNESCO, Bangkok, 2004, IMPACT: The Effects of Tourism on Culture and the Environment in Asia and the Pacific: Tourism and Heritage Site Management in Luang Prabang, Lao PDR. 11

4.7 对中国冰雪文化传承的研究 Research on Inheritance of China's Ice and Snow Culture

于立强 Yu Liqiang (CHN)

个人简介 Brief Introduction

于立强，男，中国籍，吉林体育学院冰雪学院院长，吉林省冰雪文化研究基地副主任，教授，教育学博士，硕士研究生导师。花样滑冰专业运动员出身，现为花样滑冰和花样轮滑双料国际级裁判，国家体育总局学术带头人，吉林省教学名师。

Liqiang Yu, male, Chinese, He is the dean of the School of ice and snow, Jilin Institute of Physical Education and the vice director of Jinlin ice and snow cultural research base. He is a professor, doctor of philosophy in education and postgraduate tutor. He was a professional figure skating athlete and now is the international class referee of figure skating and figure roller skating, academic leader of General administration of Sport of China and a great teacher of Jilin province.

中文论文：

对中国冰雪文化传承的研究

于立强

摘要：为了传承中国冰雪文化，本文采用文献资料法等对中国冰雪文化的形成历史进行了梳理，主要结论：阐明了传承中国冰雪文化的重要意义；对整理和保护中国冰雪民俗历史文化遗产，建构和升华中国冰雪艺术文化内涵进行了综合分析；建议：应尽快建立中国冰雪文化博物馆和成立专门机构，对冰雪文化进行深层次研究，创建中国冰雪文化公共事业服务体系，为中国冰雪文化的不断发展和繁荣做贡献。

关键词：中国；冰雪文化；传承

1. 研究目的

冰雪文化是世界性区域生态特色文化。王凯宏2012年在黑龙江冰雪艺术产业化发展对策研究一文中提出，广义的冰雪文化，是指人类在冰天雪地的自然环境从事社会实践过程中所获得的物质、精神的生产能力和以冰雪为内容创造的物质财富与精神财富的总和，狭义的冰雪文化特指体育、艺术、文学、旅游、科技等精神财富。具有极大的经济社会价值与人文社科价值。冰雪文化作为一种地域文化现象存在时间久远，它产生于寒冷地区各民族人民的生活、生产活动中。

为此，本文遵循历史，本着面向社会和未来，面向中国和世界，引领全民关注并参与，研究和挖掘中国冰雪文化遗产，传承中国冰雪文化的精髓，促进中国冰雪文化的不断发展。

2. 研究方法

（1）文献资料法

本文充分利用了图书馆、网络等资源进行文献收集，并认真查阅相关的文献，充分了解中国冰雪文化的历史、现状，为进一步的传承和发展中国冰雪文化奠定了理论基础。

（2）逻辑分析法

采用逻辑学的相关理论对所查阅的有关文献进行总结归纳、综合分析，确定了研究范围和方向，为本论文的研究提供了依据。

3. 研究结果

（1）中国冰雪文化的发展历程

中国冰雪文化按其发展历程可分为自然生成、应用发展、独立活动、全民参与四个阶段。

① 中国冰雪文化的自然生成阶段

为追溯冰雪文化的源头，单兆鉴、王博主编的人类滑雪起源地（2011）一书中研究发现：中国考古学家在新疆阿勒泰地区发现一组距今1.2万年人类滑雪姿态的岩画，上海大世界吉尼斯总部正式确认中国为人类冰雪文化的发祥地，奠定了中国在世界冰雪文化的历史地位。

② 中国冰雪文化的应用发展阶段

中国北方地区人们长期生活在寒冷天气里总结出了与冰雪环境相适应的生产方式与生活习俗，冬捕、冬狩、冬伐等生产方式以及狗、马拉爬犁、滑雪交通运输工具等生活方式便是冰雪文化应用发展阶段的雏形。

③ 中国冰雪文化的独立活动阶段

中国寒冷地区人们在生产、生活之余为了丰富精神生活而创造出冰灯、冰雪音乐、冰雪舞蹈等艺术形式和抽冰猴、单脚驴、冰滑子、滑爬犁等活动形式，最终将冰雪活动升华为冰雪文化。

④ 中国冰雪文化的全民参与阶段

随着冰雪运动的不断普及，人们对其认识由竞技项目逐步过渡到全民健身参与阶段。现代化规模的各种滑雪场、滑冰场的修建和多元化、复合型冰雪旅游产品的开发，推动了冰雪文化产业的形成，提高了全民健身参与冰雪运动的意识，促进了冰雪文化的发展。

（2）中国冰雪文化传承的意义

① 中国冰雪文化遗产的挖掘与保护

中国北方地区是一个多民族、多民俗、历史悠久的地区，其中鄂温克族、鄂伦春族、柯尔克孜族、赫哲族的人数较少，他们使用的语言及冰雪民俗文化活动处于濒临灭绝的境地，因而保护与发展、研究和发掘各族文化遗产，具有重要意义。

② 中国冰雪文化传统的渗透与现代的融合

中国各历史阶段的冰雪文化系统的形成是由各民族文化融合的结果，不同民族和地域的冰雪民俗体育文化之间也存在相互渗透的现实关系。传统的冰雪文化注重民俗情感和群体参与，现代冰雪文化突出个性发展和科学实践。因此我们必须相互借鉴，有机结合，构建具有传统民俗历史文化和现代科学发展的冰雪文化，促进中国冰雪文化多元性和相互交流与传播。实现传统与现代冰雪文化的融合 。

③ 中国冰雪文化精华的继承与发扬

中国冰雪文化的传承是体现垂直式的民俗体育文化的联系，是后人对前人所创造的民俗体育文化成果的吸收和推进。胡小明2005年主编的《民族体育》一书中指出：在人类历史生产活动中，祖辈所创造的体育文化成果、以符号或物化的形式做为后辈进行体育文化活动的条件而遗传下来。因此，我们要打破传统冰雪文化的地域封闭性，充分发挥主观能动性，打破血缘、地缘的界限，提升业缘文化，形成独特的文化特色。让中国冰雪文化走出国门去了解世界，展开交流，兼收并蓄，不断汲取其他文化的精华，丰富自己，保持冰雪文化的独特魅力。积累能量，继承和弘扬中华民族文化的精髓。

（3）中国冰雪民俗文化的传承

① 中国冰雪民俗文化的产生

李艳茹，汪普健等在 2007 年我国民俗体育文化及其资源的开发研究一文中研究得出：民俗文化又称民间文化，它是由一个民族或一个群体在长期生产实践和生活中逐渐形成并世代相传的生活文化。中国冰雪民俗文化它涉及的内容非常广泛，存在于生活的各个方面。是各民族人们在冰雪自然环境中从事日常生产、生活，以冰雪生态环境与民族习惯为基础所采用和创造的，具有冰雪符号的生活方式。是一种区域性文化，具有独特的文化属性。

② 中国冰雪民俗文化的内容与表现形式

中国冰雪民俗文化形式多样，内容丰富。包括了冰雪自然环境中的各民族、各地区人民在冬季里进行的；包括服饰、饮食、居住，生产、交通运输，岁时、节令、礼仪、精神、宗教、信仰、语言、文学艺术等生活习惯以及游艺竞技等多种形式活动。

中国冰雪文化活动的表现形式：它以强身健体为基本目的，有广泛而深厚的群众基础。具有健身性和娱乐性、表演性。项目内容较多，如抽冰猴、单脚驴、冰滑子、滑爬犁等等，丰富了人们的业余生活。2011 年孙一在吉林省冰雪旅游产业发展探究一文研究指出：北方地区的渔猎、鹰猎文化等形成了独具特色的冰雪民俗活动，最具代表性的吉林省松原“查干湖冬捕”，它保留的不仅是原始的捕捞方式，更是蒙古民族世代相传的对养育自己的天、地、湖、鱼的敬重，它利用了当地民俗风情，诠释了中国冰雪文化的历史。

③ 中国冰雪民俗文化的研究与推广

冰雪民俗体育文化具有重要的社会文化价值，是一种待开发的文化资源，其源远流长的历史、丰富的内容，蕴含的精神思想与思维方式以及有效的存在发展形式，对人的发展，社会的发展都有着深刻的启发和借鉴作用。冰雪民俗体育文化的根本在于它的健身性和娱乐性，广泛流传于民间。

因此，对冰雪民俗体育活动项目的开发和利用将成为中国体育事业发展的巨大潜力，更有利于促进文明建设。而继承和发展中国冰雪民俗体育文化的重要任务，应尽快成立专门机构、有专人对其进行不断研究，加强宣传和引导，弘扬其健康向上的优秀传统文化思想内涵和养生健身的科学方法，积极向大众体育、学校体育、健身体育推广。完善中国冰雪民俗体育理论，健全其内容结构和组织形式，走科学化发展道路，不断改革拓展，让世界各国、各民族人民能够接受、喜爱并参与。

(4) 中国冰雪艺术文化的传承

① 中国冰雪艺术文化的形成

艺术是随着人类生活的需要，在生产活动中形成的一种特定形式，并在满足人类的审美生活需要过程中形成了光辉灿烂的文明成果。凡是含有技巧和思想的冰雪活动和冰雪产品皆可以称之为冰雪艺术。可以说冰雪艺术是人们高层次的生活需求，它普遍存在于人们的衣、食、住、行、育、乐的领域中。据中国《辽史》中《仪卫志》记载："上古之人，网罟禽兽，食肉衣皮，以俪韦掩前后，契丹转居荐草之间，去邃古之风犹远也"。服装首先是人类生存的必须品，它为人类的生活、生产、劳动提供最基本的保护。随着文化的诞生、变迁和发展，冰雪服装就成了反映人们文化符号的艺术品了。可以说，冰雪服装反映了朝代的文明形式和文明程度，随着人们的生活水平的不断提高，对冰雪艺术的需求越殷切。冰雪艺术活动是拓展、充实与提升寒地人们冬季生活品质的重要活动。

② 中国冰雪艺术文化的范围与形式

中国冰雪艺术文化的主要范围包括冰灯、冰窗花、雪塑、冰景致、冰盆景、冰雕塑、冰建筑等，其形式繁多。同时，中国冰雪艺术文化还通过歌曲、舞蹈、冰雕、雪雕、邮票、书画、影视等艺术形式表现出来，更易于被人们的视觉、感觉和听觉所接受，冰雪艺术文化从理论层面外延到现实生活当中，使之更加生动和形象，渗透于社会的各个领域，从而不断丰富人们的业余文化生活，提高严寒地区人们的艺术鉴赏水平。冰雪艺术文化，如同一切社会产品一样，有其自身的结构与形态，内容与形式。但冰雪艺术作品，既不同于一般的物质产品，也不同于一般的精神产品，它是一种特殊的社会产品。创造冰雪艺术作品的目的，一般来说是为了使人们获得美感享受。但其客观效应已远远超越了自身的审美价值，而成为招商引资、繁荣经贸、吸引游客、勃兴旅游、友好往来、文化交流的重要媒介。

③ 中国冰雪文化艺术景观的开发与利用

冰雪艺术景观作为旅游资源，具有很大的开发利用价值。中国在春节、元宵节等节假日期间，冰雪景观（冰雕、雪雕、雾凇）和各种滑雪场、滑冰场的修建及多元化、复合型冰雪旅游产品的开发，吸引着无数的冰雪旅游爱好者及冰雪运动爱好者。冬季的一些民俗习惯（看冰灯、秧歌舞、贴窗花）成为北方地区人们艺术文化生活的重要内容，同时，冰雪艺术文化为人们提供了满足室外社交活动的适宜环境，所有冰雪艺术形式都具有开发和利用的广阔空间。

④ 中国冰雪文化主题公园和博物馆的建立与开发

构建以冰雪文化为主题的体育公园，在冬季将传统的民俗体育活动内容，如滑雪、滑冰、单腿驴、滑爬犁、抽冰猴等大众参与性项目融入其中。既丰富了大众体育的活动方式，又能亲身感受到中国北方冬季民俗体育的独特魅力。尽快建立中国冰雪文化博物馆，使各种冰雪艺术景观，传统民俗体育活动形式及器具、场景等以微缩、仿制的形式进入室内，一年四季都可供游客观赏，同时开设冰雪艺术摄影展、冰雪产品展示等，延伸中国冰雪文化的产业链，创建中国冰雪文化公共事业服务平台。

4. 结论与建议

（1）结论

中国冰雪文化作为一种地域文化现象存在时间久远，它产生于寒冷地区各民族人民的生活、生产活动中。通过分析中国冰雪文化的形成与发展历程，阐明了对中国冰雪文化保护、开发和传承、利用的重要意义。重点研究了中国冰雪民俗文化和冰雪艺术文化的传承。挖掘和整理中国冰雪民俗文化精髓，提炼和开发中国冰雪艺术文化内涵，建构和延伸中国冰雪文化的产业链。

（2）建议

应尽快建立中国冰雪文化博物馆和成立专门机构，对冰雪文化进行深层次研究，创建中国冰雪文化公共事业服务体系，扩大中国冰雪文化在国内外的影响力，为传播和发展中国冰雪特色文化，促进中国冰雪文化可持续发展 。

【参考文献】

1. 王凯宏．黑龙江冰雪艺术产业化发展对策研究［J］．人民论坛，2012,(32).

2. 单兆鉴，王博．人类滑雪起源地——中国．新疆．阿勒泰［M］．人民体育出版社 2011.

3. 胡小明．主编:《民族体育》［M］．广西师大出版社，2005.

4. 李艳茹，汪普健，张黎．我国民俗体育文化及其资源的开发研究［J］．体育文化导刊. 2007. 7.

5. 孙一．吉林省冰雪旅游产业发展探究［J］．体育科学. 2011 年（第 31 卷）第 6 期

6. 张海鹰．关东民俗文化旅游资源开发的策略探究［J］，理论观察. 2009. 6.

7. 张晓光．我国东北民族民俗中的冰雪文化［J］．黑河学刊. 2008. 5.

8. 刘建廷．冰雪文化的传统性与现代性［J］．牡丹江师范学院学报（哲社

版）2007.1.

9. 王子阳．打造冰世界做足雪文章——吉林省冰雪旅游特色鲜明主题突出[N]．吉林日报，2007，01，10（7）．

10. 李欣，关晶晶．东北地区冰雪体育旅游发展研究探索［J］．理论观察．2013（02）．

English paper:

Research on Inheritance of China's Ice and Snow Culture

Yu Liqiang

Abstract

In order to inherit China's ice and snow culture, this article uses literature and other methods to sort out the formation history of China's ice and snow culture, and the main conclusions: clarify the important significant of China's ice and snow culture; comprehensively analyzing the organization and protection for heritage of Chinese ice and snow folk history and culture and the construction and sublimation for connotation of Chinese ice and snow artistic culture. Recommendations: China should establish the China's ice and snow culture museum and the specialized agencies, to conduct in-depth study on the ice and snow culture and create the public utilities service system of China's ice and snow culture, which makes contributions to the continuous development and prosperity of China's ice and snow culture.

Key Words: China, Ice and Snow Culture, Inheritance

1. Research Purpose

Ice and snow culture is a worldwide regionally ecological characteristic culture. Kaihong Wang proposed in the article of Countermeasure Research on Heilongjiang Ice and Snow Art Industrial Development in 2012that the generalized ice and snow culture refers to the sum of the material and spiritual production capacity which human beings acquire by engaging in social practical progress in the natural environment of ice and snow and the material and spiritual wealth created by the contents of ice and snow, while the narrow sense of ice and snow culture refers to sport, art, literature, tourism, technology and other spiritual wealth. It has a greateconomic and social value and a value of humanities and social sciences. Ice and snow culture, as a geographical and cultural phenomenon, has gone through a long time, and it is produced in the life and production activity of the people of all ethnic groups in cold regions.

Therefore, this article follows the history, and, based on facing to the community and the future and facing to China and the while world, leads the universal attention and participation, while studying and digging out China's ice and snow cultural heritage, inheriting the essence of China's ice and snow culture and promoting the continuous development of China's ice and snow culture.

2. Research Methods

(1) Method of Literature

This article fully uses the library, internet and other resource to collect the literature and seriously consults there levant literature to fully understand China's ice and snow history and status quo, which lays a theoretica lfoundation for further inheriting and developing China's ice and snow culture.

(2) Method of Logical Analysis

It adopts the relevant theories of logic to conclude, summarize and comprehensively analyze the consultedliterature, to determine the research range and direction, which provides the reference for the research of this Article.

3. Research Result

(1) Development History of China's Ice and Snow Culture

China's ice and snow culture can be divided into four stages of natural generation, application development, independent activities and national involvement according to its course of development.

① Natural Generation Stage of China's Ice and Snow Culture

In order to trace the source of ice and snow culture, it studies and found in the book of Human Ski Origin (2011) edited by Zhaojian Shan and Bo Wang that Chinese archaeologists had discovered a group of rock paintings inAltay Prefecture, Xinjiang, which had been dating back 1.2 million years, and Shanghai Great World Guinness headquarters officially recognized that China was the birthplace of humanity ice and snow culture, laying the historical position of China in the world ice and snow culture.

② Application Development Stage of China's Ice and Snow Culture

Northern Chinese people living in cold weather for a long time summed up the production style and life habit closely adapting to ice and snow environment, and winter fishing, winter hunting, winter cutting and other methods of production, as well as a dog, horse-drawn sledge, the means of transportation such as ski and other living style, are the prototype of the application development stage of ice and snow culture.

③ Independent Activities Stage of China's Ice and Snow Culture

In order to enrich the spiritual life, the people in Chinese cold regions created ice light, ice and snow music, ice and snow dance and other art forms, as well as pumping ice monkey, single donkey leg, ice slider, slide sledge and other forms of activities, eventually sublimating ice and snow activities to ice and snow culture.

④ National Involvement Stage of China's Ice and Snow Culture

With the growing popularity of ice and snow sport, people's awareness to it develops gradually from competitive events to stage of national fitness participation. The construction of various skiing park and skating rink in modern scale and the development of diversified and complex ice and snow tourist products promote the formation of ice and snow culture industry, which improves the awareness of national fitness participate in ice and snow sport and promotes the development of ice and snow culture.

(2) Significance of Inheriting China's Ice and Snow Culture

① Exploration and Protection of China's Ice and Snow Culture Heritage

Northern China is a multi-ethnic and multi folklore area with a long history, where the number of Evenki Nationality, Oroqen Nationality, Kirgiz Nationality and Hoche Nationality is small, while their language and ice and snow folk cultural activities have already been in the verge of extinction, so protecting, developing, Studying and exploring the cultural heritage of all ethnic groups havean important significance.

② Traditional Penetration and Modern Integration of China's Ice and Snow Culture

Formation of China's ice and snow culture system in various historical stages is the result of integration between various national cultures, and ice and snow folk sport culture of different nations and regions also has the reality relationship of the mutual penetration. The traditional ice and snow culture emphasizes on folk emotion and group participation, and modern ice and snow culture highlights personality development and scientific practices. Therefore, we must learn from each other with organic combination to build an ice and snow culture with the traditional folk history and culture and the modern scientific development, promoting diversification and mutual exchange and propaganda of China's ice and snow culture. Achieve fusion between traditional and modern ice and snow culture.

③ Inheritance and Promotion of China's Ice and Snow Cultural Essence

The inheritance of China's ice and snow culture reflects the link of vertical folk sports culture and is also absorption and propulsion of descendants to the folk sports cultural achievement created by predecessors. The book of Ethnic Sports edited by Xiaoming Hu in 2005 pointed out that, in the human historical activity of production, the sports cultural achievements created by ancestors have been inherited in symbol or materialized form as the condition that descendants implement the sports cultural activities. Therefore, we must break the geographical closeness of the traditional ice and snow culture, give full play to subjective initiative to break the blood and geopolitical boundaries, and enhance business culture to form a unique cultural characteristic. Let China's ice and snow culture go abroad to learn about the world, expand exchanges to absorb anything and everything, and continue to learn the essence of other cultures to enrich themselves and maintain the unique charm of ice and snow culture. Accumulate energy and inherit and carry forward the essence of Chinese culture.

(3) Inheritance of China's Ice and Snow Folk Culture

① Generation of China's Ice and Snow Folk Culture

Yanfu Li, Pujian Wang and others studied and concluded in the article of Development and Research on Chinese Folk Sports Culture and Its Resource that folk culture is also known as social culture, a life culture gradually formed and inherited by a nation or a group living in long-term production practice and life. Contents that China's ice and snow folk culture involved are a very extensive, existing in all aspects of life. It is a livingstyle with an ice and snow symbol, which is adopted and created by all ethnic people who engaged in the daily production and living in the winter natural environment based on ice and snow ecological environment and national habits. It is a regional culture with a unique cultural attribute.

② Contents and Performing Forms of China's Ice and Snow Folk Culture

The forms of China's ice and snow folk culture are rich, including each nation and people in each regionconducting in ice and snow natural environment; including clothing, food, housing, production, transportation, age, seasons, ritual, spirit, religion, belief, language, literature and art and other living habits, as well as recreation, competitive practices and other forms of activities. The performing form of China's ice and snow folk culture: it is based on fitness as the basic purpose and owns abroad and deep mass basis. It has fitness, entertainment and performance. It has a lot of contents, such as pumping ice monkey, donkey leg, ice slider, sliding sledge, etc. , enriching people's leisure life. In 2011, Yi Sun pointed out in the research of Development and Exploration of Ice and Snow Tourism Industry in Jilin Province that: fishing hunting and falconry culture in the northern region form a unique ice and snow folk activity, while the most representative is "Winter Hunting in Chagan Lake" in Songyuan Province, which not only retains the original fishing methods, but also is the respect to the nature, earth, lake and the fish from Mongolian generations, and it takes advantage of the local customs to interpret the history of China's ice and snow culture.

③ Research and Propaganda of China's Ice and Snow Folk Culture

Ice and snow folk sports culture has important social cultural values and is a cultural resource to be developed, while its long history, rich contents, contained spiritual thoughts and ways of thinking, and effective existing form of development have a profound inspiration and reference for human development and social development. The root of ice and snow folk sports culture lies in its fitness and entertainment, which are widely spread in the community.

Therefore, the development and utilization of ice and snow folk sports activities will become a huge potential of China's sports development, which is more conducive to promoting construction of civilization. Continuing and developing China's ice and snow folk sports culture are the important tasks, so it should set up an specialized agencies and specialized person as soon as possible to conduct an ongoing research, enhance publicity and guidance, promote ideological connotations of its healthy and outstanding traditional culture and scientific methods of fitness and regimen, and actively propagate it to mass sport, school sport and fitness sport. China's ice and snow folk sports theory should be improved and its content structure and organization form should be enhanced, taking the road of scientific development and continuously reforming and expanding, so as to make people of all nationalities accept, love and participate it.

(4) Inheritance of China's Ice and Snow Art Culture

① Formation of China's Ice and Snow Art Culture

Art is a specific form created in activity of production with the needs of human life and forms the splendida chievements of civilization in the process of meeting human needs for aesthetic life. Any ice and snow activities and products containing tips and ideas all can be called as ice and snow art. Ice and snow art can be said as people's life demand at a high level, and it is commonly found in people's clothing, food, housing, transportation, education and entertainment. According to records in Yi Wei Annual in History of Liao Dynasty in China that "the ancient people hunted animals to eat meat and take the fur as clothes, covering body with Li Wei, while Qidan than moved to the grasslands and their old habits have disappeared gradually". Clothing firstly is necessities of human survival, which provides basic protection for human life, production and labor. With the birth, transformation and development of culture, ice and snow clothes become the art work reflecting people's cultural symbol. It can say that the ice and snow clothes reflects the form and degree of civilization of dynasties, while, with the continuous improvement of people's living standards, their demand for ice and snow art becomes more ardent. Ice and snow art activity is the important activity to develop, enrich and enhance people's life quality of cold region in the winter.

② Scope and Form of China's Ice and Snow Art Culture

The main scope of China's ice and snow art culture include ice snow, ice paper-cut, snow sculpture, ice scenery, ice bonsai, ice sculptures, ice architecture and other many forms. Meanwhile, China's ice and snow art culture also is manifested by songs, dance, ice sculpture, snow sculpture, stamps, paintings, film and other artistic forms, which can be more easily accepted by people's vision, hearing and feeling, while ice and snow art culture is extended from the theoretical level to real life, which makes it more vivid and iconic, permeating into all areas of society, so as to continuously enrich people's leisure cultural life and to improve the art appreciation level of people in cold area. Ice and snow art culture, as all social products, has its own structure, form, content and pattern. But ice and snow art works is different from general material products or the general spiritual product, and it is a special kind of social product. The purpose of creating ice and snow art work, ingeneral, is to make people enjoy the beauty. However, its objective effect is far beyond its own aesthetic value and becomes an important medium of investment promotion, prosperity of economy and trade, attracting tourists, flourishing tourism, friendly exchanges and cultural exchanges.

③ Development and Utilization of Art Landscape of China's Ice and Snow Culture

Ice and snow art landscape, as a resource of tourism, has a great value of development and utilization. During the Spring Festival holidays, the Lantern Festival and other holidays, the ice and snow landscapes (ice sculpture, snow sculpture and rime), construction and diversification of various skiing parks and skating rink and development of complex ice and snow tourist products attract countless fans of ice and snow tourism and enthusiasts of ice and snow sport. Some folk customs in Winter (seeing ice light, yangko dance, sticking grilles) become the important content of people's artistic and cultural life in the northern region, while ice and snow art culture provides an appropriate environment suitable for outdoor social activities for people, and all ice and snow art forms have vast space for development and utilization.

④ Establishment and Development of Theme Parks and Museums of China's Ice and Snow Culture

A sports park with ice and snow culture as a theme can be constructed, which, in the winter, the folk sports activities, such as skiing, skating, single leg donkey, sliding sledge, pumping ice monkeys and other mass participatory projects are integrated into. It not only enriches the activity way of mass sports activities, but also makes people personally feel the unique charm of the northern Chinese folk sport in winter. It should establish the China's Ice and Snow Culture Museumas soon as possible, bring ingvarious ice and snow art landscapes, traditional forms of folk sports activities, equipment, scenes and others into the room in form of miniature and imitation, which can be provided for visitor to visit all year round. Ice and snow art photography exhibition and ice and snow product exhibition are also opened at the same time to extend the industrial chain of China's ice and snow culture and to create the public utility service platform of China's ice and snow culture.

4. Conclusion and Suggestion

(1) Conclusion

China ice and snow culture, as a geographical and cultural phenomenon, has existed for a long time, while it is produced in the lives and production activity of people of all ethnic groups in cold regions. By analyzing the formation and development course of China's ice and snow culture, it expounds the significance of protection, development, inheritance and utilization of China's ice and snow culture. It focuses on studying the inheritance of China's ice and snow folk culture ice and ice and snow art culture. It explores and collects China's ice and snow folk cultural essence, refines and develops the connotation of China's ice and snow art culture, and builds and extends industrial chain of China's ice and snow culture.

(2) Suggestion

It should set up China's Ice and Snow Culture Museum and establish a specialized agency, conduct in-depth study on the ice and snow culture, create a public utility service system of China's ice and snow culture, and expand the influence of China's ice and snow culture at home and abroad, in order to propagate and develop China's ice and snow characteristic culture and promote a sustainable development of China's ice and snow culture.

Reference:

1. KaihongWang, Research on Countermeasure of Industrial Development of Heilongjiang Ice and Snow Art [J], Peoples Forum, 2012, (32)

2. Zhaojian Shan, Bo Wang, Origin of Human Ski——Altay Area, Xinjiang,

China [M], People's Sports Publishing House 2011

3. XiaomingHu, Ethnic Sport [M], Guangxi Normal University Press, 2005

4. YanruLi, Pujian Wang, Li Zhang, Research on China's Folk Sports Culture and Its Resource Development [J], Sports Culture Guide, 2007. 7

5. Yi Sun, Exploration on Development of Ice and Snow Tourism Industry in Jilin Province [J], Sport Science, 2011 (Volume 31) Section 6

6. HaiyingZhang, Exploration on Strategy of Northeast Chinese Folk Culture Tourist Resources Development [J], Theoretical Observation, 2009. 6

7. XiaoguangZhang, Ice and Snow Culture in Northeast Ethnic Folk Custom of China [J], Heihe Science Journal, 2008. 5

8. Jianting Liu, Tradition and Modernity of Ice and Snow Culture [J], Academic Journal of Mudanjiang Normal College (Philosophy and Social Science) 2007. 1

9. Ziyang Wang, Breaking Ice World to Make Enough Snow Article——Distinctive Features and ProminentTheme of Ice and SnowTourist in Jilin Province [N], Jilin Daily, 2007, 01, 10 (7)

10. Xin Li, Jingjing Guan, Research and Exploration on Development of Ice and Snow Sports Tourism in Northeast Region [J], Theoretical Observation, 2013 (02)

4.8 人类滑雪起源地古老滑雪文化传承与推广 The Inheritance and Promotion of Ancient Skiing Culture in Altay-the Cradle of Human Skiing

于洋 Yu Yang (CHN)

个人简介 Brief Introduction

于洋，女，1977年9月9日，吉林大学公共关系学士学位。

2007至今任北京卡宾雪行天下滑雪场规划设计有限公司总经理，从事冰雪产业近十年，2007年开始投身于冰雪产业；2010年开始为滑雪场做全面规划设计；

- 开创国内“滑雪场冰雪旅游产品设计”的规划思路，为滑雪场及滑雪度假区做冰雪兼非雪季旅游产品全面设计；
- 开创国内冰雪行业“经营方案设计”的规划思路，为初次投资滑雪场的投资商提供滑雪场经营管理方案；

● 开创国内冰雪行业专业的“雪场营销活动“的策划思路，为雪场经营期提供新颖的大型活动和赛事策划。

● 热衷于滑雪产业各领域关系的研究与实践，投身于中国滑雪行业集团化的尝试与推广，并取得成果；

● 对阿勒泰人类最古老的滑雪地域古老滑雪文化的传承及赞助每年举办的阿勒泰古老毛皮滑雪板的比赛十分担心，并作出了重要贡献。

Yu Yang, Female, 9th, Sep. 1977, Bachelor of Public Relations, Jilin University.

2007-present: General Manager, Beijing Carving Group

● Dedicated pursuer of ski industry for 10 years; engaged in master planning for ski resorts since 2010;

● Pioneer of the idea of snow tourism products design for ski resorts in China;

● Creator of the idea of management plan design for ski resorts in China's ski industry, provided management plans for rookie investors in ski resorts

● Pathfinder of the idea of marketing campaign for ski resorts in China's ski industry, supplied novel plans to large-scale activities and events

● Keen on the studies and research on the relationships between different areas of ski industry; devoted to the attempt and promotion of the collectivization of China's ski industry and made achievements

● Advocate of the inheritance of Altay ancient skiing culture; sponsor and contributor of the annual Altay ancient fur skis competition

中文论文：

人类滑雪起源地古老滑雪文化传承与推广

单兆鉴先生于1993年首先提出“滑雪的发源地可能在中国阿勒泰地区”，并经过长达十余年的艰难考察，在2006年起草并发布了《阿勒泰宣言》向世界宣布“中国·新疆·阿勒泰是人类滑雪最早起源地”。2015年，单兆鉴先生又亲自组织发起中国阿勒泰国际古老滑雪文化交流研讨会，全世界近20个国家的专家和学者参加了此次盛会，并参与了“北京卡宾杯中国新疆阿勒泰第十届古老滑雪比赛”。让世界各国对中国传承至今的古老滑雪有了更直观的认识，对中国古老滑雪文化的推广起到了积极的推动作用。

从《阿勒泰宣言》至今近十年间中国新疆阿勒泰已逐渐揭开神秘的面纱，让越来越多的人认识了这块神奇的土地，这是中国历史文化瑰宝中闪亮的一页。我们应该怀着一颗虔诚的心传承并发扬中国古老滑雪文化，从我做起，力所能及的为中国滑雪文化走向世界做一点事情。

现就中国古老滑雪文化传承和发扬，从我做起谈一下几点看法。

一、中国古老滑雪文化在国内的传承和发扬

1. 滑雪文化展示

(1) 展示场所

① 滑雪场

在中国尽可能多的滑雪场服务大厅内或者配套服务区，设置滑雪文化展示推广区，展示和介绍世界滑雪起源地中国新疆阿勒泰地区的古老滑雪文化，古老滑雪与中国近代滑雪文化的发展历程。通过在雪场内外设置的小品，营造雪场滑雪文化氛围，让更多的滑雪爱好者了解中国的滑雪文化，了解世界滑雪文化的发展和变迁。利用古老滑雪文化的特有符号展示雪场的个性和风格，用文化打动人，并沉淀属于每个雪场独特的风格。

② 中国与滑雪有关的博物馆

作为世界滑雪起源地——新疆阿勒泰是每个与滑雪有关的博物馆中不能忽略的重要一块，加大在中国各大滑雪博物馆的推广，是强化新疆阿勒泰古老滑雪起源地文化非常重要的一步。制作新疆阿勒泰滑雪起源地在博物馆展示方案和建议，方便博物馆拿到实物和图片影像素材后更全面系统的展示。阿勒泰政府应尽快联系各大博物馆，积极提供相关素材及实物，大型的博物馆可以有正式的捐赠仪式。让所有与滑雪有关的中国博物馆都有新疆阿勒泰的浓重一笔，让所有观看博物馆的游客、专家、学者等都知道“世界的滑雪起源地在中国新疆阿勒泰”。

③ 申冬奥委员会工作场所及未来冬奥会现场

追溯中国申冬奥的历史渊源，讲述世界滑雪起源地的神秘滑雪故事。中国与滑雪的历史渊源，中国人对滑雪的认识和发展历程。让世界认识中国，认识中国的滑雪，了解中国的滑雪文化。我们是世界滑雪的起源地，我们有着上万年的滑雪历史。在岁月的长河中，滑雪从人们必备的生存生活技能到如今的休闲时尚运动，在不同的历史时期，滑雪扮演着怎样的角色。用更丰富的手法将中国滑雪起源地源远流长的文化展现给全世界。滑雪起源地的古老文化是属于全人类的，今天，作为滑雪起源地国家——中国，向全世界讲述这个滑雪故事。

这需要从现在开始准备相关的素材和实物，为申冬奥工作积累必要的滑雪文化素材，为滑雪起源地文化走向全世界打好基础。这是一个让全世界人关注中国新疆阿勒泰的最好机会，由此产生的一系列积极影响对中国新疆阿勒泰是无法估量的，积极充分的展示滑雪起源地古老滑雪文化会让新疆阿勒泰成为本次活动的受益者。

（2）展示方式及内容

滑雪文化展示方式要多样化、全面化，根据现场情况和配套风格效果选择不同的内容，古老滑雪文化主要有以下几方面内容可以展示：

① 滑雪、狩猎相关器具和服饰

展示器具主要有：毛皮滑雪板及雪杖、木头弓箭及毛皮箭靶、滑雪起源地特色民族服装、毛皮靴子、毛皮手套、皮具水袋或酒袋、近现代滑雪板等；部分内容可以进行制作环节细化展示。如毛皮滑雪板制作过程展示，从木材的选择开始，分解制作过程，每个过程用对应的实物做详细图解和说明，让更多人了解毛皮滑雪板制作工艺，将这一古老的制作工艺更完整的保留和传承下来。伴随着古阿勒泰人毛皮滑雪板同时出现的是木头弓箭和毛皮箭靶等，当时滑雪是生存生产的基本劳动技能。

用场景展示的方式，讲述古老滑雪运动在人们生产、生活中扮演的重要角色，让参观者有场景感，更真切的体会到滑雪曾作为人们生存必备技能而存在的特殊历史时期独有的魅力。并通过声光电等方式立体多元化展示，古老的狩猎生产时代浮现在眼前。

② 纪录片、图片等资料

古老滑雪狩猎民谣，国内或外国专家和爱好者及新闻媒体拍摄的关于古老毛皮滑雪板制作及在人们日常生活场景中滑行的纪录片，关于古老滑雪文化探索和考证的相关纪录片，阿勒泰古老滑雪比赛的片子等；影像可以更深入的剖析和展示古老滑雪文化原汁原味的色彩。这种记录片可以在电视台、网络等各个平台进行多重展示，让古老滑雪文化绽放在人们面前。

照片可搜集整理新疆阿勒泰古老滑雪岩画、古老滑雪比赛现场、新疆阿勒泰人使用毛皮滑雪板进行日常生活、生产的场景等，人类滑雪起源地被认证的过程和重要节点活动颁奖及发布会等照片；人类滑雪起源地国际论坛等照片，用图片讲述和记录了古老滑雪文化发掘、传承及发扬的足迹。

各种相关研发的书籍也是推广的重要历史记载，在雪场、博物馆及图书馆等场所更广泛的普及和推广。多种文字让全世界人认识中国，认识中国新疆阿勒泰。

2. 古老滑雪文化体验

文化的感知除了视觉上的、听觉上的，很重要的一个体验是参与实践式的。直接参与互动的古老毛皮滑雪板滑雪体验，才能更加深入理解和体会传承万年的古老滑雪文化的神奇与魅力。

（1）古老滑雪比赛的传承和推广

中国新疆阿勒泰古老滑雪比赛，是古老滑雪文化传承最直接的展示，应不断传承和保留。让更多人参与比赛，将比赛的场地从新疆阿勒泰走向中国更多的地区，更广泛的范围内将这种原汁原味具有深厚历史沉淀的滑雪文化展示给更多的人。这种古老滑雪文化传承至今是值得我们每一个人尊重和敬仰的，这是最朴实的中国古阿勒泰人留给全世界人类的文明瑰宝。

(2) 国内滑雪场古老滑雪体验

有条件的雪场可开辟古老毛皮滑雪体验区，模拟中国新疆阿勒泰地区的地域和滑雪特点在雪场开辟体验区，让更多的游客和滑雪爱好者，通过直观的体验和参与更深刻的理解古老滑雪文化和狩猎文化。将中国宝贵的古老滑雪文化用这种体验的方式鲜活的保存下去。

对滑雪爱好者和游客而言这是种新奇的尝试，也是一种地域文化的参与体验过程，让更多人认识毛皮滑雪板，并知道世界滑雪起源地来自中国新疆阿勒泰，从而对滑雪这项运动有更深刻的认识和理解，油然而生一种自豪感。

二、中国古老滑雪文化在世界的推广

加强与国外滑雪文化的交流和研讨，追溯世界滑雪起源地古老滑雪文化走向全世界的发展轨迹和发展变化。作为世界滑雪文化的起点，我们随着传承的步伐应该将起源地的古老滑雪文化向所有传承地推广。让现代滑雪较先进的欧美等地有机会品尝到来自滑雪起源地的文化大餐。我们有义务和责任，将中国新疆阿勒泰滑雪起源地的源远流长的历史传承和发扬到全世界。

阿勒泰政府作为古老滑雪起源地的行政管理机构，应积极准备相关资料和实物，尤其是当地传承下来的古老毛皮滑雪板制作的实物，给世界知名的滑雪文化博物馆保留惠存，并标注这是来自世界滑雪起源地中国新疆阿勒泰，让全世界的滑雪爱好者都知道中国在滑雪文化历史发展过程中所扮演的滑雪朝圣地的重要角色。通过古老滑雪文化的推广，推动中国滑雪产业发展，扩大中国在世界滑雪领域的影响，奠定中国滑雪文化在世界范围的重要地位。

这是一段动人的滑雪起源故事，讲述了全人类如何利用自己的智慧在这片神奇的土地上繁衍生息。今天，滑雪变成了一种时尚的运动，让我们用一颗虔诚的心倾听它的故事，品味它的芬芳，分享它的乐趣。

English paper:

The Inheritance and Promotion of Ancient Skiing Culture in Altay-the Cradle of Human Skiing

As Mr. Shan Zhaojian firstly proposed in 1993, the cradle of human skiing may be somewhere in Altay Prefecture of Xinjiang, China. Through decades of hard work, he drafted and released *Altay Declaration* in 2006, through which he officially announced that Altay of Xinjiang, China is the cradle of human skiing. And in 2015, Shan initiated the Altay International Ancient Skiing Cultural Conference that attracted experts and researchers from over twenty countries, during which they also participated in the "Beijing Carving Cup" Altay 10th Ancient Skiing Competitions. This has not only brought great visual sense of China's well-inherited ancient skiing to the world but made positive impact on its promotion.

Altay has debunked its myths for the last ten years since *Altay Declaration* was released, which, as one of the most sparkling treasures throughout the Chinese history, has exposed this mystical land to more and more people. It is a common hope that we should inherit and carry forward Chinese ancient skiing culture and make our own effort to contribute to the globalization of Chinese skiing.

The followings are my points on the inheritance and promotion of Chinese ancient skiing culture.

First, Inheritance and Promotion of Chinese Ancient Skiing Culture at Home

I. Skiing Culture Display

1. Site Display

(1) Ski Areas and Resorts

To display and introduce theAltay ancient skiing, its culture and its development history of modern China as much as possible in ski service halls, supporting service areas or skiing culture promotion areas to be set. Specially planned sketch comedy in ski areas are supposed to lighten up the atmosphere so that more and more ski enthusiasts can get access to the Chinese skiing culture as well as the development and changes of the world skiing culture. Meanwhile, try to use the specific signs of ancient skiing culture to exhibit the uniqueness and styles of ski areas, find the characteristics of each ski area, and try to move people with culture.

(2) Museums about Skiing in China

As the cradle of human skiing, Altay is a non-neglectable part in every ski related museum in China. To strengthen the promotion in each ski museum in China is an important step to enhance the Altay ancient skiing culture. It is necessary to make an exhibition scheme and proposal on this cradle of human skiing so that museums can give all-round exhibition after they get real objects, pictures and videos. Altay Government is expected to contact related museums as soon as possible and offer relevant materials and exhibits. Some of the big museums are also encouraged to hold official donation ceremony. The aim is to highlight Altay in all the ski related museums in China and make it globally known.

(3) Workplace for Olympic Winter Games Bid Committee and Future Winter Games Venues

To trace the source of China's bid for Olympic Winter Games and tell the mysterious story of the cradle of human skiing to let the world know about China, China's ski sports and China's skiing culture. We are the origin of human skiing withthousands of years of history. In the long history of the world, skiing has evolved from the originally essential living skills to today's leisure and fashion sport and plays different roles in different periods. More abundant methods should be applied to exhibit the long-standing culture of the cradle of human skiing to the whole world, as this culture belongs to all human beings. Now, China, the country where skiing was originated, will tell this story to the world.

To this end, we need to prepare related materials and exhibits now, by which necessary skiing culture materials will be accumulated for Winter Games bid and good foundation will be laid for the globalization of the cradle of human skiing. This is absolutely the best chance for Altay to be internationally noticed, the positive effect exerted by which was beyond measure. Altay is bound to be the biggest winner in this event.

2. Patterns and Contents

The patterns of skiing culture exhibition emphasizes diversity and comprehensiveness and contents can be based on the real situations and supporting styles. Ancient skiing culture can be exhibited in the following ways:

(1) Exhibition Supplies and Clothing about Skiing and Hunting

The main supplies include: fur skis and poles, wooden bows and arrows, fur arrows and targets, national costumes of the original place, fur boots and gloves, feather water bags or wine bags and modern skis. Some of them can be specifically exhibited. For example, the process of making fur skis, by starting from timber choosing, manufacturing details throughout toelaborations. In this way, people will familiarize themselves with the process of fur making and pass this great ancient craftsmanship down from generation to generation. Along with the ancient Altai people's fur skis, there appeared wooden bows and arrows and fur arrows and targets, for skiing was one of the basic living skills back then.

Scenario display is another way to introduce the culture by telling the vital role that ancient skiing has played inpeople's daily production and life, creating a real sense for visitors to experience its unique charm in that age. Stereoscopic and diverse exhibitions by means of sound and photoelectricity will make you part of those ski hunters in the ancient time.

(2) Documentaries, Pictures and so on

Ancient ski hunting ballads, documentaries about ancient fur ski making and people daily skiing made by experts and enthusiasts at home and abroad and even news media, documentaries about ancient skiing culture exploration and research, films about Altay ancient skiing competition videos are sufficient to analyze and show the very authenticity of ancient skiing culture. Documentaries like these can be well exhibited through platforms like TV stations and internet.

Pictures can be about Altay ancient rock paintings, ancient skiing competition venues, Altai people's using fur skis in their daily production and life. We could also choose pictures about the process of authentication and major events in terms of the original place of human skiing, as well as those about the Altay International Ancient Skiing Cultural Conference. These pictures were expected to tell and record the footsteps of the exploration, inheritance and promotion of the ancient skiing culture.

All the related books are also a great way to promote and popularize major historical documents in a wide range of ski areas, museums and libraries.

II. Experience Ancient Skiing Culture

Cultural awareness consists of experience visually, acoustically and practically. Direct participation and interaction in skiing with ancient fur skis will do good to deepening the understanding of the myths and real charm of ancient skiing culture.

1. Inheritance and Promotion of the Ancient Skiing Competitions

Altay ancient skiing competition as the most direct way to reflect the inheritance of ancient skiing culture should be well conserved and passed down. More people are encouraged to involve in the competition and the venues are supposed to spread all over China, so that more and more people can know about this original and historically significant culture. We are really proud of this time-honored treasure that Altai people have left for all human beings.

2. Experience Ancient Skiing in Ski Areas and Resorts at Home

It is highly suggested that ski areas open up ancient fur skiing experience zone by simulating the territory and skiing features in Altay to let more tourists and ski enthusiasts get familiar with the ancient skiing and hunting cultures. This is without doubt a great way to preserve this Chinese treasure for generations.

This is not only a new attempt for a wide range of tourists and ski enthusiasts, but an involvement and experience of a regional culture. For this reason, more and more people will know about fur skis and Altay, the original place of human skiing.

Second, Inheritance and Promotion of Chinese Ancient Skiing Culture at Abroad

It is necessary to enhance skiing cultural exchange and seminar with abroad and track the development and changes of ancient skiing in its globalization. At the cradle of world skiing, we, following the footsteps of inheritance, should promote the oldest ski tracks of Altay, hoping that those European countries boasting advanced modern skiing to involve in this great cultural event. It is our duty to pass this history down and make it world-renowned.

Altay Government as the local authority is obliged to actively prepare relevant materials and exhibits, especially those local ancient fur skis for world-famous skiingculture museums to preserve and to be labeled the origin of Altay. In this way, hopefully, ski enthusiasts from the world will get to know the vital role that China has been playing in the history as the enduring shrine of ski sports. The promotion of China's ancient skiing means not only better development of Chinese ski sports but greater influences on world skiing.

This moving story of the origin of skiing tells us how human beings have been living and reproducing on this magical land with their wisdom. Today, skiing has already turned into a fashion sport. Let us listen to this story with a pure mind, feel its excellence and share its joy.

4.9 阿勒泰乌梁海部与古老式“察纳”滑雪板关系　A Study of Relations between Altay Uriyanghai Tribe and Ancient “Chana” Skis

巴图巴雅尔 & 那音塔（中国）　Ba · Batubayaer & Nayinta (CHN)

个人简介　Brief Introduction

巴·巴图巴雅尔，男，新疆师范大学文学院副教授，硕士生导师。中国江格尔研究学会常务副秘书长，新疆卫拉特蒙古研究学会秘书长，国家《清史工程文献整理项目：托忒文文献整理》终审专家。从事卫拉特蒙古档案文献与口头传承研究工作。在蒙古国、俄罗斯、日本和国内发表50篇学术论文。主持国家社科基金项目2项、省部级和厅级课题3项，

出版专著2部，主编论文集3部。

Ba · Batubayaer, male, is the associate professor and master tutor of college of arts in Xinjiang Normal University. He is the deputy vice secretary-general of China Jianggeer Research Institute, secretary-general of Xinjiang Weilate Mongolian Research Institute, and the expert to final judge *Literature Arrangement of Qing Dynast National Qing Dynasty History Project*: *Literature Arrangement of Todo uzug*. He works on the research of Weilate Mongolia archival document and oral inheritance and has published 50 academic papers in Mongolia, Russia, Japan and China. He is also in charge of 2 national social science fund projects and 3 provincial and departmental research project. And he has published 2 monographs and is the editor of 3 proceedings.

个人简介 Brief Introduction

那音塔，男，蒙古族，1972年7月出生，新疆阿勒泰人，中共党员。新疆卫拉特蒙古研究学会理事、新疆作家协会会员、新疆民间文艺家协会会员。1995年7月，毕业于新疆师范大学中文系蒙古语言文学专业，学士学位。1995年9月至今，在新疆教育学院工作。2013年3月—2015年7月，毕业于蒙古国科布多大学历史系，研究生学位。1991年起，通过实地调查搜集到了大量的有关民间文学、民俗、民歌方面的第一手资料，并在国内外发表30余篇论文。

Nayinta, Male, Mongolian, July 1972, Nayinta is born in Altay, Xinjiang, and a member of the Communist Party. He is also a member of Xinjiang Weilate Mongolian Research Association, a member of XinJiang Uyghur Autonomous Region Writer Association (XWA) and a member of The Xinjiang Uygur Autonomous Region Folk Literature and Art Association. July 1995, he graduates from the major of Chinese Department of Mongolian Languageand Literature in Xinjiang Normal University and obtains the Bachelor Degree. Sept. 1995-present, he works in Xinjiang Education Academy. March 2013-July 2015, he graduates from the Department of History in Mongolian Cob Duo University and obtains the Master Degree. From 1991, he collects a great many first information about folk literature, folk customs and folk songs through field work and publishes more than 30 essays at home and abroad.

中文论文：

乌梁海是蒙古语 uriyanghai 的音写，汉意为“灵巧的人”、“饲养驯鹿的人”。历史上还有其他多种称谓，如把乌梁海又译为“兀良哈”、“兀良罕”、“兀哴孩”、”兀良辉子”、“斡朗改”、“乌浪汗”等。新疆卫拉特蒙古乌梁海部至今还保留着传统的古老式“察纳”滑雪板、“冰上射箭”、“呼麦”、“潮尔”、“叶克勒”等宝贵的文化传统。阿勒泰乌梁海部至今使用自制的马皮包底的木质“察纳”滑雪板。他们使用“察纳”滑雪板具有悠久的历史。

阿勒泰乌梁海部落是卫拉特蒙古的重要组成部分，他们现在主要居住在新疆阿勒泰地区阿勒泰市汗德尕特乡、布尔津县禾木哈纳斯蒙古民族乡，以及分布于哈巴河县、青河县、福海县、富蕴县四县。此外在蒙古国科布多省都图县、孟克海日汗县、吉尔格楞图县、布音图县，巴彦乌力盖省布尔根县、布音图县、阿勒腾楚格楚县、托力布县、青格力县等地也有分布。清乾隆年间，阿勒泰乌梁海约有九千人，至清末，约一万三千人。民国以后，战事频繁，该部大多流散他处，至解放初，所剩不多。现新疆阿勒泰乌梁海约七千多人，蒙古国阿勒泰乌梁海大约两万六千多人。清代阿勒泰乌梁海部每年缴纳貂皮二张，还有戍边边界、驻守站台的义务。

古时，乌梁海部被称为“森林百姓”，生活在森林茂密、山脉高耸、冰雪覆盖、气候严寒的地方。乌梁海部很早就使用“察纳”滑雪板可见于历史记载。十三世纪波斯史学家拉施特在他的《史集》中写道：“因为在他们（乌梁海）国内，山和森林很多，而且雪下得很大，所以冬天他们在雪面上打到许多野兽。他们制造一种叫做察纳的特别的板子，站立在那板上；用皮带做成缰绳，将它拴在板的前端。然后手拿着木竿，以木竿撑地，滑行于雪面上，有如水上行舟。他们就这样用察纳滑雪板驰逐于原野上下，追杀野牛等动物。除自己踏着的察纳外，他们还拖着联接起来的另一些滑行板，他们将打杀的野兽放在上面。即使放上两、三千曼重荷，花不了多大力气就可以轻快地行走在雪层上。如果是一个不熟练的人，那么，他的两腿就会分叉而撕裂，尤其是在下降和疾驰时。受过训练的人则奔驰的极其轻快。没有见过的人，谁也不相信这点。苏丹喀赞（十四世纪初的波斯蒙古可汗）听说有这等事，将他们的人叫来，看到他们的技艺后才知道人们的传说是真的。”

[1]这里所说的“联接起来的另一些［滑行板］”，就是阿勒泰乌梁海部至今还在使用的用山羊皮制造的装狩猎用品的皮套—“齐尔格”。乌梁海部在山羊皮制造的“齐尔格”里装上口粮，衣物、兽皮或兽肉拖着走。乌梁海人历史上很早就会使用“察纳”滑雪板的事实，还可见十三世纪意大利旅行家鲁布鲁克在自己的《蒙古游记》里记载：“……北面同样没有城镇，只有一支放牧的民族，……有乌梁海部，他们足底缚着磨光的骨头，在冻结的冰雪上行走，速度之快可及飞禽走兽。”[2]“……蒙古‘森林百姓’部落用兽皮做衣服，在雪上使用滑雪板和雪橇，喝树汁……”[3]。上述记载是外国学者关于乌梁海部很早就熟练使用“察

纳”滑雪板的记载。

这样的记载，形象地描述了十三世纪之前古代蒙古人使用“察纳”滑雪板和雪杖滑雪的情形。这与现在阿勒泰乌梁海部使用的“察纳”滑雪板相符。将古代乌梁海部使用的“察纳”滑雪板和滑雪杖与现代体育运动使用的滑雪板和雪杖相比，虽然在制作材料和制作工艺方面有差别，但在形状、用途、使用方式方面大致一样。

以上历史文献里详细记载了有关乌梁海部“察纳”文化，说明十三世纪初包括乌梁海部在内的蒙古人已经熟练使用“察纳”滑雪板，并掌握了制造“察纳”滑雪板的技术和工艺。因此可以说，十三世纪初“察纳”文化已经在乌梁海部里形成，甚至更早。如果说蒙古人那时刚开始学会滑雪绝不会如此熟练“奔驰的极其轻快”，用“察纳”滑雪板打猎，用雪橇拉运猎物。因此，“我们可以肯定蒙古人使用“察纳”滑雪板和雪杖滑雪的历史，会早于十三世纪，在十三世纪已经进入熟练使用的阶段”[4]。

在古代狩猎和“察纳”滑雪板有着密切的关系。乌梁海部是出色的猎人，他们的狩猎知识和能力非常突出。古代的乌梁海先人以机敏的智慧，灵巧的双手制作木质的和骨质的粗大“察纳”滑雪板，用来打猎和交通，维持自己的日常生活。

现在阿尔泰乌梁海部使用的“察纳”滑雪板，还保留着这种雪板的形状。制作“察纳”滑雪板是有讲究的，乌梁海部现在使用的木质“察纳”滑雪板是由优质木板，最好的马皮、牛皮条、短铁钉（古时候不用铁钉，而用木钉或细皮条）、木竿等构成的。木质“察纳”原来主要用松木制作，有时也用松树皮制作。由于杨木轻，使用起来省劲，也有用杨木制作。“察纳”长约 1.8 米-2 米，宽约 15 厘米-20 厘米，顶部细宽约 5 厘米，板中央厚度 2 厘米，板两侧边沿厚 1 厘米，顶端向上弯起 30 度左右。“察纳”滑雪板底部主要专用马皮，选用马皮中最好的部位（主要是马腿和胯部位置）经水浸泡，到可以拉动的程度时，铺到弯好的木板底面（古时用木钉或细皮条扯住马皮绑于木板上），用铁钉从板的上面将其钉牢。马皮毛短而粗硬，并且倒向一方，这样顺毛的方向人易向前滑动，爬坡时又可以防止向后倒滑，有逆向制动作用。将滑雪板捆绑固定于脚部的是细长的牛皮条，将其用动物脂肪涂抹后使用。用动物脂肪涂抹过的牛皮条，不怕被雪水浸湿损坏，无论捆绑或解开都很方便，不容易断。雪杖一般将生长着的幼龄杨木、柳木、松木砍下晒干制作。雪杖长约 2 米以上，粗细直径约 3 厘米-6 厘米，顶端直径约 4 厘米。雪杖短了深雪中撑不牢。乌梁海部的“察纳”滑雪板只使用单只雪杖。有些猎人在雪杖的一头包上铁套，可以用于打伤猎物[5]。

阿勒泰乌梁海部认为大家有一副轻巧结实，敷着好皮子的“察纳”滑雪板，就好比猎人有了打猎的好帮手，方能显出男子汉的豪气，绝不会空手而归的。阿勒泰乌梁海部在打猎或参加比赛前有这样的传统习俗：在“察纳”滑雪板的顶端涂上奶皮或酥油，预祝圆满成功，表达美好心态。阿勒泰乌梁海部将孩子从小就领到野外山上打猎、打柴，即使严酷的冬天也在野外山洞、树洞过夜，无论高山峻岭还是林海雪原，都要前去追寻猎物，锻炼他们的智慧、意志和克服艰难险阻的能力。直到现在，仍然保存着这个习俗。不会使用“察纳”的人不能去野外打猎，去打猎的人都是身强力壮，会使用“察纳”的人。他们在深山打猎时，身手敏捷，从两、三米高的悬崖峭壁上踩着“察纳”滑雪板一跃而过。在林海里滑行如飞。乌梁海部在祖先的家园—富饶阿勒泰的美好山林里自给自足、自立更生地生活，享用着大自然的恩赐。从古至今，在阿勒泰的蒙古民族就从事狩猎，使用“察纳”滑雪板[6]。

改革开放以来，旅游业得到极大发展。现在阿勒泰市汗德尕特蒙古民族乡的乌梁海部每年冬季都举办古老式传统“察纳”滑雪比赛。近几年来，乌梁海部的古老式“察纳”滑雪引起了国内外旅游者和研究者的注意。由于阿勒泰乌梁海部的古老式“察纳”滑雪声名大振，原来不会制作使用“察纳”滑雪板的许多人也积极学习掌握“察纳”滑雪。

我们知道“任何一个民族的风俗习惯，都在一定度上保存了该民族的文化特点”[7]。我们研究民族文化时，应该从一个民族、部族的起源、生存环境、居住地点、社会历史、生活习俗、饮食、宗教信仰、语言等许多方面进行脚踏实地有根据的研究，这样才能得到科学的证据。

“虽然随着人类历史潮流进入了一个社会新阶段，但从祖先传承下来的传统文化是不会被原样抛弃的。”[8]阿勒泰乌梁海部除经营农业、牧业外，还是擅长狩猎的人群。阿勒泰乌梁海部自古以来在冬季上山打猎时使用“察纳”滑雪板，他们以弓箭猎取野猪、貂、狐狸、松鼠等动物。此外阿勒泰乌梁海部民间中有着口传的猎人专用的《猎人之歌》。

阿勒泰乌梁海部冬季踩上古老式“察纳”滑雪板，驰骋于阿尔泰山脉，祈求于阿勒泰先祖，赞颂“阿勒泰颂歌”，下夹设套，捕野猪、猎狐狸、狼、貂、松鼠、享用阿尔泰山水所赐的精华，满足生活和生产的需求，与大自然和谐相处，直到今天仍是如此。应该知道，从古至今，古老式“察纳”滑雪板是阿勒泰乌梁海部传承下来的生活重要工具，他们在与大自然的长期相处中，不断适应环境对其加以改进使用，将其传承到现在科学技术如此发达的今天。这些都是可以用阿勒泰乌梁海部的历史、风俗习惯和传统文化来证明的。

阿勒泰乌梁海部从古阿勒泰人那里，进化和传承着古老式“察纳”滑雪文化是该民族灿烂传统文化的一部分，也是新疆非物质文化遗产的重要部分。完整无损地保护和继承古阿勒泰人传统下来的古老式“察纳”文化是我们每一个人的不可推卸责任。

【注释】

[1]［波斯］拉施特:《史集》第一卷第一分册, 北京, 商务印书馆, 1997年, 第203页。

[2]［意大利］普兰卡尔宾 , 维廉 鲁布鲁克著; 格尔乐朝克图蒙译:《蒙古游记》, 呼和浩特, 内蒙古教育出版社, 1983年, 第446页。

[3]［苏］B·Y·符拉基米尔佐夫:《蒙古社会制度史》, 北京, 民族出版社, 1981年, 第87页。

[4] 呼和布音:《蒙古民俗志》, 呼和浩特, 内蒙古文化出版社, 1988年, 第437-400页。

[5][6] 那音塔:《阿勒泰乌梁海部古老式“察纳”文化初探》,《卫拉特研究》, 1996年第4期。

[7][8] 色音:《蒙古民俗学》, 北京, 民族出版社, 1996年, 第26页。

English paper:

Uriyanghai is a Mongolian sound, meaning “deft people”, “reindeer-feeding people” . In ancient history, they have many titles. Weilate Uriyanghai tribe in Xinjiang still reserves traditional “Chana” skis, “ice archery” and other traditional excellence. Altay Uriyanghai tribe still has been using wooden “Chana” skis with horsehide bottomed, which has a long history.

Altay Uriyanghai tribe mainly settles in Altay Prefecture Handegate Mongolian township and Burqin county Hemu-kanas Mongolian township. At the end of Qing dynasty, the tribe has about 13, 000 people. After the Republic of China, the tribe is scattered in many places because of frequent wars. To the Liberation, there haven't so many people left. Xinjiang Altay Uriyanghai has 7, 000 people now, Mongolia Altay Uriyanghai tribe approximately about 26, 000 people.

In ancient times, the Uriyanghai tribe is called “forest people”, living in a place with dense forest, towering mountains, ice and snow and cold climate. Uriyanghai tribe can use the skis very early which can be seen in historical records. In the 13th century, a Persian historian Rashid al-Din has recorded in his *Jami'al-Tarikh* : “ Due to a large amount of mountains and forest, people (Uriyanghai) have to hunt for wild animals in snow in the winter. They make a special board, standing on it, taking leather as rein, binding it in the front. Then they take a wooden pole in hand, landing the ground with wooden pole, sliding on the snow surface, like sailing a boat on water. They just use this kind of skis to run up and down in the wilderness, to kill buffaloes and other animals. In addition to its own stepping of "Chana" skis, they also drag some other connected boards to put killed animals on them."

[1] The above mentioned "connected boards" is still be used in the Altay Uriyanghai tribe, and the connected boards are actually leather cases for packing animals, made from goat skin and titled "Qierge". Uriyanghai people put food, clothes, animal skin and venison in "Qierge". The fact that Uriyanghai tribe can use the skis can also be seen in the record "*Adventures in Mongolia*" by an Italian traveler in the 13th century, "…there has no towns in the north, but a nomadic tribe, …the Uriyanghai tribe, they walk on frozen ice and snow tied with polished bone, speeding up like animals and birds."[2] "…Mongolian "forest people" tribe make clothes with animal skin, using skis and sleds on snow, drinking myron…".[3] The above records are the demonstrations about the early using of "Chana" skis, supplied by foreign scholars.

Such records vividly describe the situation of the ancient Mongolian people using skis and ski poles in the 13th century. This now is consistent with the present using "Chana" skis in Altay Uriyanghai. Compared with skis and ski poles in modern sports, the ancient Uriyanghai skis and ski poles though have different production material and production process, but they are roughly the same in shape, use and operation methods.

The above historical records with details states that Mongolian, including Uriyanghai have been deft at using skis and mastered the manufacturing technique and craft in the he early 13th century. Thus it can be said that in the early 13th century "Chana" culture has been formed in the Uriyanghaiuri tribe, or even earlier. If the mongols just start to learn to ski at that time, never so skilled to slide quickly to use skis for hunting, to carry prey with skis. As a result, "we can be sure that the the history of Mongolian people using the skis and poles is far earlier than the 13th century, and it perhaps has entered the stage of skillful use before the 13th century"

The ancient hunting has a close relation with "Chana" skis. The Uriyanghaiuri are excellent hunters with outstanding hunting knowledge and ability. Ancient Uriyanghaiuri ancestors with astute wisdom, dexterous hands make wooden and bone bulky skis for hunting and traffic to maintain their daily life.

The present used "Chana" skis by Altay Uriyanghaiuri tribe still remain the similar shape of the previous skis. The production of the skis is exquisite, they are made up of high quality wood, best horse leather, cowhide, short nails (ancient times without nails, but wooden nail or fine leather strap), wooden poles, etc. The skis originally are mainly made of pine wood because of its light quality and accessible power. Some of them are also made of poplar wood. The "Chana" ski has length about about 1.8-2m, width about 15-20cm, the top about 5 cm wide, the central thickness about 2cm, 1cm thick on both plate sides of the edge, the top bending up 30 degrees or so. The bottom of "Chana" ski is mainly made in special horsehide, choosing the best parts of horsehide (mainly the horse legs and hips location), soaking by water to the point that it can be pulled, spreading to the bottom of curved wood, fastening it with nails from the above. The horse fur is short and thick and backward side, so the forwarding-facing direction can easily slide forward. The skis can prevent from being slippery when climbing slopes, having reverse braking action. The house leather strap is used to fasten feet to the ski and used after daubing with animal fat. The daubed leather strap can stand melted snow water, and it is easy to bundle or unfasten and not easy to break. Ski poles are generally made from young poplar wood, willow and pine wood. Poles are about 2m long, about 3cm-6cm in diameter, thickness at the top about 4cm in diameter. If the poles are short, they cannot support in snow. Uriyanghaiuri tribe "Chana" ski only use a single pole. Some hunters wrap iron cover to the pole head, using it to wound prey[5].

Altay Uriyanghaiuri tribe believes that if you have a pair of light and strong skis, good leather, it is just like a hunter having a good helper for hunting, which can show the heroism of the hunter and he will never come back empty-handed. Altay Uriyanghaiuri tribe has such a tradition before hunting or taking part in the game: daubing skis at the top with creme or ghee to wish a complete success and express good state of mind. In Altay Uriyanghaiuri tribe, children from an early age begin to learn how to hunt in the wild mountain for firewood in spite of the harsh winter. They have to hunt for prey in cave, tree holes at night, exercising their wisdom, will and ability to overcome difficulties and obstacles. Until now, the custom is still kept. People who cannot use "Chana" skis can't go to the wild to hunt, and the hunters are always strong to use the skis. When huntsmen are hunting in the deep mountains, they are agile to leap over skis from two to three meters high cliffs, sliding in the beautiful scenery like a bird. Altay Uriyanghaiuri tribe in ancestral home is rich in the beauty of Altai Mountains with self-sufficiency and self-reliance life, enjoying the gift of nature. Historically, Mongolian nation is engaged in hunting since ancient times, using the "Chana" skis[6].

Now the Uriyanghaiuri tribe in Handegate Mongolian nationality township hold the old traditional "Chana" ski racing every winter. In recent years, the old type of ski racing has attracted the attention of tourists and researchers both at home and abroad. As the old type of skis gain prominence, those people who originally cannot make and use skis are learning how to ski. The Uriyanghaiuriwu own ancestors have inherited the old skis from ancient times. We know that "any habits and customs of a nation contains at a certain degree the national cultural characteristics.

We know that "to some extent, any ethnic customs retain the nation's cultural characteristics"[7]. When we are researching the national culture, we should make a down-to-earth study based on multi-aspect, such as the nation and tribe's origin, living environment, social history, lifestyle and custom, diet religion and language, etc. Only in this way, can we get scientific evidence.

"Although human history is bound to enter a new stage of a society, traditional culture passed down from ancestry will not be abandoned as original shape."[8] In addition to the operation of agriculture, animal husbandry, Altay Uriyanghaiuri tribe is good at hunting. Since the ancient times, Altay Uriyanghaiuri tribe go uphill hunting in winter while using "Chana" skis, and they hunt for wild boar, mink, fox, squirrels and other animals with bow and arrow. In addition, the Uriyanghaiuri tribe has a special folk *Ballad of Hunters* in oral form.

In winter, Altay Uriyanghaiuri tribe used ancient "Chana" skis to travel through Altay Mountain. They prayed to Altay ancestors and sang Altay ode as well as set traps to catch wild boar and hunt fox, wolf, marten and squirrel. They enjoyed the water provide by Altay which satisfies the demand of life and production. They live in harmony with nature. It is still today. It is well known that ancient "Chana" skis are the important life tool inherited from Altay Uriyanghaiuri tribe. They constantly improved the skis in their long-term relationship with nature and passed them to modern society with well developed science and technology. All of these can be proved by the history, customs and traditional culture of Altay Uriyanghaiuri tribe.

The Altay Uriyanghaiuri tribe has evolved and inherited ancient style "Chana" skiing culture, which is part of the splendid traditional culture and is also an important part of intangible cultural heritage in Xinjiang. To protect and inherit traditional culture intactly is the unavoidable responsibility of each one of us.

[1] [Persia] Rashid al-Din. *Jami'al-Tarikh* , vol. 1. Beijing: The Commercial Press, 1997, p. 203.

[2] [Italy] Alvin Carl, Wilhelm Lubrooke (writer), Le ChaoKeTu (translator). *Adventures in Mongolia*. Hohhot. The Inner Mongolia Education Press, 1983, p. 446.

[3] [Soviet Union] B·Y· Vladimir Zoff. *The History of Mongolian Social System*. Beijing: The Nationalities Publishing House, 1981, p. 87.

4.10 人类滑雪起源地——见证阿勒泰冬季旅游之崛起 Cradle of human skiing——witness rising of the winter tourism in Altay

史志强 Shi Zhiqiang (CHN)

个人简介 Brief Introduction

史志强，男，汉，山东省招远市人，1972 年 9 出生，中共党员，本科学历，1992 年参加工作，现任阿勒泰市旅游局局长。

Shi Zhiqiang, male, was born in Sep. 1972 in Zhaoyuan City Shandong Province. Being a communist with bachelor degree, he started working in 1992, and is the director of Altay Tourism Bureau. He is a signing photographer of the Xinhua News Agency, People's network and China News network.

中文论文：

人类滑雪起源地

——见证阿勒泰冬季旅游之崛起

一、"阿勒泰是人类滑雪起源地"学说 13 年艰苦认证历程

中国滑雪专家单兆鉴开创人类滑雪起源地中国学说研究，为中国以及世界滑雪运动做出重大贡献，为阿勒泰冬季旅游产业发展提供动力及坚实的后盾。1993 年，单老在其所著《怎样练习滑雪》中在国内首次提出"阿勒泰地区是人类滑雪起源地"学说。1994 年，中国滑雪协会、国家体委体育文史工作委员会审编的《中国滑雪运动史》中再次提出这一学说。1994 年，刘永年受单兆鉴的委托，主笔撰写了《新疆阿尔泰地域是人类滑雪发祥地之一》的文章，经单兆鉴推荐刊登于国家体委学术刊物《体育文史》1994 年第四期。1994－2004 年间，单兆鉴陆续收集国内外滑雪历史有关资料并反复地学习、梳理、研究、总结以及艰难地实际考察，于 2004 年完成了"人类滑雪起源应具备的基本条件"的研究，并最终完成了《中国新疆阿勒泰地区具备了人类滑雪起源的一切基本条件》的研究，与《阿勒泰璀璨的滑雪文化》一起在中国滑雪协会网上发布，为“中国新疆阿勒泰地区是人类滑雪最早起源地”学说的最后确立，奠定了理论基础。同年，单兆鉴编著的《滑雪运动指南》中多次提到阿勒泰地域是人类滑雪发源地。2005年8月出版的我国第一本《高山滑雪初级教程》(由单兆鉴、王石安为主编，王揖涛、任洪国为主、副审，中国滑雪协会审定的）中明确阐述“中国新疆的阿勒泰地域是人类滑雪的发源地”。2006年1月16日，“中国·新疆·阿勒泰地区是世界滑雪最早起源地”的《阿勒泰宣言》正式提出并向世人宣布。同年阿勒泰市确立“人类滑雪最早起源地纪念日”为每年1月16日。2006年12月15日，阿勒泰市人民政府和中国滑雪协会共同在北京人民大会堂举行新闻发布会，发布会的主题是：中国新疆阿勒泰是人类滑雪最早起源地。2007年1月16日，“阿勒泰是人类滑雪起源地”获得上海大世界基尼斯认证，品牌最终得到确认。

2001年起，时任阿勒泰市外宣办主任的我开始参与“阿勒泰是人类滑雪起源地”学说认证的全过程，2002年1月份撰写了当地第一篇有关滑雪起源的新闻报导，刊登在《阿勒泰日报》上。2006年，组织筹备并参与了“人类滑雪起源地——阿勒泰宣言”在北京人民大会堂召开的新闻发布会并撰写发表“北京人民大会堂见证历史性时刻阿勒泰：人类滑雪最早起源地”新闻稿。2008年，参与申报的项目“阿勒泰是人类滑雪最早起源地”获得大世界基尼斯之最最佳项目奖。2010年，积极申报并获得“中国滑雪之都”称号。

二、借助“人类滑雪起源地”品牌，阿勒泰冬季旅游蓬勃发展

在市委领导的关心和重视下，自学说认证以来，阿勒泰市冬季旅游，尤其是冰雪运动方面快速发展并带动阿勒泰市旅游产业经济发展进一步提升的可喜局面。目前，阿勒泰市共有星级酒店6家，A级景区6处（3A级景区有桦林公园，2A级景区有克兰大峡谷风景区、驼峰景区、塘巴湖景区、红石头景区、文物博物馆)；国际、国内旅行社21家；旅游汽车公司4家；S级滑雪场2家，其中将军山滑雪场为5S级滑雪场；阿勒泰市直接或间接从事旅游商品生产销售的企业、公司达310家；民俗农家乐60家，星级农家乐22家；特色餐饮店400余家。旅游从业人员达4000余名。

1. 冰雪经济提升

2014-2015年雪季，阿勒泰市以第四季中国阿勒泰国际冰雪游暨第十二届阿勒泰市冰雪风情游为载体，取得了良好成效，接待游客58万人次，实现综合收入3.3亿元，同比增长34%和73%，宾馆酒店入住率达85%。其中将军山滑雪场进场人次18万人，接待滑雪游客共计59707人次，同比增长252%和35%；将军山滑雪场营业额406万元，同比增长103%。

2. 旅游产品发展

自学说认证以来，我市狠抓冬季旅游基础设施建设。一是斥资亿元成功打造5S级滑雪场——将军山滑雪场。目前将军山滑雪场1号、2号雪道获得国际雪联认证，具备了举办国际赛事的资格。已开发雪道18条，总长度20公里，其中超长中级道长3公里，是新疆目前最长的一条中级道。滑雪场滑雪条件优越，设备精良，服务优质，是“全国高山滑雪训练基地”、“自治区高山滑雪训练基地”。二是打造全疆规模最大的冰雪大世界（冰雪雕园）。连续10年打造全疆规模最大的冰雪风情园。2014/2015雪季更使这一冰雪产品提升了规格，成就了“阿勒泰冰雪大世界”接待游客18万人。三是启动阿依海国际滑雪度假村建设，力争将其打造成为能够承办国际赛事的国际高端滑雪旅游目的地。

3. 冰雪活动丰富

自“人类滑雪起源地”学说认证以来，阿勒泰市将每年的1月16日确定为“人类滑雪起源地纪念日”并举办“古老滑雪比赛、滑冰比赛、美食大赛”等纪念日系列庆典活动，以丰富品牌的内涵及更好的传承与光大滑雪文化。自2003年起，阿勒泰市大规模、高水准地连续举办了十二届“中国新疆阿勒泰冰雪风情游”活动，全面奠定了我市在新疆冬季旅游中的“领头雁、带头羊”地位，极大的丰富了品牌内涵。作为冬季旅游活动载体的“中国新疆阿勒泰冰雪风情游”活动承办了全国性的大型滑雪赛事—2010-2011年度全国高山滑雪青少年锦标赛、2010-2011新疆大众滑雪铁杆系列赛、“绿野网”滑雪挑战赛、中国新疆冰雪旅游节阿勒泰滑雪节暨阿勒泰市人类滑雪起源地纪念日庆典活动、雪地摩托车拉力赛、滑雪滑冰普及活动、古老滑雪比赛、元宵灯会、祝福祖国—大型孔明灯放飞活动，庆典民俗歌舞晚会、书画摄影比赛、青少年滑冰、成人滑雪比赛比赛等活动，吸引了更多的游客来到阿勒泰。

4. 滑雪运动的普及

自“人类滑雪起源地”学说认证以来，我市致力于滑雪运动的普及。为全市中小学生发放4万册《阿勒泰市青少年滑雪滑冰知识普及读本》，并开设滑雪学习课程，从娃娃抓起滑雪的普及。地市工会、旅游局、文体局、文明办、妇联、团委等6部门联合发文，在全地区广大干部职工中开展滑雪拓展训练，近2年滑雪培训受训面达到75%。同时针对广大市民开办滑雪培训班、上传学滑雪视频、开展全民冰雪健身活动等多种方式展开滑雪滑冰的普及活动，使滑雪滑冰普及活动取得了广泛而又深入的成效。

5. 人类滑雪起源地魅力提升

冬季的阿勒泰市，冰雪文化源远流长，冰雪运动如火如荼，冰雪风光如诗如画，冰雪产品丰富多彩，冰雪民俗淳朴悠长，冰雪旅游日新月异。看，阿勒泰市冰雪旅游吉祥物“雪宝”，正脚踏毛皮滑雪板，神采奕奕的奔向未来，走向世界。随着冰雪旅游的快速发展，冰雪运动的大力开展，阿勒泰市滑雪产业的明天，将更加辉煌，未来的世界滑雪冠军领奖台上，必定会有阿勒泰人的出现。

阿勒泰市旅游局　史志强

English paper:

Cradle ofHuman Skiing
——witness rising of the winter tourism in Altay

I. 13 years' of tough process to the theory of "Altay-cradle of human skiing"

Chinese excellent skiing expert, Shan Zhaojian, created the theory of "cradle of human skiing", which laid a solid foundation to promote winter tourism in Altay.

In 1993, Mr Shan put forward his theory of "Altay is the cradle of ancient skiing" in his works *How to sk*.; In 1994, China Skiing Association, Historical accounts of the work committee from National Sports Association mentioned it once again.; In 1994, Liu Yongnian, commissioned by Mr Shan, wrote the article *Xinjiang Altay is the cradle of human skiing*, recommended by Mr Shan, and published in the 4th *Academic journal of National Sports Association*.; From 1994 to 2004, Mr Shan collected the related reference both at home and abroad. After studying, sorting, researching, and concluding time and time again, He finally finished the study of *The basic conditions to origin human skiing*, and therefore, accomplished the study of *China Xinjiang Altay Possessed the Basic Conditions to Origin Human Skiing*, was published in the web of China Skiing Association, together with *Profound culture in Altay*, which provided the solid convincing theory to affirm that Altay is the original place of human skiing. In the same year, Mr Shan mentioned Altay as the cradle of ancient skiing; In Aug of 2005, the first book in China *Primary Tutorial of Alpine Skiing* (Edited by Shan Zhaojian and Wang Shian, Checked by Wang Jitao, Ren Hongguo, Reviewed by China Skiing association) explained clearly that Altay is the cradle of ancient skiing. On the 16th of January in 2006, *Declaration of Altay* was issued formally to the world, in the same year, Altay named the date as Memorial Day of cradle of ancient skiing. On the 15th of December in 2006, The government of Altay City and China Skiing Association held a press conference in People's Great Hall, the theme is China Xinjiang Altay is the cradle of ancient skiing. On the 16th of January of 2007, the saying of Altay is the cradle of ancient skiing won the Shanghai Great World Guinness Certificate.

From 2001, I, working as director ofthe Altay International communication office, took part in the whole process. In January of 2002, I wrote the first local news about the cradle of ancient skiing, published in Altay Daily.

In 2006, I organized and took part in the Press Conference of Altay Declaration held in People's Great Hall in Beijing. And Wrote the Article: Witness the historical time in Beijing People's Great Hall.

In 2008, I took part in delivering the project of Altay, the cradle of ancient skiing, and gained the best project award by Great World Guinness. In 2010, we succeeded in delivering the fame of Hometown of Skiing in China.

II. Winter tourism flourished with the trademark of Altay-cradle of ancient human skiing.

The government attached great importance to Altay winter tourism, after the theory was certificated, winter tourism has fostered tourism industry and economic development.

At present, there are 6 star-rated hotels, 6 A-rated Scenic Areas (AAA Scenic Spot: Birch Park; AA Scenic Spots: KelanGrand Canyon, Hump Scenic Spot, Tangbahu Scenic Spot, Red Stones Scenic Spot and Relics Museum); 21 International and domestic travel agencies; 4 tourism vehicle companies; 2 S-rated ski resorts, including General Mountain Ski Resort, which is SSSSS-ski resort; 310 enterprises and companies, directly or indirectly engaged in tourism commodity production and marketing ; 60 Folk Farm Houses, among which, 22 are star-rated; more than 400 restaurants, and more than 4000 workers are related to tourism.

1. Economy promotion

In Winter of 2014-2015, Altay city successfully hosted the 4th China Altay International Snow and Ice Tourism and the 12th Altay city Snow and Ice Tourism, with 580, 000 tourists, and a total income about 330 million RMB, which increased 34% and 73% separately, besides, hotels occupancy rate was up to 85%. Take General Mountain Ski Resort for example, the total attendance for the resort reached 180000, among them, there were 59707 skiing guests, increasing up by 252% and 35% separately; Compared with last year, the annual turnover is 4, 060, 000 RMB, up by 103% . Influenced by winter tourism, in the first quarter, the enterprises above designated size in accommodation and catering achieved rapid growth. By the end of March, the business volume from the enterprises above designated size in accommodation and catering had totaled 15,270,000 RMB, an increase of 26.6%. Among the business volume, the Rooms Revenue was 5,232,000 RMB, an increase of 12.4%, the Catering Revenue reached 8,568,000 RMB, an increase of 24.5%; the other revenues was 1,302,000 RMB, an increase of 304.3%.

2. Tourism products development

Altay paid so much attention to the development of tourism facilities. On the one hand, the government invested a hundred million to build 5S skiing resort, now, No. 1 and No. 2 Slopes have got the homologation by FIS, and have the quality to hold international competition. There are 18 slopes, with the total length of 20km, among which, intermediate slopes are 3 km, is the longest intermediate slope in Xinjiang. The Skiing resort is equipped with high quality facilities and best service, and it is the Training center of National Alpine skiing. And Training center of Alpine skiing in Xinjiang Vygur Autonomous region.

On the other hand, build the largest scale Snow and Ice Park, For ten years, we built the largest scale Snow and Ice Park. This winter, we promoted the level of the park, and built World of Snow and Ice.

3. Colorful winter activities

Altay has named the 16th of Jan as a memorial day of Cradle of human skiing. Ancient skiing competition, Food contest, skating competition, etc, are held to celebrated the day, to enrich the trademark.

From 2003, the successful 12th China Xinjiang Altay Snow and Ice Tourism laid a solid foundation for Altay tourism in Xinjiang.

We held national Skiing competition, National Alpine Youth Skiing Competition, Xinjiang public skiing competition, Green Web Skiing Challenge, Celebrations on China Xinjiang Altay Snow and Ice tourism Festival, Snow motorcycle relay race, ancient skiing competition, Temples, lantern carnival, Flying kongming light activity, folklore party, paintings and photos competition, Youth skating competition, Adults Skating competition, etc, which attract a large number of tourists to Altay.

4. Popularize winter sports

The government is always adhering to popularizing winter sports. 40, 000 books *Altay Youth Skiing Booklet* have been handed out to the students in primary and middle schools. Six departments under the administration of government called on the masses of the whole city to take part in the exercise of skiing. More than 75% have been trained about skiing, at the same time, the popularizing of skiing got great achievement by various ways.

5. Promoted charm of Altay

Altay in winter, rich in snow and ice culture, flourishing winter sports, beautiful scenery, abundant snow and ice products, simple but profound custom, is making progress day by day.

Look, "All love" the mascot of Altay snow and Ice tourism, is skiing on the leather skis, to the future, to the world. With the development of snow and Ice tourism, the future of Altay skiing industry is sure to be more shining, I am confident to say that sooner or later, Altay skier will stand on the Champion podium in the world skiing competition.

4.11 史前岩画研究的新视角——以基因信息为基点 The New View of Researching Prehistorical Petrogram—Based on the Genic Information

史晓明 Shi Xiaoming (CHN)

个人简介 Brief Introduction

史晓明，男，1956 年生，1984-1997 年在克孜尔石窟工作，1997 年 9 月-2014 年在新疆艺术学院美术系任教，教授，至今共出版学术专著、画集 7 本。

Shi Xiaoming, born in 1956, he works in kizil grottoes from 1984 to 1997. From September 1997 to 2014, he works in Fine Arts Department of Xinjiang Arts University Xinjiang, and has published 7 monographs album of paintings so far.

中文论文：

史前岩画研究的新视角
——以基因信息为基点

史晓明

人类史前艺术史的研究方法，自进入 21 世纪以来，一个最值得关注的学术新视野莫过于将生命科学的前沿知识与艺术史问题有机地迅捷联系起来。这个历史机遇得益于近 30 年来生物技术、分子遗传学、进化生物学、个体生态学、脑神经科学、认知心理学等生命科学相关领域的划时代突破性进展，而且这个前景还会向纵深发展，并不断地随时涌现出自然科学之外的惊喜和希望。

当然，生物学问题的基础性研究成果受益的不仅是艺术史学，包括文化研究的各个领域及人性善恶伦理等难症难结都会受到潜移默化的冲击与影响。就连高更名画题目的名言“我们从哪里来，我们到哪里去”的终极思考的解答恐怕都没有什么问题。甚至全世界的每一个个体人的身世来历，也可以通过 DNA 测试弄明白自己的祖先及家族曾源自何方。本人于 2012 年 3 月就测试出自己的基因信息本源于西部的游牧部族，而我命中注定是必须要返回西域，上世纪 50 年代我仅 3 岁时就从中原“荣归故里”至今。

本文的基本思路依然是自 1997 年以来自我对生命问题的阶段性思索。即通过基因数据特意将问题的视角朝向艺术史的路径，尤其是对史前岩画的图像作者的来龙去脉做一试探性的梳理。因为就目前而言，比起其他相关学科，运用人类基因图谱的信息来讨论史前文化确实有着特殊的针对性优势。

众所周知，2000 年以来，研究生命与基因的科学家们已经帮助我们画出了一幅相对完整的人类基因图谱，也大致勾勒出了“非洲夏娃”走出非洲之后的路线及分布图，具体地说就是他们（一群基因标记为父系 M168 和母系 L3a 的“非非洲人”的后裔）引领和创造了地球上六万年以来的所有“先进文化”。无疑，现代智人的基因遗传信息源可以追溯至东非大裂谷的人类摇篮，关键是最近的冰河期以来的造型艺术的源头却与 M343 的基因标记的克罗马农人有关。而克罗马农人却是来自亚洲中部的、基因标记为 M45 单倍群的、4 万年前的族群后裔。也就是说，克罗马农人（即现代的欧洲人）是 35000 前从中亚往西至欧洲，而不是从中东直接北上，他们在到达欧洲的中部之后，后来又被冰河期的严寒逼迫到温暖的欧洲南部的伊比利亚半岛、意大利和巴尔干地区。在那里至少从公元前 30000 年前开始，他们留下了数百个绘制了大量绘画的岩石洞穴，这些艺术与非洲、澳大利亚、南北美洲所发现的各种岩石艺术交相辉映，共同构造了人类史前艺术的辉煌。

本文的问题是：在现在的蒙古国西部的阿尔泰山的孟汉区和新疆阿勒泰、伊犁地区，均发现了旧石器时代的洞穴岩壁绘画，既然中亚是又一个人类迁徙的集散地，那么，中亚东北面这些区域的洞穴岩壁绘画是本地土著的遗留还是后来从西边传过来的？因为这一带的旧石器时代的艺术曾长期地被艺术史研究者所忽略。就人类基因图谱的分布与早期人类迁徙的路线来看，也应当可以环顾到中亚东北面及新疆北部地区旧石器时代的原始艺术的曙光。

我们还期待今后科学家们的更加详细的人类基因图谱的研究成果来帮助我们进一步地认清和佐证人类史前艺术史的谜团。

【主要参考文献】

A. H. 丹尼、V. M. 马松，中亚文明史第一卷，中国对外翻译出版有限公司，2002 年。

[美] 弗雷德·S·克莱纳等，加德纳世界艺术史，中国青年出版社，2007 年 6 月。

[美] 史蒂夫·奥尔森，人类基因的历史地图，生活·读书·新知 三联书店，2008 年 6 月。

史晓明，艺术学研究方法的新视野——以生物学为基点，新疆艺术学院学报，2011 年第 3 期。

张振，人类六万年，时代出版传媒股份有限公司、安徽人民出版社，2013 年 1 月。

苏北海，新疆岩刻画，新疆美术摄影出版社，2013 年 11 月。

English paper:

The New View of Researching Prehistorical Petrogram

—Based on the Genic Information

Concerning about the researching method of Ogygian Art History, one of the most notable academic views should be the swift organic combination of the pioneering life sciences knowledge and art history. This historic opportunity benefits from the breaking development of biotechnology, molecular genetics, evolutionary biology, autecology, neuroscience, cognitive psychology and other relative subjects over the 30 years. Furthermore, this background is still moving on tending to a longitunal tendency where there will be more surprise and hope emerging out of the natural science.

Certainly, the beneficiary from the basic research of biology does not only include art history but also includes the impact to few fields of cutural researches and ethicsproblems. It might not be quite a ultimate question which is in the title of Gauguin's masterpiece "Where do we come from? where are we going to?" . Even every individuals all over the world can figure out their ancestors or origins of whole family. Take the author as an instance, the genetic information began in a western nomad, and it's doomed to return the west. Consequently, the author "came back" from the middle of China at the age of 3 in 1950s.

This essay is still focusing on the interim ponder about lives of ourselves since 1997. That is to say, the problem will be specially perspective towards the path of art history by genetic data, especially towards the genetic pectination of prehistorical petrograms' authors. It is the reason that comparing with other related disciplines, using human-gene-map information to discuss prehistoric culture does have special superiority.

As is known to all, scientists devoting to life and gene has already helped us to sketch in a pretty complete gene map of human beings, and the general outline of the "African eve's" route leaving from Africa and its distribution, which is specifically their leading to create all the "advantage culture" over 60000 years on the earth. There is no doubt that the genetic inheritance of modern homo sapiens information source can be traced back to the human the cradle of the east African rift valley, the key is the nearest the source of the plastic arts since the ice age was associated with M343 grams Roman farmer of genetic markers. While the grams Roman farmer from central Asia, the M45 haploid group of genetic markers, and 40000 years ago the ethnic descent. That is to say, the Roman farmer was from central Asia to the west to Europe before 35000, rather than directly from the Middle East, north after they arrive in Europe in the middle of the later was ice cold persecuted to the warmth of the Iberian peninsula in southern Europe, Italyand the Balkans. Where at least since 30000 BC, they left behind hundreds of draw a large amount of rock cave paintings, these art with Africa, Australia, north and South America have found all kinds of rock art in photograph reflect, the common structure of the human prehistoric art.

The question of this essay locates on: In the Meng Han area of Altai Mountains of western Mongoliaand Xinjiang Altay, Yili region, paleolithic cave wall paintings all can be found. Since the central Asia is also a distributing center of human migration, was the petrograms in northeast region of central Asiathe legacy of native or the exotic later from the west? Because the paleolithic art in this area had long been neglected by the researchers. Considering the distribution of the human genome and early human migratory routes, it can also refers to the dawn of paleolithic primitive art in the northeast and central Asiaregion in northern Xinjiang.

The hereafter scientists are really expected to obtain the result of more specific human gene maps, which can urgely help us to recognize and prove the mistery of prehistorical human art in a more profound level.

4.12 流传于阿尔泰山中的古老滑雪民谣及传说故事 Ancient Ski Ballad and Legend in the Altai Mountains

尼克·尼咏梅 Nick Ni Yongmei

个人简介 Brief Introduction

尼克·尼咏梅，女、蒙古族、新疆阿勒泰市人。1973年10月出生，1992年09月参加工作。中共党员。大学本科学历。曾任阿勒泰市汗德尕特乡副乡长，为人类滑雪起源的研究作出了贡献。现任阿勒泰市归国华侨联合会副主席。

Nick Ni Yongmei, female, Mongolian, people in Altay City in Sinjiang. Born in October 1973, she takes the job in September 1992. Member of the Communist Party of China. Bachelor's Degree. She used to be the deputy township head of Khan's essential township, and has made contribution to the research on the origin of human skiing. Now she is the deputy president of Federation of returned overseas Chinese in Altay City.

中文论文：

流传于阿尔泰山中的古老滑雪民谣及传说故事

阿勒泰山脉，有着悠久的人类文明史，产生了许多口传的故事传说、民谣……

“打猎人之歌”（又称“滑雪狩猎民谣”）。这首古老滑雪民谣，广泛流传于阿勒泰乌梁海蒙古族和蒙古族图瓦人中，历史源远流长，有着几千年的历史。它也是构成了阿勒泰游牧民族文化历史的口传史诗，具有重要的研究价值和传承价值。

2003年11月初，我来到了阿勒泰市汗德尕特蒙古民族乡人民政府担任副乡长一职。我在开展入户调查时，来到阿尔恰特村村民欧吉省（现为阿勒泰地区文物局文物保护员）家里，和他们一家人聊天，当我说乡里有没有什么关于岩画一类的地方时，欧吉省说起了他小时候家住在敦德布拉克，一天他与附近的蒙古族牧民小朋友一起在山中玩耍，为了避雨便躲进了一处洞穴里，在洞里看到画在洞穴石壁上的彩色图画有人，有动物。我感到非常稀奇，在这里还有涂在石头洞里的岩画吗？于是我和欧吉省相约第二天去洞穴所在地——敦德布拉克看个究竟。

第二天天不亮，七点钟我们就出发了。在敦德布拉克洞穴里那些颜色鲜艳图画使我惊呆，使我浮想联翩，不知道用什么来形容所看到的情景！自问是什么人留下的这些彩色的杰作？我看着山洞外面，场地宽敞，适合祭祀，便幻想画中这些屈膝的人会不会是古人在跳祭祀舞蹈，祈祷自己打到更多的猎物呢？我激动地告诉他们这是真的彩色洞穴岩绘画时，欧吉省他们高兴起来。这时候有一个蒙古族牧民掏出奶酒，唱起了蒙古长调，并围着雪敖包做起了祭祀仪式。我听着这首蒙古长调觉得非常好听，就问他蒙古长调的名字叫什么时，他说是小时候听到村里的老人们经常在冬天唱起这首长调，意思是赞美踩着滑雪板远去打猎的猎人的“打猎人之歌”。

在回来的路上，我们去拜访了一下会演唱这首“打猎人之歌”的民间艺人奴德娜西老人，听到了七十多岁的老人唱起的这首从母亲那里传下来的完整版的“打猎人之歌”。同时也得知了当地还有很多老人家都会演唱这首“打猎人之歌”，如祖鲁加、克西塔、乌鲁木赞、阔什肯白等。老人告诉我，冬天善于狩猎的乌梁海人会远去阿尔泰山中狩猎，他们会呆在山里 2、3 个月，直到临近春节前才满载而归，同家人过一个丰衣足食的春节。留在家里的亲人们会每天祈祷，在祈祷祭祀时就会唱起“打猎人之歌”，希望家人打到猎物平安回家。“打猎人之歌”其实也是一个祭祀之歌，不是在任何场合都能演唱的。当时“打猎人之歌”在汗德尕特乡也属于濒临失传的民间艺术，一方面由于“禁猎”，另一方面也因为当今的社会发展，交通便利等情况，使毛皮滑雪板失去了“用武之地”，毛皮滑雪板渐渐就不再使用了。

在当初，我们没有哪一个人会想到敦德布拉克洞穴彩绘里隐藏着后来这么大的秘密和天机，更没有想到它竟是“中国新疆阿勒泰成为人类最早滑雪起源地”的证据之一。在 2006 年 12 月 15 日，当在北京人民大会堂新闻发布会宣布中国新疆阿勒泰是人类最早滑雪起源地时，整个汗德尕特乡沸腾了，成为了歌的海洋，大家载歌载舞欢庆着这个好消息。如今“打猎人之歌”已成为阿勒泰地区蒙古族群众很喜欢的一首民谣，到处传唱着，也成为了汗德尕特乡的“乡歌”，年轻人也在传唱着。

在那高高的阿尔泰杭盖（蒙古语，意即高高的山的意思）山中，
身上背着柳木制作的弓箭，
双手斜推着滑雪棒的，
脚踩红松、白松木制作的滑雪板，
很快地滑着奔跑在松树林中的，
身后拖着山羊皮囊的，
是那勇敢而又灵活、聪明的猎人。

看那个猎人啊!
就像阿尔泰杭盖山中的羚羊一样奔跑得快,
来回在松林中奔跑着,
怎么样也抓不到他,
善射的射箭手是那猎人啊,
射到了一个又一个的猎物,
猎物是那汗德尕（即：麋鹿）和狍子。
斜推的滑雪棒啊!
把身边的雪推成了一个个小雪球,
那个小雪球，滚呀滚呀,
变成了大大的圆球,
它在和猎人赛跑,
追随着猎人奔跑。
踩着毛皮滑雪板的猎人呀,
他把它早就远远地丢在了身后面。

多年来，我一直在研究古老滑雪民谣，也从汗德尕特乡以及禾木哈纳斯、白哈巴等地的民间艺人那里收集到一些古老传说故事。这些在各地流传的版本都有本地的特色，丰富多彩。但是最大的特色还是离不开阿尔泰山一带游牧民族文化特色。

关于“野人”的传说。这是流传于阿勒泰山地游牧民族的典型传说故事。说的是阿尔泰山的古老先民在深山中狩猎时，无论是在冬季还是在春秋季都会遇见“野人”，特别是在冬季行猎之中，遇见可怕的“野人”是一件非常难办的事情，“野人”分成了雄雌。猎人在遇见雄性“野人”时，就会往山顶跑，古老滑雪板可以“抓”雪上山，会很快的跑到山顶，逃脱雄性“野人”的伤害。因为雄性“野人”额头高，眼睛深深地凹在高高的额头下，看不到头顶上的任何东西。当猎人看到雌性“野人”时，则必须往山下滑，雌性“野人”因为乳房长及下腹，总喜欢把长乳放在肩头上，以方便抓在身后的幼子哺乳，雌性“野人”在下山时要时常停下来整理长乳，把它放在肩头后，猎人乘时逃离。因此，每当狩猎人从可怕的“野人”身边逃脱后，都会来到“敖包”那里，祭祀救了自己性命的古老滑雪板。

关于“祭祀祈福”的传说。很多老人家说起古老滑雪民谣时，都会以非常神圣、端庄的态度去诉说，把它作为一个神圣的事情去看待。因为古老滑雪民谣凝聚着先民们在战胜大自然中的雪崩、猛兽奇袭、“野人”突袭、大雪封山、饥饿等磨难的经验与教训。古老滑雪民谣也是先民们向上天祭祀活动的前奏。一个村的老百姓聚在一起，围着“敖包”高唱古老滑雪民谣，抛洒着洁白的鲜奶，把古老滑雪板摆放在祭台上，磕头祭拜，向天祈祷在深山里行猎的亲人们猎到很多的猎物，平安的回到家里团聚。在亲人们凯旋而归时，众人还要来到“敖包”边，做祭祀祈福仪式，把打到的猎物摆放在祭台上，感恩上天怜悯，希望来年更加富饶。

关于“英雄悲歌”的传说。老人们经常说起在准噶尔战乱时期，乌梁海人和准噶尔人进行部族战争，在冬天作战时，乌梁海人总是胜利，因为善于狩猎的乌梁海人在阿尔泰山中踩着古老滑雪板同准噶尔人作战，把身陷深雪之中无法动弹的准噶尔人一网打尽。在秋夏季乌梁海人总打败仗，因为善战的准噶尔人兵壮马肥，善于在马背上作战。因此，每当乌梁海人唱起古老滑雪民谣时总是把对英勇战死的族人在深山中行猎的形象演唱出来，对他们寄予哀思之情。

关于“神灵所赐”的传说。古老滑雪板使用的材质一般都是阿尔泰山中的红松、白松等，以及鹿皮、野猪皮、马匹等为滑行底质，行猎棒（单杆滑雪杖）一般也用红松、白松和柳木制作。古老弓箭材质也是用以上材料构成的。乌梁海人在古籍里被称为“森林中的百姓”“狩猎人”，也是一个古老的民族，在历史上还有“打铁人”的称呼，因为阿尔泰山盛产铁，乌梁海人善于使用铁器打造冷兵器而著称。在成吉思汗西征的战争中，打造出了很多的作战兵器而备受重用。乌梁海人把古老滑雪板作为神圣的狩猎及交通工具，并在古时就把它作为神灵所赐的神物而倍加珍爱和祭拜，传唱出在“敖包”祭祀时，专门为祭拜古老滑雪板所唱的古老滑雪民谣，流传至今。

关于“庇护神”的传说。在世居阿尔泰山的老猎人会说起关于一个“铜爪女”的传说。“铜爪女”是一个可怕的专门伤害猎人的女魔头，在白天她会化成美貌少女来到猎人们的临时狩猎居住地，猎人们会防备她，故意用尖锐的长烤肉叉子和一般的猎刀插上肉递到她的手中，这时候，深藏在长袖中的女魔头的铜爪子会同猎刀相碰发出清脆的声音。此时，猎人们就会辨别她就是吸人血的女魔头。在深夜，女魔头会再次来到猎人们的居住地，从门缝里钻进去，猎人们全都藏在雪堆中密切关注着女魔头，女魔头发着恐怖的吼声把长长的铜爪一下子扎入到猎人的皮袍被子里，她的铜爪子被藏在皮被里的古老滑雪板夹得死死的，不能动弹，女魔头就这样被猎人们杀死了，只剩下了一副可怕的铜爪消失了。古老滑雪板是猎人们的保护神，只有沾了动物毛皮和鲜血的古老滑雪板才能制服一切可怕的东西。在古老滑雪民谣里猎人们还加入了古老的“呼麦”发音，利用“呼麦”来模仿古老滑雪板在滑行中摩擦雪和山石、树林发出的美妙的声音。民间艺人在传唱民谣时还会用讲述故事的方式先说出故事情节，然后用长调赞美聪明机智的猎人们战胜艰难险阻的情景。

关于“九色仙鹿”的传说。由于古代先民们狩猎过度，使得阿尔泰山山神动怒，山神就化成了一只“九色仙鹿”来到山中，故意叫贪婪的猎人们看到，猎人们被“九色仙鹿”的鹿角发出的九色光芒所吸引，聚集在一起把“九色仙鹿”活捉了，把它的发着九色光的鹿角割下来。有个老猎人在夜里受到山神启示要他带着族人离开是非之地，这个老猎人把山神的启示告诉族人，并带着族人离开了深山。但是有几个猎人受到蛊惑，不愿意离开，他们在夜晚偷偷地离开族人的队伍，回到了深山，继续对“九色仙鹿”进行围捕，身负重伤的“九色仙鹿”在临终时，把厚重的发着九色光的头角轻轻地放在了树杈间。猎人们把九色鹿角割了下来，来到草原卖了鹿角，过起了逍遥快乐的日子。没有几年，这几个猎人们忽然走到了末路，他们逃到了深山里，被林中的动物所围捕，死无葬身之地。在他们临死时看到了九色鹿顶着九色角在林中飞跃着。他们知道他们被诅咒了，非常懊悔，希望山神不要震怒于他们的族人，他们愿化成动物，供猎人们猎捕，直到诅咒解除之日。山神答应了他们的临终请求，把他们化成了美味的猎物被猎人们和动物们所猎捕，毛皮被永世踩在深山里。猎人们的族人重新回到了深山继续生活着，他们用山神赐予的动物毛皮制作各种雪板，就像九色鹿、羚羊一样跳跃奔驰在阿尔泰山中，他们也得到了山神的赐福，每次行猎都能满载而归。在林中，他们行走途中所有的山石、树木都会主动让行，并保护着猎人们不受到妖魔鬼怪的伤害。猎人们传唱着古老滑雪民谣也是在感恩山神的赐福，希望猎人们能够遵循大自然的规律，不可以过度狩猎伤害山中的神灵。

古老滑雪民谣，顾名思义不仅是民歌的一种，也是融入了传说故事、原始宗教、历史传说的素材。但是它的故事都是和阿尔泰山不可分开的，也是和当地民俗风情相适应的，它是当地群众在千百年来延续的生活、生产密不可分的文化遗迹。

English paper:

Ancient Ski Ballad and Legend in the Altai Mountains

The Altai Mountains has a long history of human civilization and has produced many oral legend story and ballads.

Skier and Hunters' Ditty (a. k. a. *Hunting Song*)

This ancient Ski Ballad is widely circulated in Altai Uriankhai Mongolian and the Mongolian Tuvans, which has a long history of several thousand years. It also constitutes the Altai oral epic in the history of nomadic culture, and have important research value and heritage value.

In early November 2003, I came to the Handegate Mongolian nationality township's government of Altay as a deputy head position. When I was into conduct household surveys, I came into Alqiate Village, and visited villager Oujishen's house, who is now looking after cultural relics in the Cultural Relics Bureau. When we talked about if there are any places might have rock paintings, Oujishen said, when he was young, he lived in Dundebulake. One day, he played with a nearby Mongolian nomads children in the mountains. They hid in a cave for taking shelter from rain, and saw there were colorful pictures of people and animals on the wall. I felt very curious——are there rock paintings in the cave? Thus, I decided to come to the cave with him to see what it is. The next day, we set out at seven o 'clock before dawn. I was shocked by the colorful pictures in the cave, thoughts thronged my mind, and lost my words to describe them. I asked myself, who left these colorful masterpiece? Looking outside the cave, where is commodious and suitable for sacrifice, I imagined that those people on the wall may be the ancient people dancing the sacrificial dance, prying for more prey. Oujishen was very happy when I told him these were real colored rock cave paintings.

At this time, there was a Mongolian herdsman, who took out milk wine, sang Mongolian long-tune, and sacrificed around the snow Ovoo. I listened to the Mongolian long-tune, and felt very nice. I asked him for the name of the Mongolian long-tune. He said that he often hears the old villagers sang this tune in winter, which means *the skier and Hunters' Ditty* of praising the hunter who step on ski to go hunting.

On the way back, we went to visit the old folk artist Nudenuoxi who could sing the *the skier and Hunters' Ditty* , and I heard this seventy-year-old artist singing the full version of this song passing down from her mother. And I also heard that there are many old people who can sing *the skier and Hunters' Ditty* . The old woman told me that in winter Uryankhai will go for hunting in Altai. They will stay in the mountains for about two to three months, until the Spring Festival. They will come back with fruitful results and spend a happy festival. Staying at home, their families will pray every day, and sing *the skier and Hunters' Ditty* for a good luck. *the skier and Hunters' Ditty* is actually a song of worship, not singing any occasion. At that time *the skier and Hunters' Ditty* also belongs to the brink of extinction folk art in Handegate. On the one hand due to the prohibition of hunting, on the other hand because of the development of social today and transport facilities, etc. , to make fur skis lose their use, fur skis gradually no longer use.

In the beginning, none of us thought Dundebulake Cave Paintings has so many secrets, and nobody thought it was one of the evidences of Altay's becoming "the earliest human skiing origin" . On December 15, 2006, when the Great Hall News Conference in Beijing announced Altay to be the earliest human skiing origins, the whole village is boiling, becoming the song of the sea. Everyone singing and dancing to celebrate the good news. Today, *the skier and Hunters' Ditty* has become a ballad which liked by many Mongolians, and it has also become the song which exemplify Handegate, passing on generation after generation:

Within the mighty and high Mountains,
With bow and arrow made of willow trees carried on his back,
Inclined ski stick is pushed with both hands,
Skis made of the red pine tree and tied to the feet,
Gliding among the pine forest rapidly,
The one who pulls the sheepskin sled on the back,
He is the brave, skillful and wise hunter.
Look at that hunter!
He can run as fast as the antelope in the grand and mighty Mountains,
Traveling to and fro among the pine forest,
It's not possible to catch him,
That hunter is an excellent archer,
Shooting prey one after another,
And the preys are deer and elk.
Inclined ski stick is pushed!
Snow rolls into small balls,
And the balls, rolling and rolling,
Become a much bigger one,
It seems to be racing with the hunter,
Rolling and chasing the hunter,
While the hunter strides on fur covered skis
The snowballs fall behind such a great distance.

Senior artists in Altay are singing the Skier and Hunters' Ditty

I have been studying ancient folk skiing for many years, and also collecting some ancient legends from folk artists of Handegate, Hemu Kanas village, White-Haba and other places.

Legend of "Savages"

This is a typical of legend circulating in mountain nomads in Altay. The ancient ancestors, which hunting in Altai Mountain, both in winter or in spring and autumn. Especially in the winter, they meet the dreaded "savage" . which is a very difficult thing to deal with. "Savage" divided into male and female. When hunters met male "savages", they would run to the top of the hill. Ancient skis can "catch" snow mountain, thus they would soon go to the top of the mountain, escaping the harm of male "savages" . They can not see anything on the head because male "savages" have high foreheads and their eyes are deeply concave at high forehead. When the hunters saw the female "savages", they must slide down the hill. Because the female "savages" have long-breasts to abdomen, thus they always stop and put the long-breasts on the shoulders tolet their cubs to grasp. Therefore, people could escape from the dreaded "savages" . After that, they would come to "Ovoo", sacrificing the ancient skis for saving their lives.

Legend of "Sacrificing and Praying"

While many old people talking about ancient skiing balled, they are very sacred, dignified, regarding it as a holy thing. Because ancient skiing balled embodied ancestors' experience and lessons of overcoming hardships such as avalanche, attacking of beasts, "savage" attack, heavy snow, hunger and so on. Ancient skiing balled is a prelude to pray. The people of the village get together around the "Ovoo", singing around ancient Ski Ballad, sprinkled with white milk, and bowed to pray that their relatives in the mountain could hunt more and go home peacefully. When the relatives triumphantly return, they would crowd to "Ovoo" edge, doing ritual blessing ceremony, puting the pries on the altar to thank the God for having mercy, and hope to be more fertile in the coming year.

Legend of "Hero Elegy"

Old people often talk about the old times of war in Junggar, Uryankhai often fight against Junggar. In winter, Uryankhai always win because they are good at hunting and stepping on the ancient skis to fight against Junggar. They catch the Junggar who were caught deeply in snow and could not move anymore easily. In summer and autumn, Uryankhai people are always defeated, because skilled people at this time are the Junggar soldiers who have strong horse, and are they are good at fighting on horsebacks. Therefore, whenever Uryankhai people sing ancient Ski Ballad, they always sing about the image of hunting of the people who are died heroically during the tribel war to placing the feelings of grief for those heroes.

Legend of "Gifted by Gods"

The materials of the ancient skis are red pine, white pine, deerskin, wild boar skin, horse skin, and so on in the Altai Mountains. Hunting rods (single-pole ski pole) generally made by red pine, white pine and willow; ancient bows are also made by the materials above. Uryankhai are called "people in forest" or "hunting people" in ancient books. Uryankhai is also an ancient nationality in the history with the title of "blacksmith" for they are famous of good at using iron to build cold weapons. In the war of Genghis Khan first west conquest, they are highly reusable for creating a lot of weapons. Uryankhai have old skis as a kind of hunting and transport instrument, and in ancient times they took it as a gift of the gods. And it is said that the ancient Ski Ballad are dedicated to the worship of those Ancient skis at the "Ovoo" worship.

Legend of "Numen"

Old native hunters in Altai Mountain always tell a legend about a "Copper Claw Girl". "Copper Claw Girl" was a She-Devil that hurt hunters especially. During the day she would change into a beautiful girl and sneak into hunters' hunting temporary residence. Hunters would have long skewers or sharp knifes and the meat plugged into her hands, at that time, the copper claws she hid in the long sleeves would collide with knife and cause clear sound. Thus, hunters would know she is the "Copper Claw Girl". In the midnight, "Copper Claw Girl" would come to hunters' residence again and get into from the door drill. The hunters were all hiding in snowbanks, taking a close spy on the copper claw she-devil. The "Copper Claw Girl" plunged her copper claws into the hunter's sheepskin quilt suddenly with a terrible voice, but the ancient skis hidden in the quilt griped the copper claws tightly, thus the She-Devil could not escape anymore. "Copper Claw Girl" was killed by hunters, and her claws left only. Ancient skis is the patron saint of hunters, but only those skis with the blood of animal and their fur could protect hunters from all the terrible things. In ancient skiing balled hunters also joined the ancient "Khoomei" pronunciation to imitate the sound that skis rubbed with snow, rocks and woods. Folk artists will tell the story first with singing ballads, and then use the long-song to praise the scen of clever hunters who overcome all kinds of difficulties.

Legend of "A Deer of Nine Colors"

Since ancient ancestors were hunting over in the Altai Mountains, which made the god of mountains was so angry that he turned himself into a "Deer of Nine Colors" and came into the mountains. He let those hunters who were greedy see him deliberately. Those greedy hunters were attracted by his deer horns which had the light of nine colors. They got together to catch the nine-color deer, and cut the deer horn which had nine colors. There was an old hunter who was told to leave with his clansmen in the night by the god of mountains, then he told his clansmen and left mountains together. But there are a few hunters were deluded, and they were reluctant to leave. They secretly left the clansmen in the night, returned to the mountains and rounded the "Deer of Nine Colors" up. Seriously wounded in dying, the deer placed the nine-color deer horns gently between the tree branches. The greedy hunters cut them and went to thegrasslands to sell, living up freely and easily. However, few years later, they were rounded up by animals and died without a burial place. They saw the "Deer of Nine Colors" wore nine-color horn leaping in the forest when they are dying. They found they were cursed and felt very remorseful. They begged to the god of mountains to forgive their clansmen, and they were willing to be animals which hunted by hunters, till the curse was removed. The god of mountains granted their dying request, and turned them into delicious prey which hunted by hunters and animals. Their fur was buried into mountains forever. The hunters' clansmen returned to mountains, using animal fur gifted by gods to make skis, jumping through the forests like the nine-color deer and antelopes. They also got the blessings from the god of mountains and rewarded a lot after their hunting. In the forest, all the rocks, the trees would give way to them and protect hunters from hunt by demons. Hunters also sang *the Skier and Hunters' Ditty* to express their appreciation to the god of mountains and they wanted to exhort their future generations to follow the laws of nature, and did not over-hunting in the mountains for the fear of hurting the gods in the mountains.

The Ancient Ski Ballad, as the name suggests, is not only folk songs, but also blended into folklores, primitive religions, historical legends and so on. In the meantime, its stories are inseparable with the Altai Mountains, fitting with the local customs and habits. Most importantly, it is a kind of cultural relic that inextricably tied with the local people's living and production for thousands of years.

4.13 以申办冬奥会为契机，推动我国冰雪运动的发展 Taking the bidding for the Winter Olympic Games as an opportunity to promote the development of ice and snow sports

吕韶钧 LV Shaojun（CHN）

个人简介 Brief Introduction

吕韶钧，男，1963年11月生，博士，教授，博士生导师。现任职于北京体育大学民族民间体育教研室主任，北京市非物质文化遗产保护专家委员会委员。主要从事中国民族传统体育的教学、训练和科研工作。曾担任菲律宾、新加坡、巴西等国家武术队主教练工作。

Shaojun Lv, male, Chinese, was born on November 1963. He is a doctor, professor and doctoral tutor. At present, he is the director of folk sports teaching and research section in Beijing Sport University and a member of the intangible cultural heritage protection expert committee of Beijing. He mainly engages in the teaching, training and scientific research of Chinese traditional sports. He is a former chief coach in national Wushu team in Philippine, Singapore and Brazil etc.

论文 Paper:

以申办冬奥会为契机，推动我国冰雪运动的发展

摘要：在当前我国积极申办冬奥会之际，一方面应该积极做好对我国固有冰雪项目的挖掘整理和推广普及工作，让世界人民进一步了解我国古老的冰雪运动；另一方面也应该整合我们现有的冰雪资源，并进行合理地配置，使我国具有鲜明地域特色的冰雪资源能够有效地被利用与开发，从而全面促进我国冰雪事业和冰雪产业的协调发展。

关键词：冬奥会；冰雪事业；冰雪产业

Abstract: While our country is actively bidding for the Winter Olympics, it should, on one hand, positively discover and promote our country's inherent winter sports event to give the world a better understanding of our ancient winter sports; on the other hand, it should integrate the existing ice and snow resource and make a reasonable disposition to make sure the ice and snow resource which has distinct characteristics can be explored and utilized. Thus, it can promote the coordinated development of our country's winter sports cause and industry.

Key words: Winter Olympics, winter sports cause, winter sports industry

2013 年 11 月 3 日，中国奥委会已于当日正式致函国际奥委会，提出以北京市名义申办 2022 年冬奥会。此刻开始，北京冬奥会申办之路正式启程。纵观奥运会承办历史，还从未有 1 个城市曾先后举办过夏奥会和冬奥会。如果 2022 年冬奥会能够落户北京，那么，中国北京将成为首座同时举办过“冬夏”两季奥运会的城市，此举将永载奥运辉煌史册。但是，我们也应该看到，冰雪运动在我国仍然是处于起步阶段，许多工作需要我们去认真思考和踏实努力。那么，如何在申办冬奥会期间，更好地突出我国冰雪运动的民族特色，推动我国冰雪运动的发展呢？我认为可以从两方面来考虑，一方面是我国固有的冰雪项目的挖掘整理和推广普及，让世界人民了解我国古老的冰雪运动；另一方面是对我国古老的地域性冰雪资源的合理开发与利用，使我国的冰雪事业和冰雪产业能够协调发展。因此，本文将围绕我国冰雪运动的普及与提高，以及资源开发与利用两个部分展开分析，以期借北京申办冬奥会之际，为我国冰雪运动的整体发展提出必要的思考。

一、处理好冰雪运动普及与提高的关系

冰雪运动在我国的体育版图中并不占有十分明显的优势，普及度不高。这一方面是由于受到我国地域和气候季节的限制所致，另一方面，也与我国对冰雪运动的挖掘提升，以及宣传推广不足有着直接关系。但是随着我国经济实力的不断增强，人们生活水平的不断提高，冰雪运动也成为了现代人们追崇的时尚运动了，越来越多的人开始走进冰雪场亲身体会冰雪运动的乐趣。据了解，目前在北京、上海、广州等地都兴建了不少大型室内滑冰场，但中小城市室内冰场仍然缺乏，这在一定程度上也制约了冰上运动的进一步普及。冰雪上运动是冬奥会上的主要项目，普及冰雪运动有利于为冬奥会储备大量的人才。

任何体育项目的发展都必须要经历过普及的阶段，才有可能得到长足的发展。可以说新中国成立后直到 1952 年赫尔辛基第 15 届奥运会之前，努力推进群众体育的普及和经常化，增强人民群众的休质健康实际上是当时中国体育唯一的任务。因此，毛泽东主席在 1952 年 6 月 20 日为中华全国体总成立题写了“发展体育运动，增强人民体质”的题词，其言简义赅地指出了新中国体育事业的性质与发展方向，于是一个群众性的体育普及运动在 960 万平方公里的神州大地兴起。而现如今面临冬奥会的申办，中国冰雪运动的发展面临着前所未有的机遇，也给中国冰雪运动的普及带来了千载难逢的机会。

我国地域辽阔，南北气候的差异性很大。冰雪运动受地域影响很大，在北方

相对普及程度较高。冬季运动管理中心主任赵英刚在接受记者采访时说，“不同项目在不同地区受欢迎的程度不同，目前花样滑冰和速度滑冰已经被更多的观众所接受，一些爱好者学会了如何欣赏和体验这些极具魅力的运动。但目前制约我国冰雪运动发展的主要原因是室内冰场过少。”据了解2005年以前，全国只有25个室内冰场，我国所拥有的室内滑冰馆不如欧美一个大城市所拥有的多，像加拿大的温哥华就有20几个场馆，而瑞典人口700万，就有室内滑冰馆40多个。“现在我国的冰场有所增加，同时也修建了一批高标准场馆，但这些场馆仍集中在北方地区，就现状而言，南方地区场馆的缺乏阻碍了我国群众冰雪运动的进一步普及。”赵英刚表示，只有运动项目走向大众，那么这项运动最大的优势才能发挥出来。一些项目的普及与我国运动员在国际赛事上取得的成绩不无关系，运动员带动了人们参与冰雪运动的兴趣。

然而，对于中国冰雪运动而言，更为重要的是普及提高绝不仅仅只是把国外成熟的冰雪项目采取“拿来主义”的办法，在我国普及推广。而更为重要的是如何把我国固有的，有着较好普及度的冰雪运动通过规范、整理奉献给世界，这应该是我们需要认真思考的一个具有战略意义的问题。从我国冰雪运动的开展而言，冰上项目的开展要好于雪上项目的开展，而在冬奥会上，雪上项目相对较为丰富，这样就形成了我国冰雪项目与冬奥会项目配置上的反差，这也对我们开展雪上项目提出了新的挑战。我们认为，在我国冰雪运动项目中，既要保持冰上项目的发展优势，也必须积极地开展雪上项目的提高。同时也应该积极地挖掘我们自身传统的冰上项目，加以规范化、标准化，为冬奥会提供具有东方魅力的冰上项目，以弥补冬奥会冰上项目的匮乏。应该说申办冬奥会这千载难逢的机会，也是我国冰雪运动全面发展的绝佳机遇。我们应全面思考，宏观谋划，把我国冰雪运动的普及与提高工作做好。

二、处理好冰雪运动资源与旅游开发的关系

冰雪是一种独特的自然资源，独特的地理环境，寒冷的气候，为北方地区提供了丰富的冰雪资源，因此冰雪资源也就成为北方地区一项重要的优势资源。而冰雪文化作为一种区域性文化，它是以自然资源冰雪为载体，具有独特的文化属性。

冰雪文化也是一种生态文化，是和冰雪自然和谐的区域文化中的特色文化。冰雪旅游是一种依托冰雪资源，集参与性、趣味性、刺激性于一体的旅游产品。在我国，冰雪旅游业发展比较晚，起步于上个世纪90年代，主要集中在黑龙江和吉林两省，之后在北京、河北、内蒙、新疆等地也逐渐发展起来。随着我国经济的不断发展，人们的生活方式发生着巨大的改变，我国旅游业也取得了长足的发展，旅游者正在从单一的观光型旅游向度假及各种专项旅游如体育旅游转化。

冰雪旅游作为一项新兴的度假旅游品，开始受到人们越来越多的关注，并日益突现出在中国旅游市场上的重要性。冰雪运动有着极强的休闲娱乐功能，它的内容和形式多种多样，但身体活动则是最主要的手段和方式，对于不同年龄者的身体健康都有积极的促进作用。

从健康城市的角度看，健康是社会进步和经济发展的强大资源，也是社会与经济发展、物质与精神丰富的重要体现。1977 年 5 月，第 30 届世界卫生大会提出了各国政府和 WHO 在未来数十年中的主要社会目标，即"人人健康"（health for all，HFA）。1979 年 11 月，联合国大会又通过了"关于健康是社会发展的一个组成部分的决议"。尽管健康城市一开始是由 WHO 倡导提出来的，但是在当今世界，其内涵和意义已经远远超出了卫生的范畴。可以说健康社会与健康人群、健康环境共同构成了健康城市的三大核心内容，而冰雪运动恰恰具有这样一些功能。我们认为，开展一些冰雪休闲娱乐的体育活动有助于调节人的身心健康，它不仅具有调节人体紧张情绪的作用，而且还可以改善生理和心理状态，有助于恢复体力和精力，是人们生活的重要内容。同时冰雪休闲娱乐体育活动还有助于促进人际交往，冰雪休闲体育不仅是休闲娱乐、健身的载体，也是消除孤独寂寞、拓展交际、增进情感交流及交友的润滑剂。人们通过冰雪休闲体育运动可以结识许多不同身份、年龄、性别的人，丰富精神生活和增进相互间的感情交流。因此，它将在构建和谐社会中发挥出积极的作用。

从一个城市的文化建设来看，城市的文化个性也是一个城市的文化资源。冰雪项目就具有突出的文化个性，它带向鲜明的地域特征，也是一个城市重要的文化名片。如阿勒泰是世界公认的"人类滑雪发源地"之一，新疆的丝绸之路，历史文化悠久，少数民族风情浓郁，有着中西方文化交融的重要特征。因此，如何充分挖掘这一地域自身的冰雪运动资源，打造城市冰雪运动的文化品牌，提升自身冰雪运动的文化影响力和文化竞争力，也是城市文化建设的重要战略举措。如：打造具有新疆阿勒泰特色的世界级冰雪节；举办国际冰雪运动的品牌赛事等等。总之，"城市的发展也需要创造核心竞争力，核心竞争力既需要依赖于城市核心资源系统的开发与创造。更需要全新意义上的城市经济与文化要素的创新，特别是更具有特殊性和实用价值的文化要素的创新。"如此说来，要打造一个城市的文化品牌，重要的是要依赖城市的文化资源。

三、结束语

我国申办冬奥会对于中国的冰雪事业发展也提出了新的要求，这不仅强调要通过冰雪事业来带动我国经济的飞速发展，而且也更加重视以此来促进国民体质的增强。冰雪事业的发展，关系到国民的身心健康，关系到我国精神文明建设。我们认为，在当前我国积极申办冬奥会之际，我们一方面应该积极做好对我国固有冰雪项目的挖掘整理和推广普及工作，让世界人民进一步了解我国古老的冰雪运动；另一方面也应该整合我们现有的冰雪资源，并进行合理地配置，使我国具有鲜明地域特色的冰雪资源能够有效地被利用与开发，从而全面促进我国冰雪事业和冰雪产业的协调发展。当然，不可否认现阶段我国的冰雪运动仍存在着许多问题，如经费严重不足，冰雪运动的“自给”能力还十分有限等等，因此就更应该加强自身的“造血”功能，早日实现“以体养体”。总之，冰雪运动作为体育的重要组成部分，在市场经济条件下必然走产业化发展道路，实现冰雪运动资源的合理配置，从而促进冰雪运动的繁荣发展。

4.14 哈尔滨体育学院滑雪学科的建设 Establishment ofSki Subject in Harbin Institute of Physical Education

朱志强　王东海　Zhu Zhiqiang &Wang Donghai (CHN)

个人简介　Brief Introduction

朱志强教授，男，1960年12月生人。哈尔滨体育学院院长，教育学博士，荣获多次嘉奖，身兼多职。从事冬季运动教学、科研、训练工作30余年，在冬季运动、体育社会学方面取得了丰富的学术研究和工作成果。

Professor Zhu Zhiqiang, born in December 1960. He is the Director of Harbin Institute of Physical Education. He is also Doctor of Education, and has won the award for many times, wearing many different hats. Working for winter sports teaching, scientific research and training more than 30 years. He has achieved rich academic research and fruitful research in in the winter sports, sports sociology.

个人简介　Brief Introduction

王东海，男，1963年10月生人。哈尔滨体育学院黑龙江省滑雪学校校长，副研究员。

Wang Donghai, born in October 1963. The President of Ski School of Harbin Institute of Physical Education, associate professor.

中文论文：

哈尔滨体育学院滑雪学科的建设

各位专家、各位同仁：

大家好！

首先感谢单兆鉴先生的热情相邀，单先生对中国滑雪运动发展投入的巨大精力与突出贡献学界有目共睹，作为同行，我十分敬佩。今天，作为一名高校工作者，我结合自身工作实践，介绍一下哈尔滨体育学院滑雪特色学科建设的情况，跟大家共同探讨高等教育如何助推中国滑雪事业发展。

哈尔滨体育学院是我国唯一一所以冰雪项目为特色的体育院校，多年来学校学科建设始终围绕冰雪特色进行。滑雪学科的建设始于 1989 年学校在全国率先开设滑雪课程，1999 年学校进一步在帽儿山第二教学区投建滑雪场，加大了对滑雪学科投建的力度。经过二十五年的发展建设，滑雪学科已成为特色鲜明、优势突出的品牌学科，主要从以下几方面加以介绍：

一、滑雪人才培养方面

首先，学校建立了以滑雪项目为重点的教学、训练体系，开创了冬夏结合，雪、陆一体化的教学与训练模式，为国家培养了众多竞技滑雪人才，现任国家单板滑雪运动队主教练是我校教师，国家单板滑雪运动队主力队员 70%以上来自我校；包括张义威、刘佳宇等冠军选手。

其次，学校成立了冬季奥林匹克学院，专门培养冰雪项目的管理人才及各类技术人才。我国参加世界大学生冬季运动会的代表团队伍，大都是由我校师生组成，目前国内从事冬季项目发展的管理人员大部分出自我校。

再次，在后备人才培养方面，哈尔滨体育学院是我国滑雪后备人才主要的培养基地，下辖的黑龙江省滑雪学校是我国第一所专门培养滑雪人才的学校。

此外，我校目前已形成冰雪项目“硕士—博士—博士后”一体化人才培养体系，拥有全国唯一的冰雪项目博士导师及唯一的冰雪项目博士后工作站，实现了国内冰雪项目最高研究层次人才的培养。

二、科研助推滑雪运动发展方面

学校从自然科学和社会科学两个领域推进滑雪运动研究。首先，利用实验室的设备和师资优势连续多年承担奥运攻关课题，为国家队备战温哥华及索契冬奥会提供科技支撑。2009 年，学校承担的科技部科技支撑计划项目《冬奥会项目陆地与冰（雪）上训练科学衔接及有效性的研究与应用》直接针对我国冬奥会重点项目关键技术的突破进行研究，成果已应用于 2014 年索契冬奥会。

其次，在社会科学研究领域，学校一直围绕着“滑雪运动的历史与当代”进行研究。先后出版了《中国冬季运动史》、《冬季奥林匹克运动》等专著。并围绕着滑雪旅游、滑雪产业等热点问题进行了大量的研究与实践，完成了国家科技部软件科学项目《建设冰雪体育产业强国的发展战略研究》等重大课题。

三、“产、学、研”一体化的特色办学

学校的帽儿山滑雪场是2009年世界大冬会雪上项目主赛区。在日常教学工作之余，一直为国家滑雪队训练提供场地、技术服务；并承担各类滑雪培训、赛事活动。同时，雪场已开放运营十多年，为推动滑雪旅游产业，促进地方经济社会发展做出贡献。2013年，哈尔滨体育学院正式被批准设立冰雪项目博士后科研工作站。经过多年的办学实践，哈尔滨体育学院滑雪学科已成为集教学、训练、竞赛、科研、产业与社会服务五位一体的特色鲜明的学科平台。

此外，哈尔滨体育学院已正式被黑龙江省学位委员会确立为冰雪研究生创新培养示范基地，我校研究生的实习实践将直接与地方旅游名牌企业“冰雪大世界”合作，实现了人才培养与市场需求的紧密挂钩，凸显了产学研一体化的办学效果。

四、打造国内滑雪运动研究权威平台

近五年来，哈尔滨体育学院滑雪学科建设屡有突破。学院的高山滑雪教学团队被教育部评为国家级优秀教学团队，以研究滑雪产业和雪上项目竞训为核心的两个团队获批为黑龙江省领军人才梯队；成果《我国冬季奥林匹克特色专业研究生课程体系建设研究》获国家级教学成果二等奖。此外，学校建有国内唯一一座冰雪运动文史馆，收录了解放后我国冰雪运动发展的相关实物、照片和文献资料，为冰雪运动历史的传承及冰雪文化的发展搭建了研究咨询平台。经过多年办学实践的积累，哈尔滨体育学院滑雪特色学科已成为供政府、企业决策咨询的权威人才机构与服务平台，在冬季运动发展领域占有不可替代的地位。

伴随着我国申办2022年冬奥会战略的实施，习近平总书记发出了“冰雪运动在中国还不普及，不出山海关”的感慨，提出“先在关内推广，带动两三亿人，通过奥运会点燃冰雪运动火炬的作用”。这一战略的提出，预示着未来我国滑雪运动的发展将迎来新的机遇与挑战。一方面，2022年冬奥会是我国发展冬季项目，解决“冬夏失衡、冰强雪弱”问题的大好时机，滑雪项目有望在冬奥会上实现成绩的飞跃。另一方面，冬奥会的申办必将掀起中国大众对滑雪运动的热情及滑雪旅游市场的投资热潮，但同时国际资本的关注和流入也将对国内市场产生巨大的冲击。这是中国滑雪旅游市场与国际接轨的必经阶段，必须经受国际标准的检验。由此，可以断言，未来中国滑雪旅游产业格局将面临重构。作为国内冰雪运动权威学科，哈尔滨体育学院将立足时代前沿，不断提升办学实力、深化“产、学、研”一体化道路，充分发挥智库作用，为推动我国滑雪运动大发展献计献策。

我的发言就到这里，谢谢大家 。

English paper:

Establishment ofSki Subject in Harbin Institute of Physical Education

Dear Experts and Colleagues,

Greetings!

First of all, I would like to extend my thanks to the warm invitation from Mr. Shan Zhaojian. The huge efforts and outstanding contributions from Mr. Shan to the development of skiing in China are obvious to all, and I admire him very much as a peer. Today, I will introduce the construction of the featured subject of skiing at Harbin Institute of Physical Education in combination with my own practices in work as a university staff, and will discuss how to accelerate the development of skiing in China together with you.

Harbin Institute of Physical Education is the only physical education institute in China with ice and snow sports as features, and the subject construction is always centering with the ice and snow features over many years. The construction of skiing subject is started since the institute taking the lead in offering the course of skiing in China in 1989, the skiing ground is further established in No. 2 Teaching Area at Maoer Mt. by the institute in 1999, and more efforts are made toward the skiing subject construction. The skiing subject has become a brand subject with distinct features and prominent advantages after development and construction over twenty-five years, and the introduction is mainly undertaken from the following several aspects.

I. Cultivation of Skiing Talents

First of all, the institute has established teaching and training system focusing on skiing events, has initiated the teaching and training pattern combining with winter and summer and integrating with snow and land, has cultivated many skiing athletic talents for the country. The current head coach of national snowboarding sport team is a teacher of our institute, above 70% leading players of the national snowboarding sport team come from our institute; including the champion players like Zhang Yiwei, and Liu Jiayu, et al.

Secondly, the institute has established the Winter Olympics College specialized in training ice and snow event management talents and all kinds of technical personnel. Most of the delegation of China attending the World University Winter Games consists of teachers and students from our institute, and currently most management personnel in China undertaking winter events development come out of our institute.

Thirdly, as for cultivation of back-up talents, Harbin Institute of Physical Education is a primary base of China for training of back-up skiing talents, and the Heilongjiang Province Skiing School affiliated to the institute is the first school specialized in training skiing talents in China.

In addition, currently, the integrated talent cultivation system of "master-doctor-postdoctor" has been established by our institute for ice and snow events, with the only doctoral supervisor of ice and snow event and the only ice and snow event postdoctoral workstation in China, and the institute has realized the cultivation of highest level research level talents for ice and snow events in China.

II. Acceleration of Skiing Sports Development by Scientific Research

The institute is accelerating the skiing sport research from two fields, natural science and social science. First of all, we have assumed the key problem tackling tasks by employing the laboratory equipment and advantage in teachers continuously for many years, and have provided a scientific support to the national team to prepare for the Olympic Winter Games in Vancouver and Sochi. The project of "Research and Application on Scientific Connection between Land Training and Ice (Snow) Training and Its Effectiveness" assumed by the institute in 2009 within the scientific support program from Ministry of Science and Technology is directly targeting at breakthrough research toward the critical technologies to key events on Olympic Winter Games, and its achievements have been applied on the Olympic Winter Games of 2014 in Sochi.

Secondly, as for the social science research field, the institute is always performing research by centering with "The History and Contemporary of Skiing Sports". The monographs successively published by the institute including "The History of Winter Sports in China" and "The Olympic Winter Sports", etc. A lots of researches and practices are conducted by centering with the hot issues as skiing tour, and skiing industry, etc, and the important tasks are accomplished like the project of "Research on Development Strategy to Construction of A Country Powerful in Ice and Snow Physical Education Industry" under software science subsidy from the Ministry of Science and Technology of the People's Republic of China, and so on.

III. Featured School Running of "Production, Learning and Research" Integration

The Maoer Mt. Skiing Ground of the Institute is a main competition area for snow events on World Winter Universiade in 2009. This ground is always offering ground and technical services to the training from the national skiing team besides the routine teaching tasks; is assuming various skiing training and events. Meanwhile, the skiing ground has been operated for more than ten years, and it has made outstandingcontributions to accelerate the skiing tourism industry and to promote the local economic and social development. Harbin Institute of Physical Education is formally approved for establishment of ice and snow events postdoctoral scientific research workstation in 2013. The skiing subject of Harbin Institute of Physical Education has become a subject platform of five-in-one distinct features integrated with teaching, training, competition, scientific research, industry and social services after school running practices for many years.

In addition, Harbin Institute of Physical Education has been formally designated to be the innovative cultivation pilot base for ice and snow event postgraduates by Heilongjiang Province Academic Degree Committee, the practices of postgraduates at our institute will directly cooperate with the local famous tourist enterprise "Ice and Snow World", has realized the close linkage between talent cultivation and market demands, and has highlighted the school running effect of production, learning and research integration.

IV. Shaping A Domestic Authoritative Platform for Skiing Sports Research

Frequent breakthroughs have been achieved in the skiing subject construction of Harbin Institute of Physical Education over the recent five years. The alpine skiing teaching team of the institute is appraised by the Ministry of Education to be a national-level outstanding teaching team, and two teams focusing on the research of skiing industry and snow events competition and training are approved to be the leading talent echelons of Heilongjiang Province; the achievement "Research on Construction of Professional Postgraduate Course System with Olympic Winter Features in China" is awarded with national-level second class prize for teaching achievements. In addition, the only Research Institute for Ice and Snow Sports Culture and History in China is established at the institute, it collects the relevant physical objects, photos and documentations to ice and snow sports development in China after liberation, and it has put up a research and consulting platform for the inheritance of ice and snow sports history and the development of ice and snow culture. After accumulations of school running practices over many years, the featured skiing subject of Harbin Institute of Physical Education has become an authoritative talent organization and service platform to decision-making and consulting from the government and enterprises, and it occupies an irreplaceable position in the field of winter sports development.

With the implementation of China's strategy in bidding the Olympic Winter Games in 2022, General Secretary Xi Jinping signs with the emotion "ice and snow sports are not popularized in China yet, it still stays outside Shanhaiguan Pass", and puts forward to "first to popularize inside Shanhaiguan Pass, to mobilize two hundred million to three hundred million people, and to ignite the torch function of ice and snow sports by means of the Olympic Games". The putting-forward of this strategy predicts the development of skiing sports in China will usher in the new opportunities and challenges. On one hand, the Olympic Winter Games in 2022 is a great opportunity for China to develop winter events and to solve the problem of "unbalance between winter events and summer events and strong in ice events but weak in snow events", and it's expected to realize a leap of scores by skiing events on the Olympic Winter Games. On the other hand, the bidding of Olympic Winter Games must raise the passions from the public in China toward skiing sports and pose an investment upsurge on the skiing tourist market, however, the attention and inflow from the international capital will also pose a huge impact to the domestic market. This is a necessary stage for the skiing tourist market in China to connect with theinternational market, and it must be tested by the international standards. Therefore, it can be asserted that the pattern of future skiing tourism in China will face the reconstruction. As an authoritative subject of ice and snow sports in China, Harbin Institute of Physical Education will keep a foothold before the times, will continuously improve the school running strength and deepen the road of "production, learning and research" integration, will fully exert the role of think tank, and will contribute ideas and exert efforts for accelerating the sound development of skiing sports in China.

That's the end of my speech, and thanks for your cooperation!

4.15 中国冬季奥林匹克运动发展分析 Analysis of the Development of Winter Olympic Games of China

李欲刚 Li Yugang (CHN)

个人简介 Brief Introduction

李欲刚，1974 年出生，硕士，讲师。现任吉林体育学院校办公室主任。参编教材 2 部，发表论文 10 篇。

Li Yugang (lecturer, master) is Office Director of JiLin Institute of Physical. He has published two books and ten papers.

摘要：从1980年至2014年，中国冬季奥林匹克运动项目发展经历十届冬奥会，不管是群众冰雪运动还是竞技水平都有很大提高。本文通过文献资料法、数理统计法、对比分析法研究中国冬季奥林匹克运动的发展情况，包括中国参加冬奥会发展历程、中国冰雪运动发展形成的冰强雪弱、北强南弱、女强男弱的特点，同时发现仍然存在的一些问题，以期为中国冰雪运动更加协调持续发展提供理论参考。

关键词：中国；冬季奥林匹克；发展；分析

中文论文：

中国冬季奥林匹克运动发展分析

中国的冰雪项目起步晚、基础差、底子薄，但是进步很大，不管是群众冰雪运动还是竞技水平都有很大提高，这与冬奥会的发展是密不可分的。然而与夏季奥运会成绩相比，中国运动员在冬季奥运会取得的战绩相对“薄弱”，与美国、加拿大、欧洲等体育强国存在着明显差距，中国欲跻身世界体育强国之林，在冰雪运动范畴内，还需要更大的提高。

一、中国参加冬奥会历程概况

截至2014年，中国共参加冬季奥林匹克运动会10届，由表1中国参加历届冬奥会的情况，可以看出中国冰雪项目发展历程和取得的成绩。

表1　中国参加历届冬奥会情况一览表

时间	届次	运动员人数	金牌数	银牌数	铜牌数
1980	13	28	0	0	0
1984	14	37	0	0	0
1988	15	15	0	0	0
1992	16	34	0	3	0
1994	17	27	0	1	2
1998	18	60	0	6	2
2002	19	72	2	2	4
2006	20	78	2	4	5
2010	21	91	5	2	4
2014	22	66	3	4	2

1980 年 2 月 13 日至 24 日，第十三届冬季奥林匹克运动会在美国的普莱西德湖举行，中国派出体育代表团参加。这也是中国自从恢复国际奥委会合法权利和地位之后首次参加奥运会。在这次冬季奥运会中，中国共有 28 名运动员参加了滑冰、滑雪、现代冬季两项等 18 个单项的比赛，与世界先进水平有较大的差距，无一人进入前 10 名。

1984 年萨拉热窝第 14 届冬奥会 中国运动员第二次参加冬奥会，37 名选手参加了速度滑冰、花样滑冰、越野滑雪、高山滑雪、冬季两项等五个大项的比赛，中国队仅仅获得了团体总分五分，在 49 个参赛代表团中排第 23 位。

1988 年卡尔加里第 15 届冬奥会，中国队派出了 15 名运动员，参加了速度滑冰、花样滑冰和越野滑雪 3 大项 18 个小项的比赛，但是运动员成绩与世界一流的成绩相差较大，中国运动员的最好名次为 14 名。

1992 年阿尔贝维尔第 16 届冬奥会，中国终于在本届实现了奖牌“零的突破”，参加比赛的 34 名运动员，一共获得了 3 枚银牌 2 个第四名。

1994 年利勒哈默尔第 17 届冬奥会，中国派出了 27 名运动员，参加了速度滑冰、短道速滑、花样滑冰、冬季两项和自由滑雪等大项的比赛，获得一枚宝贵的银牌，两枚铜牌。

1998 年长野第 18 届冬奥会，中国代表团参加了滑冰、冰球、越野滑雪、冬季两项四大项 40 个小项的比赛。中国选手在本届冬奥会上一共获得了 6 枚银牌和 2 枚铜牌，遗憾的是，没有能够实现金牌“零的突破”。

2002 年盐湖城第 19 届冬奥会，中国代表团实现了中国参加冬奥会以来零的突破，杨扬一人独得女子 500 米短道速滑和 1000 米短道速滑 2 枚金牌，此外，中国代表团还获得了 2 枚银牌和 4 枚铜牌。

2006 年意大利都灵冬奥会，中国派出 153 人组成的代表团，78 名运动员参加了 3 大类、9 个分项、47 个小项的比赛，雪上项目参赛人数首次超过冰上项目。获得 2 金 4 银 5 铜，奖牌榜名列第 14 位，奖牌总数超过历届。韩晓鹏则打破了欧美人的垄断，获得男子自由式滑雪空中技巧金牌，实现了中国雪上项目以及男子项目在冬奥会上金牌“零的突破”。

2010 年加拿大温哥华冬季奥运会，中国代表团在本届冬奥会上获得 5 枚金牌、4 枚银牌和 2 枚铜牌，11 枚奖牌的成绩平了 2006 年都灵冬奥会时的最高纪录，而金牌数则创造了历史最高。中国所获得的 5 枚金牌都来自冰上项目，并都有女选手的功劳，5 枚金牌来自花样滑冰和短道速滑两个大项。

2014 年俄罗斯索契冬奥会，是中国第十次参加冬奥会。共有 66 名运动员参加了 4 个大项、49 个小项的比赛，共获得 3 枚金牌、4 枚银牌和 2 枚铜牌，在奖牌榜上列第 11 位。

二、中国冬奥会项目发展特点

从表1可以看出中国冬季奥林匹克项目在2002年后有了快速的提高，在不断的发展过程中也形成了中国冰雪运动项目“冰强雪弱”、“北强南弱”、“女强男弱”的特点。

1. 中国冰雪项目“冰强雪弱”的特点

中国选手迄今夺得的12枚冬奥会金牌，仅1枚来自于雪上项目，其他来自冰上项目短道速滑、速度滑冰和花样滑冰。近30年，中国军团在冬奥会夺牌面不断扩大，但绝大多数雪上项目一直未有明显改观，而且中国军团有较强竞争力的雪上项目——自由式滑雪空中技巧、单板滑雪U型槽均非主流项目。相反，像高山滑雪、跳台滑雪、越野滑雪、北欧两项这类传统项目，成绩并不理想，而三个雪橇项目国内至今仍未开展。

根据金牌榜位置，中国可以称得上冰雪运动二流国家。事实上，中国还配不上这个头衔，因为中国冰雪军团存在着明显的冰强雪弱现象。冬奥会15大项目中滑冰项目仅有5项，其他10项均是雪上项目，不少雪上项目是冬奥会的主流项目，但中国在一些传统项目上还很弱势，如果想在冬奥会上有更好的成绩，必须大力发展好雪上项目。

2. 中国冰雪项目“女强男弱”的特点

从中国冬季奥运会奖牌榜成绩可以看出，中国冰雪运动成绩主要来自女运动员，呈现“女强男弱”的特点。例如1994年冬奥会，中国派出了27名运动员参加，其中女选手就19名，3枚奖牌均有女运动员获得，张艳梅获得500米短道速滑银牌、叶乔波获得1000米速滑铜牌、陈露获得花样滑冰女子单人滑铜牌。从表2纵观中国冬奥会奖牌榜也可以看出，中国冰雪运动项目在冬奥会上取得的成绩有金牌12枚，几乎全部为女运动员获得，其中男子仅一枚；银牌22枚，男子4枚；银牌19枚，男子6枚。因此中国男子项目距离世界最高水平还需要进一步加强，以争取更广阔的奖牌空间。

表2 中国参加冬奥会奖牌男女分布情况

时间	金牌	银牌	铜牌
1992	0	3（女）	0
1994	0	1（女）	2（女）
1998	0	6（男2女4）	2（女1男1）
2002	2（女）	2（女）	4（女2男1、双人滑）
2006	2（女1男1）	4（女3、双人滑）	5（女3、男1、双人滑、）

时间	金牌	银牌	铜牌
2010	5（女4、双人滑）	2（女1、双人滑）	4（女3、男1）
2014	3（女）	4（2女、2男）	2（男）

3. 中国冰雪项目“北强南弱”的特点

由于气候、地域等条件的影响，中国冬季体育的人才培养目前仍以东北地区为主，主要集中在黑龙江、吉林两省。虽然中国旨在消除地域属性的“北冰南展”计划已持续了30多年，且大大小小的滑雪场已经超过400家，遍布中国28个省市，但拥有冬季项目队伍的南方城市却增长缓慢。虽然目前冰雪运动已经向辽宁、河北、新疆等地快速发展，但就运动成绩而言仍然呈现“北强南弱”的特点。

三、冬季奥林匹克运动会发展状况及趋势

1. 冬奥会参与范围不断增加

当今世界各国，包括第三世界国家，纷纷强化了对竞技体育的管理和支持，各国更加重视奥运成绩和排名。1992年第16届冬奥会以来，参加冬奥会的国家、地区及运动员人数逐届增多，获奖牌的国家也在不断增加，如表3所示，至第22届俄罗斯索契冬奥会参与冬奥会的国家和地区已经有88个，参与运动员也逐年增多。

表3　16-22届冬奥会各届次参赛单位、参赛运动员情况

奥运年	参赛单位数	参赛运动员人数
1992	64	1801
1994	67	1737
1998	72	2176
2002	78	2399
2006	80	2508
2010	82	2629
2014	88	2887

2. 冬奥会项目发展不断增多

由表4可以看出，近20年冬奥会单项总数呈继续增加的趋势，平均每届冬奥会增加5.4个单项。综合各方面因素考虑，同夏季奥运会相比，冬奥会单项发展的空间相对较大。目前，经国际奥委会承认的国际冬季运动组织有7个，他们共管辖25个大项168个小项，其中有15个大项98小项相继被纳入冬奥会，占目前开展的冬季项目的50%。未来冬奥会比赛项目总数还有很大的增加空间，未来冬奥会比赛项目总数的增加也将带来参赛国家、地区及运动员人数增加的可能性。

表4 16-22届冬奥会各届次金牌、奖牌及单项变化

奥运年	金牌总数	奖牌总数	单项总数
1992	57	171	57
1994	61	183	61
1998	69	205	68
2002	80	234	78
2006	84	252	84
2010	86	258	86
2014	99	295	98

同时，由于传统项目如速度滑冰、越野滑雪等发展的空间越来越小，冬奥会未来项目的增设将主要集中于一些新兴的冬季项目。按照项目规划预测，到2024年，冬奥会项目将由现在的98个小项发展到100个小项，新增项目中新兴项目将占80%以上。冬奥会发展的另一个趋势就是项目的增设越发倾向于更具观赏性、刺激性和竞争激烈的比赛项目，以适应冬季运动与现代大众传媒深人结合的需要。例如2002年冬奥会单板滑雪在项目设置中，以更具观赏性和刺激性的平行大回转代替了1998年冬奥会中的大回转。单板滑雪中最近几年才兴起的多人雪道障碍赛则被率先纳入2006年都灵冬奥会比赛。中国冬季运动的优势项目短道速滑、花样滑冰发展的空间基本饱和，那么要想在冬奥会获得好成绩，在项目布局时就要对新兴项目的重视，在一些新兴的项目取得重大的突破。

3. 冬奥会运动成绩中的科技含量将继续加大

现代科学技术的发展大大地促进了体育科技的进步，体育科技的地位和作用日益强化，体育科研系统形成面向社会、面向世界的开放体系，体育科研的多学科综合性趋势不断加强，同时针对优秀运动员的、具有个性化的研究也将不断深入。现代冬奥会在很大程度上是参赛国之间的科技较量，它涉及到生物学、信息科学、材料科学等前沿学科领域内的高新技术成果对冰雪运动的介入和影响。这将不断改变冰雪运动的面貌，促使运动成绩向着更高的层次迈进。特别是高科技手段、科研成果在训练方法、运动器材和运动员康复等方面的积极探索与运用，推动了各个运动项目运动技术的快速改进、提高与发展，使运动成绩不断提高，世界记录不断被刷新。例如，速度滑冰项目在第 18 届冬奥会后，15 项世界记录已被刷新了 12 项，占 80%。自由式滑雪项目的技术动作难度不断提高，原 6. 70 的主流难度指数已基本被淘汰出局。有关冰雪运动科研方面的竞争必将更加激烈，冰雪运动的科学性将更加突出，运动成绩中的科技含量将继续加大。

四、制约中国冬奥会项目发展问题分析

1. 中国冬奥会项目发展水平与夏季奥运发展水平不协调

根据中国冬季冰雪运动发展现状的实际，中国仍属于基础实力薄弱、整体水平不高的冰雪运动弱国与中国夏季奥运会体育大国的地位形成极大反差，反映了中国冬季奥运发展水平与夏季奥运发展水平的不协调。

2. 中国冬奥会竞技成绩与群众冰雪运动基础不协调

中国目前所取得的奥运奖牌多来自短道速滑、花样滑冰和自由式滑雪空中技巧，除速度滑冰从事人群较多外，其他项目在中国的群众基础都很薄弱，自由式项目在中国群众中了解并参与的人为之甚少。夏季乒乓球的竞技成绩与群众基础就基本协调，反映了竞技冰雪运动发展与群众冰雪运动发展的不协调。

3. 中国冬奥会项目发展实际与未来体育强国战略不协调

我国目前冰雪运动的条件虽有改善，但与美国、加拿大和欧洲国家相比，冬季项目无论从场地、群众参与度还是器材设施自主研发来看，都与未来实现体育强国战略目标的要求存在极大的差距，反映了我国竞技冰雪运动水平与体育强国战略目标的不协调。

五、中国未来冰雪运动发展建议

1. 全面快速发展中国全民健身冰雪运动，努力实现其与整个全民健身计划协调发展。

2. 实现中国冬季冰雪运动管理体制和运行机制、运动训练、竞赛、体育产业经营等系统内部的全面、协调和可持续发展。

3. 在举国体质协调下，做好冰雪优势项目的成绩保持，努力计划和开展新增项目，争取更好的竞技成绩。

4. 发展构建良好的国际和国内冰雪运动的人文和生态环境，为中国冬季冰雪运动系统可持续发展打好基础。

5. 申办与筹备奥运会将是启动经济高速发展，促进社会、经济良性运行的有利契机。成功举办冬季奥运会将是中国冬季运动项目发展战略的转折点，必将提升冰雪运动社会化程度，构建冰雪运动发展的新平台。

【参考文献】

[1] 王仁周，朱志强．冬季奥林匹克运动［M］．人民体育出版社．2005

[2] 吴晓华，于立强．从加拿大看中国冬季运动发展［J］．体育文化导刊，2013，（12）38-40

[3] 刘仁辉，李玉新，吴 颖．欧美滑雪文化的流变及对中国滑雪文化传承与传播的启示［J］．沈阳体育学院学报，2014，04，56-62.

[4] 于立强．中国冬季运动项目北冰南移可持续发展战略研究［J］．天津体育学院学报，2004，4（19-22）

[5] 郭亦农．对我国冬季运动项目发展的理性思考［J］．沈阳体育学院学报，2001，2，52-56

[6] 张新华．对我国冰雪运动发展战略存在的问题分析［J］．齐齐哈尔大学学报，2005，11，33-35

[7] 颜彤丹，周宝伦．中国参加冬奥会竞技项目战略分析［J］．哈尔滨体育学院学报，2005，5，39-42

[8] 崔爱博．对我国冬季运动项目发展战略的思考［J］．冰雪运动，2006，10（5），36-40

English paper:

Abstract: From 1980 to 2014, China Winter Olympic sports events have experienced ten sessions of Winter Olympics, whether the masses winter sport or the competitive level has greatly been improved. Through methods of literature data, mathematical statistics and comparative analysis, it studies the development of Chinese Winter Olympic Games, including the development process of China's participation in the Winter Olympics and the features of strong ice sport and weak snow sport, Strong North and Weak South and strong women and weak men formed in the development of China's winter sport, while some problems have also been found, in order to provide the theoretical reference for the more coordinated and sustainable development of Chinese winter sport.

Keywords: China; Winter Olympics; development; analysis

Analysis of the Development of Winter Olympic Games of China

Ⅰ. Introduction

China's winter sport starts late, the infrastructure is poor and the base is weak, but it has made a great progress, whether the mass winter sport or competitive level have been greatly improved, which is inextricably linked with the development of the Winter

Olympics. However, compared with the results of Summer Olympics, the records that Chinese athletes achieved in Winter Olympics is a relatively "weak", with an obvious gap from the United States, Canada, Europe and other sports powers. If China wants to rank among the world sports powers, within winter sports area, it also needs a greater improvement.

Ⅱ. General Historical Situation of China's Participation in the Winter Olympic Games

As of 2014, China totally took part in the 10 sessions of Winter Olympic Games, and condition of China's participation in all previous sessions of Olympic Winter Games is shown in Table 1, we can see the development process and achievements of China's winter sports events.

From February 13th to 24th, 1980, the 13th session of Winter Olympic Games was held in the Lake Placid, United States, and China sent a delegation to participate in the game. This is also the first Olympic Game that China participated in since recovering the legal rights and status of the International Olympic Committee. In this Winter Olympics, totally 28 Chinese athletes participated in skating, skiing, biathlon and other 18individual competitions, due to the large gap from the world's advanced level, no one ranked in the top 10.

In the 14thSarajevo Winter Olympics in 1984, Chinese athletes participated in the Winter Olympics for the second time, and 37 players took part in the speed skating, figure skating, cross-country skiing, alpine skiing, and biathlon, the five major items, but Chinese team only won five scores in total weight of team, ranking No. 23 in the 49 delegations.

In 1988 Calgary 15th Olympic Winter Games, Chinese team sent 15 athletes to participate in the speed skating, figure skating and cross-country skiing, the three major competitions with 18 small items, but athletes' scores were greatly different from the world-class performance, and the best rank of Chinese athletes was 14th. In 1992 Albertville 16thWinter Olympic Games, China finally realized the "Zero Breakthrough" of medals, while 34 athletes won a total of three silver medals and two fourth ranks in the competition.

In 1994 Lille-hammer 17th Olympic Winter Games, China sent 27 athletes to participate in the speed skating, short track speed skating, figure skating, biathlon and freestyle skiing, winning a valuable silver medal and two bronze medals.

In 1998 Nagano 18thOlympic Winter Games, Chinese delegation participated in skating, ice hockey, cross-country skiing, and biathlon race, totally four major items with 40 small items. Chinese athletes in the Games won a total of six silver medals and two bronze medals; unfortunately, it has not been able to achieve the "Zero Breakthrough" of gold medal.

In 2002 Salt Lake City 19th Olympic Winter Games, Chinese delegation realized the "Zero" breakthrough since Chinese delegation has participated in the Winter Olympics, Yang Yang won the gold medals of women 500meters short track speed skating and woman's 1000 meters short track speed skating, in addition, the Chinesedelegation also won two silver medals and four bronze medals.

In 2006 Winter Olympics in Turin, Italy, China sent a delegation consisting of 153 people, while 78 athletes participated in the three categories, nine sub-race and 47 small items, and the number of people who participated in snow projects exceeded the people in ice project for the first time. They won 2 gold medals, 4 silver medals and 5 bronze medals, ranking No. 14 in the medals standing, and the number of medal exceeded over that in the previous sessions. Xiaopeng Han then broke the monopoly of Europeans and Americans and won the gold medal of men freestyle skiing aerials, as well as achieving the "Zero Breakthrough" in Chinese snow items and men events in the Winter Olympic Games.

Table 1 List of China's Participation in All Previous Sessions of Winter Olympic Games

Time	Session	Number of Athletes	Number of Gold Medals	Number of Silver Medals	Number of Bronze Medal
1980	13	28	0	0	0
1984	14	37	0	0	0
1988	15	15	0	0	0
1992	16	34	0	3	0
1994	17	27	0	1	2
1998	18	60	0	6	2
2002	19	72	2	2	4
2006	20	78	2	4	5
2010	21	91	5	2	4
2014	22	66	3	4	2

In 2010 Vancouver Winter Olympics, the Chinese delegation won five gold medals, four silver and two bronze medals at the Games, while the achievement of 11 medals equaled to the record in 2006 Winter Olympics in Turin, and gold medals created a historical number. Five gold medals gained by China all came from ice project with efforts of female athletes, and five gold medals came from the figure skating and short track speed skating, these two major items.

The 2014 So-chi Winter Olympics was the 10th Winter Olympic Game that China participated in. A total of 66 athletes participated in the four major items and 49 small items, winning three gold medals, four silver medals and two bronze medals, ranking NO. 11 in the medal standings.

Ⅲ. Characteristics of China's Winter Olympic Event Development

From Table 1, it can see that China's winter Olympic events have been rapidly improved since 2002, and in the continuing process of development, it also formed the features of Chinese winter sports project about "strong ice and weak snow events", "Strong North and Weak South" and "strong women and weak men" . .

1. Characteristics of China's Winter Project "Strong Ice and Weak Snow"

Chinese athletes totally won the 12 gold medals of Winter Olympics, only one from snow project and others from the ice projects that are short track speed skating, speed skating and figure skating. In nearly 30 years, the Chinese Army keeps expanding on seizing the medals in the Winter Olympics, but the vast majority of the snow projects have been not significantly improved, and the Chinese army's snow projects with strong competitive power——freestyle skiing aerials, snowboarding U-grooves are the non-mainstream projects. Instead, like alpine skiing, ski jumping, cross-country skiing, Nordic Combined and such traditional items, we do not have ideal results, but three sled projects have not yet carried out domestically.

According to the position in gold medal standing, China can be called a second-rate country of winter sport. In fact, China has even not deserved this title, because China winter army obviously is weak in snow projects, but being strong in ice projects. Among 15 major projects in the Winter Olympics, only five items are skating events, and other 10 projects are snow events, while a lot of snow events are the mainstream projects in the Winter Olympics, but China has still been vulnerable in some traditional items. If China wants to achieve better grades in the Winter Olympics, it has to develop the snow projects greatly.

2. Characteristics of China's Winter Project "Strong Women and Weak Men"

As can be seen from the China's score in the medal standing in Olympic Winter Games, China's winter sports achievements mainly come from female athletes, presenting the characteristic of "strong women and weak men" . For example, in 1994 Winter Olympics, China has sent 27 athletes to participate in, including 19 female athletes, while three medals were obtained by female athletes. Yanmei Zhang obtained the silver medal of 500 meters short track speed skating, Qiaobo Ye got the bronze medal of 1000 meters speed skating, and LuChenobtained the bronze medal of female solo figure skating. From Table 2, it can see from the medal standing of Chinese Winter Olympic Games that the scores achieved by China winter sports project at the Winter Olympics have 12 gold medals, almost of which are obtained by female athletes, the men only get one piece; 22silver medals, men only get 4; 19 bronze medals, men only get 6. So China's men events need to be further strengthened compared with the world's highest level, in order to gain a broader space of medals.

3. Characteristics of China's Winter Project "Strong North and Weak South"

Due to the effects of climate, geographical and other conditions, the talent cultivation of Chinese winter sports is currently still based on northeastern region, mainly concentrating in Heilongjiang and Jilin province.

Although the plan of "Extending Northern Ice Project to Southern" that China aims to eliminate geographical attributes has already been going on for over 30 years, and large and small ski areas have exceeded more than 400, covering 28 provinces and cities across China, but the southern cities with winter sports teams still grow slowly. Although currently the winter sport has already rapidly developed towards Liaoning, Hebei, Xinjiang and other places, in terms of athletic performance, it is still showing the characteristic of "Strong North and Weak South" .

Ⅳ. Development Condition and Trend of Winter Olympic Games

1. Increasing Participation Ranges of Winter Olympic Games

Countries in the world, including the Third World countries, have successively strengthened the management and support to competitive sport, and each country pays more attention to the scores and rankings of Olympics.

Since 1992 16th Olympic Winter Games, the countries, regions and number of athletes participating in the Winter Olympics are growing, and the number of countries obtaining medals is also increasing, as shown in Table 3, until the 22nd Sochi Winter Olympics, there has been already 88 countries and regions participating in the Winter Olympics, and the athletes who participate in Olympics are also increasing year by year.

Table 2 Men and Women Distribution of Chinese Medal in Winter Olympics

Time	Gold Medal	Silver Medal	Bronze Medal
1992	0	3 (Women)	0
1994	0	1 (Women)	2 (Women)
1998	0	6 (2 Men and 4Women)	2 (1Woman and 1Man)
2002	2 (Women)	2 (Women)	4 (1 Woman, 2 Men and Pair Skating)
2006	2 (1Woman and 1 Man)	4 (3 Women and Pair Skating)	5 (3 Woman, 1 Men and Pair Skating)
2010	5 (4 Women and Pair Skating)	2 (1 Women and Pair Skating)	4 (3 Women and 1 Man)
2014	3 (Women)	4 (2 Women and 2 Men)	2 (Man)

Table 3 Entries Units and Competitors Condition in 16th—22nd Winter Olympic Games

Olympic Year	Entries Units	Number of Competitors
1992	64	1801
1994	67	1737
1998	72	2176
2002	78	2399
2006	80	2508
2010	82	2629
2014	88	2887

2. Constantly Increasing Development of Winter Olympic Events

It can be seen from Table 4 that in the past 20 years, the total number of individual events in Winter Olympics has been on an increasing trend, with an average increase of 5.4 individual events in each Winter Olympics. Taking all factors considered, compared with the Summer Olympics, the space of Winter Olympics individual development space is relatively large. Currently, the international winter sports organizations recognized by the International Olympic Committee are seven, while they totally administer 25 major items with 168 small items, and 15 major items with 98 small items have been included in the Winter Olympics successively, occupying 50% of the ongoing winter projects. The total number of future Winter Olympic events still has a great increasing space, and the increase of events of future Olympic Winter Games will also bring a possibility of an increase in the total number of countries, regions and athletes participating in competition. Also, because the development space of traditional items such as speed skating, cross-country skiing and others is getting smaller and smaller, the additional events in future Winter Olympics will focus on some emerging winter projects. According to the predicts and planning of project, by 2024, the Winter Olympic projects will develop from the current 98 small items to 100 small items, and the emerging events in the new projects will account for more than 80%. Another trend of Winter Olympic development is that the additional projects incline to be the more ornamental, irritating and highly competitive competitions, in order to adapt the requirement of combination between winter sports and the modern mass media. For example, in event setting of 2002 Winter Olympics, the snowboarding used the more ornamental and irritating parallel giant slalom to replace the giant slalom in 1998 Winter Olympics. In recent years, the multiple-people ski track steeplechase emerging in snowboarding was firstly included into the 2006 Turin Olympic Games. The advantageous project of Chinese wintersport is short track speed skating and figure skating, which are basically saturated, so in order to obtain good results in the Winter Olympics, we must attach importance to the emerging project in the layout of events and achieve significant breakthrough in a number of emerging projects.

3. Continuously Increasing Scientific and Technological Contents in Winter Olympic Games

Sports Results. The development of modern science and technology has greatly promoted the advancement of sports science and technology, the position and role of sports science and technology have increasingly strengthened, sports scientific research systems will form the open system to the society and the world, and the comprehensive trend of multidisciplinary of sports scientific research continue to strengthen, while the researches for the outstanding athletes with a personality will also be deepened. Modern Winter Olympic Game is largely the technologicalcontest between participating countries, which relates to the involvement and influence of biology, information science, materials science and other high and new technology achievements in the frontier discipline areas to the winter sport. It will continue to change the face of winter sports, promoting the athletic performance to develop toward a higher level. Especially the positive exploration and utilization of high-tech means and achievements of scientific research in training methods, sports equipment and rehabilitation of athletes promote the rapid improvement and development of various sports events and sports technology, making the athletic performance continues to improve and the world record continue to be refreshed. For example, after the 18thOlympic Winter Games, 12among the 15 world records of the speed skating event had been refreshed, accounting for 80%. Technical movement difficulty of freestyle skiing continues to be improved, and the mainstream difficulty index of original 6.70 had basically been eliminated. Competition in the relevant scientific research on winter sport is bound to become more intense, the scientific nature in the winter sport will become more prominent, and the scientific and technological contents in the sports scores will continue to increase.

Table 4 Change in Gold Medals, Medals and Individual Event in Each Session from16 to 22 Winter Olympic Games

Olympic Year	Number of Gold Medal	Total Number of Medals	Total Number of Individual Events
1992	57	171	57
1994	61	183	61
1998	69	205	68
2002	80	234	78
2006	84	252	84
2010	86	258	86
2014	99	295	98

V. Analysis on Problems of Restricting Development of Chinese Winter Olympic Events

1. In coordination of Development Level between Chinese Winter Olympic Events and Summer Olympic Events

According to the actual development status of Chinese winter sport, China is still the weak winter sport country with weak basis of the strength and low overall level, forming a great contrast to status of China's Summer Olympics sports power, which reflects the disharmony between China's development level of the Winter Olympic

Game and Summer Olympic Games.

2. In coordination between Athletic Score of China's Winter Olympic Game and Mass Winter Sports Basis

The Olympic medals that China currently obtained are mostly from the short track speed skating, figure skating and freestyle skiing aerials, in addition that many people engage in the speed skating, the mass basis of other projects in China is weak, while even less Chinese people know and participate in the freestyle project. Athletic achievements of summer table tennis basically coordinate with the mass basis, reflecting the in coordination between the development of competitive winter sport and the development of mass winter sport.

3. In coordination between Development Reality of China's Winter Olympic Events and Strategy of Future Sports Power

Even though China's current conditions of winter sports has been improved, compared with the United States, Canada and European countries, no matter from stadiums and people's participation or independent research on equipment and facilities, the winter sport is lagging behind the requirement of strategic objectives of achieving

future sports power, reflecting the in coordination between China's competitive winter sports level and strategic objective of sports power.

Ⅵ. Development Suggestions of China's Future Winter Sports

1. Comprehensively and rapidly develop China's national fitness of winter sport, and strive to achieve the coordinated development with the national fitness program.

2. Achieve the comprehensive, coordinated and sustainable development of management system, operational mechanism, sports training, competitions, sports industry management and other internal systems of China's winter sport.

3. Under the coordination of the whole national physique, keep the score of winter advantageous project swell, make effort to plan and carry out new projects, and strive for a better athletic performance.

4. Develop and construct a good international and domestic winter sports humanistic and ecological environment, to lay the foundation for sustainable development of China's winter sports system.

5. Bid and preparations for the Olympic Games will be a favorable opportunity to start the rapid economic development and promote the healthy operation of society and economy. Successful host of the Winter Olympics will be the turning point in the development strategy of China's winter sports events, which will enhance the socialization degree

of winter sport and build a new platform for the development of winter sport.

Reference

[1] RenzhouWang, ZhiqiangZhu, Winter Olympic Movement [M], People's Sports Publishing House, 2005

[2] XiaohuaWu, Liqiang Yu, SeeingChina's Winter Sports Development from Canada [J], Physical Culture Guide, 2013, (12) 38-40

[3] Lingling Wei, Consideration on the Sustainable Development of China's Winter Sport [J], Iceand Snow Sport, 2006, 12 (6); 51-53

[4] Liqiang Yu, Research on Strategic for Sustainable Development of China's Winter Sports Evnet Moving Northern Ice to South [J], Academic Journal of Tianjin Institute of Physical Education, 2004, 4 (19-22)

[5] YinongGuo, Rational Reflections on Development of China's Winter Sports Event [J], Academic Journal of Shenyang Institute of Physical Education, 2001, 2

[6] XinhuaZhang, Analysis on Existing Problems of Development Strategy of China's Winter Sport [J], Academic Journal of Qiqihar University, 2005, 11

[7] Tongdan Yan, Baolun Zhou, Analysis on Strategy of China's Participation in the Winter Olympic Athletics Events [J], Academic Journal of Harbin Institute of Physical Education, 2005, 5

[8] Aibo Cui, Thoughton Strategy ofChina's Winter Sports Development [J], Ice and Snow Sport, 2006, 10 (5)

4.16 滑雪运动起源的思辨——由阿勒泰史前岩画引发的思考
Speculation on Origin of Skiing——Reflection from Altay Prehistoric Rock Carving

吴晓华 Wu Xiaohua (CHN)

个人简介 Brief Introduction

吴晓华，女，中国籍，1980年9月生人，讲师士，本科就读于哈尔滨体育学院，研究生就读于苏州大学体育学院，现任吉林体育学院冰雪学院滑雪教研室主任，国家统编教材编委，一直从事冰雪运动项目教学、科研工作，发表论文20余篇。

Xiaohua Wu, female, Chinese, was born in September, 1980. She is a lecturer and a master. Her bachelor degree was obtained in Harbin Sport University while her master degree was obtained in the College of Physical Education of Soochow University. At present, she is the director of skiing teaching and research section in School of ice and snow, Jilin Institute of Physical Education and the member of the national state-compiled textbook editorial board. She has been engaged in the teaching and scientific research of the project of ice-snow sport with more than 20 thesis published.

论文 Paper:

滑雪运动起源的思辨——由阿勒泰史前岩画引发的思考

摘要：本文对专家论证得出“中国古代滑雪起源于新疆阿勒泰地区”的结论，谈了赞同的理由。采用文献法对目前世界上关于滑雪起源时间和起源地点几种学说进行了总结，认为古老滑雪运动有多民族、多地域的特点。同时对古老滑雪文化的挖掘、保护和传承，古老滑雪与现代滑雪的不同，中国现代滑雪发展出现的问题等进行了思考和讨论。

关键词：滑雪 起源 推论 思考

滑雪是一项古老的的运动项目之一，滑雪运动的产生动因与花样滑冰、冰球以及冰壶运动等冬季运动项目有所不同，它的产生不是出于娱乐和兴趣，而是起源于人类生存和与自然作斗争的需要。

滑雪板的使用可以追溯到远古时代。在其演化过程，人类总是知道用什么方法来让自已适应周边的地理环境和气候。为了确保自己的生存，人类必须在非常恶劣的地形穿梭，必须为了食物而在野外打猎，也正是古人文明智慧的所在。

滑雪运动早在公元前五世纪的文献中就已经有了记载。但一般来说，历史文献的记载相对考古发现还是要晚许多，所以追溯滑雪的起源得用考古资料。原始的滑雪板是用木、皮制作的，容易腐朽，在考古发掘中很难找到，这为滑雪的科学探源带来了许多困难。从人类保留的考古遗迹发现的古老滑雪运动有多民族、多个地点、多项社会活动的特点。

Speculation on Origin of Skiing-Reflection from Altay Prehistoric Rock Carving

Abstract: in this thesis, the reasons for the approval of the conclusion that the ancient Chinese skiing originates from Xinjiang Altay Prefecture are discussed and the conclusion is obtained through expert argumentation. The documentary method is applied to summarize the theories of origin time and area of skiing in the world and it is believed that the ancient skiing has the multiethnic and multiregional characteristics. Meanwhile, the reflection and discussion are made on the excavation, protection and inheritance of ancient skiing culture, the difference between ancient skiing and modern skiing and the problems appearing during the development of Chinese modern skiing.

Key Words: Skiing; Origin; Inference; Reflection

Skiing is one of the ancient sport events and its producing motivation is different from that of figure skating, ice hockey, curling and other winter sports; it does not originate from recreation and interest, instead, it derives from the need for human survival and struggle against nature.

The use of skis could go back to the ancient times. During its evolutionary process, mankind always knew the methods to accommodate to the surrounding geographical environment and climate. In order to survive, mankind must pass through the rough topography and hunt in the wild for food, which was the wisdom of ancient civilization.

Skiing has been recorded since the fifth century BC. Generally speaking, the record in the historical document is much later than archaeological discovery and thus the origin of skiing should be traced through the archaeological materials. The original skis are made of wood and fur and are easy to decay and thus it is difficult to find during the archaeological excavation, which brings a lot of difficulty to the scientific study on the origin of skiing. It is found from the reserved archaeological sites that the ancient skiing is characterized by multiple nationalities, multiple locations and multiple social activities.

一、北欧滑雪起源的考古学推论

关于滑雪的起源地，以往比较盛行的说法是起源于北欧。因为在挪威北部边远的小岛发现过一幅公元前 2500 年左右的岩刻画，上面雕刻着一个穿着巨大滑雪板滑雪的人，他手持一根木棍，双脚踏着滑雪板，靠一根滑雪杆向前滑行，滑行姿势相为身体前倾、双膝弯曲（如图 1）。此外，1921 年，人们在瑞典中部那姆特兰省靠近西博滕省交界处的泥岗地理发现了一具保存完好的古代滑雪板，经鉴定这幅滑雪板已经有 4500 年的历史，这一发现更加坚定了滑雪起源于北欧的说法。

此外，欧洲是近代滑雪、现代滑雪的兴起之地，有很多世界滑雪运动的“之最”、“第一”都在这里产生，多项滑雪运动在这里得到普及和推广，在国际上挪威被誉为“滑雪运动的故乡”，奥地利被誉为“滑雪王国”等。因此，滑雪起源于北欧的观点更容易被广泛认可。

图 1 挪威岩刻画中脚踏巨大滑雪板的人

Figure 1 Person with Gigantic Skis under Feet in Norwegian Rock Carving

I. Archaeological Inference of Skiing Origin in Northern Europe

For the origin of skiing, there was a popular saying that it originated from Northern Europe. A rock carving around 2500 BC was found in a small remote island on the north of Norway and a skier with the gigantic skis was engraved on it; he held a wooden stick with the skis under the feet and slid forward against a ski pole and he leaned forward and bended knees (as shown in figure 1). In addition, in 1921, a pair of well-preserved ancient skis was discovered in the mud downland next to the juncture of Vaesterbotten Laen in Jamtland County in central Sweden and it had a history of 4500 years, which firmed the saying that the skiing originated from Northern Europe.

The modern skiing sprang up in Europe and thus Europe had many "best" and "first" of skiing; besides, many skiing sports were popularized and generalized here and Norway was honored as "Hometown of Skiing" and Austria as "Skiing Kingdom". Hence, the opinion that skiing originated from Northern Europe was much easier to be widely accepted.

二、俄罗斯滑雪起源的考古学推论

"北欧说"一直持续到了 20 世纪 60 年代。俄罗斯考古人员对这一学说提出质疑，并且提出了确凿的证据。当时，在俄罗斯东北部乌拉尔山脉维斯一地的泥炭沼中，发现了 8000 年前石器时代制作的滑雪板残片。滑雪板为弯曲状，雕刻有驼鹿头状的"制动器"。这件滑雪板已相当进步，可以想像当时的居民已能够进行急速滑行了。同时，据 1985 年出版的吉尼斯大全记载，1934 年苏联一位考古学家在苏联别索维斯列德基（Bessovysledki）发现了公元前 6000 年一个滑雪者的石雕像，使用的滑雪板是由动物骨骼制成的。这证明俄罗斯人早在 8000 年前就已经学会了使用滑雪板，其滑雪形成时间要早于北欧。但这一考古信息虽然已经历半个世纪，但人们仍然很陌生，尚没有得到普遍的传播和公认。

II. Archaeological Inference of Skiing Origin in Russia

The "Doctrine of Northern Europe" lasted until the 1960s. The Russian archaeologists raised doubts on such doctrine and put forward the hard evidence. Atthat time, the relics of skis made 8000 years ago during the Stone Age was discovered in the peat bog in Vis of Ural Mountains in northeastern Russia. The skis were curved with the moose-head-shape "brake" engraved on it. Such skis were really progressive and it could be imaged that the residents could glide fast. Meanwhile, according to the Guinness Book of Records published in 1985, a soviet archaeologist discovered a stone statue of skier in 6000 B. C. in Bessovysledki and the skis were made of animal bones, which proved that the Russians had knew how to use the skis 8000 years ago and it was earlier than Northern Europe. Although such archaeological information had appeared for half a century, it was still unfamiliar to human beings and was not universally spread and accepted.

三、中国新疆阿勒泰滑雪起源的考古学推论

近年来，来自中国的单兆鉴等多名专家从不同的角度论证了中国新疆阿勒泰作为人类滑雪最早起源地这一观点。比以往其他国家发现的人类滑雪岩刻岩画以及滑雪板残片所反映的年代至少提前2000年以上。

专家们还谈到在日本札幌的冬季运动博物馆内保留着一幅古老的挂图，在这幅图中清楚地画出了滑雪运动最早出现在阿勒泰地区，并标出了由这里向北欧和北美洲扩展的路线图。

图2　日本札幌市冬季运动博物馆滑雪起源及传播路线图

Figure2　Skiing Origin in Sapporo Winter Sports Museum and its Propagation Route Map

前苏联的一本《滑雪运动教科书》在"滑雪运动史"一节中称："最早的滑雪板是在哪个区域出现的，准确的讲，还没有定论，但普遍认为最早采用滑雪板作为代步工具的是生活在西伯利亚地区（从贝加尔湖到阿勒泰地区）的人们。随着人类的迁移，又扩展到了阿拉斯加东部、日本和斯堪的纳维亚半岛西部与西北

部，直到欧洲中部。”这一说法当时依据的还是上个世纪60年代在其境内乌拉尔山脉发现的距今8000年前的滑雪板残片。今天的发现与这本教科书的描述仍然吻合，只不过敦德布拉克岩画的历史更久远些罢了。

考古学家发现在新疆阿勒泰市汗德尕特蒙古族乡的敦德布拉克1号岩画棚内，有滑雪人物岩画：从阿尔泰山地草原文化发展及岩棚画的情况看，它应属于旧石器时代晚期的岩棚画，距今约1~2万年。单兆鉴等多名滑雪专家对岩画中第3组人物的动作进行了鉴定分析，认为岩画中的人物姿势基本呈站立式，脚下有延长物，上体前倾，膝部前屈，而且动感明显，符合滑雪人的姿态要求。岩画中几个人脚踏雪板，有的还手持单杆，滑雪人的动作形态栩栩如生，与现今阿勒泰地区农牧民穿用古老滑雪器具滑雪姿态，有着惊人的相似之处。

阿勒泰乡村居民至今仍使用的“毛皮滑雪板”，与8000年前俄罗斯的滑雪板残片一样非常原始。阿勒泰地处我国西北角，西北与哈萨克斯坦、俄罗斯相接，这里山地面积占近1/3，丘陵河谷面积也很大，过去一直是我国北方民族的游牧地之一。由于地域相对封闭，到上个世纪末，这里仍是一个以畜牧业经济为主的区域，人们对阿勒泰的了解也仅限于雪山草原和牛羊。直到现在，一项“阿勒泰是人类滑雪最早起源地”的研究报告的发布让这里成为世人瞩目的焦点。

图3 一万年前的新疆阿勒泰的滑雪人岩画
Figure 3 Rock Carving for Skier in Altay, Xinjiang Ten Thousand Years Ago

西北大学考古学系主任、西北大学文化遗产保护与考古学研究中心主任王建新从更专业的角度进行了论述。王建新说，敦德布拉克岩画是使用颜料绘制的，岩绘岩画主要流行于欧洲和印度等地的旧石器时代晚期，在中国境内只有广西花山和阿尔泰山区有少量分布。最早的岩绘作品出现于欧亚大陆西部的法国和西班牙的岩洞中，一般认为最早可达距今3万年。印度的岩绘距今约两万年。敦德布拉克人物岩绘的形式和颜色与印度皮摩波特卡山区晚期的岩绘较为接近。敦德布拉克的岩绘虽然并不是同一时期的，但均应早于游牧文化的岩刻。根据现有的资料，王建新更倾向于将人物岩绘的年代初步推定在距今1万年左右，动物岩绘的年代还应早一些。

在敦德布拉克人物形象的岩绘中，的确可以看出有的脚下有很像滑雪板的长条形物。此外，部分人物岩绘为弯腰、撅臀的形象，很像是在做滑雪动作。从已知的与滑雪相关的考古资料看，欧洲的挪威、瑞典、奥地利等国最早的资料都在距今4000多年前，而俄罗斯的资料则早到距今8000年前，距今1万年左右的敦德布拉克岩画的滑雪形象应该是目前已知年代最早的与滑雪相关的考古资料。

专家们引用了中国古代地理书《山海经·海内经》中的记载："有丁令国，其民自膝下有毛，马蹄善走。"并解释所谓丁令国，即当时贝加尔湖以南直到阿勒泰山一带从事游牧的我国北方少数民族。

专家们提到其实希腊史学家希罗多德在其所著《世界史》第四卷中的一段描述："住在阿勒泰地区的人们拥有山羊角，冬季在雪中奔跑。"形容当地人借助传统滑雪器具在雪地疾走的场面。

虽经漫长的时代变迁，现阿勒泰居民仍广泛沿袭脚踏自制的"毛皮滑雪板"、手持单只木杆在雪地里滑行的古老传统。阿勒泰乡村居民使用的非常原始的"毛皮滑雪板"，与记载的唐代滑雪板形状非常相似。这种"毛皮滑雪板"相比于8000年前俄罗斯东北部乌拉尔山脉维斯发现的滑雪板残片还要原始。古老的滑雪板流传至今，不仅说明历史上阿勒泰地区相对来说有些封闭，同时也反映出阿勒泰地区滑雪的历史也非常古老。

III. Archaeological Inference of Skiing Origin in Altay, Xinjiang

In recent years, Shan Zhaojianand other experts from China demonstrated that Altay in Xinjiang was the earliest origin of skiing from different angles. It was at least 2000 years earlier than the ages reflected on the rock carvings and relics of skis discovered by other countries.

The experts also talked about the ancient wall map in the Sapporo winter sports museum, which showed clearly that skiing first appeared in Altay Prefecture and the route map from here to Northern Europe and North America was also designated on it.

In the section of "Skiing History" in *Textbook of Skiing* by former Soviet Union, it is declared: "accurately speaking, there is no final conclusion on the origin of skis, however, it is widely believed that the earliest people to use skis as transportation tools are the people living in Siberia (from Baikal to Altay). Along with human migration, the scope is expanded to Eastern Alaska, Japan, west and northwest parts of Scandinavian Peninsula and Central Europe." Such statement was based on the 8000-year-old relics of skis discovered in Ural Mountains in the 1960s. The discovery today is identical to the description in this textbook; however, the Dundebulake rock carving has a more ancient history.

The archaeologists found that there were rock carvings of skiers in No. 1 Dundebulake rock carving dolmen in Handegate village of Altay City in Xinjiang: According to the prairie culture development of Altay Mountain and the condition of rock carving, it should belong to the rock carving during the Upper Paleolithic Period, which was about 10 to 20 thousand years ago. Shan Zhaojian and other skiing experts identified and analyzed the movements of the people in the third group in the rock carving and thought that the people were standing with continuations under feet and the upper bodies and the knees were forward with the sense of movement, which confirmed to the posture requirements of skiers. In the rock carving, several people were stamping on the skis with both feet and some were holding single poles; the movements and shapes of the skiers were lively and were similar to the skiing postures of the farmers and herdsmen with ancient skiing tools in modern Altay.

The villagers in Altay still use the "fur skis" which is as original as the Russian skis relics 8000 years ago. Altay is located in the northwest corner of China and is bordered by Kazakhstan and Russia on the northwest; the mountainous area accounts for 1/3 of the total area and the area of hills and river valleys is also large; in the past, it was one of the nomadic lands of northern ethnic groups; since this region was relatively closed, it was still a region with animal husbandry economy as the principal until the end of last century and understanding on Altay was restricted to snow-capped mountains and marshlands and flocks and herds. Due to the release of a research report that Altay is the earliest origin of skiing, it becomes the spotlight today.

Wang Jianxin, the chairman in department of archaeology in Northwest University and the director of cultural heritage protection and archaeology research center of Northwest University, expounded from more professional angles. Wang Jianxin said that the Dundebulake rock carving was painted through pigment and the rock carving was mainly popular in Europe and India during the Upper Palaeolithic Age and in China, it was only distributed in Guangxi Huashan and Altay Mountains in small amount. The earliest rock carving appeared in the caves of France and Spain in the western Eurasia and it was generally acknowledged that the earliest one was about 30 thousand years old. The Indian rock carving was about twenty thousand years old. The form and color of Dundebulake rock carving of figure was similar to that of Pimobokate mountainous area during the late period. Although the Dundebulake rock carvings were not in the same period, they were earlier than the rock carving of nomadic culture. According to the existing materials, Wang Jianxin tends to infer that the rock carving of figure is about ten thousand years old and that of the animal is much older.

In the Dundebulake rock carvings of figures, it was observed that there were long and narrow objects under the feet, which were similar to the skis. In addition, some people were stooping and sticking up asses, as if they were skiing. According to the known archaeological materials related with skiing, the earliest materials of Norway, Sweden and Austria appeared more than 4000 years ago and the materials of Russia appeared 8000 years ago, therefore, the skiing figure in the Dundebulake rock carving ten thousand years ago should be the earliest archaeological materials related with skiing that was known.

The experts cited the record in the ancient Chinese geography book of *The Classic of Mountains and Rivers* that there was a state named Dingling and people in this country were adept in running due to the leg hairs under the knees and the feet like horse hooves." It was explained that the Dingling State referred to the northern minorities who were engaged in nomadic activities between the south of Baikal and Altay Mountains.

The experts also proposed a description in the fourth volume of *World History* written by the Greek historian Herodotus that the human beings living in Altay had goat horns and could ran on the snow, which described the scene that the local people trotted on the snow with the traditional skiing tools.

After the change of time, the residents in Altay still follow the ancient tradition to slide on the snow with the home-made "fur skis" under feet and single wooden poles in hand. The "fur skis" used by the villagers in Altay is similar to the recorded skis of Tang Dynasty. Such kind of "fur skis" is even more primitive than the ski relics found in Vis of Ural Mountains in northeastern Russia 8000 years ago. The ancient skis are spread up to now, which not only declares that Altay is closed in history, but also reflects that history of skiing in Altay is very old.

四、从新疆阿勒泰滑雪起源引发的思考

1. 古老滑雪运动被再次挖掘、保护和传承

在众多专家学者研究考察滑雪起源的过程中，古老滑雪运动的足迹被现代人重新挖掘，发现了滑雪运动在 8000-10000 年前就已经在多个地域出现，并有确凿的考古依据和文献记载。同时，这一古老运动经过世世代代传承，在一些地域

还能一直长久原貌般的保留下来，弥足珍贵，已经成为中国乃至世界滑雪文化的宝贵遗产。同时各国相关政府部门也通过制定规范、修建博物馆、举行纪念节日等措施对古老滑雪运动进行保护和传承，让现代人类早起生存、滑雪文明的起源、古老运动的历史有了新的了解和认识。

2. 原始古代滑雪与当代滑雪的差异

由于人类文明的发展阶段、进化程度、劳动工具、材料来源等因素所限，原始古代滑雪首先解决的是使双腿不下陷于雪中困难，很可能用树枝、树皮捆绑在脚底，使其具有现代仍使用的“雪踏”的功能。古人在实践中不断改进用具，从雪地走动演变成滑动，并且逐渐学会运用滑雪杖。

随着人类文明的进步和科技的发展，滑雪的实用性逐渐由狩猎、军事、交通向健身、娱乐、兴趣发展，当代很多新的滑雪项目如单板滑雪、自由式滑雪就是人们休闲娱乐的衍生项目，当代滑雪也一跃成为当今的四大贵族运动之一。

3. 阿勒泰古老滑雪掀起滑雪旅游新热点

伴随着中国新疆阿勒泰地区是人类滑雪最早起源地《阿勒泰宣言》的成功发布，阿勒泰地区的古老滑雪运动也被广泛的传播。阿勒泰地区每年举办古老毛皮滑雪板比赛已经成为当地的盛大节日，吸引了众多海内外游客到此参观、考察和体验，而这无疑推动了该地区乃至新疆滑雪旅游产业的发展，新疆阿勒泰已经成为举世瞩目的滑雪旅游新热点。

经历半个世纪，但人们仍然很陌生，尚没有得到普遍的传播和公认。

IV. Reflection from Skiing Origin in Altay, Xinjiang

1. Excavation, protection and inheritance of ancient skiing

During the process that the experts and scholars investigated the origin of skiing, the track of ancient skiing was excavated again; it was discovered that skiing appeared in many regions 8000 to 10000 years ago and there were valid archaeological foundation and documentary records. Meanwhile, such an ancient sport event was inherited from generation to generation and some even remained in the original appearance, which was really precious, therefore, it became the legacy of Chinese and world skiing culture. Simultaneously, the relevant government sectors ofvarious countries also protected and inherited the ancient skiing through formulating criteria, constructing museums and holding anniversaries so that the modern people could understand and know the origin of skiing civilization and the history of ancient sport.

2. Difference between original ancient skiing and contemporary skiing

Since the ancient skiing was restricted by the development phase of human civilization, evolution degree, instruments of labor and source of materials, the first problem to be solved was that the both legs should not be caught in snow and thus the branches and bark might be bundled under feet so that it could have the function of "snow tread" which was still used by modern people. The ancients improved the tools during the practice, transforming from walking in the snow to sliding and gradually grasped the methods to use ski poles.

Along with progress of human civilization and technological development, the application of skiing is developed from hunting, military and transportation to fitness, recreation and interest and many novel skiing events are the derivative events of leisure and recreation, such as snowboarding and freestyle skiing and the modern skiing has become one of the four noble sports.

3. Hot spot of skiing tourism raised by Altay ancient skiing

After the successful release of *Declaration of Altay* that Xinjiang Altay is the earliest origin of skiing, the ancient skiing of Altay is also extensively propagated. The ancient fur ski competition is held in Altay each year, which is a grand festival that attracts tourists from home and abroad to visit, explore and experience; undoubtedly, the ski tourism industry of this region and even Xinjiang is promoted and thus Xinjiang Altay becomes the hot spot of ski tourism.

五、中国现代滑雪运动的发展

1. 1930年-1949年前中国的雪上运动

虽然在一万年之前中国就已经有了滑雪的足迹，但是非常遗憾，这项运动没能很好的流传下来。中国的现代滑雪运动始于20世纪30年代初期，由俄罗斯和日本传入。当时旅居在东北的白俄罗斯人在哈尔滨市的玉泉北山建立了中国第一个滑雪场，用于冬季室外健身和娱乐，其后在1940年代由日本人接手经营，主要为日本占领军和日本在黑龙江的铁路员工服务。另外还有吉林省通化市的千叶湖滑雪场，也是在日伪时期修建的滑雪场。

2. 新中国成立后雪上运动的兴起

1949年新中国成立后，群众性的滑雪运动得到进一步的发展。他们在非常简陋的滑雪场进行训练，没有造雪机和压雪机、甚至没有拖牵。1957年中国第一次滑雪比赛在吉林省通化市举行，1959年2月在吉林市举办了第一届全国冬季运动会。1961年及1963年，中国人民解放军滑雪队先后两次出国参加滑雪比赛。1980年，中国滑雪队参加了在美国普莱西德湖举行的第13届冬季奥林匹克运动会。1996年亚洲冬季运动会以后，现代滑雪运动在中国广泛开展起来。

3. 中国滑雪运动存在的问题

虽然中国的滑雪运动在1996年以后快速发展，但与欧美等国还存在一定差距。第一，中国滑雪场的数量多但规模小。雪场数量虽多，到目前为止，中国大大小小的滑雪场数量已经突破450家，但规模与欧美存在巨大差异，配备高空缆车，符合欧美标准的不超过50个。第二，滑雪人口标准差异，高级滑雪者比例低。中国滑雪人口在2011年已经突破1000万，并且每年以20%的速度递增。但关于滑雪人口，中国的统计标准是一生只滑大于或等于一次的人，而欧美统计标准是连续两年中，每年冬季至少有一次滑雪活动的，才能被计入滑雪人口。因此中国滑雪人口的转化率还有待提高。

4. 吉林省滑雪运动发展概况

30年代的滑雪运动：邮递员冬季送信时用过滑雪板，冬季巡查线路的变电工人用过滑雪板，师范校的学生也玩过滑雪板。但这个时期的滑雪活动范围小、规模窄。1957年在吉林省通化市举行第一届全国滑雪比赛。从1958年-1990年，全国举办的大型滑雪赛事有2/3都在吉林省举行。2003年瓦萨国际滑雪节入住吉林省长春市，经过十几年时间在2014年被列入国际瓦萨罗佩特组织。目前吉林省拥有可以承办大型赛事的滑雪场有北大湖滑雪场、长白山万达滑雪场、松花湖滑雪场、净月潭滑雪场等。

伴随阿勒泰地区的古老滑雪运动被人们挖掘、保护和传承，以及中国目前滑雪发展的现状，都充分说明中国滑雪产业的发展充满着巨大的空间。特别是中国申办冬奥会一旦成功，滑雪运动在中国的发展必将是史无前例的。

V. Chinese Modern Skiing Development

1. Chinese snow sports between 1930 and 1949

Although skiing appeared in China ten thousand years ago, it did not come down. The Chinese modern skiing started in the early 1930s and was introduced by Russia and Japan. The Belorussian living in northeast established the first ski field in Yuquan Beishan of Harbin for outdoor fitness and recreation in winter and then it was taken over by the Japanese in the 1940s to serve the Japanese occupation armies and railway personnel in Heilongjiang. In addition, Qianyehu ski field in Tonghua city of Jilin province was also built during Japanese puppet regime period.

2. Rising of snow sports after the establishment of New China

After the establishment of New China in 1949, the mass skiing was further developed. They were trained in the rough ski field without snowmaker, snow-packing machine and towing. The first skiing competition was held in Tonghua city of Jilin province in 1957 and the First National Winter Games was held in Jilin City in February, 1959. In 1961 and 1963, the Skiing Team of the Chinese People's Liberation Army went abroad to compete in the skiing competitions. The Chinese skiing team attended the 13th

Winter Olympic Games in Lake Placid of the United States in 1980. After the Asian Winter Games in 1996, the modern skiing was widely developed in China.

3. Existing problems of Chinese skiing

Although Chinese skiing has developed rapidly since 1996, there is still a certain gap compared with Europe and America. Firstly, the ski field in China is characterized by large quantity and small scale. So far, there are 450 ski fields in China, however, there is a huge gap in the scale compared with Europe and America; there are no more than 50 fields equipped with chairlifts and conforming to European and American standard. Secondly, there is the standard difference in the skiing population and the proportion of advanced skiers is low. The skiing population in China has reached 10 million in 2011 and is growing at the rate of 20% each year. The statistical standard for skiing population in China is the person who skies more than or equal to once for the whole life, however, that of Europe and America is the person who skies at least once in each winter season during two consecutive years. Hence, the percent conversion of Chinese skiing population should be improved.

4. General situation of skiing development in Jilin province

Skiing in the 1930s: the postmen used the skis when delivering letters in winter and the electricians used the skis when inspecting the lines in winter and the students in normal colleges played with the skis. However, during this period, the range and scale of skiing activity was small. In 1957, the first skiing competition was held in Tonghua city of Jilin province. From 1958 to 1990, 2/3 of the major skiing competitions were held in Jilin province. Vaasa International Skiing Festival came to Changchun of Jilin province in 2003 and it was listed in the International Vaasa Loppet Organization in 2014. At present, the ski fields that can hold major sport events include Beidahu Ski Field, Changbai Mountain Wanda Ski Field, Songhua Lake Ski Field and Jingyuetan Ski Field.

The excavation, protection and inheritance of ancient skiing in Altay Prefecture and the current situation of skiing development both clearlyshow that the development of Chinese skiing industry has huge space. Once China succeeds in the bid for Olympic Winter Games, the development of skiing in China will be unprecedented.

【参考文献】

[1] 单兆鉴，王博．人类滑雪起源地——中国·新疆·阿勒泰［M］，人民体育出版社，2005

［2］王石安．冰雪运动［M］，人民体育出版社，2000
［3］王仁周，朱志强．冬季奥林匹克运动［M］，人民体育出版社，2005
［4］吴晓华，于立强．从加拿大看中国冬季运动发展［J］，体育文化导刊，2013，（12）38-40
［5］张兴华．中国冬季运动发展战略研究［J］，齐齐哈尔大学学报，2005，11

References

［1］ZhaojianShan，BoWang，［M］，People's Sports Publishing House，2005
［2］ShianWang，Ice and Snow Sports［M］，People's Sports Publishing House，2000
［3］RenzhouWang，ZhiqiangZhu，Winter Olympic Movement［M］，People's Sports Publishing House，2005
［4］XiaohuaWu，Liqiang Yu，Seeing China's Winter Sports Development from Canada［J］，Physical Culture Guide，2013，（12）38-40
［5］XinhuaZhang，Analysis on Existing Problems of Development Strategy of China'sWinter Sport［J］，Academic Journal of Qiqihar University，2005，11

4.17　以滑雪板为例的——滑雪器材演化研究　Study on the Evolution of Skiing Equipment——Taking the Snowboard as an Example

张贵海　Zhang Guihai（CHN）

个人简介　Brief Introduction

张贵海，博士，男，1964年11月生，籍贯：辽宁省凌源市。黑龙江省经济管理干部学院、黑龙江职业学院教授，黑龙江省冰雪产业研究院院长，黑龙江省科学顾问委员会宏观经济组专家、旅游专家组专家，主要研究领域为中国冰雪产业。

Doctor Zhang Guihai，Male，born in Nov. 1964 in Lingyuan，Liaoning，professor of Heijlongjiang Province Cadre School of Economical Management and Heilongjiang Polytechnic，and President of HJL Provincial Institute of Ice-Snow Industries，an expert of HLJ Scientific Advisory Committee in microeconomics and tourism，whose main research field is the ice & snow industries in China.

中文论文：

滑雪器材演化研究
——以滑雪板为例

摘要： 滑雪器材是滑雪者的重要工具，是完成滑雪动作的物质保证。滑雪器材的组合和演化是科技成果的体现。滑雪器材的开发和生产，形成了庞大的滑雪产业集群。本文仅以滑雪板为例，重点探讨了滑雪板演化的因素，滑雪板演化的维度和市场方向。通过探讨滑雪板的起源，重点介绍了滑雪板的结构、材料、外型态和科技元素。提出科技是滑雪板演化的内生推动力，市场是滑雪板演化的外在牵引力。

关键词： 滑雪器材　滑雪板　演化

中国有句成语“工欲善其事，必先利其器”。对于滑雪爱好者或者运动员而言，滑雪器材是其滑雪成功和享受的重要工具。每位滑雪个体都很关注滑雪器具的品牌、功能和使用效果。对于滑雪板的研发单位或制作厂家，更会迎合市场导向，不断的改进滑雪器材，以满足滑雪爱好者的需求或者偏好。

滑雪本是人类适应自然的一种生活方式，起源于寒冷地区，或者说多雪地区，有观点认为距今已有几千年的历史。考证滑雪的起源说，现在专家们莫衷一是。一说是源于斯堪的纳维亚半岛，又有说北高加索山脉，以考古学的视角看，基本是以出土文物或者文字记载为考证依据。不过，仅以现在发现的资料分析，中国的新疆阿勒泰地区应该是最早的滑雪发源地，其中已经发现的岩画图案中有若干组近似滑雪动作和器具的图形，证明滑雪已经在文字发明之前被该地域人们所使用。该地域至今保留着用传统方式制作和使用毛皮雪板，更间接证明滑雪文化的历史传承和起源。

滑雪作为高寒地区人类出行方式虽然久远，但是滑雪成为运动和旅游方式的时间并不太长。大约在 19 世纪中叶，英国人在瑞士才建有第一家高山滑雪场，北欧的越野滑雪比高山滑雪还要早一些。不过，滑雪被国际雪联纳入冬季奥运会项目，仅仅开始于 1924 年在法国举办的冬季运动会。由于滑雪运动的兴起，滑雪由贵族运动、时尚运动成为普通人的冬季首选项目，随之带动滑雪器材的工业化生产。

一、滑雪板的雏形

我们今天看到的滑雪板大多是工业化、大机器化的产物，工业化的特点就是规模化，标准化和市场化。但是，在上世纪初滑雪板大都是手工制作，为了与现在的滑雪板制作区别，笔者分别称之为工艺板和工业板。工艺板的材料一般首选木材，也有用竹材或者藤材制作的。在木材选择上，为了加工方便，一般选择木质松软、木纤维长、韧性好、不易变形的木材，比如，松木、杨木等等。以一块完整的木材为基材，按照不同人的脚形大小，配套雪板的紧固度和舒适度，确定板子的长度、宽度和厚度。滑雪板的形状由方头过渡到圆头，又改进到尖头。人们在使用滑雪板过程中，逐渐意识到滑雪板摩擦力对滑行的影响，于是，在木条上包一层动物皮毛，以动物毛皮的逆、顺来调整滑行时的速度、转弯等动作，既安全又实用。挪威和新疆阿勒泰都有按照原始模式制作滑雪板的工艺和作坊。在欧洲的滑雪博物馆，我们也会看到这类滑雪板的雏形。

二、影响滑雪板演化的市场因素

随着工业科技的不断发展，科技对滑雪板的演化改进起到了巨大的推动作用。首先，滑雪运动的目标是“更快、更高、更强”，滑雪运动员作为滑雪板的使用者和消费者，拉动着滑雪板的不断创新演化，以达到这一目标。滑雪运动员除了加强自身的素质和体能训练，转而加大技术、技巧的训练。随着滑雪技术的提升，运动员对滑雪板的要求也在不断提高。于是，滑雪板在上世纪进入演化的快车道，以此满足运动员和滑雪爱好者的挑剔需求。其演化主要集中在以下几个方面，第一是材料演化，第二是外形态演化，第三是结构演化，第四是科技演化。其次，滑雪板的制造商为了占有更多市场份额、降低制造成本、提高工业化生产效率，从供给的角度也在推动滑雪板的演化。再次，市场竞争的加剧，要求生产厂家要不断创新。特别在上世纪 30 年代，欧洲的工业文明已经成型，工业化格局已经深入到社会的各个方面，很多滑雪板的制造商，最初都是以生产木器为主的，比如奥地利的 KNEISSL、日本的小贺坂（OGASAKA）最初都是木工坊，原来是制造木制马车、爬犁或者农用工具的作坊，生产滑雪板仅仅是一个附属项目。但是，随着滑雪不断被世人所接受，滑雪市场的需求出现井喷式增长，滑雪板制造渐渐成为他们的主营业务，滑雪板也成为主要产品。上世纪 50 年代末，进入到滑雪板制造领域的人不断增加，大公司、大财团分别进入滑雪板制造领域，成就了很多家喻户晓的品牌，如 SALOMON、ATOMIC、ROSSIGNOL、FISCHER、VOLKL、HEAD、K2、ELAN、NORDICA、DYNASTAR、HART、BLIZZARD、VECTOR-GLIDE、LINE 等等，在欧洲和美国形成了专业性更强的滑雪板制造商。

三、滑雪板演化分析

前面已介绍滑雪板的演化的四个维度，其演化过程也可分成四个时间节点，可以定义为古代滑雪板、近代滑雪板、现代滑雪板和时代滑雪板。滑雪板的演化是先从使用材料开始的，随着现代冶炼技术的发展，原来由木材制作的滑雪板可以用金属制作，后来发展为用复合材料制作，也可以将化工材料应用到滑雪板上。比如，UV 材料、工程塑料、工程橡胶、石墨材料等，现在，航空材料也正在应用到滑雪板制造上。材料的改进是对木材单一材料的补充，更在于追求滑雪板的轻便、韧性好，便于操控。雪板芯材大多仍然以木材为主，对于初级板，已经有复合材料作为芯材使用。原始的雪板是一块木材制作，现在的雪板只有芯材使用木材。即便是芯材使用木材，也很少有一体的木材了，现在的芯材大多是集成材。通过木材加工的指接、拼接、胶合工艺形成滑雪板的芯材模块。上下板面通过浇注、成型、层压，镶嵌等方式，制作成完整的滑雪板。

板刃材料有钢铁、铜、合金钢、铬金属、钛金属、钛铝合金等，主要是防止滑雪板边刃的锈蚀，提高良好的切雪操控能力。现在很少使用钢铁的，一般都是合金材料，如锰铬合金，钛合金等等，这些材料硬度大、耐磨、切削力强。

板底面最早用毛皮，继之是金属条，即中国东北俗称的脚滑子。在北欧地区，以越野滑雪板为主，也充分考虑滑雪板底面的摩擦力和可操控性。现代的高山滑雪板底面大多采用石墨材料，也有用硬化塑胶的。不过，为了持久耐磨，一般都选用耐磨好的材质。

板面是保护滑雪板的外在保护罩，除了美观的图案和性能注释，更在于和基材的紧密结合。由于固定器要经过板面与板体固定在一起，板面的抗冲击性和握钉力更为重要。现在的板面一般分三层，即保护膜、板结层和纤维层。随着新材料、新技术、新工艺的应用，滑雪板的表层材料也在与时俱进地改进中。

上世纪40年代，HEAD发明了金属板底，开创了金属和木材的结合，制造了金属滑雪板，将滑雪板的制造技能提高到工业水准，而法国的ROSSIGNOL又将这一技术发扬光大。60年代开始，KNEISSL将化工材料和木材结合，制作不同材料复合滑雪板，使滑雪板的材料选择更加多元化，滑雪板厂家的创新不断诞生出滑雪板演化的新纪录。

其次，滑雪板演化的第二特征是滑雪板外形态的改变。最早的滑雪板主要是手工制作，或者具体地说是手工定做，没有固定的数字比例。其实，科学研究发现，除了滑雪板的长度外，还有滑雪板的“三围”指标，即板头、板腰，板尾的宽度，这些数字的组合，产生不同功能的滑雪板。比如，大回转、小回转、速降、自由式，野雪等功能性雪板，其对应的滑雪板形状是不同的。现代滑雪板，由于雪质不同，其滑雪板功能对应性更加细分。比如，NORDICA品牌滑雪板，对不同雪道的雪质比例，其选择的板型都有差别。由此可见，雪板的精细化功能决定了板型的演化。在1990年前，全球使用滑雪板都属于狭长形的，板头、板腰、板尾差距的比例很小。对于初学滑雪或者非专业人员而言不好操控，影响了市场的认知度。1990年后，滑雪板外形发生了一次深刻的革命，适应CAMBER滑雪技术而出现了卡宾板型，长度缩短，板头、板腰、板尾加大比例，这种雪板拥有腰线（SIDECUT）滑行者只要施加压力，让其变形成弓形，雪板就可以自行转弯，特别适合初学者和非专业运动员使用，给低迷的国际滑雪市场注入一针兴奋剂，使大众滑雪的普及程度变得更快。这就是我们俗称的大头板，它加快了滑雪由专业运动向大众运动的过渡。

上世纪 80 年代，美国人 BURTON 发明了单板，为滑雪板家族增加了新的成员。发明之初不受滑雪场青睐的单板项目，最后成为与双板平分天下的时尚运动，吸引了一批年轻人参与这项近乎极限和表演的运动方式，它是对滑雪板一次颠覆性的改变，虽然灵感来自于冲浪板，但是雪地驰骋跳跃的乐趣给与滑雪者更好的享受。其外形宽度是高山滑雪板的 3-5 倍，并且双脚在同一块板面上，虽然增加了滑雪的难度，但更多地创造了滑雪的乐趣。

进入 21 世纪，单板和双板在演化中互相借鉴，开始由欧洲兴起“大脚板”迷你板，美国又出现了俗称“西瓜皮”的迷你圆片板，吸引更多的人参与到滑雪之中。研究发现，滑雪板外形态的每次改变都会产生巨大的市场推动力。

再次，滑雪板的结构演化应该得益于现代的 3D 技术和空间结构理念。长达一个多世纪的滑雪板制造之路进入到 21 世纪后，3D 滑雪板逐渐展现头角。从结构力学的角度研发滑雪板，成为最近 20 年的主要项目。由于滑雪板厚度有限，在滑雪板的结构改动方面，更多地考虑滑雪板滑行中力的传导和减震效果，降低阻尼系数。由于结构的内外差别，最早尝试结构演化基本是以外部镶嵌式为主。我们可以看看阿托米克（ATOMIC）品牌的早期滑雪板，在固定器前部镶嵌隆起传导带。后来，不同的厂家都在开发不同结构的滑雪板，比如，筛管结构、褶皱结构、蜂窝结构等等，也由外部镶嵌变成内置插入。结构的改变不仅提升滑雪板的功能和驾驭效果，也更加美观，更受到消费者的喜爱。

同时，非对称概念也进入滑雪板的研发之中，滑雪板的形状、颜色也变得千奇百怪。为了减少滑雪板的阻尼系数，滑雪板板头的外包形态、材料、工艺也在发生变化。我们看到市面上有裸头板和包头板。包头材料采用橡胶包头，金属包头；包头工艺有内熔型和旋入型；包头形状有侧口包头、圆口包头和偏口包头、孔隙包头。滑雪板板尾改进中充分借鉴高山滑雪、跳台滑雪、花样滑雪的优点，滑雪板出现了平头板尾、圆头板尾、翘头板尾、燕尾板尾等，给予滑雪者更多的选择。

总之，科技的发展在促进着滑雪板的演化，科技发展推动新材料和新工艺的不断创新，新材料和新技术正在应用到滑雪板的制造之中，新材料如航空材料、石墨片材、复合材料、碳纤维，压电陶瓷等，新技术如纳米技术、光电技术，热耦合技术等。

随着滑雪运动由专业化向大众转变，滑雪板的娱乐功能也正在加大，不断被人们所接受，如热敏板、音频震动片、感应器、LED 光源正在和滑雪板充分组合，现在流行的眩光板、LED 滑雪服等产品就是滑雪和最新科技相融合的结果。在我们可预见的将来，GPS 定位模块、界面感应装置、温度测试，风阻测试、速度记录器、雪地巡航技术等都将会得到融合与应用，智能滑雪板将会大行其道。

纵观滑雪发展史，滑雪板的每次巨大演化无不引来市场震荡和产业嬗变。滑雪器材是多功能组合体，主要为了满足滑雪动作的连续和舒适。滑雪板的演化仅是器材优化的一个方面，除了滑雪技术的不断创新，滑雪鞋、固定器、滑雪杖、垫板需要进行优化组合，特别说明的是在滑雪中其他辅助用品也不能忽视，比如雪镜、头盔等等。但是，滑雪并不是器材的简单组合，而在于滑雪者本身技术和心态，购买和使用滑雪器材，不能心为物役。滑雪器材的演化是为滑雪者服务，需求是滑雪板演化的牵引力，科技是滑雪板演化的核心推动力。在信息化时代，滑雪板的信息化智能化特征将会越来越受到市场的欢迎。

【参考文献】

1. www. winter-sports. cn/home/backup/2012-05-21/377828. html
2. www. skiworld. cn
3. 单兆鉴 高山滑雪教程 2010. 1. 8 中国滑雪协会
4. 曾五一 滑雪板材料制作工艺的演变（J）文体用品与科技/SPORTING GOODS & BUSINESS 2006.（11）
5. 元荪 模压塑料滑雪板及其制作工艺（J）文体用品与科技/SPORTING GOODS & BUSINESS 2007.（1）
6. 单兆鉴 王博 人类滑雪起源地—中国新疆阿勒泰（M）人民教育出版社 2011. 1
7. www. sfi-ski. com

English paper:

Study on the Evolution of Skiing Equipment—Taking the Snowboard as an Example

Abstract As a physical support for the action of skiing, the corresponding equipment is essential, the organization and evolution of which have embodied the achievement in science and technology. The development and production of skiing equipment has made up a huge industrial cluster. Taking snowboard as an example, this paper focuses on investigating into the influence elements, dimensions and market orientation of the snowboard. By looking into the source of the snowboard, the paper introduces its composition, material, configuration and the scientific and technological elements. It concludes that science and technology are the inherent motivation and market is the external pull for the evolution of the snowboard.

Key words: skiing equipment, snowboard, evolution

In China, there is an old saying that a handy tool makes a handy man. For a skiing enthusiast or player, skiing equipment is an important tool to make them succeed in and enjoy the skiing. Everyone of them attaches great importance to the brand, function and application effects of the equipment, while the research and development sectors or manufacturers try their best to meet the demands of the market segment and make continuous improvement on the skiing equipment to satisfy the former.

As one of the living styles for people to survive and with a history of thousands of years, skiing indeed originates in cold areas or where there was a lot of snow. Experts have not agreed on the origin of skiing and identified a variety of perspectives, including that from Scandinavian Peninsula or Northern Caucasus, based on unearthed relics or written records. However, according to existing documents, Altay Prefecture of Xinjiang Province in China has more evidence to support itself as the source of skiing. For example, the discovered cliff paintings have presented several sets of designs as skiing actions and tools, which means people had skied before writing was invented. So far the traditional fur made snowboards have been maintained in this area, an obvious proof of the cultural passage in history.

In spite of its long history of skiing as a travel mode for people in cold areas, it is not a long time before skiing became a sport and tourism activity. It was not until middle 1800s that the first alpine skiing field had been established in Switzerland by the British, a little bit later than the cross-country skiing happening in Northern Europe. In 1924 when the winter Olympics was held in France, skiing was included as an Olympic sport by the International Ski Federation. Since its start, skiing has evolved from a noble and fashion sport to an activity favored by ordinary people in winter, thus is the industrialized production of skiing equipment.

I. Prototype of Snowboard

The snowboard we see now is basically the production from industrialized assembly line, which is characterized with scale, standardization and market orientation. However, at the beginning of last century, most of snowboards were handmade. To make it clear, we call it craftwork boards (CB) while the former as industrial boards (IB) . CB usually chooses timber wood as the primary material, though some also use bamboo or vine. To make the processing convenient, the soft wood with long fibre, toughness and not easy to deformed is generally given priority in selection, such as pine or poplar. With a complete piece of wood as the base material, the board's length, width and thickness are decided according to different sizes of feet and corresponding tightness and comfort. The shape of the board starts as a square head, then in round, and now ends in a pointed tip. In the course of its application, it has been gradually realized that the friction force of the board impacts running. A layer of animal fur was covered around the wood to adjust the running speed and turning action according to the fur'sgrowing direction. It adds to the safety and practicability. There have been the traditional craftwork and workshops run in Norway and Altay Prefecture of Xinjiang Province in China. The similar snowboard prototypes could also be found in ski museums in Europe.

II. The Market Elements Influencing the Evolution of Snowboard

With the incessant development of industrial science and technology, snowboard evolution has been highly motivated. Skiing sports are held aiming at being faster, better and stronger. As the users and consumers of snowboard, athletes have led the constant innovation of the equipment. In addition to improvement of their own qualities and physical fitness training, they resort to more application of technology and skills, thus is the high demand for quality snowboard. Last century has witnessed a rapid evolution of snowboard so as to satisfy athletes and skiing fans' critical requirement. The evolution mainly goes in the aspects of materials, external forms, structures and scientific technologies. To occupy a market segment, manufacturers try to reduce the cost in production and increase industrial productivity, which contributes to the evolution of snowboard from the perspective of suppliers. On the other hand, the increasing market competition pushes the manufacturers to make innovations, especially in 1930s when the industrial civilization had become mature and embodied in various aspects of the society. Most snowboard manufacturers focused on wood products at the very beginning, such as KNEISSL in Austria and OGASAKA wood workshop in Japan, which used to produce wood carriage, sledge or agricultural tools, with snowboard making as a subsidiary item. However, with worldwide popularity of skiing followed by the rapid increase of the market, snowboard making gradually became the primary business. At the end of 1950s, more and more companies and financial groups went into the field of snowboard manufacturing, creating a variety of well-known brands, such as SALOMON、ATOMIC、ROSSIGNOL、FISCHER、VOLKL、HEAD、K2、ELAN、NORDICA、DYNASTAR、

HART、BLIZZARD、VECTOR-GLIDE、LINE, to name a few, with more professional businesses developed in Europe and the USA.

III. Analysis of Snowboard Evolution

Beside the four dimensions of snowboard evolution mentioned above, there are another four timeline milestones in the course, namely, ancient snowboard, modern snowboard, contemporary snowboard, and fashion snowboard. The evolution started from the materials used. With the development modern smelting technology, the original wood made snowboard was replaced by metal, then by composite or chemical materials, including but not limited to UV, engineering rubber, plastics, or graphite. At present, aerial material has also been used in snowboard making. Material improvement has compensated for the shortage in material selection and helps with the ideal of light, convenient and malleable use and control of snowboard. Compared to the original application of a complete wood piece for a snowboard, the present one only has the core material made in wood, which is often made of laminated wood due to the scarcity of complete wood pieces. The basic module is usually formed after such craftwork as finger joint, splicing and gluing, with the upper and lower surfaces of the snowboard developed under teeming, shaping, laminating and inlaying.

The ski edges used to be made of steel, copper, alloy steel, chromium or titanium metals, so as to protect against corrosion and increase snow-cutting control. Now steel is seldom used and replaced by alloy materials, such as manganese chromium ortitanium alloy because of their high hardness, abrasion resistance and strong cutting abilities.

The board bottom used to be covered by animal furs, which is replaced by metal strips, which is locally named as Foot Slider in Northeast of China. In the mountain areas of Northern Europe, the making of popular cross-country skiing board has also taken into consideration of the friction force and controllability of the snowboard bottom. Contemporary alpine snowboard bottom is mostly made of graphite materials, with some using hardened plastics to make it lasting and abrasion resistant.

As the external protective cover of snowboard, the board surface is not only beautifully designed and functionally interpreted, but also tightly combined with the base materials. With the fixer having to pass across the board surface and be fixed with the board, it is critically important for the board surface to be of shock resistance and able to hold the nails tightly. The present board surface is often composed of three layers- protective film, hardened layer and fibrous coat, which are under ceaseless improvement with the application of new materials, technology and arts.

In 1940s, HEAD started the production of metal snowboard by combining wood with metal to make board bottoms, pushing the snowboard manufacturing technique to an industrial level, which was further enhanced by ROSSIGNOL in France. In 1960s, chemical materials were used together with wood to produce snowboard by KNEISSL, which led to a variety of materials applied in the field, followed by continuous innovations in the evolution of snowboard manufacturing.

Another characteristic of this evolution is the change of snowboard expressions. In comparison to the original hand-made or customized board without fixed numerical proportions, the later products embody the achievement in science and technology. In addition to the change in length, there are vital statistics for the width of the board head, waist and end. Based on different digital combination, snowboards present different functions. For instance, various sports actions including giant slalom, slalom, prompt drop, freestyle, to name a few, can be fulfilled under the help of different shapes of snowboard. Contemporary snowboards are produced in more detailed fragmentation according to different snow qualities. The products by NORDICA are an example, which would choose different board shapes based on different snow qualities in different trails. Before 1990, snowboards around the world were featured by being narrow and long, with small differences in the width of board head, waist and end, which was difficult to control for the beginners or amateurs, seriously impacting the market. After 1990, a breakthrough took place in the snowboard shape. In response to the skiing technology of CAMBER, there occurred a kind of snowboard with shortened length and increased proportion in board head, waist and end, more suitable for the beginners and amateurs, strongly stimulating the spread and development of mass skiing activities when the world skiing market was under depression. This is what we often called big head snowboard, a contribution to mass sports' popularity from professional ones.

In 1980s, an American, BOTAN, invented single plate snowboard. In spite of their being ignored at the very beginning, single plate boards were soon popular among young people and have been applied in various cutting-edge performances, become a fashionable sport, caused subversive change in snowboard, inspired surfing, and above all, brought more enjoyment for skiers when they jump and run in the snowfield. The single plate snowboard is 3-5 times wider than alpine snowboard. Although players have to put both feet on the same board, they have more fun under the challenge.

Since 2000, single and double plate snowboards have evolved with reference to each other. "Big Foot" mini board becomes popular in Europe, while the so-called

"Water Mellon Peel" round mini board spreads in the US, attracting more people in the snow world. According to research, each change of the snowboard shape has greatly impacted the market.

The structural evolution of snowboard has benefitted a lot from the three dimensional technology and the idea of spacial structures. In the course of more than 100 years' snowboard manufacturing, it was not until after 2000 that 3D snowboard had come into being. The study and development of snowboard from the perspective of structural mechanics have gained more attention. Given the limitation of the board thickness, the effects of power transmission and shock absorption have to be taken into more consideration in improving the structure of snowboard so as to reduce damping coefficient. The earliest attempt in structure modification focused on external inlaying because of the inside and outside differences. For example, the earlier snowboard under the brand of ATOMIC was inset by swelled conduction band at the front of fixer. Later, different manufacturers developed different structures, such as those of screen pipe, wrinkle or cell. Some also turn the external inlaying into internal insertion. All the modification have not only greatly improved the function and controlling effects of the snowboard, but also made it more beautiful and popular.

Meanwhile, asymmetrical idea has been introduced in the study and development of snowboard, leading to variety of shapes and colors applied. To reduce the damping factor, changes happened in the sourcing, material and craftwork of the board head. We can see bare or covered heads in the market. The cover is usually done by rubber or metal with techniques of inside welding or screw-in, applied as side-cover, round mouth cover, flat cover or gap cover. The reform of the board end has referred more to the strengths in alpine skiing, ski jumping and free style skiing, resulting in the shapes of flat, round, nose and forked ends, leaving more choices to the players.

The last primary contributor to the snowboard evolution is the development science and technology, which have greatly encouraged endless innovation in materials and craftwork. More and more new materials and technologies have been applied in the production of snowboard, especially aerial, graphite, alloy, carbon fibre and piezoelectric ceramics materials, or such technologies as nanometer, photoelectronics and thermo coupling. The spread of skiing sport has aroused more entertaining functions to the sport, thus is the wide acceptance of thermo sensing board, audio vibration piece, sensor and LED being integrated into snowboard making. For example, the contemporarily popular dazzling plate and LED ski suit derive from combining skiing with the latest scientific technology. In the foreseeable future, more technologies like GPS module, interface sensing device, temperature and wind resistance meters, speed recorder, trail navigation, to name a few, would be introduced and applied in snowboard making. Smart snowboard should dominate the market soon.

A review of the ski history presents that snowboard evolution has brought great changes in the related market and industry. As a multi-function complex, skiing equipment targets at making the players' actions inherent and comfortable. Snowboard evolution is only one aspect of the equipment optimization. More improvement and combination should also be done in skiing shoes, fixers, sticks and backing plates, as well as the subsidiaries of glasses and helmet. However, skiing is more than a simple combination of equipments. It has more to do with the player's skills and attitude, procurement and application of ski equipment without his/her heart being enslaved. The evolution of skiing equipment aims at serving the players, pulled by the market and pushed by science and technologies. In the time of information and network, intellectual and informed snowboard would be more popular.

Reference

1. www. winter-sports. cn/home/backup/2012-05-21/377828. html
2. www. skiworld. cn
3. Shan Zhaojian A Course in Alpine Skiing 2010. 1. 8 Chinese Ski Association
4. Zeng Wuyi The Evolving of Materials of Skis (J) SPORTING GOODS & BUSINESS 2006. (11)
5. Yuan Sun Molding Plastic Skis and Concerning Techniques (J) SPORTING GOODS & BUSINESS 2007. (1)
6. Shan Zhaojian Wang Bo The Original Place of Skiing-Altay Prefecture of Xingiang, China (M) People's Education Press 2011. 1
7. www. sfi-ski. com

4.18 毛皮滑雪板滑过阿勒泰 Skiing in Altay by Ancient Fur Skis

周磊 Zhou Lei (CHN)

个人简介 Brief Introduction

周磊，女，中国籍，供职新疆乌鲁木齐晚报，旅游文化记者十余载，跑遍新疆山山水水，被称作专家型的记者。专注阿勒泰古老毛皮滑雪板十年，从岩画记录、滑雪歌，到阿勒泰角角落落的毛皮滑雪板痕迹，挖掘本土古老滑雪文化，挖掘古老毛皮滑雪板与今天的生产生活的关系，从而热爱阿勒泰，热爱古老毛皮滑雪板，热爱喀纳斯景区，更热爱着使用毛皮滑雪板的牧民们。

Zhou Lei, female, who works at Sinkiang Urumqi Evening Paper as a cultural reporter on tourism, she has been to most of the places in Sinkiang, thus is called reporter of "expert" level. She has been dedicated to ancient fur skis for ten years, from cliff painting records and ski song to the traces of fur skis here and there in Altay. She further studied the local ancient ski culture, the relations between ancient fur skis and nowadays' production and living. Thus she is crazy for ancient fur skis, and for Kanasi Scenic Region, and, moreover, for those herdsmen who use fur skis.

中文论文：

毛皮滑雪板滑过阿勒泰

专家考证，中国新疆的阿勒泰是世界滑雪起源地，使用滑雪板的历史已有1万余年。阿尔泰山南麓的蒙古族乌梁海部落，使用毛皮雪板最为出色，其左支是图瓦人，聚居在禾木村、喀纳斯村、白哈巴村，右支在阿勒泰市汗德尕特乡，他们仍与1万年前的祖先一样，脚踏毛皮雪板穿越七个月的漫长冬季。

起初，我是出于对毛皮雪板的好奇而进入这些隐于深山的村庄，如今，我已经在那些山路上往返了上百次，从来也没有厌倦，甚至想留在那里，和牧民们一起生活。每次走进村子，图瓦大妈和姐妹们都上前和我拥抱，那份朴实的热情能赶走任何寒冷。回到城里，一个人静下来的时候也会想，舒开老人的黑蜂怎么样了？喇嘛忙着去谁家念经呢？玛力琴又在给谁做毛皮雪板？星花姑娘是不是已经约会待嫁？

随着旅游开发，外来的经营者开始进入村庄，看着古朴小村的变化，心里也有几分遗憾。好在一到冬天，村中便又恢复了平静，山里的积雪将近两米，牧民们又开始撑着毛皮雪板走出木屋，四周的高山上，雪板留下的两道痕迹从山顶一直延伸到山脚。

一、与毛皮滑雪板的不解之缘

我第一次见到毛皮雪板，是在八年前。

2006年6月6日傍晚，我来到喀纳斯景区白哈巴村，准备参加两天后的敖包节。夕阳的余辉给村里一幢幢木屋镀上了金边，炊烟正袅袅升起，路边有三三两两归家的牛马，一切都显得那样宁静、安详。据说，一百多年前，喀纳斯湖畔来了许多俄罗斯人，把盖木屋的技艺传授给了当地牧民，村里的蒙古族图瓦人和哈萨克人住的都是这样的木屋。我住在牧民梅花家里，举着相机一遍一遍地拍她家的房子，梅花看我兴致勃勃的样子，笑着说：还有屋顶的三角阁楼没拍呢。她的爱人帮忙搬来木梯子，我爬上阁楼一看，原来是一个储物间，用不着的农具、过时的家具、孩子的旧玩具堆得满满当当。梅花从阁楼最里面取出一对积满厚厚灰尘的毛皮雪板，说这是他们冬天出行必不可少的交通工具，当时我对这个灰头土脸的家伙有些不以为然：不就是一块裹着动物毛皮的木板嘛。

就在那年冬天，我学会了滑雪，也真正了解了梅花家那副毛皮雪板背后的渊源。

2007年1月16日是阿勒泰市的“人类滑雪起源地纪念日”，当地举办了一系列古老滑雪与现代滑雪的表演赛，之后，阿勒泰市临时组建了古老毛皮滑雪队，我成了负责组织古老毛皮滑雪队的“队长”，队员都来自周边的村子，最小的18岁，最大的43岁。我们的对手是乌鲁木齐附近各个滑雪场的教练们，双方各派出6名队员在雪道上进行接力赛。下滑时，两队速度不相上下，上行时，我们的队员轻松地在雪道上跑步，教练们则用雪板踏着内八字，十分吃力。有个教练提出互换用具，想藉此扳回一局，但毛皮雪板可不是那么好驾驭的，他们用木棍左戳右捣，雪板就像是一头倔驴，不为所动。这场“古今大对决”，古老毛皮滑雪队最终完胜，队员们高兴极了，他们中间有的人还是第一次出远门，第一次看见火车，一路上好奇地跟我打听：为什么那么多人要住在拥挤的城市里，村子里一望无际的林子多好啊。我想，或许正是因为他们的生活如此单纯、闭塞，古老的滑雪习俗才得以完好地保留至今。

在阿勒泰市的各个乡镇，会滑雪和会制作毛皮雪板的人并不多，许多牧民家里已看不到毛皮雪板的影子。但在喀纳斯景区的村庄里，毛皮雪板的制作非常普及。

从布尔津县前往喀纳斯景区禾木村的道路并不通畅，整个冬季都是大雪封山，近百公里山路只能依靠马爬犁往返，我们走了两天两夜才进入禾木村，现在回想起来，那真像是一次生与死的考验。

出发前被当地朋友再三叮嘱：山里的温度是-40℃，一定要注意保暖。我是全副武装爬上马爬犁的：两套保暖内衣，两件抓绒上衣，一件专业羽绒服，两件和当地部队借的皮大衣，一条厚厚的滑雪裤，三双超厚的专业徒步袜，一双宽大的毡筒靴，一顶抓绒帽，一顶皮帽子，一副滑雪眼镜，一副抓绒手套，一副棉手套，外加一个羽绒睡袋。

坐在马爬犁上，那种冷只能用“彻骨”来形容。正午时分，竟然没有太阳，温度仿佛一直在下降，不到一小时，人都彻底冻透了，里三层外三层的衣物如同无物，风像锥子般直刺肌肤，灌满骨缝，心仿佛只是在惯性跳动。我唯一的想法就是捂得严实点、再严实点，保证手指与脚趾有知觉，否则极易冻掉。

我在第一天下午差点失去一个脚趾头，冻的发乌，幸好及时到达牧民的木屋，

一路上的风景是极美的，沿途的风光宛如一幅幅水墨山水画，长长的卷轴随着我的脚步慢慢打开：一会儿是一片雪蘑菇群，一会儿是一排树挂，一会儿又是玉树临风的雪松，连路边的草都朦朦胧胧地罩上了晶莹剔透的外衣；偶尔路过几户人家，炊烟缭绕的木房子置身于空旷的雪地之中，像是童话小屋。

就这样在深山里走了整整两天，我们终于到达了禾木村。小村被群山环绕着，山坡上常能看到两道长长的雪板痕迹，从山顶一直延伸到山谷，旁边点缀有牛马的蹄印。村里的小坡上，一群孩子正用小型的毛皮雪板滑雪，不少木屋门口靠着刚用过的雪板，我仿佛回到了万年前的阿尔泰山，那时的人们都脚踏着毛皮雪板，滑过七个月的漫长冬季。村里的喇嘛巴依尔说：“禾木冬天雪大得很，我们进山拉烧火的木头，去草场拉草垛子，去邻近的亲戚家串门，都要穿上毛皮雪板，有时侯和几个朋友一起爬上高高的禾木峰，唱起古老的图瓦调，然后跟着风一起‘呼’地滑下来。”

禾木夜晚的星空极美，闪烁的群星仿佛伸手可及。我最喜欢静静聆听深藏在村边森林中的自然之音，想象着林中雪兔灵巧地快跑觅食，狼和狐狸巡视着领地，隐隐约约还有哈熊的吼叫……

当年的艰辛依稀记得，如今进入禾木道路畅通，仅仅四个小时就到了，道路的便捷吸引了越来越多的滑雪爱好者。

在多年的毛皮滑雪板挖掘与报道过程中，与美国人尼尔森不期而遇，更让我深深感到尼尔森是我遇到过的最执着的滑雪者，他当过世界冠军，深深爱着古老的滑雪方式。尼尔森是美国的职业滑雪教练，一直从事滑雪历史的研究，因为从

12 岁开始滑雪，虽然早已年过 50，但是看上去只有 40 多岁。

十几年前，尼尔森开始看 19 世纪加拿大历史专家戴维森关于雪踏的著作，戴维森一生最重要的研究成果，是肯定了“雪踏是雪板的前身”，他曾经在阿勒泰附近发现迄今为止世界上最古老的雪踏。戴维森认为，印第安人、爱斯基摩人、北欧人都是从阿勒泰山脉迁出的。后来新疆社会科学院的学者也得出相同的结论，即“中亚人类向北迁徙到西伯利亚后，一支向东迁徙到美洲，另一支迁徙到欧洲。”

进入喀纳斯时，已经翻阅了大量关于中国滑雪的资料，古时的阿尔泰山系，到处奔跑着鹿、野马、贝加尔牦牛、条纹羚羊，冬天正是狩猎、滑雪的好时机，古代生活在阿尔泰山系的丁令人，把滑雪板叫做“马蹄”或“山羊脚”，这些都引发了尼尔森的向往。七年多以来，尼尔森不断到访阿勒泰，经过无数次考察，他更加坚定了自己的观点——大约两万年前，阿勒泰山系雪踏盛行，印第安人从阿勒泰山系迁出，抵达较为平坦的美洲，完整保留了雪踏，而阿勒泰山系的原住民则在穿越山林狩猎的过程中，将雪踏升级为雪板。

一系列关于阿勒泰古老滑雪的研究成果令尼尔森无比兴奋，他像候鸟一样，一到冬天便进入阿勒泰，和翻译阿尔肯一起，背上行囊，踏上越野滑雪板，在山林中穿行。有时，他会特意沿着毛皮雪板滑过的痕迹，追随当地牧民的脚步。有人曾经告诉尼尔森，阿勒泰的原住民滑雪时可以从数米高的岩石上跃过去，尼尔森将信将疑，直到在禾木村附近与几个年轻人一起滑雪时，才见识到他们类似的高超技巧。

2013 年春节前，尼尔森早早来到喀纳斯的阿夏布拉克村，住在图瓦猎人巴彦家里。几年前，尼尔森曾与巴彦的两个儿子把提和巴特一起踩着毛皮雪板上山。对于居住在喀纳斯湖畔高地上的少年来说，滑雪是一项必备的生存技能，尼尔森还记得，当年 17 岁的把提第一次穿上现代雪板，就朝山下飞速滑了下去，毫无生疏之感；15 岁的巴特起初略显羞涩，稍稍学习过后，也穿着滑雪板猛冲下山。这就是阿勒泰人的天性。

二、图瓦牧民的滑雪冠军梦

阿勒泰地区的喀纳斯景区是蒙古族图瓦人在中国的唯一聚居地。

800 年来，在喀纳斯每年长达 7 个月的冬季里，图瓦人脚踏古老的毛皮滑雪板，身背自制的弓箭，在高高的阿尔泰山追逐猎物；20 年来，实施禁猎后的图瓦人并没有将毛皮滑雪板束之高阁，而是将它当做日常交通工具；2008 年至今，图瓦牧民在当地举办的古老毛皮滑雪板比赛中频频取得优异成绩，在新疆乃至亚洲滑雪登山大会上接连取得冠军。滑雪成为图瓦人新的凝聚动力，促使图瓦人思想观念产生悄然变化。

如今，图瓦人又有了新的目标：选派图瓦牧民去参加世界滑雪比赛。这将是图瓦人更大的光荣，是“滑雪”和“图瓦人”紧密相连的最有力证明。

那么，图瓦牧民的毛皮滑雪板究竟有着怎样的历史？图瓦牧民又是怎样走出深山参加滑雪比赛的？喀纳斯景区和禾木喀纳斯蒙古族乡对此项运动给予了怎样的鼓励和支持？滑雪对图瓦人将产生哪些深远影响？

这还得从喀纳斯景区禾木哈纳斯蒙古民族乡的玛力琴说起，从 2009 年 1 月到 2012 年 3 月，玛力琴 3 年获得 11 个滑雪冠军，其中包括由亚洲滑雪登山联盟和中国登山协会共同主办的 2011 年亚洲滑雪登山比赛极限组冠军。“玛力琴”这个名字几乎成为图瓦英雄的代名词，玛力琴说：“这是我们部落的传统，最好的猎人都在我们部落，滑雪冠军也应该在我们部落。”

我是 2009 年在首届“禾木杯”古老滑雪板狩猎比赛上第一次见到玛力琴的，当时他 31 岁，黑黝黝的脸上总是挂着憨厚的笑容，1 米 78 的身高，在图瓦人中算是数一数二的大高个了。玛力琴原是禾木村有名的木匠，从木头房子到毛皮雪板、弓箭，以及木碗、木头玩具，只要是用木头能做的他都会做。过去，禾木的图瓦男子都是出色的猎人，玛力琴的家族中每一代都产生过出色的猎人，对喀纳斯的山山水水熟悉得如同自己的掌纹。每一位图瓦牧民提到玛力琴，都会竖起大拇指：玛力琴，滑雪冠军！

图瓦人与雪有着不解之缘。村里的老人常常回忆 20 年前的情景：当地木屋的门清一色是朝里开的，早上拉开门，迎面就是一堵雪墙，男主人会铲出一条通向马厩的路，然后与马一起为孩子踏出一条上学的路。村里每家都有这样一条踏出来的雪道，错综的小雪道汇聚到主路上的大雪道，最后通向学校。我可以想象出这样的场景：二十多匹马在厚达一两米的雪地上奋起扬蹄，远远望去，唯见马头高高扬起，鬃毛飞扬；跑出近百米后，领头的马一声长嘶，往一侧的雪墙上靠，让出位置，后面的马立刻顶了上来，紧跟其后的是几辆马爬犁，几十公里路就这样踩出了一条雪道。

如果你问一个图瓦男人几岁开始滑雪，他会用手比划到一米高的位置：“这么高的时候就开始了。”你再问他到现在一共用了多少副毛皮滑雪板，他会很认真地扳着指头计算，最少也有四五副。玛力琴告诉我，他从四岁开始滑雪，如今已经用了八副雪板，算是相当多的。我故意问他：为什么你比别人用得费啊？他憨厚地回答：因为我是滑雪冠军啊。

然而，玛力琴的冠军之路并不平坦。

2008 年 1 月 16 日，禾木喀纳斯蒙古族乡政府首次派出牧民，代表喀纳斯景区前往阿勒泰参加第三届古老毛皮滑雪板比赛。当时，阿勒泰地区各县市共有 9 支代表队 80 名运动员参赛，禾木喀纳斯蒙古族乡的选手未能进入前 10 名，玛力琴的成绩是第18名。

玛力琴说："那时候我们就像刚从山里出来的马，没有训练过，胖胖的，跑不动。"

那次经历后，玛力琴开始加强训练，每天至少跑5公里。用他的话来说，目标是要让自己成为一匹冠军赛马。

2009年1月3日，喀纳斯景区在禾木举办首届"禾木杯"古老滑雪狩猎邀请赛。来自阿勒泰地区的5支代表队50名运动员参赛，玛力琴取得冠军。这是玛力琴的第一个滑雪冠军。2010年1月16日，玛力琴又在阿勒泰古老毛皮滑雪板比赛中取得冠军。

每得一次冠军，玛力琴都会得到一副现代雪板的奖品。于是，从单板、高山双板到越野双板，玛力琴都有。

比赛结束回到村里，玛力琴和村上的图瓦青年们一起相约上山，带上古老的毛皮滑雪板和现代雪板，练习更复杂的滑雪技巧。

禾木喀纳斯蒙古族乡为了挖掘图瓦人的滑雪潜质，2010年1月选送10名牧民前往乌鲁木齐丝绸之路滑雪场，进行为期10天的单板和双板滑雪学习。

学习期间，乡上领导得知1月31日将举办新疆滑雪登山比赛，便抱着试试看的态度派出玛力琴和胡恩台参赛。没想到，图瓦牧民很轻松地包揽了冠亚军。从此，滑雪比赛为图瓦牧民开启了一扇通向外界的大门。

2011年3月10日，由亚洲滑雪登山联盟和中国登山协会共同主办的亚洲滑雪登山大会开赛，共有来自亚洲各国的48名选手参加比赛。禾木喀纳斯蒙古族乡争取到两个名额，派玛力琴和托合达参赛。此次图瓦牧民也是代表新疆队出征，他们又一次包揽了冠亚军。

亚洲滑雪登山联盟主席、大韩山岳联盟滑雪登山项目主管柳汉奎先生对这两位图瓦牧民产生了浓厚兴趣。他说，在此之前，一直以为人类滑雪起源地在欧洲，玛力琴和托合达带来了家乡的毛皮滑雪板，他这才知道，早在2005年，国际学术界通过论证已证实"人类滑雪起源地在中国阿勒泰"。这不仅是玛力琴家乡的骄傲，更是亚洲的骄傲，当然也是滑雪人的骄傲。

中国登山协会新项目部部长李文茂认为，玛力琴具备了专业滑雪登山运动员的素质，而滑雪登山这项运动在欧洲成绩好的运动员几乎都在30岁至40岁之间。近几年，我国有关部门一直在筹备成立滑雪登山国家队，玛力琴将是首选的运动员，玛力琴的家乡将是我国今后选拔滑雪登山运动员的重要基地。

登山滑雪与毛皮滑雪板滑雪的原理相似，赛程相似，有利于发挥图瓦人与生俱来的攀登优势，为图瓦人开启了一扇通向世界滑雪赛事的大门。

接受采访时，汪海峰先为我们描述了第一次看到毛皮滑雪板的心情：震撼！

他拿着毛皮滑雪板翻来覆去地看，还跟着牧民脚踏毛皮滑雪板学习驾驭，当时就有一种很奇妙的感觉，认为毛皮滑雪板与自己将产生千丝万缕的关系。

汪海峰告诉记者，早在上世纪 50 年代，禾木牧民索伦加布曾经代表阿勒泰地区去东北参加滑雪比赛，并取得第 4 名的好成绩。

2007 年，在叶木盖山坡上，汪海峰组织牧民开展毛皮滑雪板赛事。当时，喀纳斯冬季旅游并没有真正开展，这次赛事只是为冬季旅游宣传打基础。

2008 年元旦，喀纳斯首届冰雪摄影节开幕。在此之前于 2006 年 12 月 15 日，《阿勒泰宣言》在北京人民大会堂向全世界宣布：中国新疆阿勒泰是世界滑雪最早起源地。

2008 年的首届冰雪摄影节刚结束，汪海峰就开始筹备去阿勒泰参加第三届古老毛皮滑雪板比赛。然而，未能进入前 10 名的比赛成绩，给了汪海峰一记重击。但即使如此，也没能动摇他推进古老毛皮滑雪板运动的决心。

在喀纳斯景区管委会的支持下，汪海峰开始筹备 2009 年 1 月 3 日的首届“禾木杯”古老滑雪狩猎邀请赛，同时为参加第四届阿勒泰古老毛皮滑雪板比赛积极做准备。

当时禾木牧民在喀纳斯景区铁列沙汗训练，汪海峰亲自陪同，并为牧民们鼓劲加油：我们一定要培养自己的滑雪职业选手，若干年后，在世界滑雪赛场上，将会出现禾木的图瓦选手！

这一年正逢温哥华冬季奥运会，汪海峰显然是话中有话。然而，牧民们只是一笑而过。直到 2011 年图瓦牧民取得亚洲滑雪登山大会的冠亚军，玛力琴和托合达对汪海峰的这一番话语才真正领悟。

2011 年 11 月 22 日，自治区体育局接到国家体育局通知：2016 年全国冬运会将由新疆承办。得到这一消息，汪海峰和自治区体育局体训一大队的郭志鹏书记不约而同地想到滑雪登山项目，提出将滑雪登山项目列入 2016 年全国冬运会项目。

郭志鹏解释，按照惯例，新疆作为冬运会承办方，可以加入新的赛事项目，而滑雪登山赛事正是新疆的优势，也是图瓦人的优势。

面对毛皮滑雪板的未来，汪海峰信心满怀：“过去毛皮滑雪板走不出阿尔泰山，即使走出去了，也只剩下表演的意义。但凭借毛皮滑雪板练就的滑雪本领，却可以走向冬运会乃至奥运会。经过一代人或者两代、三代人的努力，禾木的图瓦人一定能迈进奥运会赛场！对于图瓦人来说，其意义当然不是单纯的滑雪比赛了！”

禾木喀纳斯蒙古族乡隶属于喀纳斯景区，仅有 2 个村庄，即禾木村和喀纳斯村，共有 500 余户 2300 人，其中 54%是蒙古族图瓦人。

在以往漫长的岁月里，每年长达7个月的冬天，图瓦人沉醉于自酿的奶酒。进入2000年，外来的经营户开始在禾木村经营小卖部，销售几元钱一瓶的白酒。

喀纳斯旅游进入大开发、大发展时期后，禾木的哈萨克族牧民开始融入到旅游经营中，而图瓦牧民的生活却波澜不惊。

滑雪冠军玛力琴的两个哥哥阿得力和加尼木汗，滑雪水平与玛力琴不相上下，但他们不愿意进村居住，而是选择在距离禾木村10公里左右的也买盖提牧业点生活，家里的木屋建造在高高的阿尔泰山半山腰上。玛力琴的父亲特恩特克曾经是图瓦人中最出色的猎人，习惯了在深山密林中行走，也不愿意进入日益变得喧闹的村庄。对于他们来说，村上路修不修，电通不通，有没有自来水，电视信号能收多少个台，手机有没有信号，似乎都和他们没有太大关系。

然而，随着图瓦人频频取得滑雪冠军载誉而归，这一切开始了悄然的转变。

从景区的赛事到地区的赛事，再到新疆的赛事、亚洲的赛事，那副普通的毛皮滑雪板，成为凝聚图瓦人的核心。

住在自然村和牧业点上的小伙子们踏着毛皮滑雪板来到村里要求参加比赛，就连距离村庄最远的牧业点的图瓦牧民，也会前往禾木古老滑雪狩猎邀请赛场观看，甚至跟随参加比赛的图瓦小伙子们前去阿勒泰市，为图瓦运动员加油。图瓦人中最尊贵的长者用传统礼性，为图瓦运动员们祈福。

图瓦人仿佛一夜之间觉醒，认识到喀纳斯景区这几年的民生工程实施后为生活带来的方便。很少来到村里的牧民们，发现修建的公路真的很方便，从禾木到喀纳斯看古老滑雪狩猎比赛，以前要骑一天马才能到，现在坐汽车两个多小时就到了。就是骑摩托车，三四个小时也到了。

牧业点上的图瓦人还惊奇地发现，居住在村庄的人家每天晚上亮起了电灯，全家人可以在电视机前观看玛力琴他们参加比赛的场面，还可以看许多频道，以前电力不足时电视屏幕满是雪花，只能“听电视”的时代永远地过去了。

图瓦人还发现，当自家亲戚前去参加某项滑雪比赛，拨通手机就能知道获得的奖项。

对来自阿尔泰山以外的新事物，图瓦牧民从漠然到接受，滑雪赛事起到至关重要的促进作用。

看到图瓦牧民的转变，乡领导喜在心间。通过乡里积极争取，自治区体育局体训一大队新疆单板队教练和领导来到禾木，选拔走3名12岁左右的学生。2011年5月19日，在中国第一个旅游日，自治区体育局正式授牌禾木喀纳斯蒙古族乡为新疆滑雪之乡，同时成立喀纳斯景区古老滑雪队，首批队员30名，大多是禾木的牧民。

看到古老滑雪队的成立，汪海峰终于舒了一口气，但接踵而来的还有更艰巨的任务。

当 2011 年 3 月取得亚洲滑雪比赛冠亚军后，汪海峰就认为，是进行图瓦人毛皮滑雪板申遗工作的时候了。

2011 年夏季开始，汪海峰组建申遗小组，文字采集和视频图片采集同步进行。如今申遗在申报中，先地区后自治区，最后申报国家级和世界级非物质文化遗产。这些将和图瓦人参加世界滑雪比赛同步进行。

今天，当你于晨光熹微时走进禾木，在村里的山坡上会看到图瓦孩子们在玩单板；去图瓦人家做客，也可以看到四五岁的小男孩脚踏小毛皮滑雪板，撑着长棍子在滑着行走；走进山里，则可以看到高高的阿尔泰山上，两道雪板留下的痕迹从山顶一直延伸到山脚下。

这是新疆的滑雪之乡，是古老毛皮滑雪板保留最完整的村庄；这是图瓦人的家乡，是冰雪激情永不消退的地方。

English paper:

Skiing in Altay by Fur Skis

According to some experts' research, Altay in Xinjiang, China is the birth place of skiing in the word, and fur skis have been used for more than 10, 000 years. Mongolian Uriankhai tribe living at the south foot of Altay Mountains was the most outstanding in the use of fur skis, with the left branch Tuvas in Hemu Village, Kanas Village, Baihaba Village and the right branch in Handegate Township, Altay City. They passed through a winter which was as long as seven months by fur skis as their ancestors did 10, 000 years ago.

At the beginning, I came to this village hidden in the deep mountains for being curious about fur skis. Now I have gone there and back for over one hundred times and I never felt tired of it, and even wanted to stay there, living together with herdsmen. Whenever I entered into the village, Tuva aunts and sisters came to embrace with me, and their simplicity and enthusiasm could drive away cold. When I came back to the city, I would think in quiet how the black bees raised by grandpa Shukai were? In which family Lama was chanting scriptures? Whose fur skis Ma Liqin made for? Whether the girl Xinghua has got an appointment and waited to get married?

With the development of tourism, outside operators entered into the village. I felt a bit pity when I saw changes took place in this plain village. Fortunately, the village restored to tranquility when the winter approached, the snow was nearly two meters deep and herdsmen could go out of their wooden houses with fur skis, with two lines of traces extending to the foot of the mountains from the top.

Ⅰ. The indissoluble bound with fur skis

It was eight years ago when I met fur skis for the first time.

In the evening of June 6, 2006, I came to Bahaba Village where Kanas Scenic Spot was located for participating in the Aobao Festival which would be held two days later. After flow of the setting sun embedded wooden houses with golden edge, smoke from kitchen chimneys was curling upwards, cattle and horses at the roadside returned home in twos and threes, all were full of peace and tranquility. It was said that a number of Russians came to Kanas Lakeside more than a hundred years ago and they passed on the technology to build wooden houses to local herdsmen, and thus Mongolian Tuvas and Kazakh lived in wooden houses like these. I resided in a herdsman Meihua's house, she said: you hadn't photograph that triangle loft yet with smile when I took pictures of her house. Her husband help to carry a wooden ladder and I climbed up the loft, I saw a

storeroom which was filled with useless farm tools, old-fashioned furniture and old children toys. Meihua took a pair of fur skis covered with many inches of dust from the loft, and said it essential tools for transportation in winter when going out. Looking at this dust-covered tool, I didn't think so and I thought it was just a piece of wooden board wrapped with animal fur.

Just in that winter, I learnt to ski and knew the source of that pair of fur skis in Meihua's house. January 16, 2007 is the Memorial Day of the Birthplace of Human Skiing held in Altay City. The local people held a series of ancient skiing and modern skiing performance competition. Afterwards, a fur skis team was set up temporarily in Altay and I was the leader. Most of team members came from the neighboring villages, the youngest one was 18 years old and the eldest one 43. Our opponent was instructors; the two sides dispatch 6 members for relay race on the trail. When skiing down, the speed of the two teams was the same. When skiing up, our team membersran easily on the trail but those instructors skied very hard with in-toeing gait. An instructor put forward that skiing tools would be exchanged to break back. But fur skis were not easy to control, they tried very hard, but skis were stubborn as donkeys, remaining unmoved. In the competition of ancient skiing VS modern skiing, old fur skis finally won the game. Our tem members were very happy. Some of us went on a long journey for the first time. When they saw a train, they would ask me about curiously why so many people lived in a crowded city. How wonderful the village with a vast stretch of trees was! I think, perhaps, just because of their simple and isolated lifestyle, ancient skiing customs can be retained perfectly till today.

In all the townships and towns of Altay City, there were a few people who could ski or make fur skis. And in many herdsmen's family, fur skis couldn't be seen. However, in the village where Kanas Scenic Spot located, the making of fur skis was popular.

The road from Burqin County to Hemu Village where Kanas Scenic Spot located was not smooth, and it was blocked by the snow throughout the winter.

We only pass through nearly one hundred li of highway by sleigh. Two days later, I arrived in Hemu Village. When I recall it now, it was really like a test of life and death.

A local friend urged once and again before departure that the temperature in the mountains was −40℃, so be certain to keep warm. I was heavily armed before taking sleigh: wearing two suits of thermal underwear, two articles fleece coats, a article of professional down jacket, two articles of fur coats borrowed from local troops, a thick ski pants, three pairs of super−thick professional socks for hiking, a pair of large felt boots, a fleece hat, a pair of ski glasses, a pair of fleece gloves and a down−filled sleeping bag.

When I was on the sleigh, that kind of cold could be described as "ice cold". At noon, there was no sun, and the temperature kept dropping. In less than one hour, I got chilled, the much more thick I wore were not helpful. Wind penetrated through my skin like an awl, filled with my suturas and my heart seemed to beat as inertia. My only idea was keeping warmer to ensure my fingers and toes had perception, otherwise, they would be frozen off.

I almost lost a toe which was purple because of cold in the first afternoon. Luckily, I arrived at a herdsman's wooden house. The scenery on the way was magnificent, like an ink landscape painting. The long picture scroll spread with my footsteps: sometimes it was snow mushrooms, sometimes it was a line of rime and some times it was cedar and the grass at roadside was covered with crystal clear coat. When I passed by some households occasionally, wooden houses with smoke from kitchen chimneys curling up were in open snowfield, like those in a fairy tale.

I walked for entire two days in the deep mountains and finally arrived in Hemu Village. This village was surrounded by mountains and two line traces of skis could be seen on the slope, extending from the top of mountains to the valley, with hoofprint of cattle and horses. On the slope of village, a group of children were skiing with small fur skis and skis which were just used lean against the door of many wooden houses, I felt as if

I returned to Altay Mountains which was ten thousand years ago. At that time, people pedaled fur skis and slid a seven-month long winter. Lamabayir in the village said: "The snow in Hemu in winter was very heavy, we had to take fur skis when carrying back woods from the mountains for making a fire, or laystack from meadow or dropping around in neighboring relatives. Sometimes, we climbed up the high Hemu Peak with friends, singing old Tuva melody, and then slid down with the wind."

Hemu's starry sky was nice and twinkling stars seemed to be within reach. I liked listening to sound of nature deep inside the mountains by the village, imaging snow hare running deftly in the mountains for foraging quietly and wolf and fox inspecting their territory and hearing Ha bear's roar faintly…….

Hardships I made in those years I could remember vaguely. Today, the road leading to Hemu is smooth and it only takes four hours to arrive there. The convenience of the road attracts more and more ski lovers.

In many years of fur skis exploration and report, I met American Nielsen by chance, he was the most clinging skier I ever met. He was ever world champion and deeply loved the old skiing mode. He was a professional American skiing instructor. He had been engaged in the research of skiing history. He looks like only 40 years old although he was actually over 50, that was because he began learning skiing when he was 12.

A dozen years ago, Nielsen began reading the works of Davison on snow pedal written by a Canadian history expert in the 19th century. His most significant research achievement in his life was the recognition of the snowboard being original snow pedal. He ever found the oldest snow pedal in the world till today nearby Altay. He thought the Indians, Eskimos and Nordic emigrated from Altay Mountains. Later, Xinjiang Academy of Social Sciences drew the same conclusion, namely one branch migrating eastward and to America and another branch Europe after Central Asians migrating northward and to Siberia.

Before entering the Kanas, I have looked through a great deal of data about skiing in China. In ancient Altay Mountains, deer, wild horses, Baikal yak and koodoo run here and there. In winter, it was the best time to hunt and ski. And ancient Dingling people living in Altay Mountains called snow board as "horse hoof" or "goat hoof", which triggered Nielsen's interest. In more than seven years, he visited Altay continuously, and was firmer about his opinion that about 20, 000 years ago, skiing in Altay Mountains was popular, Indians completely retained the snow pedal when emigrating from Altay Mountains to flat America while indigenous people in Altay Mountains upgraded snow pedal to snow board in the course of hunting when passing through the forest.

A series of the research result about ancient skiing in Altay made Nielsen excited. Just like a migrant bird, he came to Altay, packed his travelling bag and pedaled wild snowboard with the interpreter Arken when winter approached. Sometimes, he would ski along the traces left by fur skis, or followed the footsteps of local herdsmen. Someone ever told Nielsen that indigenous people in Altay could ski over rocks of several meters high. Nielsen was dubious of it until he witnessed their similar excellent skills when skiing with several young men living in Hemu Village nearby.

Before the Spring Festival of 2013, Nielsen came to Axiabulake Village earlier and lived in Tuva hunter Bayan's house. Several years ago, Nielsen ever went up the mountains by fur skis with Bayan's two sons, Bati and Bate. For the juvenile living in highland at Kanas Lakeside, skiing was a necessary survival skill. Nielsen still remembered Bati slid down the mountains at full speed by pedaling modern snow board for the first time when he was 17 years old without any unfamiliarity; the 15-year-old Bate was a little shy at the beginning and also slid down the mountains very fast after learning how to ski for a little while. That was the nature of Altay people.

Ⅱ. Tuva herdsmen's champion dream in the skiing

Kanas Scenic Spot in Altay Prefecture is the only place populated by Mongolian Tuvas.

In the past 800 years, Tuvas went hunting in high Altay Mountains by ancient fur skis in 7-month-long winter and with self-made bow and arrow. Over past two decades, Tuvas didn't lay up the fur skis after the hunting was prohibited but took them as daily transportation tools. From 2008 till today, Tuva herdsmen have achieved excellent results repeatedly at the local ancient fur skis competition and won the title consecutively at Xinjiang even Asia Skiing & Mountaineering Exchange Conference. Skiing has become Tuvas' new cohesion and has promoted the change of their ideology quietly.

Today, Tuvas have a new target: selecting Tuva herdsmen to participate in the World

Skiing Competition. This will be great glory for Tuvas and will be a powerful demonstration that "skiing" and "Tuvas" are closely connected.

But what was the history of Tuva Herdsmen's fur skis? How did they go out of the mountains for the skiing competition? How did Kanas Scenic Spot and Hemu Kanas

Mongolian Township encourage and support this sport? What effect will the skiing bring to the Tuvas?

It started with Ma Liqin in Hemu Kanas Mongolian Township, from January 2009 to March 2012, he won the skiing title 11 times, including champion of X-sports Group at 2011 Asia Ski Mountaineering Competition held by Asian Ski Mountaineering Federation and Chinese Mountaineering Association. And the name of "Maliqin" was almost the synonym for Tuva hero. Ma Liqin said:" This was our tribe's tradition, the best hunter was in our tribe and skiing champion would be in our tribe as well."

I recognized Ma Liqin on the First Hemu Cup Ancient Snowboard Hunting Competition in 2009 when he was 31 years old with simple and honest smile on his dark face. He is 1.78m high, one of the top high in Tuvas. He was once a famous carpenter in Hemu Village and he could make wooden houses, fur snowboards, bows and arrows, wooden bowls, wooden tools and other wooden things. In the past, All Tuvas in Hemu were excellent hunters. There are outstanding hunters in each generation of Maliqin's family, who know about mountains and rivers of Kanas just as their own palm prints. Each Tuva herdsman will thumb up when talking about him: Maliqin, the ski champion!

Tuvas have an indissoluble bound with snow. The aged in the village always recalled scenes in 20 years before: all local wooden doors were opened from inside. There was a snow wall when opening the door in the morning, then the host would shovel a road toward the stable to send his child to school on the horse. This was the same for each family. All these small tricky snow roads lead to the main large snow road and to the school. I can image that more than twenty horses are running on snowfield in one to two width with heads up and horsehair flying. After running for about a hundred meters, the leading horse gives a loud neigh and stands near the snow wall on one side, then horses behind come over, next are several sleighs. A snow road is treaded in a few tens of kilometers long.

When you ask a Tuva man how old does he begin to ski, "Just when I was at this height", he will say with hand pointing out one-meter height. When you ask how many skis has he used, he will say four or five at least, counting seriously by his fingers. Ma Liqin told me that he began to ski from four year old and he has used eight skis, which is quite large number. "Why do you use them more than others", I asked deliberately. "Because I am a champion", he answered honestly.

However, his champion road is not smooth.

Herdsmen were appointed by Hemu Kanas Mongolian Township government to take part in the Third Ancient Fur Skis Competition in Altay representing Kanasscenic spot for the first time on Jan. 16, 2008. There were 9 representative teams totally 80 athletes in the competition from counties and cities of Altay prefecture. Athletes of Hemu Kanas Mongolian Township were not in the top ten, and Ma Liqin was in the 18th position.

"We just like fresh horses coming from mountains at that time, without training and fat", he said.

He began to enhance training after that, running 5km at least each day. The champion was regarded as his target.

The First Hemu Cup Ancient Skiing and Hunting Invitational Tournament in Hemu by Kanas Scenic Spot on Jan. 3, 2009. There were 5 representative teams totally 50 athletes taking part in the competition. Ma Liqin achieved the champion, which was his first skiing champion. He got champion again in Altay Ancient Fur Skis Competition on Jan. 16, 2010.

He will achieve a pair of modern skis as a prize for each champion. So he has snowboard, downhill skis and cross-country skis.

After returning village from competition, he experiences more complex skiing skills using ancient fur skis and modern skis with Tuva youth of the village.

10 herdsmen were sent to Urumqi Silk Road Ski Field for a 10-day study of snowboard and skis in Jan 2010 by Mongolian Township to exploit their potentials.

During the study, township leaders knew that there would be a Xinjiang Skiing and Mountaineering Competition on Jan. 31, so they appointed Ma Liqin and Huentai to participate as a trial. It was unexpected that they won the first and second place easily. From then on, skiing competition has opened a door to the outside for Tuva herdsmen.

There were 48 competitors from Asia taking part in the Asia Skiing and Mountaineering Competition held by Asia Skiing and Mountaineering Association and Chinese Mountaineering Association on March 10, 2011. Mongolian Township strived for two quotas for Ma Liqin and Tuoheda representing Xinjiang Team, and they won the first and second place again.

Mr. Liu Hankui, the director of Korean Alpine Federation Skiing and Mountaineering Project and chairman of Asia Skiing and Mountaineering Association, had a strong interest in these two Tuva herdsmen. He said he had always thought that the origin of human skiing was in Europe until they brought fur skis from their hometown, then he knew that "the origin of human skiing was in Altay, China" had been verified by international academic circles in 2005. This is not only the pride of Maliqin's hometown, but also the Asia and kanonen.

Li Wenmao, new project department director of Chinese Mountaineering Association, said that Ma Liqin has professional quality of skiing and mountaineering athletes, while excellent European athletes for this sport are among 30 to 40 years old. In recent years, relevant authorities in our country have been preparing national skiing and mountaineering team. Ma Liqin is the first choice and his hometown will be an important base for selecting skiing and mountaineering athletes.

Mountaineering skiing has the similar principle and schedule with fur skis skiing, which is conducive to play Tuvas inherent climbing advantage to open a door to the world skiing events for them.

During the interview, Wang Haifeng firstly described his mood when he saw fur skis for the first time: shocking! He looked at it over and over and learned it from herdsmen. There was a strange feeling that there would be a complex relation between them.

He told the reporter that Hemu herdsman Solon Gabe had ever taken part inskiing competition in the northeast representing Altay prefecture in 1950s and got the fourth place.

He organized herdsmen to hold fur skis competition on Yemugai mountain slope in 2007. This competition aimed to lay a foundation for winter tourist propaganda for winter tourism of Kanas had not really developed at that time.

The First Kanas Ice and Snow Photography Festival was opened on the New Year's Day of 2008. Before this, on 15th December, 2006, *Altay Declaration* was announced to the whole world in the Great Hall of the People in Beijing that Xinjiang Altay of China is the earliest origin of skiing in the world.

He began to prepare to take part in the third ancient fur skis competition in Altay as soon as the festival was completed. Failed to enter the top 10 of the competition gave him a heavy blow. Even so, this did not shake his determination to promote ancient fur skis sports.

He started to prepare the First Hemu Cup Ancient Skiing and Hunting Invitational Tournament on Jan. 3, 2009 under the support of Kanas scenic spot management committee, and also to actively prepare for the Fourth Altay Ancient Fur Skis Competition.

He accompanied with Hemu herdsmen and encouraged them when they were trained at Tielieshahan of Kanas scenic spot. "We must train our own professional skiing athletes. There is going to be Tuva athletes in the world skiing race several years later", he said.

Vancouver Winter Olympics was going to be opened this year, so it was obvious that there were overtones in his words. While herdsmen just laughed it off. This was really understood by Ma Liqin and Tuoheda until Tuva herdsmen won the first and second place on Asia Skiing and Mountaineering Assembly in 2011.

Sports Bureau of Autonomous Region received a notice from General Administration of Sport of China on Nov. 22, 2011 that the National Winter Games 2016 is going to be held in Xinjiang. After hearing the news, both Guo Zhipeng, the director of Sports Training Team 1 of Sports Bureau of Autonomous Region, and he thought the skiing and mountaineering project, proposing to list the project into the Games.

Guo Zhipeng explained that as an organizer, Xinjiang can add new project, and the skiing and mountaineering competition is just the advantage of Xinjiang, and also of Tuvas.

Wang Haifeng has full confidence in the future of fur skis: "Fur skis can not pass through Altay Mountains in the past. Even it can, it is only viewed as a performance. But skiing skill by fur skis can go to the Winter Sports or even the Winter Olympics. Tuvas in Hemu are bound to participate in the Olympic Games through endeavor of one, two or more generations! Its meaning is not just a pure skiing competition for Tuvas!

Hemu Kanas Mongolian Township belongs to Kanas scenic spot. There are only two villages, Hemu village and Kanas villages, with more than 500 families and 2300 people in total, 54% of which are Mongolian Tuvas.

Tuvas are intoxicated with milk liquor made by their own during 7-month long winter in the past. Outside businessmen began to sell white spirit in several Yuan a bottle in Hemu village from 2000.

Kazak herdsmen in Hemu began to manage tourism when Kanas tourism entered a large-scale development stage, while Tuva herdsmen's life was still unchanged.

His two brothers, Adeli and Jianimuhan, almost have the same skiing level with Maliqin, while they do not want to live in the village, but live in Yemaigaiti grazing station about 10km away from Hemu village. Their wooden houses are built on thehillside of Altay Mountains. His father Teenteke used to be the most excellent hunter among Tuvas, and he is not willing to live in the increasingly noisy village after accustoming to deep mountains and forests. Whether there are roads, electricity, tap water, TV signals or phone signals, these may have no relation with them.

However, all of these begin to change quietly as more championships are won by Tuvas.

That pair of ordinary fur skis has become the core condensing Tuvas together from competitions of scenic spot to the local, and even to Xinjiang and Asia.

Youth living in natural villages and grazing stations request for taking part in the competition with their fur skis, even Tuva herdsmen living most far away from the village will go to watch Hemu Ancient Skiing and Hunting Invitational Tournament on the site. They also even accompany with competitors to Altay City and encourage for them. The most honorable elder pray for competitors with traditional etiquette.

It seemed that Tuvas realized the convenience brought by livelihood projects of Kanas scenic spot during these years overnight. Herdsmen several come back to the village found that highways are very convenient. It cost one day by riding before from Hemu to Kanas to watch ancient skiing and hunting competition, while it costs only more than two hours by bus, and just three or four hours for motorcycle.

They also surprisingly found that there were lamps in the houses of village every night. The whole family could not only watch the competition Ma Liqin and other competitors participated in on the TV, but also many channels. The era of listening TV because of poor electric power has gone forever.

Tuvas also found that you can know his result by making a call when their relative completed his skiing competition.

Skiing competitions have played a crucial role in promoting Tuva herdsmen to accept new things outside of Altay Mountains from indifference.

Township leaders were delighted when they saw the change of Tuva herdsmen. Three students about 12 years old in Hemu were selected by coach and leaders of Xinjiang snowboard team in Sports Training Team 1 of Sports Bureau of Autonomous Region through active endeavor of the Township. Hemu Kanas Mongolian Township was awarded Hometown of Xinjiang Skiing by autonomous region at the first Chinese Tourism Day on May 19, 2011. Kanas scenic spot ancient skiing team was set up at the same time with 30 members at first, most of whom are Hemu herdsmen.

Wang Haifeng finally sighed with relief when he saw the establishment of the team, while there were more arduous tasks following one by one.

He recognized that it was the time to apply for world heritage for Tuvas fur skis after wining the first and second place on the Asia Skiing Competition in March 2011.

He set up an application team to collect words, videos and pictures from the summer of 2011. And now, the application is being declared from region to autonomous region, and then national level and world-level intangible cultural heritage, which will be carried out simultaneously with world skiing competition taken part in by Tuvas.

Today, when you walk into Hemu at dawn, you will see Tuva children playing snowboards on hillside; when you visit Tuva family, you will see four or five-year old boys are skiing on small fur skis supporting by long sticks; when you walk into the Altay Mountains, you will see traces left by two skis extending from the top to the foot.

This is the hometown of Xinjiang skiing, a village with the most complete ancient fur skis; this is the hometown of Tuvas, a place with ice and snow passionnever gone.

4.19 推动滑雪运动发展—吉林体育学院不甘人后 In Promoting the Development of Snow Sports, Jilin Sport University Makes Great Effort

赵志军 Zhao Zhijun (CHN)

个人简介 Brief Introduction

赵志军，男，吉林体育学院党委书记，博士，教授，博士生导师，吉林省教学名师，吉林省高级专家，吉林省有突出贡献的中青年专业技术人才，国务院津贴获得者。教育部义务教育监测项目专家组成员；吉林省教育学会副会长，中国教育管理学学会副会长。主编、参编著作 30 多本；发表论文 100 余篇。

Zhijun Zhao, male, Chinese, He is the party secretary of Jilin Institute of Physical Education, doctor, professor, doctoral supervisor, senior expert of Jilin province, the professionally young and middle aged technical talent of Jilin province who makes outstanding contributions and the State Council allowance gainer. He is a member of the expert group of compulsory education monitoring project of Ministry of Education, vice chairman of Jilin Educational Society and the China Institute of Educational Administration. He has edited and subedited more than 30 works and published over 100 papers.

论文 Paper：

推动滑雪运动发展——吉林体育学院不甘人后

大家好，我是吉林体育学院的党委书记赵志军，在2014年下旬我接到了单兆鉴老先生发出的邀请，心中非常激动，作为一个体育院校的党委书记，来到人类滑雪起源地深感荣幸。

小时候我就特别爱体育运动。对于东北人来说，冰雪运动是我们的天然优势。2012年我到吉林体育学院工作，不仅喜欢，而且有条件参加滑雪运动，对滑雪有了更深的理解。滑雪从人类的不得已而为之，到成为一种体育项目，再到今天成为大众运动、娱乐、休闲、产业消费的重要方式，体现了社会的进步和文化的发展。阿勒泰市政府举办本次古老滑雪文化交流研讨会，追朔滑雪起源，发展滑雪运动，传承滑雪文化意义重大。

今天我主要想通过本人的经历，谈谈对推动冰雪运动的感受。主要用四个词来概括：压力、激动、兴奋、期待。

In Promoting the Development of Snow Sports, Jilin Sport University Makes Great Effort

At first people had to ski for survival, then it became a sports event, and now it has become the important part of public sports, entertainment, leisure and consumption. The process shows the progress of society and the development of the culture. Altay Municipal Government holds this seminar on the old skiing culture to trace the origin of skiing, develop skiing and inherit the skiing culture. It's of greatsignificance.

一、压力

我到吉林体育学院伊始，要用一个词来形容我的心情应该是压力。吉林体育学院是吉林省唯一一所培养体育人才的专业院校，建院历史近六十年来，培养了100多名世界冠军，特别是冰雪项目更是成绩卓著，叶乔波，陈露、李佳军，栾正荣等一大批世界和洲际冠军。在上一周我校学生宁琴等又在全国自由式雪上技巧比赛中包揽三甲，包括我们这次会议的发起人单兆鉴老先生也是吉林体院最优秀的毕业生之一。

在这样一个有着辉煌成绩和悠久历史的院校，怎样能进一步努力，创造新的成绩、成果，做出新的贡献，我心中盘算的同时很有几分压力。

1. Stress

One word to describe my feeling when I first came to Jilin Sport University should be stressed. Jilin Sport University is the only professional college to cultivate the sports talents. Over 100 world champions have been cultivated since the university was founded about 60 years ago. The achievements are outstanding especially for the snow sports. Ye Qiaobo, Chen Lu, Li Jiajun, Luan Zhengrong and many other world and intercontinental champions have won the awards for our country. Last week, Ning Qin and other students of our university won the first, second and third prizes in the national moguls competition. Even Mr Shan who initiated this seminar is one of the best graduates of Jilin Sport University.

In such a university with brilliant achievements and a long history, I'm always thinking about how to make a further effort, to create better achievements and to make new contributions. At the same time, I feel kind of stressed.

二、激动

当我在吉林体育学院工作一段时间以后，再用一个词来形容我的心情就是激动。吉林体院借助地域优势，突出发展冰雪特色，为了更好的挖掘、保护、传承和发展冰雪运动，在我的推动下，2013 年我们建立了吉林省冰雪文化研究基地，后又被评为国家级冰雪文化研究基地。

基地包括冰雪运动、冰雪民俗、冰雪艺术和冰雪产业四个研究方向，每个方向也对应一个展览室，共有展品万余件，例如冰雪运动展室有古老冰刀、毛皮滑雪板、奥运火炬、奖杯奖牌等。

基地开幕式　Opening ceremony

吉林省冰雪文化研究中心展

Jilin Province Ice and Snow Culture Research Base

我们通过基地争取了科研项目，并开展了一些活动，收到了社会各界尤其是同行们的认可和肯定，为吉林体育学院冰雪特色发展助力，在此过程中我更多的感到激动。

2. Excitement

After I worked in Jilin Sport University for a period of time, another word to describe my feeling is excited. With the help of the geographical advantages, Jilin Sport University has made the snow sports as its specialty. In order to better explore, protect, inherit and develop snow sports, Jilin Province Ice and Snow Culture Research Base was founded in 2013 with my promotion and effort. Then it was appraised as the national snow culture research base.

In the base there are four research fields including snow sports, snow customs, snow arts and snow industry. There are altogether over 10, 000 exhibits. For example, the old ice skate blade, fur skiing board, Olympic torch, cups and medals for prizes. Through the base we did some research projects and implemented some activities, which got the approval and recognition of all walks of life, especially our peers. This has added more color to the special snow sports development of Jilin Sport University. During the process I have felt more excitement.

三、兴奋

2014年2月7日 习近平总书记在看望我国参加索契冬奥会的体育健儿时，讲了这样一个观点，就是受气候条件影响，中国冰雪运动还不够普及，不进山海关，关外才1亿人。如果在关内推广冰雪项目，会带动两三亿人从事冰雪运动。随着中国国内生产总值和人均生活水平不断提高，中国越来越具备普及冰雪运动的条件，更多群众可以体验冰雪运动带来的快乐。我们具备这个条件，如果能办一届冬奥会，就可以起到点燃冰雪运动火炬的作用。

总书记的这段话让我深有感触，作为北方体育院校，吉林体院责任重大，应该为中国冰雪运动的开展做点事情。

长春大众冰雪季大型冰雪公益活动 Changchun Ice and Snow Season Public Service Activities

2015年1月3日，由吉林体育学院主办的“冬奥梦、冰雪情”长春大众冰雪季大型冰雪公益活动，在长春城市湿地公园拉开序幕。

活动当天我们开展了千人雪地徒步、滑雪体验、爬犁赛、雪上拔河、抽冰猴、冰上自行车、滚雪圈、冰球射小门、冰上保龄球等15项具有传统特色，又具有趣味性的冰雪健身活动。所有活动项目都是免费的，市民参与热情高，参与人数万余人。

吉林体育学院有义务充分利用独有的冰雪资源，传承冰雪体育传统，推动冰雪体育运动的普及。长春大众冰雪季大型公益活动的举行，为更多人群参与冬季体育搭建了平台、创造了机会，也是学校在用实际行动助力我国申办2022年冬奥会。同时也是为了拉动冰雪旅游，推动长春市民进行冰雪活动，带动全民健身，达到增强市民体质的目的。能够为申奥出一份力，让我很兴奋，吉林体院人也很兴奋，整个中国都为中国能申办冬奥会而兴奋。

3. Delight

On February 7. 2014, when Chairman Xi Jinping was visiting the Chinese players who took part in the Sochi Winter Olympics, he talked about his ideas. Influenced by the climate, the Chinese snow sports are not popular enough. Only 100 million people are outside Shanhaiguan Pass. If snow sports are promoted inside it, maybe 200 or 300 million people will do snow sports. With the improvement of Chinese GDP and the per capita living standards, the conditions to popularize the snow sports are almost ready. More people can experience the pleasure brought by snow sports. We can do this. If one Winter Olympics is held in China, it will work as the torch to fire and promote the snow sports.

On January 3, 2015, the big-scale Changchun People Snow Season Public Benefit Activities named Dream of Winter Olympics, Feelings for Snow which were hosted by Jilin Sport University, were started in Changchun Wetland Park.

On that day, we had 15 snow and ice fitness activities with the traditional specialty and enjoyment, such as one thousand people snow hiking, skiing experience, sledge race, tug-of-war on the snow, top spinning, bike riding on the snow, snow tubing, ice ball shooting, ice bowling. All the activities were free and the people were very enthusiastic and thousands of people took part in them.

Jilin Sport University has the duty to fully make use of its special snow resources, inherit the snow sports traditions and promote the popularization of snow sports. Changchun People Snow Season Large-Scale Public Benefit Activities provided the platform and created the chance for more people to join in the winter sports. It is also our actual action to support our bid for 2022 Winter Olympics. At the same time, snow and ice tourism is promoted and the aim of encouraging people to do snow sports and live a healthy life has been achieved. It made me, teachers and students of Jilin Sport University, feel delighted to make our own contribution to bidding for Winter Olympics. All Chinese people will be delighted if the Winter Olympics can be held in China.

四、期待

在新年到来之际，我怀着很多期待，对祖国美好未来的期待，对2022中国成功举办冬奥会的期待，对吉林体院在传承和发展冰雪运动的期待。

在此，欢迎大家到吉林省，到吉林体育学院参观指导。

4. Expectation

As the new year has come, I have more expectations, expect the bright future of China, expect 2022 Winter Olympics will be held in China successfully, and expect the new contribution Jilin Sport University will make in inheriting and developing snow sports.

Here, welcome to Jilin province, welcome to Jilin Sport University and give us some suggest.

4.20 中哈两国哈萨克草原文化旅游合作的思路与对策 The Ideas and Countermeasures of Cooperation of Grassland Culture Tourism Between China and Kazakhstan

高春惠　Gao Chunhui (CHN)

个人简历　Brief Introduction

高春惠，女，中国籍，新疆伊犁哈萨克自治州文物局副局长，伊犁哈萨克自治州博物馆馆长。

研究方向：博物馆学、文物保护法执法研究。著有《在丝绸之路经济带建设中加强文物工作的思考》、《中哈两国哈萨克草原文化旅游合作前景探析》等。

Gao Chunhui, Chinese, female, is the deputy director of Cultural Relics Bureau in Kazak Autonomous Prefecture in Yili Sinkiang, and curator of Museum in Kazak Autonomous Prefecture in Yili Sinkiang.

Research direction: museology, research on enforcement of the cultural relics protection law. He has written "Strengthening the Thinking in Protecting Cultural Relics While Developing Silk Road Economic Belt" and "Discussions and Analyses on the prospects of Kazakhstan steppe cultural tourism cooperation between Kazakhstan and China".

中文论文：

中哈两国哈萨克草原文化旅游合作的思路与对策

中哈两国都有着丰富的旅游资源和巨大的旅游潜力。两国间政治的不断加深，经济的联系性和互补性不断增强，历史文化上的同一性和差异性为两国旅游业的发展提供了必要的条件。针对两国旅游业未来发展状况，建议做好以下方面工作：

一、以哈萨克草原文化旅游为纽带促进丝绸之路经济带的健康发展

文化是联系心灵的纽带，共同的文化可以产生共同的认同感和归属感。通过大力发展哈萨克草原文化旅游，使中哈两国民众感受到两者历史文化联系的源远流长，为习近平总书记提出共建“丝绸之路经济带”的“政策沟通、道路联通、贸易畅通、货币流通、人心相通”总体思路的“人心相通”奠定思想基础，推动丝绸之路经济带的健康发展。

二、以共同举办哈萨克斯坦“中国旅游年”活动为契机加快发展两国出入境旅游

两国互办“旅游年”活动，既是两国巨大的旅游盛事，也是两国发展全面战略合作伙伴关系的重大外交活动，将两国旅游发展战略提高到国家战略的地位。新疆和伊犁州各级政府和旅游部门应高度重视做好配合哈萨克斯坦“中国旅游年”的准备工作，争取将伊犁州作为哈萨克斯坦“中国旅游年”的分会场和国际游客中转基地，借助伊宁机场与北京直航的条件，承担从哈萨克斯坦到伊犁旅游区国际游客前往北京的中转任务；同时承担从北京等全国各地前往哈萨克斯坦参加“中国旅游年”游客的中转接待工作，以此拉动伊犁国际旅游谷乃至整个新疆的国际旅游产业跨越式发展。

三、配合国家开展全球性“丝绸之路文化大篷车”工程，以国际文化旅游产业合作方式提高国家文化软实力

一是建议国家文化部组织国内丝绸之路沿线十四个城市开展中国“丝绸之路大篷车”国际宣传交流活动。国内各城市每个城市组装一台文化大篷车，统一由国家“丝绸之路大篷车”组委会与丝绸之路沿线国家联络安排。每到一个国家的重要城市均开展社区中华文化宣传和艺术团体演出活动及文博展览活动，分别于所在城市和文艺团体开展学术交流活动，并签订文化艺术合作协议，为将来更高层次、更大规模的国际文化交流合作创造条件。

二是建议国家文化部、国家旅游总局通过上海合作组织，邀请丝绸之路沿线的中亚和欧洲国家，向中国境内的丝绸之路沿线城市派遣文化大篷车，向中国公民宣传本国为丝绸之路做出的贡献和本国的文化艺术，并与中国各城市和文化团体签订丝绸之路文化旅游产业国际合作协议，使中国公民能够通过丝绸之路沿线的中亚和欧洲国家的宣传，了解丝绸之路沿线国家的经济、社会、民族、历史、文化、艺术发展情况。

English Paper:

The Ideas and Countermeasures of Cooperation of Grassland Culture Tourism Between China and Kazakhstan

Both China and Kazakhstan are rich in tourism resources and have enormous potential for tourism. With the development of politics and economics, the similarities and differences of history and culture have provided essential condition for the tourism between two countries. Considering the future development of the tourism, here are some suggestions:

1. To promote the Silk Road economy's sound development with the Kazak Grassland Culture Tourism as a link

Culture is a bridge, so the common culture generates the common sense of identity and belonging. By developing the Kazak Grassland Culture Tourism, the people in both countries can feel the long history of the connection between our two countries, laying ideological foundation for the guideline of "the heart is interlinked" put forward by Mr XiJinping to "build the Silk Road economy zone together" through policy communication, road connection, currency flowing and heart interlinking and promoting the Silk Road economy's sound development.

2. To speed up the development of the in-and out-bound travel between two countries with jointly organizing China Tourism Year in Kazakhstan as a chance.

It is not only a wonderful tourism spectacle but diplomatic events as well for the two countries to organize Tourism Year for each other, raising the strategy of tourism development to the status of a national development. The governments and tourism sectors in YiLi and XinJiang should attach great importance to the preparations for the China Tourism Year in Kazakhstan, striving to make YiLi as a session of the China Tourism Year in Kazakhstan and the transferring base of international tourism. With the help of the direct flight between YiNing airport to Beijing, YiLi can transfer international tourists from Kazakhstan via YiLi to Beijing and also thepassengers from Beijing or all over the country to participate in the China Tourism Year in Kazakhstan, which can push the leap development of the international tourism in YiLi and even XinJiang.

3. To improve the national culture soft power with the cooperation of international culture tourism and the coordination of "Silk Road culture Caravan" project

On the one hand, it is suggested that China Ministry of Culture require 14 cities on Silk Road to organize international Silk Road Culture Caravan publicity campaigns. Each city is advised to exhibit a Silk Road culture caravan to cities in Central Asia and European countries on Silk Road with the cooperation of Silk Road Culture Caravan Committee and countries on Silk Road. On arriving an important city, an exhibition of Chinese culture, artistic performances and historical relics should be followed. And for further international culture communication and cooperation, it is strongly recommended that academic exchange with local culture organization be organized and cooperation agreement be signed.

On the other hand, it is suggested that China Ministry of Culture and National Tourism Administration invite Central Asia and European countries on Silk Road send Silk Road Culture Caravan to Chinese cities on Silk Road and international cooperation agreement of Silk Road tourism with Chinese cities and culture organization be signed, displaying their culture and contributions made to Silk Road and helping Chinese people know the economy, society, ethnic groups, history, culture and art of these countries.

4.21 中国古代北方民族滑雪狩猎文化与黑龙江冰雪丝绸之路变迁研究 The Study on ancient ski hunting in northern china and changes of Heilongjiang Ice & Snow Silk Road

唐云松 Tang Yunsong (CHN)

个人简介 Brief Introduction

唐云松，男，中国籍，教授，硕士生导师，中国体育科学学会会员、教育部人文社科、省社科、省教育厅项目评审专家；省直事业单位公开招聘面试考官；省冰雪文化研究基地教授、省滑雪研究院首席专家，黑龙江大学体育学术带头人。研究方向为冰雪体育产业、少数民族体育与现代时尚休闲运动资源开发，主编4部著作、主持完成省部级立项6项、发表30余篇论文，获省自然科学技术二等奖、省社科三等奖。

Tang Yunsong, male, as professor, master's supervisor, member of Chinese Sports and Science Academy, evaluation expert of Humanities and Social Science Academy of Ministry of Education, expert of Provincial Social Science Academy, and expert of provincial education department project; the interviewer of provincial public institutions, professor of provincial research base of ice and snow culture, chief expert of provincial ski institute and academic leader of sports in Heilongjiang University. The research direction is ice and snow sports industry, the minority sports industry and modern fashion and leisure sports resources exploration. He has edited 4 famous works as chief editor, accomplished 6 provincial projects, released more than 30 papers, and won the second prize of provincial Academy science and technology of n the third prize of provincial Academy of Science and Technology.

中文论文：

中国古代北方民族滑雪狩猎文化与黑龙江冰雪丝绸之路变迁研究

滑雪活动作为古代北方民族交通、狩猎必不可少的一种生存生活方式，滑雪狩猎是冬季狩猎生产中所采用的一种主要的狩猎手段，滑雪狩猎文化是一种世界范围的文化，并形成了独特滑雪狩猎文化带。古代人类滑雪活动密集遗迹出现在中国大阿尔泰地域、在斯堪的纳维亚半岛、贝加尔湖以及北美等地区。我国滑雪狩猎文化带从东北的长白山（白云峰以北）开始一直向北，包括大小兴安岭，最后沿着蒙古高原的北部延伸到阿尔泰山脉，这在当地民族历史文化和现实生活中都曾产生重要影响。用地方特产和冬季狩猎的经济猎物朝贡和贸易，形成了黑龙江冰雪丝绸之路，它促进了黑龙江世居民族与中原文明的交流、互补、融合与升华，在不同时期起到加强渔猎、游牧、农耕等不同社会经济类型民族间的交往，推动民族融合、经济繁荣、文化丰富、边疆稳定，推动中华民族对外开放。黑龙江冰雪丝绸之路以不争的事实说明，黑龙江流域是与黄河、长江中华文明的发源地之一。

一、中国古代滑雪起源

中国古代滑雪的文字记载始见于《山海经》，古代丁零民族是有文字记载，中国从事滑雪活动最早的民族。古丁零民族在公元四、五世纪改称铁勒，又称高车，公元六世纪被唐册封改称为回绝，公元九世纪中期，分为三支，一支迁河西走廊，两支迁新疆，《史记．匈奴传》记载其因战争的原因被迫于公元前二千年至公元前一千年初迁徙至西伯利亚和贝加尔湖地区。古代丁零民族是有文字记载，中国从事滑雪活动最早的民族，从事滑雪活动的时间不应晚于战国时期，地点在西伯利亚和贝加尔湖地区。丁零民族在不同的时期的称谓是有所不同的，随着丁零民族的迁移，与其他民族的融合，在不同的历史时期，丁零民族的滑雪活动有了新的发展。隋唐时期，从事滑雪活动的古代北方民族主要有丁零后裔都播、拨野古、拨悉弥部族，以及坚昆后裔黠戛斯和北室韦等部族，历经肃慎（帝舜时-战国）、挹娄（战国后）、勿吉（南北朝后）、靺鞨（隋唐后）、女真（宋后）。我国古代北方民族滑雪活动的区域大约在北纬44—58，东经80 一 148 之间，即西起阿尔泰山、额尔齐斯河和乌伦古河森林地带，东至日本海包括库页岛，北抵贝加尔湖、勒拿河流域，南达牡丹江、松花江流域的广大区域，17世纪-19世纪40年代，鄂伦春、鄂温克、达斡尔、赫哲等族继承了古代北方民族滑雪活动的习俗，并将这种习俗保留至解放后。鄂伦春族称滑雪板为亭那、鄂温克族称滑雪板为金勒、达斡尔族称滑雪板为肯古楞、满族也称滑雪板为恰尔奇克，赫哲族称滑雪板为克依俄勒或恰尔气刻、齐纳楞，每个猎人都准备一条桦皮船、一副滑雪板，每个家庭必须准备一个狗拉雪橇。

二、中国古代滑雪狩猎文化和贡貂制度的形成

滑雪狩猎文化是雪原、山林、狩猎生产三者综合铸就的文化，有平原狩猎、山岭森林狩猎。滑雪狩猎文化严重依赖自然环境，具有超稳定的内部结构，具有长期性、多元性。在地形复杂的山岭之中，在茂密的林海之中，在冰封大地的雪原之上，较之骑乘的马、驯鹿、狗拉爬犁、大轱辘车等其他交通工具，滑雪板具有无比的优越性。滑雪板非常实用、便捷，雪越大，越显优势。自古以来各民族都利用滑雪板在雪中行走便捷和快速的特点，在狩猎中穿在脚上追逐野兽。每年的十一、十二月到次年的二三月雪大、雪深是利用滑雪板滑行速度快、野兽跑不动狩猎的最好时节。野兽打得多，把两个滑雪板并在一起，制成了爬犁，把猎物放在上面，拉着滑雪板走。

狩猎猎物分为两类：一类是供人食用的肉类动物，主要以野猪、狍子、鹿和熊等；另一类是供给人皮毛的皮毛动物，如狐、貉、獾、灰鼠、水獭、紫貂。当天寒降雪，猎取细毛兽，兽中以貂为贵。只有有中国、苏联、蒙古产貂。在我国，貂主要产于大小兴安岭及长白山脉，紫貂喜居长白山针叶林与阔叶林混交林地带，气候愈寒则毛色愈纯厚，冬季有雪时行之，因有踪可觅故也。猎人于深雪中追捕，跟貂，张网捕之。作为特种经济动物，貂给人们带来巨大财富。貂皮自古以来就是向中央王朝纳贡交往的重要方物，在我国政治经济发展上起过重要作用。《后汉书》、《三国志》、《魏书》、《晋书》及后世史籍中均有记载，并时断时续，史不绝书。从肃慎时期（战国）起，弓矢（楛矢石砮）和貂皮就是东北少数民族和中央王朝保持联系的重要物质媒介。我国东北貂皮贸易在东汉时代就已经发展起来了，当时称之为挹娄貂，到唐代（7-10世纪），黑龙江和乌苏里江流域民族向外国市场贩卖的极为贵重的黑貂皮等商品大受欢迎。元代皮毛贡赋多用貂皮作基数，一张虎皮折50张貂皮，一张豹皮折40张貂皮，一张狐皮折2张貂皮。清初十六七张貂皮可换一匹马，实际上是把貂皮作货币用了，清朝进行了贡貂赏乌绫制度，是女真（满洲）征服者与东北边疆其他各族维持臣属关系的一项传统制度。正如在农耕文化的国度中向属民征收实物税粮食等产品一样，对狩猎民族所属居民征收兽皮，毫无疑问具有相同的作用。清政府每年动用数万金，自盛京解往之乌绫等件，还有对贡貂人设宴款待、颁发路米，是特殊的政治制度而不是商业贸易。其为为东北各族人民的贸易活动创造了必要的条件，不仅提供了丰富的货源，而且提供了集中交易的时间和场所。

三、贡赏贸易与冰雪丝绸之路历史变迁

中国传统的朝贡及贡赏贸易，有贡有赏，表现了政治上的臣服与归属关系，同时也完成了相互需要的物资交换，周边民族都能在中原得到丝绸及其制品，所贡之物与所赏之物及数量也与后来基本相当，中原朝廷与历代东北先民就有朝贡的历史。肃慎先民通过遥远的水路或陆路与中原商、周王朝已有了交往。据先秦《竹书纪年》、《大戴礼记》、《史记》等古籍记载，典籍中关于“肃慎氏之贡矢”“北土”贡品楛矢石砮足以佐证。黑龙江地区历史上的少数民族肃慎为了修好中原，于公元前2249年开辟的以贡赏贸易为主的黑龙江冰雪丝绸之路，至今已有4260多年的历史。《黑龙江省志．大事记》也有如下记载：公元前2249年（帝舜二十五年），分布在黑龙江东部地区的肃慎先民派使者前往中原地区，向华夏部落大联盟的首领帝舜贡献弓矢。历代形成了唐代渤海国贡道（有朝贡道、日本道、营州道和契丹道）、辽代海东青、金代鹰路、元代站赤与东北路、明代海西东水路城战及永宁寺碑、明钦差亦失哈十下奴儿干开拓东北亚丝绸之路、清代赏乌绫制度、戍边卡伦及丝绸之路。

“丝绸之路”是中国历史上黄河、长江流域的中央王朝与周边地区，并延伸到更远地区的贸易通道的称谓。中国历史上的丝绸之路主要有四条：西北的沙漠丝绸之路、草原丝绸之路、海上丝绸之路和西南丝绸之路。作为欧亚大陆频繁的政治、经济、文化往来的见证，丝绸之路不仅成为中国积极的对外关系的浓缩，也成为全人类共同的文化遗产，被纳入到了世界遗产体系之中。黑龙江冰雪丝绸之路经历了漫长而久远的历史进程，经过了多次的更辙变迁。东北边疆的少数民族与中原的历代王朝，就是通过这条交通线实现沟通联络、朝贡赏赉、商务交往。由于年代久远，时代变迁，这条经过无数次更迭逐渐形成的连接东北与中原的古老通道早已鲜为人知，许多历史事件也被湮没在浩瀚的典籍之中。但这条路是实实在在、真真切切存在的，它承载着松花江、黑龙江流域那悠远而漫长的历史，记录着跌宕起伏、影响深远、引起转折甚至剧变的历史事件。几千年来，黑龙江冰雪丝绸之路一直是连接东北边疆与中原内地的桥梁与纽带。

四、黑龙江冰雪丝绸之路线路

历史上黑龙江地区曾经有一条繁荣了几千年的“冰雪丝绸之路”。之所以称之为冰雪丝绸之路，是因为黑龙江地区每年有六个月左右的冰封期，无论是从黑龙江地区向中原朝贡，还是中原历代王朝的赏赉；无论是走陆路、走水路的商贸，还是各类人员之间的往来，都会有将近半年的冰雪路面，而中原的赏赉及商品以丝绸为大宗，黑龙江冰雪丝绸之路由此而得名。黑龙江冰雪丝绸之路是我国东北边疆与中原通道的最东北段。

这条冰雪丝绸之路主线依江而设，源头长白山的松花江汇入黑龙江，连接黑龙江中、下游，直通黑龙江东北端入海口的鄂霍次克海，再上库页岛的神奇之路，横贯整个东北大地的千里交通线，成为连接中原与东北边疆的桥梁和纽带。它是典型的平原河川，这成就了水路、陆路两种通道，蜿蜒曲折数千里，直通今天的库页岛。东北地区每年有半年左右的冰封期，独特的地理环境与气候条件，在这条遥遥数千里的水陆大通道上，夏日宽阔平缓的江面之上可用舟船运送货物；冬季则在千里冰封的江面上利用爬犁搭人载物，于是又形成了冰雪通道。黑龙江冰雪丝绸之路有多条线路，延伸、拓展的地域大致“包括今天的中国华北东部、东北部，内蒙古的东部、东北部，东北三省；蒙古人民共和国东部；俄罗斯的东西伯利亚的东南部和远东地区的北部（包括东北西伯利亚）、滨海省、库页岛（又称桦太岛或萨哈林岛）；日本的北部、东北部有日本（虾夷锦）；朝鲜半岛的北部和东北边远的地区”（温跃宽）。在这一广阔的地域内，不同历史时期，有过许多条以贡赏、商业和贸易为主的交通路线，由于从内地来的丝绸为主要货物，故有些学者将其称为东北亚丝绸之路。如果“以经纬度划，东北亚地区大致在东经 114°以东直至亚美分界线，北纬 38°以北的亚洲地域内”（温跃宽）。

五、冰雪代丝绸之路的当代启示

当年在这一庞大、交错的交通渠道上，冰雪丝绸之路上，居住在松花江流域、黑龙江中下游广大地区的我国东北边疆少数民族，利用舟楫航船、狗拉爬犁或马拉爬犁，通过这条交通线运送东北地区的东北三宝、稀奇珍宝、土特产品到中原朝贡，并带去了东北边疆的民间习俗、风土人情；而历代朝廷出于安定边疆、招抚边民的目的，以金银米粮、工艺饰物、丝绸棉帛作为“赏赉”，广布朝廷“天恩”，使这条天然具有文化色彩的通道具有了更多文化的侵染，并通过不同的方式呈现在世人面前。这条“路”是人类文明史和进步史的有力见证。冰雪丝绸之路再一次走进了时代，其海纳百川的博大胸襟，开拓进取的人文气质和文化底蕴将被再一次释放，其文化符号将再一次被世人揣摩，其价值将再一次得到弘扬和提升。

这有助于实现了边地与内地相互交流地域文明、丰富祖国文化宝库、传播中华文明之目标。冰雪丝绸之路上丝绸产品的交流形式不仅有由中国向域外单向输出的形式，而且也有互相交换而成为双向交流。在经济、文化上有很大的互补性，具有互相取长补短，共同合作发展经济的良好条件和悠久历史，而且这种合作的有效性也被历史所充分证明。今后我们应当发扬冰雪丝绸之路上形成的这种传统，在平等互利的基础上开拓合作领域。那么，东北亚地区的经济必将因有更大更快的发展而令世界瞩目。

2013年习近平总书记提出"一带一路"的战略构想建设，将其作为一项"造福沿途各国人民的大事业"，作为典型的泛亚贸易交通网络，互通互联和贸易投资是现代丝绸之路的基本尺度，是新式深度合作的新链接范式，冰雪丝绸之路在人类社会的经济、文化等各项活动中长期扮演着重要的角色，对当今东北亚的商品交易、人文交流都产生了深远的影响。

English Paper:

The Study on ancient ski hunting in northern china and changes of Heilongjiang Ice & Snow Silk Road

Skiing is one of the indispensable lifestyles to the ancient residents in the North of China for transportation and hunting. The culture of ski hunting is an importantway of hunting in winter, which is a worldwide culture and has formed unique zones. The historical relics of ancient skiing mainly appear in Altay China, Scandinavian Peninsula, Lake Baikal and North America. In China, the zone of hunting by skiing starts from Changbaishan Mountain in Northern China, passing Daxing'anling and Xiaoxing'anling, extending along the north of Mongolian Plat and ends in the Altay mountains, which plays a significant role in the history of ethnic culture and modern life. Heilongjiang Icy Silk Road came into being by trading and paying tribute of local speciality and prey, which promoted communication and unity between the native ethnic in Heilongjiang and those in the central plains of China. The zone also strengthened communication among the different ethnics in fishing and hunting, nomady and faming, promoted mutual fusion、flourished economic、enriched culture, consolidated the border areas and promoted the opening up.

There is no doubt that Heilongjiang Icy Silk Road is one of origin places of civilization of Yellow River and Yangtze River.

1. Origin of ancient skiing in China

Ancient skiing in China was recorded in ShanHaiChing, and according to the record of DingLing, an ancient ethnic, China is the first nation that undertook skiing. Ancient DingLing was called Tieke in 4, 5 DC, and GaoChe as well, HuiJue in 6DC, In the middle of the 9th century, it was divided into three branches, one branch moved to the HeXi Corridor, and the other two branches moved to Xinjiang Historical Records-The Huns shows the cause of the war and that they were forced to migrate to

Siberia and the Lake Baikal region in early two thousand BC to one thousand BC. As is recorded, ancient DingLing, is the ethnic groups of China's earliest engaged in skiing, skiing activities should not be later than the warring states period of time in Siberia and the Lake Baikal region. The titles of DingLing varied in different periods. With the migration and mutual fusion of the group, skiing developed greatly. During Sui and Tang Dynasties, the ancient northern ethnics engaged in skiing mainly are tribesof Dubo、BaYeGu、BaXiMi—the generations of DingLing,, and the generations of JianKun—AnJiaSi and BeiShiWei, followed by SuShen, YiLou, WuJi, MoHe, NvZhen. The area for Chinese ancient northern ethnics to engage ski activities is around north latitude 44 to 58, east longitud e 80 to148, that is, starts from Altai, Irtysh River and WuLunGu forest belt in the west, to the sea of Japan including the Sakhalin island in the east, Lake Baikal, Lena basin in the north, south of Mudanjiang, large areas of Songhua river basin in the south. From the 17th century to the 1840 s, the nationalities of Oroqen, Ewenki, Daur, Hezhe inherited the ancient custom of the northern national ski activities, and the custom was kept until after liberation. Oroqen people call skis Lingna, Ewenki call them Jingle, Daur—Kenhuleng, Man—Qia'erqike, and HeZhe—Keyi'ele or Qia'erqike, Qinaleng. Each hunter had to prepare a birchbark boat, a pair of skis, and every family must be ready to hang a dog sledding.

2. Ski hunting culture in ancient China and the formation of paying tribute sables system

Ski hunting culture is the production of snow skiing, mountain forest, hunting, consisting of plain hunting and mountain hunting. Ski hunting culture relies heavily on the natural environment, having a super stable internal structure, which has features of long-term and diversity. In the complex terrain of the mountains, in the thick of the forest, on the plains of frozen earth, snowboarding has incomparable superiority than riding horses, dogs, reindeer pulling sledge, big wheeled carriages and other vehicles. The skis are very practical and convenient, the heavier the snow is, the more superiority they will have. Since the ancient times, all ethnic groups have taken advantage of the skis in the snow, which is convenient and rapid, they wear skis on the feet while chasing in the hunting wild animals. From November to March in the following year is the best time to make use of skis, when the wild animals run slowly while hunters can ski rapidly. The skis can be combined together to form a sledge if the hunter gets many prey. Hunting prey is divided into two kinds: one kind is animals for people to eat, mainly wild boar, deer, and bear, etc.; Another kind is fur animals to supply people with fur, such as fox, raccoon, badger, squirrel, otter, sable. In the cold snow, hunt for fuzz beasts, among, beast with mink is the most expensive. It is only in China, the Soviet Union, Mongolia that have sables. In our country, the sable mainly live in DaXingAnLing, XiaoXinAnLing and ChangbaiShan Mountains, sables enjoy living in coniferous and broad-leaved mixed forest zone in ChangBaiShan Mountain, where it is cold, the colder, the better quality will its fur have. As a special economic animal, sables bring great wealth. Mink as tribute to the central dynasty is since the ancient times an important party, played an important part in the political and economic development in China. *History of Latter Han*, *History of the three Kingdoms*, *Book of Wei Dynasty*, *Book of Jin Dynasty* and the later history books recorded constantly that sables benefit economy a lot.

3. Tribute and reward trade with the historical changes of Ice&snow Silk road

The traditional trade of ancient China's tribute and reward trade is formed by two parts. tribute to the emperor and the reward from him, through which, it shows the political relationship of obedience and territorial entitlement (or the relationship of administrative subordination) . what's more, it also completed the need in exchanging the goods form both sides, the neighborhood nations may all get silk and silk productions from central China. The tribute and the reward had kept a balance in exchange rate of kind and amount, later on, it is almost the same. The central China government have kept a long term of being tributed relationship with the ancient northeast landers. The ancient Sushen people who had the trade relationship between central China can date back to Shang and Chou Dynasty. According to the Tsin Dynasty's works, such as "ZhuShuJiNian", "DaDaiLiJi", "ShihChi" etc. The archeological discovery of Hu and Stone Arrows from 'northland' proves what was written on the book of 'Sushen people tributes arrow' true. The ancient Sushen people in Heilongjiang district opened up the Icy Silk Road aiming at tribute trade in 2249 B. C, which has a history of 4260 years, only to foster cordial relations between Sushen and central China. it is also written in 'Heilongjiang almanac: Events' that 2249, B. C. (year of 25th Emperor Shun) the Sushen people, who lived in east of Heilongjiang had send emissaries to central China tributing arrows to the leader of Huashai tribe Emperor Shun. Throughout dynasties, there are Bohai State tribute road (tributing road, Japan road, Yingzhou road and Khitan road included) in Tang Dynasty, Haidongqing road in Liao Dynasty, hawk road in Jin Dynasty, Zhanchi and northeast road in Yuan Dynasty, East Haixi waterway station and Yongning temple monument in Ming Dynasty came into being, northeast silk road opened up by Imperial envoy Yishihashixianuergan, also, forged the WuLing reward and KaLun guarding the frontier system along with the silk road in Tsing dynasty.

'Silk road' is the name of trade route from central empire located in Yellow river and Yangtze river drainage area to surrounding area. There are 4 major silk roads in ancient China: the desert silk road in northwest, grassland silk road, sea silk road and the southwest silk road. As a witness of frequent exchange in politics, economic and culture between Asia and Europe, Silk road is not only an epitome of China's positive external relations, but also a legacy of human culture, which has been listed into the World Cultural Relic Reservation. The Heilongjiang Icy Silk Road has experienced a long history, throughout many times of changes. Through dynasties, people of ethnic groups in northeast frontier were using this route to achieve communication, tribute and reward trade as well as business activities. The road now is lost in the mists of antiquity, and many history of the road are lost in books. But the road is real, it carries the long history of Songhuajiang river and Heilongjiang river drainage area, and witnesses the dramatic historic events reaches far. For hundreds of years, the Icy Silk Road has always been the tie form northeast frontier to the central China.

4. The Route of Ice&snow Silk Road in Heilongjiang

There used to be a trade route prospered for hundreds of years called Icy Silk Road, for there are 6 months' frozen period in Heilongjiang river drainage area, so no matter how the tribute to the central China government, or to get reward from it, no matter by which mean the trade is made through, land or waterway, it also happened when all the people make exchange, there always would be at least half a year that the merchants were going on a road of ice to the central China, basically in exchanging the silk, and that is why this route is called Icy Silk Road. The Icy Silk Road is the most farthest part of the channel which connects the northeast frontier to the central China.

The Icy Silk Road was built along the rivers, from Songhua river whose source is in the Changbaishan Mount, flows into Heilongjiang river, connecting the middle and lower reaches of Heilongjiang river, through its northeastern mouth into the sea of Okhotsk. Then together with the magic road in Saghalien, the hundreds miles of traffic lines in the northeast frontier is playing a role as the bridge and link from the central China to the northeast frontier. It is a typical plain river, which formed two channels: the waterway as well as the land path meandering thousands of miles to the Sakhalin Island.

Every year, there are about half of the year is freezing period. This unique climatic conditions and geographical environment allows merchants to deliver goods through thousands of miles long channels, in summer on the wide flat river, by boats and sledges in the winter, forming the icy channel. The icy silk roads have many routes, which covers the land including the northern part of east and northeast of China, east and northeast of inner Mongolia, the three Northeastern Provinces of China, east of The Republic of Mongolia, Russia's East Siberia and Far East region of southeastern North (including the Northeast Siberia), coastal province, Sakhalin Island (also known as Karafuto); Northern and northeast Japan; north of the Korean peninsula and northeast rural areas. In this vast region, throughout history, there have been many tribute tours, commercial and trade oriented traffic routes, because people mainly trade the silk from the mainland, so some scholars called it the Northeast Asian Silk Road. If to show the area by latitude and longitude, the Northeast Asia area is roughly the area from 114°E until the Asian American boundary line, 38°N north the region in Asia. (Yuekuan Wen)

5. The Contemporary Enlightenment of Ice&snow Silk Road

In this huge, staggered traffic channels, throughout Icy Silk Road, the ancient Northeast ethnic minorities living in the Songhua River basin and the middle and lower reaches of Heilongjiang river, used water transport, sled dogs or horses pulling a sledge, carrying the Northeast Sambo, rare treasures, native products to the central China for a tribute trade, bringing customs from the northeast frontier; Through history, The central government for the stability of the border areas, and the purpose of offer amnesty and enlistment to frontier landers, reward them with gold and silver ornaments, rice, silk cotton silk process as " the emperor's kindness ", widely showing the central government's "grace", that made the born cultural colored channel infected more culture, and showing it by different ways to the world, This "road" is a powerful witness to the history of human civilization and progress of history. Again, the Icy silk road entered a new era. Its broad mind that all rivers run into sea, pioneering and enterprising culture temperament and culture will be released again, its cultural symbol will once again be the mysterious of the world, and its value will once again be promoted and enhanced. The Icy Silk Road would again help us to achieve the goal of mutual exchange the rich cultural heritage between the mainland and the frontier, the dissemination of Chinese civilization. The silk products on the Icy Silk Road in exchanging is not only by the Chinese to extraterritorial one-way output form, but also the exchange and become a two-way communication. There is a great complementarity in economy as well as in culture, with learning from each other, it provides good conditions for economic cooperation development through a long history, and the effectiveness of this collaboration has been fully proved by history.

General Secretary Xi Jinping proposed the strategic concept of building "One Belt and One Road" project in 2013, in a concept that "a huge undertaking of benefiting the people of all countries along the way", also building it as a typical Pan Asian trade transportation network, interconnection and trade and investment is the basic scale of Modern Silk Road, it is the new depth of cooperation as a new link paradigm, icy silk road plays an important role in the human society economic, cultural and other activities in a long term, have a profound influence throughout the current northeast inferior commodity trading, cultural exchanges.

4.22 新疆克尔木齐墓地出土双联器初步研究中探索阿勒泰滑雪的起源 The Tentative Discussion about Twin Ware Excavated From Keermuqi

鲁礼鹏 Lu Lipeng (CHN)

个人简介 Brief Introduction

鲁礼鹏，男，中国籍，生于1972年11月10日。1996年毕业于西北大学历史系考古学专业，同年7月进入新疆博物馆工作至今，现任新疆博物馆考古部主任、副研究员，主要从事新疆青铜时代至早期铁器时代文化研究。曾于1996年、1998年两次参加新疆且末扎滚鲁克古墓群发掘，2006年参加新疆吐鲁番阿斯塔那古墓群发掘，2008年主持温宿县博孜墩墓地的发掘。先后发表发掘简报、论文等20余篇。

Lu Lipeng, male, was born on the 10th of November, 1972. He graduated from Northwest University majored in archaeology. Since the same year, he has been working in Museum of Xinjiang Uygur Autonomous Region till now, and works as director and associate research fellow of Archaeology Department of Xinjiang Museum. He mainly engages in the research work on the culture from Bronze Age to the Early Iron Age of Xinjiang. He participated in the excavation of ancient Zaghunluq Cemetery in Qiemo County twice in 1996 and in 1998. He participated in the excavation of ancient Astana Cemetery in Turpan of Xinjiang in 2006. He conducted the excavation of Bozidun Cemetery in Wensu County in 2008. During his work years, he successively published over 20 excavation newsletters and papers.

中文论文：

新疆克尔木齐墓地出土双联器初步研究中探索阿勒泰滑雪的起源

关键词： 新疆　克尔木齐墓地　双联器　初步研究　阿勒泰滑雪起源

内容提要： 目前，在新疆出土的考古资料中，发现有一种很奇特的随葬器物“双联器”。这种特殊器物是在制作时均用质地相同的材质整体加工出相连的两件形制相同的器物，故称之为“双联器”。

1963 年下半年，前新疆维吾尔民族研究所考古组在阿勒泰县的克尔木齐公社发掘了 32 座墓葬，在 3 号石棺墓中出土了仅有的一件双联杯。

通过年代讨论，克尔木齐墓地出土双联杯当为青铜时期至早期铁器时代。在这个时期的阿勒泰地区，滑雪技术应该早已成为居住在这块土地上的人们在日常生活中必不可少的一项生活技能。

另外，翻检新疆考古资料，目前出土双联器的墓地除了克尔木齐墓地以外，还有鄯善县洋海墓地、托克逊县鱼儿沟墓地及且末县扎滚鲁克墓地等。

本文尝试通过新疆克尔木齐墓地出土的这种器物双联器，及新疆境内其他墓地出土的双联器，结合内地中原出土的类似器物，来探讨其内涵、功用及发展源流，并论述阿勒泰滑雪起源。

2004 年 9 月对阿勒泰地区进行的中外联合调查结果表明，在阿尔泰山丘陵地带发现了较多的旧石器时代晚期的遗存，距今 1 万~3 万年。2006 年 1 月年底在阿勒泰市举行的第一次滑雪起源地论证会结束后，在发布的《阿勒泰宣言》中的第三条已经“证实古阿勒泰人早在距今一万年左右就已经开始了滑雪活动。”

敦德布拉克岩绘画　Rock Paintings in Dundebulake

因此，可以说阿勒泰地区在旧石器时代的中晚期就已经有了居民活动，而且至迟在距今一万年左右就开始了滑雪狩猎经济。狩猎是一种非常古老的生产方式，而且在整个旧石器时代的第四纪期间，因受自然环境的制约，阿尔泰山地居民都是以狩猎经济为生的。至于新石器时代，分布在地势平坦的河流沿岸的居民，在保留滑雪狩猎习俗的同时，也发展了渔猎经济，如哈巴河县的额尔齐斯河沿岸。直到春秋时期马具的出土，证明阿勒泰地区的居民已经逐渐走上了游牧经济的道路，而滑雪狩猎则渐趋衰落，成为日常生活中辅助性的生产方式。

English Paper:

The Tentative Discussion about Twin Ware Excavated From Keermuqi Cemetery in Xinjiang

Key Word: Xinjiang Keermuqi cemetery Twin ware Tentative discussion origin of skiing in Altay

Abstract: So far, among the archaeological materials in Xinjiang province, there is a unique funeral object—twin ware. A same piece of material was used to make two joined identical wares. So we call it "twin ware".

In the lower half year of 1963, the archaeological group of the former Xinjiang Uygur National Institute excavated 32 tombs in Keermuqi commune. A twin stone cup was found in the stone coffin of tomb No. 3.

Through the argumentation about the time, the time of the couple-connected stone cups unearthed from Kermuqi Cemetery was from the Bronze Age to the early Stone Age. During this period, the ski technique in Altay had become an inseparable part of the locals' daily life.

Twin ware also was unearthed in other cemeteries, such as Yanghai cemetery in Shanshan County, Yuergou cemetery in Tuokexun County and Zagunluke cemetery in Qiemo County.

By comparing the twin stone cup of Keermuqi with other twin wares found in other cemeteries both in Xinjiang and in central China, this article tries to discuss the connotation, function, origin and development of twin ware, and make an exploration about the origin of skiing in Altay.

In September 2004, a joint investigation result by Chinese and foreign experts shows that these remains in the Old Stone Age, discovered in the Altai Mountains foothills, has a history dating back to 10000-30000 years ago (38). At the end of January 2006, after the first discussion meeting on the origin of skiing held in Altay, the article 3 from *Altay Declaration* has confirmed that the ancient Altay people have started skiing activities as early as ten thousand years or so ago.

Therefore, it is fair to say there already has residence activities in Altay region at the middle of Old Stone Age, and at least starting hunting economy around ten thousand years ago. Hunting is a very old way of production, and in the old Stone Age of the Quaternary period the Altai Mountains residents are mainly engaged in hunting economy because of the restriction of the natural environment. As for the New Stone Age, residents distributing in the flat river coast, have saved the tradition of skiing and also developed the fishing and hunting economy, such as Irtysh River coast in Habahe county. Until the unearthed harness in the Spring and Autumn period, that has demonstrated that residents of Altay region has gradually stepped on the path of nomadic economy. Then skiing hunting gradually declines, becoming accessory production mode in daily life.

4.23　雪面上滑雪雕刻的弧线　CUrves On The Ski-Carving on Snow

阿诺·科莱恩（奥地利）　Arno Klien（AUT）

个人简介　Personal information

Arno Klien was born in the heart of the Wine quarter" in Lower Austria in 1940. His father, originating from the Alpine region in Western Austria, was a childhood friend of Anton Kaestle, the famous racing ski-producer in Vorarlberg.

Arno Klien studied geography and sports science at Vienna University. Subsequently he worked as a coach for track and field as well as for basketball.

Together with his wife he was the first skiers couple to be awarded the Austrian ski instructor's license.

For over 30 years Arno Klien has been involved in Telemark-skiing, He taught the technique at Vienna Universty where he developed the process of state - examations. Furthermore, Klien undertook methodical and biomechanical research in freeheel-skiing, in historical skiing movies and skiing history. He shared his expertise as a speaker at 5 INTERSKI-congresses and as the author of three books as well as of numerous articles.

阿诺克莱恩，男，1940 年出生于下奥地利州“葡萄酒节”中心地区。

阿诺克莱恩在维也纳大学学习地理和运动科学。

他和他的妻子是奥地利第一对获得滑雪教练执照的夫妇。

克莱恩采用了系统的生物力学方法来研究随心所欲的滑雪方式，研究历史性的滑雪电影和滑雪历史。

作为三本滑雪书籍及大量滑雪文章的作者，他在第五届国际滑雪大会上作为嘉宾和大家分享了自己的专业知识。

Speech 发言稿

编者说明：

这是阿诺·科莱恩先生提供的珍贵的滑雪历史图片，由于历史久远，内涵深邃，标注的语种多，一般的翻译难于胜任并难以保障原意，故此文基本按原稿收录于此。

Editor's note：

These are Mr Arno Klien's precious skiing historical pictures，but many translations of them are beyond his original meaning because of long history，deep content and various connotation. Therefore，this article is compiled according to his original manuscript.

CURVES on SKIS

CARVING on SNOW

Evolution

of

Hardware and Software

Origin of Skis

Bindings

Qualities，Attributes

Curves…

Skiing / Carving…

雪板上的曲线

雪上的卡宾

硬件软件双改革

固定器质量，特性，曲线…

滑雪/卡宾…

7-6. Millenium BC：Vis / Russia（Burov/1959，2004）

6300 BC：Lake Sandor / Russia

5100 BC：Oldest Ski /Vefsn Nordland Ski / NOR（Steinar Sörenson）

4000 BC：Rock carvings from Böla / NOR（Rune Flaten）

3000 BC：Kalvträsk / Sweden

2500 BC：Hoting / Sweden

3000-2500 BC：Rödöy / NOR……

公元前 7-6 世纪：俄罗斯 Vis（Burov/1959，2004）

公元前 6300 年：俄罗斯 Sandor 湖

公元前 5100 年：最古老雪板/ Vefsn Nordland 雪板/挪威（Steinar Sörenson）

公元前 4000 年：来自 Böla 的岩刻画 Rock carvings/挪威（Rune Flaten）

公元前 3000 年：瑞典 Kalvträsk

公元前 2500 年：瑞典 Hoting

公元前 3000-2500 年：挪威 Rödöy……

……

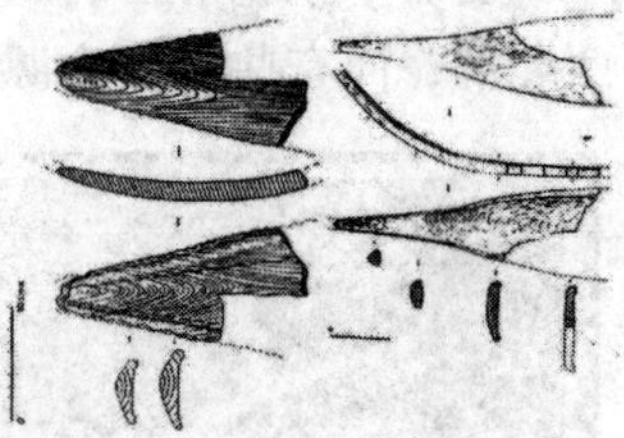

Oldest Skis（Burov 1959，2004）

Russland / Vis

Mesolithikum 7-6. Millenium BC

最古老的雪板（Burov 1959，2004）

俄罗斯/ Vis

公元前 7-6 世纪中石器时代

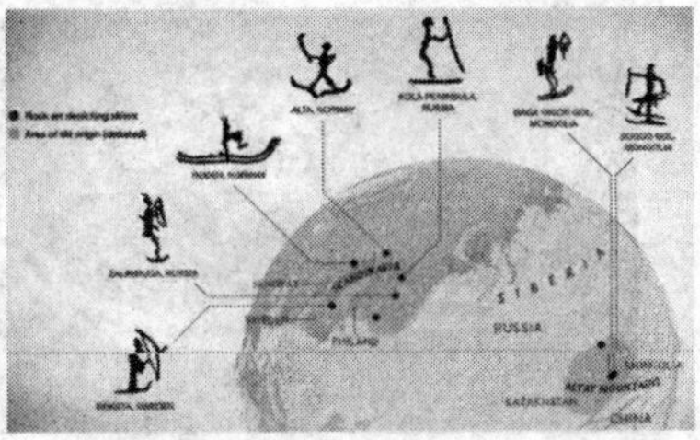

>>> **RÖDÖY**！

描绘滑雪者的岩画艺术

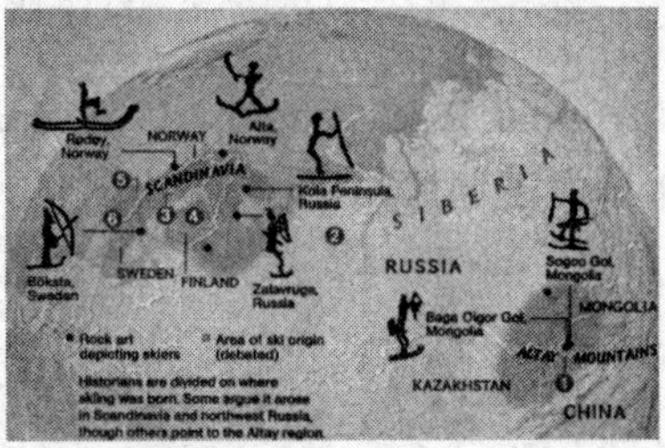

滑雪起源地区（有争论）

Skihaserl of Rödöy ca. 2500-3000 BC
Rödöyca 的滑雪初学者：约公元前 2500-3000 年

Almost same time：in Moors：HOTING and KALVTRÄSK Sweden 4500 and 5500 Years old

几乎同一时期，在瑞典的 HOTING 和 KALVTRÄSK 也发现了滑雪文化痕迹，距今 4500 至 5500 年。

历史学家就滑雪的诞生地有分歧，一些人认为起源于斯堪的纳维亚和俄罗斯西北部，而有些人认为源于阿勒泰地区。

Camber nice high Shovel Twin Tipps Skiing Position，Downhill Well bent Joints
拱形滑板 前端高翘 双翘滑板用于高山滑雪，弧形固定器

The original Rock Carving revealed 1929
1929 年发现原版岩石雕刻

4. Century AD：Villa Romana del Casale lose to Piazza Armerina，Sicilia
公元 4 世纪：靠近西西里岛亚美林娜小镇的卡萨莱古罗马别墅

Powderski　1300 Years old　172cm　145mm　Leatherstraps　Oppland fot. /NOR　Rune Hole Powderski
1300 年历史　长 172cm　宽 145mm　皮带式固定　发现于奥普兰郡/挪威神秘洞穴

Leonardo da Vinci　1452-1519
列奥纳多·达·芬奇　1452-1519

Fridtjof Nansen　Snowsailing　1888/89
伟大的探险家弗里德约夫·南森雪上航行　1888/89 年

BINDINGS:

固定器:

除了上文中提到的皮带式固定器（Leatherstraps）之外，研究中还发现了各类材质的固定器:

Willowtwigs:

柳条固定器:

Sondr A. Norheim ca. 1860

Meerrohr, "Rohrstaberl" reed

Metal-Toepiece:

镶有防磨金属的鞋头的固定器:

Huitfeldt 1897（1894）
Lilienfeld-Steelplate-Binding
Huitfeldt 1897（1894）
利林菲尔德钢板固定器

图片为配带靴子和不配带靴子情况下的固定器外观

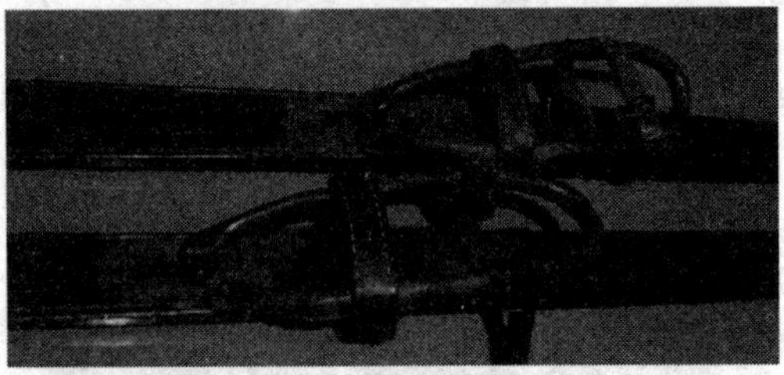

Rohrstaberl - Binding：Franz Reisch with Skis up the Kitzbüheler Horn 1893
Rohrstaberl 固定器：1893 年发现基茨比尔山

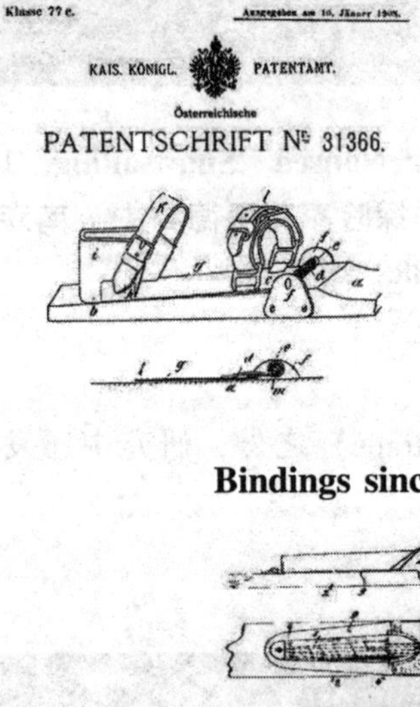

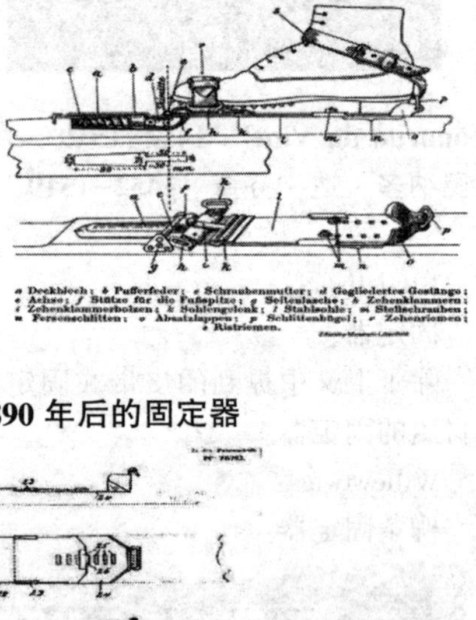

Bindings since 1890 1890 年后的固定器

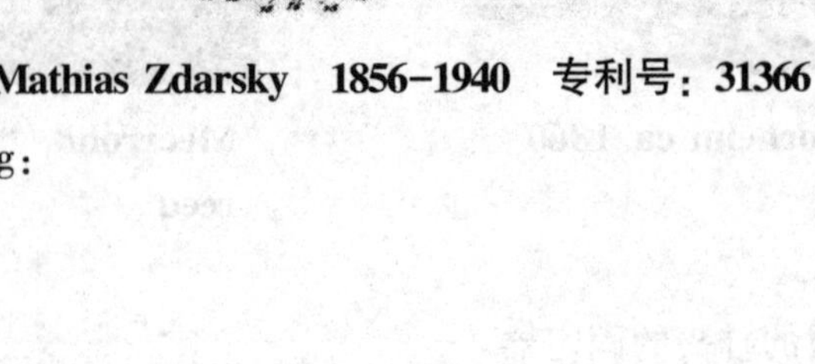

Mathias Zdarsky 1856-1940 专利号：31366

Military-Binding：
军事固定器：

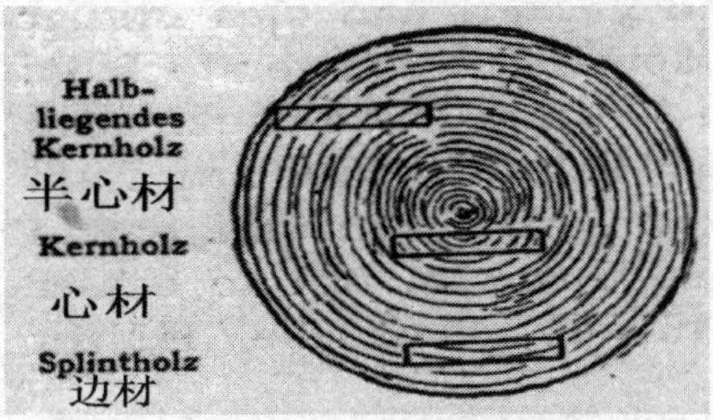

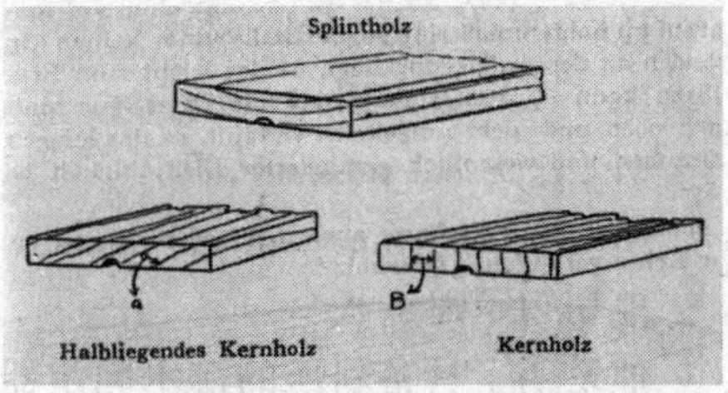

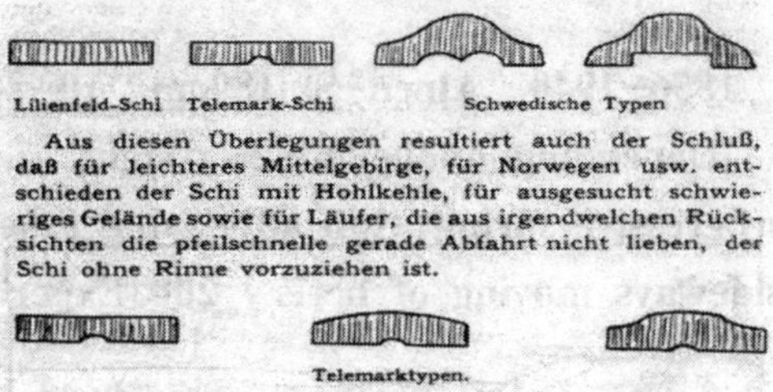

Aus diesen Überlegungen resultiert auch der Schluß, daß für leichteres Mittelgebirge, für Norwegen usw. entschieden der Schi mit Hohlkehle, für ausgesucht schwieriges Gelände sowie für Läufer, die aus irgendwelchen Rücksichten die pfeilschnelle gerade Abfahrt nicht lieben, der Schi ohne Rinne vorzuziehen ist.

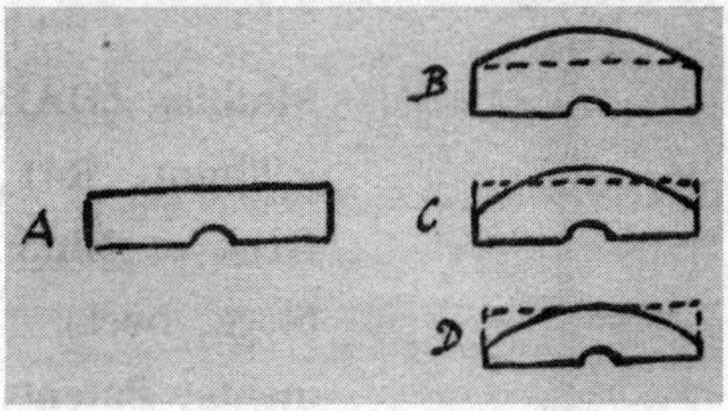

由这些想法可得出结论，带弧形饰的滑雪板适用于小的山丘、挪威以及其他地区。对于极其困难的山地以及出于任何的考虑不喜欢极速的顺坡滑行的运动者更喜欢不带凹槽的滑雪板。

The CURVEs on Skis

滑雪板上的历史人物

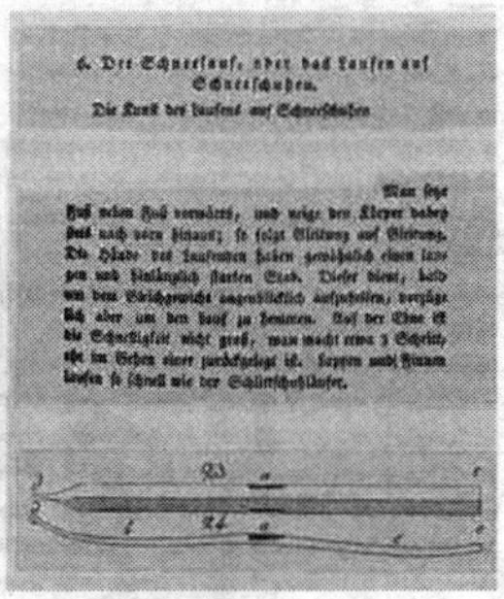

6. Der Schneelauf, oder das Laufen auf Schneeschuhen.

Die Kunst des Laufens auf Schneeschuhen

C. F. GutsMuths：1804

Urcarver　最早的卡宾滑雪板（1825-1897）

Sondre A. NORHEIM ca. 1860　L 235cm，84-69-76mm，Side-cut，15mm>R=74m 长 235cm，84-69-76mm，三围 15mm>R=74m

He cut-shortened the skis
He invented Willow-Binding
with diagonal pressure
He skied for fun, with the Kids…
他切短了滑雪板
他发明了具备斜压的柳木固定器
他和小孩一起滑雪，对他来说，滑雪只是为了好玩。

Mathias ZDARSKY 1856-1940 Alpen-Ski180cm 10-80-90mm, R41, 6m Depending on height & weight, no Groove Binding: progressive spring, full adjustable (toe-piece, heel) no sideways moving of heels 200 Experiments, Patents…

Mathias ZDARSKY1856-1940 高山滑雪板：长度 180cm，10-80-90mm，R41，6m，取决于高度和重量，无凹槽
固定器：改良型弹簧，安全可调节（鞋头，脚后跟），鞋跟不向侧边移动，200 项实验，专利……

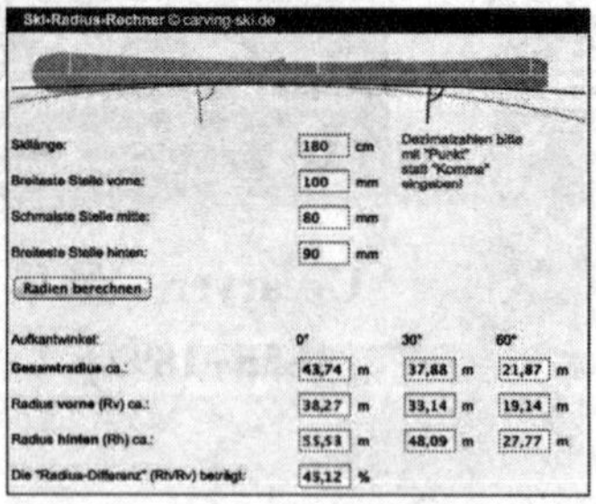

Alpen-Ski 高山滑雪

Mathias Zdarsky
since 1893

- Shortened the Norwegian Skis to some Standard
- as for do-it-yourself
- Variable for individual Bodymass and Weight
- No groove on the running surface！（>> Gleitski，Fahrski）
- 100-80-90 mm
- L 180 cm，R 41，6m

Mathias Zdarsky
自 1893 年起

- 按照一定标准缩短挪威滑雪板
- 同时也确定个人手工做板的标准
- 根据体重有多样的选择
- 雪板表层无凹槽（>> Gleitski，Fahrski）
- 100-80-90mm
- 长 180cm，R=41，6m

Etbin Henrik，Schollmayer，Klagenfurt 1893

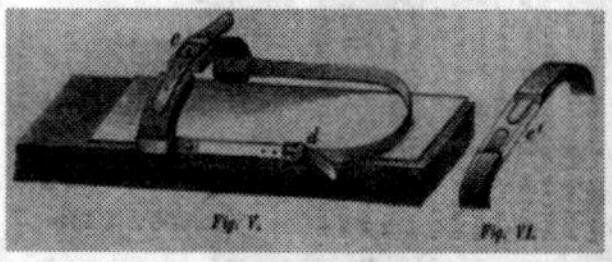

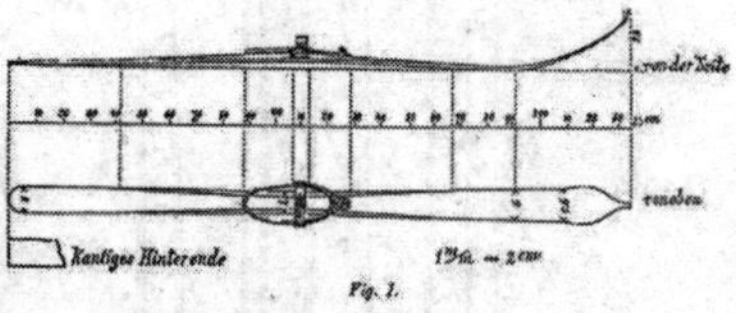

L 235cm，90-70-80mm，R 62m（74，56 Overall-Radius）
长 235cm，90-70-80mm，半径 62m（74，56 整体半径）

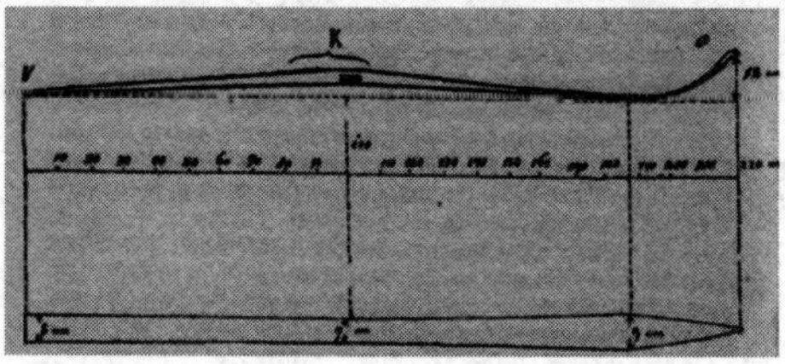

Hungary 1896：90 - 70 - 80mm，L 220cm Wood：in Center f. ex. 30mm thick R 65，34 m > 56，59 m（30°）> 32，67 m（60°）

匈牙利 1896：90-70-80mm，长 220cm 木制：中部 30 mm 厚度 半径：65，34m>56，59m（30°）> 32，67m（60°）

1922：EDSBYN-SKI CARVER　117mm　96　114
L= 178，5cm，R=28，5m，Oct. 2002，Vienna 1922
埃斯宾-卡宾滑雪板　117mm　96　114　长=178，5cm　半径=28，5m　2002年10月，维也纳

Rudolf Lettner：Steel-Edges：Patent 1926
Rudolf Lettner：钢边：专利 1926 年

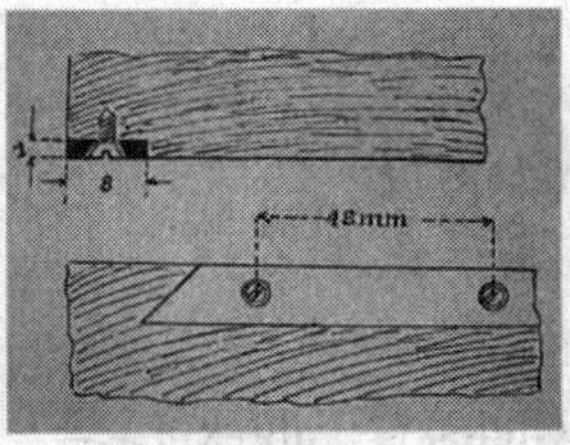

Edges-sharpen-machine　磨边机器

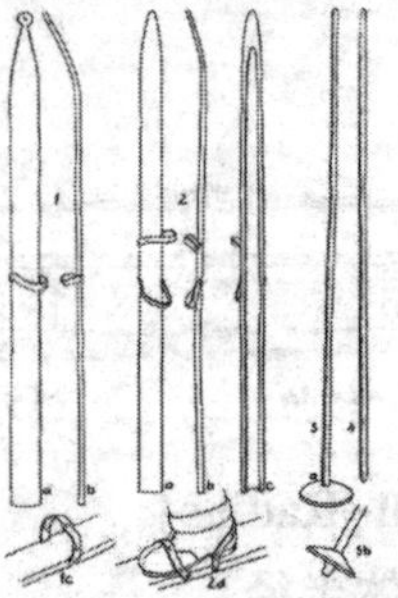

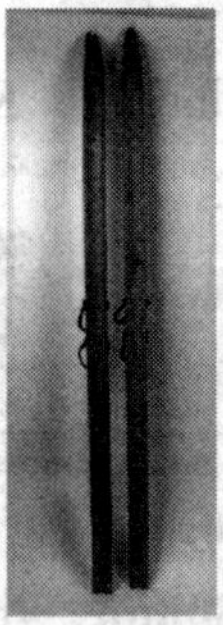

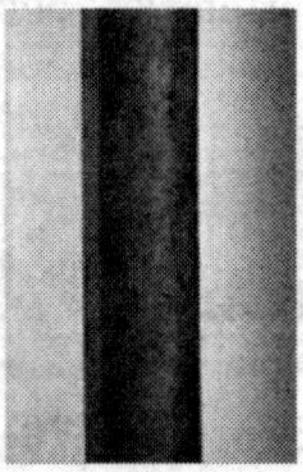

Pohorje-Skis　Pohorje-滑雪板　Running Surface　流线型表面处理工艺

The CURVEs on Skis　滑雪板上的历史

AAndré Girier 1983　安德烈 吉利耶 1983 年

Since 1992 Fa. Lacroix：
Patent for asymmetric Waist（Morpho Logic Concept）-Also Fa. Aasnes/N
Since 1995 Fa. Fischer（Gottschlich）：
Radarc；til 2002 produced；and again since 2004
Oktober 2001 found in France：

Urcarver of Abel Rossignol, Voiron (1909):

91-65-78mm, L 170 cm, R=28m

Fa. Lacroix：始于 1992 年，不对称腰部专利（变形逻辑概念），

Fa. Aasnes/N 原理相同

Fa. Fischer (Gottschlich)：始于 1995 年

Radarc2002 年生产：2004 年再一次生产

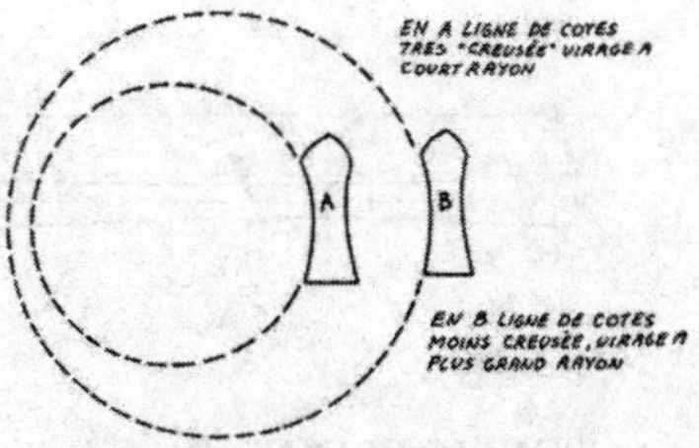

2001 年 10 月在法国发现 Abel Rossignol, Voiron (1909) 古老的卡宾滑雪板，91-65-78mm，长 170cm，半径=28m

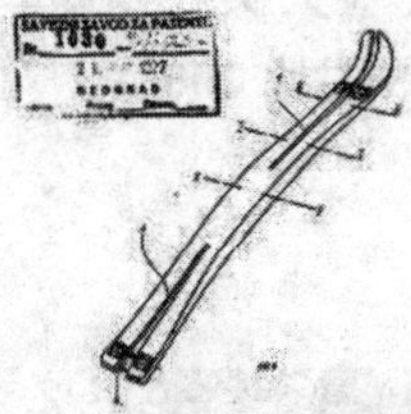

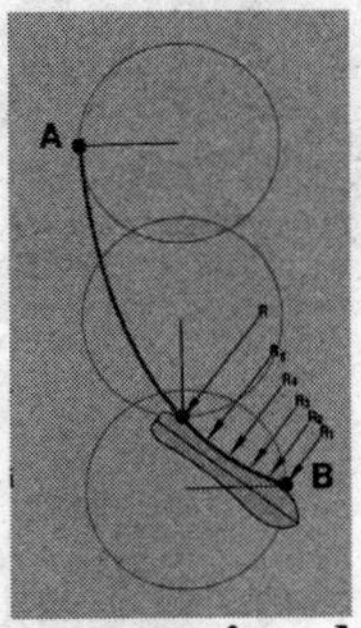

VSS-Variable Sidecut System

VSS-可变侧切系统

ELAN Andrej Robic 1977

Multiradial: progressiv, degressiv…

转弯半径：多半径结构，半径持续递减

UR-SNOWRIDER Reinhard Fischer

初期的（大头板）滑雪板

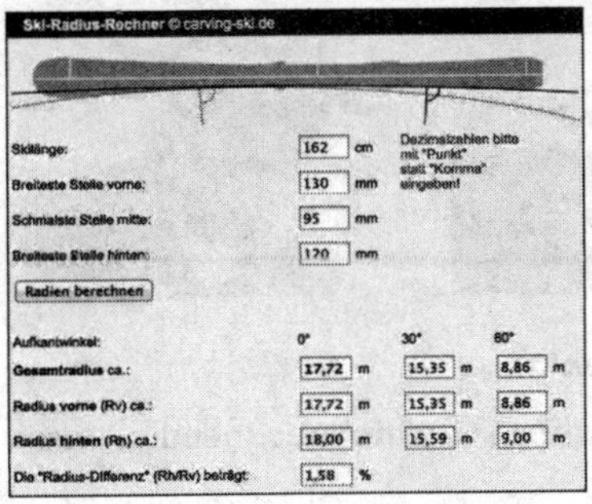

雪板长：162cm 前端最宽处：130mm 中间最窄处：95mm 尾部最宽处：120mm

半径尺寸

边角弧度：0°，30°，60° 整体半径：约 17.72m，15.35m，8.86m 前端半径（Rh）：约 17.72m，15.35m，8.86m 后端半径（Rv）：约 18.00m，15.59m，9.00m 半径差值（Rh/Rv）变化百分比：1.58%

SNOWRIDER 1993 （大头）滑板1993年

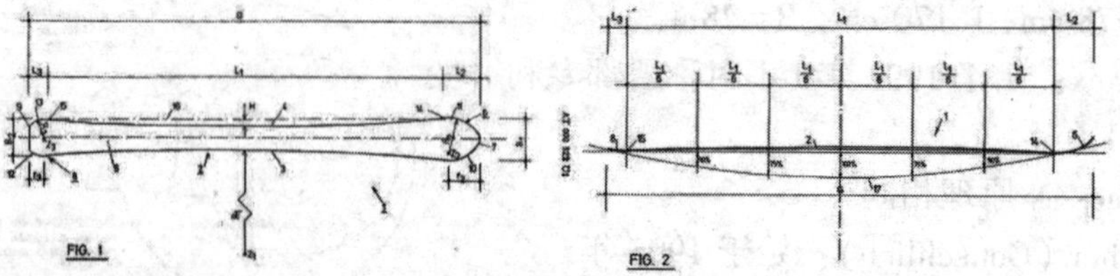

TENSIONLINES Biegelinien 滑板弯曲曲线

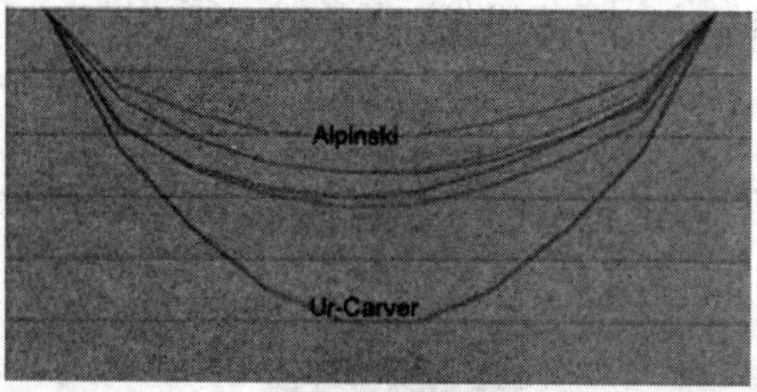

ALPIN-SKI-SNOWRIDER 2008 高山滑雪板、（大头）滑板与卡宾滑雪板的弯曲曲线对比 2008

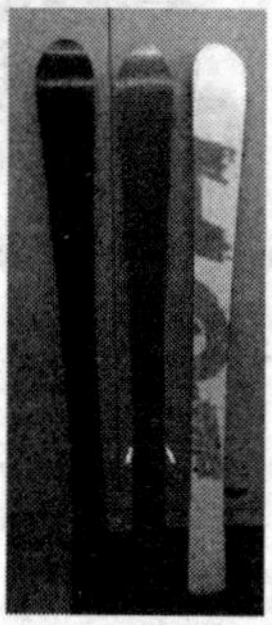

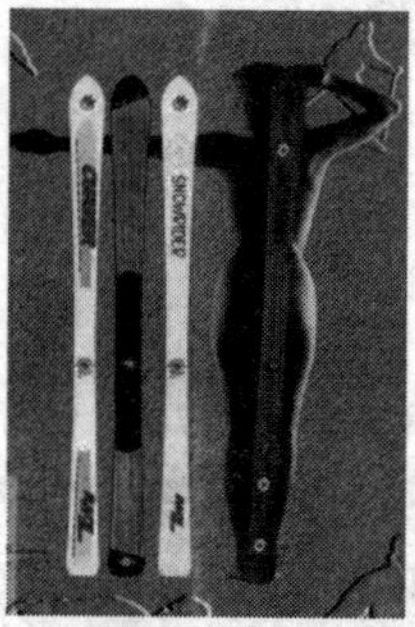

1989-90 ASYMMETRIC：14cm alpin

不对称：14cm alpin 28 Telemark 泰勒马克

Die KURVEN am Ski Curves on Skis

- Since 1977-Reinhard FISCHER / Ö Accelerating-Technique, needed more Sidecut, like Snowboard…
- 1990 SNOWRIDERR = 10-14m
- Ivan PETKOV / BG：S-Ski

- 1990-KNEISSL：Big Foot / R = 3，9 m（H. Mölg）
- 1992-ERGO，R=15m
- 1993 - ELAN：PARABOLIC Experiments with *variable* Sidecut（VSS / A. Robic）since 1977
- 自 1977 年-Reinhard FISCHER / Ö 加强的技术，需要更多的侧切，像单板一样…
- 1990 SNOWRIDER　R = 10-14 m
- Ivan PETKOV / BG：　S-Ski
- 1990-KNEISSL：Big Foot / R = 3，9 m（H. Mölg）
- 1992-ERGO，R = 15m
- 1993-ELAN：PARABOLIC 自 1977 年已做可变侧切（VSS /A. Robic）测试

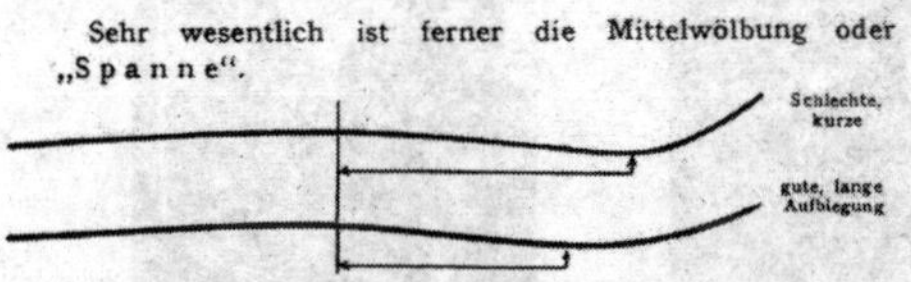

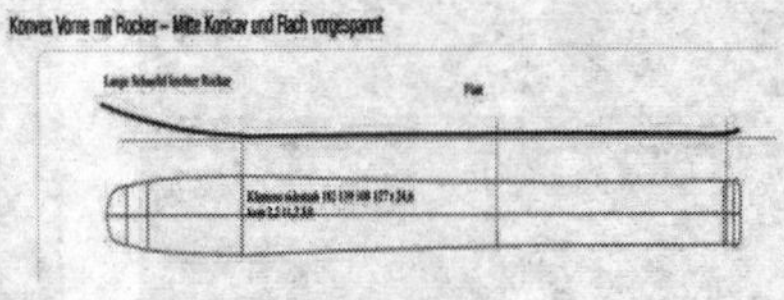

Faster learning，no Plough，safer，self confidence，Fun-Character
特点：学的更快，没有耕地，更安全，自信，有趣

1948，1951-	**1950，1961-**	**1967-**	**1966**
Firngleiter	**goon**	**GER**	**FRA**
Kurzski	**Short-ee-skis**		
Kitzbuehel	**GLM**		

INTERSKI 1971 G-P　Source：Kenneth Lawler 1994

Short Ski direct　短滑雪板

Tröndelag 1880
特伦德拉格 1880

Pohorje Kids-Ski
波霍尔耶山脉儿童板

Tubek 2005
Irkutsk　Listwanjka

Lake Baikal 贝加尔湖

Das Kurven fahren mit Ski

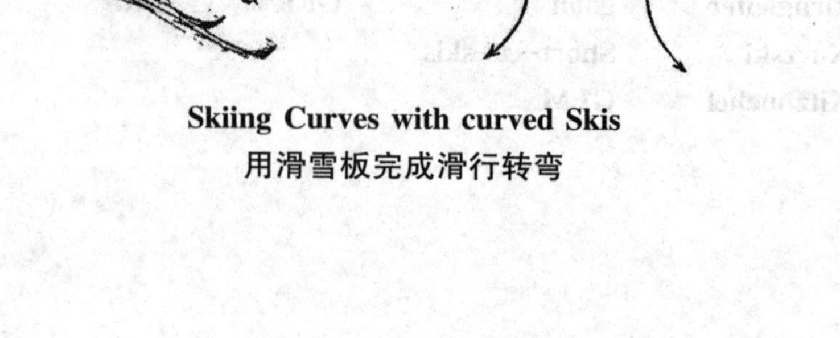

Skiing Curves with curved Skis
用滑雪板完成滑行转弯

E. C. RICHARDSON 1904 E. C. 理查森 1904 Kristiania Telemark Huitfeldt 1907 Snowboard：frontside–Telemark backside–Kristiania 奥斯陆 泰勒马克 Huitfeldt 1907

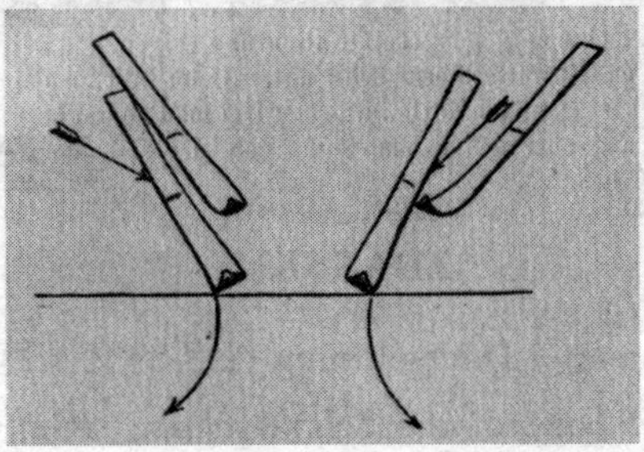

单板：正面–泰勒马克，背面–奥斯陆

- Kombiniertes Schwingen / Bilgeri 1922：
- Combined Turns：组合转弯
- Stemmbogen–Telemark–Kristiania

Combined Technique / *Luther* 1930 组合技术 *Luther* 1930

- *Doppelschwüinge*, *Doubleturns*, *since Huitfeldt* 1896…双弧形，双旋转，自从 1896 年
- Hybridturns, Paramarc…/ Parker 多旋转

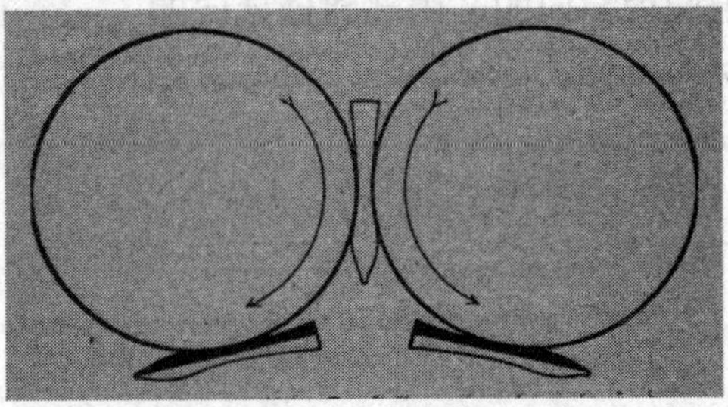

Carl J. Luther, 1913 *Bogenlaufende Wirkung des gekanteten Ski*："*Carving*"
滑雪曲度效应："卡宾"

The CURVEs on Skis Sondre A. NORHEIM-ca. 1860, *Urcarver*

L 235*cm*, 84-69-76*mm*, *Side-cut of* 15*mm* >*R*=74*m*

Carl J. LUTHER-1913; bzw. 1920

滑雪曲线　雪鞋的弧度效应　按照法律规定的滑雪形式所指定的滑雪向导

"die bogenlaufende Wirkung des gekanteten　Schneeschuhs"

ZARN / BARBLAN-1922

"Eigenführung der Ski, abhängig von der　Gesetzmäßigkeit der Skiform."

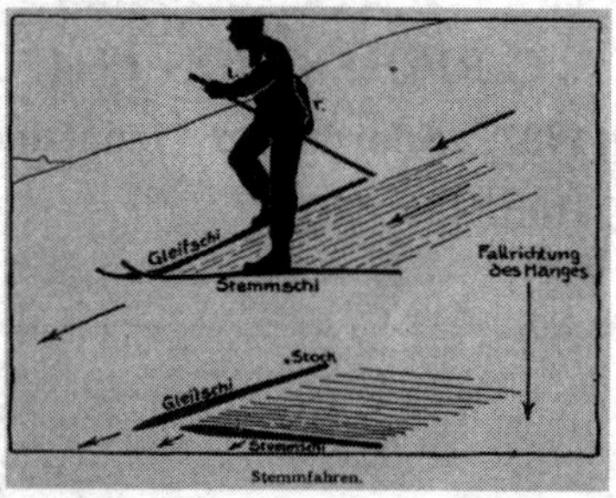

CAULFEILD 1911　　**ZDARSKY**　　**HOEK 1911**

- Luther 1920: gesteuerter Querschwung 控制的交叉跑动

"…bei ihm steuert der bogeninnere Schneeschuh; 内部带有弧度的雪鞋在他的控制之下

er wird auswärts gekantet…" 他在对方场地用滑雪板的边缘滑雪

- Henry Hoek 1921: Kristiania　　挪威式转弯 Kristiania

"…ein Bogen auf der Außenkante des führenden inneren Skis." 一个位于起主导作用的内部的滑雪板的外缘之上的弧度

- Zarn / Barblan 1922: „ *…beim Kanten*, …
- *die wie Messer　s c h n e i d e n…* " 磨去棱角，就像用刀切割一样
- A. Fanck / H. Schneider 1925: System- *außenbein-innenbeinorientiert*; *Movie-picture-sequencies*　外部腿做导向的，内部腿做导向的

Motionanalysis, *Slowmotion*, *Timelaps-Fotography*, …动作分析

A. Fanck　H. Schneider

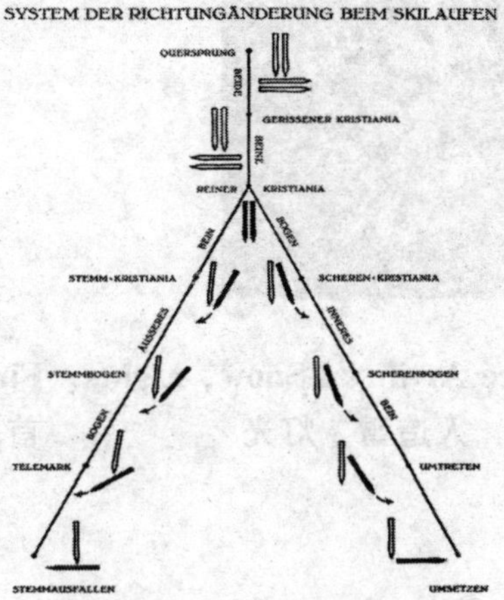

滑雪时改变方向的体系

"*Stem*" *swing*：停止旋转

Winkelstellung–Ausfallschritt–Innenlage Telemark >>Snowplough >> Christiania

角度设置—停止步骤—内部装置　特勒马克旋转>>梨式滑雪>>挪威式转弯

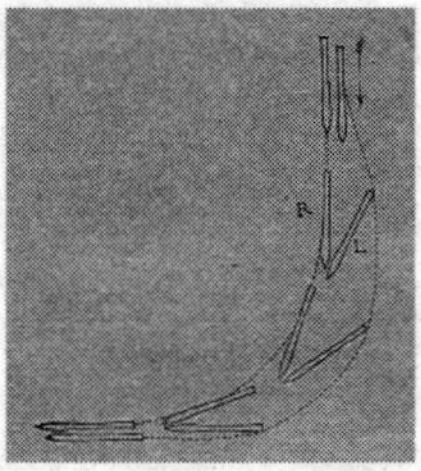

Bilgeri 1922

Schneider 1925

First SKIHALL 第一个雪具大厅

1936　Kunstpiste　1936
人工雪道

1927 Viennese Snowpalace Artificial Snow, Lights　First time Alpin-Disciplines

1929 年 维纳斯滑雪大厅　人造雪、灯光　　　　首次高山滑雪训练

二战后参考文献：

…after the WW II：

Frank HARPER 1949 *Skiing Naturally*

Karl KOLLER 1951, Clif TAYLOR 1955, M. PUCHTLER 1966, …

Walter FOEGER 1958 *Natur Teknik*

Morten LUND 1958 *Skiers Bible*

Fritz REICHERT 1958：*Skis with more sidecut*

Ramon TOSTADO 1965 *Skiing with the Shovel*

Dieter KINDL 1968 *Ski Tips*, 1971 *INTERSKI GP*：*Carving IPS*

Warren WITHERELL　1972 *How the Racers Ski*

Raimund SOBOTKA 1974 *Experiments with Skimodel*

Helmut GOTTSCHLICH + Hans ZEHETMAYER 1978

Andrej ROBIC 1977 *VSS-ELAN*

John HOWE 1979, 1981 ：*NTR-HEAD*

George TWARDOKENS 1983 , Shiro SHIMIZU 1989 ：*Models*

Reinhard FISCHER 1990 *Snowrider*

Harry MOELG 1990 *BigFoo* t　　　　　…Seth MASHIA doc

wedge turn

parallel turn

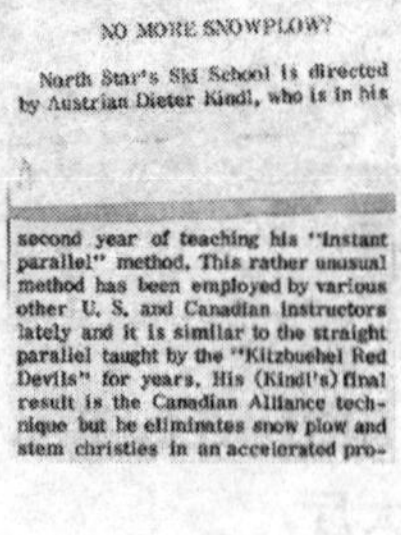

NO MORE SNOWPLOW?

North Star's Ski School is directed by Austrian Dieter Kindl, who is in his

second year of teaching his "Instant parallel" method. This rather unusual method has been employed by various other U. S. and Canadian instructors lately and it is similar to the straight parallel taught by the "Kitzbuehel Red Devils" for years. His (Kindl's) final result is the Canadian Alliance technique but he eliminates snow plow and stem christies in an accelerated pro-

Stop：Snowplough, Leaning out, "Stem" turn

Dieter Kindl：1967 Instant Parallel IPS with skis more waisted

停止动作：犁式慢动作

Dieter Kindl：平行式转弯

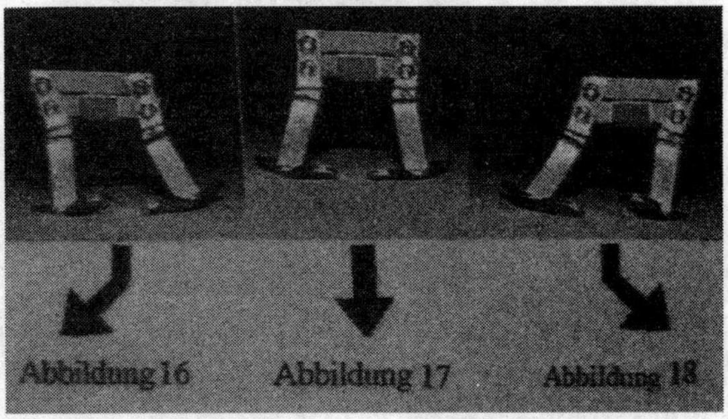

Sobotka 1974，Vienna
索博特卡 1974，维也纳

Helmut Gottschlich–Hans Zehetmayer

Georges JOUBERT 1970

生物（人）& 机械（模型）

The front–ski "makes" the turn

…der jeweils vordere Ski macht die Kurve

er leitet sie ein！

Huitfeldt, 1907：*…der vordere, kurveninnere Ski leitet beim Kristiania auf der Kleinzehenkante in die Kurve hinein.*

前方的滑雪板完成转弯前面的、位于弧度内侧的滑雪板引导在挪威式转弯时在小角度情况下进入弯道

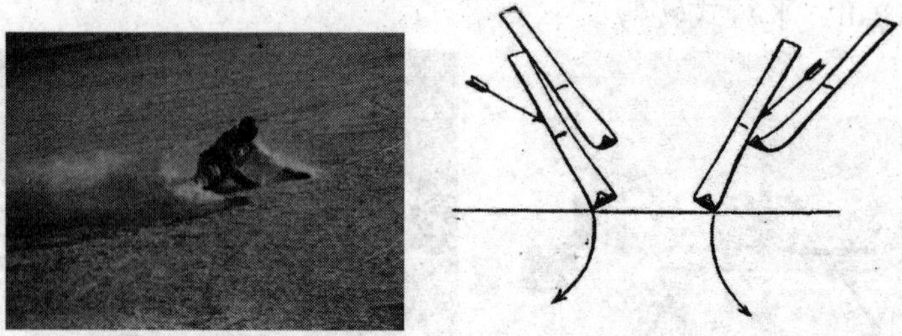

TeleBodyCarving-Geri Tumbasz, H

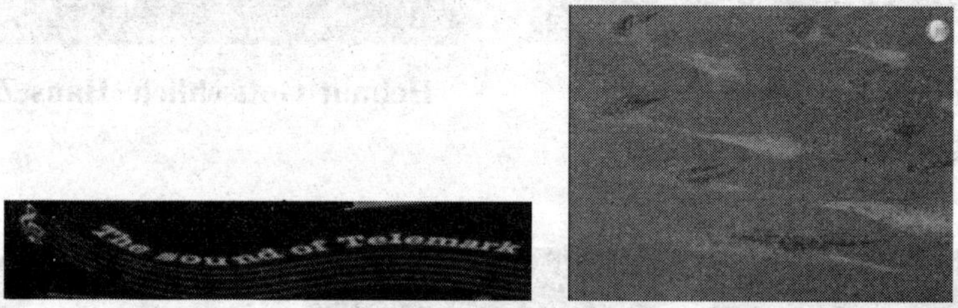

Pavel Stancl: FrühlingsstimmenWaltz *Modern Snowsports*, PI-NÖ / Cz 2005
现代滑雪运动

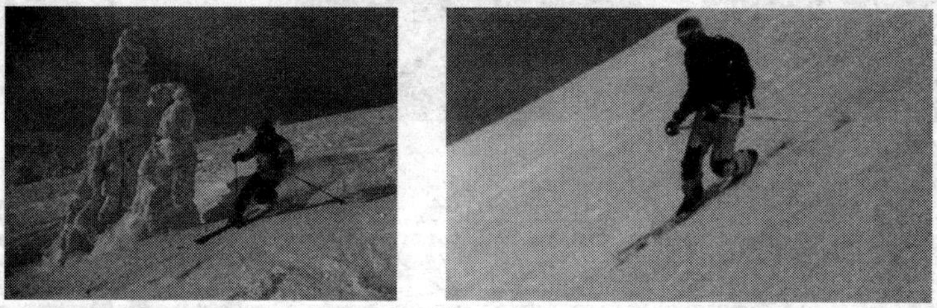

Martinske Hole, Slovakia schifoan……skiiiing……

Thankx.

arno. klien@ telemark-austria. at telemark freiferseln Freeheeling free heels & hills, mind & soul

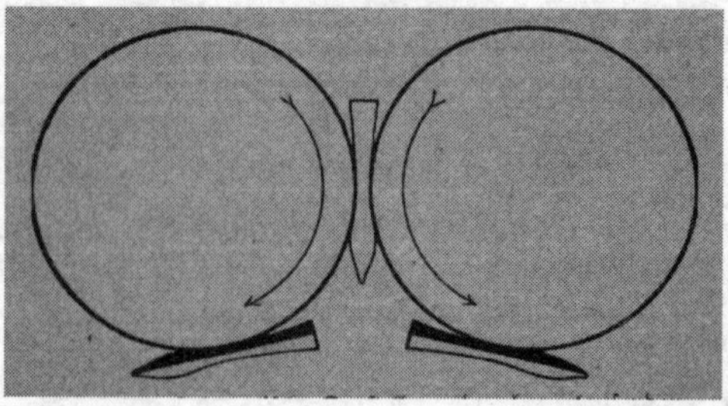

Carl J. Luther, 1913 Bogenlaufende Wirkung des gekanteten Ski: "Carving"
卡宾滑雪的日常弧度效应

Wildwest-Skier：Skier Cross…Table Rock/Cal. 1863，more than 100 kmh
西部滑雪者：滑雪交叉…平顶岩/Cal. 1863，时速超过 100 千米

Elk-Hunting，Sibiria 狩猎麋鹿，西伯利亚

English Paper：

CURVES ON THE SKI-CARVING on SNOW Altay 2015

Arno J. Klien

Any ski has a multitude of curves-you can see them from above，one at the tip，even at the tails，the side cut or the waist. As viewed from the side-like a soft wave，coming up at the tip，more or less tension at the center as seen by the camber，upturns at the tail and several functional roundings at the cross section. But the most significant and obvious conditions of the geometry are the telemark coving，as the waist is often described based on historic roots. This coving can be significantly modified by the edging，loading and flexing as well as the torsional stability of the ski. These technical advances allowed the development of other winter sports equipment，which allow more or less curved movements，wherby the radius of these curves resulted in a significant factor in the construction of this equipment.

This feature of the tool "ski" is probably much older than commonly acknowledged. Traditional and discovered parts of skis do not directly point at these conditions as do，however，the intentional use of wood as the edge，following the outside of a tree trunk. The analysis of the surprising depiction of the "ski rabbit" of Rödöy allow these assumptions: rounded tips, tension and camber at the center, curved tails-almost perfect twin tips. Not only are the tips at front upturned like a Viking ship, also the back tips, just as we have them nowadays, are turned up. Also the connection of man to ski with only straps can be assumed, which of course allows the free heel way of skiing.

The German sports teacher GutsMuths spoke already of the waist in his book *Gymnastics for Youth* (1804), which allows the statement that "the waist of a ski was mentioned only later" to be viewed in new light. As interim finding are skis which are somewhat wider at the tip, which would allow the use of willow twigs as binding without damaging those during forward movement. An example exists in skis from Oslo, about 1900-1910, with measurements 110-80-80mm and a length of 195cm. But Fridtjof Nansen had already used 9 pairs of skis for his Greenland expedition of 1888 with measurements 92-80-80mm and a length of 230cm, which allows a calculated radius of 178.5 m. Only the tip was wider, which allowed tracking in deep snow while protecting the bindings under the boots.

Ever since-aside from "rocker skis" -are skis somewhat wider at front than in the back, which also relates to the shape of the foot and this trapezoid shape allows the initiation of an easier turn on skis.

Only at the time of Sondre Norheim (1825-1897) was the intentional use of a curve like waist on skis introduced. He reduced the overall length of them, then generally used skis to about 243cm and introduced a side cut of 15mm (84-69-76), which resulted in a radius of 74.71m. With this "telemark curving" on his original carver skis he started the basic boom of modern skiing.

His willow binding with diagonal installed twigs resulted in better sideways stability, which allowed some jumping even for cross country skiing, which often also consisted of a final turn at the end of a run. We still call this "ab-kristeln", a derivative of the Nordic type of skiing. This final turn often resulted in a short uphill movement, so that you could save a little bit of climbing back up the hill. These resulting double type turns, known as Telemark or Kristiania turns, were dependent on the use of the wider tip of the advanced ski, or, based on the preference for one side by the skier.

Fritz Huitfeldt in 1907 wrote about it aptly when he said "*…the advanced, inside ski leads during a Kristiania the little toe edge in to the turn*". His patent for a metal binding toe piece from 1894 is another milestone.

Already Mathias Zdarsky spoke in his first book on the teaching of skiing in 1896: *"The edge of the ski is part of a circular curve. From this form results the direction of the turn. Additionally the tip leads into the turn as soon as it recognizes resistance."* Zdarsky reduced the length of the Norwegian skis to 180cm, eliminated the groove and used for his alpine ski the measurements 100-80-90mm, which he varied depending on the body height and weight of the skier. This resulted in an approximately same radius of 41.6m.

His patented sideways stabilized platform metal-bindings allowed the effective use of the characteristics of the ski; it influenced the fixed heel, progressive springs and adjustable binding systems to this day.

Why the use of edges in skiing develops into "carving" and how important the waist of the ski is, Zdarsky wrote very clearly about in his 1896 book:

"Let's try to determine how the curving towards uphill develops…The design of the ski is such that the width under the boot is narrowest, the tail end is 1cm wider, the widest part at the tip, where the tip starts lifting, is again 1cm wider than the tail end. The edge is therefore part of a circular curve. As the pressure is acted against the ski, this curve is ever more similar to the circle. From this edging develops the curving direction of the track. But as you think, that we can move the center of mass (balance point) into the direction of the center of this circle, that we can create a resistance with the pole, and that eventually the raised tip, as it is reacts to the resistance, also must turn towards the uphill, we realize that, through a combination of all these factors, a curving track must evolve."

In 1907 he wrote in his abstract *Methodical exercises for skiing*: "*Any deviation from a straight track will be called ' turn, which leads to conflicting interpretations. The simplest type of turn develops, when, leaning sideways, we edge the skis simultaneously.*"

At the Holmenkollen Ski Museum in Oslo we can find several skis with emphasized waist dated 1860, for example a pair called "Arena" and the measurements 104-60-98mm with a length of 205cm, radius 21m or another ski from Jostedalen with 104-59-72mm and 181cm length-a carving ski with a radius of 23m. A patent lawsuit with Rossignol was dismissed because of that in 1997.

Based on the International Hunting Exposition in Kleve/Niederrhein in Germany (former Netherlands) in 1881, where the Norwegians introduced the use of skis in forested areas, land owners, hunters and woodmen in Austria purchased several pairs. These "pre-nansen" concepts led to Gusswerk near Mariazell/Austria, where already in 1886 skiinstructions were held for the forest rangers of major land owners in Styria as well as Slovenia, then part of the Austrian-Hungarian Empire. This was even the origin of the so-called *Pohorje skis* , which only disappeared after the Second World War.

The oldest known example of an exact survey on skis was made by the forest ranger Andreas Scheliessnig of the monestary of St. Lambrecht/Styria, dated April 1, 1892. It is included in the first Austrian book on skiing by Etbin Henrik Schollmayer from 1893. That ski had a reed binding, was 235cm long and had the Zdarsky similar measurements of 90-70-80mm, which resulted in a radius of 62m.

Similar measurements-but with a length of 220cm-can be found in the first Hungarian book on skis, dated 1896, which also includes the thickness of the wood at the binding as 3cm. (p. 18: Chernelhazi Chernel, Istvan: A Labszankosas Kezikonyve. Lampel, Budapest 1896)

A short ski, which was made from a model by Sondre A. Norheim in Frankfurt an der Oder/Germany in 1904, had the measurements 80-60-60 (!) with a length of only 150cm. An original French carver was found in 2001, with the name "Abel Rossignol Voiron" recognizable at the tip, dated 1909 and with measurements 91-65-78mm, with a length of 170cm and a radius of 28m.

How the development of the waist in ski design influenced the technique of the day can be seen in a few literary excepts: In 1908 the first race of the newly formed Ski Club of Great Britain was held in Kitzbuehel, which was won by its president E. C. Richardson and where the founding member W. Rickmer Rickmers in a Combined Curving and Speed Race showed a remarkable run of 30 turns in perfect Zdarsky's Lilienfeld technique, using Zdarsky's Alpine-Ski and Platform metal-binding.

C. J. Luther (1914; 1920, 34) writes about *"the curving effect of the edged snow shoe"* , which he substantiated with his remarkable graphics. Also Henry Hoek mentions " *the edgewise curving of the ski favors the start of a turn*" , makes it "turning"; or with his description of the effects even more concise and shorter: *"a curve along the exterior edge of the inner directing ski"* . Hoek recommends these measurements for the telemark ski with 240cm long, 9-10mm/7-8mm/and 7.5-8.5mm, radius 93m (1921, 8) .

The Swiss Zarn-Barblan speak of " *the self tracking of the ski*, *depending on the established rules of the form of the ski*", where a first mention of the possible tracking appears: *"with edging, which CUT like knives…"* They describe the ski as "track", whereby all construction details developed are to increase the independent tracking of the ski along its longitudinal axis.

Similar statements come from Vivian Caulfeild in his book SKI－ING TURNS (1922): *"Turning by edging [carving} and turning by skidding are…. two incompatible processes"*. But even he has realized that the inner ski during a drifting turn is less on edge as the outer ski, but requires a stronger edging to achieve a carved turn. This is the first description of "carving" in an English book. A comparison to the tracking description by M. Zdarsky comes to mind. Of interest is also his comparison to an ice skate, whose turn on ice is dependent on the angle to the inside of a turn.

Then a relative calm set in for a while.

During the time of the wooden ski the grain of the wood was of great importance, whereby the bulging of the top surface influenced the weight, elasticity and stiffness: narrower skis were often preferred also because of the use in cross country skiing.

In October 2002 the author was able to make an extremely interesting discovery. During the closing of the traditional *Berko* Sports Shop in Vienna/Austria, at whose founding the British ski pioneer Rickmer Rickmers was involved, a collection of antique skis was offered for purchase to the antiquities dealer Patrick Kovacs. Among the many valuable items emerged a few skis of the same type: wide, short, carvers with tight radius, a mortised hole, squared 2.5cm groove, with measurements 117－95－115mm and 178.5cm length, side cut 22mm, radius of 28.5m. Bindings were apparently never installed, the weighted balance point is located about 1cm behind the 3cm wide mortised hole. Maybe these skis were a bit too radical in design for Vienna at the time and could not be sold? They came from Edsbyn, Central Sweden, in 1922, were fitted with a shield "ES Trademark" and the emblem Edsbyns Skidfabrik Sweden. These factory－new models had features, which would be typical for a contemporary Carver or Free Rider ski: short, wide and with accented waist.

The invention of the segmented metal edges for skis by Rudolf Lettner of Werfenweg/Salzburg, for which he received a patent in 1926, emphasized the effects of the waist, for which ski racers back then and to this day are convinced.

After the Second World War Frank Harper of the USA wrote about Carving Skis in his 1949 book "Skiing Naturally". Clif Taylor (1921－2005) put his students already in the winter of 1950 on " Goon－Skis", taught starting in 1955 in Hogback/Vermont on short skis and produced 1959 his "Shor－tee skis"; he published his ideas in "Instant Skiing－On Short Skis" (1961) and later his book "Ski in a Day" (1964) with short cut off alpine skis for "first time skiers". He promoted the elimination of poles and developed the GLM (Graduated Length Method), a new term and acronym by

Morten Lund (Frey 1998, 7), as well as in "GLM–The New Way to Ski" (1973).

First use of the term "Carving" was established by Ramon Tostado of the ski school Snow Summit/California in October 1965 in his publication by the title "Skiing with the Shovel". A most appropriate way to describe the effects of the proven design! Incidentally Sepp Ortner from Austria follows that line by saying, during a conversation on September 2, 2013, that the inner ski has the larger responsibility for the turns between gates. As Klien formulates–with respect to telemark, "the leading ski which is in front is responsible for the initiation of the turn".

The first major article in a trade magazine (SKI, January 1967) was published with the title "Moments of Truth on Skis", to which also Pepi Stiegler and Othmar Schneider had added articles. Dieter Kindl, back then member of the Canadian demo team at the INTERSKI Congress in Garmisch–Partenkirchen 1971, emphasized the term "carved turns", which he had already used 3 years prior in the US magazine under "Ski Tips". His successful teaching method "Instant Parallel", known as IPS, did away with the plough, while Walter Foeger's "Natur Teknik" had already dispensed the angled position with his "Hop Approach" in 1958. Morten Lund expressed in his "Skiers Bible" (1968), that the highest goal for a skier should be "a long, carved, parallel turn".

Warren Witherell recognized and described early on in his book "How the racers ski" (1972) the importance of "carving turns" and the connection of Skidding (Andriften) of Turns (Schwuenge) and Carving (Schneiden), including their mix, which he called Steering (Steuern). A year later he formulated the words "Edge–then Carve" combined with inside canting and was therefore ahead of his time.

In the meantime in Austria appeared an interview with Dieter Kindl, returning from Canada, in the media, while in Kitzbuehel Karl Koller, after the introduction of the Kurzski, worked with what he called Jet–Turn. You could read that as a precondition for carving would be, specifically cut, narrow waist skis, which are much narrower in the middle portion than at the tip or at the tail. The avoidance of the plough position would lead directly to parallel skiing. However, in Austria, ski schools held on to extreme weighing of the outside ski in a plough position (Nach–aussen–Kippen).

Reinhard Fischer was told about that, visited with Dieter Kindl at Obertauern and was fascinated with the thought of skis with an emphasized waist.

The scientific, however barely recognized breakthrough, was successful with Fritz Reichert (1925–2011) in then–Eastern Germany with his dissertation " The Influence of theForm of the Ski on the Directional Changes during a Downhill Ski-Run" (Leipzig 1956), in which he recommended skis with smaller waist for racers.

At the University of Vienna experiments were conducted with distribution of body weight on the ski inside vs. outside and front vs. back (Raimund Sobotka, 1974), leading to determinations of the effects of weight on the edges. Results: the studied model completed the test with the lowest contact to the snow after the shortest time, at the slowest tempo in a turn of the smallest radius.

In the US George Twardokens worked on the phenomenon of Brachistochrone Curve (1988) transposed on the downhill track according to the slogan "Longer line-shorter time".

The *Viennese ski models* of Helmut Gottschlich and Hans Zehetmayer supported these findings with constructions of heavily emphasized waists, which "drive" by themselves around curves. Even on YouTube one can see impressive demonstrations of carving on skis. These experiments started in Vienna in 1978, in 1983 by George Twardokens in the US and independently 1989 in Japan by Shiro Shimizu.

At Elan Andrej Robic started experimenting in 1975 on skis with variable radii as VSS (Variable Sidecut System), which received a patent in 1977.

Sohler Company of Wangen/Allgaeu built in 1984 in cooperation with the Department of Sports Sciences at the University of Hamburg (Horst Tiwald), the "Sohler Galopp", which was thought of as the first "Curver Ski".

Reinhard Fischer had developed his *acceleration technique* starting in the mid-seventies, which allowed racers to gain up to 3 seconds in the gates over their competitors. Looking for skis better equipped for this purpose, he tried to get the attention of any of the Austrian ski manufacturers to produce skis with shorter radii, however, except for a few prototypes, no real cooperation developed and he ended up in financial disaster.

At a summer race on grass for a mountain-bike-snowboard event on October 22, 1989 at Hinterbruehl near Vienna, he came into contact with the snowboarder "Big Otto" Lorenz. His son Gusi (Christian Fischer) used a Kneissl prototype with the measurements 93-63-83mm, length 200cm and radius 32.4m. Based on that R. Fischer, in the early winter of 1990, acquired from OttoLorenz/New Sports of Vienna, initially an asymmetrical Hot-Logical snowboard and later another one, but a Hot-Revolution of symmetrical layout. He then cut these 2 snowboards with the help of Josef Sladohlawek at the shop of their carpenter friend Peter Heller on his band saw with the conviction, that the smaller radii of 10-14m of the then popular snowboards would allow more radical turns. This way he ended up with 2 pairs of wide and short skis with extreme small radii, however with one steel edge only. His first tries in February 1990 convinced him of his idea.

Meanwhile, at the University of Vienna, a biomechanical pilot study proposed by Herbert Janko was conducted by Herbert Hatze, which contributed to the further development of the *Snow Rider*. The original Carver of 1990 had the measurements of 130-95-120mm with a length of 162cm and a radius of 12m.

This ski was initially proposed by *Pale* but since 1993 is being produce by *Roland Voigt* based on R. Fischer's trade mark, which he had obtained on December 23, 1993, including the name *Snow Rider* , the design of the Flintstone type lettering and the Edelweiss wood design.

The Bulgarian Ivan Petkov (1953-2012) had come to the US as ski instructor in Aspen. This former ski racer had previously successfully developed sail boards "Bora", worked with Robbie Naish and decided to build a carving ski. In 1992 he returned to Tschepelare/Pamporovo, Bulgaria, where Atomic had transferred the production of lower-priced skis too. There he built a few pairs of 113-61-91mm and 187cm length. Back in the US he tested these at Mt. Hood, was positively surprised and called them "S-Ski" . He applied for international patents for this geometry, built in the lengths of 183 and 193cm andeven Warren Witherell (How the racers ski) was enthusiastic. The 183cm model had 115-61-85mm with a side cut of 19.5mm and a radius of 15m. In 1994 he reduced the length to 163 and 178cm and sold 1200 pairs. This development resulted in the same area of contact at a reduced length.

Because the quality in Tschepelare was not satisfactory he negotiated with Blizzard. Even Atomic, Fischer and Head had understood the trends and started producing skis with 15mm side cut. At Fischer the model was called Revolution Ice (92-62-92), at Head it was the Cyber (94-61-90) and at Atomic there were the same products under different names.

Back in 1990, when Solomon had captured the world with their Cap-Monocoque-Technique many manufacturers experienced problems and even Rossignol did not yet have a radical ski in their program. Several companies, including Blizzard, got into distress while competing with Solomon in 1994/95. Despite having the formula on the geometry from Petkov they developed their own version of the Cap ski, while Tschepelare/Bulgaria built for other companies with the original Petkov dimensions. But when Blizzard used his formula, Petkov contacted K2 to no avail and when nobody wanted to accept his patent, his *S-Ski* disappeared altogether.

There was an earlier story about the former Yugoslavia. The mountaineer Dr. Franc Novak in 1960 ordered from Zvone Debeljak (Kranji/Slovenia) skis with a length of 160cm for easier traversing cross country terrain. These ski were called KANIN, had a pronounced side cut, 90-67-78mm with 160cm length and a radius of 30. 5m.

George Joubert in 1966 wrote about the "virage coupe" . Ciril Pracek and Ales Gucek, both former members of the Slovenian national team, met with their traditional skis in Kranska Gora to try out these virage coupe (carved turns) . This worked so well that Pracek reported about it in the Slovenian magazine DELO and Gucek even in the "Academic Sports Revue" . With this experience they visited Elan in order to explore the possibility for further development of the side cut, but were rejected. Later, Andrej Robic took on these ideas at Elan and introduced the "Uniline" for all skis. This resulted in the models "Servo" and "Retro", and the VSS (Variable-Sidecut-System) with front and back adjustable side cut waist, including the patent of 1977. He actually used several different radii.

In the development department at Elan Jurij Franco and Pavol Skofic worked on a computer generated form, based on which starting in 1988, skis were built with bigger side cut. With one of these Ole Furuseth outraced all competitors 1989 in Park City. Marjan Stele demonstrated this type of skiing with the new SCX (SideCutExtreme), the "Ski of the Year" 1995 in the US, as well as at the INTERSKI in Nozawa Onsen/Japan, for which he had already in 1984 prepared a manual, which was even recommended by UNESCO as the method for young skiers.

Horst Abraham, the CEO of the US Skiing Technique Commission (1983), had produced this sketch demonstrating the difference between carved and drifted turns.

Another story is the one on Martin Puchtler. It is only indirectly related to the waist of the ski, but indicates what in the Sixties was proposed to allow new skiers to learn the new type of skiing. This ski instructor from Bischofsgruen in the Fichtelgebirge/Germany gavc his last student a pair of children's skis, who-to everybody's surprise-came in first at the final race of the day. So he himself parked his 210s in the corner and switched to 180s. He then visited the "Largest Ski Instructors School in the World" in Kitzbuehel, where aleady after the Second World War Karl Koller had worked with disabled war veterans, older people and beginner skiers using shorter skis of 150 to 170cm lengths. Later on he flew to the US where in Aspen/Colorado he studied the short ski method by Clif Taylor. Similar to the GLM (Graduated Length Method, also called Gliding Length

Method) Taylor used skis from 65cm through 160cm in accordance with the slogan: half the length in accordance with lower speed, preferably without poles. While the press, TV and his students were excited, there wascontinued resistance by the German Ski Association (DSV) and the professional ski instructors. But Prof. Kruckenhauser, the Austrian Army and the Swiss skiers showed interest on his graduated teaching system.

Excitement also produced the Kneissl *Bigfoot* , a creation by Harry Moelg, which is patterned after ones actual foot, toes included. This became almost a cult item with its radical geometry and was produced in 1 million pairs. Heinz Petanjek even wrote an instruction booklet patterned after a small school. This ski had a radius of 3. 9m and an easy to use toe binding (1990) . This model influenced the development of the *Ergo* , which was introduced at the Fall-ISPO in 1992 and then marketed as 100-62-100 with a radius of 14m and a sidecut of 19mm.

At Elan the *Parabolic* was introduced at the Spring-ISPO 1993 in Munich, after Ingemar Stenmark had already used skis with emphasized waist the prior year. The skis were then still longer, when he demonstrated his Step-over-Technique on 205cm long skis with 81-67-70mm and a radius of 100m; however, with a 60 degree edge angle the radius is about half that amount. Elan writes on their website: "Ever since Elan has changed skiing with the invention of Carving forever, there are new expectations." Nowadays they are working with different angles, which should minimize unintentional canting, developing a combination of Rocker and Camber, called Triple-Base-Technology (TBT) and used preliminarily for freestyle and powder skiing.

In April 1993 one saw the prototype Elan SCX at the ISPO in Europe and Mike Adams, the US Marketing Director received 4 pairs for testing, as well as the Kneissl ERGO; both caused some stir in a positive way, as Seth Masia reports. Jurij Franco and Pavol Skofic worked through the summer on a shorter version with the same radius of 15m, but only 163cm long.

At Head John Howe in about 1979 had already used the radius as the differentiating element for his skis and since 1981 had marked that information as NTR (Natural Turning Radius) on top of the ski. A gray Ladies' RS ski of Inge Klien was marked as NTR 56m. Today this type of information has become standard with many ski companies showing measurements of the waist and is often visible on the side wall. This idea of J. Howe and his marketing manager Gary Kiedaisch was realized on the Head Yahoo with a length of 180cm, a sidecut of 7. 3mm and a radius of 35m, while the factory still did not dare to use smaller radii. Of interest is the pocket-sized model made by Kiedaisch, a moving aluminum model made for his sales staff to demonstrate the effects of carved turns with extremely short radius. When shown people would ask why one could not get normal sized skis with a similar small radius.

At this point it is unknown if the experiments by George Twardokens and the "Viennese Ski Models" by Helmut Gottschlich and Hans Zehetmayer were known to the rest of the ski world and cannot be proven by this author.

Additional Historic Notes on Specific Subjects:

ASYMETRIC SKIS:

These were always of great interest and subject to experimentation by several ski companies. ASNES produced 1996 a *Telemark-Pradator* racing ski, which was intended to get around the regulations: the measurements were 73-57-67mm, however the sidecut on the inner edge of the ski was larger than that on the outer edge. The problem arose during production and the subsequent automated completion. The same occurs in the model lineup at G3 for 2014/15, which have a smaller radius on the inside edge compared to the outside edge on the big-toe of the same ski, similar to different size of tracks from the wheels on a car.

VOELKL in 1995 introduced the P9RSL, which was intended to be a Slalom ski on one side and a Giant slalom ski on the other side. Similarly the ATOMIC Beta Race 9.28 (radius 28/30m) and the Beta Carve 9.11 (radius 10/11m) were available until 2001/2002.

FISCHER produced the RadArc from 1995 to 2002 as influenced by Helmut Gottschlich with the finding that the turn-inner ski takes a tighter track than the turn-outer ski.

LACROIX in 1992 had obtained a patent for an asymmetrical waist (Morpho-Logic-Concept), where the sidecut is offset in accordance with the shape of the foot.

SCOTTY BOB/USA produces telemark skis with a marked offset of the sidecut, unequal long edge pieces in accordance with the larger stride position of telemark skiing. Scott Robert Carlson works in a vacant old electric plant in Silverton, within the San Juan Mountains of Colorado. When he worked as ski instructor for telemark he noticed that ski companies concentrated on materials but not on the design of skis, which based on production requirements is symmetrical. In the late 1990s he started experimenting with asymmetrical designs and invented the *Bob-Tail* ski. It has edge pieces of different lengths on inner and outer edges of the ski, making it asymmetrical, improving control and turning ability. For the telemark ski he uses an offset of 28cm, for the alpine ski he uses 14cm. This way he corresponds to the mechanism of the typical stride and is the only ski manufacturer to offer this design. Even the top-surface of the skis can be ordered individually by the purchaser, with selections of wood grain, colors and limited graphics.

ROCKER SKIS FOR 2015:

A new development for skis include more convex forms of skis-ROCKERS. George Twardokens experimented in 2000 with reverse camber and described the effects of that design. Further development by ST. Drake-C. Bonay led to the first fitting of a reverse camber for 30cm to the tip portion of their skis, complemented by a reverse sidecut. That resulted in a pronounced shift of the contact point towards the center of the ski thereby reducing the exposed length of the edging. The rebound of the camber cannot be replaced, which makes this type of ski ideal for off-piste skiing and increases the trend for 2 pairs of skis. This development continues today with skis from Drake-Peter Turner (DPT), with Stephen Drake having been responsible for naming this type of ski "ROCKER", a term which he borrowed from surfing.

The current development of the geometry of skis goes into many directions, including the convex forms as shown in the rockers, even mixed forms of convex/concave designs. Depending on the intended use of the equipment, the tip of the ski becomes most meaningful, which is shown on a reversed rocker. The length of the shovel tip, contact points and the camber or reversed camber (rocker), combined with torsional stability and flexural properties become the determining factors for choosing the appropriate model, for example from BLIZZARD or DPD.

COMMENTS ON SIDECUT:

The waist determines the sidecut of the ski. It is always a part of the total concept of a ski design and is determined by the proposed use. The radius is not only determined by the geometry-the length of the ski and sidecut, but also by the depth at the contact with the snow and the angle at which the ski is placed against the snow. All of this depends on the mechanical properties of the ski (bending and torsional stiffness, flexing and rebounding), loading components (weight, centrifugal force) and the mechanical properties of the snow. The stiffnesses influence the ski like the chassis and damping properties of a car, which reminds one of the words by Georg Kassat "…because the piste turns the ski".

The table below shows the calculation of the radius of the original Snow Rider according to the Sagitta formula, which is not entirely correct but still is quite meaningful.

Examples of Skis with the same width at the tip as at the tail:

Kneissl Ur-Ergo 100-62-100 with 180cm, R=18m and 94.5-62-94.5 with 160cm, R=16m

Fischer: Revolution Ice 92-62-92 with 170cm, R=19.5m

Shorter Skis:

Zdarsky (Alpen-Ski), Bilgeri (Jagdski/160cm, Summerski 100-160cm), Hoek (Glacierski), Firngleiter, Karl Koller (Learning Ski), Clif Taylor (GLM), Sigi Engel of Kitzbuehel, since 1952 used in Sun Valley, Puchtler, Foeger, „Shorties", Sohler Galopp, Hoppichler (Comfort Ski) …

During the winter of 1938 the figure skater Jimmy Madden of Boston drew with children-skis a few figures on snow at Mt. Cranmore. In order to be able to ski backwards Thor Groswold of Denver built him a pair with upturned ends-they called them "goon-skis" and are the first twin-tip skis since the ski rabbit of Roedoey of about 4000 BC.

At the end of the 1930s the Swiss Streuli Frères encouraged the ski schools to use 120cm skis for beginners and then to let them use 130 to 160cm skis. In 1938 Zogg used a 130cm long "glacier ski" with double grooves. In 1962 Authier introduced his solid wood "Liliput" ski for little money, but was apparently 10 years too early for the market. Even Attenhofer had a short ski in the 1960s with 170cm, 90-80-85 and a radius of 78m.

Karl Koller started using shorter skis at his ski school in1951 made by Michael Ober, who already made *Firngleiter* since 1948. Sigi Engl exported those to Sun Valley in 1952 and the American Peter Scully, who had written an article "Short Skis for You?", took these skis down the Streif in Kitzbuehel in 1954 as the "Kitzbuehel-GLM". 145 winter sport towns in the Alpine Region then took over this Short-Ski-Method.

Eight Percent of the output of all ski companies were produced as short skis with lengths of 150-175cm, predominantly for inexperienced and older skiers. Fischer of Ried/Austria, the largest ski producer worldwide, produced 15, 000 pairs of these short skis for the 1970/71 season, Arnsteiner even exceeded that with 18, 000 pairs. Austria equipped its army, ski patrol and border patrol with 170cm skis.

As the newer carver skis were more accepted in the mid-1990 the request for shorter skis increased, also because of the BigFoot by Kneissl. The fun factor, the decrease of knee injuries because of the shorter lever and the faster learning curve caused the rapidly increased production. Fun-or Short Carvers like the Carvellinos/Blizzard or the Snowblades/Salomon were the top models. Added to that were not only snow boards but also hybrids like Monoski, Skwal, Snowdeck, etc. Even Telemarkers discovered the All-Mountain and Freeride skis and got away for the narrow slats. The last novelty are Altai skis (AS) by Nils Larsen, model HOK (125cm, 124-110-122mm, R=24.3m) and KOEM (162cm, 124-98-119mm, R=22.6m), available at www.altaiskis.com.

A strong signal for the new carver skis came from the racing circuit. Here is where the story of Bode Miller (born 1977) rocked the scene. During his senior year in high school he got into contact with the development specialist at K2. They already started experimenting with an emphasized waist, which Bode could relate to based on his snow board style of racing. He started winning races in 1995 in New Hampshire and competed in 1996 with a new model K2 Four at the US-Junior championships in Sugarloaf/ME. He not only won downhill, super-G and giant slalom but also came in second in the slalom. With these successes he contributed the breakthrough of the carving ski with racers, which now was no longer relegated to the free-rider crowd. He was the first one to win, they were just made fir his racing style and catapulted him to the top of world ski racing. 2001 he became World Cup champion for slalom and giant slalom, and in 2008 he was the only racer ever who had won in all 5 disciplines 5 times. Additionally he became world champion in 4 disciplines and was Combined Olympic Champion (2010). He is also known for his ruthless critique of skiing organizations and their officials.

In the meantime the FIS has revised its previous regulations on the design on carver skis and has revised the 2011 radii by increasing them from 27m to 35m, in addition to lengthening the skis to make them less aggressive. But the existing equipment from 2014may still be used for the 2015 season.

Werner Woerndle (1996, 2005) actually said that the breakthrough for the carver skis came from the US. Because of the former better preparation of the ski areas with artificial snow and modern grooming machines as compared to Central European locations, the skiing surfaces are harder and more like racing conditions. That was the reason that even the recreational skier took easier to the new type of ski which allowed a more controlled use on hard prepared surfaces as provided by the ability to negotiate tight turns with the carver ski.

Hermann Wallner (2008), who wrote several books on this subject, formulates this with the statement that "…while making turns the self induced turning power of the skis with the emphasized waist is being used".

And Walter Kuchler (2011), who has spent considerable time with the subject "carver" has developed this credo "…the skis turn by themselves, if you just let them. That was my first realization. Since then I am talking about the auto-kinetic properties of the ski, their self-regulating turns. I experience skiing as the intelligent cooperation with the ski and as synergy of operator and ski." Many discussions on carving and carver skis become mute when you can see the *Vienna models of skiing* in motion.

What the curves on a ski do, can be demonstrated with the models by Helmut Gottschlich and Hans Zehetmayer: the small, exactly detailed metal figurines follow at contact with the surface with their edges, flexible hinged body parts allow tilting downwards, initiating the next turn. The fact that Helmut Gottschlich, after some soft prodding, developed a similar model for telemark, the "Telemaxl", only emphasizes the appropriateness of the application, indicating how skis with strongly emphasized waist, independent of the actual technique, can be used to demonstrate carving turns.

This now shows the span of development from the circular and snake like turns of Mathias Zdarsky in 1896, past the "Schematic Demonstration of the Turning Power of the tilted Snow Shoe…" by C. J. Luther in 1920 up to the current carved tracks in snow. For the recreational skier as well as for the racing enthusiast.

This circle closes when you see the skiers of the Altai with their long boards, sometimes with a soft convex center portion, just like today's Freeriders schussing down the hill, then you know: "OIS WAR SHO AMOL DO!" I. e.: "Everything has been here already!" *Alles schon da gewesen!*"

Translation by Wolfgang J. Klien, Arizona/US

Sources are to be seen in the German Original Version of the Author's lecture in his Book *"Reinhard Fischer-Schneiden im Schnee. Ein Visionär ist Achtzig", p. 115-137*

ISBN 978-3-902111-52-4

arno. klien@ telemark-austria. at　0043 (0) 664 2204595

中文论文：

雪面上滑雪雕刻的弧线

任何滑雪都有诸多弧线——你能从上面、尖端甚至尾部、侧面和腰部看到他们。从旁边看的时候像一条柔软的曲线，向尖端滑去，能看到弧形中间或多或少的紧张感，尾部的翻转和在雪面上交叉的几个功能性环绕。但这个几何图形最重要和引人瞩目的情况是屈膝旋转法的“拱”，因为其腰部的描述往往基于历史根源。这种拱可以通过雪板的边缘、负荷、弯曲性和扭转稳定性等大幅改动。这些技术进步促进了其他冬季运动装备的发展，允许了或多或少弧线运动的发生，这些弧形的半径构成了这种装备生产的重要因素。

滑雪工具的特点可能比普遍认知的要早很多，雪板的传统部分和发现部分并未直接指向这些条件，然而刻意使用树干外部的木质来做雪板边缘。对 Rödöy“雪兔”惊人描述的分析认可了以下假设：圆形尖端、弧形中心、紧张感和弧形的尾部——几近完美的双重尖端。不仅前部的尖端旋转时像“维京船”形式，就像我们目前所拥有的一样，后部也出现了尖端。而且可以联想到只使用固定器滑雪的男人，当然这允许了脚跟自由的滑雪方式。

德国运动老师 GutsMuths 已经在其《青年体操》（1804）一书中提到过腰（中部），使大家从一个崭新的角度审视这种说法“只有在后来才提到滑雪（板）的腰（中部）”临时发现显示雪板尖端有点宽，因此允许使用柳条作为约束物且在前行的过程中不损坏他们。约 1900-1910 期间，奥斯陆的一款雪板是一个例子，其尺寸为 110-80-80mm，长为 195cm。但 Fridtjof Nansen 已经在其 1888 年的格陵兰探险中使用了 9 副雪板，雪板尺寸为 92-80-80mm，长度为 230cm，可接受的计算半径为 178. 5 m。只有尖端更宽，才能在保护雪靴下面固定器的同时允许在深雪中滑进。

除了摇臂滑雪板，自此以后雪板前边都比后边宽一些，这也与鞋的形状相关，这种梯形使雪板转身更容易。

但只有在 Sondre Norheim（1825-1897）的时代，才开始刻意引进雪板中部的弧度。他减小了他们的总体长度，然后使用 243cm 的滑雪板，并引进 15mm（84-69-76）的侧切，结果转弯半径是 74. 71m。作为屈膝旋转法（泰勒马克）的鼻祖，它开启了现代滑雪最初的繁荣阶段。

其对角安置树枝的柳条绑定法增强了侧面的稳定性，甚至在越野滑雪中允许加入一些跳跃动作，往往会在最终进行一个转身。我们称之为北欧滑雪类型的衍生物“ab-kristeln”。最终的转身导致短暂的上坡动作，这样你就节省了一些上山后退的空间。这导致两种类型的转身，分别是屈膝旋转法和克里斯提娜旋转，依赖于高级滑雪的广泛使用或者基于滑雪者对一侧的偏好。

1907，Fritz Huitfeldt 这样写道，他说：“在克里斯缇娜旋转中，高级内部滑雪领头，小脚趾缓缓旋转” 1894 年，其金属固定脚趾的专利是另一个里程碑。

1896 年，Mathias Zdarsky 已经在其教授滑雪的第一本书中写到：雪板的边缘是圆形曲线的一部分，从形式中得出旋转的方向。除此之外，当他认识到阻力之时，雪板尖端部分开始引导转身。Zdarsky 将挪威雪板长度减至 180cm，去除了底面沟槽，并用于高山滑雪的测量数据 100-80-90mm，而该数据的确定值取决于滑雪者的身高和重量。这导致了大约相同的 41. 6m 的半径。

他的专利侧滑稳定了金属绑定的平台，允许了对雪板特点的有效使用；至今都影响固定的鞋跟，渐进的弹簧和可调节的绑定系统。

在 1896 年，Zdarsky 清晰的写到：雪板边缘的使用为什么发展成了“雕刻”以及雪板中部的重要性。

让我们努力去决定曲线是如何向上坡发展的，雪板的设计是这样的情况，雪靴下边的部分是最窄的，尾部边缘比它宽 1cm，雪板两端头部最宽，且雪板前端头部以上开始向上弯曲，且前端头部比尾端部分还宽 1cm。因此边缘部分又构成了一个圆形弧度的一部分。而且由于雪板所承受的压力，所构成的弧线就更像圆形的一部分。也由此在雪道上划出的弧线方向得到了发展。但我们可以把平衡点的中心移向该圆形中心的方向，我们可以用孔创造一种阻力，因为提高的前段部分会和产生阻力的孔发生反应，因此，最终提高的部分必须向山上移动。此时，所有这些因素的结合使我们意识到弧线轨道产生的必然性。1907 年，他在滑雪方法概要中写到：任何竖滑直轨道的偏离都叫作转弯，他的这种说法引发了许多争议性的解释，最简单的转弯方法就是当我们向旁边倾斜的时候，雪板的轨迹自然的形成了弧度。

在奥斯陆的霍门科伦滑雪博物馆，我们可以看到 1860 年的中部加强版的滑雪板。例如，有一副雪板名为“Arena”，尺寸为 104-60-98mm，其长度为 205cm，半径 21m，还有一种来自 Jostedalen 的雪板尺寸为 104-59-72mm，长为 181cm，是半径为 23m 的雕刻雪板。且由此，1997 年的一场和 Rossignol 专利诉讼案被取消。1881 年德国克莱纳和下莱茵河举办国际狩猎展览，在此基础上，挪威人在林荫地区引进了滑雪板的使用，奥地利的地主、猎户和樵夫均购买了几副。这些比南森超前的概念导致奥地利玛利亚采尔的 Gusswerk，1886 年，首先在施帝力尔和施洛文迪亚已经为林区居民的大地主们进行了滑雪建设，其后在奥匈帝国的部分地区。这甚至就是波或耶尔山脉滑雪的起源，但仅在二战之后就消失了。

根据准确的雪板调查，最早的雪板调查于 1892 年 4 月 1 日，产生于兰布雷西特或施帝力尔修道院，由一名名为 Andreas Scheliessnig 的人制作完成，在 1893 年由 Etbin Henrik Schollmayer 编写的奥地利第一本关于滑雪的书籍上也有提及。该雪板有编箝机，长 235cm，而且还有 Zdarsky，其尺寸为 90-70-80mm，导致其半径为 62m。

同样尺寸，但长为 220cm 的该部分可以在匈牙利第一本滑雪书籍中找到，这要追溯到 1896 年，还包括当时的绑定结构的木板厚度为 3cm（18 页：Chernelhazi Chernel, Istvan: A Labszankosas Kezikonyve. Lampel，布达佩斯 1896）。

一条短板，在 1904 年由德国奥德河畔法兰克福市的模型制成，尺寸为 80-60-60 而长度仅为 150cm。2001 年发现一件原始的法国卡弗，在顶尖处发现其名为“Abel Rossignol Voiron”，追溯到1909年，尺寸为91-65-78mm，长度为170cm，半径为28m.

可以从一些文学节选中发现雪板腰身设计的发展如何影响当时的技术：1908年，新形成的滑雪俱乐部的第一场滑雪比赛在基基茨比尔举行，且其总裁E. C. 理查森赢得了比赛，也是在那里创始人之一的W. Rickmer Rickmers以组合曲线和速度比赛，以完美的Zdarsky's Lilienfeld技艺，通过使用Zdarsky's高山滑雪和金属固定平台，展示了惊为天人的30次转弯。

C. J. 路德（1914；1920，34）写到*“小幅雪鞋的曲线效果”*，且他通过自身卓越的制图学证实了这一点。同时亨利胡克也提到”雪板边缘的曲线有利于转弯的开始”使其成为转折点；或者他对效果的描述更为精确和简短：“雪板引导外部边缘形成的曲线”胡克提议的屈膝旋转法滑雪板的尺寸长240cm，尺寸为9-10mm/7-8mm/7.5-8.5mm，半径为93m（1921，8）。

瑞士Zarn-Barblan谈到“滑雪自身形成的踪迹依赖于滑雪方式固有的规则”，此处可能是第一次滑雪轨迹出现的地方：“带有边缘部分，形状像刀子”他们将滑雪描述成“轨迹”，在这种轨迹里所有发展的实施细节均为提高沿纵轴滑雪形成的独立轨迹。

Vivian Caulfeild在其书《滑雪转弯》（1992）中也作出了类似的陈述：“通过边缘（曲线）转弯和侧滑滑行进行转弯是两种不兼容的过程”。但他甚至意识到了在漂移转弯期间内板比外板紧张度要低，但需要一个更强的边缘来实现曲线转弯。这是第一次在英文书中描述“曲线”。映入脑海的还有与M. Zdarsky关于轨迹的描述，有趣的是他与溜冰鞋进行了对比，溜冰时的转弯依赖于转弯内部的角度。此后相对平静了一段时间。

在运用木质雪板期间，木制的纹理十分重要，因为上层表面的膨胀影响重量、弹性和硬度，更窄些的雪板更受欢迎，因为可用于越野滑雪。

2002年10月，作者有一个十分有趣的发现。在奥地利维也纳百鹤高体育用品店要关门的时候，发现英国滑雪先锋0Rickmer Rickmers，故向他推荐了大量古董雪板，由董商Patrick Kovacs购买。在这些珍贵的物件中出现了一些同类的雪板：宽的、短的、带有紧凑半径的弯曲度，带卯孔的，2.5cm沟槽的，尺寸为117-95-115mm，长178.5cm，侧壁切削22mm，半径28.5m。很明显是没有安装绑定结构的，重量的平衡点在3cm宽的卯孔后面1cm部分。或许在当时的维也纳这些雪板的设计有些太过激进，有可能卖不出去，他们1922年来自瑞典中部埃斯宾，配有防护物“ES商标”并且标有Edsbyns Skidfabrik Sweden。这些工厂新制作的型号有现代雪板或自由滑雪者喜爱的典型特点，既短又宽，腰部较重。

Werfenweg/Salzburg（地名）地区的Rudolf Lettner因其发明的分段金属边缘

雪板于1926年获得专利，他强调了雪板腰部（中部）的作用，并以此说服着当时的滑雪比赛者及当今的人们。

第二次世界大战之后，美国的弗兰克哈珀在其1949年的书中写到卡宾技术《自然滑雪》。Frank Harper of the USA wrote about Carving Skis in his 1949 book "Skiing Naturally". 克里夫泰勒（1921-2005）于1950年冬天开始使其学生了解" Goon-Skis"，在1955年Hogback/Vermont（地名）开始教授短板，1959年诞生了"Shor-tee skis"；于1961年在《即时滑雪-短板滑雪》和后来的书《一日滑雪》（1964）中谈及了其想法为"初次滑雪者"提供短的高山雪板的指导，发展了《滑雪板长度渐进法》（GLM），这是由Morten Lund（弗雷1998，7）在《滑雪板长度渐进法-滑雪新方法》（1973）提出的新术语和缩略词。

加州雪峰会滑雪学校的Ramon Tostado1965年在其出版的名为《以铲子滑雪》一书中首次使用"卡宾"一词。描述证实的设计最合适的方法。2013年9月2日，奥地利的Sepp Ortner偶然的在一次谈话中沿着这条线说道在门中间转弯时内侧滑雪承担更大的责任。正如克莱恩规定的那样，屈膝转弯法中转弯的开始由前部负责。

第一篇主要文章出版于一本贸易杂志（滑雪，1967年1月），名为"滑雪真实瞬间"。后来Pepi Stiegler和Othmar Schneider亦在此添加了文章。Dieter Kindl，曾是加拿大演示队的成员之一，1971在Garmisch-Partenkirchen（地名）强调了"卡宾转弯"这个术语，他优先美国杂志"滑雪技巧"三年使用这一词。其成功的授课方法"即时平行法"被称为"诱导多能性"，同犁式一同减弱，而1958年Walter Foeger的"自然技巧"已经开始分配角度位置和"跳的方法，Morten Lund表达了他的"滑雪者圣经"（1968），对于滑雪者而言，最大目标应是"长的、卡宾的平行转弯"。

Warren Witherell认识到这一点并很早在其《比赛者如何滑雪》（1968）一书中描述了"卡宾转弯"的重要性，转弯的侧滑滑行与卡宾（包括他们的混合，他称之为转向）之间的关系。一年之后，它提出了这些"先侧向移动，然后转弯"结合内侧倾斜的方法，因此，在当时比较前卫。

同时，在奥地利的媒体中出现了从加拿大回来的Dieter Kindl的采访，而在Kitzbuehel Karl Koller（地名），在介绍 了 Kurzski之后，随后与其所谓的喷射转弯合作。你可将其视为卡宾技术的前提，专门设计，窄小的雪板腰身，中间腰身部比顶部或尾部窄很多。避开犁式姿势将直接导致平行滑雪。然而，在奥地利，滑雪学校坚持以犁式姿势滑雪。

Reinhard Fischer谈起和Dieter Kindl在Obertauern见面的事，并且对强调雪板腰部的想法极其感兴趣。

然而，几乎没有人认可的这种突破在当时东部德国 Fritz Reichert（1925-2011）的论文中成功了，论文名为《下坡雪道上滑雪方式对方向转变的影响》（Leipzig 1956），在论文中他为滑雪比赛者推荐了腰部较小的雪板。

在维也纳大学进行了雪板内、外、前、后身体重量的分配情况，（Raimund Sobotka, 1974），得出体重对边缘影响的程度。结果：研究模型以最短的时间，在最小的转弯半径中，以最慢的速度和雪进行最少的接触。

在美国，根据“长线-短时间”的口号 George Twardokens 研究最速曲线（1988）根据“长线-短时间”的口号向下坡轨道转换的现象。

The *Viennese ski models* of Helmut Gottschlich and Hans Zehetmayer 的滑雪模型支持这些带有加重强调腰身的发现，且这种雪板在曲线附近有“驱动”的功能。甚至在土豆网你也可以看见关于雪板卡宾技术的形象解释。这些实验始于 1978 年的维也纳，1983 年美国的 George Twardokens 和 1989 年日本的 Shiro Shimizu。

在 Elan，1975 年 Andrej Robic 开始带有可变半径（可变侧切系统，于 1977 年获得专利）雪板的实验。

Sohler Company of Wangen/Allgaeu 汉堡大学的运动科学系和“Sohler Galopp”（曲线滑雪第一人）于 1984 年合作成立了 Wangen/Allgaeu Sohler 公司。

Reinhard Fischer 在七十年代中期发展了加速技巧，相较于竞争者，为比赛者在起点赢得了约三秒的时间。为了寻找能更好满足这种需求、装备更优良的雪板，他尽力取得所有奥地利短半径雪板生产厂商的注意，然而，除了一些原型之外并未取得真正的合作且以经济困难而告终。

1989 年 10 月 22 日，在维也纳旁的 Hinterbruehl 地区一场夏季高山自行车雪板草上比赛中，他和雪板商“Big Otto”Lorenz 取得联系。他的儿子 Gusi（Christian Fischer）使用了一种 尺寸为 93-63-83mm，长度为 200cm 和半径为 32.4mKneissl 原型。在此基础上 R. Fischer，在 1990 年早冬，从维也纳 OttoLorenz 或新运动开始了非对称热逻辑雪板，而后又有一个带有对称格局的热改革。然后他在 Josef Sladohlawek 的帮助之下，在他们的木匠朋友 Peter Heller 的店中切了这两个雪板，他们的朋友确信后来流行的半径为 10-14 米的将允许更多的激进式转弯。结果他制作了两幅半径极小、宽而短的雪板，然而，只有一边是钢边。1990 年 2 月他的首次尝试证实了他的想法。

同时，在维也纳大学，Herbert Janko 提出的生物力学试验研究由 Herbert Hatze 进行，促进了滑雪进一步的发展。1990 年最初的卡弗尺寸为 130-95-120mm 长度为 162cm，半径为 12m。

这种雪板最初由 Pale 提出，但自从 1993 由 *Roland Voigt* 在 R. Fischer 商标的基础上进行生产，1993 年 12 月 23 日他获得了雪花骑士的称呼，摩登原始人类刻字和雪绒花木质设计。

保加利亚的 Ivan Petkov（1953-2012）作为阿斯彭的滑雪教练来到美国。这位前滑雪比赛者曾和 Robbie Naish 成功发展了帆板“Bora”随后决定建立“卡宾”滑雪。1992 年，他回到保加利亚 Tschepelare/Pamporovo，在那里 Atomic（原子）也转移了低价雪板的生产。在那里他建立几副尺寸为 113-61-91mm，长度为 187cm。回到美国他在胡德山检测了这些，结果令人大吃一惊，他将他们称为“S-滑雪”。为了这个几何图形，他申请了国家专利，长为 183cm 和 193cm，甚至 Warren Witherell（滑雪比赛者如何滑雪）也十分热情。183cm 型号的尺寸为 115-61-85mm，侧切面为 19.5mm 半径为 15m。1994 年，他将长度减至 163 cm 和 178cm 且销售了 1200 副。这项发展使得同一地区的联系较少。

Tschepelare 地区的质量不太令人满意，他和 Blizzard 商量过。甚至 Even Atomic，Fischer 和 Head 也理解了这些趋势并且开始生产侧切为 15mm 的雪板。在 Fischer 这种型号称为冰革命（92-62-92），在 Head 是 Cyber（网络），在 Atomic 不同的名称下是同样的产品。

回到 1990 年，当所罗门以硬壳结构技术占领世界时，很多生产商发现了问题，甚至罗西尼奥尔在他们项目中还没有激进滑雪。几家公司包括 Blizzard 在内，在 1994/95 年和所罗门竞争陷入困境。尽管有塞特科夫的几何公式，他们发展了滑雪帽（Cap ski）自己的版本。而 Tschepelare/Bulgaria 已最初的 Petkov 规格建立了其他的公司。但当 Blizzard 使用其公式时，Petkov 联系了 K2，但无济于事，当时没有人想要接受其专利，他的 S 滑雪一起消失。

很早之前有一个关于前南斯拉夫的故事。1960 年，登山家法郎诺瓦克博士从 Zvone Debeljak（Kranji/Slovenia）订购了长为 160cm 的雪板为更容易地跨越跨国领土。这些雪板名为 KANIN，有显著的侧切，尺寸为 90-67-78mm，长为 160cm 半径为 30.5m。

1966 年 George Joubert 写“virage coupe”时写道 Ciril Pracek 和 Ales Gucek，两位前苏联国家队成员在 Kranska 偶然遇见他们的传统雪板并进行了尝试。他们觉得效果很好，所以 Pracek 在苏联杂志 DELO 和 Gucek 上报道，甚至在学术运动杂志上进行了报道。在这样经验的基础上，他们去拜访了埃朗，目的是探索进一步发展侧切的可能，但遭到了拒绝。后来，Andrej Robic 像埃朗讲了这些想法，并且引进了雪板的单行线路。导致“Servo”和“Retro”模型，VSS（可变侧切系统），带有前后可调的侧切腰身，包括 1977 年的专利。事实上它使用了几种半径。

Elan Jurij Franco 和 Pavol Skofic 基于 1988 年开始的加大雪板侧切情况在发展部研究一种电脑生成形式。1989 年 Rruseth 基于此在公园城市超越了所有的竞争对手。Marjan Stele 用崭新的（侧切极限）来阐述这种类型的滑雪。在 1995 年美国的“年度滑雪”，Nozawa Onsen/日本 INTERSKI 的滑雪，1984 年已举办过，准备了手册，甚至联合国教科文组织将其推荐为指导青年滑雪者的方法手册。

Horst Abraham 美国滑雪技术委员会的总裁（1983）通过素描的方式来对解释卡宾转弯和漂流转弯之间的差异。

另一个是 Martin Puchtler 的故事。他只是间接与雪板腰部相关的故事，但暗示出六十年代提出的允许新滑雪爱好者学习新的滑雪方法。来自 Bischofsgruen 的滑雪教练在德国菲柯特高原送给他最后一名学生一副儿童雪板，令所有人吃惊的是在那天的比赛中，他成了第一名。所以他将自己的 210s 放在了角落并换成了 180s。然后他拜访了位于基次比尔的“世界上最大的滑雪教练学校”。二战后，Karl Koller 在那里和一些战后残疾的老兵共事，老人或滑雪初学者使用长为 150-170cm 的短板。后来他飞到美国阿斯彭和科罗拉多去研究 Clif Taylor 的短板滑行方法。与 GLM（滑雪板长度渐进训练法，亦称为滑行长度法）相似的是，与标语相呼应，Taylor 使用长度为从 65cm 到 160cm 的雪板；一般长度对应更慢的速度，最好没有两端。尽管媒体界、电视界和他的学生们都很激动，仍然有大量来自德国滑雪协会和专业滑雪教练的阻碍。但奥地利军人和瑞士滑雪者对他的这套系统展现出了极大的兴趣。

这种激动也产生了 Kneissl Bigfoot，Harry Moelg 创造的产物，以实际的脚型和脚趾为基础，这已经成为一种崇拜性物品带有几何图形，并生产了 100 万副。Heinz Petanjek 甚至在一个小学派出了一本指导手册。这种雪板半径为 3.9m，易于使用脚趾绑定。这种模型影响了 Ergo 的发展，于 1992 年 ISPO 秋天引进，进入市场的尺寸为 100-62-100，半径为 14m，侧切为 19mm。

在 Ingemar Stenmark 已经使用腰部加强雪板之后的前一年，埃朗在 1993 年慕尼黑春季 ISPO 引进了“抛物线”。当时的雪板更长些，当他解释后续技术时，长为 205cm 尺寸为 81-67-70mm 半径为 100m；然而，60 度的边角的半径约为其一半。Elan 在网站上写道：“自从开创了卡宾滑雪技术，Elan 就整个改变了滑雪，并期待更多”目前，他们正研究多角度，最小化非刻意倾斜，发展摇臂和外倾角的结合，我们将其称之为“三步科技（TBT）”，而且主要适用于自由滑雪和粉雪中滑雪。

1993 年 4 月，有人在欧洲 ISPO 看到 Elan SCX 原型，而且，美国市场总监麦克亚当时接受了 4 副的测试，还有 Kneissl ERGO；赛斯玛西亚报道，两者都在积极的方面激起了波动，Jurij Franco 和 Pavol Skofic 整个夏天都在研究在相同半径 15 米的情况下，仅为 163 厘米长的是短板。

在 Head，约 1979 年，John Howe 已经将雪板半径的长短作为区分雪板的元素，且自 1981 年将其作为滑雪时的头号标志称为“自然转弯半径”英奇克莱恩的灰色女士的 RS 雪板的自然转弯半径为 56 米。当今，这种标志已经成为许多展现雪板腰部尺寸的标准，而且往往在外侧清晰可见。J. Howe 和他的市场经理 Gary Kiedaisch 的这种想法已经在 head 雅虎上被意识到，其长为 180cm，侧切为 7. 3mm 半径为 35m，而工厂仍然不敢使用更小的半径。令人感兴趣的是 Kiedaisch 制作的口袋尺寸模型，一款可移动的铝制模型，用于工作人员展示带有极短半径的卡宾转弯效果。当向人们展示的时候，人们会问为什么不买一款拥有相同半径的普通尺寸的雪板呢?

此时，如果 George Twardokens 的实验是未知的，和 Helmut Gottschlich 和 Hans Zehetmayer 的“维纳斯滑雪模型”是被雪界以外的人所熟知的，但不能被此作者证明。

关于具体对象的额外历史备注：

对称雪板：

这些总是很令人感兴趣，且总是几家滑雪公司争相进行实验的对象。1996 年 ASNES 生产了屈膝旋转法赛用雪板，目的是有办法应付各种规定：尺寸为 73-57-67mm，而雪板内边侧切比外边侧切大。在生产过程和后续的自动完成过程中问题出现了。同样的问题出现在 2014/ 15 年的 G3 模型阵容中，在同样雪板的“大脚趾”上内边半径比外边半径小，相当于同一辆车论拥有不同尺寸的轨道。

VOELKL 1995 印记了 P9RSL，一方面是要成为回转滑雪板，另一方面要成为障碍滑雪板。类似情况，ATOMIC Beta 比赛 9. 28（半径 28/30m）和 Beta 卡宾 9. 11（半径 10/11m）直到 2001/2002 可用。

Helmut Gottschlich 发现了内转雪板比外转雪板的轨道紧，受他的影响，FISCHER 从 1995 到 2002 生产了 RadArc 。

LACROIX 1992 年获得了腰部不对称（生物力学逻辑概念）的专利，其侧切可以根据脚型进行抵消。

美国 SCOTTY BOB 根据屈膝旋转法的大跨度位置对应的不平衡长边生产了带有明显侧切抵消功能的屈膝旋转法雪板。Scott Robert Carlson 在在科罗拉多的圣胡安山脉西佛敦的一座空虚老电厂里工作。当他在做屈膝旋转法教练指导员的时候，根据生产要求的不对称性他发现滑雪公司只注重雪板的材料，而不关注雪板的设计。1990 年代后期，他开始进行不对称设计实验，并且发明了鲍勃-尾部雪板。其雪板边缘内部和外部边缘部分的不同长度使它不对称，提高了控制和转弯的能力。对于屈膝旋转法滑雪他采用 28cm 进行抵消，因为高山滑雪使用的是 14cm。这种方法与典型的机械进行了对应且是唯一一家提供这种设计的雪板生产厂商。甚至雪板的顶端表面可以由购买者进行独特订购可以自行选择木质纹理、颜色和限制图案。

2015 年摇臂滑雪板：

雪板的新发展包括更多的凸状形式-摇臂雪板。2000 年 George Twardokens 利用反向弧面体验和描述了这种设计的效果。ST. Drake-C. Bonay 进一步发展了这种设计，它实现了雪板尖部 30 厘米的反向弧线的首次拟合，完成了反向侧切。导致连接点向雪板中心的明显转变从而减少了边缘部分的暴露长度。弧线的回升不能被取代，因此使其成为非滑雪场地滑雪使用的理想雪板类型，且提高了两副雪板的趋势。Drake-Peter Turner（DPT）认为，如今这种雪板的发展依旧，他和 Stephen Drake 对命名这种雪板为“摇臂式雪板”负责，因为这是从冲浪界引借的一个术语。目前雪板的几何性发展有许多方向，包括摇臂式中的凸面形式，甚至还包括凹凸面设计，根据对设备的刻意使用雪板尖部成为了最有意义的部分，从反向摇臂式雪板可以分析得出。铲子前端的长度连接点、弧度或反向弧度，与扭转稳定性和灵活性向结合成为了选择合适型号雪板的决定性因素，如选择 BLIZZARD 或者 DPD。

对“侧切”的评价：

雪板腰部决定雪板的侧切。他一直是雪板设计概念的一部分，且由用途来决定。半径不仅由几何性-雪板的长度和侧切来决定，还有和雪接触的深度、雪板与雪放置的角度来决定。所有的这些都依赖于雪板的机械特性（弯曲性扭转性，灵活性和反弹性）、装载成分（重量和离心力）及力学的机械特性决定。弹性进度系数影响雪板的原理和减震对汽车的影响是一个道理，提醒我想起 Georg Kassat 说的一句话：“因为雪场影响滑雪”。

根据 Sagitta 的计算，未必精确，但有参考价值，下表是“雪花骑士”最初半径的计算。

在尖端和尾部具有相同宽度雪板的例子：

Kneissl Ur-Ergo 尺寸为 100-62-100，长为 180cm，半径为 18m。尺寸为 94.5-62-94.5，长为 160cm，半径为 16m。

Fischer：Revolution Ice 尺寸为 92-62-92，长度为 170cm，半径为 19.5m 更短的雪板 Zdarsky（高山滑雪），Bilgeri（Jagdski/160cm，夏季滑雪 100-160cm），Hoek（冰山滑雪），Firngleiter，Karl Koller（学习滑雪），Clif Taylor（GLM），Sigi Engel of Kitzbuehel，自 1952 年在太阳谷使用，Pchtler，Foeger，„ Shorties “，Sohler Galopp，Hoppichler（舒适滑雪）…

在 1938 年冬天，波士顿的滑冰者 Jimmy Madden 想出了 Cranmore 山上儿童滑雪的一些形象 。为了能够向后滑雪，Thor Groswold of Denver 给了他一副向上翻转边的雪板，他们称之为“goon-skis” 自从公元 4000 年前 Roedoey 雪兔之后的第一个双尖雪板。

在 1930 年代末瑞士的 Streuli Frères 鼓励滑雪学校使用 120cm 的雪板供初学者使用，然后再让他们逐渐改用 130－160cm 的雪板。1938 年，Zogg 使用了 130cm 的带有双凹槽的“冰川雪板”。1962 年，Authier 用较少的钱引进了“Lilliput”实木雪板，但很明显比市场需求早了十年。在 1960 年代 Attenhofer 有一个短雪板，长为 170cm，尺寸为 90-80-85cm ，半径为 78m。1948 年制作了 *Firngleiter*。Sigi Engl。1952 年将这些出口到太阳谷和美国 Peter Scully，他曾写过一篇文章，名为“为你设计的短板”，1954 年在 Streif Kitzbuehel 将其全部买下，并将其称为“Kitzbuehel-GLM”。后来高山区域的 145 冬季运动城接手了他的短板滑雪方法。

所有滑雪公司 8%的输出均源于 150-175cm 的短板，主题消费人群为没经验的初学者或稍有经验的初学者。奥地利莱德市的 Fischer 公司是世界上最大的雪板厂商，在 1970/ 71 季节生产 15000 副这样的短雪板。Arnsteiner 甚至用 18000 副超过了他们。奥地利用 170cm 的雪板武装了其军队，加强了武装巡逻和边境巡逻。

随着 1990 年代中期，崭新的卡弗滑雪板更为人们所接受时，也因为 Kneissl 的 Bigfoot ，对短板的需求与日俱增。有趣的因素是，由于杠杆更短，学习曲线加快，膝盖受伤情况降低，导致雪板产量大大提升。有趣或短卡弗如 Carvellinos/ Blizzard 、hSnowblades/Salomon 是顶级型号。此外，不仅有单板，还有如 Monoski，Skwal，Snowdeck 的混合产品等。甚至屈膝旋转法的滑雪者发现了所有山地和自由滑雪的雪板已经远离窄木条。最后一个新颖之处就是 Nils Larsen 的阿尔泰滑雪板，新制作的模型 HOK（125cm，124－110－122mm，R＝24. 3m）和 KOEM（162cm，124-98-119mm，R=22. 6m），参考 www. altaiskis. com。

还有一种说法即新的卡弗雪板来自于比赛场地。以下就是 Bode Miller（出生于 1977）震撼的故事。在他高中的时候联系上了 K2 的发展专家。基于比赛风格的雪板，他们已经开始着重腰部的实验。1995 年，他在新罕布什尔开始赢得比赛，并于 1996 年在 Sugarloaf/ME 美国青年锦标赛完成了新模型 K2 四号 。它不仅在下坡、障碍滑雪、大回转中取得了好成绩，而且在大回转中取得了第二名的成绩。在这些成功的基础之上，他为比赛者的卡宾滑雪做出了突出贡献，现在不将其归入自由滑雪人群。他适应的这项比赛的第一人，刚刚形成了自己的比赛风格，迅速成为世界顶级滑雪比赛选手。2001 他成为世界杯大回转和障碍滑雪的冠军。2008 年，他是有史以来唯一一个赢得 5 次 5 项的比赛者。除此之外，他成为 4 项世界冠军，且获得了 2010 年联合奥林匹克冠军。他也因其对滑雪组织和官员的无情批判而闻名。

同时 FIS 已经修订了卡弗雪板设计之前的种种规定，且通过将半径从 27 米增至 35 米，修订了 2011 年的半径。除此之外，延长雪板降低了他们的危险性。但 2014 年目前现存的设备可能仍然会被用于 2015 季。

实际上 Werner Woerndle（1996，2005）说卡弗雪板的突破源于美国。因为前期较好的准备，如滑雪区域的人工雪，当代压雪机，与中欧地区相较而言，雪面更硬，更符合比赛条件。这就是为什么甚至娱乐性滑雪者都更容易接受新滑雪方式的原因，使得雪板在较坚硬的雪面更好控制，提高运用卡弗雪板进行急转弯的能力。

Hermann Wallner（2008）已经写了几本关于这个话题的书，他这样陈述："在转弯的时候使用了雪板加强的腰部自我引导转弯的能力"。

Walter Kuchler（2011）已经在"卡弗"这个话题上花费了了大量的时间，且发展了这个信条"如果你让雪板转弯，他们会自行进行，这是我最初的认识"后来我就开始谈论雪板的自动性能，他们的自律性转弯。我认为滑雪是滑雪者、雪板运营商和雪板之间的智能协作。当你看到动态的维也纳滑雪模型时，很多关于卡弗和卡弗滑雪的讨论都烟消云散了。

可以通过 Helmut Gottschlich 和 Hans Zehetmayer 的模型来解释滑雪形成什么样的曲线：小而细节精确的金属雕像不断接触边缘，柔韧铰链的肢体部分允许向下倾斜，开始下一个转弯。Helmut Gottschlich 经过一些了解之后，提出了和屈膝旋转类似的模型"Telemaxl"模型，他强调使用的舒适性，阐释了腰部加强的雪板和独立的实际技巧如何一起用来解释卡宾转弯。

现在他展示了 1986 年 Mathias Zdarsky 的圈形和蛇形转弯发展阶段，由 C. J. Luther 于 1920 年对"倾斜雪鞋转弯时的原理演示"之后至今的雪上卡弗轨道。适用于娱乐性滑雪者或比赛爱好者。

美国艾利桑那州 Wolfgang J. Klien，当你看到阿尔泰的滑雪者拿着他们的滑雪板，有时带着软凸中心部分，就像今天的自由滑雪者进行高山直线下滑一样时，完整的一圈就圆满了。"一切都曾经存在过！"

来源请参考德国作者原版的演讲"Reinhard Fischer-Schneiden im Schnee. Ein Visionär ist Achtzig"，115-137 页 ISBN 978-3-902111-52-4

arno. klien@ telemark-austria. at　0043（0）664 2204595

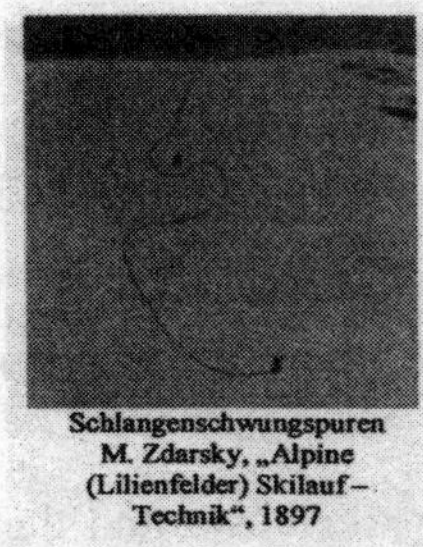

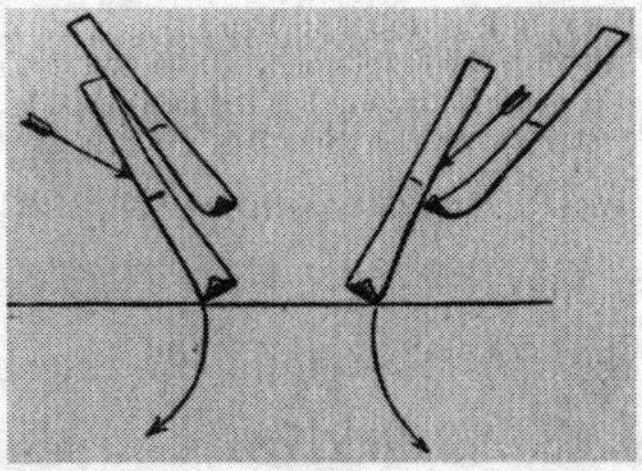

M. Zdarsky，阿尔匹斯山，滑雪技术，1897　　**Huitfeldt 1907　蛇舞痕迹（百合天地）**

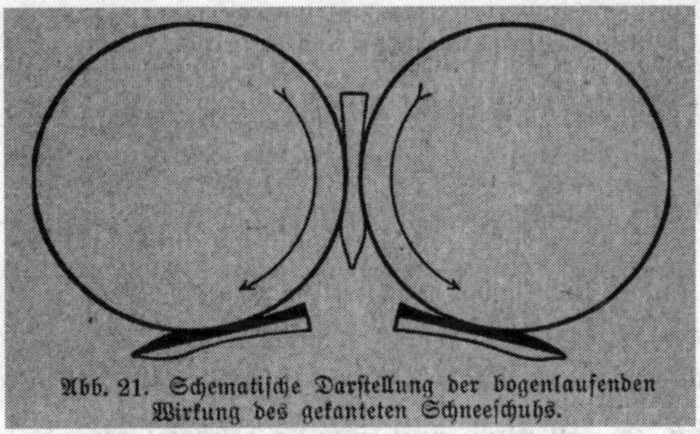

C. J. 路德 1913

4.24　关于阿勒泰滑雪历史文化的感悟　Inspirations on Altay ski historic culture

艾瑞克·本桑（瑞士）　Bengt Erik Bengtsson（SUI）

个人简介　PersonalInformation

国际滑雪联合会北欧滑雪技术官员，北欧滑雪委员会负责人，滑雪文化研究学者。

Nordic skiing technical official of International Ski Federation, The head of ski committee in Northern Europe, Researcher of skiing culture.

Speech　发言稿：

Dear ski friends

It was a great honour for me to be invited to the International Ancient Skiing Cultural Exchange and Seminar in Altay City some time ago.

During my 20 year long service at the international ski federation my interest for the skiing history has grown. What I really remember was a night in Holmenkollen in Oslo when I was invited to coffee at the table of King Olaf together with the well known ski historian Jakob Vaage. King Olaf talked among other interesting things on the introduction of the new Rottefella binding and how his mother the queen tried to forbid him to use it as this binding destroyed his ski boots.

Now to the Altai region. It was early said that the skis were invented there. Why not Scandinavia? The question is simple to explain. At this time Scandinavia was covered by snow and ice and no people lived there.

Just about 10 years ago wall paintings were found (see picture1) and today these paintings are examined to be the oldest sign of skiing.

It was very, very interesting to look at the paintings and feel the history behind. Welcome to come to Kandegate and look.

We also had the possibility to see skiers in action (see picture2) . About100 skiers (only men) started, all with old homemade skis and with one long pole. All of the competition was possible to watch as the track was laid out in a stadium. It is really impressing that the ski tradition is still alive and can be studied also today. Here you have another reason to come and look.

Especially I want to thank my old friend from Changchun Mr. Shan Zhaojian and our real chief Mr. Ayiken Jiashan for their devoted work.

图1　滑雪岩画

Fig. 1　Skiing rocking paintings

图2　古老滑雪比赛

Fig. 2　Ancient skiing race

亲爱的滑雪界朋友：

很荣幸受邀参加了这次在阿勒泰举行的国际古老滑雪文化交流和研讨会。

我在国际滑雪联合会工作了20年，我对滑雪历史的兴趣与日俱增。让我记忆深刻的是在奥斯陆霍门科伦的一个晚上，我受邀和著名的滑雪历史学家Jakob Vaage一同与国王奥拉夫喝咖啡。国王奥拉夫讲述了一些趣事，其中一件事便是有关使用一种 Rottefella binding 新的固定器，由于使用这种固定器不当，损坏了他的雪鞋，他的母亲，也就是女王，硬性试图禁止他继续使用 Rottefella binding。导致他不能如愿去滑雪。

现在来说阿勒泰地区。滑雪为什么能起源于此地，而不是在斯堪的纳维亚呢？很简单，那时斯堪的纳维亚被冰雪覆盖，无人居住。

大约 10 年前，人们在阿勒泰市汗德尕特乡发现了古老滑雪狩猎岩画（图 1）。经考证，这些岩画标志着最古老的滑雪痕迹。

观看这些岩画，亲眼感受其背后的历史，极其有趣。欢迎我的朋友来汗德尕特乡观看。在这里，我们有机会看到正在使用古老滑雪器具的滑雪者（图 2）。

阿勒泰市的古老毛皮滑雪板比赛开始约有 100 余名滑雪者参加（只有男士），全都配有古老的自制滑雪板和一个长杆，在雪山中奋力滑进，雪面上刻留着雪板的痕迹，站在山坡上可以看到所有的比赛。古老滑雪传统保留至今，并且还可以供我们加以研究，让人印象深刻。我们又有了一个来此观看的理由。

在此特别感谢在中国长春相识的老朋友单兆鉴先生以及我们的新朋友阿依肯·加山先生，感谢他们无私的辛勤付出，精心策划了这次世界滑雪文化活动。

4.25　连接传统民俗滑雪与现代国家认同的滑雪：斯洛文尼亚案例　Connecting traditional folk skiing with modern national identity skiing: Slovene case

布鲁特·巴塔力（斯洛文尼亚）　Borut Batagelj（SLO）

个人简介　Personal Information

Borut Batagelj (born 1976) did PhD at History department of Faculty of Arts, Ljubljana University (Slovenia, EU) in 2009. In 2010 dissertation was issued as book titled "Izum smučarske zgodovine: kulturna zgodovina smučanja na Slovenskem until 1941" (The invention of skiing tradition: Cultural history of skiing in Slovenia until 1941) which was nominated for national ski award in Histriography. Batagelj took part in several ski history conferences aruond the world and is reguraly publishing papers from the field of sport history, cultural history and archives. His working as a director of Historcal Archives Celje.

Borut Batagelj 生于 1976 年，2009 后取得卢布尔雅那大学（斯洛文尼亚）文学院历史系博士学位。2010 年以专著形式发表论文，名为《滑雪传统的由来：

1941 年之前斯洛文尼亚的滑雪文化历史》，此书被提名为国家滑雪编史奖。Batagelj 参加了各国的滑雪历史研讨会，定期发表体育历史，滑雪文化历史和档案领域的论文。并且他还是采列历史档案的负责人。

English Paper

Connecting traditional folk skiing with modern national identity skiing: Slovene case

In the long term process, when the history of skiing, including the present Conference in Altay is paving a path to a comprehensive global interpretations and the pieces of previously unknown episodes ski history are combining in a mosaic of the world's ski history, there can be simultaneously observed between some separate stories also some similarities. A modern example of detecting pre-history of skiing in the area of Altay may in some segments show similarities to the beginnings of discovering ancient folk skiing in small isolated plateau Bloke (Slovenia). Traditional folk Bloke skiing (for the first time in written sources described in 1689) became more and more popular with spreading of modern skiing in Slovenia at the beginning of the 20th century. Before that almost no one knew anything about that isolated premodern skiing phenomena. When Bloke folk skiing was newly discovered, represented one of the anchors of creating the Slovenian national ski identity. Individual pioneers of modern skiing in Slovenia and in particular the Yugoslav winter-sports association (founded in Ljubljana, 1922) recognized in Bloke skiing the great advantage and opportunity that Slovenian (then Yugoslav) skiing would become known and recognized in the world. Strive for the development of modern skiing in Bloke was seen in organizing excursions, courses and competitions there and finally, they listened to the initiatives scientifically explore Bloke folk skiing, which meant that the Bloke skiing after1930 bacame known to the world readers of all eminent skiing serials (Der Winter, The British Ski Year Book…). The question that arises for itself when presenting a paper at a conference in Altay is how many similarities can be found between the process of building the Slovenian national skiing identity around 1930 (and later) with contemporary occurring situation in modern China, when the world's superpower with splendid examples of ancient skiing is on the way to be placed finally on the global ski (historical) map.

中文论文：

连接传统民俗滑雪与现代国家认同的滑雪：斯洛文尼亚案例

在长期过程中，当前滑雪的历史，包括目前在阿勒泰的会议正为对滑雪全球性的认知和解释以前支离破碎的滑雪片段铺平道路，进而为拼接式的世界滑雪历史做出诠释。同时我们可以观察到在一些分离的滑雪故事中也有一些相似之处。一个现代性的例子，检测到的阿勒泰部分的史前滑雪历史在某些方面可能与在一个与世隔绝的布洛克高原（斯洛文尼亚）发现的古老民间滑雪的开端有相似之处。

在20世纪初，传统的民间布洛克滑雪（第一次书面性的描述可追溯到1689年）随着现代滑雪在斯洛文尼亚的传播而越来越受欢迎。在这之前，几乎没有人知道任何关于孤立的前现代滑雪现象。新发现的布洛克民间滑雪，代表着创建斯洛文尼亚全国性滑雪的身份的一个锚点。斯洛文尼亚的现代滑雪的先驱者，尤其南斯拉夫的冬季体育协会（1922年成立于卢布尔雅那）认为布洛克滑雪有优势和机会让世界认可斯洛文尼亚（当时的南斯拉夫）的滑雪地位。这种滑雪的优势和机会使斯洛文尼亚滑雪将达到已知的和公认的世界水平。争取发展布洛克的现代滑雪的努力表现在组织远足、课程和比赛。最后，他们倾听了科学探索布洛克民间滑雪的倡议，这意味着在1930年之后布洛克滑雪已为世界上所有著名的滑雪系列的读者所知（《冬季》、《英国滑雪年鉴》等）。

当在阿勒泰会议上呈现一篇论文时，问题本身在于在创建斯洛文尼亚国家滑雪身份约1930年（后来）的过程中如何发掘它与当代中国现代滑雪所发生的情况中的更多的相似性。而在此时，拥有古老辉煌滑雪史的世界超级大国正走在并入世界滑雪（历史）地图的路上。

4.26 哈萨克斯坦地区滑雪发展历史 The history of the development of skiing of kazakhstan

柏克蓓（哈萨克斯坦） Burkitbay G. Ayagan（KAZ）

个人简介 Personal information

Director of the Institute of State History, Science Committee, Ministry of Education and Science of the Republic of Kazakhstan, Prof. Dr. Burkitbay Ayagan

国家历史科学委员会研究所主任，哈萨克斯坦联合国教育科学部部长，柏克蓓·阿亚干博士

English Paper:

The history of the development of skiing of kazakhstan

Many European scientists may not know a thing-on the ancient time of Turks Khanate and the Empire of Genghis Khan, the territory of Kazakh people covered theSouth Siberia and the Altai region. And this region was very cold and the winter was very long. The long winters' snow was very thick and there lived many animals such as wolf, fox, sables, squirrels, etc.

The ski arts in Kazakhstan were not very popular in the places as Shymkent, Tashkent, Taraz, but in the places of north Kazakhstan as Astana, Kostanay, Kokshetau, Petropavlovsk (Kyzyljar), Pavlodar, Oskemen, Semey, Karagandy, the ski arts have been developed since the ancient time. On the ancient time, the ski was especially used for hunting. The skis of Hunters and snipers were very short (1.5-2 meters), and they were made by flat boards of wood.

The ski arts spread to Kazakh people should from the people of Siberia-as Evenk, Yakut, Tatar, Komi, Mordovians. As we know, the etymology of the word "ski" in Kazakh language as "Shanggy" itself shows that this word is from the ancient time. As well as the word "ski" in Russian language is "lyzhi" (лыжи), the Russian came to Kazakh land was happened in the 18th-20th century. And in the 20th century, the number of skiers has increased sharply - because many special training centers of skiers were opened during the Soviet-Finnish War and the World War II, and many young people and students were involved in there.

The ski racing in Kazakhstan has been systematically started in the 50s-60s of ×× century. For example, when I was at school (1967-1972) there always have been ski racings among young people of schools, villages, and I was always been a part of them and got prizes.

On that time, there were many types of ski in Kazakhstan appeared. As we said the ski for hunters, which was sharp and made by flat boards of wood; as well as the ski for the children and the school students. And also on that time, most of the local people were going hunting or go into forest by using horses or ski during whole winter.

Generally in Kazakhstan, until now people are still using the most environmentally hunting way-using the eagles, golden eagle or falcon. Of course, as we know, unfortunately people nowadays are also using rifles, jeep cars or even the helicopters.

And now, the ski racing is including the ski jumping, cross-country, slalom, biathlon and etc.

As far as we know the first official ski race was held in 1767 in Norway. And after that several special ski clubs opened in Norway（1874），Finland（1886），Germany（1891），Austria and Switzerland（1892）and Russia（1895）. And also the Olympic Games in 1929，the World Cup in 1924，the Winter Games which were held in Asia in 1987.

The first championship of skiing in Kazakhstan was held in 1934 in Kyzyljar（Petropavlovsk）. In 1968，A. Suslov from Kazakhstan became the champion of the USSR，and I. Garanin won the bronze medal at the 1967 Winter Olympic Games.

A. Artyomenko and M. Husainov were the absolute champions of the USSR by the alpine skiing. And the famous V. Smirnov was the champion of the Olympic Games in 1989 and1994.（I. Garanin，V. Smirnov. K. Nogambaev，L. Turgyn etc.）In 2011，the Kazakhstan skiers have reached a great success in the Asian Winter Games of Almaty. At the moment，the ski sports of Kazakhstan are developing at schools，colleges，universities，as well as sports clubs. Besides that，there are thousands of children playing ski as a hobby.

中文论文：

哈萨克斯坦地区滑雪发展历史

很多欧洲科学家可能不知道一件事，即在土耳其汗国和成吉思汗帝国时期，哈萨克人统治西伯利亚和阿勒泰地区。这一地区极其寒冷且冬天十分漫长。冬季的雪很厚，这里栖息着很多动物比如狼、狐狸、貂、松鼠等等。

滑雪在哈萨克斯坦的什姆肯特、塔什干以及塔拉兹地区并不十分流行，但在哈萨克斯坦北部，如阿斯塔纳、库斯塔奈州、科克舍套、彼得巴甫洛夫斯克、巴普洛达尔、厄斯克门、塞米、卡拉甘达地区，滑雪在古代时就得到了发展。滑雪板在古代只用于打猎。猎人和狙击兵的滑雪板特别短（1.5-2 米），是由木板制成的。

滑雪应该是由西伯利亚的鄂温克人，雅库特人，鞑靼人，科米人以及莫尔多瓦人传给哈萨克族人。“ski”这一词在哈萨克语中为“Shanggy”，该词的词源显示其源自古代。“ski”在俄语中为“lyzhi”（лыжи），俄罗斯人到哈萨克是在 18-20 世纪。在 20 世纪时，滑雪者数量突然急剧增加。原因就在于在苏芬战争以及二战期间这里开办了很多滑雪者训练中心，很多年轻人和学生加入其中。

哈萨克斯坦的滑雪比赛在 20 世纪 50-60 年代有条不紊的开始了。比如，当我上学期间（1967-1972）学校以及村庄的青年之间经常举办滑雪比赛，我总是参与其中并赢得奖项。

那时，哈萨克斯坦出现了很多类型的滑雪板。正如我们所说的，猎人用的滑雪板是尖头且由平滑的木板制成的，以及孩子和学生用的滑雪板，也是在那个时候，大多数的当地人在冬天时会去打猎或凭借马或滑雪板进入森林。

在哈萨克斯坦，直到现在人们仍然使用这种最环保的狩猎方式，即使用鹰、金鹰或猎鹰狩猎。当然，就我们所知，不幸的是，人们现在也在使用步枪、吉普车甚至是直升飞机打猎。

现在，滑雪比赛包含跳台滑雪、越野赛跑、回转滑雪、冬季两项等等。

就我们所知，第一场正式滑雪比赛是在1767年在挪威举行的。在那之后，几个滑雪俱乐部在挪威开办（1874），芬兰（1886）、德国（1891）、奥地利和瑞士（1892）、俄罗斯（1895）、以及奥林匹克运动会（1929）、世界杯赛（1924）和在亚洲举办的冬季运动会（1987）。

巴萨克斯坦的第一届滑雪锦标赛是1934年在彼得巴甫洛夫斯克举办的。在1968年，来自于哈萨克斯坦的A. Suslov成为了苏联的冠军，I. Garanin赢得了1967年冬季奥林匹克运动会的铜牌。Artyomenko和M. Husainov是苏联高山滑雪的绝对冠军。著名的V. Smirnov是1989年和1994年奥林匹克运动会的冠军（I. Garanin，V. Smirnov. K. Nogambaev，L. Turgyn等等）。在2011年，哈萨克斯坦的滑雪者在阿拉木图的亚洲冬季运动会上取得了巨大的成功。现在，哈萨克斯坦的滑雪运动在中小学、大学、以及运动俱乐部发展。除此之外，有成千上万的孩子把滑雪作为一种兴趣。

4.27 尤通黑门山高级路线—“古老滑道的新转机” Jotunheimen Haute Route-“New Turns in Old Tracks”

贝克（挪威） Dag Inge Bakke（NOR）

个人简介 Personal Information

Dag Inge Bakke（38），Vågå，Norway

Nature Interpreter（guide）employed by Klimapark 2469 AS

Academic：Nature and culture-guiding（Hedemark College 2011），Bachelor in outdoor studies（Nord-Trøndelag College 2010），Natural Resource Management（Nord-Trøndelag College 2000），Sport

-studies（Meråker High School 1995）

Courses：NSA-ski instructor，NF-mountain guide，Red Cross Rescue-Technical manager Avalanche，Personal experience，Grown up on the foothills of the Jotunheimen Mountains in southern Norway，skiing has always been a central part of my life. Skis are used for playing，sports and for transportation，and they are always in reach from late Octoberuntil June. I competed in cross-country skiing in my youth but converted later to telemark-skiing and alpine-skiing. I have long experience as a mountain guide，and special ski-touring. Avalanche safety and rescue techniques have been a main focus in my work. I have also worked as a reindeers-herdsman and Park Ranger.

达格·英奇·贝克—挪威考古学家、山地指导员、滑雪教练

教育背景：自然与文化指导（赫德马克学院，2011），户外研究学士（北特伦德拉格学院，2010），自然资源管理（北特伦德拉格学院，2000），体育研究（梅罗克高中，1995）

社会实践：NSA-滑雪教练，NF-山地指导员，红十字会救援-雪崩技术经理

个人经历：贝克成长于挪威南部的 Jotunheimen 山麓，滑雪一直是他生活中的核心部分。滑雪板可用于玩耍、运动和运输，雪板在十月底至次年六月是一直可以用的。年轻时，贝克参加过越野滑雪，但后来转为泰勒马克滑雪和高山滑雪。我对于高山滑雪和特殊滑雪旅游有着长期丰富的经验。雪崩的安全和救援技术一直是我工作的重点。我也当过驯鹿放牧员和公园护林员。

English Paper：

Jotunheimen Haute Route- "New turns in old tracks"

Ski-tracks have cut through the snow-covered Jotunheimen Mountains for thousands of years. Who were the first people that challenged the rough nature? What did they look like? What kind of skis did they use? These are questions we will probably never get precise answers to. However，the ancient ski history still follows us when we are making turns through fresh snow today.

The mountains can be both rough and demanding，and especially so in the winter. However，the mountains are also filled with resources. For many people up north，reindeer was the main source of living. Those who were most skilled in dealing with the challenge of the mountains also had the best chance to survive.

Reindeer are snow-loving animals，specially developed through thousands of generations to handle snow and freezing in all forms. In contrast，we humans are a potential tragedy in the snow standing on two narrow and naked legs. We developed as a species made for the savanna and tropic temperatures. However, generations of experience, specialized technology, and our great ability to learn and adapt, makes it possible for us to live in almost any environment.

The development of skis and skiing must have been a great revolution for man. A nomadic life with a seasonal migration from the mountains in the summer down to the valleys or out to the coastline for a winter stay could finally change. With skis humans could travel easily through deep snow, and even quicker than on bare ground. Skis opened up new areas for living, and enabled a new way of hunting. Tracking animals in snow could be an efficient way to hunt down big game like deer and moose, especially so if it is downhill and the snow is soft and deep. The invention of the ski transformed humans from being helpless in snow to being one of the best adapted creatures on snow.

It might be 10 000 years since the first skier slipped through the snow-covered landscape for the first time. Even with this long distance in time I am convinced that we still can share some of the same satisfaction of being able to stay on top of the snow for the first time. It is a little bit like flying, we are not made for it, and not supposed to do it by nature, but we can do it anyway! We are floating on top, and can go where others struggle to move.

1. Hunting on skis

Hunting on skis has a long tradition in Norway. Skis were used to move around and track animals, but also to hunt them in slopes-using the speed going downhill to get close to the animals for shooting an arrow or throwing a spear. Already in a 13th century source we hear about hunters who ski downhill, get close to the reindeer and manage to kill them with spears. The truthfulness of these old sources has been questioned. Is it even possible to "ski in" a reindeer? How good control of the skis is it possible to get on the traditional wooden skis, with simple bindings and soft leather boots? However, there are also newer stories, dating back to 17th century, that describe similar techniques. This type of hunting has also taken place in modern times using guns.

2. From a vital tool in subsistence to fun and amusement

Why is it so popular to ski downhill today? And why is it accepted to take great risk, doing something so "meaningless" as skiing down a steep mountain? If you wanted to be a great hunter back in the days, you also had to be a really good skier-not only cross country, but also downhill. A lot of practice is the key to becoming a good skier. And a successful hunt depends on great skills used at the right moment.

A successful hunt can give the hunter and his family a lot of food from a short effort. Hunting is, however, not only based on skills, sometimes it is also based on luck. So in general, compared to agriculture, which is depending more on good planning, systematic and hard work, hunting has more of a spirit of gambling.

To be a good skier, you need to spend a lot of time on your skis, and you have to challenge yourself. Ski-play probably was a key to becoming a competent skier. Who could go fastest? Run quickest? Jump of the steepest cliff and just stay upright down the bumpy downhill?

The best skiers today may get a price and a goblet, but back in the days, the best skier was the one who could provide plenty of food for his family. To be a good skier is still a very honorable title in Norway. Skiing is the national sport, and it has a long tradition as a sport, going back to the 18th century.

3. Ski-touring in ancient ski-tracks

The Jotunheimen Haute Route is a five to six days ski-tour in the heart of Jotunheimen, established after the model of the classical Haute Route in the Alps. This "high route" takes you to some of the wildest and most beautiful mountain terrain in southern Norway. As an aside, it is worth mentioning that the name Jotunheimen actually means "Home of the Giants" and is a description for the "outside world" in the Old Norse mythology. The route goes over peaks and mountain passes, including the two highest peaks in Norway, Galdhøpiggen and Glittertind, which are higher than 2400 m. It also goes through a landscape with a lot of history.

The first known winter "mountaineers" in Jotunheimen were of course hunters. A story from the 19th century tells us about the well-known hunter Jo Gjende who was hunting for reindeer close to the second highest peak in Norway, Glittertind, when a reindeer bull ran all the way up to the top. The stubborn Jo said to his companion Gullbrand that if the reindeer could do it, so would he! The story also says that he left a reindeer antler on the highest peak, and on the next day Gullbrand went up, and brought the antler back down to Jo.

Jotunheimen has always been an area with a lot of resources. Up here the reindeer-herds roamed freely. You can still see them today. The sheep and cattle feast on the best grass and herbs during the summer, and melting ice and snow brings water down to the drier valleys around. However, the mountain range has always been a barrier between east and west. Trading routes went over many of these mountain passes, and a crossing could involve great risk, especially if the weather turned bad during the journey. Melting ice is now bringing some of those stories back. With all the history and tradition going back to the ancient hunters, a journey through this landscape is given an extra dimension. It might even put life in a new perspective when you "struggle" the last meters forward to the next accommodation, based in a luxuriously staffed lodge with drinks, food and a warm bed.

The Jotunheimen Haute Route is designed to give the skiers some of the best downhill skiing, so it does not follow the old trade routes in general. Instead it brings the skiers over some of the highest and most beautiful peaks in Jotunheimen. It requires good weather and favorable snow conditions, and often a strong effort to complete this route.

Most people prefer to bring a guide on this trip. The route goes over high peaks, glaciers, avalanche hazard areas and includes an unpredictable weather. A qualified guide with local knowledge can make the all difference between success and failure. The main task for a modern ski guide is of course to bring all his clients safely from A to B and give them a positive and happy journey. Good snow, challenging terrain and a nice view, could be some cues, but don't forget to put it all in a context. The guide can provide interesting information about history and nature, which opens up for a new perspective in addition to the actual skiing, and brings the whole experience to a higher level.

4. Modern skis-old shape and technology

Today alpine touring skis (randoneè) or telemark skis are mainly used on this kind of trips. Light skis make the climbing more comfortable, but many skiers will prefer a more "solid" ski on the downhill. The ideal ski for this kind of trip is light, but still stabile. Climbing skins are used to get good grip to the snow on the way up, but are removed for the downhill skiing. It is very interesting to see how some of the modern deep-snow loving powder skis have a lot in common with some of the prehistorically skis that have been found, and are still used in some places. With a full reverse sidecut and continuous curve rocker, these skis offer a powder skiing experience unmatched to skis with any other shape. They are not good for carving, and can be a real challenge when to traversing on hard packed snow, but in the soft snow you can really go surfing on these boards.

If we go ten years back, there was no market for this type of skitouring in Norway. Most Norwegians used their "mountain skis" or light telemark skis, and had no interest, skills or equipment for steep skiing in the mountains. Alpine skiing was a sport reserved for lift-based alpine resorts. New equipment and a new wave of interest for the mountains have changed this quickly and profoundly. Today many people are eager to climb the mountain before they can make turns down in virgin powder with a great joy. “To earn your turns” is a well used expression.

Norway has a big national marked for this kind of skitouring. In the Alp Region of Europe this type of skiing has been popular for decades. Alpine skitouring are also very popular in North America. Skiing is the national sport in Norway, and everyone “does it”. If just a small number of the alpine or cross country skiers convert to alpine skitouring, it will quickly become crowded up in the mountains…

As a conclusion: Successful skiing naturally depends on the skiers skills. The ancient hunter had to perform on an impressive level, combining high speed, good balance and perfect precision to achieve any success. Today we do steep skiing just for the excitement and for the fun of it, and the motivation is thus slightly different. However, if you like to ski the Jotunheimen Haute Route, and plan to do it in a controlled and safe way, the terrain here demands skiing on a high level, based on years of training. Many of us love skiing, and we love to practice and challenge ourselves to become better skiers. I like to believe this has a historical reason-maybe as a small “ski-gene” hidden somewhere in our DNA? -programmed to always convince us about the unquestionable fact that skiing is great fun!

中文论文：

尤通黑门山高级路线—“古老滑道的新转机”

数千年前白雪皑皑的尤通黑门山上就遍布了雪道。谁是向自然挑战的第一拨人？他们长什么样？使用什么样的滑雪板？这些问题也许永远得不到准确的答案，但是如今当我们在新雪上做回转动作时依然有古老滑雪的历史痕迹。

山上生活艰苦并且条件苛刻，冬天尤甚。但是山上资源丰富，对北部的很多人来说，驯鹿是生活的主要来源。那些擅长应对深山恶劣环境的人往往拥有最好的生存机会。

驯鹿是喜欢雪的动物，经过数千代的发展进化，其能应对各样的雪地及寒冷条件。而我们人类凭借纤细的两条腿，在雪地条件中就是一个潜在的悲剧。人类已进化成适应热带草原及热带气候，不过通过几代人积累的经验，精湛的技术以及强大的学习适应能力，人类几乎可以在所有的条件下生活。

游牧生活常常进行季节性的迁移，夏季人们从山上迁到山谷，冬季从山上迁到海岸线，滑雪板和滑雪运动的发展对人类来说是一场伟大的革新，这种游牧生活终于可以改变。利用滑雪板，可以轻松的穿过厚厚的积雪，甚至比走在裸地上还要快。滑雪板打开了人类生活的新领域，实现了一种新的打猎方式。在雪地上追踪猎物是捕获大型动物如鹿和麋鹿的有效方式，特别是在雪质松软深厚的下坡。雪板的出现使得人类成了最适应雪地生活的生物，而在此之前人类在雪地中完全无计可施。

大概早在10000年前，第一个滑雪者首次滑过了白雪覆盖的山脉。尽管这么久远，我相信我们依然可以感受到第一次能待在雪顶的激动心情。这有点像飞翔的感觉，我们天生不会做也不应该做的事情，最终我们做到了，我们可以在雪顶漂浮，可以去他人难以动弹的地方。

一、滑雪板打猎

滑雪板打猎在挪威有着悠久的传统。滑雪板被用来四处移动和追踪动物，但在斜坡处也用来猎杀动物，借助下坡的速度接近猎物，用箭或长矛将其射杀。在十三世纪传说中，我们就听说猎人滑雪下坡，接近驯鹿，用长矛将其杀死。这种传说的真实性有待确认，利用滑雪板追逐驯鹿真的有可能吗？传统的木制雪板只有简易的固定器和软皮靴雪板，需要多好的控制力才能操控这种雪板？

二、从重要的生存工具到娱乐

如今为什么速降滑雪这么受欢迎？人们为什么能接受这么大的风险，做这么“没有意义”的事情，从陡峭的山下滑下来？在过去如果你想成为一个极好的猎人，你必须得是一个优秀的滑雪者，不仅是越野式，也包括速降。大量练习是成为优秀滑雪者的关键，成功的狩猎取决于在合适的时刻使用正确的技巧。

成功的狩猎可以让猎人和其家人在短期内获取大量的食物。但是，打猎靠的不光是技术，有时也要看运气。农业主要依赖于良好的规划，系统的劳作和努力，与农业相比，狩猎更具有赌博精神。

要成为一名优秀的滑雪者，需要花费大量的时间练习，并且不断的挑战自己。参加滑雪比赛是成为优秀滑雪者的关键所在，最终看谁能滑的最快？看谁能从最陡峭的峭壁滑下，并保持在崎岖的下坡直接滑行？

现今最好的滑雪者可能得到奖金和奖杯，但在过去，最好的滑雪者为其家人提供充足的食物。在挪威，成为一个优秀的滑雪者仍然是一个光荣的头衔，滑雪是一项国家运动，作为一项体育项目，其历史可追溯到18世纪。

三、在古老的滑雪道上滑野雪

尤通黑门山高级路线是在尤通黑门山中心区域为期5到6天的滑雪行程，根据阿尔卑斯山经典高级路线模式建立。这种“高级路线”可以带你去到挪威南部最原始最美丽的山区，另外值得一提的是尤通黑门山这个名字实际上意味着“巨人之家”，在北欧神州中描述“外部世界”。此路线经过许多山顶和山道，包括挪威两大最高峰 Galdhøpiggen 和 Glittertind，高于2400米，还穿过历史悠久的景观。

尤通黑门山第一批为人所知的“登山者”当然是猎人。19 世纪流传的故事讲述了一位著名的猎人 Jo Gjende，在靠近挪威第二高峰 Glittertind 处猎鹿，驯鹿一路跑到了山顶。顽固的 Jo 对他的同伴 Gullbrand 说如果驯鹿能到达山顶，他也能。这个故事还说到他把一只鹿角留在了最高峰，第二天 Gullbrand 登到山顶，将鹿角取回，交给了 Jo。

尤通黑门山具有丰富的资源。在这里，鹿群自由漫步，今天依然能够看到他们。夏季牛羊享用最好的牧草，融化的冰雪给干燥的山谷带来大量的水源。但是山脉一直是东西方之间的障碍。贸易线穿过很多山道，横道充满风险，尤其是旅途中天气变得不好时。如今融化的冰雪使一些故事在现实中重现，所有的历史和传统重现古老的猎人，旅行穿越这片风景将会带来更多的感受。在最后几米，当你步履艰难地走向下一个住处时，住处就是一个配置豪华的别墅，有饮料、美食和温暖的大床，你可能会得到新的人生观。

尤通黑门山高级路线目的在于给滑雪者提供最好的速降滑雪，所以此路线整体上并没有沿用古老的贸易路线，而是交将滑雪者带到了尤通黑门山一些最高最美的山峰上。完成这条路线，需要良好的天气条件和有利的雪质条件，并且通常还需要滑雪者强大的努力。

大多数人会选择带一个导游。这条路线穿过山峰、冰川、雪崩危险区域，还有不可预测的天气，一个具备当地知识的专业导游是成败的重要因素。现代滑雪导游主要的任务无疑是把客户安全地从 A 带到 B，给客户一个积极快乐的旅行。优良的雪质，具有挑战性的地形，美丽的景观都是提示，但别忘了将其融合在一起，导游可以提供有趣的历史和自然信息，除了真正的滑雪外，这些都打开了一个新的视角，并将整个体验提升到更高的水平。

四、现代滑雪板—古老形状和科技

如今高山野雪板和泰勒马克滑雪板主要用于这种长涉中。轻质的雪板使登山更加的舒适，但许多滑雪者在下坡时更加喜欢“坚硬”的雪板。这种旅行的理想用板应该重量轻，但仍稳定。止滑带能保证在上坡时良好的抓雪力，在下坡滑雪时去除。有趣的是一些适用于深厚粉雪的现代滑雪板和古老滑雪板有大量的共同点，并仍然在一些地方使用。这些雪板带有完整的逆向侧切和连续的曲线 rocker，其所提供的粉雪滑雪体验是其他板型无法比拟的。此类雪板不适用 carving，并且在坚硬的积雪上使用也是一种挑战，但在松软的雪上，这些板子可以滑行自如。

十年前，在挪威这种野雪板完全没有市场，大部分挪威人都用他们的“山地板”或轻质泰勒马克滑雪板，对陡峭的山地滑雪不感兴趣，并且也没有相应的技术和装备。高山滑雪是 lift-based 高山度假地的专有运动，新型装备和新一轮对高山运动兴趣的兴起，快速深远地改变了这一状况。如今能在原始粉雪上做回转动作之前，许多人已经迫不及待地登上了山。“实现这种回转”成了常用的追求方式。

挪威有一个大型的区域，就是以这种野雪滑雪为标志。在欧洲高山地区，这种滑雪方式已经流行了几十年，其在北美也很受欢迎。滑雪在挪威是国家运动，每个人都滑雪。如果仅仅一小部分高山或越野滑雪转变为高山野雪滑雪，那么高山上很快就会挤满人群。

总结：成功的滑雪一般取决于滑雪者的滑雪技术。古老的猎人要想获得任何成功，必须有惊人的滑雪水平，高速、良好的平衡力和完美的精密度。如今，我们在陡峭的高山滑雪只是为了获得刺激和乐趣，因此目的稍有不同。但是，如果你喜欢在尤通黑门山高级路线滑雪，并且想确保安全可控性，这里的地形特点要求较高的滑雪水平，这基于多年的训练。我们很多人都热爱滑雪，喜欢练习并不断地挑战自己，成为一个更好的滑雪者。我相信这有一个历史原因—也许是由于我们 DNA 里藏有“滑雪基因”—这些基因使我们信服滑雪超级有趣，这是一个毫无疑问的事实。

4.28 中亚的滑雪历史 The history of ski in central asia

达木丁苏荣·策往道尔吉（蒙古国）
Damudingsurong · cewangdaoerji (MON)

个人简介 Personal information

Damdinsuren TSEVEENDORJ, Mongolian, male, Born on May 16th in 1949 in Mongolia;

He used to conduct academic exchanges in universities and Science Academy in Mongolia and several related countries. Between 1973 and 2014, he published over 488 works in more than 10 countries, including 38 monographs, 50 collaborative works, 400 scientific articles and reports.

At present, Director of Institute of Archaeology, Mongolian Academy of Sciences, Vice President of Mongolian Academy of the Humanity Sciences, Mongolian Academy of Sciences

达木丁苏荣·策往道尔吉，蒙古，男，1949 年 5 月 16 号出生在蒙古，教授、高级研究员。

曾在蒙古国内以及多个相关国家的大学、科学院学术交流。

在1973年和2014年之间他出版了38部专著，50份合作作品，400篇学术论文和报告，总计488份作品在数十个国家发行。

目前，蒙古科学院考古研究所所长，蒙古科学院蒙古人文科学院的副校长。

English Paper：

THE HISTORY OF Mongolia is a country of steppe nomads. It is famous with its strong horses, two-humped camels-theships of the desert, and yaks-potentates of high snow-capped mountains and etc. All of these means of transportations are widely used in economic traditions of Central Asian steppe nomads.

Once, envoy of King Louis IX William of Rubruck, who visited the Great Mongol Empirein 1253, with great surprise wrote about the big Yurts - traditional Mongolian housing. According to his words, "the Mongols constructed huge Tergengers (yurt with a cart). Big-ger yurt was constructed on a huge cart, the length of the axis of which reached 20 feet. Two rows of 22 oxen were harnessed in such carts. Rich Mongols had between 100 and 200 of these covered wagons. It is known that Bat Khan had 26 wives. Each wife owned one of these, in which she lived. In addition, there were about 200 small covered wagons that maids lived in".

On the other types of transportation as skis, sleds and boats remained very little information in the historical chronicles, and the real relics or images are almost unknown. Only in the "Compendium of Chronicles" Rashid ad-Din writes that "They (the Mongols-D. TS) make special boards, which are called "chané", and they set leather reins in it, sliding on snow cover, abut a stick in the ground, same way as floating by boat on water.

Speed on thechané (ski) in the steppe and the plain, on ascent and descent, is high enough so that skiers can overtake mountain bull and other animals. Hunters dragged more other skies in order to stack killed wildfowls. If a considerable number ofloads are carried on them, then a little effort would be needed to go easily on the snow crust. If someone inexperienced would try to ski on this, then his legs would definitely disperse apart or fall, especially on slopes and during rapid run-up. Indeed, a trained man would run on this with a great ease. No one will believe this until it has been seen.

The Chane is known in most areas of Turkestan and Moghulistan. Especially this is more popular inBargudzhin-Tocumen, and among tribes Kori, Kirgiz, Urasut, Telengut and Tumat.

Since 1994, "Ancient Altai" project have been organized in the Mongolian Altai by joint Mongolian - American - Russian team led by D. Tseveendorj, E. Jacobson and V. D. Kubarev-Institute of Archaeology, MAS, University of Oregon (USA) and Institute of Archaeology and Ethnography (Russia) respectively.

For over 6 field seasons the field team have been discovered dozens of petroglyphic sites, burial mounds, khirgisuurs, stone fences, steles, deer stones and stone sculptures. One of the largest petroglyphic sites is located in the area of BagaOigor, where we have reviewed and analyzed approximately five thousand scenes. Among them, there is only image of a hunter who put a pair of skis on. Ahead of the hunter a mountain goat (ibex) runs with huge curved horns of which ends reach the small tail. There are more than twenty ridges on the horns and it has small and rounded ears, and little elongated muzzle. Also, its neck is long, which is SKI IN CENTRAL ASIA * shown straight up, torso is long as well, and legs are bent inward at the time of the jump.

The hunter chases the goat sliding on the snow on skis, which are medium sized and front ends are curved up. Legs of the hunter are slightly bent at the knees, expressing the movement of not only the hunter but also, the rapid skiing. There is a long and wide quiver attached on the hunter's belt. In front of him, he keeps a ready to shoot bow and arrow. The bow is small and short.

Moreover, there is a dog with a long snout and a large open mouth running beside the hunter. She has thin ears, a thick neck, a powerful and concise body, a thin tail with a curved end-male gender is marked clearly. Legs are stretched in full length and shown in full jump. The movement of this man and the dog is illustrated with a great ability. All rapidly run forward with their full might. The goat is on the brink of life and death, and the hunter This form of bow and quiver was broadly spread during the Bronze Age. It is possible to consider that this image was made in the Bronze Age, according to the depiction style of the man, the goat, the dog and the weapons. This petroglyph scene from the river valley Baga Oygorbears atestimony to the fact that skis have been used in the high snowy regions of Central Asia (Northern and Western Mongolia, also present Tuva, Altai and Buryatia, and others) since ancient times, in this case, since the Bronze Age. This type of transport and its role in life of the 13thcentury Mongolian people of Central Asia, though, it is short, but are clearly recorded in the collection of the historical chronicles. and dog run for good luck.

中文论文：

古时的中亚有不同形式的交通方式，比如雪板、雪橇和船等，关于它们的历史记载很少，并且关于它们的真实的遗迹或图像大多也是不得而知的。仅仅 Rashid ad-Din 在《记录刚要》中提到："他们（蒙古人）制作特别的木板，叫做'chané'，并且他们把皮革绳设定在上面，在雪地上滑行，滑杆紧插着地，滑行的方式就像船在水上运行一样。"

雪板在草地、平原上，在上坡和下坡时的速度都比较快，所以滑雪者能够超过山牛和其他动物。为了堆起更多猎杀的野禽，猎人会拖带更多的雪板。如果只有相当数量的负载，雪板在雪地上很轻轻松地就可以滑行。如果没有经验的人想要乘雪板滑雪，那他的双腿一定会分开或摔倒，尤其是在坡道上或速滑时。事实上，一个训练有素的滑雪者可以轻松滑行。

"Chane"这种雪板在突厥斯坦和蒙古的大部分地区都为人所知。尤其是在 Bargudzhin-Tocumen 地区及 Kori，Kirgiz，Urasut，Telengut 和 Tumat 部落比较盛行。

自 1994 年，联合团队蒙古—美国—俄罗斯已在阿勒泰组织了"古老阿尔泰"项目课题组。该团队由 D. Tseveendorj，E. Jacobson 和 V. D. Kubarev-考古研究所，MAS，俄勒冈大学（美国）和考古和民族志研究所（俄罗斯）领导。

通过小组 6 年多的现场实地勘探，已发现数十个岩石壁画地点，墓地群，石围栏、石碑、鹿石头和石雕塑。其中一个最大的岩石壁画地点位于 BagaOigor，这里有接近 5000 处现场被考察和分析。在它们当中，只有一幅猎人踏雪板的图画。在猎人的前面是一只奔跑的山羊，山羊的弯曲大角的末端顶着自己的尾巴。角上有多于 20 处的粗纹路，尾巴又小又圆，伸长的口鼻也很小，脖子也很长，直立着，躯干也很长，腿在跳跃之际向内弯曲。

猎人在雪板上滑行着抓住山羊，雪板是中等大小，前部末尾有弧度。猎人的腿在膝盖处微微弯曲，这显示出猎人运动的姿势和快速的滑行。有一个箭袋系在猎人的腰间。猎人展现出欲拉弓射箭的姿势，所用的弓小而短。

而且，一条有着长鼻子和口部大开的猎犬在猎人旁边奔跑着。这条猎犬有着薄薄的耳朵、粗重的脖子、强大简洁的身体和一条小尾巴。腿部完全伸展开，展现出尽力跳跃的姿势。这个猎人和这条猎犬的运动姿势都彰显出巨大的力量，在向前快速奔跑中展现出全身的能量。山羊处在生死之际，而猎人和猎犬是在为好运气而奔跑。

在青铜器时代，这种形式的弓和箭袋广泛传播。我们从对猎人、山羊、猎犬和武器的描述中可以推断出这幅图画成于青铜器时代。来自于 BagaOygor 河谷的岩石壁画场景证实了这样一个事实，即自从青铜器时期，雪板以用于中亚的高山雪地区域（蒙古的北部和西部，也就是现在的图瓦、阿尔泰、布里亚特和其他地方)。尽管这种交通方式及其在 13 世纪的中亚蒙古人生活中的作用不是那么大，但是它们却被明确地载入史册。

4.29 穿着雪鞋的汤姆森 塞拉的雪地邮递员 Snowshoe Thompson: Sierra's Skiing Mailman

格兰·保尔森（美国） Glen Poulsen（USA）

个人简介 Brief Introduction

Name（full name）: Glen forest Poulsen, Gender: M, Passport No: C10236815, Occupation: Ski Guide, property manager, Postal address: Po Box 2637, Olympic Valley, Ca USA, back ground information:（what kind of ski related race and had experiences or success you have, and your goal）: Active ski guide in polar regions, arctic, Antarctic. Veteran of euroloppet races including vasaloppet, birkiebiener and 5 other euroloppet races. Skied on all continents. Decades of competition in alpine, Nordic, and ski jumping…Ihave managed and operated three small ski areas. I am excited to spend time with and learn the ancient methods of skiing, meet the indigenous people and promote xinjian as the cradle of skiing in the world…

格兰·保尔森，男，滑雪教练，地产经理，背景信息：活跃于极地地区的滑雪教练，曾走过各大洲体验滑雪。数十年间曾在高山滑雪、北欧两项、跳台滑雪项目中任教等。曾经管理过三个小型的滑雪场，乐于学习传统的滑雪技巧，与当地人交谈，致力于推广新疆阿勒泰是世界滑雪摇篮的理念。

English Paper:

Snowshoe Thompson: Sierra's Skiing Mailman

Out of all the skiers who have carved the slopes around Lake Tahoe, the most famous is undoubtedly John "Snowshoe" Thompson, the legendary skiing mailman of the Sierra Nevada.（In the 19th century skis were often called snowshoes in the California mining camps.）

Born Jon Torsteinson-Rue in Telemark, Norway, "John" was 10 years old when his family immigrated to the U. S. Midwest in 1837. In 1851, the 24-year-old farm boy was bit by gold fever and he ran off to California. He found no gold, but he did Americanize his name to John A. Thompson and settled in Placerville, about 30 miles east of Sacramento. Thompson farmed in the summer and cut commercial firewood in the winter. In 1855 Thompson saw an ad published in the *Sacramento Union* : People Lost to the World: Uncle Sam Needs Carrier. The Placerville postmaster needed someone to carry mail 90 miles east, up and over the Sierra range to Utah Territory, in the dead of winter. There weren't any takers until Thompson, who used to ski to school as a child in Norway, decided to answer the call to duty. It took him 3 days to ski across the rugged peaks and arrive in the settlement of Genoa, just south of present-day Carson City, Nevada. No one in the region had seen skis before Thompson showed them his homemade long boards and single brake pole.

Twice a month for 20 years Snowshoe hauled an 80-100 pound rucksack full of letters, newspapers, medicine, and other supplies through the mountains. His skis were 10 feet long and weighed 25 pounds. For personal protection, he carried only matches, some beef jerky, crackers and biscuits — no blanket, no gun, no camping gear or compass. Snowshoe rarely stopped and it took him only 48 hours to return to California with the lighter pack. He tried to charge $1 per letter, but some people wouldn't pay and demanded their mail anyway. Naive in the ways of government, he had not signed a contract with the U. S. Postal Service, but Thompson wasn't worried and said, "If I do my job and get the mail to the people, Uncle Sam will pay me." Unfortunately, Thompson was never paid despite an 1869 appeal by the Nevada Legislature to the federal government for $6000 in compensation.

Thompson's skiing ability was legendary. After famed Comstock journalist Dan De Quille watched Snowshoe perform, he wrote: "He flew down the mountainside. He did not ride astride his pole or drag it to one side as was the practice of other snowshoers, but held it horizontally before him after the manner of a tightrope walker. His appearance was graceful, swaying his balance pole to one side and the other in the manner that a soaring eagle dips its wings."

Subject: A additional account of California ski history…

Eighty-eight miles per hour! (150km) No speed record you say? Try telling that to Cornish Bob, the world's first champion speed skier. It was near La Porte, on the snow-covered slopes of Lexington Hill in February of 1867 that he fairly flew to victory over the 1, 804 foot track on twelve foot long wooden skis. Using the magic "dope" concoction of Bill Church, Cornish Bob covered the distance from a standing start in fourteen seconds, leaving his competitors far behind.

"Norway skates," or skis, were first introduced to the mining camps in 1853. Due to the remoteness and altitude of the Plumas and Sierra county camps, skis were the perfect vehicle for winter transportation. Sporting fellows soon began racing and the following year Hugh "Buckskin" Porter began turning out a lengthened and improved version at his Saw Pit Flat workshop.

In 1861, the first organized ski club races were held at Onion Valley, between Quincy and La Porte, giving birth to the sport of downhill ski racing in the western hemisphere.

For the next twelve years races were held between various camps such as Onion Valley, Saw Pit, La Porte, Howland Flat, Port Wine and Gibsonville. In late 1866, the Alturas Snowshoe Club was formed at La Porte to reinvigorate and to bring about a modicum of respectability to the sport. In February, 1867, they held their first formal race and It wasn't until ten years later that a similar ski meet was held in Norway. For the next twenty years or so, organized meets with fifty or more participants, 500 spectators and purses of \$500 to \$1000 (\$50000 today) were held. The racers, representing their towns, made the winter circuit from La Porte, Johnsville, Jamison City, Poker Flat, Sierra City, Monte Cristo and smaller camps.

The skis these early speed demons rode were commonly called "snowshoes" or "Iongboards" and were constructed of tight, vertical-grained Douglas fir. The skis were shaped with planes, the groove on the bottom with a special "grooving" plane, and the tips bent by a long steaming process. Traveling skis were generally eight to ten feet long, while the racing skis were a minimum of ten feet and might reach an unwieldy length of fifteen feet! In both cases however, the binding consisted only of two pieces of leather attached to the sides with three or four holes on each side for lacing tight. A small block of wood was attached to the ski to hold the heel in place.

For starting and stopping, a six foot long single stout pole with a wood block at one end was employed. Starting was accomplished by making three or four strong lunging thrusts, while stopping was a matter of sitting on the pole to apply pressure, creating a drag and at the same time, a spectacular "rooster tail" of snow.

Although a strong start is definitely a plus in this style of racing, the wax or "dope" applied to the base is equally or more important. The recipes to create these substances were closely guarded by the dopemaker, and even today, though the recipes have been handed down, the cooking times were not. Materials used in the brewing of a batch of dope included spermaceti, a waxy substance from the brow of the sperm whale, oil of cedar, Venice turpentine, oil of tar, wintergreen, soapstone, balsam of fir, pine pitch, and in one instance, melted Edison cylindrical records! Thespeeds the dope produced led to slogans such as "Sierra Lightning" and "Dope is King!"

The early generations of longboarders continued the sport until the last race in 1917. During the 1930s there was a small revival, then a much stronger one in the 1950s, another hiatus, and now the present revival, started in 1990. In the spirit of the 19th century racers, three longboard races are now held annually at the Plumas Eureka Ski Bowl at Johnsville. The racers must be dressed in period style clothing, and only dope from authentic recipes and ingredients may be used on the skis. As in the original races, they are gender based, and participants must climb the hill on foot to the starting line. Once a squad of three to four racers is lined up and poised, the gong is sounded and the race is on. The strongest start and the straightest line (along with the best dope and best balance) generally determines the winner.

中文论文：

穿着雪鞋的汤姆森　塞拉的雪地邮递员

滑过雪地和穿过太浩湖的滑雪者中最有名的莫过于穿着雪鞋的约翰·汤姆森了，他是穿越内华达山的传奇邮递员（在 19 世纪，雪板在加州采矿营地常被称为雪鞋）。

Jon Torsteinson-Rue 出生在挪威的特里马，在 1839 年时，John 十岁，他的家人移民到了美国的中西部。在 1851 年，这个 24 岁的农场小伙子受到当时“淘金热”的影响，就跑到了加利福尼亚州。他在那里没有淘到金子，但是却把他的名字美国化成为 John A. Thompson，并且定居在了普莱瑟维尔，在萨克拉门托以东约 30 英里的地方。Thompson 在夏季种植作物，在冬季砍伐商业木柴。在 1855 年，Thompson 在《萨克拉门托联合报》上看到一则广告：人们丢失了世界，山姆大叔需要运送者。普莱瑟维尔邮局需要邮递员在寒冷的冬季向东 90 英里沿途穿过内华达山到犹他州境内发送包裹信物。Thompson 儿时在挪威曾上过滑雪学校，他决定接下这个责任，而在这之前没有人曾做过这件事。滑雪穿过崎岖的山顶到达定居地热那亚（现在内华达卡森城的南部）需要 3 天时间。Thompson 给这里的人们展示了家里使用的长板和单木杆，而在这之前，他们从未见过雪板。

Thompson 穿着雪鞋拉着载满信件、报纸、药品和其他供应物的重 80-100 英镑的帆布背包穿过雪山，这在 20 年前运送频率是一月两次。他的滑雪板是 10 英尺长，重达25磅。从自我保护的角度，他只携带火柴，一些牛肉干和饼干——没有毯子，没有枪，没有野营装备或指南针。雪鞋很少停下来，他只用了48小时便带着轻便的装备回到加州。他试图每封信收取1美元，但有些人不会支付，并且索要他们的邮件。他以天真的方式与政府打交道，没有与美国邮政总局（U. S. Postal Service）签署合同。但汤普森并不担心地说："如果我完成我的工作，把邮件送到目的地。山姆大叔会付钱给我的"。不幸的是，汤普森从未得到。尽管内华达州议会1869年上诉联邦政府得到6000美元的赔偿。

Thompson的滑雪本领是传奇的。著名的康斯托克记者Dan De Quille看到他的滑雪表演后写到："他飞下了山坡。他没有骑着他的雪杆或将其拖到一边，就像其他的雪板驾驭者一样，而是水平地抓着它，以走钢丝的方式一样踩着雪板。他的外表优雅，摇曳着平衡到另一边，而另一边就像一只雄鹰翅膀翱翔着向下飞行。"

主题：对加利福尼亚州滑雪历史的附加说明……

每小时88英里（150km）！没有更快的速度记录！试着告诉康沃尔郡的Bob—世界上第一个速度滑雪冠军。1867年2月，拉波特附近，在白雪覆盖的列克星敦山的山坡上，他踏在12英尺长的木制雪板上，相当快地飞跃1804英尺长的雪道。使用比尔教堂的魔法"涂料"的混合物，Bob鲍勃从开始在14秒内完成所有路程，把他的对手远远抛在后面。"挪威滑冰"或者是滑雪，在1853年被首次介绍到采矿营地。由于普卢默斯县和塞拉营地地处偏远和海拔较高，雪板是冬季运输的完美工具。运动项目不久就也随之而来。次年，Hugh "Buckskin" Porter开始在他的Saw Pit Flat工作间延长和改进现有的比赛项目。

在1861年，首次有组织的滑雪俱乐部比赛在洋葱山谷（在昆西和拉普特之间）举行，自此山地滑雪比赛在西半球诞生。

接下来的12年的滑雪比赛在不同的营地举行，比如Onion Valley, Saw Pit, La Porte, Howland Flat, Port Wine和Gibsonville等地举行。在1866年下半年，Alturas Snowshoe俱乐部在拉普特成立，目的是为了重振该地的体育及表示对体育运动的尊重。在1867年2月，他们举办了第一场正式的滑雪比赛。自此10年之后挪威才举行另一场类似的滑雪运动会。接下来的20年左右的时间里，组织50人或更多的参与者，500名观众和收益达500至1000美元（现在的50000美元）的比赛举行了多次。代表他们的城镇的选手，在La Porte Johnsville, Jamison City, Poker Flat, Sierra City, Monte Cristo和一些小营地间回环滑行。

这些早期的滑雪板通常被称为"雪鞋"或"长板"，它们由木质紧密、垂直生长的道格拉斯冷杉制成。滑雪板塑形时带有平面，槽底部有一种特殊的"凹槽"平面，顶部由于长期蒸的过程而变得弯曲。旅行滑板通常是8到10英尺长，而比赛用的雪板最小也要有十英尺长，并有可能达到笨拙的15英尺长！然而，在这两种情况下固定器都只有两块绑在两边的皮革，每边有两三个孔以让皮革系得更紧些。一小块木头附加到滑雪板上以固定鞋跟位置。对于雪撬的开始和停止，雪板的一边使用一个一根六英尺长的单一粗壮的杆，并带有一块木板。开始时是向雪地用力刺插三四下，停止时是坐在杆上施加压力，创造一个阻力，与此同时是一个壮观的雪地“鸡尾”的场景。

尽管开局强劲绝对是这种比赛的一种助推，或许这种打蜡或“涂加”是同等重要的。做食物的方法一般都被制作者严密保存，即使是今天也是这样的。尽管秘诀被代代相传，而烹煮食物的时间是不一样的。用于涂抹的一批涂料包括鲸蜡、从抹香鲸的额头取得的蜡状物质、雪松油、威尼斯松节油、石油沥青等，有一个实例，就像融合的爱迪生圆筒唱片！混合的速度产生了一批口号，如“塞拉闪电”和“涂抹助推为王！”

早期的长板时代把这项体育运动延续至1917年。在20世纪30年代有个小的复苏期，而在20世纪50年代出现了更强劲的复兴。之后复苏进程一度中断，现在又出现了复苏，始于1990年。延续19世纪比赛选手的精神，长板滑雪比赛每年在约翰斯维尔市的普卢默斯尤里卡 Ski Bowl 滑雪胜地举行一次。参赛者必须穿着时代风格的服装，只能选取真实的涂料配方和成分可以应用到滑雪板上。在原始的种族中，参与者以性别为分组基础，他们必须徒步爬上山坡到达起跑线上。一次球队的三到四个选手排队准备，锣声响后比赛开始。开局强劲和滑行笔直（连同最好的添加技巧和最佳平衡）对比赛者的输赢起决定作用。

4.30　滑雪人　Skiing People

哈特维格·伯克利（挪威）　Hartving Birkely（NOR）

个人简介　Brief Introduction

Famous Sami author, Researcher of skiing culture, He has wrote many books and essays on skiing.

萨米地域著名作家，滑雪文化研究学者，著有多部滑雪书籍和论文。

English Paper:

"Skiing Samis" (*skrithifinni*), as an early Nordic writer called the Samis ——Skiing people

1. When I met Ayiken in Alta he wondered whether there was a linguistic connection between Alta and Altai.

2. Presumed area of Sami settlement about 2000 years ago and today (Solbakk 1994: 14) .

From the earliest times Samis lived in hunting communities, in which hunting wild reindeer and fishing were the most important economic resources. Probably, they had already tamed some reindeer. A few tame reindeer were an important aid for families in their hunting way of life and they could be used as draught and pack animals and to lure wild reindeer into traps.

As the basis for hunting communities was changing from 1500–1700 Samis began to adapt to other livelihoods. However, some Eastern Samis maintained their hunting and fishing way of life into the 19th century. While tame reindeer herding, cultivation and keeping livestock took over, it was still in combination with the utilisation of outfield resources, hunting, fishing and gathering, which remained part of the economic base. At the same time Coastal Samis began utilising marine resources, the catching and selling of fish and sea mammals becoming important income. This was also combined with outfield activities. However, already 1500 years ago Iron Age Sami hunting communities were consuming dairy products by keeping a few tame female reindeer.

3. The map shows the Suoŋil–*siida* (a small community of reindeer herding families) way of life (Bureukson after Salengena from 1601) .

Notice the Sami hunting wild reindeer, a child shooting at a target, a reindeer sleigh and a shaman in a sacrificial séance.

4. The inside cover of Schefferus' famous book (1674) . Notice the sleigh, a pair of skis of different length and a person sewing a boat.

5. This is how Schefferus portrays Sami outfield life in the 17th century. Dutch print in Solbakk (1994) .

The sub–arctic area is characterised by long winters. People living there adapted their tools and technology to be able to utilise their resources in winter. With this in mind they made use of skis, sledges and sleighs. A similar adaption also appears in the language. The Sami linguist Israel Ruong (1969) notes that in Finnmark Sami dialects the verb *johtit* (to move, to glide) has 8 different meanings. Likewise the Sami language has about 200 words for snow, many describing the exact condition of the snow. Sami ski terminology has many old and natural words, for example, *sabet*, *ĉipma og beađŋŋis* (a ski, the curved tip of a ski, the place of the foot on a ski), plus *ĉuoigat* (to go skiing) (Aikio 1992: 52, Nesheim 1966: 27). There are 17 words with different meanings derived from the verb *ĉuoigat*, such as *ĉuiggastuvvat* (to desire to go skiing). Skis have several names in Sami. I will explain some of the words later. With such a large vocabulary it is much easier for me to handle the theme of winter and snow in Sami, both orally and in writing.

Harald Gaski (1991: 29) refers to the myth of the birth of Kallen's sons (*gállá bártnit*). According to the story Kallen's sons were the first 3 Samis. They were excellent elk hunters and invented skiing. So as not to be forgotten, they were lifted into the sky after they died.

6. Parts of the Sami night sky (Berit Åse Johnsen 1990). Kallen's sons, the Elk, the Skier with his dog and *fávdna* with his bow (English, the Plough). *Fávdna* with his bow and the Skier with his dog are both hunting the same elk.

We have seen that the Samis inhabited a large geographical area, stretching over several climatic zones. Therefore the technical functionality of skis differs from place to place. In order to exploit the resources of the terrain at different places the Samis developed skis for various uses and landscapes. In a description in DAUM from 1931 it is stated that Sorsele Samis in the Umeå Sami area used the following types of skis: 1. *Såkki-träokka* (birch skis) for autumn use and mid-winter. 2. *Majnekk-träokka* (skis made from extra hard pine wood) that may be used on crusted snow in late winter and also on the first snow of autumn when skis may still scrape on stony ground. 3. *Bjätsäk-träokka* (pine skis), 20cm wide and light for use in hunting wolves. 4. *Bjätsäk-majnekk-träokka* (skis made from extra hard pine wood) that have different ski lengths, the short one for "kicking" to gain motion and the long one for gliding along. Two short skis were also employed using a diagonal technique and two ski poles. A pair with two ski lengths using the kicking technique and one ski pole was effective for hunting wild reindeer on crusted snow since they were very fast.

7. A pair of skis with different lengths and the relevant skiing technique (Schefferus 1674, Arvidsson's photo in Berg 1950).

A Sami with skis of different lengths. Bergs reproduction of the skiing technique.

Skiing in Sami hunting culture

Many ways of catching prey were used. One of the most efficient methods, describing the Kemi Sami community (Tegengren 1952: 106), was to harass wild reindeer on skis. Together with the method of using fences to trap reindeer, hunting reindeer on skis, especially after the introduction of the rifle, led to a reduction in the number of wild reindeer herds.

Tegengren (ibid 103) also relates that Kemi Samis caught wild reindeer on crusted snow in late winter. They used skis and spears. Knud Leem (1776), an 18th century missionary in my home place of Porsanger, recounts the same method of hunting there. He relates that though late crusted snow could no longer carry a reindeer's weight, it would still carry a skier's weight. As the wild reindeer sank into the softer snow under the crust the skiers could quickly catch up and kill them.

8. Elk hunters in Zalavruoga on the White Sea (Sørensen 1997: 26 with reference to Savvatejevi).

Here the rock carvings are located in an area that also East Samis are assumed to have inhabited previously. The carvings are estimated to be 3500 - 4000 years old. Possibly the figures of skiers are using short, wide skin-covered skis like the northern Siberian peoples do, something that Sørensen (1997: 26) believes a couple of rock carvings in Alta also depict. The Alta carvings are thought to be 6200-5600 years old.

9. A Sami bow (Vorren/Manker 1974) mounted with a spike and basket for use as a ski pole.

The rock carving scene at Zalavruoga appears to confirm that the skiers have used two ski poles. In some hunting methods the Samis also used two poles when required. The main pole was the spear, mounted with a spike and basket. When more speed was needed the bow was used as well, also mounted with a spike and basket.

10. A skier camouflaging a pitfall, as interpreted by Sørensen (ibid: 30)

Ruong (1969: 16) cites the 17th century clergyman Tornæus, who refers to another method of hunting, namely *čiegarbivdu* (trapping wild reindeer on a migration route). In late winter when wild reindeer fall through the snow and can't easily move, they eat and trample in the deep snow making the snow hard (čiegarduvvá) in a limited area. Hunters could exploit such a situation. As the sun softened up the snow and the cold returned in the evening a thin crust formed (*moaráda*) that could carry the weight of a skier and his dog. Hunters would immediately seek out such migration places (čiehkara) where the wild reindeer were. At dawn they would sneak out and lay traps (*beartošiid*) along all the reindeer routes (*čiegarmohkiid*) that the wild reindeer had trampled down in their search for lichen. When the sun had risen dogs were let loose along the routes (*ĉiegar*) to frighten the reindeer into the traps. Tornæus relates that reindeer that did not run into the traps would be chased by skiers and dogs and then shot with bows and arrows or speared. Dogs would attack any remaining reindeer, biting the neck until they died.

11. Skis with convex soles (*ĉigarsabehat*) for use in areas of reindeer migration.

Skiing in reindeer herding

The adjustment of Samis to a nomadic way of life based on tame reindeer herding brought about new challenges that entailed different ways of utilising the land. The private ownership of larger and larger reindeer herds required greater need for protection from predatory animals and the chance of herds mixing with otherherds. The reindeer herder had different problems to face than the hunter. He had to adapt to the habits of the reindeer, follow its migration in search of varied pastures and use the landscape differently. The need for different types of pasture land forced some groups of herders to move through several types of landscape and climatic zones, which again influenced the usage of skis. In winter all movement before the motorisation of reindeer herding was made on gliding equipment, such sleighs, sledges and skis. A Pite Sami reindeer herding group had a migration route of about 1, 000 km between summer and winter pasture lands. They moved between the Gulf of Bothnia and Salten in Norway, roughly half the distance on gliding equipment.

12. Reindeer herder Nils Hotti, Karesuando (Sweden), describes the life of nomadic herders in a *luohti* (the Sami traditional song form) .

13. Tame reindeer migrating (Turi 1910: 2)

During his travels in Finnmark in 1872 professor JA Friis sketches the life of a reindeer herding family. He reports that herders continually had to watch over the herd by day and night throughout the winter to prevent wolves, alone or in packs, from attacking the animals. Every15 minutes a herder and his dog would ski around the herd to gather any animals that may have strayed. He would shout, scream and fire his gun, making as much noise as possible so wolves near and far would know there were people with the herd. A starving wolf stops at nothing! But with sufficient vigilance a wolf would usually keep its distance because it knew and feared Samis on skis in deep snow, says Friis (Friis 872, Turi 1910) .

Skiing and hunting wolves.

Because of the damage they could do to a herd of reindeer, wolves were a reindeer herder's greatest enemy. They were hated and despised beasts. Proof of this is that the wolf has more than 200 nicknames! The spear, which also served as a ski pole, was the only weapon used for wolf hunting in the old days, according to Sjulsson. He notes that Samis were not inclined to use a rifle when hunting wolves, because they thought a bullet too mild a way of killing a wolf that had ravaged a reindeer herd.

14. Wolf and bear hunting (Berg 1950: 55, D. Von Gogguer 1828).

Sjulsson (Pettersson 1979) relates more about wolf hunting. When the hunting team found wolf tracks they removed their heaviest clothing and rucksacks. Then they set off on skis one after another, changing who was the lead skier making the track for the others. The slowest skier's job was to pick up clothing the others discarded as the tracking continued and put it into a rucksack. One piece of clothing after another would be cast off. Weather conditions and the type of terrain determined how long it took to reach the wolf pack. The hunt might last for several days skiing over 100 km before the last wolf was killed. The hunters approached the pack side by side, competing to see who could be first to spear a wolf. The rucksack carrier also took part in the competition. If he managed to overtake the next last hunter in the file he would give the rucksack of cloths to him instead. Such long hunting trips on skis made Samis into good skiers. Perhaps the best in the world? Zetterberg (1981: 1) wrote about a wolf hunting team that went after a pack of wolves on skis in 1889. He names the mountains they passed. The hunt lasted a whole week, skiing about 1100 km.

After killing a wolf it was skinned. According to Sjulsson, it was customary for the skier who had first speared the wolf to skin the wolf's head, the second skier to reach the pack skinning the neck and so on. The hunter who reached the pack last, the poorest skier, was given the detestable job of pulling the skin off the tail.

15. Skijoring (Manker 1975: 195).

16. Skijoring pictures, rock carving (Manker 1954: 125, 126).

17. 5000 year old find in a bog from Kalvträsk, northern Sweden, and Eastern Sami leather clad skis (Berg 1950, Itkonen 1848).

18. Skier on a Sami shaman's drum (Manker 1963: 71).

19. Sami children practising skiing (Leem 1756).

20. South Sami Tomasson's pair of skis of unequal length (Tomasson 1928).

21. Sami child's and woman's skis (Granlund 1941).

Literature

Luohti text

Such is the life of a Lapp:
Skis on his feet,
a lasso over his shoulder,
and a dog behind.
Far did he travel
through the night on crusted snow,
and he halted,
when he found pasture.

中文论文：

滑雪的萨米人，一个早期的北欧作家称其为萨米人
——滑雪人

当我在阿尔塔遇到阿依肯的时候，他想知道在阿尔塔和阿尔泰之间是否有一个语言联系。

萨米人2000年前和现在的大概定居地方。

最早的时候，萨米人生活在狩猎社会，在那里狩猎野生鹿和钓鱼是他们最重要的经济来源。也许，那时他们已经驯服了一些鹿。一些驯鹿是他们狩猎生活中的一项重要帮助，它们可以用来运输动物，并可以引诱野生驯鹿进入陷阱。

狩猎社会的基础是从1500-1700年开始进行改变，萨米人开始去适应其他的生计模式。然而，一些东部的萨米人直到第十九世纪仍然保持他们的狩猎和捕鱼的生活方式。驯鹿放牧，种植和饲养牲畜，它依然是与外部资源相结合，狩猎，捕鱼和采集，这仍然是经济基础的一部分。同时沿海的萨米人开始利用海洋资源，捕捉并贩卖鱼和海洋哺乳动物成为重要的经济来源。这也是一项与外部资源结合的活动。1500年前的铁器时代，狩猎群落的萨米人通过饲养一些驯服的母鹿来消费乳制品。

3. 地图显示了Suoŋil-*siida*（驯鹿放牧家庭）的生活方式。（1601年Salengena之后的Bureukson）应注意萨米狩猎野生驯鹿，孩子射向目标，驯鹿雪橇和降神的巫师。

4. Schefferus名著（1674）的内封面。注意雪橇，衣服不同长度的雪板和缝船。

5. 这就是十七世纪Schefferus对萨米户外生活的描述。印刷于荷兰Solbakk。

极地气候区以漫长冬日为特色。生活在那里的人们充分将冬日的资源应用于他们的工具和科技。出于这种考虑，他们开始使用雪板、爬犁和雪橇。同样的适

用性也发生在语言上。萨米语言学家 Israel Ruong（1969）注意到在芬马克郡萨米人的方言中动词“移动、滑行”具有 8 种不同的含义。相似的，在萨米语中，有约 200 个词表示雪的含义，许多表示雪的准确状态。萨米滑雪术语有许多古老而自然的词汇。例如，*sabet*，*ĉipma og beađŋŋis*（雪板，雪板弯曲的一端和雪板尾端），加上 *ĉuoigat*（去滑雪）（Aikio 1992：52，Nesheim 1966：27）。从 *ĉuoigat* 这*个词衍生出了 17 个具有不同含义的词，例如，ĉuiggastuvvat*（想要去滑雪）。在萨米语中，雪板有很多种称呼。稍后我会对其中的一些进行解释，如此大量的词汇使得把握萨米冬雪主题变得更加简单，无论是从口语中还是书面语中。

6. Harald Gaski（1991：29）指的是 Kallen 的儿子出生的神话。根据神话故事，Kallen 的三个儿子是第一批萨米人。他们是优秀的麋鹿猎人并发明了滑雪。为了不被人们遗忘，他们死后升天。萨米人夜空的部分（Berit Åse Johnsen 1990），Kallen 的儿子们，在狩猎麋鹿时，是与带着狗的滑雪者和带着弓的 *fávdna*（英语，北斗星）都在狩猎同一只麋鹿 。

我们知道萨米人的生活空间占据着大范围的地理面积，延展到几个气候区域。因此雪板的技术功能因区域的不同有较大的差异。为了在不同的地区开发土地资源，萨米人研究具有不同用途和适用于不同地形的雪板。1931 年 DAUM 的描述中写到在乌米萨米地区的 Sorsele 萨米人使用以下几种雪板：1. *Såkki-träokka*（桦木雪板）用于秋天和越冬中期。2. *Majnekk-träokka*（ 极硬松木制作）适用于晚冬的陈雪和秋天的第一场雪，但当雪板滑行于多石地面时仍会出现划痕。3. *Bjätsäk-träokka*（松木雪板）20 米宽，在狩猎狼的时候雪板较轻。4. *Bjätsäk-majnekk-träokka*（极硬松木制作）具有不同的滑雪长度，短的通过“踢”来动起来，而长的则用于滑行。通过使用斜技术和两个雪杖来应用两款短雪板。

使用“踢”技术和一个雪杖，带有两个滑雪长度的组合在陈雪上狩猎野生驯鹿时十分有效因为他们速度很快。

7. 一副带有不同长度的雪板和相关的滑雪技巧（Schefferus 1674，Arvidsson1950 年在冰山的照片）

A Sami with skis of different lengths. Bergs reproduction of the skiing technique.

带有不同长度雪板的萨米人，滑雪技巧的冰山复制。

萨米狩猎文化中的滑雪

使用很多方法捕捉猎物。描述在凯米萨米社区（Tegengren 1952：106）最有效的方法之一，即在雪板上骚扰野生驯鹿。连同使用围起栅栏来困住驯鹿的方法在雪板上捕捉驯鹿。尤其在引进步枪之后，导致野生驯鹿群数量大大减少。

Tegengren（ibid 103）也联系到凯米萨米人在晚冬的陈雪上捕捉驯鹿。他们使用雪板和矛。Knud Leem（1776），我家乡 Porsanger 地区 18 世纪的传教士陈述道，在那儿同样的狩猎方法。他说道尽管久积陈雪不能承受驯鹿的重量，他能够承受滑雪者的重量。随着野生驯鹿陷入雪壳下松软雪的部分，滑雪者们可以快度地追上并杀掉他们。

8. 在白海的 Zalavruoga 地区的麋鹿猎人（Sørensen 1997：26 参考 Savvatejevi）。

在这里，岩石雕刻所在的位置亦有人称是曾经东部萨米人居住的地区。据估计，这些雕刻有约 3500-4000 年的历史。有可能滑雪者使用短的、表面被大范围覆盖的雪板，就像北部西伯利亚人民使用的一样。Sørensen（1997：26）相信在阿尔塔的一些岩石雕刻也有所描绘。阿尔塔雕刻被认为有 6200-5600 年的历史。

9. 一只萨米弓（Vorren/Manker 1974）在尖部有像篮子形状的箭头，这种弓可作为雪杖使用。在 Zalavruoga 的岩石雕刻景观似乎确认了滑雪者曾经使用了两种雪杖。在一些狩猎方法中，需要时萨米人曾使用过两种雪杖。主要的雪杖在尖部有像篮子形状的箭头。当对速度需求更高时，也会使用弓，在其尖部有像篮子形状的箭头。

10. Sørensen 解释道滑雪者伪装成一个陷阱。

Ruong（1969：16）引用了 17 世纪牧师 Tornæus 的话，指的是另外一种狩猎方法，即 ŋ̌ĉĉiegarbivdu（在迁徙路线中困住野生驯鹿）。深冬季节，野生驯鹿陷入雪中不能轻易移动。他们在雪中进食，在雪中踩踏导致一定区域内的雪变硬。猎户可以寻找这样的区域。当太阳将硬雪部分软化，而夜间温度降低形成一层薄壳，这层薄壳可以承受滑雪者及其猎犬的重量。狩猎者会立即找出这样的驯鹿迁徙区域。黎明时分他们会偷偷出来埋伏好并沿着驯鹿迁徙的路线设下陷阱，这样在驯鹿寻找苔藓时就会被困住。当太阳升起，狩猎者会松开猎狗将驯鹿吓到提前设好的陷阱里。Tornæus 说到，滑雪者和猎狗会追逐没有进入陷阱的驯鹿，并用弓箭或矛来射杀他们。猎狗会攻击剩下的驯鹿，咬住他们的脖子直至死亡。

11. Skis with convex soles (*ĉigarsabehat*) for use in areas of reindeer migration。

带有凸底的雪板（ *ĉigarsabehat* ），用于驯鹿迁徙的区域在驯鹿群中滑雪。

在温顺的驯鹿群的基础之上，萨米人向游牧生活方式的转变带来了新的挑战，要求将土地用于多种用途。随着个人所有的驯鹿群的不断壮大，需要更好地保护驯鹿群不为掠食性动物所伤，同时还要防止和其他人家的鹿群混淆。相对狩猎者而言，放牧驯鹿的牧人所要面对的问题要更多。他必须适应驯鹿的生活习惯，为寻找不同的牧场，追随他的迁徙路线，更大可能的运用地形优势。对不同类型牧场的需求使放牧者不得不穿过不同的地形和气候区，这在无形之中也会影响雪板的使用。在冬季，驯鹿放牧机械化之前使用的均为滑行设备，如雪橇，爬犁和雪板。一个皮提萨米驯鹿放牧群冬夏季沿着驯鹿迁徙路线所跨越的牧场土地之间的距离为 1000 公里。他们在波的尼亚湾和挪威的 Salten 地区间移动，大约一半的行程是在滑行设备上完成的。

12. 驯鹿牧民 Nils Hotti，Karesuando（瑞典）在 *luohti*（萨米传统歌曲形式）中描述了游牧牧民的生活。

13. 1872 年，JA Friis 教授在芬马克游历之时描绘了驯鹿放牧家庭的生活。他说道整个冬天放牧者都必须日夜不停地看着驯鹿群以防个别狼或狼群侵袭。每隔十五分钟放牧者和猎狗就必须整理一次动物以防驯鹿走失。他会通过大喊、狂叫、开枪来发出尽可能大的噪声来告知狼群驯鹿群旁有人，以防狼群靠近。当然，遇到饿狼就没有办法了。但 Friis（Friis 872，Turi 1910）说通过足够的警告，狼会保持一定的距离，因为在深雪中他们知道且害怕雪板上的萨米人。

滑雪和捕狼

由于可能给驯鹿群带来的伤害，所以狼狈驯鹿放牧者视为大敌，是被憎恶受歧视的野兽。从狼具有 200 多个绰号就可以看出这一点。据 Sjulsson 说，矛，也作为雪杖的一种，在过去是捕狼唯一的武器。他强调到萨米人不倾向于使用步枪来射杀狼，因为他们觉得用枪来射杀蹂躏了驯鹿群的野兽对他们来说太过慈祥了。

14. 狼和猎熊（Berg 1950：55，D. Von Gogguer 1828）

Sjulsson（Pettersson 1979）讲到更多关于捕狼的事情。当狩猎团队发现狼的踪迹他们会丢掉最重的衣服和背囊。他们会一个接着一个滑雪板出发，改变带头滑雪者以为其他队伍人员制造印记。最慢的滑雪者的工作就是捡起沿途其他人丢弃的衣物放进背囊。一件又一件的衣物会被丢弃。天气状况和地形决定了要到达狼群处所需的时间。猎户们会从不同的方向接近狼群，相互竞争着看谁会是第一个插死一只狼的人。携带背囊的人也会参加到这个比赛中来。如果他能成功赢过队伍中倒数第二位的猎户他就可以将装有衣物的背囊交给他。这样漫长的雪板之上的狩猎行程使萨米人个个擅长滑雪。他们会为他们经过的山命名。那次的狩猎持续了整整一周，滑行距离为 1100 公里。

杀完狼会剥掉狼的皮。据 Sjulsson 说，萨米人有个惯例，即由第一位杀死狼的人来剥狼头部的皮，第二位到达狼群的猎户来剥颈部的皮等等。最后一位到达狼群的可怜人就只能轮到剥最令人厌恶的尾巴的皮。

15. 马爬犁运动（Manker 1975：195）

16. 马爬犁运动图片，岩石雕刻（Manker 1954：125，126）

17. 发现于北部瑞典 Kalvträsk 地区的沼泽，具有 5000 年历史，东部萨米毛皮雪板（Berg 1950，Itkonen 1848）

18. 在萨米萨满的鼓上的滑雪者（Manker 1963：71）

19. 萨米的孩子练习滑雪（Leem 1756）
20. 南萨米 Tomasson 长度不同的一副雪板（Tomasson 1928）
21. 萨米孩子和女人的雪板（Granlund 1941）

文学

Luohti 文本（萨米传统歌曲形式）

这就是拉普兰人的生活
脚下踩着雪板
肩上扛着套索
身后一条猎狗
他行走于深夜的陈雪中
很远很远
当他找到牧场时
他停顿了一下（请参阅下面相关图片和信息）

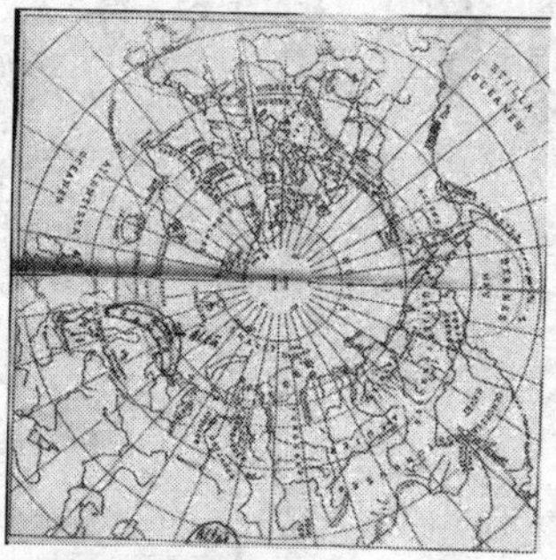

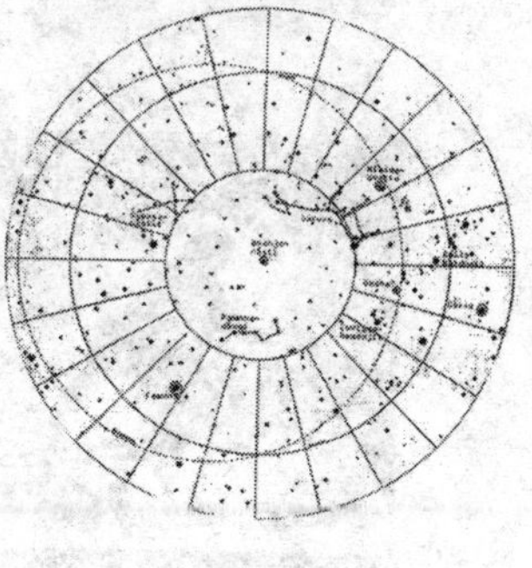

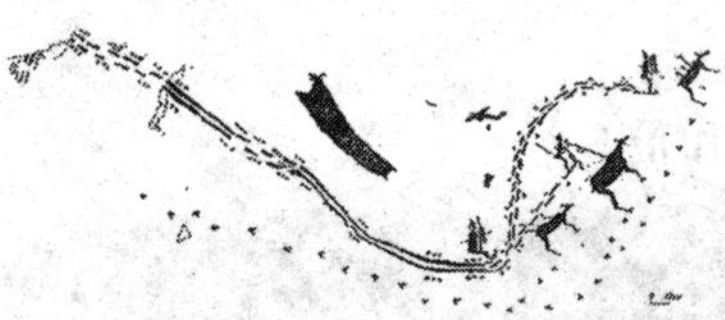

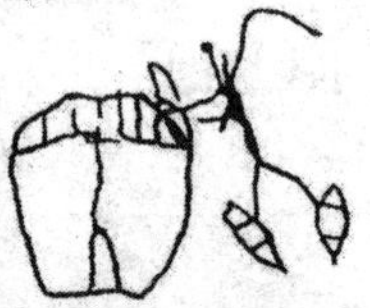

Fig.8. Figurscene fra Alta, hvor det trolig vises en skiløper som dekker over en fangstgrav.

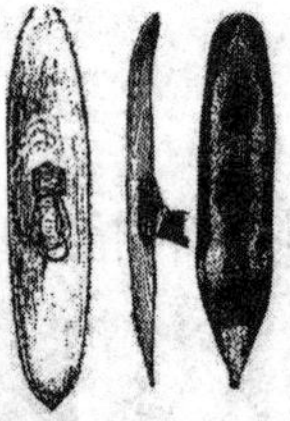

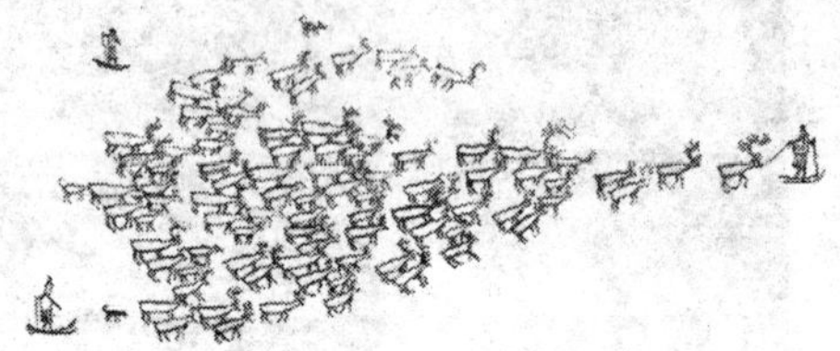

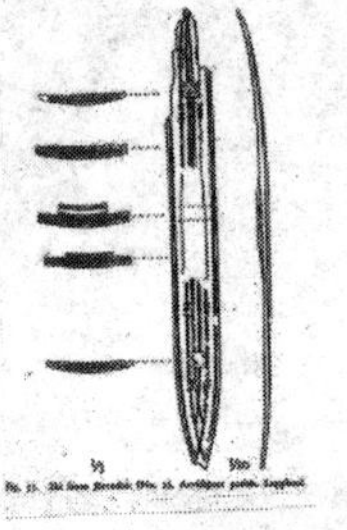

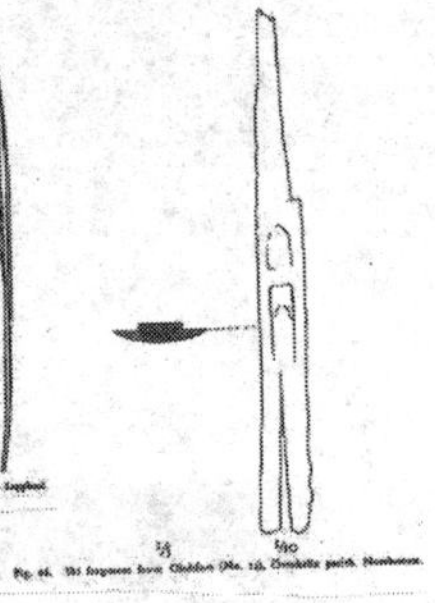

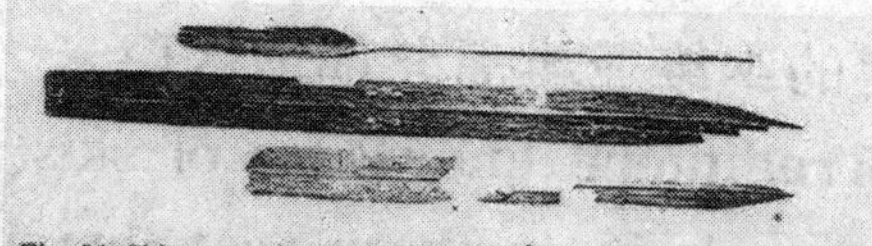

Fig. 54: Ski og stav fra Kalvträsk. Etter Åstrtröm/Nordberg (1984).

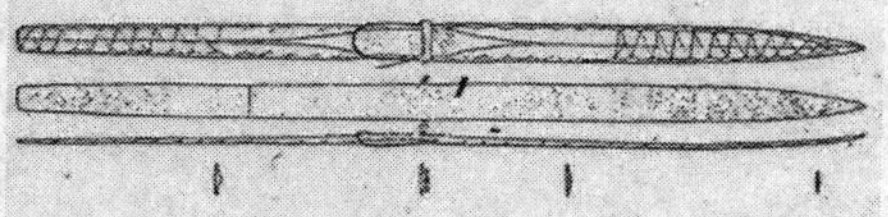

Fig. 55: Østsamiske ski (Itkonen 1948).

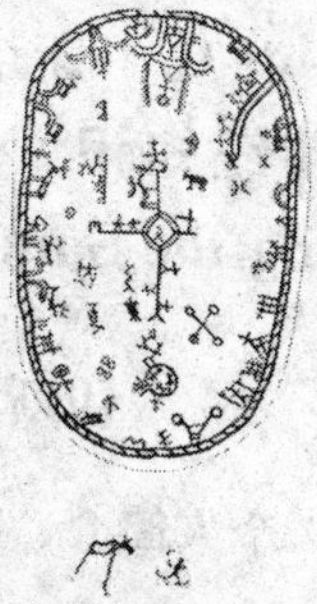

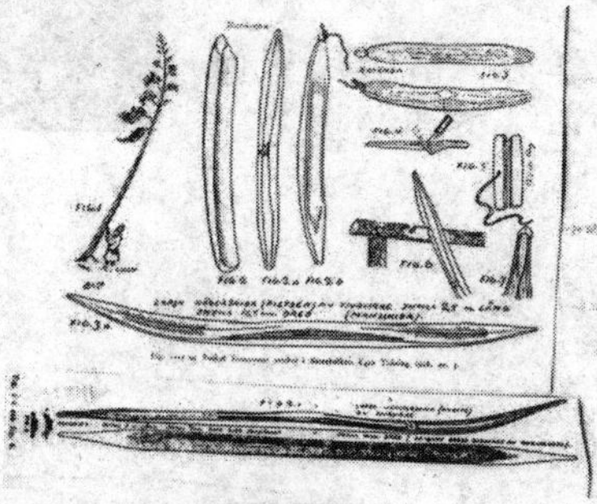

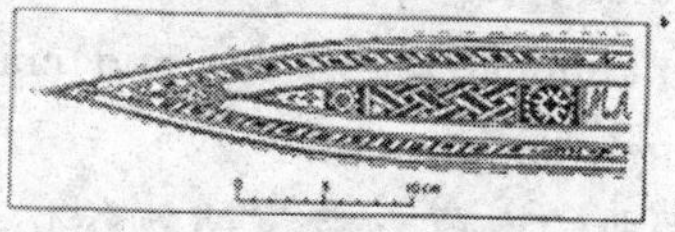

Bild 25. Framdel av skida från Jokkmokks socken, Luleå lappmark, Lappland. Tillverkad år 1894 av medlemmar av lappfamiljen Mattsson Rimpi som högtidsgåva till en kvinnlig medlem av familjen i Åliloukta. Ovansidan med rundad rygg, som begränsas av låga åsar. Av björk. Längd 219 cm, bredd mellan 8,4 och 7,9 cm. Svenska skidmuseets acc.nr 701 b (utst.nr 481.

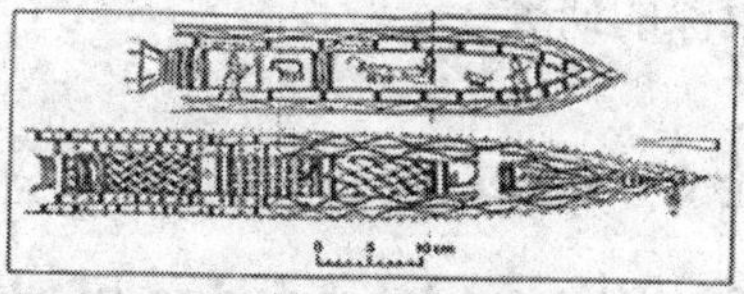

Bild 3. Barnskida från Västerbottens lappmarker. Tillverkad omkring 1870. Ovansidan med svagt välvd rygg. Linjegrupperna korsade enligt bild 1 b. Av björk. Längd 135 cm, bredd 8,4 cm. Svenska skidmuseets acc. nr 328 b (utst.nr 661.

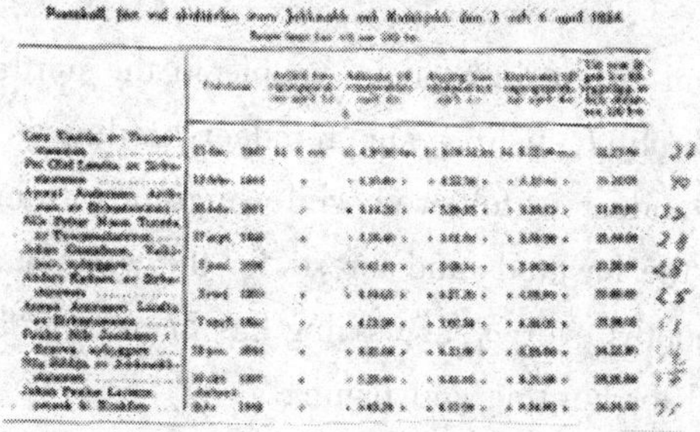

4.31 斯堪的纳维亚半岛北部地区萨米人关于滑雪板和滑雪技艺的传统知识 Traditional knowledge of skis and skiing techniques among the Sámi people in northern Scandinavia

伊斯·伊斯拉埃尔松（瑞典） Isse Israelsson（SWE）

个人简介 Brief Introduction

Curator at Ájtte Museum, Jokkmokk, Sweden, Archaeologist; traditional knowledge and crafts, enviromental history, old building restoration

瑞典约克莫克滑雪博物馆馆长，考古学家，滑雪历史研究专家，同时对传统知识和工艺、环境历史、古建筑修复等也有很深的研究。

论文 Paper:

Traditional knowledge of skis and skiing techniques among the Sámi people in northern Scandinavia.

The Sámi are an indigenous people in the northern part of Fennoscandia and Kola Peninsula. Hunting, fishing and reindeer herding is still the main occupation. The domesticated reindeer is followed while migrating from the summer pastures in the high mountain to the lowlands and forests for the winterstay. Since the ground is covered with snow 7-8 months every year, skiing has been of great importance, both for moving with the herd and for hunting and fishing.

斯堪的纳维亚半岛北部地区萨米人关于滑雪板和滑雪技艺的传统知识

萨米人是芬诺斯坎底亚和科拉半岛北部地区的原住民。在那里，狩猎、钓鱼和驯鹿放牧仍是主业。为过冬从夏季高山牧场迁移至低地和森林时，驯养驯鹿是必备的伙伴。因为在当地一年中有7-8个月地表均被大雪覆盖，因此，无论是为放牧、狩猎或是钓鱼，滑雪都十分重要。

YngveRyd

This paper reveals some traditional knowledge of skiing, based on interviews with old Sámi men, bornin the early 1900. They were herders and built skis the traditional way, a knowledge passed through several generations. Since the 1950s the reindeers are followed with modern transportation like snowmobile, helicopter etc, skiing and making of skis has declined in importance.

In the early 1900 many hundred skis were found in peat bogs in Fennoscandia, most of them were made of pine. Scholars soon began trying to classify them. The oldest ski in Sweden, *Kalvträskskidan*, 5200 BP, was called the Arctic type, still in use in east Eurasia. The type with vertical holes for binding strap has probably been covered with fur.

The second oldest ski, *Hotingskidan*, 3500 BP, is of another type, called the Botnic. From 3500 BP and to modern time this type has been in use. The Botnic ski has raised footstep and horizontal hole for binding strap, and is still a common type among hunters and herders. It is often called the Sámi Ski, since almost every bog find of skis come from the Sámi winter area in the forests.

基于对出生于二十世纪九十年代的萨米老者的采访，本文揭示了一些关于滑雪的传统知识。他们是牧羊人，他们用传统的方法制作滑雪板，这种技艺历经了几代人的传承。自从二十世纪五十年代现代交通工具如雪地摩托车及直升飞机等取代了驯鹿、滑雪和滑雪工具制作，重要性有所下降。

二十世纪初期，在芬诺斯坎底亚的泥炭沼泽发现大量滑雪工具，其中大多数由松木制成。很快，学者开始对他们进行分类。最古老的滑雪板在瑞典 *Kalvträskskidan*, 5200 BP，被称为北极类，目前在欧亚大陆东部地区仍在使用。带有垂直钻孔来系绑定带的那类可能曾经被皮毛覆盖。

第二古老的滑雪板在 *Hotingskidan*, 3500 BP，它属于另一种，名为 Botnic. 从 3500 BP 至今，此类滑雪板一直在使用当中。Botnic 滑雪板提高了脚底，用水平钻孔来系绑定带，目前该法仍广泛应用于猎户和放牧者当中。它亦被称为萨米滑雪板，因为几乎每一个发现滑雪板的沼泽均位于萨米冬日的森林地区。

Botnic 滑雪板，提高了脚底，用水平钻孔来系绑定带

滑雪板制作者 Bo Östergrenwith 与 Botnic 桦木制滑雪板，与 Kalvträsk 北极滑雪板的副本，附雪杖 5200 BP.

Isse Israelsson

IsseIsraelsson

One hundred years ago everyone had several skis, made of different wood with specific qualities, for skiing in loose snow or on crust, for work or festivities. Skis made of pine were only one of many pairs of skis every man and woman used. Notordinary pine, but pines growing a bit curved have a special hard wood. Skis made of this compression wood from pine outrank all others for skiing on hard crust, a condition most common in the late winter/early spring. But to remain in the right shape, skis of pine had to be stored for summer in peat bogs, they were deliberately placed and stored there.

一百年前，每个人都有数副滑雪板，由专门质量的木材制作，分别适用于松散的雪质或较硬的雪质，适合工作或节日。松木滑雪板是每个男人和女人均使用过的多副滑雪板之中必备的一套。不是普通的松木，而是长得有些弯曲的松木，由于这样的木质较坚硬。由这种松木的密实木性材制作的滑雪板在硬雪上的地位高于其他雪板。这种情况在晚冬和初春较为常见。但为了保持原来的形状，松木制滑雪板必须在夏天保存于泥炭沼泽之中，他们是被故意放在那里保存的。

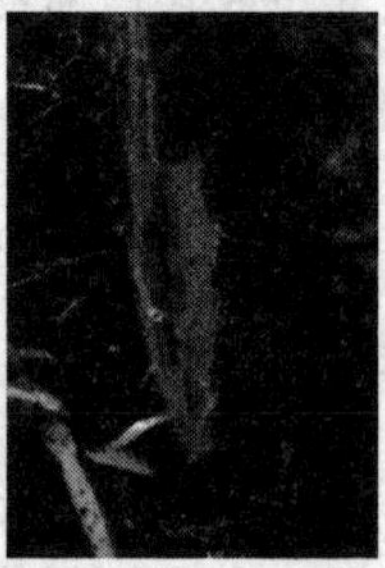

带有密实材质的松木，YngveRyd

For skiing in loose deep snow, the normal snow conditions in the winter forest, skis made of birch is still preferred. These skis are long and with little width, ca 8-12 cm. To compensate for the slenderness the ski is rather long, over 3 m is not unusual. The birch ski is different from modern skis in many ways. While the modern plastic ski is short, stiff, has a significant arching, the birch ski is not so hard, has a small span and a long and softly curved brim. The brim can be as long and 50 cm, and is the reason why birch skis seem to flow on the deep snow. The fronttip of the ski is always above the snow.

When the snow is wet and tends to stick on the birch ski, skis of aspen is often better. Aspen wood has very little weight, and the skis can therefore sometimes have more width than the birch skis.

When skiing in old days, often only one ski stick was used. The stick found together with the oldest Swedish ski, 5200 BP, is of a type still in use among herders. The shovel makes it possible to dig and check under snow if the pasture is good for the reindeers. The stick is a help to slow down when skiing downhill. Unlike modern skiing, the stick seldom helps to forge ahead. Instead it supports side, so the skier would not fall when there are sudden voids or obstacles in the snow.

Another type of stick could be a bow or a spear for hunting. Many stories are told about the brave huntsmen who managed to run with skis in order to overtake a running wolf. The best condition for hunting wolf is when the snow is very loose, like powder, then breathing is hard, either you are a hunter or a wolf. Several hunters follow the wolf for a very long time. When the wolf is exhausted and rather near, maybe 100 m, the best hunter starts to run on the skis. The stick serves as a third leg, almost like pole vault. This three leg running leaves traces not like ordinary skiing but instead deep holes in the snow. When the wolf is caught up the hunter uses the spear stick.

冬日森林中的正常雪况，在松散的深雪中滑行时桦木制的滑雪板更受青睐。这种滑雪板较长，且宽度较小，大约 8-12 厘米。为弥补它纤细的特点，这种雪板相当长，长度大于三米并不罕见。桦木制雪板与现代雪板在很多方面均有差异。现代雪板短，坚硬有很好的弯度。而桦木雪板不那么坚硬，弯度较小，且前部弯曲部分长而柔软。弯曲部分可长达 50 厘米，这也是为什么桦木雪板能在深雪中滑行的原因。前部弯曲部分总位于雪之上。

湿雪容易粘在桦木雪板之上，此时，山羊木质雪板则更受欢迎。山羊木木质更轻，其雪板相较于桦木雪板更宽。

过去滑雪时，经常只使用一根雪杖。5200BP，与最古老的瑞典雪板一起发现的还有雪杖，是目前放牧人仍在使用的雪杖的一种。雪铲可以向下挖掘并检查雪下的情况以判断这片牧场是否适合驯鹿。在下坡滑行时雪杖有助于减速，不同于现代滑雪，雪杖很少帮助前行。相反，它起到支持的作用，当雪中突然出现空洞或障碍时，滑雪者不会摔倒。

另一种雪杖可以是狩猎中的弓或矛。有很多关于勇敢的猎户的故事，讲述他们设法通过滑雪追赶并猎下一头狼的故事。猎狼最好的条件就是雪松的像粉一样时，对于猎户和狼来讲，呼吸都是困难的。几个猎户要追踪狼很长一段时间，当狼已经疲惫，且距离我们已很近时，最好的猎户将开始在雪上滑行，雪杖的作用是充当第三条腿，有点像撑杆跳。三条腿跑时留下的痕迹不同于普通滑雪留下的痕迹，会在雪中留下深洞，抓住狼之后猎户会使用矛杖进行刺杀。

雪杖和弓的组合

IsseIsraelsson

Key words：

Traditional knowledge，Sámi，ski，hunting

References

Ryd，Y. 1994. Varför hittar man skidor i myrar? Forntida Teknik 1994：2

Ryd，Y. 1998 Bo Östergren，skidmakare. Hemslöjden 1998：1

Ryd，Y. Snö. Ordfront，Stockholm，2001

Åström，K & Norberg，O. 1984. Förhistoriska och medeltida skidor. Västerbotten 2：84.

Key words：

传统知识；萨米；滑雪；狩猎

【参考文献】

Ryd，Y. 1994. Varför hittar man skidor i myrar? Forntida Teknik 1994：2

Ryd，Y. 1998 Bo Östergren，skidmakare. Hemslöjden 1998：1

Ryd，Y. Snö. Ordfront，Stockholm，2001

Åström，K & Norberg，O. 1984. Förhistoriska och medeltida skidor. Västerbotten 2：84.

4.32　青铜时代的雪——冬天在青铜器时代传播创新的作用 There was snow in The bronze age-The role of winter in spreading innovations in The bronze age

杰西皮克（芬兰）　J-P. Taavitsainen（FIN）

个人简介　Brief Introduction

(also: . J. -P. Taavitsainen, born 1951) is a professor of archaeology at the University of Turku. He has studied in particular the Finnish prehistory and the Middle Ages. 2000s Taavitsainen has examined in particular the relics of medieval Turku Cathedral. [1] Taavitsainen has since 2000 Finnish Historical Society, a scientific member [2], and since 2004 a full member of the Finnish Academy of Science. Now he is the professor of archaeology at the University of Turku.

杰西皮克是芬兰图尔库大学的考古学教授，曾专注于芬兰史前和中世纪的研究。Taavitsainen 还特别研究了中世纪图尔库教堂的遗址。Taavitsainen 从 2000 年就是芬兰历史协会的一员，2004 年成为芬兰科学院的正式一员。

论文　Paper:

There was snow in The bronze aGe-The role of winTer in sPreadinG innovaTions in The bronze aGe
青铜时代的雪——冬天在青铜器时代传播创新的作用

Jussi-Pekka Taavitsainen and Timo Kuokkanen Means of transport are the measure of culture. The nations that have been able to make most use of them have been in the forefront of history, while those whose means of transport have been limited in comparison with others have been left behind both economically and culturally.

交通方式是文化的测量器。能充分利用交通工具的国家便能走到时代的前列，而运输方式受局限的国家在经济和文化上便会被时代所抛弃。

Väinö Voionmaa (1933)

Abstract: Pastoral and mobile economies have been given a leading role in Eurasian prehistory, with a focus on their development from cattle herders with wagons to horse riders, and on related equipment and technology. Eurasia, however, also has taiga and tundra zones, with winter conditions prevailing throughout most of the year. With their hunting-fishing economies, these areas were integrated into the Bronze Age network by the mid-second millennium BC. Mutually distant communities also maintained and developed their social ties in winter, as facilitated by frozen waterways and bogs. Developed winter transport equipment, such as skis and sledges, was a further precondition. The article presents different types of Bronze Age sledges, with an emphasis on economic background factors. Expanding commerce required the improved transport of wilderness products to middlemen and markets.

Keywords: Winter transport, sledges, reconstructions, Eurasia, Fennoscandia, Bronze Age

摘要：田园和移动式经济体在欧亚前期历史中占有主导地位，关注于牧民用马车负重到骑马的转变以及相关的设备和技术。当全年大部分进入冬季环境时，欧亚大陆也有针叶林和苔原地带。随着狩猎捕鱼业的发展，在公元前第二个千年的中期，那些林原地带也被纳入青铜器时代的网中。在冬季，由于冻结的水路和沼泽的便捷，相距遥远的社区的人们也维持和发展了他们的社会关系。不断发展的冬季交通设备，如雪板和雪橇，是其前提条件。这篇文章将呈现青铜器时代不同种类的雪橇，主要侧重于其背后的经济因素。电子商务的扩展需要改善交通状况将偏僻地区的产品输送至有需求的中间商和市场。

关键词：冬季交通，雪橇，复原，欧亚大陆，芬诺斯坎底亚，青铜时代

Travel and the transmission of knowledge provide the main theme of Kristian Kristiansen's and Thomas B. Larsson's book *The Rise of Bronze Age Society. Travels, Transmission and Transformations* (2005). The presentation of the monograph begins with following words: 'Beginning with state formation and urbanization in the Near East c. 3000 BC and ending in central and northern Europe c. 1000-500 BC, the Bronze Age marks a heroic age of travels and transformations throughout Europe' (Kristiansen & Larsson 2005). The central role in the technology of travel is usually given to the wheel. Wheeled transportation has clearly had a huge impact on social and economic development. Its importance as an innovation and a transmitter of languages, populations and innovations is distinctively underlined for example by the title of David W. Anthony's seminal work *The Horse, the Wheel, and Language. How Bronze-Age Riders from the Eurasian steppes Shaped the Modern World* (Anthony 2007; see also Kristiansen 2008). On the other hand, the importance of the period, the Bronze Age, is stressed not only by archaeologists. The social anthropologist Jack Goody has recently discussed 'the relative unity of the European and Asian continents rather than their differences, a relative unity that began with the Bronze Age Revolution'（Goody 2010：1）.

旅游和知识传播是 Kristian Kristiansen's 和 Thomas B. Larsson 所著一书《青铜器时代社会的兴起：旅游、传播和转变》的主题。这本专著以下面这样一段话开篇："始于公元前 3000 年前近东国家的形成与城市化，终于公元前 1000-500 年前中北欧，这段青铜器时代是标志整个欧洲的旅游和转变的英雄时代"（Kristiansen & Larsson 2005）。车轮在旅行技术中据核心角色。轮式交通对社会和经济的发展具有重大影响，它的重要性还体现在创新性、语言的传播和人口的流动方面。创新性显要体现在 David W. Anthony 具有开创性的一书《马、车轮和语言，欧亚大陆草原上的青铜器骑者如何塑造现代世界》（Anthony 2007；Kristiansen 2008）。另一方面，不只考古学家强调青铜器时代的重要性。社会学家 Jack Goody 最近提到"欧亚大陆的相对统一而不是分歧是始于青铜器时代的革命"（Goody 2010：1）。

This contribution is about technology and techniques of transport equipment, the prerequisites of travel and transmissions of products, ideas and genes in the northern parts of Eurasia and especially in Fennoscandia. It also takes into consideration the usually ignored severe winters of the Bronze Age in Eurasia（Kristiansen 1998：27-31）and the fact that winter transport equipment was, in fact, the wheel of the Eurasian tundra and taiga zone. Overlooking movement over snow-covered terrain has unfortunately led to the invisibility of winter transport equipment and its importance in major archaeological syntheses ever since J. G. D. Clark's classic *The Prehistoric Europe*: *the Economic Basis*（Clark 1952：293-301）. When discussing the spread of various eastern artefacts and technologies, such as Mälar axes, textile pottery, asbestos ceramics, Ananino celts etc. during the Bronze Age and Early Iron Age in the circumpolar zone from the Russian steppes and the Urals to Scandinavia（Denmark excluded）, the question arises of the role of winter and winter vehicles such as sledges and skis in this process.

交通技术和技巧的发展，旅行及新产品和新观点传播的前提条件主要在于欧洲北部地区，尤其在芬诺斯坎底亚（包括芬兰、挪威、瑞典和俄罗斯部分）地区，还要考虑到欧亚大陆青铜器时代严酷的冬季（Kristiansen 1998：27-31）。冬季的交通设备实际上是欧亚大陆苔原和针叶林区域的轮式交通。自从 J. G. D. Clark 的经典著作《欧洲前史：经济基础》，人们从对积雪覆盖地区的眺望运动想到运用冬季滑雪设备的局限不可见性和整合重大考古发现的重要性。当在谈论东部的手工艺品和技术时，比如黀骨轴、纺织陶瓷、陶瓷石棉等，从俄罗斯大草原的半极地区和乌拉尔到斯堪的纳维亚地区（丹麦除外）的青铜时代和铁器早期时代，冬季及冬季交通（雪橇和雪板）的角色在这一过程中显现出来。

The importance of winter for moving and transport in Eurasia

冬季运动和交通在欧亚大陆的重要性

In summer conditions, land transport routes did not exist in the same sense as today. Easily passable terrain such as ridges, heaths and long surface outcrops of bedrock were used for travelling. Naturally, also long and forked bodies of water served as roads and transport ways. Hilly and wooded terrain, bogs, rivers and lakes cutting the land routes were obstacles during the snowless period. During the long journeys even carrying personal equipment and provisions was a heavy task, not to mention merchandise. On longer journeys in particular, the most convenient way to transport goods was by water.

在夏季条件下，陆上交通线路并不像今天这样存在。便于通行的地区，如山脊、荒地、基岩的表面被用于旅行。自然地，绵长而又有分叉的水域也被作为道路和交通方式。丘陵和森林地形、沼泽、切割陆路的河流和湖泊在无雪的时期会成为交通的障碍。携带个人装备和食物的长途旅行是一项沉重的任务，更不用提购买商品了。在特别长的旅程中，水运是最便捷的交通运输方式。

The winter changed the situation dramatically. Impassable bogs became good winter roads. Lakes and rivers could also be used in winter. Easier travelling saved time and energy. In wintry forested terrain it was easier to transport catches of game, camping equipment as well as merchandise.

冬季巨大地改变了交通不便的状况。不可跨越的沼泽在冬季也能成为便利的交通方式，河流和湖泊在冬季也能用于交通。便利的交通方式节省了人们的时间和精力。在寒冷的森林地形中，运输猎物、野营装备和商品就比较容易些。

Heavily loaded sledges were easy to draw on snow, especially when using dogs. In fact, during the winter, the prerequisites for people moving and travelling were far better and more versatile than in the summer. Even the range of travelling was longer in the winter despite suitable water routes that could also be used in the summer.

负载量较重的雪橇在雪地上比较容易滑行，尤其是用雪橇犬拉动时。事实上，人们在冬季比在夏季出行得更远，交通方式也更灵活多变。尽管水运线路在夏季也适于利用，但人们在冬季的旅行范围更宽泛些。

Winter was also an active period for social life. Collecting and storing foodstuffs was less intensive than in the spring, summer and autumn. In winter there was more time to maintain social ties. Our idea about distances, whatever the season was, is totally different today. Ethnographic examples tell us, how e. g. Eskimos could journey thousands of kilometres to visit other groups. It has been estimated that under favourable conditions objects from the Eskimos of the Bering Strait might reach their kinsfolk on Hudson Bay within two-and-a-half years (Birket-Smith 1972: 384, 392).

冬季的社会生活也比较活跃。较之春季、夏季和秋季，冬季搜集和储藏食物没有那么迫切。人们在冬季也有更多的时间维持社会生活。现在，我们对于距离的看法，无论在哪个季节，都大大不同以往。人类学的例子告诉我们爱斯基摩人可以行走千里去拜访其他族群。据估计，在有利的交通条件下，居住在白令海峡的爱斯基摩人可能需要两年半的时间到住在哈德逊湾亲属家（Birket-Smith 1972：384，392）。

Examining the prerequisites of travel on water in northern Russia and Siberia we notice how most of the rivers of this vast region run from south to north. This is not an advantage in east-west travel and traffic in the summer months. In the winter, the situation is and was totally different. Snow and the freezing of the terrain and bodies of water made movement possible even in surroundings that were inaccessible in the summer. Vast areas of bogs and wetlands are good examples of this.

考察过俄罗斯北部及西伯利亚的水域运行的先决条件，我们注意到这个大片区域的河流走势大都从南向北。在夏季，这对于东西走向的交通是不利的。而在冬季，这种情况是完全不同的。由于雪和冻结的地形、水域，那些在夏季无法通行的区域在冬季就变得有可能通行。大片的沼泽和湿地便是有效的证明。

We have no exact knowledge about prehistoric winter traffic. We do not know how the distances were travelled by expeditions. Were objects and goods moved in stages over shorter distances relay-style, by different expeditions, or did a single expedition travel all the way? Travellers may have moved from one village to another enjoying reciprocal hospitality. This meant that it was not necessary to carry a large quantity of foodstuffs for people and dogs. Nor was there a need to spend time acquiring nutrients. Moreover, travel also became faster, because it was not necessary to set up one's own camp every night.

我们对于史前历史的冬季交通没有确切的材料。我们不知道探险游行进的距离和方式。是对象和货物在不同的探险中以短距离接力赛的形式还是单一的旅行方式移动？我们对此不得而知。旅行者可能需要从一个村庄到另一个村庄去享受互惠的招待。这意味着行者和雪橇犬不必要携带大量的东西，也不需要花费大量时间获取营养。而且，旅行也更快捷，这就不需要每晚都搭起营帐。

We may assume that in the Bronze Age expeditions consisted of a few sledges. We can further guess that the expedition was headed by an experienced man who also knew the route. Other participants were individuals or people in good health. Skiing was their way to move forward and the speed was that of easy walking. There was no point in hurrying in untouched snow. The guide skied first, orientated and opened the trail for the dogs which made the going easier. One of the authors (TK) once helped the dogs by using snowshoes. An exceptionally good period to travel was late winter. All people living in these climatic conditions, know that the crusted snow of the season makes travelling faster because the frozen crust on the snow bears skiers as well as dogs and their sledges.

我们可能认为青铜器时代的远游会用一些雪橇。我们还可以进一步猜想远游的行程会有一位有经验的人带路。而其他的参与者都是一些体格健壮的个人。滑雪是他们远行的一种方式，并且速度也比较快。其中的一位作者（TK）曾帮助雪橇犬穿上雪鞋。特别好的远行时段是在深冬。住在严寒天气条件下的人们都知道在压实的雪上可以滑行得更快，因为冻结的雪层能有效的支撑起滑雪者、雪犬和雪橇。

Sledge types of the Bronze Age
青铜器时代不同种类的雪橇

Finland's bogs and lakes have revealed some 200 finds of sledge runners, boat sledges and other parts of sledges. Chronologically, sledge runners extend from the Mesolithic Stone Age to historically documented times. This contribution discusses the types used during the Bronze Age. Skis are excluded from this article (on skis, see e.g. Taavitsainen et al. 2007: 64–75).

人们在芬兰的沼泽和湖泊里发现大约200件雪板、船形雪橇和雪橇的其他部分。按时间顺序，雪板可追溯到中石器时代至有史料记载的时期。这篇文章主要讨论雪橇不同种类，而不是关于雪板的具体研究（关于雪板的详情请看 Taavitsainen et al. 2007: 64–75）。

In Finland general transportation and its history have been treated by U. T. Sirelius (1919), Väinö Voionmaa (1933), Kustaa Vilkuna (1934), T. I. Itkonen (1934) and Ilmari Manninen (1934), to name a few ethnologists and historians. Important for Finnish studies is also Gösta Berg's (1935) classic *Sledges and Wheeled Vehicles*.

关于芬兰的交通及其历史已有许多民族学家和史学家研究过。比如 U. T. Sirelius (1919), Väinö Voionmaa (1933), Kustaa Vilkuna (1934), T. I. Itkonen (1934) 和 Ilmari Manninen (1934)。比较重要的还有 Gösta Berg's (1935) 的经典著作《雪橇和轮式车辆》。

Prehistoric sledge runners have been studied most actively by U. T. Sirelius (1918), T. I. Itkonen (1931, 1932, 1935. 1938, 1949) and Ville Luho (e. g. 1945, 1948, 1951, 1957). Later scholars, Aarne Kopisto (1964), Unto Salo (1965, 1967,

1984), Janne Vilkuna (1986), Hannu Kotivuori (1996) and Timo Kuokkanen (1999, 2000) have made either reconstructions or proposals for reconstructions of sledges based on runner finds. New radiocarbon dates of old finds as well as new material and the *Stand der Forschung* have also been presented and discussed (e. g. Seger 1988, 1991; Taavitsainen et al. 2007: 76-81).

对史前雪橇研究比较深入的主要有 T. Sirelius (1918), T. I. Itkonen (1931, 1932, 1935. 1938, 1949) 和 Ville Luho (e. g. 1945, 1948, 1951, 1957)。近期的学者主要 Aarne Kopisto (1964), Unto Salo (1965, 1967, 1984), Janne Vilkuna (1986), Hannu Kotivuori (1996) and Timo Kuokkanen (1999, 2000), 他们在已有的发现的雪板的基础上对雪橇提出了重构。新放射时期的旧发现和新材料和 *Stand der Forschung* 已被展现出来和讨论过（比如 Seger 1988, 1991; Taavitsainen et al. 2007: 76-81）。

The typology of Finnish runner finds has been constructed on the basis of the structural features of runners and ethnological analogies. The typology applied here follows on from the work of T. I. Itkonen (1938: 28) and Ville Luho (1949: 13) and it is supported by 14C dates. The general terminology of sledges is presented in Fig. 1.

芬兰滑雪板的分类是在雪板的结构特征和民族类别的基础上构建出来的。雪撬的分类也以 T. I. Itkonen (1938: 28) 和 Ville Luho (1949: 13) 的作品为依据，并以十四世纪的历史为支撑。雪橇的一般性分类展现在下面的图 1 中。

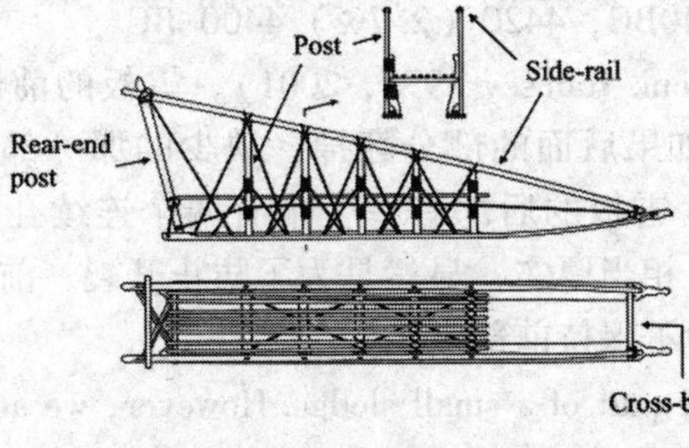

Fig. 1 The applied terminology (Berg 1935). Drawing: T. Kuokkanen.

图 1 使用的术语 (Berg 1935). 绘画：许道嵩

There are three runner/sledge types in Finland that were, or could have been, used during the Bronze Age. They are presented in the following with particular focus on the so-called ridged type sledge and its reconstructions. As far as we know, the ridged type sledge has been found only in Finland.

青铜器时代，芬兰有三种雪橇。下面的文章会将他们一一呈现出来，主要聚焦于脊形雪橇及其复原。据目前所知，脊形雪橇仅仅在芬兰发现。

The Kuusamo runner（KM/eh 20248）. An interesting small runner was found in Kuusamo, central north-east Finland（Fig. 2）. The date is 5690+110 BP（Hel-1159），cal 4690 BC（65.5%）4440BC，4420（2.7%）4400 BC（Reimer et al. 2004；Bronk Ramsey 1995，2001）. The fore part of the runner has a high curving shape（Fig. 3）. The length of the runner is 83 cm. If the rear part has broken off, the missing part was apparently short. The width of the fore part is 14.2 cm，narrowing towards the rear. On the rear part there is a high ridge with two consecutive holes. The tip of the fore part may represent an animal and is quite thick，apparently to prevent splitting. Two parallel holes in the fore part were made for the binding which kept the fore part up.

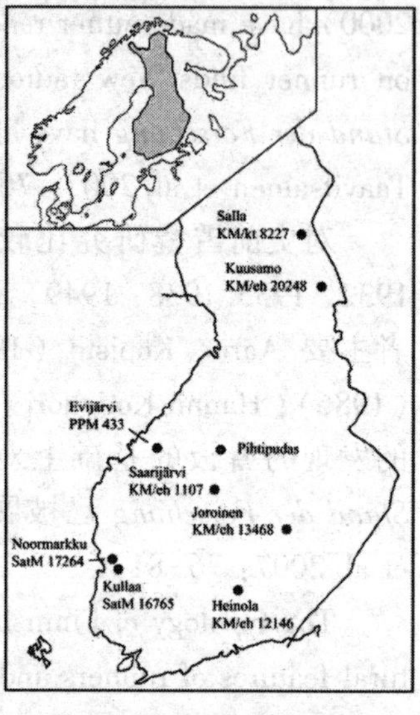

Fig. 2　The find locations of Salla，Kuusamo and ridged runner finds.

图 2　萨拉，库萨莫和脊形雪板的发现地

库萨莫滑雪板 *The Kuusamo runner*（*KM/eh* 20248)，是在芬兰中部和东北部的库萨莫发现的一只有趣的雪板，时期在 5690+110 BP（Hel-1159），cal 4690 BC（65.5%）4440BC，4420（2.7%）4400 BC（Reimer et al. 2004；Bronk Ramsey 1995，2001）。雪板的前部有一个高度的弧形（图 3），长 83 厘米。如果后面的部分坏掉，缺少的那一部分就会变短。雪板宽 14.2 厘米，向后变窄。雪板的后部有一个带有两个连续孔的高脊。前部尖端部分可能代表一种动物，相当厚实，显然是为了防止开裂。前部的两个平行的孔是为了设置固定器，是为了保持前部向上。

The runner could be part of a small sledge. However，we are inclined to think that it is a sledge as such. Berg（1935：Plate II，fig. 3）has presented a small ethnographic runner that resembles the Kuusamo runner（Fig. 4）. The Sami have used it to drag *kota*（tepee）poles. How was this done? We have not seen a description but we can easily present an interpretation. The slender ends of the poles are bound on both sides of the ridge, and the fore part of the runner prevents the bundle from sinking into snow. The runner must be upright all the time. A stick spreader connecting the outer poles would serve this function（Fig. 5）. Although we lack Bronze Age finds，we can assume that similar small runners were used in the Finnish north and interior regions between the

Stone Age and historical times.

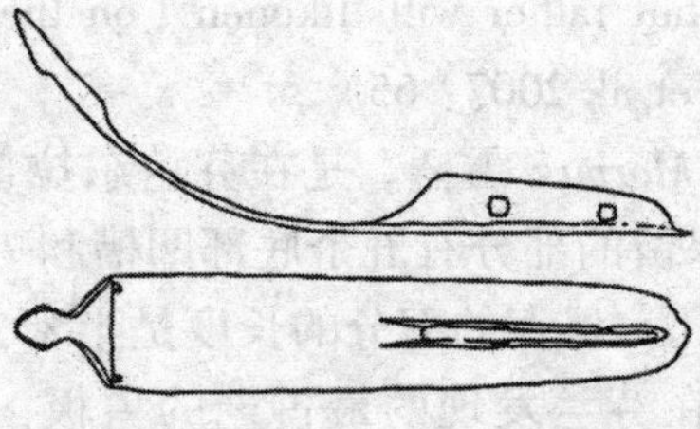

Fig. 3 Kuusamo runner（KM/eh 20248）.
图 3 库萨莫滑雪板

雪板可能只是一只雪橇的一部分。但是，我们都倾向于一只雪橇大概也就是这样的。伯格（1935：Plate II，图 3）曾展现出来一只与库萨莫滑雪板相似的民族特色雪板。萨米人用它来拖动圆锥帐篷。这是怎样做到的呢？我们没有找到有具体描述的史料，但我们可以轻易地推断出来。雪杆细长的末端固定在脊的两边，板头能防止货品沉入雪中。雪板必须是一直指向前方的。连接雪杆的棍形吊具会起到这种功能（图 5）。尽管我们在青铜器时代发现很少这样的滑雪板，但是我们可以推测在石器时代和历史时期，芬兰的北部和内陆地区用过相似的小滑雪板。

Fig. 4 Swedish tent-pole runner. Simplified drawing after Berg
图 4 瑞典帐篷柱滑雪板。Berg 基础上简易绘画

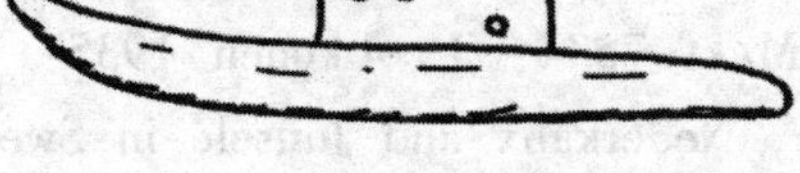

Fig. 5 Suggested interpretation of how tent-poles were drawn.
图 5 如何绘画帐篷柱滑雪板的建议

The ski-sledge, also known as the Morjärv type sledge. An early ski-sledge runner was found in Salla, Eastern Lapland, Finland（Fig. 2）. The preserved part of thc runner has five bottom grooves and one post-hole（Fig. 6）. On both sides of the post-hole there are holes for binding or inserting plugs. The length of the preserved parts is half a metre, but the original length was much greater. The Salla runner（KM/kt 8227）is the oldest dated ski-sledge runner in Finland, with a radiocarbon date of 4470+110（Hel-1330），cal 3020BC（68. 2%）2920BC（Reimer et al. 2004；Bronk Ramsay 2005）. Eero Naskali（1989：12，1999：296，301-302）has suggested that this find, identified by Itkonen (1938: 19-20) as a sledge runner, could be a ski. We do not agree with Naskali's identification but rather with Itkonen (on the criticism, see Kuokkanen 1999: 33-34; Taavitsainen et al. 2007: 65).

滑雪雪橇，也被称为 *Morjärv* 雪橇。是在芬兰东拉普兰的萨拉发现的一只早期的雪橇（图二）。雪橇保留的部分有五个底部凹槽和一个后孔（图6）。后孔的两侧有固定或插入塞子的孔。保存的部分的长度是半米，但原长度要长得多。萨利雪板（KM/kt 8227）是在芬兰发现的最古老的雪板，4470+110（Hel-1330），cal 3020BC（68.2%）2920BC（Reimer et al. 2004；Bronk Ramsay 2005）的放射性碳时期。Eero Naskali（1989：12，1999：296，301-302）认为这一发现可能是一只雪板，而 Itkonen（1938：19-20）认为是一只雪橇。我们认同 Naskali 的看法而不是 Itkonen 的看法（相关评论请看 Kuokkanen 1999：33-34；Taavitsainen et al. 2007：65）。

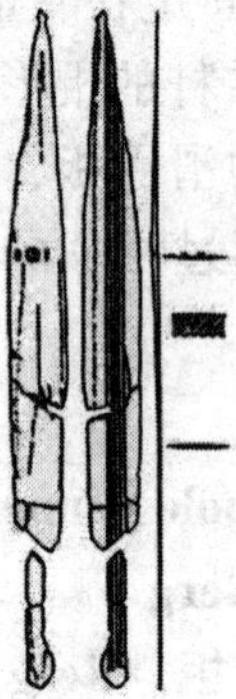

Fig. 6　The Salla ski-sledge runner (Itkonen 1938: 21, fig. 4B)

图6　萨拉滑雪板（Itkonen 1938：21，fig. 4B）

The function of the bottom grooves is clear, preventing the sledge from sliding sideways on inclined surfaces. Several other ski-sledge runner finds have a post-hole structure comparable to the Sodankylä runner (KM/kt 7534: 1, Itkonen 1935: 11, Fig. 5C) as well as the runners from Lycksele, Nederkalix and Junsele in Sweden (Berg1935: Figs 17, 18, 20). The eventual 14C dates of these finds are unknown to the authors.

雪橇底部的凹槽的功能是显而易见的，就是阻止雪橇从倾斜的表面滑向路边。其他几个雪橇有一个后空结构，相比较于索丹基拉（KM/kt 7534：1，Itkonen 1935：11，Fig. 5C）和瑞典（Berg 1935：Figs 17，18，20）的莱克塞勒等地的雪橇。而对于14世纪关于雪橇的这些发现作者还不得而知。

The next-oldest Finnish ski-sledge find is dated to the Bronze Age. The date for the Enontekiö runner (KM/kt 8153 Itkonen 1938: 22-24, k. 5B) is 2960+80 (Hel-3925), cal 1300BC (68.2%) 1050 BC. The dated ski-sledge find from Laukaa is from the Early Iron Age, its calibrated age being 380-120 BC (Vilkuna 1986: 12). The age of the youngest ski-sledge find, from Saarijärvi, is cal AD 120-380 (Vilkuna 1986: 12). The authors know of 14 Finnish finds, 11 from Sweden and several from Russia (so-called Novgorod type). After this stage, a new sledge type, the boat sledge, apparently displaced the ski-sledge in Finland (Taavitsainen 1999: 312). In northern Russia and Siberia the ski-sledge remained in use until modern times.

另一个古老的雪橇可追溯到青铜器时代。Enontekiö 雪橇（KM/kt 8153 Itkonen 1938：22-24, k. 5B）的时期是 2960+80（Hel-3925），cal 1300BC（68.2%）1050 BC。从 Laukaa 发现的雪橇的时间是青铜器的早期。它的校正时期是公元前 380-120 年（Vilkuna 1986：12）。从 Saarijärvi 发现的最年轻的雪橇大约是公元 120-380 年（Vilkuna 1986：12）。作者所知道的 14 类雪橇，11 个来自瑞典，其他几个来自俄罗斯（所谓的 Novgorod 型）。这个时期之后，是一个新的雪橇类型—船形雪橇，显然它取代了在芬兰的滑板雪橇（Taavitsainen 1999：312）。在俄罗斯北部和西伯利亚，滑板雪橇至现代时期还在使用。

The sledge of ridged type. The ridged runner is a continuation of the so-called central-grooved runner type of the Stone Age (Kuokkanen 1999, 2000). The structure of the ridged runner was simplified and improved. Besides runners, other parts of the sledge have been found. The ridged type has been dated from the Late Stone Age to the Early Iron Age. Preceding central-grooved runners have been found in a wide region, from Sweden to the Ural Mountains. The ridged type, however, seems to be a local Finnish type.

Runners. At present, seven ridged runner finds are known (Table 1). All of these have been found in the southern and central parts of Finland (Fig. 2).

脊型雪橇。脊型雪橇是石器时代所谓的中部凹槽雪橇的继续发展的一种雪橇。脊型雪橇被不断加以简化和改进。除了雪板也发现了雪橇的其他部分。脊型雪橇可追溯到石器时代晚期和铁器时代早期。之前的中部有凹槽的雪橇是在一片广泛的地区发现的，从瑞典到乌拉尔山。然而，脊型雪橇似乎是一种芬兰的本地型雪橇。现今，已发现的的脊型雪橇有七种（表 1）。所有的这些雪橇都是在芬兰的南部和中部发现的（图 2）。

Counterpoint: Essays in Archaeology and Heritage Studies

Three runners have been 14C-dated. The age of the Heinola runnner (KM/eh 12146, 12923: 1-2) is 3600+175 BP (Hel-659), cal 2200 BC (68.2%) 1650 BC. That of Noormarkku (SatM 17264; Salo 1967) is 3530+110BP (I-1921), 2020 BC (66.0%) 1730 BC and 1710 BC (2.2%) 1690 BC. The age of Kullaa (SatM

16765：1-5；Salo 1965）is 2390+160BP（Tx-125，A-254）= 770 BC（68.2%）360 BC. The problem of the dates is not only their large uncertainties which cause problems in placing the runners in the Stone，Bronze or Iron Age. This is further hampered by the fact that we do not know how and where the dated samples were taken and whether they are from the outer or inner wood of the piece. Estimates of how many year rings were cut or carved away while constructing the sledge are also lacking. In any case，the dates are too old.

三种雪板发现于 14 世纪。Heinola 雪板（KM/eh 12146，12923：1-2）的时间大约是 3600+175 BP（Hel-659），cal 2200 BC（68.2%）1650 BC.。Noormarkku 雪板（SatM 17264；Salo 1967）的时间大约在 3530+110BP（I-1921），2020 BC（66.0%）1730 BC and 1710 BC（2.2%）1690 BC。Kullaa（SatM 16765：1-5；Salo 1965）雪板的时间大约是 2390+160BP（Tx-125，A-254）= 770 BC（68.2%）360 BC。它们出现时间的极大不确定性致使不知将它们定位在石器时代、青铜器时代还是铁器时代。我们不知道这些样品雪板是怎样取得，在哪儿取得，它们是来自外木片还是内木片，这也进一步增加了时期的不确定性。制作雪橇时对年轮的刻雕的估算也缺乏证据。无论如何，它们的年代是很久远的。

On the runner there is a ridge through which the binding holes were made. The forepart is flat like a board and its thickness is approximately the same as that of the ridged portion. The rear end has one or two holes for the rear-end posts. Only three runners have been preserved unbroken. The length of the Evijärvi runner（Fig. 7a）is 290cm（Itkonen 1932：60-62）. The Heinola and Kullaa runners mentioned above are 288 cm and 213 cm long respectively. The breadth of the three runners is 10-13.3cm. The other runners are more or less fragmentary. The central part of the Saarijärvi runner is missing if we assume that the discovered fore part and rear part belong to the same runner. The fore part of the Joroinen runner is missing almost completely. Only the fore part and a small portion of the ridge of the abovementioned Noormarkku runner have been preserved. The Pihtipudas runner has only a rear part 123cm long.

雪板上有一个脊，在脊上制作了许多装订孔。前部扁平像板，厚度接近脊的部分。板尾有一两个孔。仅仅有三块板防开裂。Evijärvi 雪板（图 7a）是 290 厘米（Itkonen 1932：60-62）。上面提到的 Heinola 和 Kullaa 雪板分别是 288 厘米和 213 厘米长。它们的长度范围是 10-13.3 厘米。其他的雪板或多或少是残缺不全的。如果我们认为发现的前部和后部属于同一只雪板，那么 Saarijärvi 雪板的中间部分是缺失的。Joroinen 雪板的前部几乎是完全缺失的。只有前面提到的 Noormarkku 雪板的前部和脊的一小部分是保存完整的。Pihtipudas 雪板只有一段长

123 厘米的后半部分。

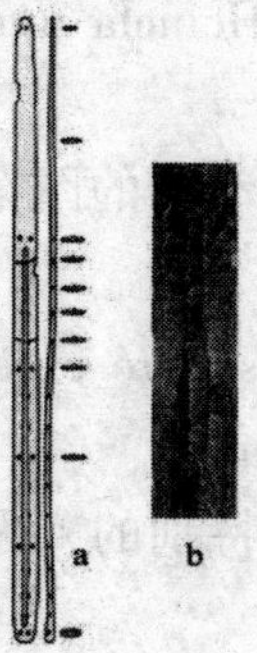

Fig. 7　a-the evijarvi ridged runner（itkonen 1932：60，fig. 2B）；b-The Heinola ridged runner（Edgren 1984：54）.
图 7　Evijarvi 脊形滑雪板

Ridged runners have numerous and varying structural features（Fig. 8）. This ridge is continuous except in the Heinola runner where it was made only at the location of the binding holes（Fig. 7b）. As for the ridge of the Noormarkku runner, we know nothing. The post-holes were made on both sides of the ridge except in the Heinola runner where the ridge is missing at the location of the post-holes.

脊型雪板由许多变化多样的结构特征（图 8）。除了 Heinola 板脊，一般的板脊都是持续的。Heinola 雪板的板脊只在固定孔的位置（图 7b）。至于 Noormarkku 雪板的板脊，我们一无所知。一般雪板的后空都在脊的两边，而 Heinola 雪板后空的脊则是缺失的。

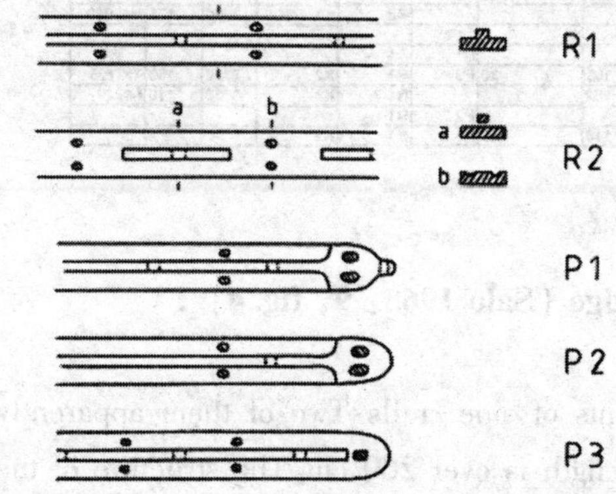

Fig. 8　Structural features of the ridged type runners（combinations-see Table 1）. K 1-3 = Forms of the fore part, R 1-2 = Ridged part and post holes, P1-3=Forms of the rear part.
图 8　脊形滑雪板的结构特征

The board-like fore part is approximately one metre long. Two of runners display carved animal art in tips of the fore part: a bear's head in the Heinola runner and an elk's head in the Noormarkku runner.

雪板像板形的前部分接近一米长。两只雪板的前头刻有动物的图案：一个熊头在 Heinolar 雪板上，一个麋鹿头在 Noormarkku 雪板上。

Other parts of ridged sledges. The Kullaa and Joroinen finds were exceptional because other parts of the sledges were found together with the runners.

至于脊形雪橇的其他部分。Kullaa 和 Joroinen 的发现是特别的，因为所发现的雪橇的其他部分都带有雪板

Two side-rails and a rear-end post were found with the Kullaa runner (Fig. 9). One of the side rails is complete and 252 cm long. Below the side-rail there is a groove resembling an inverted letter V. In the groove there are several long holes for the upper ends of the posts. The aft end of the side-rail has a large hole for the rear-end post. The other side rail is similar but fragmentary. The upper end of the rear-end post is curved and was situated in the rear hole of the side-rail when found.

Kullaa 雪板有两个侧轨和一个后桩（图 9）。一侧面的板轨是完整，252 厘米长。侧轨下面有一个类似倒置字母 V 的凹槽。在凹槽上有几个长孔是为了固定底部上方的桩。侧轨的后端有一个长孔是为了固定板尾的桩。后端桩的上方是弯曲的，位于侧轨的后孔里。

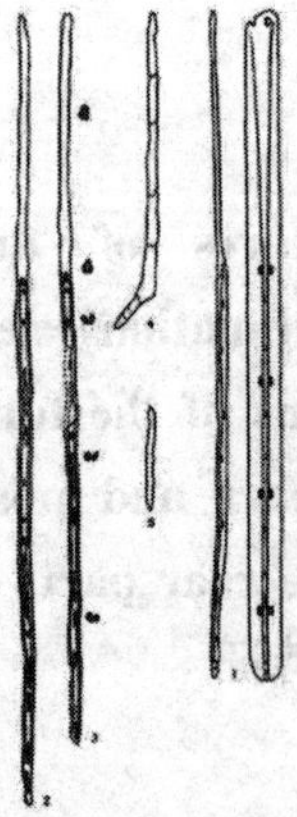

CATALOG NUMBER			PARISH	LENGTH OF COMPLETE RUNNER MM	BREATH MM	THICKNESS MM	STRUCTURAL FEATURES REAR	MIDDLE	FORE	14C DATE	± σ	LAB NO
KM/eh	20248		Kuusamo	820	142					5690	110	Hel-1159
KM/kt	8227		Salla		136	18				4470	110	Hel-1330
RIDGED RUNNERS												
PHM	433		Evijärvi	2900	110	35	P2	R1	K1			
KM/eh	12146		Heinola	2880				R2	K3	3600	175	Hel-659
	12923	1,2										
KM/eh	13468	1 - 5	Joroinen				P1	R1				
SatM	16765	1 - 5	Kullaa	2130	105	30	P3	R1	K2	2390	160	TX-125
SatM	17264		Noormarkku		102			R1 ?	K3	3530	110	I-1921
	–		Pihtipudas				P2 ?	R1				
KM/eh	1107		Saarijärvi		115	35	P1	R1	K2			

Fig. 9 Parts of the Kullaa ridged sledge (Salo 1965: 9, fig. 4).

图 9 库拉脊形滑雪板部分展示

The Joroinen find included three fragments of side-rails. Two of them apparently belong to the same side-rail. The combined length is over 260 cm. The structure of the Joroinen side-rails is similar to the Kullaa side-rails (Fig. 10a). The side-rails were made of the wood of a young tree (Fig. 10b) . The V-groove was made to support the posts, but it also prevents splitting when the wood dries.

Joroinen 地区发现的雪板包括三个侧护栏的片段，其中两个显然属于同一侧边，合并后的长度超过 260 厘米。Joroinen 雪板的侧边与 Kullaa 侧边的结构相似 (图 10a)。侧边是由年轻的树木做成（图 1b），V 型槽的制作是为了支撑后桩，但是它也阻止树木边干后开裂。

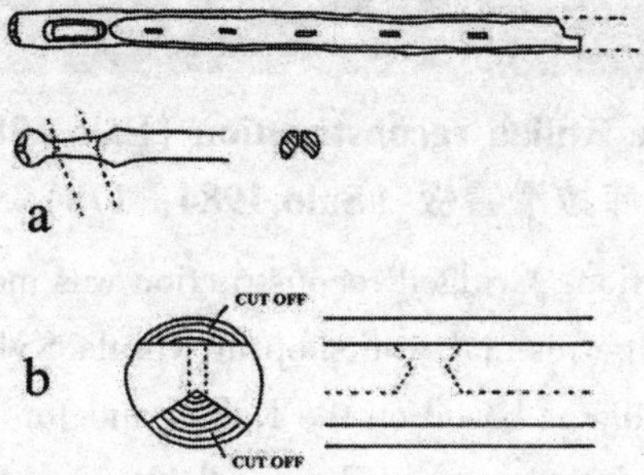

Fig. 10　Side-rail structure of the Joroinen ridged sledge. Drawing: T. Kuokkanen.

图 10　Joroinen 脊形雪板的构造 绘画：T. Kuokkanen.

Reconstructions of the ridged type sledges. The ridged runner type has no clear ethnographic counterparts. The preceding Stone Age central-grooved sledge type seems to have been two-legged (Kuokkanen 1999, 2000), and the ridged sledge is an improved version of it. Because of this and the ridged sledge parts we can assume that the ridged sledge was also two-legged.

脊型雪橇的复原。脊型雪橇没有明确的民族特色的对应体，前面的石器时代的中央凹槽式雪橇似乎有两条腿（Kuokkanen 1999, 2000），脊形雪橇是它的一种改进的版本。因为这一点和脊形雪橇的其他部分，我们可以假定脊形雪橇也是两条腿。

The Kullaa reconstruction. A reconstruction based on the Kullaa finds was made at the Satakunta Museum in 1963 (Salo 1965) . The reconstruction greatly resembles the modern dog sledge (Fig. 11) . The structure is functional except the cross-bar, which should be placed above the runners.

Kullaa 雪橇的复原。这种重构是建立在 1963 年 Satakunta 博物馆中关于 Kullaa 雪橇的发现（Salo 1965）。复员后的这种雪橇与现在的犬拉式雪橇有极大的相似（图 11）。这种结构是功能性的，除了横杆，横杆应该被放置在雪板之上的。

Fig. 11 The Kullaa reconstruction (Salo 1984: 178).
图 11 重造库拉滑雪板 (Salo 1984: 178).

The Kurala reconstruction. A ridged reconstruction was made in the winter of 1991-92 in the archaeological experimental workshop at Kurala Kylämäki (part of the Turku Museum Centre). The sledge is based on the Kullaa and Joroinen finds with some modifications. The fore parts of the runners have elk heads after the Noormarkku find (Fig. 12).

Kurala 雪橇的复原。这种脊形的复原是建立在 KuralaKylämäki 地区（图尔库博物馆中心的一部分）的 1991/1992 年冬天考古实验工作小组的基础上的，这种雪撬的复原是基于 Kullaa 和 Joroinen 雪橇的发现及一些修改而建立起来的，在 Noormarkkudiqu 地区之后发现的雪板的前部都有麋鹿头像（图 12）。

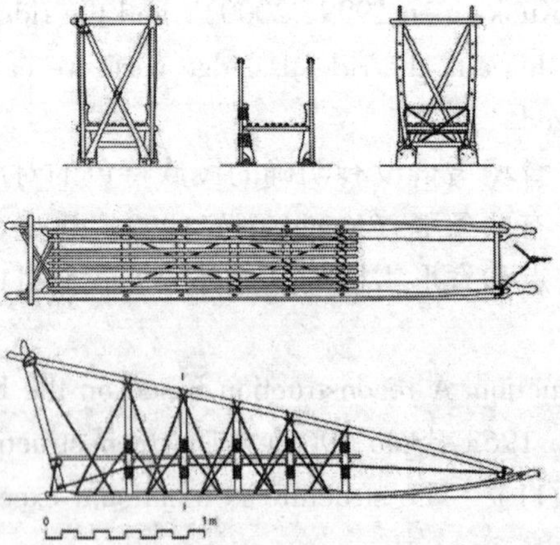

Fig. 12 The Kurala reconstruction as tested at Saarijärvi. Drawing T. Kuokkanen.

图 12 在 Saarijärvi 测试的库拉滑雪板重造 绘画 T. Kuokkanen

Because of winter and scanty resources it was not possible to use curved woodor chosen branches. For this reason, the inner post structure is more complicated than that of the Kullaa reconstruction（Fig. 13b）. There are more bindings. Instead of rawhide, sisal string had to be used.

由于冬天的到来和资源的匮乏，不能再利用木块和树枝制作雪板。由于这个原因，Kurala 地区发现的雪橇比 Kullaa（图 13b）地区发现的雪橇的内部结构的复原更为复杂。因为它有更多的固定器，要用更多的剑麻绳而不是生牛皮。

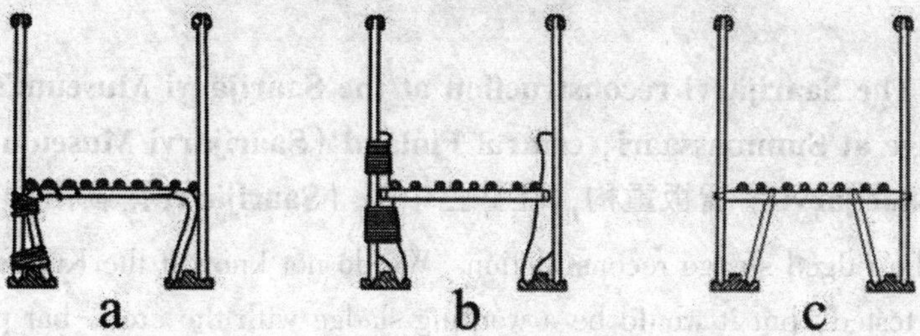

Fig. 13　Post structure of the ridged sledge reconstructions. a－The Kullaa reconstruction, b－The Kurala reconstruction and c－The Saarijärvi reconstruction. Drawing: T. Kuokkanen.

图 13 脊形滑雪板重构的板尾结构。a－The Kullaa 滑雪板重构，b－The Kurala 滑雪板重构和 c－TSaarijärvi 滑雪板重构 绘图：T. Kuokkanen.

In the Kullaa reconstruction the inner posts were branches which were bound together（Fig. 13a）. A comparable structure could be made by using two bent wooden strakes bound together. The weight of the Kurala reconstruction is 25 kg.

在 Kullaa 雪橇重建过程中，内部的杆的分支被连接到一起（图 13a），把两个弯曲的木板绑在一起就可以制成一个比较稳定的结构。Kurala 雪橇复原后的重量是 25 千克。

The Saarijärvi reconstruction. A new ridged sledge was made in 2000 for the Saarijärvi Museum. The inner post structure is simpler and the inner posts are slanted（Fig 13c）which makes the structure more rigid. The bindings were made of wet elk rawhide. Many fewer bindings were needed（Fig. 14）. The straps tightened while drying.

Saarijärvi 的复原。Saarijärvi 雪橇在 2000 年为 Saarijärvi 博物馆重构成的一只新脊型雪橇，内杆制作简单，倾斜的角度使结构更加坚固（图 13c），固定器是由湿麋鹿皮制成，所需要的固定器也更少（图 14），当是麋鹿皮边干后，束带就变得紧固。

Fig. 14　The Saarijärvi reconstruction at the Saarijärvi Museum's Stone Age village at Summassaari, central Finland (Saarijärvi Museum).

图 14　Saarijärvi 滑雪板重构，在芬兰中部（Saarijärvi 博物馆）

Testing the ridged sledge reconstructions. We do not know if the Kullaa reconstruction has been tested, but it would be a working sledge with the cross-bar placed above the runners. The Kurala reconstruction was tested in 1992 at the Saarijärvi Museum's Stone Age Village in Summassaari, central Finland. The test cargo was light, only a single elk hide. Because the total weight of the sledge and cargo was small, only two dogs were used to haul the sledge. A short test drive showed that the sledge was quite handy and resembled a modern cargo sledge. There were numerous lashings in the sledge and we can assume that during long trip those lashings would have loosened making their tightening necessary.

检测脊型雪橇的复原。我们不知道 Kullaa 雪橇的复原是否已经通过测试，但是在雪板上摆放一个横杆它就能够运行。Kurala 雪橇复原的检测是在 1992 进行的，地点是在芬兰中部 Summassaari 的 Saarijärvi 博物馆的石器时代村落。该测试物是较轻的，只有一块麋鹿皮。由于雪橇和测试物的总重量很小，只有两条狗被用来拖拉雪橇。一个简短的试驾表明，雪橇相当方便，类似于现代拉货雪橇。雪橇中有许多绳索，我们可以假设，这些绳索在长途旅行中，会使有所松动地方让紧缩，这是非常必要的。

The Saarijärvi reconstruction was tested briefly at the Saarijärvi Museum's Stone Age Village in 2001. The structure of the sledge was much better than that of the Kurala sledge.

Saarijärvi 复原后的检测主要是在 2001 年的 Saarijärvi 博物馆的石器时代村落。这种雪橇的结构比 Kurala 雪橇的结构更优化。

Unfortunately, the testing of the different reconstructions under real conditions has been too superficial. We can, however, summarize and state that the structure of the Kurala reconstruction is too complicated and its binding material is modern. The Kullaa and Saarijärvi reconstructions are probably closer to the originals. They seem to function better than the Kurala reconstruction in natural conditions and their structures seem to bear more strain in the tests. However, we do not know yet how functional they will eventually be. Only thorough tests with full loads will provide the final word.

不幸的是，复原后的不同的雪橇在真实条件下的检测是肤浅的。然而，我们能总结出 Kurala 雪橇的重构结构太复杂，它的固定器的材料也是较现代的。Kullaa 雪橇和 Saarijärvi 雪橇的复原可能是接近原样的，在自然条件下，它们的比复原的 Kurala 雪橇的功能性更好，它们的结构在检测中似乎也能承受更多的压力。然而，我们不知道它们最终的功能怎样，只有用完全的重量去测试，它们才能提供出最终的承载量。

Conclusions: what lies behind the change of types?

结论：雪橇类型改变的背后动因是什么？

As far as we know the ridged runners have been found only inFinland. Why? We must remind the reader that, naturally, it is possible that ridged runners outside Finland may still remain to be found. On the other hand, ridged sledges may have been a local tradition. In Russia, the ski-sledge apparently replaced the earlier Stone Age central-grooved sledge. In Sweden there are some interesting runner finds: two runners from Hälsingland (Oldeberg 1974, Hälsingland 2879 & 2881) and one from Jämtland (Oldeberg 1974, Jämtland 2891). The runners somewhat resemble central-grooved runners but are apparently their own type; in particular Hälsingland 2882 and Jämtland 2891 look similar (Oldeberg 1974). Both deserve a closer look in future work.

据我们所知，脊形雪橇仅发现于芬兰，为什么呢？我们必须提醒读者脊形雪橇在芬兰以外的其他地方还有待发现。另一方面，脊型雪橇可能是当地的一个传统。在俄罗斯，雪板雪橇显然取代了石器时代早期的中部凹槽雪橇。瑞典有几个关于雪板的有趣发现：两只来自于 Hälsingland 的雪板（Oldeberg 1974, Hälsingland 2879 & 2881）和一只来自于 Jämtland 的雪板（Oldeberg 1974, Jämtland 2891）。这些雪板有点与中部有凹槽的雪板相似，但是它们各自又都有自己的风格。尤其是 Hälsingland 2882 和 Jämtland 2891 雪板，它们看起来相似（Oldcberg 1974），它们都值得进一步探究。

The ridged sledge is quite rigid. The driver can push the sledge in difficult terrain and it is not necessary to fasten the cargo. On the other hand, the sledge must be hauled by a man or dogs. The driver cannot use skis or snow shoes, nor can he stand on the runners, but has to walk behind the sledge. Hands on the handle bar and the cargo tend to press down the rear of the sledge. This raises the fore part slightly. It seems probable that the fore parts were quite low, making the sledge glide easily in soft snow. The ridged sledge was perhaps used for long journeys, seal-hunting trips and winter net fishing where large cargo capacity was needed. In immediate surroundings a small ski-sledge was more practical.

脊型雪橇是相当坚硬的。驾驭者崎岖的能够在崎岖的地形中推动雪橇，并且不用固定货物。另一方面，雪橇必须由人或犬拉动，驾驭者不能使用雪板或雪鞋，也不能站在雪橇上，而是必须要走在雪橇的后面。在扶手和货物上的手要按住雪橇后部，这样雪橇的前部就稍稍抬起。看起来雪橇的前部相当低，使雪橇在松软的雪地上轻易地滑行。这种坚固的雪橇或许适用于长距离的旅行、猎捕海豹的行程和冬钓，它们都需要大量货物的运输。在中间的环境中，小雪橇是更实用的。

Why did the ridged sledge disappear? We are inclined to think that the ski-sledge replaced it. The ski-sledge is a versatile all-round sledge and it is easier to make. The smaller ski-sledge is good for hunting and fishing activities, while the larger one is good for longer journeys.

为什么脊型雪橇消失了？我们倾向于认为是雪板雪橇取代了它。雪板雪橇是一种多功能全方位的雪橇，容易驾驶。小点儿的雪橇适用于捕猎和捕鱼活动，而大点儿的雪橇适用于长距离的旅途。

We can consider the example an Iron Age boat type known as the Mekrijärvi type boat. It has been suggested that the expansion of commerce during the Viking Age demanded a more effective means to transport wilderness products to middlemen and the markets. The buoyancy of the boats used in the lakes and rivers of the interior of Finland had to increase. The time was ripe for a new boat type consisting of five main parts: a hollowed-out keel timber that was spread out, a V-shaped hollowed-out fore and aft staves, and two side strakes which add considerably to the buoyancy of the boat type. The construction was strengthened with ribs fastened to the keel timber by lashing through ‘ears’ left on the keel. This type, based on stern and sternpost construction, is regarded as an intermediary stage in the development of the clinker-built boat from the dug-out to the stave-built type with several clinker-built strakes (Taavitsainen 1998: 153, note 1; Taavitsainen et al. 2007: 52-54 and references).

我们可以想到铁器时代船形雪橇一例，Mekrijärvi 船形雪橇。船形雪橇的出现说明北欧海盗时代商业的扩展，因为商业的发展需要更有限的交通运输方式把偏僻地区的商品运给中介人和商品。芬兰内陆地区的水运船只也要增加。船形雪橇时代的成熟包括以下五个主要方面：一种龙骨木材的扩散，v 型前后部镂空船的棍子，和两边的底板大大增添船的浮力。通过把左侧的“耳朵”系到龙骨上而将船肋骨固定到龙骨上来加强构建结构。建构是加强肋骨固定在龙骨木材上，并用绳系住“耳朵”的龙骨。人们认为这种类型是叠接式构造而成的船从挖掘手法而造的船到层叠式低板窄板船的一个中间发展的阶段（Taavitsainen 1998：153，note 1；Taavitsainen et al. 2007：52-54 和其他参考）。

The development also affected the means of Iron Age winter transport. The clinker technique used in the Mekrijärvi boats was naturally applied to winter vehicles, resulting in the *ahkio* sledge. The Viking Age is the most probable date for the oldest

representatives of this Lapp sledge（Taavitsainen 1999：312）.

这种发展历程也影响了铁器时代冬季的交通运输方式。用于建造 Mekrijärvi 船的叠加技术自然也运用到冬季的交通工具中，从而 Ahkio 雪橇便应运而生。北欧海盗时代是最有可能出现古老的 Lapp 雪橇代表的时期（Taavitsainen 1999：312）。

Owing to the uncertainties of the few radiocarbon dates and the lack of further dating we cannot discuss the development and changes of the Bronze Age sledge types in more detail. Activity in the circumpolar regions increased during the Bronze Age, during the ‘heroic age of travels and transformations’, apparently in connection with a more efficient linking of the circumpolar areas with the networks of ‘international’ trade of the time. Increased demand for the products of the taiga and tundra regions required the more efficient transport of larger quantities of products than previously. It became necessary to construct more serviceable winter transport equipment. It is to be anticipated that when more detailed study of sledges with new 14C dates will emerge, some of the changes to be discovered in winter transport equipment are to be connected with the development of Bronze Age trading networks and needs associated with this web of interconnectivity.

由于为数不多的放射性碳年代测定的不确定性，我们不能对青铜器时代的雪橇类型作进一步的细节讨论。在“旅行和转换的英雄时代”，极地附近地区的活动增加了，显然那个时期的“国际”贸易网有效地连接了极地附近的地区。社会产品的需求增加，使得针叶林和苔原地区产品需求的增加，需要比以前更高效的交通来运输大总量的商品。这就必要构造更有用的冬季运输设备。我们可以预见到新的 14 世纪关于雪橇具体种类的研究将会出现，在冬季交通运输工具中会发现一些变化，这些变化与青铜器时代贸易的发展和需求有内在的相关性。

Jussi-Pekka Taavitsainen：ustaa@ utu. fi（Corresponding author）

Jussi-Pekka Taavitsainen：ustaa@ utu. fi（通讯作者）

Abbreviations 缩写

KM/eh = National Museum of Finland/prehistoric collections（芬兰国家博物馆/史前收藏品）

KM/kt = National Museum of Finland/ethnographic collections 芬兰国家博物馆/民族志收藏品

SatM = Satakunta Museum（萨塔昆塔博物馆）

References 参考文献

AALTO, M., J.-P. TAAVITSAINEN and I. VUORELA, 1981. Palaeobotanical Investigations at the Site of a Sledge Runner Find, Dated to about 4900 BP, in Noormarkku, SW Finland. *Suomen Museo* 1980: 41-65.

ANTHONY, D. W., 2007. *The Horse, the Wheel, and Language. How Bronze-Age Riders from the Eurasian steppes shaped the Modern World*. Princeton & Oxford: Princeton University Press.

BERG, G., 1935. *Sledges and wheeled vehicles. Ethnological studies from the view point of Sweden*. Stockholm: Fritze (Nordiska museet handlingar 4).

BIRKET-SMITH, K., 1972. *Kulttuurin tiet* 1. Porvoo & Helsinki: WSOY.

CLARK, J. G. D., 1952. *The Prehistoric Europe: the Economic Basis*. London: Menthuen.

Bronk Ramsey, C., 1995. Radiocarbon Calibration and Analysis of Stratigraphy: The OxCal Program. *Radiocarbon* 37 (2): 425-430.

Bronk Ramsey, C., 2001. Development of the Radiocarbon Program OxCal. *Radiocarbon* 43 (2): 355-363.

EDGREN, T., 1984. Kivikausi. *Suomen historia* 1: 8-97. Espoo: Weilin+Göös.

GOODY, J., 2010. *The Eurasian Miracle*. Cambridge: Polity.

ITKONEN, T. I., 1931. Muinaissuksia ja-jalaksia. *Suomen Museo* 1930: 82-90.

ITKONEN, T. I., 1932. Muinaissuksia ja-jalaksia. II. *Suomen Museo* 1931-1932: 50-63.

ITKONEN, T. I., 1934. Vesikulkuneuvot. In T. I. Itkonen (ed.), *Vanhaa Hauhoa*: 256-261. Vammala: Tyrvään Kirjapaino Oy (Kansatieteellinen arkisto 1).

ITKONEN, T. I., 1935. Muinaissuksia ja-jalaksia. III. *Suomen Museo* 1934: 1-21.

ITKONEN, T. I., 1938. Muinaissuksia ja-jalaksia. V. *Suomen Museo* 1938: 13-34.

ITKONEN, T. I., 1949. Muinaissuksia ja-jalaksia. VIII. *Suomen Museo* 1949: 27-40.

KOPISTO, A., 1964. Uusia jalaslöytöjä. *Suomen Museo* 1964: 17-25.

KOTIVUORI, H., 1996. Pyytäjistä kaskenraivaajiksi. Rovaniemen asutus noin 6000 eKr-1300 jKr. In M. Saarnisto, H. Kotivuori, J. Vahtola and M. Enbuske (eds.), *Rovaniemen historia vuoteen* 1721: 34-125. Jyväskylä: Rovaniemen kaupunki, Rovaniemen maalaiskunta & Rovaniemen seurakunta. KRISTIANSEN, K., 1998. *Europe Before History*. Cambridge: Cambridge University Press.

KRISTIANSEN, K., 2008. Eurasia in the Bronze and early Iron Ages. *Antiquity* 82: 113-118.

KRISTIANSEN, K. and T. B. LARSSON, 2005. *The Rise of Bronze Age Society. Travels: Transmission and Transformations*. Cambridge: Cambridge University Press.

KUOKKANEN, T., 1999. *Päällyskourullinen, keskikuurnallinen ja keskiharjallinen reki. Kolme esihistoriallisen reen rekonstruktiota*. Unpublished MA-thesis. Department of Archaeology/University of Turku.

KUOKKANEN, T., 2000. Stone Age Sledges of Central-grooved type: Finnish Reconstructions. *Fennoscandia Archaeologica* XVII: 37-56.

LUHO, V., 1945. Pielaveden reenjalaksen ikä. *Suomen Museo* 1945: 82-84.

LUHO, V., 1948. Über steinzeitliche Winterverkehrsmittel in Finland. *Acta Archaeologica* XIX: 115-144.

LUHO, V., 1951. Lapinlahden jättiläisjalas. *Suomen Museo* 1951: 108-116.

LUHO, V., 1957. Eine steinzeitliche Schlittenform. *Suomen Museo* 1957: 9-16.

MANNINEN, I., 1934. Kulku-ja kuljetusneuvot. *Suomen suku* III: 209-241.

NASKALI, E., 1989. Suksi muinaislöytöjen valossa (Skis in the light of old finds). *Latua! Suomen hiihtomuseon julkaisuja* n: o 1: 12-18.

NASKALI, E., 1999. On Ancient Skis. In M. Huurre (ed.), *Dig it all. Studies dedicated to Ari* Siiriäinen: 295-306. Jyväskylä: The Finnish Antiquarian Society & The Archaeological Society of Finland.

OLDEBERG, A., 1974. Die ältere Metallzeit in Schweden I-II. Stockholm: Kungl. Vitterhets Historie och Antikvitets Akademien.

REIMER, P. J., M. G. L. BAILLIE, E. BARD, A. BAYLISS, J. W. BECK, C. J. H. BERTRAND, P. G. BLACKWELL, C. E. BUCK, G. S. BURR, K. B. CUTLER, P. E. DAMON, R. L. EDWARDS, R. G. FAIRBANKS, M. FRIEDRICH, T. P. GUILDERSON, A. G. HOGG, K. A. HUGHEN, B. KROMER, G. MCCORMAC, S. MANNING, C. BRONK RAMSEY, R. W., REIMER, S. REMMELE, J. R. SOUTHON, M. STUIVER, S. TALAMO, F. W. TAYLOR, J. VAN DER PLICHT, and C. E. WEYHENMEYER, 2004. IntCal04 Terrestrial Radiocarbon Age Calibration, 0-26 ka cal BP. *Radiocarbon* 46 (3): 1029-1058.

SALO, U., 1965. Kullaan Puiston muinaisjalas. *Suomen Museo* 1965: 5-15.

SALO, U., 1967. Die Elchkopfkufe von Noormarkku. *Suomen Museo* 1967: 42-45.

SALO, U., 1984. Pronssikausi ja rautakauden alku. In: *Suomen Historia* 1: 98-249. Espoo: Weilin+Göös.

SEGER, T., 1988. Heinolan esihistoria. In I. Wilmi (ed.), *Heinolan pitäjän historia* 1860-*luvulle*: 15-73. Jyväskylä: Heinolan maalaiskunta, Heinolan maaseurakunta, Manttaalikunnan säätiö.

SEGER, T., 1991. Ten thousand years of Finnish prehistory. A tentative calibration of the earliest radiocarbon dates. *Finskt Museum* 1990: 14-23.

SIRELIUS, U. T., 1918. Über einige prototype des Schlittens. *Suomalaisugrilaisen seuran aikakauskirja-Journal de la Sociétéfinno*-ougrienne ××× 32: 1-26.

SIRELIUS, U. T., 1919. *Suomen kansanomaista kulttuuria* I. Helsinki: Otava.

TAAVITSAINEN, J.-P., 1998. Exploitation and wilderness resources and Lapp settlement in Central and Eastern Finland. In H. Andersson, L. Ersgård and E. Svensson (eds), *Outland Use in Preindustrial Europe*: 134-155. Lund: Lunds universitet (Lund studies in medieval archaeology 20).

TAAVITSAINEN, J.-P., 1999. Wilderness commerce and the development of boat types-remains of the Hartola boat. In M. Huurre (ed.), *Dig it all. Studies dedicated to Ari Siiriäinen*: 307-

313. Jyväskylä: The Finnish Antiquarian Society & The Archaeological Society of Finland.

TAAVITSAINEN, J. -P. , J. VILKUNA and H. FORSSELL, 2007. *Suojoki at Keuruu-a mid-14th century site of wilderness culture in Central Finland*. Helsinik: Suomalaisen Tiedeakatemian toimituksia (Annales Academiae Scientarium Fennicae Humaniora 346).

VILKUNA, K. , 1934. Kulku-ja kuljetusneuvot. In T. I. Itkonen (ed.), *Vanhaa Hauhoa*: 241-255. Vammala: Tyrvään Kirjapaino Oy (Kansatieteellinen arkisto 1).

VILKUNA, J. , 1986. Kaksi muinaisten suksirekien jalasta Keski-Suomesta. *Keski-Suomi* 18: 8-16.

VOIONMAA, V. , 1933. Liikenne ja kauppa. *Suomen kulttuurihistoria* I: 434-479. Jyväskylä & Helsinki: K. J. Gummerus.

4.33 瑞典古老滑雪板介绍 Introduction of theAncient Sweden Ski

肯尼斯·阿斯特姆(瑞典) Kenneth Åström(SWE)

个人简介 Brief Introduction

Until 1998 Senior Curator and Deputy Museum Director at Västerbottens Museum and Swedish Ski Museum, Umea, Sweden Responsible for building up the new Swedish Ski Museum 1984 in UmeåFrom 1998 Museum Director at Eskilstuna Museum of Art, Eskilstuna, Sweden From 1 of January 2015 Senior Adviser Studied Ethnology at Uppsala University. Works at Eskilstuna konstmuseum Sweden. His main work is historical research and museum designer.

1984 年,任埃斯基尔斯蒂娜艺术博物馆馆长,馆址位于瑞典埃斯基尔斯蒂娜。1984 年,负责建设新瑞典滑雪博物馆,馆址位于瑞典于默奥。至 1998 年,Västerbottens 博物馆高级策划人、瑞典于默奥滑雪博物馆副馆长。2015 年 1 月 1 日,高级顾问。曾在瑞典乌普萨拉大学学习人种学。在瑞典埃斯基尔斯蒂纳的博物馆工作,他的主要工作是滑雪历史研究和博物馆设计。

论文 Paper:

Kalvträsk ski, West Bothnia, Sweden Kenneth Åström

The ski from Kalvträsk is perhaps the most remarkable archaeological object that has been found in the northern part of Sweden. It was in use approximately 5200 years ago and have since then, up until it was discovered been preserved by lying bedridden in a bog.

The ski was found in 1924 just over two kilometers outside the village of Kalvträsk when work with frost drainage of the marsh area that stretches between the villages Fäbotjälen and Nybrännet was taken place.

The finding, which contained two skis and a paddle rod, was found at a depth of about 150 cm. Both skis and the rod were seemingly whole and intact when they were discovered. But when they were picked up out of the bog and during transportation from place of discovery one ski fell into pieces.

Before the items were removed from the bog, they were measured and it showed that both skis had exactly the same dimensions. They were 204 cm long and 15. 5 cm wide. The paddle rod was 156cm.

Today, the remains of the collapsed ski consists of only fragments, just the middle portion and the front right portion are intact. The second ski is essentially complete except for minor pieces missing at the tip and at the left edge behind the footplate.

There are no processing tracks on the skis, while the paddle rod show signs of being worked on with stone tools.

The Kalvträsk ski is the only discovery in the Nordic region with the binding type which is characterized by two pairs of vertical holes through which the binding straps drawn. A firm conclusion cannot be drawn from this single finds. But the fact that a pair of skis with this special ski binding have been found in West Bothnia, may perhaps be taken as evidence of the lively cultural contacts that have taken place in an easterly direction. And within the vast area that northern Eurasia represents, where large numbers of nomadic groups lived under similar conditions. The same type of bindings is to be found in both Siberia and large parts of Asia far into our time.

The circumstances surrounding this ski find are broadly the same as for all other finds made in the Nordic countries. No skis have been found at archaeological sites and therefore cannot be linked to other discoveries or cultural relics. They are, in almost all cases preserved for posterity by ending up into a tarn, lake, marsh or bog where the otherwise perishable wood has been embedded. Chemical processes and an almost non-existent supply of air have ensured that the objects could be preserved for several thousand years.

Kalvträsk（地名）滑雪板，西波的尼亚湾，瑞典

肯尼斯　阿斯特姆

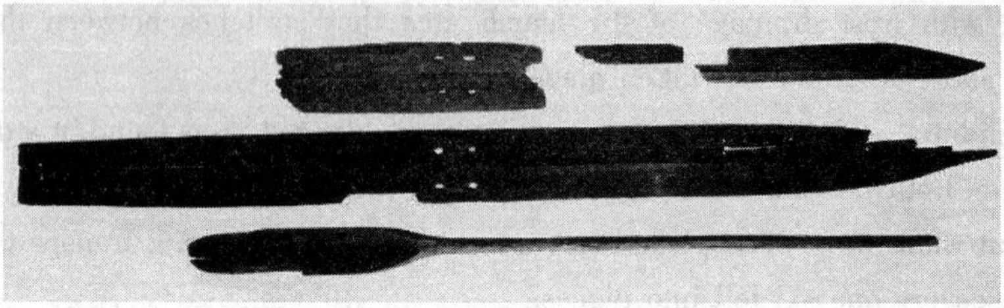

图1

Kalvträsk（地名）滑雪板或许是瑞典北部发现的最具标志性的考古对象，大约5200年前投入使用，此后至被发现之前，一直保存于一片沼泽之中。

1924年，雪板发现于Kalvträsk村庄外两千米的地方，当时正在沼泽区域建立弗罗斯特排水系统，该系统延伸到Fäbotjälen（地名）和Nybrännet（地名）两个村庄之间。当时在地下1.5米的深度处发现了两个雪板和一个划桨，发现之时雪板和划桨均完好无损。但在从沼泽中取出雪板之时及从发现地运出的过程中，一只雪板摔成了碎片。

物件被取出沼泽之前已被进行了测量，测量显示两个滑雪板的规格完全一致，长均为204cm，宽均为15.5cm，划桨长156cm。

如今，已毁雪板的残余部分就只剩下片段，只有中间部分和右前段部分完整存在。第二只雪板除去顶端和踏板右后方有少许缺失，其余基本完整。在雪板上没有处理过的痕迹，而划桨上有被石器敲击过的痕迹。

Kalvträsk雪板是北欧地区唯一带有束缚功能的雪板，雪板上有两个竖直孔用来系绑定带。目前还不能从这一单一发现得出固定结论。但在西方西面发现一副带有这种绑定带的雪板，或许可以成为向东面进行活跃文化交流的证据。在北欧北部的广袤区域内，大批的游牧部落曾居住于相似的条件之下。之后才在西伯利亚和亚洲的大部分地区发现类似的绑定装置。雪具发现地周边的环境与北欧地区其他事物发现地的环境大体相同。因为不曾在考古遗址发现过滑板，因此不能与其他发现和文化遗址联系在一起。几乎在所有情况下，他们均为子孙后代保存，最后被存放于冰斗湖，湖泊，沼泽或湿地中。否则，那里将被嵌入易腐蚀的木头，化学反应和近乎真空的环境保证其中的物品可保存数千年之久。

Dating

Any attempt to date the findings was never made in connection to the discovery. It wasn't until 1930, seven years after the findings that the museum experts came back to the site to conduct an inspection and make an analysis of the soil. By then, the peat had floated away around the ditch where the skis were found. The surrounding part of the bog had then, because of drainage, started to collapse. A drill profile was therefore made about 5 meters from the place of discovery in a similar position and at the same depth at which the ski was found.

In order to make a more reliably dating a pollen diagram was taken from the wreck site as well as from the peat residues saved from the found object. Both analyses showed such a good consistency, that the time when the ski ended up in the bog could be determined to the period around 2000 BC.

Pollen analyses have often proved unreliable; therefore, new and more reliable dating methods have been developed. One of these is the Radiocarbon dating (C 14 analysis). Today, over 90 of the nearly 200 discoveries made in the Nordic countries have been dated with this method. The performed dating's has provided some very interesting results. These include the calibrated dating of the Kalvträsk ski (sample ST 8411, 3200 BC) which gives it an age of 5200 years, in terms of tree age. Although it is assumed that the ski was made of a full-grown tree, but it will still make it older than the oldest pyramid in Egypt.

年代测定

以往从未尝试去确定与发现相关的日期。直到 1930 年，即在发现之后七年，

博物馆专家才回到发现地去进行检查，分析土壤。可那时，发现雪具的沟渠附近的泥炭已经飘走。由于排水，当时沼泽周边的环境已经开始崩溃，因此在距离发现地 5 米的地方在相似的地理位置安装了钻井装置，并且其深度与发现雪具位置的深度一致。

为得出更为可靠的日期，采取了孢粉图示法对遗址和发现地保留下来的泥炭残留进行分析。分析显示出了很好的连续性，当时雪板封存于沼泽的时间可以被限定在约公元前 2000 年。

经证实，孢粉分析的可靠性不足，因此，更多可信赖的新方法得到了发展。其中之一就是利用放射性碳（碳 14 分析）。目前，北欧的 200 多种发现中，有超过 90 种通过这种方法测定了年代。这些测定提供了一些十分有趣的结果。包括 Kalvträsk 滑雪板的标准年代测定（样品 ST 8411，公元前 3200），测定结果是雪板的木材有 5200 年的历史。即使假设当时的雪板使用的是成年树，它的历史亦比埃及最古老的金字塔更加久远。

Compression wood as ski material

In early ski research there was no link drawn between the ski's shape, the terrain and snow conditions it was used in, and a study on how the ski material is taken from the tree. Another thing missing was how the annual rings of the wood lies in relation to the ski's sliding surface, parallel or perpendicular, which affects how the sliding surface is worn in contact with the snow. In order to obtain evidence of our assumptions, we conducted a micro-siping investigation. This was done in collaboration with the Academy of Forestry in Umeå, Sweden on a number of the oldest findings contained in the Ski Museum collection. The micro-siping study gave us a clear result of how the ski was taken out of the tree.

The investigation revealed that the Kalvträsk ski was made of what we in Sweden call, (tjurved) compression wood from pine. Ski manufacturers have for many generations regarded this as a good material for skis because of its strength, endurance and glide properties.

Compression wood (reaction wood) formed when the tree's growth in some way is disturbed by unilaterally acting wind, sloping terrain, undermining of the root system or damage of the tree trunk. The result of this can be seen by looking at the trunk's shape which takes on a more oval eccentric shape than the normal symmetric circular shape. The phenomenon occurs when the resin and phenols are added as impregnation of the channels in the tree that needs to be strengthened in order not to be attacked by rot. The material becomes through this, very easily tarred and pre-waxed if you heat it over an open fire.

In the craft-rate ski manufacturing as we know since the late 1700s, compression wood has been highly sought when the manufacturer wanted to achieve a high quality product. But because the availability of compression wood was scarce it was not commonly used. When compression wood was used they added the ski bottom toward the tree marrow or vice versa. The ski material was therefore produced with lying annual rings. This gave an uneven wear with a slightly concave or convex underside depending on how the ski material was turned.

Here we can talk about the Kalvträsk ski as a solitary not only from the traditional ski production during 1800 and 1900 quarters but also from the other seven findings included in the micro-siping study. The material has namely been charged with vertical annual rings which are highly unusual when it comes to compression wood (reaction wood). (Picture 3)

The Kalvträsk ski is made with vertical annual rings. (Picture 4)

Most common was to take the compression wood with horizontal growth rings. The underside has then been turned out well against the bark or toward the marrow.

密实木材作为雪板材质

在早期的雪板调研中，雪板形状、地势、使用雪板的雪况及雪板材料从树上获得的研究之间没有任何联系。另外缺失的还有树木的年轮与雪板表面、平行线或垂直线之间的关系，它影响当雪板与雪面接触时的磨损方式。为了获得假设的证据，我们进行了一个微型沟槽调研。该调研与瑞典的于默奥林业科学研究院合作展开，对滑雪博物馆收藏的大量古老发现进行研究。研究结果清晰的解释了如何从树上获得雪板木材。调查揭示了 Kalvträsk 雪板是由瑞典称之为（tjurved）的一种密实松木木材构成。由于其坚固性、耐用性、及滑行时的特性，连续多代的雪板制造商均将这种材质视为上等雪板材质。当树的成长在某种程度上受到了破坏，如单方向的强风，斜坡地势，树根系统受损或树干受损时，密实木材（应力木）会形成，结果可以通过树干的形状体现出来，相较于正常对称的圆形，密实树干往往呈现出奇怪的椭圆形。为了防止受腐蚀，树木吸收营养的渠道需要加强，因此应加入树脂和酚类，此时会出现以上现象。通过这种方式形成的材料在明火中加热很容易变脏且体积变大。

众所周知，自从二十世纪七十年代后期，雪板制造商就一直在追求使用密实木材，因为他们意欲生产出高质量的产品。但由于密实木材不易获得，因此在雪板的使用中较为罕见。当使用密实木材时，他们沿着树髓的方向突出雪板底部，或是与之相反。雪板的材料上带有水平年轮，导致雪板底部的不均衡磨损，在某种程度上这还取决于雪板材料的来源。我们可以视 Kalvträsk 雪板为隐士，不仅因它来源于十九世纪和二十世纪的传统雪板生产，更由于微型沟渠研究包括的其他七项发现。也就是说，带有竖纹年轮的密实木材（应力木）相当罕见。

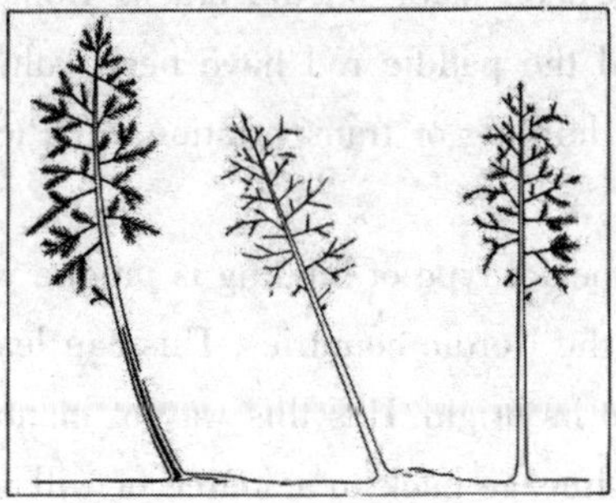

图 2　密实木材

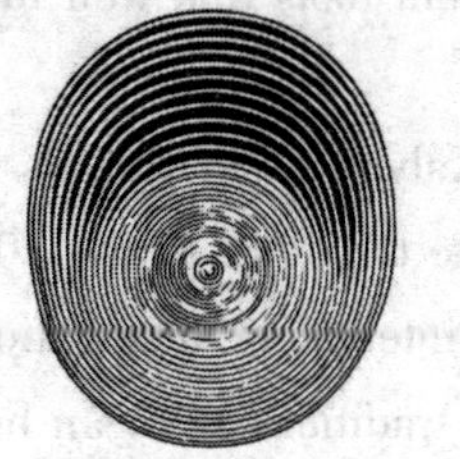

图 3　秘制木材的横截面

用带有水平年轮的密实木材制作的雪板最为常见。沿着树髓的方向突出雪板底部。如图 4 所示。

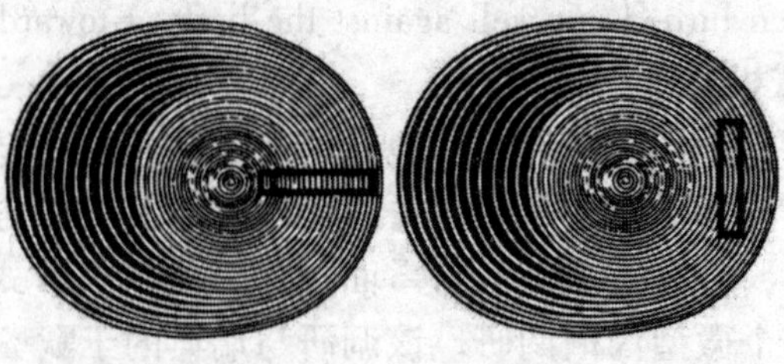

图 4　用竖纹年轮的密实木材制作的 Kalvträsk 雪板

The ski construction

The ski is very thin, with a flat underside. The top is reinforced with a narrow lightly marked, spine which stiffens and holds together the otherwise thin design. The cut back end has been thickened which reinforces it and prevents cracking.

The reinforcement makes it almost certain that we can dismiss any discussion that the ski may have been pointed at both ends. The flat and well-sharpened underside of the ski shows that it was not coated with skin. The manufacturer would not process the underside so carefully if a skin was planned to be applied.

How have they been able to achieve stability at skiing when both skin and stripe on the underside were missing? If a ski material with vertical annual rings is used, lengthwise micro tracks forms, by abrasion, on the underside of the ski. This is enough to control the ski in soft and medium-hard snow.

The choice of material and construction shows that the manufacturer had very good knowledge about the properties of wood. Many recent ski constructions are not nearly as functionally made. The meticulous repairs that has been made on the cracks front and back with straps of rawhide show that the skis and the paddle rod have been valuable and important tools that well fulfilled their roles in hunting or transportation. (Picture 5)

The Kalvträsk ski with its flat underside and special type of binding is unique when compared to the other nearly 200 findings made in the Nordic countries. This can lead to some very interesting speculations when it comes to its origin. Has this way of manufacturing skis traditions that can be traced through its lineage back to a source or will it remained a solitary exception?

Research within the field of skies was, during a long time, characterized by theories about distribution and thoughts around a place of origin for various cultural elements. A problem with this kind of speculation is that many of the conclusions drawn highly depend on what part of the ski's design the research is based on. For example did a team of Finnish researchers, who had chosen to focus on the ski's underside and the shape of the guiding stripe, come up with totally differentrelations between the various skis that had been used. One can generally say that research that has been done around the pre-historic and historical findings hasn't taken into account the possible connection between the ski's shape and the terrain and snow conditions it was used in. It is of vital importance that a new study is initialized so that we can get a clearer picture and deeper understanding of the various applications these different types of skis could have had.

The Ski from Kalvträsk is stored and displayed in the Swedish Ski Museum, Umeå, Swede

雪板建设

雪板很薄，底部是平板。顶部用窄小略微带有标记的松木巩固，用来粘住并将其他单薄设计连在一起。加厚了被削减的尾部，目的是巩固并防止开裂。这种加强使我们几乎可以确定，关于雪板可能指向两边这一问题不必再做任何讨论。雪板平坦和削尖的底部显示他们没有用动物皮毛覆盖。如果计划应用皮毛，生产者不会如此细致的处理底部。

没有底部的条形皮毛，滑雪时他们如何应用这种滑板。如果使用了带有竖直年轮的木材来制作雪板，通过雪板底部的摩擦，就会形成纵向的细微轨迹。在柔软和中等硬度的雪中可以控制雪板。

从对雪板材料和结构的选择可以看出生产者十分了解木材的特性。很多当今雪板的功能性不比从前。对带有生皮毛的雪板前后裂缝的细致维修显示，在过去的狩猎和交通中，雪板和划桨是很珍贵和重要的工具，并且两者都很好的完成了他们的任务。

图 5

与北欧国家的其他近 200 种发现相较而言，带有平坦底部和特殊绑定带的 Kalvträsk 雪板独树一帜。那么谈到其起源时就会出现十分有趣的猜测。我们会对这种生产雪板的传统方法追根溯源，或是使它继续做一个孤独的例外。

在很长的时间段内，雪板领域的研究一直以分布理论和带有多种文化元素的起源地的思想为特色。这里有一个问题，即很多得出的结论都太过依赖雪板设计的那一部分。例如，一队芬兰研究人员，选择专注研究雪板底部和引导带的形状，提出在不同种类雪板之间他们存在着完全不同的关系。大体上可以这么说，史前发现和历史发现没有考虑到雪板形状、地形和雪况之间可能存在的联系。展开一项崭新的研究，这样我们就可以更清晰深刻的了解不同类型雪板曾有过的各种应用，这至关重要。

Kalvträsk 雪板储存并展示在位于瑞典于默奥的瑞典滑雪博物馆之中。

4.34 考古学角度研究欧亚地区史前滑板及驯鹿放牧 AnArchaeological Perspective on Prehistoric Skis and Reindeer Herding in Eurasia

谢尔·阿克·安德森（瑞典） Kjell-Åke Aronsson (SWE)

个人简介 Brief Introduction

Ph. D. 1992 with the dissertation Forest reindeer herding AD 1-1800-an archaeological and palaeoecological study in northern Sweden. Prize for scientific work 1993 from The Royal Swedish Academy of Letters, History and Antiquities. Have been working with cultural heritage management during many years. Since 2005 Director at Ájtte, Swedish Mountain and Sámi Museum.

The main focus of research has been on the traces of reindeer herding in the landscape in a long-term perspective and the Eurasian context of reindeer herding. Ongoing research is also focused on the impact from climatic change on snow and ice patches in the high mountains. Traces like arrows and sledged are now melting out from snow and ice patches and give new insights in hunting technologies and the utilization of the landscape.

1992 年，凭借《森林驯鹿畜牧：公元 1-1800 年》论文取得哲学博士学位，这篇论文为瑞典北部的考古及古生态学研究。1993 年，获得瑞典皇家人文、历史及考古学院的科学工作奖。多年来一直从事文化遗产管理工作。自 2005 年以来，担任瑞典山区与萨米博物馆馆长。

他一直集中于从长期视角研究地区驯鹿放牧遗迹和欧亚地区驯鹿放牧遗迹。他正在进行的一个研究是关于环境变化对高山地区雪及冰道的影响。现在，很多遗迹比如箭和雪橇随着雪和冰道的融化而显露出来，他们为打猎技术和地形利用提供了新的视角。

论文 Paper:

AnArchaeological Perspective on Prehistoric Skis and Reindeer Herding in Eurasia

Key words:

Archaeology, prehistoric ski, reindeer herding, Eurasia

Skis in the world are archaeological finds from northern Sweden. In the area of the Gulf of Bothnia, the skis from Kalvträsk demonstrate the technique of skiing was in use in Scandinavia at least 5200 years ago. In contrast to Norway, in Sweden there is not a single depiction of a skier in the prehistoric rock art.

考古学角度研究欧亚地区史前滑板及驯鹿放牧

关键词： 考古学，史前滑雪板，驯鹿放牧，欧亚大陆

滑雪的起源和滑雪史一直以来备受争议。世界现存最古老的比较完整滑雪板是考古学家在瑞典北部发现的。波的尼亚湾的 Kalvträsk 滑雪板证明，至少在 5200 年前，斯堪的纳维亚地区人们就已使用滑雪技术。与挪威相比较，瑞典在史前时期没有关于滑雪者的岩画。在挪威最早的关于描述滑雪者的岩刻画被称为 "Rödöy man"（大约距今 6500 年），表明了斯堪的纳维亚地区古老的滑雪传统。关于这一岩画的解读不是没有争议，有些人认为这是人在独木舟中滑行的岩画。

the 'Rødøy Man'

挪威滑雪者岩画

Rock skiing painting of Norway

Rödöy in Norway, the so called "Rödöy man" (about 6500 BP) seems to indicate an old skiing tradition in Scandinavi. not undisputable and other possibilities like a man in a canoe have also been discussed. Concerning the "Böla man" in Norway from about 8000 BP an interpretation of a human being on snowshoes seems to be more likely than a depiction of a man on ski. One of the problems with rock pictures is that they not always are easy to interpret. Motives can be realistic but also fragmentary or they can represent ancient myths we can't understand today. Another problem is that dating of rock art is complicated and usually very uncertain. For pictures close to the sea the land upheaval in northern Scandinavia gives just the highest possible age. However sometimes rock art motives seem very easy to interpret. ters going on skis belongs to this categoryanother example although it can also have a mythical meaning.

In the oldest (6200–5700 BP) chronological layer of the rock–carvings in Alta, northernmost Norway we can't find any certain depiction of a skier. However in a younger layer there is a possible human on skis. Concerning the proportions between the man and the skis this picture seems to be more realistic than the Rödöy man. My conclusion is that skiing was probably unknown among the first immigrants to northern Fennoscandia at the time just a Skis were also unknown for the early immigrants to northern America. Snowshoes were their way for walking on snow as well for the early Scandinavians. Walking with snowshoes is also well depicted in the oldest rock carving in Alt clusion is that the technique of skiing was developed some time a land bridge was closed and the Bering Sea opened at about 15 000 years ago. So far the spread of skiing technique in Eurasia must be a postglacial phenomenon.

Skiing was not a part of the indigenous people's culture in Northern America. In contrast to northern Eurasia where diff erent forms of reindeer herding are widespread domestication of reindeer was also unknown in northern America until it was introduced from Scandinavia in recent time.

Arguments put forward in earlier research that knowledge of skiing is a prerequisite for reindeer herding seem plausible. So far it is a striking fact that skiing was unknown in northern America. tense debate about the origin of reindeer herding started in 1917 AD. In that year Laufer published an article based on information from Chinese literature dated to 499 AD. Dear herding people are described in the northern border areas of China. Laufer put forward the idea that reindeer herding originated in the areas surrounding Lake Baikal through the imitation of cattle and horse breeding. extent of reindeer herding is the result of diff usion. From a critical point of view it can be argued for that this was just based on speculation. Laufer did not get any support from the leading Swedish researcher Wiklund, who argued for that reindeer herding was an independent evolution in Scan–dinavihas however been discussed by other researchers like Vasilevich and Levin. Argumentation has mainly been based on comparative ethnographical data. More recently Vainshtein gave support to such ideas. Vanshtein mainly argues from an ethnographical point of view but some striking data are the rock–carvings with depictions of humans riding on reindeer like the practice is even today in Eurasiin the debate. Today this idea is supported by archaeological finds like rock carvings although data in written sources are scarce and of relatively later date.

在挪威发现的“Bölaman”（大约距今 8000 年）脚穿靴鞋，被人们解读为踩在双板上的滑雪者。关于这些岩画的其中一个问题是对其内容的解读绝非易事。

对它们的解读不完整或它们代表着古代的神秘传说，而处于当下的我们很难读懂它们。另一个问题是对岩画年代的追溯很复杂，并且是不稳定的。发现于斯堪的纳维亚北部的岩画的年代确定似乎最接近其真实的形成年代。同时，有些岩画似乎又很容易解读，例如 Zalavruga，W. Russia（4000-3500 BP）的岩画—站在滑雪板上的驼鹿狩猎者就是属于这一类。而另一个例子，位于阿尔塔地区的岩画却有着神秘的意义。

在挪威北部阿尔塔地区最古老的岩画（距今 6200—5700 年）我们没有发现关于滑雪者确切的描述。然而在稍后的距今比较近的时间层，我们发现了可能存在的关于滑雪的人的岩画。考虑到人与滑雪板的比例，这副岩画似乎比 Rödöy man 更为真实。我的结论是在冰河世纪后期的芬诺斯坎底亚北部的早期移民或许不知道怎样滑雪，而雪鞋只是他们雪地行走的工具，就像早期的斯堪的纳维亚人一样。穿着雪鞋行走的景象在阿尔塔地区的早期岩画中也有相关的描述。进一步的结论是滑雪技术是在大约 15，000 年前白令海峡大桥关闭和白令海峡开通之后发展的。到目前为止，滑雪技术在欧亚地区的传播必定是一种冰河期后出现的现象。

滑雪并不是土著北美人文化中的一部分。相对于欧亚大陆北部地区，在斯堪的纳维亚半岛近期麋鹿的不同的放牧方式才比较普遍。有人认为关于滑雪知识的早期研究以麋鹿放牧为前提的结论似乎是可信的。

雪踏痕迹
Footprints after skiing

在史前时期东西方长距离的联系的重要性是不可忽略的，其中的一个争论是麋鹿放牧的起源时期始于 1917 年。就在 1917 年 Laufer 基于中国的文献发表了一篇文章，把麋鹿放牧的年限追溯到 499 年，文中记载了放牧者主要位于中国北部边境地区，Laufer 认为麋鹿的放牧区域起源于贝加尔湖附近，这一观点主要基于移民者把麋鹿当作运输牛马和雪橇的交通工具。现今麋鹿养殖的存在是多种方式融合的结果。而这一观点是建立在主观推断的基础上。Laufer 的观点没有得到瑞典主流研究者 Wiklund 的支持，而 Wiklund 认为麋鹿的放牧是斯堪的纳维亚地区一种独立的进化方式。认为麋鹿放牧是在西伯利亚南部地区不断扩散的方式，这观点已经被许多研究者争论许久。他们的争论只要在于对相对的民族志学数据不认同。而最近 Vainshtein 对这个观点表示赞同。从民族志学的角度，Vainshtein 认为关于人骑麋鹿的岩刻画的描述在现今的欧亚地区仍然存在。麋鹿放牧这一现象仍然存在于欧亚中部地区，这一结论仍在争论中。而这一观点得到考古发现的支持，尽管考古学家发现关于岩刻画的书面记载计较少时间也比较晚。

就如上文提到的在芬诺斯坎底亚地区的史前时期没有关于麋鹿放牧的岩刻画的记载。在斯堪的纳维亚地区关于家庭饲养麋鹿的最早记录追溯到约 892 年前。萨米人饲养麋鹿的最早记录是由 Olaus Magnus 在《北欧人的历史》中提到。他认为关于家庭饲养麋鹿，挤鹿奶及把麋鹿当作交通工具是平常的生活场景，不能当作历史记录的作证 。考古研究发现斯堪的纳维亚北部地区定居方式的改变表明麋鹿养殖的方式大约在公元 200—800 年左右被介绍到这个地区，这一观点与早期的文献纪录大致吻合。

As mentioned above there are no prehistoric rock depictions indicating reindeer herding in Fenno-scandidated to about 892 AD Magnus in his History of the Nordic People from 1555 AD. His description of herding domesticated reindeer, milking of reindeer and transports with reindeer are too realistic to be regarded as only fables. Archaeological studies of changes in settlement patterns in northern Scandinavia indicates that reindeer herding was introduced in time in Scandinavia sometimes between 200 AD and 800 AD which is not contradicted by the earliest literary source.

What about the introduction of skiing to Fennoscandia? Even in this case long distance east-west contacts must be taken into consideration. Such contacts have been discussed in archaeology for many dec discussing the spread of innovations in the circumpolar area became influential. In the waves of the so called "New Archaeology" during the 1970's and early 1980's focus in Scandinavian archaeology was moved to studies of regional economic and social development. However advances of radiocar - bon dating methods also raised a new interest in dating prehistoric wooden artefacts, among them the bog finds of skis in Fennoscandia. Suddenly the supposed oldest ski from Hoting in northern Sweden became much younger stick from Kalvträsk became with new dating the oldest ski in the world dated to about 5200 BPvertical holes for binding strap of the Kalvträsk ski demonstrate similarities with skis in eastern Eurasi tal hole for the binding strap. Obviously this innovation is the starting point for development of theso called "Bothnic" or Sámi type of ski used up into modern time in Fennoscandia. It may be seen as a prototype for modern skis.

滑雪何时被介绍到芬诺斯坎底亚？东西方长距离的联系这一事实必须被考虑进去。这些联系在考古学中也被讨论了数十年。考古学家 Gjessing 在他的书 "Circumpolar Stone Age" 中提到从 1944 年滑雪在极地地区不断创造性地传播的观点具有深远影响。

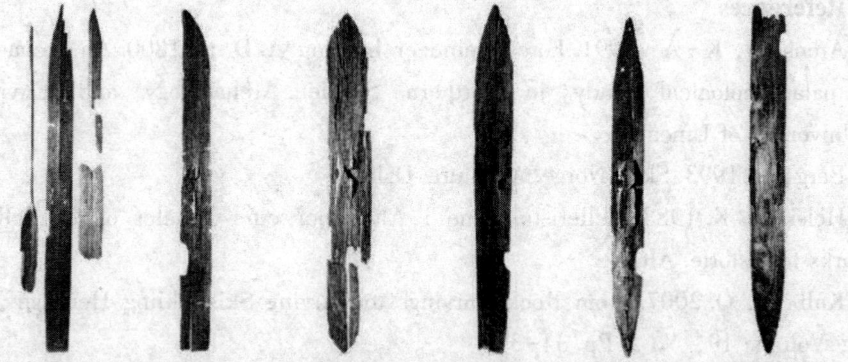

Skida från Kalv-träsk, Västerb. 5200 BP　*Skida från Hoting, Angermanland. 3500 BP*　*Skida från Stor-bäck, Västerb. 3200 BP*　*Skida från Anu-mark, Västerb. 2000 BP*　*Skida från Siika-vuopio, Norrb. 1100 BP*　*Skida från Slag-näs, Norrb. 1000 BP*

在所谓“新考古学”后期，1970s 和 1980s 早期的斯堪的纳维亚地区的考古学重点转向地区经济和社会发展的研究。然而放射性碳的研究方法催生了人们对史前木质工艺品研究的巨大兴趣，其中便包括人们在芬诺斯坎底亚地区的沼泽地中发现了滑雪板。突然之间，在瑞典北部 Hoting 发现的最古老的滑雪板的年代并非那么久远。在 Kalvträsk 地区发现的近乎完整的并带有铲子的雪板刷新了最古老雪板的年代记录，可追溯到距今约 5200 年前。Kalvträsk 地区的滑雪板固定条上垂直的孔洞与在欧亚大陆东部发现的滑雪板上的有一定的相似性。然而在 Hotin 发现的雪板上的固定器上的孔是水平方向的。很显然这种创新是所谓的“Bothnic”或萨米型滑雪板（在现今芬诺斯坎底亚地区使用的一种雪板）发展的起点，它可能是现代滑雪板的原型。

Kalvträsk 滑雪板上的用于绑带的竖排孔是与东欧滑雪板十分相似。令人惊讶的是北美的土著居民竟然都不知道滑雪板。甚至，北美土著居民的文化没有驯鹿放牧，这与广为流传着各种形式的驯鹿放牧的欧亚大陆北部是完全不同的。针对滑雪知识为驯鹿放牧的前提的研究论据似乎十分可信。这就可以解释为何驯鹿放牧没有成为北美原住民的文化。早期迁到北美的移民以及迁到芬诺斯堪的亚的移民可能都不知道滑雪板的存在。在阿尔塔的雕刻岩石的最古老年代层上，大约距今 5600-6200 年，清晰描绘了人们练习穿滑雪鞋走路的情景。滑雪知识似乎后来在这一地区得到了发展。将滑雪介绍到芬诺斯堪的亚的东西交流的影响是不容忽视的。阿尔塔地区已经被称为滑雪及驯鹿放牧的起源的创新地区。相似之处在于滑雪板上用于绑带的孔、驯鹿缰绳以及这一方向上简易类型的驯鹿驮鞍。然而，芬诺斯堪的亚的滑雪后来发展成为独立于东部地区的滑雪技术。在大约 3500 年前出现了增加脚步的用于绑带的水平孔。这被称为 Bothnic 或 Sámi 类型的滑雪板证明一种现今仍在芬诺斯堪的亚使用北部的滑雪板类型发展的开端。

References

Aronsson, K-Å, 1991. Forest reindeer herding A. D. 1-1800. An archaeological and palaeoecological study in northern Sweden. Archaeology and Environment 10. University of Umeå.

Berg, K. 1993. Ski i Norge. Aventure. Oslo.

Helskog, K. 1988. Helleristningene i Alta. Spor etter ritualer og dagligliv i Finnmarks forhistorie. Alta.

Kulberg, Ö. 2007. From Rock Carvings to Carving Skis. Skiing Heritage Journal, June, Volume 19, No 2. Pp. 34-37.

Weinstock, J. 2005. Skis and skiing from the Stone Age to the birth of the spor Press, Ltd. USA.

Åström, K & Norberg, O. 1984. Förhistoriska och medeltida skidor. Västerbotten 2: 84. Pp 82-88.

4.35 飘在雪上—关于滑雪板和滑雪的电影项目的第一步 FLOATING ON SNOW-the first steps in a great film project about skis and skiing

Kurt Skoog (SWE) 库尔特·斯科格 (瑞典)

个人简介 Brief Introduction

Kurt Skoog, lives in Östersund, Sweden. I am a film-maker and ski researcher. I make documentary films about nature and culture, often in co-production with Swedish Television. Many of the films have been awarded at international film festivals.

In the ski research field I work together with Anna Erlandsson and Micke Sundberg. Anna Erlandsson works as a painter and illustrator and is also a devoted skier. Micke Sundberg is a mountaineer and skier and has been doing ski research for many years. He also works as a nature protector.

居住在瑞典厄斯特松德，是电影制作人和滑雪研究者。经常与瑞典国家电视台合作制作有关自然和文化的纪录片，许多纪录片获得了国际电影节奖项。在滑雪研究领域中，还与 Anna Erlandsson 和 Micke Sundberg 合作共事，Anna Erlandsson 是一个画家，插图家，也是一个忠实的滑雪热爱者和参与者。Micke Sundberg

爱好登山和滑雪，滑雪研究已经做了很多年了，他还是个自然保护者。

Michael Sundberg (ski coach & skiing historian) and Anna Erlandsson (researcher of skiing culture in north Europe), as assistants of Kurt Skoog, offer great help in film project and paper writing about skis and skiing.

米奇·松德贝里是滑雪教练和滑雪历史学家；安娜·埃兰德松是北欧滑雪文化研究者，两人均是在库尔特·斯科格先生进行冰雪电影的制作和滑雪论著写作过程中的得力助手。

Michael Sundberg(米奇·松德贝里) **Anna Erlandsson(安娜·埃兰德松)**

论文 Paper:

FLOATING ON SNOW-the first steps in a great film project about skis and skiing

Background.

As an independent film maker I've made several documentary films about both culture and nature/science subjects. Some of the films were co productions with Swedish Television and they have also been screened on festivals all over the world.

Many of my nature documentaries have been about water, this fascinatin subject, the prerequisite for life on earth.

The idea of a film about the origin and history of ski came from my friend Micke Sundberg. Snow is a form of water and skiing can be seen as an expression of the relation between mankind and nature. For me that's more than enough as a base for a very interesting film project. Man, ski and snow in combination with the landscape and the terrain forms the concept of skiing that will be examined in a broad perspective in the film. What does it take to be a skier? What has skiing meant for mankind historically? Skiing as an expression of the relation man-nature, what does that mean? What is the history of ski? How to make a ski of traditional style? What is needed for a ski to be able to float on unprepared snow? What is snow? How affects different types of snow the interaction with the ski? What is the art of skiing? That's some example of questions for the film.

Focus will be on that type of skiing that took and takes place on unprepared snow which is the way skiing merely has been done historically. Skiing in prepared tracks and slopes-sometimes even with artificial snow-is a modern a very short time phenomenon in the history of skiing.

飘在雪上——关于滑雪板和滑雪的电影项目的第一步

背景

作为一个独立的电影制作人，我制作了几部关于文化与自然/科学学科的纪录片。一些电影是和瑞典电视台共同制作的，他们在节日期间在全球进行放映。

我的许多自然纪录片都是关于水的，这是一个迷人的主体，也是生命在地球上出现的先决条件。

拍一部滑雪起源和历史电影的想法来自我的朋友米克桑德博格。雪是一种水的形式，滑雪可以被看作是一种人类与自然关系的表达。对我来说更多作为一个非常有趣的电影项目的基础。人、滑雪和雪并结合风景和地形形成了滑雪的范畴，在电影中以广阔的视角来进行检验。如何才能学会滑雪？对人类来说，在历史上滑雪意味着什么？滑雪作为对人的本性的一种表达，这意味着什么？什么是滑雪史？如何制作一种传统的滑雪板？对于滑雪板来讲，如何才能让他漂浮在没有处理过的雪上？什么是雪？不同类型的雪是怎样影响与滑雪者的互动？什么是滑雪的艺术？这是电影中的一些问题。

将重点放在这类的滑雪，他们的产生是顺其自然的。滑雪的这种方式在历史上已经出现很久。而在准备好的雪道上滑雪，有时候甚至在人造雪上滑雪是一种现代的滑雪方式，在滑雪史上是非常短暂的现象。

In Scandinavia and Finland skiing has a long tradition. Many findings of very old skis have been made here. Most of these skis have been found in bogs in Sweden and Finland and nowadays many findings are made by glacier archeologists in Norway due to melting glaciers. The oldest preserved ski in the world was found on a marchland in

Kalvträsk in northern Sweden. It's dated to be 5 400 years old.

Still skiing is a common activity in Scandinavia and Finland but nowadays mostly for exercise and sports in prepared tracks and slopes with technical and advanced equipment, long from the historical models of skis. A big change happened for about 50 years ago. Before the ski was an important and common working tool for several groups in society like the Sami people and farmers and woodsmen. The change came with the introduction of the snow mobile and the increasing mechanization of the working life and society.

The predominant theory today among ski researchers is that skis were brought to Scandinavia by the Sámi people. In general nomadic people are of greatimportance when it comes to the origin and the spreading of skis. Interesting is that historically skis were only to find in a belt from inner and northern Asia to the northern parts of Europe, i. e. Finland and Scandinavia. It was Scandinavian migrants who took ski to North America and to the Alps in Europe in the 18 th and 19 th century.

斯堪的那维亚半岛古老滑雪史

在斯堪的纳维亚和芬兰，滑雪有着悠久的传统。很多研究结果显示，许多古老的滑雪板已经产生在这里。大多数这些滑雪板被发现在瑞典和芬兰的沼泽里，现在的很多发现是由冰川造成的。

由于冰川融化，挪威的考古学家在瑞典北部的边界地区发现了保存下来的最古老的滑雪板，距今已有5400年的历史。

在斯堪地纳维亚和芬兰，滑雪仍然是一项非常普及的运动，但是目前大部分的滑雪运动和训练都是借助先进的装备在准备好的雪道上进行的。大程度的改变发生在大约50年前。之前滑雪板是社会团体中一个重要和平常的工作工具，比如萨米人、农民、牧民。这些变化是随着雪的引入而来的，机械化、移动化的设备在工作生活和社会逐步增多。

滑雪研究者的主要理论是，滑雪板是由萨米人带到斯堪地纳维亚的。在一般的游牧民族中，滑雪板的传播具有重大的意义。有趣的是历史上的滑雪板，只在从中北部的亚洲和北部的欧洲，这一条带上被发现。这是由斯堪的纳维亚的移民在18、19世纪将滑雪板带到了北美和欧洲的阿尔卑斯山地区。

Visiting the Altay Mountains and meeting traditional skiers.

Following the Norwegian explorer and scientist Fridtjof Nansen's theories about the origin of skis take us to the Altay Mountains in the inner Asia, a border area where China, Mongolia, Russia and Kazakhstan meet. In the Chinese part of the Altay Mountains there are many findings of old cave paintings and stone carvings. On some of them you can see skiers. The archeologist Mr Wang Bo has analyzed one cave painting, discovered close to the village of Handegate. According to the style and the motive, a hunting scene with skiers and wild animals including wild cows, Mr Wang Bo estimate it to be at least 10 000 years old. For us Westerners it could be hard to interpret the figures in the painting as skiers but if you are familiar with the skiing style in this region it's quite obvious that they are skiers.

Now we make a second visit here but in wintertime to meet some local skiers in the Altay Mountains. And again we are going together with our excellent guide Ayiken Jiashan. The indigenous people living in this region are Kazakhs, Tuvins and Mongols. When we make a turn into the road to the small village of Khom we are facing a great view over the beautiful Altay Mountains.

In Khom lives 1200 people. Many of the families have some cows or chickens.

Horses are traditionally the most common mean for transportation. In the last years the number of cars has increased due to a new road which also is kept open in wintertime. Not long ago you had to go by horse and sledge for 100 kilometers to reach this village in wintertime. Temperature is often around – 20 degrees Celsius all winter and ground is covered by a deep layer of cold, soft snow.

阿勒泰地区最古老滑雪文化

下面谈谈我们对阿勒泰地区第二次（第一次是在前一年的秋季）的考察和访问，在冬季的阿尔泰山脉去见一些当地滑雪者，这一次我们还是和优秀的导游阿依肯·加山一起，居住在这个地区的土著人是哈萨克人和蒙古族图瓦人。

当我们转到一个叫禾木的小村庄的时候，面对着非常美丽的阿尔泰山脉风景。

在禾木，大约有 1200 个村民，许多家庭都养有牛和鸡。马是当地最普遍的运输工具，在最近的一些年，汽车的数目在增多，因为附近的一条新路在冬季也开放。不久之前你只能通过马或者雪橇来到达，这个小村庄温度通常在负 20 度左右。土地上覆盖着一层厚厚的柔软的雪。

On the first days in January every year there is a festival in Khom with traditional activities like horseracing, girl chasing and wrestling. But most of all it is a ski festival. They compete with traditional skis in a race also including archery, some sort of biathlon. The skis they use are of the same type that has been used here for thousands of years. They are made by the skiers themselves or by local craftsmen. Underneath they use fur from horse. They use one pole, downhill the pole becomes a supporting leg in a leaning back style of skiing.

At the opening ceremonies for the race all ski teams perform shamanic ceremonies for luck, power and speed. All in all around 30 skiers participate in the race. That means that the race also contribute to keep the ski making tradition alive.

每年一月份的最初几天是禾木村的节日，有一些活动比如赛马、女子追逐、摔跤会在这个时间进行。但是大部分情况下，这是一个滑雪的节日。他们比赛就是滑雪、射箭以及冬季两项。他们所使用的双板就是几千年来流传下来的那种，他们是由当地的滑雪者或者工匠制作完成的。在雪板下面他们贴上马的皮毛，他们使用一个滑雪杆，作为下山时的一个支撑。

在比赛的开幕式上，所有的滑雪队都表演萨满式的运气，力量和速度的仪式。大约会有 30 个滑雪者参加比赛。这意味着，比赛也有助于保持滑雪的传统。

The skiers go three laps around the track. For every lap there is a station for archery. The target is a fur pelt. You have three chances; if you miss you must go an extra track. This type of race is based on the traditional way of hunting. In the race the skiers also pull a skin bag where they, just as hunters used to, have blankets and some food.

After the festival in Khom we leave the village for a visit in a small settlement in a more remote area in the mountains. Here lives only seven families and they invite us to share a very living old ski tradition. They make their own skis. The skin for the ski is prepared by cutting it out.

putting it into hot water to expand and finally they nail it to the ski. Nowadays they use the skin from the front leg of a horse. The best skin however used to be the utter skin. The skis are extremely well fitted for use in the specific conditions here; the landscape with its ups and downs and the deep, cold and soft snow. The dimensions, the length, the form of the tip are all designed to make the ski flow on the snow and the skin under gives a good grip when going up and glides well downhill.

滑雪者绕雪道三圈。每一圈都有一站来进行射箭，箭靶是一张皮毛。你将会

有三次机会，如果没有射中，你必须要重返另一个雪道上。这种比赛是基于传统的狩猎方式。在比赛中，滑雪者将拉一个皮袋（就像猎人一样）来装他们的用品和食物。

禾木节日之后，我们去了在山上更偏远的地区的一个小定居点。这里只有七个家庭，他们邀请我们分享一个非常古老的滑雪传统。他们使用自己制作的滑雪板。滑雪板所使用的皮革是从马皮切割出来的，把它放入热水中使其进行扩张，然后再把它钉在滑雪板上。如今他们用一匹马的前腿上的皮。然而，最好的皮革是完整的皮。滑雪板是非常适用在这里的条件中；景观与山体的起伏、寒冷和软雪。滑雪板的尺寸，长度，形状的设计都使它更适合在雪上漂滑，板下面的毛皮革也使在上山和下山时做一个贴合和抓雪。

他们讲了很多双板该被用于狩猎的故事，滑雪去丛林里利用诱捕的方式来捕捉小动物和鸟儿。对于大型的动物，比如麋鹿，首先要对动物进行定位，然后通过滑雪的方式去到比动物所在位置更高的地方。然后他们滑雪全速前进，用套索捕捉动物，并用刀子将他们杀死。很早之前这也是居住在欧洲的萨米人常见的狩猎方式。现在这些滑雪板是用来对牛羊进行放牧以及通信。

They tell us many stories about how skis were used for hunting. It could be going by ski out in the woods to hunt small animals and birds by using snares. For bigger animals like elks they first localized the animal and get in position above the animal. Then they skied with full speed down the slope, catching the animal with a lasso and then killed it with a knife. Long ago this was a common hunting method for the Sámi people in northern Europe too. Nowadays the skis here are used for herding both cows and horses and forcommunication.

One of the most experienced skier told that the skis made today are simpler than before. In older days the skis had a narrower tip, a wide tail and the middle part was concave like today's carving skis. And the changes in the ski design are still going on. Nowadays the popular ski races tend to affect the ski design into shorter, lighter skis. You can actually talk about two types of skis, the race ski and the traditional, longer and heavier mountain ski.

All skiers we talked to learned to go by ski when they were kids. They were out skiing all winter, up and down the slopes. But nowadays that sight is becoming rarer. Modernity has reached also these remote areas, today children here like everywhere else have mobiles and computers. And when they are out in the slopes they can as well use snow boards.

Nevertheless most of the skiers believed that the traditional ski would survive at least in the Khom area. In the mountains the traditional skis often is the only effective communication tool. There is also a big traditional ski race in Altay The challenge for the future is to keep the balance between the traditions and modcity and these races could help preserve the old style of skiing. ernity. A complication that also affects the chances for keeping the old skiing tradition alive is the general ban on hunting. That law will affect the conditions for life in many respects in this region.

Tourism is often the only way for development for remote areas like this. If that will come It will be of great significance to find forms for a tourism that is based on sustainability and the locals own interests.

一位很有经验的滑雪者说，现在滑雪板的制作要比以前简单很多，在过去，滑雪板有一个很窄的前端，尾部较宽，中间部分像今天的滑板。并且这个滑雪设计中的改变一直在继续。现在最流行的滑雪比赛倾向于让滑雪板的设计更短更轻。你可以谈论两种类型的滑雪板，一种是比赛用板，一种是传统的更长更重的山地滑雪板。和我们交谈的所有的滑雪者都是在孩提时期学会了滑雪，在整个冬天，他们都在外面滑雪上山和下山。但是现在这种场景越来越少了，现代化已经到达了这个遥远偏僻的地方，现在这里的孩子们像其他地方的一样使用手机和电脑。并且，当他们在雪道上时，也可以很好地使用滑雪板。

然而大多数的滑雪者认为，至少在库目地区传统滑雪会被保存下来，在山上，传统的雪板通常是唯一的有效交流工具。在阿尔泰地区，也有一项大型的传统滑雪比赛，这些比赛有助于将滑雪的传统保存下来。

未来的挑战是如何在传统和现代化之前保持一个很好的平衡。目前禁止狩猎是影响滑雪传统生存的因素，这项法律将会影响这个地区很多的方面的生存状态。

旅游业通常是发展这种遥远村落的唯一方式，如果这个地方要发展旅游业，那么开发一种基于当地人利益及可持续发展的旅游模式将会有重大的意义。

The old cave paintings and rock carvings we could see here were indeed spectacular. But what made the greatest impression on me was to experience that the old traditional skiing is such a living culture, quite unique in the world.

That alone is a strong indication of a very old history of skiing in this region. This living tradition is also expressed in other cultural forms. It was great to hear some Mongol women singing an old traditional folksong about skiing, a moment I'll keep in my memory for ever.

我们能看到古老的雕刻画和石头雕刻是非常壮观的。但是让我印象最深刻的是古老的滑雪传统的流传，这在当今世界是非常独特的。

它是这个地区古老滑雪历史的一个见证，这种流传下来的传统在其他的文化形式中也有表现。当我们听到蒙古女人唱着古老的滑雪民歌，那种感觉非常棒，那一刻也将在我的记忆中永存。

4.36 滑雪史 SK I HISTORY

维尔纳·马格瑞特（奥地利） MAG. WERNER MARGREITER（AUT）

Brief Introduction 个人简介

Werner Ma Gerui, Austrian, with much experience in designing, managing and practicing, is an senior advisor of FIS and has participated in the designing and decision work of many competition terrains of FIS. He, as a celebrity in the ski field for his special experience, used to be several countries' ski instructor. Meanwhile, he is the president of committee of internationally renowned ski competitions. In 2012, the Winter Olympic venues designed by him are specially rewarded by FIS.

维尔纳·马格瑞特奥地利人，1954年5月8日出生，拥有丰富的滑雪场设计、管理和从业经验，是国际雪联（FIS）的资深高级顾问，国际雪联的很多比赛场地他都参与了设计工作及决策工作，他曾经担任过几个国家队的滑雪教练，经历比较特殊，是滑雪界的知名人士，同时也是国际知名滑雪赛事的组委会主席。2012 年由他设计的青年冬季奥运会场地更是受到了国际雪联的特别嘉奖。

Speech 发言稿：

SKI HISTORY 滑雪史

Austria's historic role in skiing and special aspects of tourism
奥地利在滑雪方面所扮演的历史角色和在旅游产业的进展

Margreiter Werner Altay, China January 2015
维尔纳·马格瑞特（2015 年 1 月–中国·阿勒泰）

Ski：

-equipment to move（glide）on snow or grass

-name comes from word for "split"

-thousands of years old（more than 10.000 yrs.）

-first main purpose：skis used for hunting，travel，work later also used for military reasons

-in the last 100 years developed into mass phenomenon on the slopes around the world

-findings in Scandinavia and Asia：special wooden parts（rings，boards）paintings

滑雪板—在雪地上或草地上滑动的一种设备，这一名字来源于"split"（劈开，裂缝），已有数千年的历史。以前，滑雪板主要用来打猎、游玩、工作，后来也用于军事方面。上个世纪，滑雪板发展成为在世界各地斜坡上的一种普遍现象。在斯堪的纳维亚半岛和亚洲发现特殊的滑雪板的木质部分（环，板）和图画。

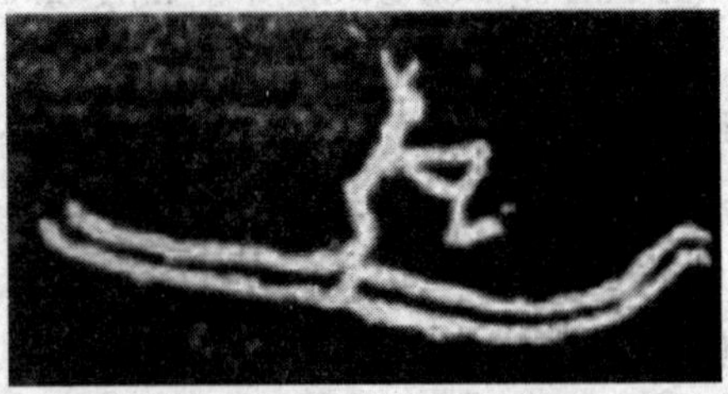

Ski：-oldest findings in area between Lake Baikal and Altay Mountains

最早的滑雪板发现于贝加尔湖和阿尔泰山脉地区。

-3 types: 1. Arctic - sibirian type: 16 - 23cm wide, 180cm long, with fur 2. Scandinavian-central nordic type: 1 long gliding ski, 1 short push off ski with fur 3. Southern type: 2 equal long skis, with tip in front, tail cut across

主要有三种：1. 北极-西伯利亚型：180 厘米长，16-23 厘米宽，有皮毛；2. 斯堪的纳维亚-中北欧型：一只长滑翔雪板，一只推动式毛皮滑雪板；3. 南方型：2 只同样长的雪板，前端锋利，后端带有尾巴；

History of skiing: -documented especially in Scandinavia -e. g.: safe of the King's son Hakon Hakonson by 2 "Birkebeiner" people-escape and return of Danish Gustav Vasa

滑雪史—主要是斯堪的纳维亚半岛地区的文献记载，例如，利用雪板逃离敌人并返回丹麦的古斯塔夫一世。

Development of nordic style in Norway

-1850 in Telemarken: Slalom-type and Downhill-type runs

-1875: 1st skiclub in Oslo-Kristiansand

-1879: 1st ski jump competition Oslo-Huseby

-1881: 1st public ski lessons in Oslo

-1888: Fridtjof Nansen: „ On Snowshoes across Greenland "Roald Amundson-South Pole

北欧式滑雪在挪威的发展：

-1850，在泰勒马克郡，回转式和滑降式滑行

-1875，首个滑雪俱乐在挪威 Oslo-Kristiansand 建立

-1879，首个跳台滑雪比赛在 Oslo-Huseby 举行

-1881，首次公众滑雪课程在挪威奥斯陆 Oslo 开设

-1888，弗里德约夫·南森滑雪横跨格陵，从罗尔德·阿蒙森-南极

History of skiing: Development of alpine style in Austria:

阿尔卑斯式滑雪在奥地利的发展：

–1990s Matthias Zdarsky：inventor of modern alpine ski technique

1990s，Matthias Zdarsky 发明现代高山滑雪技术

–1893：1st Alpine ski race in Austria

1893，首次高山滑雪赛在奥地利举行

–1893：Franz Reisch starts tourism in famous Kitzbühel

1893，Franz Reisch 开始其在基茨比厄尔的旅行

–1909/10：invention of new stem turn by Hannes Schneider–Arlberg/Austria–stem kristiania

1909/10：Hannes Schneider– Arlberg 发明停滑转动

–1920s："Arlbergschule"

–1926：Invention of steel edge（Lettner）

1926：钢边雪板出现

–1951：1st Intern. Ski Congress Zürs/Austria

1951：首次国际滑雪会议在奥地利举行

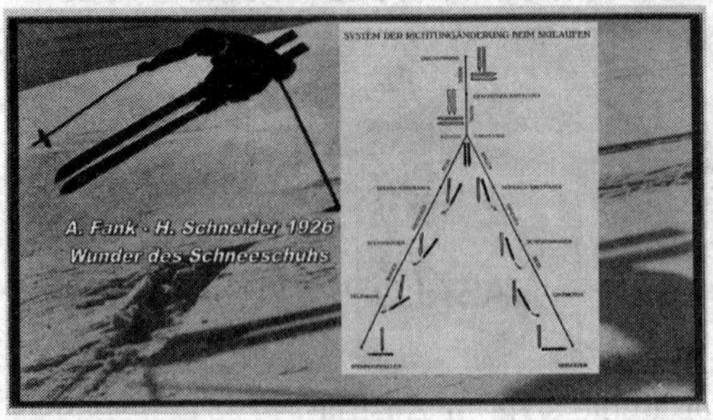

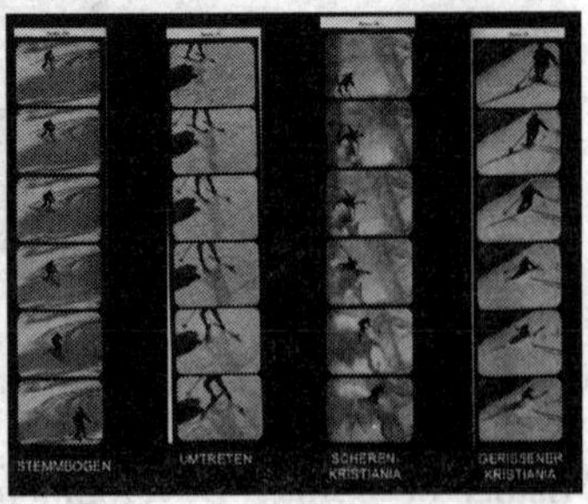

Österreichischer Skilehrplan 1956

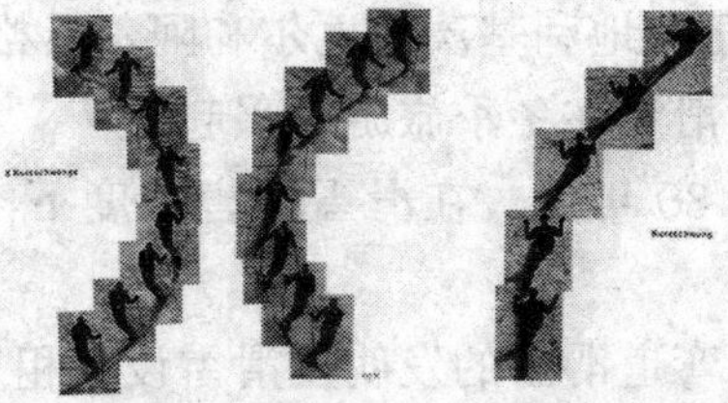

Verwinden - Counter rotation technique
developed from analyzing the best skiracers of that time !

Österreichischer Skilehrplan 1956

WEDELN… a special turn goes around the world!

Race technique becomes common for everybody!

Aspects of Skiing and Tourism

- In the early 1900s: starts in Kitzbühel and the Arlberg
- In the 1950s: enormous push in winter tourism
- 1960s-1980s: golden age for ski industry and glacier ski resort
- After that time dramatic reduction in ski sales
- 1990s: increase in ski rental business
- 1990s: invention of carving ski
- 2000s: season start 2-4 weeks earlier
- Over the years onstant improvement in snow making techniques
- 2010s: Development trends

滑雪及旅游方面：

- 20 世纪初，开始于奥地利基茨比厄尔和阿尔贝格；
- 20 世纪 50 年代，滑雪在冬季旅游中兴起；
- 20 世纪 60 年代至 80 年代，在滑雪销售极度下滑后，滑雪产业和冰山滑雪迎来黄金时期；
- 20 世纪 90 年代，弯道滑雪的发明及滑雪设备租赁业的快速发展；
- 21 世纪初，滑雪业季比以往提前 2 至 4 个周。经过数年的发展，造雪技术有了长足的发展，并呈现出新的发展趋势。

Economic Impact of Tourism

Tourism：great importance in world economy

-136-Tourism：biggest industry in the world

-137-Contribution of tourism to world economy：6，5 trillion USD（2012）

-138-In 2000：668 million tourists worldwide（393 in Europe）

-139-In 2005：73，6% of all Germans were on holidays（average 12，5 nights，total revenue 58 billion Euro）

-140-In 2020：calculated 1.560 million tourists worldwide（717 in Europe）

-141-Tourism：11，6% of gross domestic product

-142-About 10% of all employees work in tourism（260 million people in 2012；about 326 million in 2022-every 10th job in tourism）

旅游业对全球经济的发展起着举足轻重的作用，已发展成为全球最大的产业领域。旅游业对全球经济的增长在 2012 年达到 6.5 万亿美元；

2000 年：全球有 6.68 亿游客 668（其中欧洲有 3.93 亿）；

2005 年：有 73.6% 的德国人度假旅游（旅游营业总收入 580 亿欧元）；

2020 年，全球大约有 1560 万游客（其中有 717 万在欧洲）；

旅游业占国内生产总值的 11.6%，约有 10% 的雇员在旅游行业工作（2012 有 2.6 亿人；2022 年预计有 3.26 亿人）

Global Tourism as Stimulus to Growth

Development countries：bigger growth as fully developed mature economics

Average growth of international arrivals 2012-2030

Development countries：+4，4 %

Mature economics+2，2 %

Global tourism with clearly higher growth than in Austria，Tirol or Kitzbühel：

全球旅游业刺激经济的发展：

发展中国家：较大的增长并成为发展成熟的经济大国；

2012 年至 2030 年全球经济的平均增长水平：
发展中国家增长 4.4 %
发达国家增长 2.2 %
全球旅游业将比奥地利、蒂罗尔或基茨比厄尔有显著增长；

Growth of international arrivals 1995 – 2012	
Global Tourism	+95,3 %
Austrian Tourism	+40,6 %
Tyrol Tourism	+30,4 %
Kitzbühel	+31,6 %
St. Anton	+42,5 %

1995-2012 年全球旅游业的增速

全球旅游业	+95.3 %
奥地利旅游业	+40.6 %
蒂罗尔旅游业	+30.4 %
基茨比厄尔旅游业	+31.6 %
圣安东旅游业	+42.5 %

Tourism in the Alps-Tirol in Top 3

Tourism in the Alps：facts and figures
阿尔卑斯山的旅游业：实例与数据

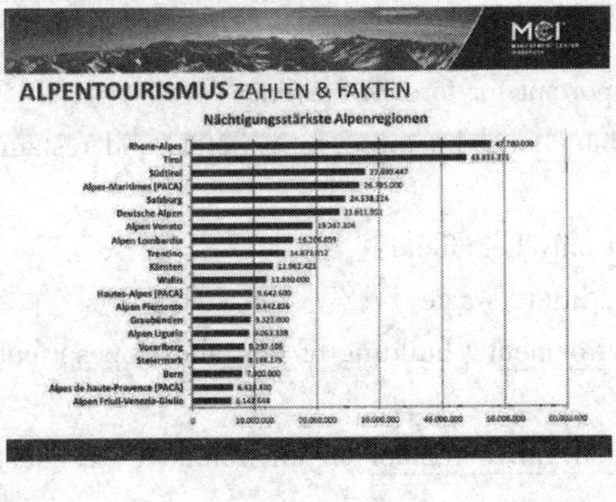

Strongest regions in the Alps

在阿尔卑斯山旅游业发展最快的地区

Winter generates 40% of all bednights in the Alps

冬天创造了阿尔卑斯山40%的客源入住量

Tourism in the Alps: facts and figures

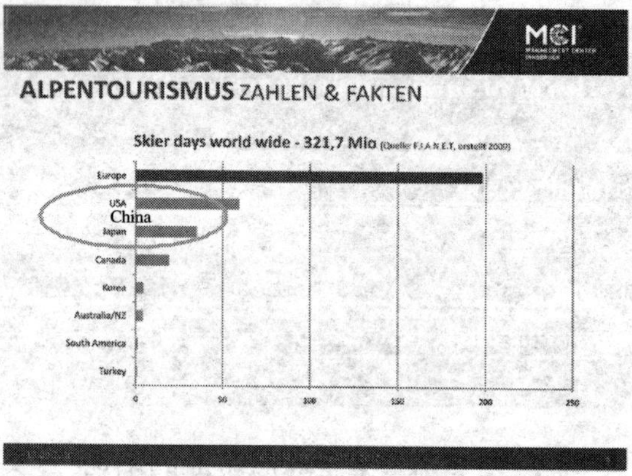

Economic Impact of a Ski Resort

- Impact on tourism destinations (irrelevant if in summer or winter):
- Generates lot of jobs in hotels, restaurants, service, lift operations…
- Higher income because tourists pay higher level of prices compared to other parts
- Additional education because languages and other skills are needed
- Tourists are used to comfort: they ask for high level in general infrastructure, public traffic (busses, taxis), communication, water, electricity etc. also beneficial for other industries and businesses like transport roads to airport, other roads, communication infrastructure (radio, TV), power, wastewater etc.
- Tourist is end-consumer (final user): leaves money in the country, that stays at the place
- Tourism is important for foreign currency
- Tourism generates local business, e. g. hotels and restaurants buy at local suppliers…
- Tourism is not only beneficial:
- More garbage, litter, waste
- Impact on environment (building of lifts and slopes) but minimal compared to land size
- generate more negative impact on environment (exhaust emissions from more

cars, busses and planes…)

- ……

滑雪场的经济影响力：

滑雪场对旅游地的影响—创造就业机会，提高当地民众的收入，增加当地人额外教育的机会（旅游业需要不同的语言和其他技巧），游客要享受舒适的服务（他们需要高水平的基础设施、交通工具、信息服务以及水和电等），游客是终端消费者（他们要在旅游地食宿和购物等）；旅游业促进外币的流通；旅游业促进当地商业的兴起；

旅游业的发展有利也有弊，旅游过程会产生垃圾废物，需要进行地形改造而建设配套设施，交通工具会排放尾气，对环境产生消极影响。

Ski sports development in China

- Relatively big number of ski resorts
- Relatively small size of ski resorts
- Now big efforts in winter tourism: big potential
- China bidding for Winter Olympic Games 2022
- Development of biggest ski resort in Asia
- vertical drop of Ayihai Resort more than 1500m in 1st stage!

滑雪运动在中国的发展：

中国已有相当数量的大型滑雪场及小型的滑雪场；

大力推进冬季旅游业的发展，有巨大的发展潜力；

中国申办 2022 年的冬奥会；

亚洲正在建设最大的滑雪场（垂直落差 1500 米的阿依海度假区一期施工正在进行）；

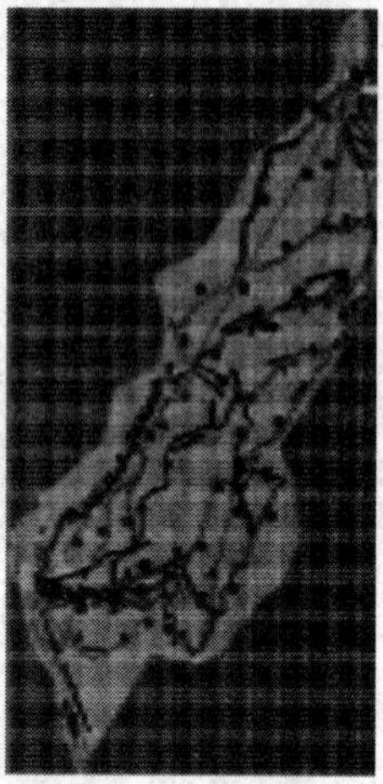

AYIHAI RESORT
阿依海度假区

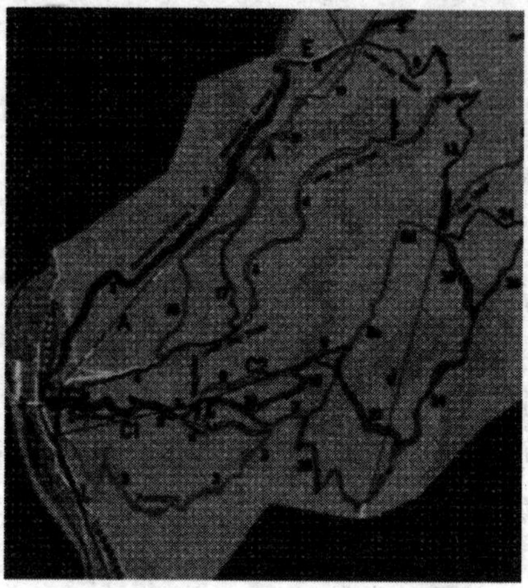

AYIHAI RESORT lower part
阿依海度假区的底部

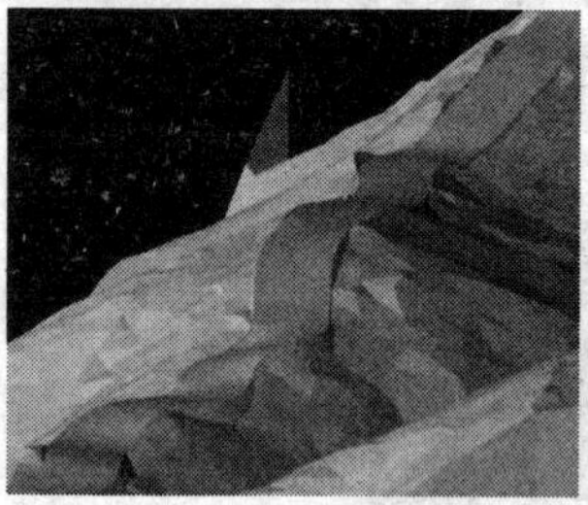

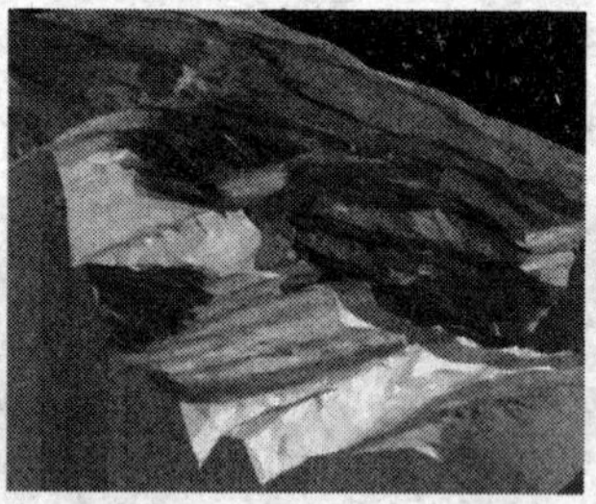

4.37 阿勒泰乌梁海的七面旗帜 档案与口述历史 The Seven Banners of Altain Urianhais: Archives and Oral History

乌恩德尔杰（捷克） Ondrej Srba（CZK）

个人简介 Brief Introduction

Doctor and Professor of Institute of South and Central Asia at Charles University in Prague, Altay historical culture specialist.

捷克布拉格市查理大学哲学院南中亚系教师、博士，阿勒泰历史文化专员。

English Paper:

The Seven Banners of Altain Urianhais: Archives and Oral History

Ondĵej Srba (Charles University in Prague, Czech republic)

Altain Urianhais are an ethnic group with two languages, an Oirat or Western Mongolian dialect and a Turkic language, almost similar to Tuvan. Both of these linguistic groups have been using an ancient Central Asian ethnonym Urianhai, at least one part of them thanks to their ethnic origin, another part presumably due to their common way of life, which was based on hunting, seasonal agriculture and originally in less important measure, nomadic husbandry. Urianhais came to Altai long before the Manchu conquest of Dzunghar Khanate in 1750s, which they also had been formerly subordinated to, and according to the region their inhabited they started to be called Altain Urianhai to be distinguished from Tannu Urianhai (present Tuva), Altan nuuriin Urianhai (present Altai Republic in RF) and Hövsgöl nuuriin Urianhai in the present Hövsgöl aimag in Mongolia. All of these Urianhai areas mixed Turkic and Mongolian speaking populations, but belonged to the larger Mongolian cultural sphere, including Buddhism and the use of Written Mongolian or Written Oirat as their literary languages. Manchu Qing administration divided Altain Urianhais into two parts subdivided in seven banners (the Left and the Right wing). Four of the banners were Mongolian speaking, three of them mostly Tuvan speaking. Six of the banners were situated in vertical belts going from north-east to the south-west through the Altain range as to allow to develop various types of economic activities and to migrate in case of need as natural disasters. This system functioned up to 1913, when the Altain Urianhain banners according to the Russian-Chinese contract became divided between the newly proclaimed Autonomous Mongolia and the Xinjiang province with a local administration of the Altai area here in Sir-a süm-e. But as far as the frontiers were almost opened until 1930s, the occasional migrations continued disregarding the protests of both Xinjiang and Mongolian authorities. At the end of the 19th century several administrative units of Kazakh's allowed by Urianhai and Manchu authorities to settle inside the Seven Banners of Altain Urianhai started to function as parallel administrative system.

The governors of the Altain Urianhai banners have neither originated in the Eastern Mongolian Golden Clan of Chinggis khan's descendants or the Dzunghar Öölöt nobility nor was their hereditary succession confirmed by the Manchu court in the official genealogies *Iledkel šastir* . In the administrative division of Altain Urianhais created between 1762-1839 after the submission of Altain Urianhais to the Qing empire in 1754, the Banner of *Jegün amban* presided over the Left wing of Altain Urianhais and its governor's rank was *sula amban* , while the title *sula amban* of the Right wing was usually held by the hereditary governor of the easternmost banner (Banner of Darqan beyise in the Autonomy period) . The other Urianhai banners were governed by general directors *bügüde -yin daruγ-a* (*uheri da*) , but all of them were in fact hereditary. Even though we are not sure, it is highly probable that at least the clans of the Mongolian speaking banners, but also of the Köke mongĉaγ's banner originated from *ijaγur-un jayisang* , the pre-Qing local rulers among the Urianhais.

My research is based on a study of archive documents in the fonds of Altain Urianhai banners in the National Central Archive of Mongolia. Similarly to all the archives from the Western Mongolia, the archives of Altain Urianhai banners have been destroyed with exception of few documents. The fonds of Altain Urianhais in theNational Central Archive of Mongolia contain accidental documents starting from *Törü gereltü* (Daoguang, 1820-1851) era and followed by more frequent documents from the *Badaraγultu törü* (Guangxu, 1871-1908) era.

In the fragmentary archives we can find documents about providing taxes in furs of sables and foxes, documents concerning levies of horses, camels and other necessities for the functioning of *örtüge* communications, but the most of the documents are of demographic character. The most extensive one is an undated census describing the populations of Jegün amban-u qosiγu and Qar-a soyun-u qosiγu (with uheri da Sengdünjab) . This detailed census mentions also clan names of the individual families, the places of their stay and one of the three main occupations of Urianhais-nomadic pastoralism, agriculture or hunting. The census was updates two years later, which is obvious from the data of age, and all the families resided in the same place as they had been two years ago. It refers to the fact that the populations of the northern and the southern sides of Altai were generally fixed, and were not migrating periodically as it was more common in the eastern Left wing of Altain Urianhais. It is also confirmed by the oral history from the both sides, which regards the two populations as two distinguished entities within one banner administration.

As far as the archive sources are so limited, we have to take into account the rich oral tradition and oral history which at least the older generation of Altain Urianhais continues to transmit up to the present days. It has created a complex of genealogies and narratives around individual members of the local nobility (banner governors, *sumun janggi*, *jakiruγĉi*, *kündü* etc.), wise monks and reincarnated holy men, legendary wrestlers, hunters, horse robbers and others.

In the following Mongolian part of my presentation I would like to mention some of the cultural phenomena in the Urianhai's oral tradition, which are becoming highly endangered and near to be forgotten. One of them is the tradition of *hara bagši* , religious specialists of the popular Mongolian Buddhism, who used to perform the collective reading of Oirat Mongolian translations of Buddhist sutras written in the Clear script, while the monks in Western Mongolian monasteries were limited to the use of Tibetan.

Altai Urianhains living at the Xinjiang side of the Mongolian Altai practised the ritual reciting of the Clear script sutras until recently. Old people still remember *hara bagši* s who as late as in the 1990s have been reading the Clear script sutras on demand of others and practising a method of detecting stolen things (usually some livestock) by a ritual arrow or a vajra. Even though a few of the Clear script manuscripts survived the Cultural Revolution and the old and middle age generations learned the Clear script in schools, in present days there is nobody regularly reciting and copying the Clear script sutras as it is practices in Mongγolküriy-e and the nearby counties.

A similar situation is at the Mongolian north-eastern side of Altai mountains, where Altain Urianhains survived as a minority among Kazakhs in Buyant, Altai, Altancögc and Bulgan sums in Bayan-ölgii aimag (except the Tuva-speaking Altai Urianhains in Cengel sum, regarded today as the Tuva nationality) and as a majority in two sums (Mönhhairhan, Duut) in Hovd aimag. During my repeated oral history research in these areas (since 2010), I have collected some few mentions about local people previously famous in their native place for their knowledge of the Clear script and reciting the Clear script sutras. The best evidence has come from the historical *Baraγun amban-u qosiγu* (called also Darqan beyise-yin qosiγu) of the Left wing of Altain Urianhains (today's Mönhhairhan and Bulgan sums and a part of Duut sum). Unlike in Xinjiang, where the Clear script was in use as the official writing system for Mongolian until early 1990s, in Western Mongolia (formerly the Hovd Frontier *Qobdu-yin kijaγar*) the Classical Mongolian script has been used for the administrative needs starting with the Manchu times (at least 19th century) and, of course, replaced by the Cyrillic during the late 1940s. The Clear script has been limited to the private use, mainly for the religious needs, and has never been taught in official schools. ① Still the books in the Clear script has been kept in a high esteem and despite the big loses caused by several forced migrations in the first half of the 20th century and the harsh anti-religious campaigns from 1940s to 1990, a large amount of the books is still kept by local families and reestablished local temples.

Unlike in Mongγolküriy-e, where the tradition of *hara bagši* is still preserved, in Baraγun amban-u qosiγu has not been any exception that it was a woman who mastered the Clear script and regularly recited the scriptures.

Türuunii Togtoh (deceased in 1963, 76 years old) belonging to the Myangat sum of the Baruun amban's banner, was known as *usanz* (skr. *upāsikā*), a lay devotee, who had undertaken certain vows, transmitted her knowledge of the Clear script and inherited her books to her daughter, Damdinii Muuja (1909-1992). ② Muuja in her older age also started to observe the precepts and the rules of an *usanz*. She has been reciting the Diamond sutra on 15th and 30th day of every month of the Mongolian calendar. She started to recite the Diamond sutra as soon as the morning tasks like the milking of cattle had been finished, lit a lamp and made an incense offering. Muuja learned the Clear script spontaneously just following her mothers reciting. She has probably never used the

① The only short time when the Clear script appeared in the archives of the Altain Urianhain banners were the late 1910s, when Altai Urianhains pertained to Chinese authorities in Sir-a süm-e (today's Altay in Xinjiang) -*Fu dutong xian Aertaishan daoyin gongshu* 副都統銜阿爾泰山道尹公署.

② Muuja's father Damdin belonged to the Oriyas elkin of Ah sumun in the Baruun ambanii hošuu. His father was Sam'ya and gradfather Baglaan (Бөххуяг 2010, 51).

Clear script for writing. ①

Another legendary wise old woman reciting the Diamond sutra was Sanjiin Naadgai from Mönhhairhan sum (Hovd aimag), who can be considered one of the most remarkable personalities in the recent past of the place. She was born in 1902/1903 as a daughter of Sanji zahiragĉi, ② presumably an assistant of the banners governor. ③

Being an old lady with a perfect memory, Naadgai has been interviewed by several researchers. In 1978, she was called to talk with prof. Jaroslav Vacek from the Charles University in Prague and Jugderiin Lubsangdorji, who went to Mönhhairhan during their dialectological research in Hovd aimag. In 1988, she provided a lot of ethnological information to the field researcher I. Lhagvasüren from the Mongolian Academy of Sciences. J. Coloo in his article about the Altai Urianhain written culture mentions the traditional names of the graphical components and individual letters in the Clear script recorded from S. Naadgai with their comparison to the names included in the written sources. ④

According to the interviews with Naadgais son Magsar and her daughter-in-law Pooluugiin Noosgoi, ⑤ Naadgai learned the Clear script from her father, forgot it through his life and brushed up her knowledge again when she was seventy, it means in 1970s. At that time she has was searching for old manuscripts preserved by others and probably collected some of them. Then she has been copying them by hand and also presenting the copies to the people.

The other topic I will mention in the Mongolian version is the relation of Altain Uri-

① According to the interview with ĉuluunoĉir, Muuja's adoptive son (son of Maidar, Nücged elkin) (14. 5. 2012, Ulaanhus bag, Bulgan sum, Bayan-ölgii aimag). The collection of manuscripts inherited by ĉuluunoĉir from his mother Muuja contains four items in the Clear Script: 1.) *Xutuqtu biligiin ĉinadu kürügsen tasuluqĉi uĉir kemēkü yeke kölgöni sudur orošibo* (26 fol., a manuscript written by *calamus* on the Russian handmade paper, presumably of the first half of the 19th century), 2.) *Zouraduin sonosōd toniluqĉi orošibo* (14 fol., written by *calamus* on the Russian handmade paper), 3.) *Altan gereliyin xurāngyui orošiboi* (4 fol., modern Russian paper), 4.) *Xutuqtu Mayidariyin tangγariqlaqsan kemēkü toqtol* (2 fol., modern Russian paper).

② Her father belonged to the Tünken *elken* (clan) in Ah *arvan* of Oorcog sumun of Baruun ambanii hošuu. Naadgai has been a resident of Bort bag in Mönhhairhan sum.

③ Otherwise, the name Sanji zahiragĉi has never been mentioned in the oral history I have collected in the region of the former banner.

④ Цолоо-Мөнхцэцэг 2008, 424-427. J. Coloo interviewed S. Naadgai in 1971.

⑤ Centre of Mönhhairhan sum, 13. 7. 2011, 27. 6. 2012, 8. 7. 2012, 20. 6. 2013, 6. 7. 2013.

anhais to their homeland places, which they were forced to abandon many times during both the older and modern history, which comes out in legends, folk-tales and songs. The others are the almost vanished traditional Urianhai agricultural, a unique tradition among Mongolian nomads, the tradition of hunters and of course, the tradition of skying.

I have come across a single mention about skying in my research of Urianhai's oral history. It links to this banner, the Banner of the Left wing's governor whose stage used to be on the northern side of Altai range next to the Sagsai river together with the banner's large monastery (Sagsain hüree), while the second monastery of the banner used to nomadize around the souther part of the banner and finally settled in Handagait. During winter season the governor used skiers for communicating official affairs to the representatives of the southern part of the banner or during the Mongolian new year to change presents and felicitation between the local officials or between the higher lamas of the banner's two monasteries. Three of the last skiers were Tüdüb, Bayan ĉaγan and Taya. Tüdüb and Bayan ĉaγan came from the southern part of Altai, because the natural conditions of the north-eastern slopes do not allow using skis. They are said to have been transporting their skis until the ĉigirtein davaa on horseback and using them just behind the mountain pass, on the southern side.

Without the plentiful sources of the oral tradition, the reconstruction of the Altain Urianhains history of the 19th and 20th centuries would be reduced to a one-sided interpretation at least there, where the archive documents are widely absent.

References:

Бөххуяг, Ш.: *Алтай сайхан нутгийн ардын ухааны амин шүтэлцээ.* Улаанбаатар, 2010.

Бөхөө, Ц.: *Түүх бүтээлцсэн ард түмэн минь.* Мөнххайрхан сум, 2007.

Luvsandordž, Dž. - Vacek, J.: *Otázky a odpovědi.* Praha, 1990.

МУЗСЭХ-Монголын угсаатны зүйн хээрийн судалгааны эх хэрэглэгдэхүүн (1988-1989) -Field reports in Mongolian ethnology (1988-1989). X. Ulaanbaatar, 2011.

Пунцагдорж, Б.: *Алтайн Урианхайн аман зохиолын цоморлиг.* Өлгий, 1990.

Пунцагдорж, Б.: *Алтай сайхан нутгийн минь ардын ухааны эрдэнэсийн хэлхээ.* Улаанбаатар, 1999.

Цолоо, З. -Мөнхцэцэг, А.: *Урианхайн өв соёл.* Улаанбаатар, 2008.

中文论文：

阿勒泰乌梁海的七面旗帜 档案与口述历史

Ondĵej Srba（捷克共和国 布拉格 查尔斯大学）

阿勒泰乌梁海是一个有两种语言的少数民族，一个卫拉特或西部蒙古方言和突厥语语言，几乎类似于图瓦语。这两种语言组织一直由一个古老的中亚部落乌梁海使用，其中至少有一部分是由于种族起源，另一部分可能由于他们的共同的生活方式，主要基于狩猎、季节性农业和原来不那么重要的游牧畜牧业。乌梁海人来到阿勒泰是在满族征服 Dzunghar 汗国之前，当时大概是 18 世纪 50 年代，当时根据他们所在的居住地而被称为阿勒泰乌梁海以区别于唐努乌梁海（现在的图瓦)、阿勒泰诺尔乌梁海（现在的阿尔泰共和国）和库苏古尔诺尔乌梁海（现在蒙古的库苏古尔)。所有这些乌梁海地区混合土耳其和蒙古人口，但属于更大的蒙古文化圈，包括佛教和使用书面蒙古语或书面卫拉特语作为他们的文学语言。满清政府把阿尔泰乌梁海划分为两部分，又细分为七面旗帜（左翼和右翼)。四个旗部说蒙语，其中三个主要说图瓦语。六个旗部位于贯穿阿尔泰地区东北到西南的垂直地带，在这里人们允许开发各种类型的经济活动和自由迁移，以防自然灾害。这个系统运行到 1913 年，当时根据中俄条约，阿勒泰乌梁海在新宣布的蒙古自治区和新疆行省中分裂，归属阿勒泰地区管辖。但是到 20 世纪 30 年代边界前沿几乎被完全打开，偶尔的迁移继续无视新疆和蒙古当局的抗议活动。19 世纪末，乌梁海和满族当局允许哈萨克斯坦的几个行政单位定居在七面族旗部落，此时阿勒泰乌梁海开始以平等的管理系统存在。

阿勒泰乌梁海族旗的首长既不是起源于东部蒙古黄金家族称为可汗的子孙或 Dzunghar Öölöt 贵族，他们也不是他们满族朝廷赋予的世袭继承。1754 年阿勒泰乌梁海臣服于清朝，之后在 1762-1839 年之间该地进行了行政区域的划分。*Jegün amban* 旗帜管辖帜左翼阿勒泰乌梁海，他们统领者的级别是 *sula amban* 。而右翼势力的统领者通常是由最东部旗部（自治时期的答剌罕旗）的统领者世袭。另外的乌梁海旗部是由一般的统领者 bugude-yin daruγ-a（uheri da）管理，但实际上都是世袭的。虽然我们不确定，但至少一些旗部是使用蒙语的，同时 Koke mongĉaγ 旗起源于 ijaγur-un jayisang，是乌梁海人中的前清当地统治者。

我的研究是一项基于究蒙古国家中央档案馆中关于阿勒泰乌梁海旗的文件档案的研究。同蒙古西部所有的档案有相似之处，关于阿勒泰乌梁海旗帜的档案在破坏中只有少数幸免。在蒙古国家中央档案馆中对于阿勒泰乌梁海旗的发现包括意外发现的从道光时期（1820–1851 年）的文档，紧随其后的是更频繁的在光绪时期的文件（1871–1908 年）。

在断断续续的档案中我们发现关于提供黑貂皮、狐狸皮毛税收的文件，及征收马、骆驼和其他必需品的文件，但是大部分是关于人口特征的文件。最广泛的一个是未标明日期的描述 Jegun amban-u qosiγu 和 Qar-a soyun-u qosiγu（uheri da Sengdunjab）人口的普查。这份详细普查也提到家族个体家庭的名字、他们居住的地方，乌梁海人从事的三个主要活动之一——游牧畜牧业、农业或打猎。人口普查两年后更新，这明显年是从年龄数据记载，所有的家庭居住在两年前的同一个地方。这表明北部和南部的阿勒泰人口通常是固定的，而东部的阿勒泰左翼那样周期性的迁移是常见的。这也证实了双方的口述历史，作为两个不同的实体而在属于同一旗部。

由于档案来源非常有限，我们不得不考虑到丰富的口头传统和口述历史，它们至少是老一代乌梁海人继续传播到现在的信息。它创造了一个复杂的家谱和描述了当地的贵族个体成员（横幅州长，*sumun janggi*，*jakiruγĉi*，*kündü* 等）、明智的僧侣和转世的圣人、传奇的摔跤手、猎人、马强盗和其他人。

在接下来的关于蒙古人的一部分我的演讲将提及乌梁海口头传统的一些文化现象，它们现在处于高度濒危和几乎被遗忘的境地。其中一个是哈拉 hara bagši 传统，宗教专家流行的蒙古佛教的宗教专家，他们曾执行佛经翻译成卫拉特蒙古语脚本的集体阅读活动，而西部蒙古修道院的僧侣限制于藏语文本的使用。

居住在新疆阿勒泰附近的阿勒泰乌梁海人直到最近还在诵读脚本佛经。当地的老人还记得 hara bagšis 在 20 世纪 90 还在他人的要求下阅读脚本佛经和通过一种使用仪式箭头或金刚的仪式方法来检测偷来的东西（通常是一些牲畜）。尽管只有一些佛经脚本经历文化大革命的洗劫而留存下来，而老中年一代在学校可以学习这些佛经。现今，几乎没有人经常诵读和摘抄佛经了，就像在 Mongγolkuriy-e 和附近的县那样。

类似的情况是在阿尔泰山的蒙古东北部，在那里阿勒泰乌梁海人幸存下来并作为少数种群散居在哈萨克人当中，主要在 Buyant，Altai，Altancögc and Bulgan sums in Bayan-ölgii aimag（除了说图瓦语的阿勒泰乌梁海人，现在被认为是图瓦族）和作为在 Hovd aimag 区域的多数种群（Mönhhairhan，Duut）。经过反复研究这些地区的口述历史（2010 年以来），我收集了一些关于当地人很少提到的以前当地人以渊博的佛经知识和诵读佛经而闻名的史实。最有力的证据来自阿勒泰乌梁海左翼的史料记载 Baraγun amban-u qosiγu（也称为 Darqan beyise-yin qosiγu）。不像在新疆，在这里直到 20 世纪 90 年代脚本佛经才在蒙古人的官方书写体系中使用；而在蒙古西部（以前的 Qobdu-yin kijaγar），经典的蒙古脚本从管理需求的角度在满清时期（至少在 19 世纪）已开始使用，在 20 世纪 40 年代末被西里尔字母取代。经典蒙语佛教脚本一直局限于私人使用，主要用于宗教需要，从未在官方学校公开教授。还有一些蒙语脚本佛经书籍被人们赋予崇高的敬意保存着，尽管 20 世纪上半页的几次被迫迁移和 20 世纪 40 年代到 90 年代的严酷的反宗教运动对其造成重大破坏，而大量的书籍还是由当地家庭和重建的寺庙保存了下来。

不像在 Mongγolkuriy-e 区域，在这里 hara bagši 的传统仍被保留着。而在 Baraγun amban-u qosiγu 地区没有任何特别的情况，在这里一位女性掌握了佛经脚本并和定期诵读经文。

Turuunii Togtoh（1963 年去世，享年 76 岁）属于 the Myangat sum of the Baruun amban's banner，也被称为 usanz（skr. upāsikā），一位信徒，曾承担一定的宣誓活动，传播她所知道的佛经知识，并把她的佛经书籍传给女儿 Damdinii Muuja（1909-1992）。2Muuja 在她年迈时也开始研究 usanz 的戒律和规则。她在蒙历的每月 15 日和 30 日都会诵读金刚经。在早上的工作完成之后，如挤牛奶，她开始诵读金刚经，点燃一盏灯，制作一个香祭。Muuja 自发跟母亲的诵读学习佛经，但她有可能从未使用佛经脚本写作。

另一个传奇聪明诵读金刚经的老妇人是 Sanjiin Naadgai，她被认为是这个地方近来具有卓越品质的伟大女性之一。她出生在 1902/1903 年，作为 Sanji zahiragĉi4 的女儿，可能是地方长官助理。

这位拥有非凡记忆的老人家-Naadgai 已经被几位研究人员采访过。在 1978 年，她被邀请与来自布拉格查尔斯大学的 Jaroslav Vacek 教授交谈。1988 年，她提供了大量的民族学的信息给来自蒙古科学院的研究员 I. Lhagvasuren。J. Coloo 在他的关于乌梁海文化的文章中提到图形组件的传统名称和佛经脚本记录中单个字母，这些记录来自于 S. Naadgai 与书面来源佛经中的名称的比较。

根据对 Naadgais 的儿子 Magsar 和儿媳 Pooluugiin Noosgoi 的采访，Naadgai 是从她父亲那里学会佛经知识。她在生活磨难中曾忘记这些知识，当她 70 岁时又再次捡起了她的佛经知识，也就是大概在 20 世纪 70 年代。当时她开始寻找由他人保存的古老手稿，并且可能收集了一些。然后她用手抄写这些手稿，也把抄写的副本送给他人。

我将提到另一个主题是阿勒泰乌梁海人与他们家乡居住地的关系，在古代和现代历史上他们多次被迫放弃自己的家园，他们的家园孕育了古老的传说、民间故事和歌谣。其他的还有濒临消失的传统乌梁海农业，蒙古游牧民族的一个独特的传统，当然也是猎人的传统，河水猛涨的传统。

在我调查乌梁海的口述历史时偶然间提及过滑雪，与左翼首领的旗相关，其活动范围在阿勒泰山脉北部，Sagsai 河旁，该旗最大的僧院（Sagsain hüree）亦位于附近。而该旗第二大的僧院曾游牧于该旗南部，而最终落户在汉德尕特。冬季，旗长会通过滑雪来和南部的代表进行官方事务交流。在蒙古新年期间，当地官员及该旗内两家僧院的高僧亦通过滑雪的方式来交换礼物或表达祝贺。最后的三位滑雪者是 Tüdüb，Bayan ĉaγan 和 Taya。Tüdüb 和 Bayan ĉaγan 来自于阿勒泰南部，因为东北部坡道的自然条件不适合使用雪板。据说他们一直在运输雪板直至马背上的 ĉigirtein davaa 开始在南部山口后面使用他们。

没有足够口述传统的资源，阿勒泰乌梁海 19 世纪和 20 世纪实际的历史重建将仅仅演化成片面的解释，因为广泛缺乏档案资料。

4.38 劳斯舞的由来 Origin of Lausdans

桑卓（托马斯之子）（挪威） SondreAslaksby（NOR）

Ancient skiing dance performers in Norway
挪威古老滑雪舞蹈表演者

Lausdans

The *Lausdans* is one of our oldest folk dances in Norway. An element of the dance, *kruking* , can be seen on ancient rock carvings. The lausdans, also known as Halling, is a half-dance, meaning a dance without a partner. During the dance it is important to show strength, flexibility, balance and rhythm, which is a sign of "leug" .

The dance is also a competition where the object is to impress a future partner. It is mainly a male dance, but it can also be danced by women. Lausdans was part of the training of military ski troops in the old times. The best laus - dancer was called Frikar. This was a title also given to the best skier.

劳斯舞

劳斯舞，是挪威最古老的民间舞蹈之一。舞蹈的因素之一，就是钩子舞（kruking），在古代岩画上可以见到它。劳斯舞，与哈林舞一样著名，是单人舞（half-dance：一半的舞），意为没有舞伴的舞蹈。在舞蹈中，显示力量、灵活性、平衡性，节奏感很重要。这也是"鲁格"（"leug"）的标志。

舞蹈，同样也是一种竞赛，目的是给未来的伴侣留下深刻的印象。它也是以男性为主的舞蹈，不过女性也可以跳。劳斯舞，是以前的滑雪部队军事训练的一部分。最好的舞者被称为弗利卡。这一称号，同样也给与最好的滑雪者。

4.39　挪威传统滑雪板制作一瞥　A Gleam into the Norwegian Tradition of Making Skis

托马斯（挪威）　Thomas Aslaksby（NOR）

个人简介　Brief Introduction

Thomas Aslaksby is a ski planner and designer. He is devoted to making research on the tradition of making skis and history and skis for many years and has made fruitful results.

托马斯是挪威知名的滑雪规划设计专家。多年来致力于滑雪板的制作和滑雪板的发展历史的研究，并在此领域取得了卓越成就。

Speech　讲演稿：

A Gleam into the Norwegian Tradition of Making Skis

First of all, let me express my heartfelt thanks for being given the opportunity to get an insight into the Altay ski tradition and to be invited to this conference.

My son Sondre and I love the winter and the snow, its form, its movement and many other aspects. This primeval soup gives us the opportunity to play and dance on skis. To be able to do that, we need knowledge of how to make skis. The Norwegian Crafts Institute and I are cooperating to achieve this knowledge. We are trying to dig deep into the ski history and ski tradition through historical records. At the same time we try to preserve and promote the knowledge, culture and professions relating to the traditional craftsmanship. We use the term "action-born knowledge" to describe the knowledge of a craft has its basis in both practice and action.

It was not the Norwegians who invented the ski, but just as the Europeans enabled wine, the Scandinavians and especially the Norwegians have enabled the ski culture and have spread it worldwide in modern times.

However, a long time ago the ski and the knowledge of ski-making were spread with the nomadic people. According to Fritjof Nansen, the famous Norwegian arctic explorer and scientist, the skis were brought to Scandinavia by the Sami people, following the reindeer. This was a long time before the Scandinavian nation states oftoday were established. There is an interesting map in Nansen's book "First Crossing of Greenland" from 1890, in the chapter called "Ski og skiløbning" . The map shows the distribution of skis and the link between genuine names for ski. Based on this he writes that the evidence "…lead us to regard the Baikal and Altai region as the probable home of ski" . In this area there is still today a fantastic living tradition of using skin-clad skis.

If we look to Norway, there was still a living tradition of making skis based on local culture 200 years ago and earlier. Skis were made on almost every farm in the mountains and other areas with winter snow. Skis were made of different kinds of wood and varied a lot in shape. Local wood was used, mostly birch and pine, which are the most widespread.

Birch glides especially well when the snow is cold. Pine provides quite light skis with decent glide on wet snow, if heartwood has been used. Sallow and willow are best on drifting snow, while tennar skis are best on crust, in addition to being very durable on hard snow, and providing good camber. Ash elm and mountain willow give good flexing strong and smooth skis. Elm and mountain willow were smooth that it was said that it was just like having the Devil behind you! Maple also yielded good skis, in Southern Norway it was considered to be among the best. Oak was also used quite a lot in Southern Norway.

Some skis were skin-clad, like here in Altay, to provide a good grip and a good glide on all kinds of snow. A special tradition is the use of a long ski and a short one. This may be a mix between two different traditions of short skin-clad skis and long tennarskis. They may have taken one ski from each pair, and used the short skin-clad one for kicking and the long one for gliding. In addition to using different kinds of wood for raw material, a large number of different types of skis were developed, both in the Norwegian and Saami tradition. Some were short and wide, others were long and narrow. The skis may have parallel sides, or be trapezoid, boat-shaped or have carving. Even staves from wooden barrels have been used for making skis, normally for children. They were good for training the balance. Later they developed into the mini-skis of today. Many of the shapes of the historical skis can still be seen in modern skis, but we have to look into history to find all of the local ski-making traditions.

Skis have a special place in Norwegian history, both as a part of the Norwegian identity and as a leisure activity. Norway was one of the earliest countries with military ski units. Skis were also important for the success of the polar expeditions of Nansen and

Amundsen. It was the Norwegians who developed the basic forms of cross-country, ski-jumping, alpine and biathlon, which are so popular today among many nations. However, the older traces of skiing must be found further east.

It is with great pleasure that Sondre and I have seen some of the oldest and most intact remains from our earliest ski history, and a very living tradition of skiing and ski-making.

中文论文：

挪威传统滑雪板制作一瞥

首先，我衷心的感谢被邀请到本次会议，感谢有机会能深入了解阿尔泰的传统滑雪。

我和我的儿子桑卓喜爱冬季和雪，以及它的形态，它的运动和其他诸多方面。这原始的汤汁使我们有机会在滑雪板上玩耍和跳舞。为了做到这一点，我们需要掌握如何制作滑雪板的知识。我们通过历史记载，努力的、深入的挖掘滑雪历史和滑雪传统。同时，我们也努力的保护和弘扬与传统手工业有关的知识和文化。我们使用“行动诞生知识”来形容一门手艺的知识，有其实践和行动的基础。

并非是挪威人发明了滑雪，但是如同欧洲人开启了酒文化，斯堪的纳维亚人尤其是挪威人开启了滑雪文化，并在近现代将它推广到全世界。

然而，很久以前滑雪和制作滑雪板的知识是通过游牧人传播的。根据挪威著名的北极探险家和科学家弗里德约夫·南森的研究成果，滑雪板是由塞米人追随驯鹿带到斯堪的纳维亚的。这是在今日斯堪的纳维亚的各个国家建立之前的很久以前。在南森1890年的著作《首次穿越格陵兰》的“Ski og skiløbning”① 章节中，有一幅有趣的地图。地图显示了滑雪板的分布并且提到了滑雪的原始名称。在他写的这些证据的基础之上，“引导我们认为贝加尔湖和阿尔泰地区是滑雪的故乡”。在这个区域内，仍然保留了使用毛皮包裹的滑雪板，这一奇妙的鲜活的传统。

我们看看挪威，这里仍然有制作滑雪板的活生生的传统，这种传统建立在200年前，甚至是更早的土著文化上。几乎山上的每一个农场和其他冬季有积雪的地区，居民都会制作滑雪板。滑雪板用不同的木材做成，形状也不尽相同。使用本地的木材，主要是桦树和松树，这是最普遍的。

---

① 这个词是挪威语，与滑雪有关。

降雪时，桦树滑雪板滑行效果特别好。松木提供的是更轻的滑雪板，如果使用树木的中心木材，则可以在湿雪上体面的滑行。蜡黄和柳木的滑雪板，在风吹雪中使用最好，同时特纳（tennar）[①]滑雪板在痂壳雪面上使用最好，除了能在硬雪上十分耐用外，它还有很好的弯曲度。灰榆和山柳可以提供良好的弯曲，结实光滑的滑雪板。榆树和山柳的滑雪板十分光滑，有句话说，就像魔鬼跟在你身后！枫木也可生产出好的滑雪板，在挪威南部，它被认为是最好的。在挪威南部，滑雪板也多用橡木制作。

一些滑雪板，包裹了皮毛，就像在阿勒泰的一样，它具有良好的抓地力以及减少了下滑的摩擦力。一个特殊的传统是使用一个长滑雪板和一个短滑雪板，这可能是短的毛皮滑雪板和长的特纳滑雪板，这是两种不同的传统的滑雪板组合。它们可能是从每双中选取一只，短的皮毛包裹的滑雪板用于踏雪，长的滑雪板用于滑行。除了使用不同种类的木材做原料，大量不同类型的滑雪板被开发出来，不论是挪威还是萨米传统。一些短而宽，一些长而窄。滑雪板可能有平行的边，或是边缘呈梯形、船型，上面有雕刻等。甚至木桶的板条被用来做滑雪板，通常为儿童而制作。它们十分有利于训练平衡。之后它们被发展成今天的迷你的滑雪板。在现代滑雪板上可见许多史前滑雪板的形状，但是我们必须回顾历史去寻找所有本地传统滑雪板的制作工艺。

滑雪板在挪威的历史上有特殊的地位，即是挪威人的身份标识，也是代表一种休闲活动。挪威是最早有滑雪军事部队的国家之一。滑雪板在南森和阿蒙森的极地探险成功中功不可没，是挪威人发展了越野滑雪、跳台滑雪、高山和冬季两项的基本形式，今日这些在许多国家都十分风靡。然而，古老滑雪的痕迹必须在更远的东部才能找到。

我和桑卓非常高兴，能够看见一些来自于我们早期滑雪历史的最古老的并且大部分都保存完好的遗存，以及观察到滑雪和滑雪板制作的鲜活的传统。

4.40 波兰滑雪的起源 The Origins of Polish Skiing

Tomasz Jagodzinski（POL）托马斯 加（波兰）

个人简介 Brief Introduction

Tomasz Jagodziński, Graduate technical mining, followed by Warsaw University-studied at the Faculty of Journalism and Political Science. He worked as an electrician,

① 是一种木材。

and since 1982 as a sports journalist. In 1991 he obtained a senator (as an independent) fromthe province Piotrkow.

He belonged to thePolish Peasant Party, on behalf of the candidate, among others, in parliamentary elections in 1997 and 2001. He served as spokesman for the Polish Football Association (e. g. during a dispute between Marian Dziurowicz and Jack Dębski) . In 2008 he was a candidate for the post of chairman of the board PZPN, but on the day of the election by the General Assembly of the Polish Football Association (30 October) resigned from applying for this function.

He is the author of a book published in 1993, *buster not mess with* dedicated aferom in Polish football. He is a director Museum of Sport and Tourism and is a member of the supervisory board GKS "Bełchatów" SSA

托马斯·加曾任教于华沙大学新闻与政治科学系，其后又研究采矿技术。他曾经当过电工和体育记者，在 1991 年取得彼得库夫省参议员的席位。在 1997 年和 2001 年的选举中代表该地的候选人参加选举。

他还是波兰足球协会的发言人。

1993 年，他发表 *Buster not mess with* 一书，主要阐述关于波兰足球的一些看法。

他还是波兰体育运动旅游博物馆的主管，还是 GKS "Bełchatów" SSA 董事会的监管理事。

Photos in his speech:

Welcome everybody

Sport and Tourism Museum in Warsaw, treasury of Polish sport, founded in 1952, is one of the oldest institutions of the Museum of sports profile. Since 2011 the Museum is part of the elite program of International Olympic Committee called Olympic Museums Network in short (OMN)

Only 22 best sports museums in the world are members of the OMN.

Museum possess 53. 5 thousands of exhibits, rich collections of the library and photographic archive. Most of the collections are gifts from private collectors, athlites, activists, as well as from associations and sports clubs. There are 2, 500 ski artifacts, of which 10 percent is the unique collection rilated to the origins of the Polish skiing.

华沙体育运动旅游博物馆成立于 1952 年，是波兰体育运动界的瑰宝，也是关于波兰体育运动档案最古老的机构之一。自从 2011 年以来，该博物馆就成为国际奥委会精英计划的一部分，就是所谓的奥林匹克博物馆网络（OMN）。在全世界，只有 22 家最好的体育运动博物馆是奥林匹克博物馆网络的成员。

博物馆拥有上千件展品，收藏品和照相存档丰富多样。大部分藏品来自于私人收藏家、运动家、活动家，以及来自协会和体育俱乐部。博物馆还有 2500 件滑雪文物，其中 10%的独特的收藏与波兰滑雪的起源有关。

The origins of Polish skiing

波兰滑雪的源头

from the collection of Sport and Tourism Museum in Warsaw

来自于华沙体育旅游博物馆的收藏品

Oldest ski equipment

最古老的滑雪工具

Tourist ski made of ash-wood, manufactured by Stanisław Barabasz with self-made bindings. Ski with groove, long head with burned engraving "S. B", 1980.

旅行滑雪板，用白蜡木制成，由 Stanisław Barabasz 自制绑定发明。滑板有凹槽，雪板头长并烧制雕刻有字母"SB"，1980 年。

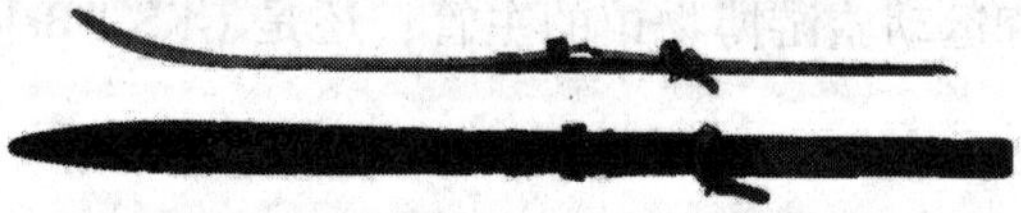

Short rocker ski made of ash-wood, manufactured by Stanisław Barabasz, used for skiing on the tampered snow, rocker covered with metal sheet.

短摇杆式滑雪板，用白蜡木制成，由 Stanisław Barabasz 发明，可在已压过的雪地上滑行，摇杆覆盖着金属片。

Ski made of beech-wood with cane bindings, lenght 1, 80m, special leather-cap mounting for shoe

雪板由山毛榉木制成，绑着藤条，长 1. 80 米，特殊的皮革固定在雪板上作为固定器。

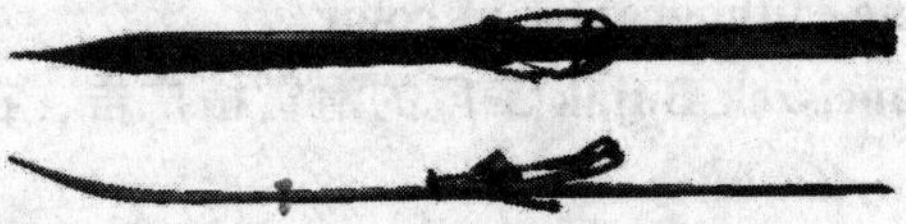

Ski made of ash-wood, double groove, “Huitfeld” bindings, circa 1905

雪板由白蜡木制成，双槽，由“Huitfeld”绑定，大约出现于 1905 年。

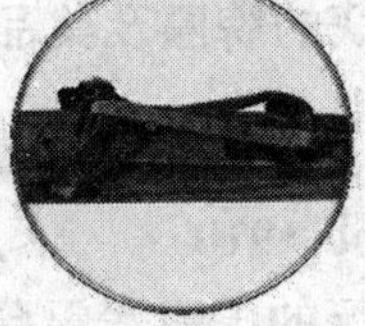

Ski poles made of bamboo, lenght 134 mm, coloured, with holes for leather hand-straps, beginning of ×× century

滑雪杆，由竹子制成，长 134 毫米，有色彩。皮革手带，有空。始于二十世纪。

BUJAK ZAKOPANE

Ski of Helena Marusarzówna-champion of ski sport from the first half of ×× century, manufactured by Franciszek Bujak

Helena Marusarzówna 滑雪板，二十世纪上半叶的滑雪运动的冠军，由 Franciszek Bujak 制成。

古老的滑雪板展示　Oldest ski advertisements

Advertisement of ski from the Franciszek Bujak Factory in Zakopane, lithography in color

Franciszek Bujak 工厂的滑雪板广告，在色彩方面采用平版印刷术。

Ski advertisement in book

书中的滑雪板广告

Plaques and prizes from oldest ski competitions organized in Poland

波兰举办古老滑雪比赛收获的牌匾及奖品

Plaque-I prize in the General Tatra Run, International Ski Meeting, Zakopane 1910

1910 年在扎科帕内举行的国际滑雪会议上获得的奖牌

Plaque-I prize in the Ski-Jumping competition, Zakopane 1914

1914 年在扎科帕举行的跳台滑雪比赛中获得的奖牌

Plaque - I prize in the Championschip of Karpaty, Sławsko 1914

1914 年在喀尔巴阡山举行的滑雪锦标赛中获得的奖牌

Madal-I prize in the Senior's Run, Sławsko 1914

1914 年在 Sławsko 举行的高级滑雪赛中获得的奖章

Badges of Polish Ski Association

波兰滑雪协会的徽章

Golden badge, openwork

镂空雕刻的金色徽章

Gold Honorary badge, made on the occasion of 20 aniversary of Polish Ski Association 1939

1939 年波兰滑雪协会成立 20 周年的而制作的金质荣誉徽章

Silver badge of mountain tourism proficiency, the first of its kind in Europe, approved by the General Board of Polish Ski Association, 1932

1932 年波兰滑雪协会董事会首批在欧洲举行的山地旅游能力赛的银质徽章

Badge of profficiency

滑雪熟练度比赛的徽章

Badges of Ski Division of Polish Tatra Society (SNPTT)

波兰塔特拉社团的滑雪分会的徽章

Membership badge

会员徽章

Membership badge, 1927

会员徽章, 1927

Membership badge, 1938

会员徽章, 1938

Badge "Zakopane Ski Division" Tatra Society, 1908

塔特拉社团的滑雪分会的徽章, 1908

Badges of the oldest ski societies and associations
古老的滑雪社团与协会的徽章

Badge of the Tatra Ski Society, 1908
塔特拉社团的徽章，1908 年

Badge of the Tatra Ski Society, before 1914
塔特拉滑雪社团的徽章，1914 年前

Membership badge of the Ski Section of Academic Tourist Club, Lwów 1911
利沃夫学术旅游俱乐部之滑雪分部的会员徽章，1911 年

Membership badge of Karpatia Ski Society in Lwów, 1907
卡尔帕提亚滑雪社团的会员徽章，1907 年

Commemorative badge from the first Championship of Poland 1921
波兰首个锦标赛的纪念徽章，1921 年

Membership badge of "Czarni" Sport Club Ski Section
滑雪运动俱乐部的徽章

Membership badge of Karpatia Ski Society in Lwów, 1907
卡尔帕提亚滑雪社团的会员徽章，1907 年

FIS Word Skiing Championship in Zakopane, 1939
1939 年扎科帕内国际滑雪联合会锦标赛

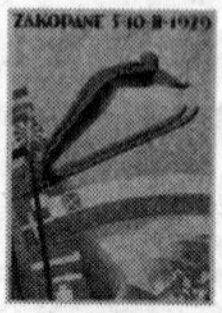

Poster by Stefan Osiecki and Jerzy Skolimowski
海报

Honorary tribune, in the middle President RP Ignacy Mošcicki
名誉论坛

Badge-I International Ski Competition
国际滑雪比赛的徽章

FIS Word Skiing Championship in Zakopane, 1939
1939 年扎科帕内国际滑雪联合会锦标赛

Official programm of competition
官方滑雪竞赛项目

Bulletin of competition
竞赛公告

Poster by Czesław Wielhorski and Leszek Piąkowski
海报

FISWord Skiing Championship in Zakopane, 1939
1939 年扎科帕内国际滑雪联合会锦标赛

Diploma of participation in championship
参加滑雪锦标赛的文书

Illustrated report from the contest
关于比赛的报道

FIS Word Skiing Championship in Zakopane, 1939

1939 年扎科帕内国际滑雪联合会锦标赛

Function badge

功能徽章

Silver badge

银质徽章

Function badge-press

功能徽章

Gold medal

金质奖章

Plaque

奖牌

Silver medal

银质奖章

FIS Word Skiing Championship in Zakopane, 1939

1939 年扎科帕内国际滑雪联合会锦标赛

Badge

徽章

Plaque-price in the Military Ski Patrols Run

军事滑雪巡逻赛中的奖牌

FIS Word Skiing Championship in Zakopane, 1939

1939 年扎科帕内国际滑雪联合会锦标赛

Postcard-ski competition

明信片-滑雪比赛

Postcard-Tatra Mountains, Five Ponds Valley
明信片-塔特拉山，五池塘谷

Post stamps of Polish Post-Office
波兰邮局的邮票

Oldest ski photographs
关于滑雪的老照片

Ski tourism, Sławsk area, East Karpaty, 1908
在东喀尔巴阡的滑雪游，1908 年

Ski tour in East Karpaty, 1907
在东喀尔巴阡的滑雪游，1907 年

Zakopane Ski Division during the ski class in Zakopane, Gubałówka mountain, 13 XII 1908
扎科帕内滑雪分会的滑雪课，1908 年

Ski Class in Sławsk, East Karpaty, 1909
在东喀尔巴阡的滑雪课，1909 年

Oldest book about skiing
关于滑雪的旧书

Józef Schneider in Tatarów, autor of the first Polish Ski Coursebook, photo 1897 Józef Schneider
波兰第一本滑雪教材的作者，**1897** 年

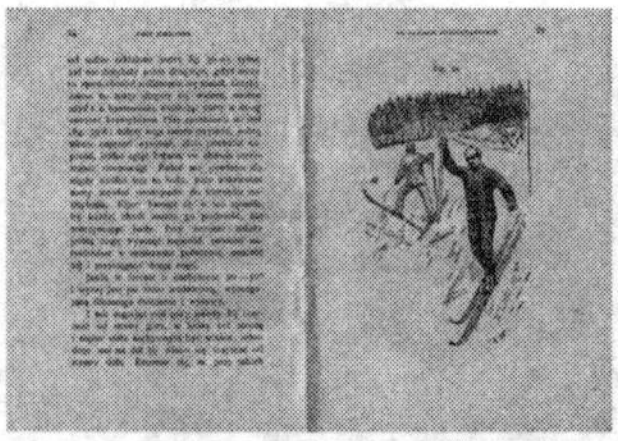

Book by Józef Schnajder "On the scandinavian ski", 1898
《关于斯堪纳维亚地区的滑雪》，**Józef Schnajder, 1898** 年

Oldest documents about skiing
关于滑雪的古老文件

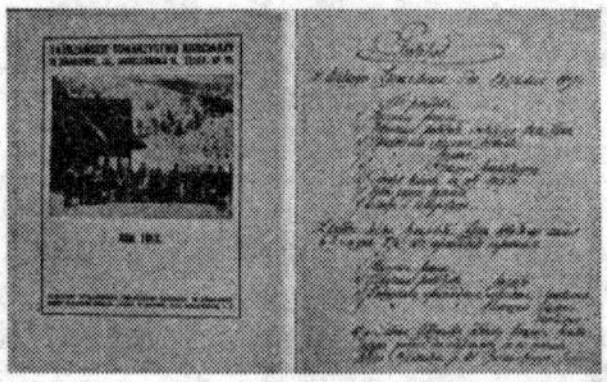

Files of the Krakow Karpatia Ski Asociation in Lwów, 1910-1921
Krakow Karpatia 滑雪协会的文件，**1910-1921** 年

Pocket ski calendar Polish Ski Association, 1928-29
波兰滑雪协会的袖珍滑雪日历，**1928-1919** 年

"Journal of the Tatra Society", yearbok 1, 1876
塔特拉协会的杂志，**1876** 年

Honorary diploma of Stanisław Facher, graduated by Tatra Ski Asociation in Kraków, 1923
荣誉证书

Identification card of Tadeusz Szumański, member of Polish Ski Association, 1930
波兰滑雪协会会员的身份证

Ski snow map issued by Polish Meteorology Institute, League of Tourism Support and Ski Propagation Society, 1936/1937
滑雪地图

Oldest skiing postcards
滑雪明信片

Lady on ski, 1980
滑雪的女士

Zakopane, Ski sport, 1910
滑雪运动，1910 年

Tatra mountains, Goryczkowy Wierch peak, 1916

"Skier" signed Z. Stryjeńska, 1937

Polish ski-sport in art
波兰滑雪运动艺术照

Portret Leonašliwińskiego w stroju narciarskim, męża Władysławy Kostakiewiczówny, autorstwa Wacława Dygmańskiego, 1932

Portrait of Władysława Kostakiewiczówna in the ski dress, the first Miss Polonia (1929), by Wacław Dygmański, 1932

"Marusarz Family", painting by Walter Gebauer, 1933

First prize in the slalom, won by Leszek Nycz during the FIS Word Skiing Championship in Zakopane, 1939
滑雪小回转比赛中获得的第一次奖品，由 Leszek Nycz 在国际滑雪联合会锦标赛中获得。1939 年

"Skier", sculpture in wood by Jan Szczepkowski, 1935
"滑雪者"木雕，由 Jan Szczepkowski 雕刻，1935 年

English Paper:

THE ORIGINS OF THE POLISH SKIING IN THE COLLECTION OF THE MUSEUM OF SPORTS AND TOURISM IN WARSAW

The Museum of Sports and Tourism in Warsaw was established in 1952. It was the first sports museum in Poland and one of the oldest ones in Europe. The main mission of the Museum was to 'collect and store cultural goods in the field of physical culture, tourism, and, in particular, the trophies, badges, awards, personal mementos, stamps, coins, posters, banners, clothes and sports equipment, travel accessories, sport-related works of art, photographs, movies, books and magazines'① .

At the end of 2014 there were 53567 artifacts on 69 sport disciplines in the collections of the Museum.

The ski collection department has gathered more than 2, 500 objects, out of which only about 100 date back until 1918 (the year of regaining independence by Poland after 123 years of captivity). This modest number of objects, however, has such a great historical and emotional significance, that it is one of the key elements of the Museum's collection.

The first historical documents on the examples of the use of skis in Poland are from the second half of the 16th century② and probably the skis were then occasionally used, but did not meet with mass acceptance.

Not until the mid-19th century there were more and more articles about Norwegian and Alpine skiing in the Polish press③. In 1892 the first articles promoting the use of

---

① Statute of the Museum of Sports and Tourism in Warsaw, 1952

② Gwagnin Aleksander, *Sarmatiae Europeae descripto* , Krakow 1578

③ *Muzeum Domowe* , 1835; *Magazyn Powszechny* , 1837; *Wędrowiec* , 1879, 1888

skis in Poland appeared. Leopold šwierz, one of the most respected members of the Tatra Society, published an article *Wycieczka do Morskiego Oka zimową porą*①, and another one about skiing②. šwierz encouraged to use skis in Zakopane, although he was not an active skier.

Józef Schnaider (1974-1959), ethnographer, woodsman and a pioneer of skiing and ski touring in the Eastern Carpathians, described his personal impressions of the first winter climb to Mount Hoverla③ in a book issued on his own, entitled *Na nartach skandynawskich. Podręcznik dla zwolenników sportu narciarskiego*④. For the first time it has included information about skiing, unknown to a Polish reader before (types of bindings, poles, shoes, clothes, know-how, skiing techniques). The publication was one of the first of its kind in the world. Today the book is rara avis and the pride of the Ski Department in the Museum's Library.

Stanisław Barabasz (1857-1949) was an architect, graduated from the Technical University of Vienna and a painter studying fine arts in Krakow and Vienna. He also had a great teaching ability, had been teaching drawing at schools for a long time. In the years 1901-1922 he led the Wood School in Zakopane, where under his guidance, the students started to produce the first Polish skis.

The name of 'Polish Pioneer of Modern Skiing' stuck to him after years of promoting skiing in the mountain resort of Zakopane, located not far from Krakow, which in the late 19th century became the first Polish winter resort.

In 1888 Barabasz made skis for himself, which were to assist him in hunting, as he was an avid hunter. In 1914, in a book *Wspomnienia narciarza*, which is an interesting contribution to the history of the origins of skiing in the Tatras, he wrote:

'This was in the eighties (19th century). No one has heard of skiing (in today's sense of the word). We knew the stories about Siberians, sleds pulled by reindeers, skis, which were used to hunt through the snow, somebody read about someone's *ski*, with the use of which the Norwegians where making miracles, so that their ski run was

---

① *Pamiętnik Tatrzański*, vol. 13, 1892; in English the title means: *Excursion to Morskie Oko lake in winter-time*

② *Kurier Zakopiański*, no. 7, 1892

③ the highest peak of the eastern Beskids in the Czarnohora range, currently the highest mountain in Ukraine, 2061 meters above sea level

④ Schnaider Józef, *Na nartach skandynawskich. Podręcznik dla zwolenników sportu narciarskiego*, Krakow, 1898; in English the title means: *On Scandinavian skis. A guide for ski sports followers*

compared to the flight of a bird'[1].

'I couldn't believe it but the more I knew, the more I wanted to possess these mysterious devices. It lasted for a few years…In December 1888 I visited my school colleague with whom I was on the hunt. In this time the huge snow had fallen, so that walking on the field was nearly impossible…With the help of the carpenter, my first pair of skis has been made. One was made of ash and the second of beech because the amount of material was not even'[2].

'My skis were very thin, in the middle of a pencil-thick, extremely flexible, adapting so easily to the bumps, and the ride was quite difficult, because it required a continuous balancing of forward and backward…I kept my feet together, heel next to heel, so the trail was tight'[3]. In Cieklin near Jaslo, where the above-mentioned events took place, a Museum of Skiing named after Stanisław Barabasz was established in 2008.

In the collection of the Museum of Sports and Tourism in Warsaw there is a single ski made of ash, signed with SB letters. It is 163 cm in length and 9, 70 cm in width. It was purchased to the Museum collection from a private person in 1963.

In 1907 three friends, Stanisław Barabasz, Mariusz Zaruski and Mieczysław Karłowicz, founded The Zakopane Skiers Section of the Tatra Society. Barabasz became its first president, Zaruski was in charge as a secretary and treasurer, and a young composer Karłowicz-as a so-called member-controller. The activities of the Zakopane Skiers Section mainly manifested in the organization of skiing courses. The first one was held in 1907, with Mariusz Zaruski as a main instructor. The course consisted of learning to walk on skis, skiing straight and taking bends, called as 'snake' by Zaruski. At the end of the course a trip was organized to test acquired skills. Zaruski trained a large number of highlanders and mountain guides in skiing techniques.

Barabasz, a friend of Mariusz Zaruski, contributed to the establishment of Mountain Volunteer Search and Rescue in 1909, after the tragic death of Mieczyslaw Karłowicz in the mountains. Zaruski became the first head of the Mountain Volunteer Search and Rescue (1909-1926). It supplied emergency shelter, rescue equipment and first aid kits, its members had been trained in first aid. The Mountain Volunteer Search and Rescue al-

---

① Barabasz Stanisław, *Wspomnienia narciarza*, Zakopane 1914, p. 10; in English the title means: The skier's memories

② Ibid., p. 11

③ Ibid., p. 13

so issued warning posters for tourists.

He was the author of the Statute of the Mountain Volunteer Search and Rescue, he wrote an oath, organized courses and personally led almost all of the emergency actions. He was also gradually completing the Book of Expeditions. The Museum possesses a manuscript of Zaruski's book entitled *Tatrzańskie Ochotnicze Pogotowie Ratunkowe*①.

Mariusz Zaruski (1867–1941) was a Renaissance figure. A prominent mountaineer and skier, athlete and instructor, sailor, creator of the Polish marine yachting, as well as s painter, writer and poet. Upon the outbreak of the World War I, he joined the army. In appreciation of bravery and significant war merits, he received numerous military decorations and was promoted from private to colonel. In 1923 he was awarded the rank of Brigadier General.

He was a supporter of skiing, which comprises the value of cognitive–grown under natural conditions, which is a test for the body and the spirit, and at the same time creates a unique opportunity to discover the beauty of nature. He was opposed to all forms of competition.

'Skiing is a sport, but it's a special branch of human activity. Skiing opens the gates of the ice mountains locked and bolted, reveals the alps covered under snow, lays open frozen lakes, shows grey–beard mountains' peaks and unveils the mystery of a winter desert in the Tatra mountains… On skis, and only on skis there is an opportunity to walk, listen and see… Besides, skiing gives health, shapes character, teaches courage and an ability to make a decision, increases the sense of beauty…'②.

Zaruski learnt to ski quite quickly, probably he came into contact with skis during his deportation to Siberia (1894–1899). The reason of his exile by the Russians was the activity in the patriotic organizations. Stanisław Barabasz was his teacher in Zakopane since 1904. He also read the books written by Mathias Zdarski–the author of Austrian school of skiing.

Zaruski soon became the author of the first Polish books dedicated to skiing. Along

---

① Zaruski Mariusz, *Tatrzańskie Ochotnicze Pogotowie Ratunkowe. Jego organizacja, dzieje i wyprawyratunkowe ze wspomnień swoich i notatek napisał Mariusz Zaruski, Naczelnik Straży Ratunkowej*, Warszawa 1922; in English the title means: *The Tatra Volunteer Search and Rescue. Its organization, history and rescue expeditions–written by Mariusz Zaruski, the chief of Rescue Brigade, on his memories and notes*

② *Zakopane*, no. 27, 1908

with Henryk Bobkowski he issued a skiing manual enriched with his paintings①. The greatest encouragement to skiing was his guide around the Tatra mountains, first issued in Polish②.

The Library of the Museum of Sports and Tourism in Warsaw possesses almost all the books written by Zaruski. Among the manuscripts (18 catalogued titles) there are also speeches and articles on skis and skiing (advice and instructions). The ink drawings on parchment (20 catalogued positions) are dedicated to marine themes.

In the collection of the Museum of Sports and Tourism there are also private souvenirs of Zaruski, ten artifacts in total-skiing, climbing and sailing equipment. Exhibits indirectly connected with skiing are: shoe warmers, canvas gloves and folding ski poles. Most of these objects are presented at the permanent exhibition of the Museum of Sports and Tourism in a glass-case dedicated to the Mountain Volunteer Search and Rescue.

The beginnings of the Polish skiing can be found in unique documentation of the Photo Archive of the Museum of Sports and Tourism. The collection of photographs before 1918 counts several dozen pieces obtained from private individuals, mostly coming from family albums. However, the most interesting are 170 glass-slides from 1905-1914, some of them presenting skiing tourism in Western Carpathians (95 objects) and other showing climbing in the Tatra mountains (75 objects).

Some of the photographs were taken by Maksymilian Dudyk, Zygmunt Klemensiewicz and Roman Kordys who signed their works with letters 'D. K. K.'. Dudyk, Klemensiewicz and Kodrys were trekking around the Tatra mountains since 1901, mostly in the companion of their friends Mieczysław Lerski and Jerzy Mašlanka. Since 1904 they had been popularizing mountain tourism and skiing in Lwow. Thanks to their efforts the propagator of the Alpine school of skiing, Mathias Zdarski came to Lwow. He responded to the invitation of The Active Games Society and under his leadership a skiing course was organized in 1906. Two weeks after the course Dudryk, Klemensiewicz, Kordys and Mašlanka organized the first expedition in Gorgany in the Eastern Carpathians, which ended up with climbing to the peak of Doboszanka (1757 m).

These unique and precious collection of visuals enriched Museum's resources in the

---

① Zaruski Mariusz, Bobkowski Henryk, *Podręcznik narciarstwa według zasad alpejskiej szkoły jazdy na nartach*, Krakow 1908

② Zaruski Mariusz, *Przewodnik po terenach narciarskich Zakopanego i Tatr Polskich*, Zakopane 1913

50s of the 20th century, thanks to an engineer Jerzy Mašlanka (1886-1961) -a great mountain climber and skier. He was a member of the Tourist Section of the Tatra Society, co-founder of the Tatra Climbers Group and Carpathian Skiers Society. In 1907-1910 he successfully made first winter ascents of some peaks in the Eastern Carpathians. He was also a photographer and one of the first to have made visuals which were later used during his lectures about the Tatra Mountains and ski tourism.

Despite some damages of the visuals, collection of the photography on glass is considered to be one of the most valuable documentary artifacts. Not every picture is technically perfest, but all of them accurately reflect the atmosphere of the origins of skiing and the specificity of the photography in the early 20th century.

The Museum of Sports and Tourism possesses an interesting collection of badges related to the first Polish skiing organizations, which were established at the beginning of the 20th century. The eldest are those belonging Carpathian Skiers Society-they date back to 1907. It is the same year that organization was established in. Among its 22 founders there were representatives of intellectual elite of that time: Kazimierz Panek, Zbigniew Klemensiewicz and Maksymilian Dudyk. Panek was the chancellor of the Medical Academy in Lwow. Klemensiewcz was a great physicist and chemist whereas Dudyk was an architect. The aim of Carpathian Skiers Society was 'to spread skiing and winter tourism in our country, to make access to the mountains available by using proper equipment and tools'. The organization also provided courses with the greatest Scandinavian skiing instructors' participation and published skiing and ski jumping guides.

The badges measure 3, 5 ×3, 5cm and are made of metal. They present 'KTN' abbreviation which stands for 'Karpackie Towarzystwo Narciarzy'① -written in a triangle. There is also a drawing of a wanderer on the skis with one pole. The badges were bought in 1966 from the representative members of the organization and whole Polish Eastern Borderlands②-Zbigniew Klemensiewicz and Wacław Kuchar.

Earlier, in 1906, the Academic Club of Tourism was established. It's was the third Polish organization of that type, after Galician Tatra Mountains Society and Polish Sightseeing Society. The Academic Club of Tourism was set up by Mieczysław Orłowicz and

① Carpathian Skiers Society

② Eastern Borderlands, in Polish: Kresy Wschodnie, were the territories very important for the Polish culture, with such cities as Lwow and Wilno; they belonged to Poland before the partitions in the end of 18th century and than in the interbellum period; Poland lost that territory to Soviet Union as a result ot the Second World War, now they belong to Ukraine, Belarus and Lithuania.

Kazimierz świtalski. They were students and graduates from the Lwow University-both rendered good service to the Polish tourism. Kazimierz świtalski was a Polish officer, politician, and the Prime Minister of Poland (1929). The club organized walking expeditions to Gorgany, Bieszczady and Tatra Mountains. In some periods of their activity the number of the members rose to even 400 persons.

In the 60s of the 20th century the collection of the Museum of Sports and Tourism was enriched with a badge from a Skiing Section of the Academic Club of Tourism. It is enameled, comes from 1911, has rectangular shape (2×3cm) and was made of metal. It presents a jumping skier against a blue background. There is an abbreviation SNAKT-'Sekcja Narciarska Akademickiego Klubu Turystycznego'①.

Skiing was also practised at the oldest Polish sports club, Czarni Lwow, which was established in 1903. Although Czarni focused mainly on football and athletics, a skiing section existed as well. The club organized the first official Polish ski jumping competition in Sławsk-Eastern Bieszczady mountains (19th January 1908). The winner was Leszek Pawłowski. Later, in 1965, he sold a badge of skiing sections of Czarni Lwow to the Muzeum of Sport and Tourism. The badge is made of metal, has got oval shape (2, 5 cm diameter) and was made before the World War I. It also presents a ski jumper in the sky.

Another significant ski jumper of that time was Jan Jarzyna (Czarni Lwow). He broke a record of Kalatówki jumping hill (15 m), which was also a Polish record of all time. In 1914, in Sławsk, Jarzyna won in jumping and running competitions during the championships in the Carpathians. In the 70s of the 20th century his family handed over his awards to the Museum of Sports and Tourism in Warsaw.

For winning at running he won a gold-plated medal of circular shape, with a diameter of 4 cm. It surprisingly depicts a ski jumper.

For winning at jumping he won a gold-plated badge. It presents a jumping skier, a mountain view and an inscription: 'Championship of the Carpathians', KTN abbreviation and the 1914 date.

The pioneering period of Polish skiing ends on 28th December 1919, when the Polish Skiing Association was established. From that moment most of the competitions were organized under its direction. The organization also provided an educational activity and led skiing courses. It was one of the first sports associations established after Poland had

① Skiing Section of the Academic Club of Tourism

restored its independence. This fact is best sign of the popularity, which skiing attracted and continues to attract in the Polish society.

The most interesting exhibits related to the origins of Polish skiing are presented on the permanent exhibition entitled 'The History of Polish Sports and Olympism'. Many others are shown on temporary exhibitions, used in educational programs, publications, as well as TV and movie productions.

Material evidence of the birth and development of the pioneering period of Polish skiing are attracting great attention of museum visitors, especially as the following years have brought a growing fashion for skiing and further rapid development of this sport discipline. In 1929 and 1939 skiing world championships were organized in Poland under the auspices of FIS. In the years before the outbreak of the World War II a great ski careers of Bronisław Czech and Stanisław Marusarz managed to develop.

Bibliography:

- Schnaider Józef, *Na nartach skandynawskich. Podręcznik dla zwolenników sportu narciarskiego*, Krakow, 1898
- Barabasz Stanisław, *Wspomnienia narciarza*, Zakopane 1914
- Zaruski Mariusz, *Tatrzańskie Ochotnicze Pogotowie Ratunkowe. Jego organizacja, dzieje i wyprawyratunkowe ze wspomnień swoich i notatek napisał Mariusz Zaruski, Naczelnik Straży Ratunkowej*, Warszawa 1922 – *written*
- Zaruski Mariusz, Bobkowski Henryk, *Podręcznik narciarstwa według zasad alpejskiej szkoły jazdy na nartach*, Krakow 1908
- Paryska Zofia, Paryski Witold, Wielka Encyklopedia Tatrzańska, Poronin 1995
- Małolepszy Eligiusz, Rak Leon, Narciarstwo Polskie 1888–2008, Jasło 2009
- Pręgowski Zenobiusz, Dzieje narciarstwa polskiego do 1914 roku, Warszawa 1994

中文论文:

波兰滑雪的起源—华沙体育和旅游博物馆的收藏

华沙体育、旅游博物馆成立于1952年，它是波兰第一个体育博物馆，同时也是欧洲最古老的博物馆之一。博物馆的主要任务是收集和存储体育、旅游领域的文化商品，特别是奖杯、徽章、奖项、个人纪念品、邮票、硬币、海报、横幅、服装、体育器材、旅行配件、体育运动相关的艺术作品、照片、电影、书籍、和杂志。

2014年年底博物馆69体育学科收集了53567件文物。

滑雪收集部门已经收集了超过2500个藏品，其中只有大约100个能追溯到1918年（这一年，历经123年封地的波兰重获独立）。然而这少许的藏品却有着伟大的历史和情感意义：它是博物馆收藏的关键因素之一。

在第一历史文献中记载波兰首次使用滑雪板是在16世纪下半叶，可能之后的滑雪板被偶尔使用，但不符合质量验收标准。

直到19世纪中叶，波兰媒体报道越来越多有关挪威和高山滑雪的文章。1892年波兰文章中首次推广使用滑雪板。Leopold świerz——最受尊敬的Tatra Society成员之一，发表了一篇《*Wycieczka do Morskiego Oka zimową porą*》和另一篇关于滑雪的文章。虽然świerz不是一名滑雪者爱好者，但他鼓励扎科帕内的人使用滑雪板。

Józef Schnaider（1974-1959），是东部喀尔巴阡山的人种学家、樵夫、滑雪以及滑雪旅游的先驱。在他发行的第一本——《*a nartach skandynawskich. Podręcznik dla zwolenników sportu narciarskiego*》书中，描述了他第一个冬天对爬Mount Hoverla山的印象。这本书中第一次提到有关滑雪的信息，这些信息波兰读者之前从未接触过，包括绑定的方式、用杆支撑、鞋子、衣服、诀窍、滑雪技术。这是世界上第一本跟滑雪有关的书籍。如今这本书被收藏在博物馆，是无价之宝，同时也是滑雪部门的骄傲。

Stanisław Barabasz（1857-1949）是一名毕业于维也纳技术大学的设计师，同时也是在克拉科夫和维也纳学习美术的一名画家。他在学校做了很久的美术老师，并且拥有很强的教学能力。1901-1922年期间他担任扎科帕内伍德学校的校长，在他的领导下，学生们开始制作第一个滑雪板。

他坚持多年在扎科帕内的山区度假胜地（位于克拉科夫，在19世纪末成为波兰第一个冬季度假胜地）推广滑雪，之后他荣获“波兰现代滑雪的先锋”称号。

Barabasz非常热爱打猎，于1888年他制作了属于自己的滑雪板，协助他打猎。1914年，在一本名为《*Wspomnienia narciarza*》（它对塔特拉的滑雪起源有着重要的历史意义）的书中，他写到：“如今是八十年代（19世纪）。我们都听说过西伯利亚的故事，用驯鹿拉雪橇，雪板（用来在雪地里打猎），有人读到关于某人的滑雪板（被使用于挪威人创造奇迹的地方），因此他们的滑雪是与一只飞鸟相比的。”

“我了解的越多，我就越不敢相信，我就越想拥有这些神秘的设备。这种情况持续了好几年，1888年我拜访了我的同学，从他那里，我得知了我正在寻找的东西。雪如此的大，因此徒步走在雪地是几乎不可能的。在木匠的帮助下，我拥有了属于自己的第一副滑雪板。因为材料有限，所以一个是由火山灰制作的，另一个是由山毛榉制作的。”

“我的滑雪板很薄，中间部位厚度如同铅笔厚度，非常灵活，也很容易适应疙瘩的雪面，但是操作会很困难，因为它需要一个可以连续向前或向后的平衡装置。我保持我的双脚在一起，脚后跟挨着脚后跟，因此对我来说，道路太狭窄。”上述事件是在紧挨着 Jaslo 的 Ciekin 发生的，继 Stanisław Barabasz 之后，于 2008 年在这里建立滑雪博物馆。

华沙体育、旅游博物馆收藏了一个由火山灰制造的单板，并带有 SB 的署名。板长 163 厘米，宽 970 厘米，该板是于 1963 年从一家私人博物馆购买的。

1907 Stanisław Barabasz, Mariusz Zaruski and Mieczysław Karłowicz 这三位好友共同成立了 Tatra Society 附属的扎科帕内滑雪俱乐部，Barabasz 担任第一位会长，Zaruski 担任秘书和司库，年轻的作曲家 Karłowicz，被称为所谓的成员控制器。扎科帕内滑雪俱乐部的活动部分主要体现在滑雪课程的组织。第一次是在 1907 年组织的，Mariusz Zaruski 是主讲师。学习的课程包括雪板在雪地滑行，直线滑，曲线滑，这被 Zaruski 称为“蛇行”。课程的尾声，会测试学员获得的滑雪技能。Zaruski 训练了大量的高地人，并且指导他们学习山地滑雪。

Mieczyslaw Karłowicz 在山中悲惨死去，由此 Mariusz Zaruski 的一位朋友 Barabasz 于 1909 年帮助成立了山地志愿者搜救队。Zaruski 领导第一任志愿者搜救队（1909-1926）。该搜救队提供应急避难所，救援设备和急救用品，也出版警示海报以此警醒游客，并且他的队员都经过急救训练。

他是《山地志愿者搜救队条例》的作者，条例中，包含誓词，课程的组织和个人应对突发事项的紧急行为。他也正逐步完善《探险》一书。博物馆拥有一份 Zaruski 的《*Tatrzańskie Ochotnicze Pogotowie Ratunkowe*》的手稿。

Mariusz Zaruski（1867-1941）是文艺复兴时期的人物。著名的登山和滑雪，运动员和教练，水手，波兰海上游艇的创造者，以及年代画家，作家和诗人。在第一次世界大战爆发后，他加入了军队，由于他的勇敢并提供了有利于战争的消息，他收到了很多军事装饰，也被提升为上校，于 1923 年被授予准将的军衔。

他是一名滑雪爱好者，包括滑雪在自然条件下认知发展的价值，这是一个考验身体和精神，同时创建一个独佳的机会去发现大自然的美。他反对一切形式的竞争。

“滑雪是一项运动，但它是人类活动的一个特殊分支。冰山滑雪打开了雪山的锁螺栓，揭示了覆盖在雪下的阿尔卑斯山脉，解封了冰冻的湖泊，显示了形象山脉的山峰和 Tatra 山峰冬天沙漠的神秘。关于滑雪板，除了听和看，只有它能在雪地里行驶。滑雪能带来健康，改善形体特征，提高勇气和做决定的能力，增加了美感。”

Zaruski 很快就学会了滑雪，他可能在西伯利亚被驱逐期间（1894-1899）接触到滑雪板。他流亡的原因是俄罗斯爱国组织的活动。Stanisław Barabasz 从 1904 年就担任 Zaruski 的老师。他也读过 Mathias Zdarski 的书《奥地利学派》。

Zaruski 很快成为波兰滑雪的第一本书的作者。随后 Henryk Bobkowski 发布了一个富含他画作的手动滑雪。滑雪最大的鼓励来源于 Tatra 山上滑雪的向导，首次发布于波兰。

华沙体育、旅游博物馆拥有 Zaruski 写的几乎所有的书。有关于滑雪板和滑雪（建议和说明）的演讲和文章达 18 篇手稿。用墨水在羊皮纸上画（20 编目岗位）是致力于海洋的主题。

体育、旅游博物馆的收藏中也有 Zaruski 个人纪念品，滑雪，登山和航海设备共计十个工件。展品中间接与滑雪有关的是：带加热器的鞋，帆布手套，滑雪折叠杆。这些工件中大多数被永久的展览在博物馆的玻璃箱中——致力于山地志愿者搜救队。

波兰滑雪的开端可以在体育、旅游博物馆的照片文档中发现。1918 年之前收集的照片有几十张来自于个人，大多数来自于家庭。然而，最有趣的是从 1905-1914年收集的 170 个照片，其中一些代表着西方喀尔巴阡山（95 个对象）滑雪旅游，其他（75 个对象）代表 Tatra 山地攀岩。

其中的一些照片是由 Maksymilian Dudyk，Zygmunt Klemensiewicz 和 Roman Kordys 拍摄的，并标有“D. K. K”字样。从 1901 年，Dudyk，Klemensiewicz 和 Kodrys 就开始在 Tatra 山地徒步旅行，主要的同伴有 Mieczysław Lerski 和 Jerzy Mašlanka. 自 1904 年以来，他们一直推广 Lwow 山地旅游和滑雪。阿尔卑斯滑雪学校以及 Mathias Zdarski 使 Lwow 人人尽皆知，这得益于他们大力的推广。他回应积极游戏社会的邀请并在他的领导下于 1906 年创立滑雪课程。两周后，Dudryk，Klemensiewicz，Kordys 和 Mašlanka 在东部喀尔巴阡山组织了第一次探险，以 Doboszanka（1757 m）高峰的攀登结束。

这些独特而宝贵的视觉效果集合了 20 世纪 50 年代博物馆的资源，得益于工程师 Jerzy Mašlanka（1886-1961）——一个伟大的登山者和滑雪者。他是 Tatra Society 旅游俱乐部的成员，同时也是 Tatra 登山集团和喀尔巴阡山滑雪者俱乐部的联合创始人。1907-1910 年他成功的第一次攀登东部喀尔巴阡山峰。他同时也是摄影师和第一位拍摄视觉效果图的人，这些图被用于他的 Tatra 山脉和滑雪旅游的讲座中。

尽管这些视觉效果图有一些损坏，但是收藏在玻璃箱中的摄影被认为是最有价值的纪录片构件之一。并不是每一个画面的拍摄技术都是完美的，但是它们准确的反映了20世纪波兰早期滑雪起源和特异性的大气层。

体育、旅游博物馆拥有20世纪初建立的波兰滑雪组织的有趣的徽章。这些最老的徽章属于喀尔巴阡山滑雪者俱乐部——它们可以追溯到1907年。同年，该俱乐部成立。其中22位创始人是那个时代的知识精英代表：Kazimierz Panek，Zbigniew Klemensiewicz 和 Maksymilian Dudyk. Panek 是医疗学院的院长。尽管 Dudyk 是一位建筑师，但是 Klemensiewcz 却是一个伟大的物理学家和化学家。喀尔巴阡山滑雪者俱乐部的目的是传播我国滑雪和冬季旅游，通过适当的设备和工具来进行山地滑雪。北欧滑雪指导员参与该组织，发表滑雪及滑雪跳台指南。

徽章规格是3. 5×3. 5厘米，金属材料。他们提出把“KTN”（Karpackie Towarzystwo Narciarzy 的缩写）写在一个三角形中，还画着一个流浪汉和单板。这枚徽章是于1966年在该组织和整个波兰东部边境地区——Zbigniew Klemensiewicz and Wacław Kuchar 的一名代表者手中购买的。

早些时候，1906年，旅游学术俱乐部成立。这是继喀尔巴阡山 Tatra 山地俱乐部和波兰观光俱乐部之后的第三个波兰此类型组织。旅游学术俱乐部是由 Mieczysław Orłowicz 和 Kazimierz świtalski 组织成立的。他们是 Lwow 大学的学生并毕业于该学校——为波兰旅游提供良好的服务。Kazimierz świtalski 是波兰官员、政客和波兰总理（1929）。俱乐部组织去 Gorgany，Bieszczady and Tatra Mountains 徒步冒险，在某一时期的活动成员的数量甚至上升到400人。

20世纪60年代的体育、旅游博物馆的收藏来自于滑雪旅游学术俱乐部。1911年的搪瓷，矩形（2×3厘米），金属材质。它提出了一个蓝色背景的跳跃滑雪。缩写为 SNAKT——‘Sekcja Narciarska Akademickiego Klubu Turystycznego’。

波兰最古老的体育俱乐部，Czarni Lwow 成立于1903年，也教授滑雪技能，尽管 Czarni 主要关注足球和田径以及滑雪。该俱乐部成立之后，于东部的 Bieszczady 山（1908年1月19日）举行第一场正式的波兰跳高滑雪比赛。获胜者是 Leszek Pawłowski。之后，于1965年，他向体育、旅游博物馆出售了这枚徽章。该徽章为金属材质，椭圆形（直径为2. 5厘米），于第一次世界大战之前制作。他同时还介绍了在天空中的跳台滑雪运动员。

另一个重要的跳台滑雪时间是1月（Czarni Lwow）。Jarzyna 打破了 Kalatówki 跳山（15米）的记录，也是波兰记录的保持者。1914年，于 Sławsk、Jarzyna 赢得了喀尔巴阡山锦标赛的跳跃和跑步比赛。20世纪70年代，他的家人将他的徽章交给华沙体育、旅游博物馆。

在跑步比赛中，他赢得了一枚镀金圆形勋章，直径为4厘米。令人惊讶的是，这枚勋章描绘了跳台滑雪。

在跳越比赛中，他赢得了一枚镀金徽章，它展示了一个跳台滑雪、山景和题字："冠军的喀尔巴阡山" KIN（缩写）以及1914年（日期）。

波兰滑雪的开拓时期截止到1919年12月28日，波兰滑雪协会于这个时候成立。从这时起，大多数比赛是在该协会组织下举行的。该组织引领滑雪课程，并提供滑雪教育活动，它是波兰恢复独立后的第一个体育协会。这一组织成立是普及的最好标志，由此滑雪吸引并将继续吸引波兰大众。

最有趣的展品是跟波兰滑雪起源有关的，被陈列在常设展厅，题为"波兰的历史、体育和奥林匹克精神"。其他展品被陈列在临时展厅，便于教育节目、出版物、以及电视和电影制作之用。

波兰滑雪创业时期的物证的诞生和发展，吸引着博物馆参观者的注意，尤其是在接下来的几年里不断发展的时尚滑雪和这种体育纪律的快速发展。1929年到1939年世界滑雪锦标赛在波兰 FIS 的赞助下举办。第二次世界大战爆发前的几年时间里 Bronisław Czech 和 Stanisław Marusarz 的滑雪职业生涯发展受限。

【参考书目】

- Schnaider Józef, *Na nartach skandynawskich. Podręcznik dla zwolenników sportu narciarskiego* , Krakow, 1898
- Barabasz Stanisław, *Wspomnienia narciarza* , Zakopane 1914
- Zaruski Mariusz, *Tatrzańskie Ochotnicze Pogotowie Ratunkowe. Jego organizacja, dzieje i wyprawyratunkowe ze wspomnień swoich i notatek napisał Mariusz Zaruski, Naczelnik Straży Ratunkowej* , Warszawa 1922 - *written*
- Zaruski Mariusz, Bobkowski Henryk, *Podręcznik narciarstwa według zasad alpejskiej szkoły jazdy na nartach* , Krakow 1908
- Paryska Zofia, Paryski Witold, Wielka Encyklopedia Tatrzańska, Poronin 1995
- Małolepszy Eligiusz, Rak Leon, Narciarstwo Polskie 1888-2008, Jasło 2009
- Pręgowski Zenobiusz, Dzieje narciarstwa polskiego do 1914 roku, Warszawa 1994

4.41 A shortHistory of Finnish Skiing 芬兰滑雪简史

托尼·艾莫尼（芬兰） Tony Ilmony（FIN）

个人简介 Brief Introduction

Tony Ilmony Journalist. Owner, Messsage Maker Media. He worked with different expedition activities. Such as Mannerheims' way cross the Middle asia by horseback to Beijing.

托尼·艾莫尼 男，曾当过记者，在多地参与过多次不同的探险活动，比如曾骑马穿过亚洲中部达到北京。

English paper:

A Short History of Finnish Skiing

It was a necessity for the people of the North to speed over the snow on extraordinary implements unknown to others. Over one thousand years ago, the first dimension of Finnish culture and heritage started with survival. Hidden in the wilderness, the original Finns strapped onto their hand-fashioned boots, little more than bowls as they moved cautiously over the snow-covered landscape. During the stone and iron ages, the men were on skis during the struggles between tribes and intruders. Historically, skis are some of the oldest pieces of equipment found in the country.

In Finland, some of the oldest artifacts discovered in bog lands (the peat bogs) have been a variety of prehistoric skis in different parts of the country. Pollen dating of peat at one of the oldest sites, at Kinnula, in the southern province of Häme, gives an age of approximately 5000 years to the skis found there.

Skis from the 6th century A. D., found in a peat bog in south-central Finland had a raised footrest and were faced with skin, which prevented snow from sticking to the ski, with a badger skin toe-strap.

The Finnish word for ski is "suksi", probably of Uralic origin, which may have evolved into the Scandinavian word "ski." The word was probably first defined in Gustaf Widegren's Svenskt och Engelskt Lexicon (Swedish-English Lexicon), published in Stockholm in 1788. "Skid: a kind of scate or wooden shoe on which they slide over the snow…"

Definite regional differences in ski shapes and names existed before the advent of mass production.

The small band of foreign travelers who wrote of their experiences in Finland in the 19th century provide some of the sharpest observations of skiing in its natural setting. Paul du Chaillu's description of skiing in Finnish Lapland serves as a model for the rest of the country. Up in the north he came across several types of ski or "the queer snowshoes of the north." He saw "short ones used in the forest…where the trees are close together; long ones, for use on soft snow " so that they can bear up the weight of a man and not sink too deeply"; skis faced with sealskin, "used in spring when the snow is soft and becomes watery; the skin prevents the snow from sticking to the ski" . Du Chaillu's reference to 'queer snowshoes' may be misleading to today's reader. However, it is certain that he means skis, not the snowshoes of the North American continent, which never caught on in Finland.

Thus, the ski was a working aid and an important means of transport in Finland from prehistoric times until the last quarter of the 19th century. A local observer in the southern parish of Hauho wrote in the 1880s that one seldom saw a ski exceptoutside the huts of foresters, who used them for the journey to and from work.

Skis served Finland in the past and particularly well during the war with Russia some 70 years ago. Without the sniper ski patrols dressed in their all white ski suits-the outcome might have been different. Skis had a big role in keeping Finland independent.

Today skis are mostly something to have fun with.

Sports and Competitions are a way of having fun and improving knowledge and skills. This too has a long tradition.

As a matter of necessity, toddlers learned to ski as they learned to crawl and walk. School children skied to school and home again, did their lessons and hopped back outside on skis. They skied and played until they had to head for their warm log homes at bedtime. Racing through the forests of Finland was a part of daily winter life. Skiing must be in the genes of the Finns.

中文论文：

芬兰滑雪简史

对于北部的人们来说，使用工具提升在雪上的运行速度是很有必要你的一件事。一千年前，芬兰文化的首要层面是生存。早期的芬兰人或躲在荒野中，或将脚绑在手工制作的靴子里，小心谨慎地在冰雪覆盖的地貌中行走。在石器和铁器时代，雪板上的人们在部落与侵略者之间挣扎。在历史时期，滑雪板是发现于这个国家最古老的工具之一。

在芬兰，发现于沼泽地中的一些古老的手工制品就是史前时期的各种各样的滑雪板。在 Häme 省南部发现了一处古老的遗址地，在此处发现的雪板大约可追溯到 5000 年前。

公元 6 世纪的雪板发现于芬兰中南部的泥炭沼泽地，雪板上有突出的搁脚物，并附有獾皮套趾皮带，以防雪粘着在雪板上。

滑雪一词的意义用芬兰语表示是“套趾雪板”，可能起源于乌拉尔语系，后又发展成为斯堪的纳维亚语“ski”。滑雪一词的定义首次出现在 Gustaf Widegren 的 Svenskt och Engelskt Lexicon（Swedish-English Lexicon），发表于 1788 年的斯德哥尔摩。在滑雪板大量生产之前，不同的地区对雪板的形状和名字有不能同的定义。

19 世纪，一群外国旅行者在芬兰的的旅行经历在自然环境方面为了解当地滑雪文化提供了大量有用信息。Paul du Chaillu 对芬兰拉普兰郡滑雪的描述为其他国家提供了一个范例。在北部地区他看到几种不同的滑雪板或“不同种类的奇怪的雪鞋”。他看到“短的雪鞋用于森林中；长的雪鞋用于粉雪中，所以它们能够承受人的体重”。附有海豹皮的雪板用于雪变得柔软且有些融化的春天。Du Chaillu 所提到的“奇怪的雪鞋”可能会误导今天的读者，但它确实表示雪板，而不是美洲大陆北部的雪鞋，它们在芬兰从未流行过。

因此，从史前时期到 19 世纪后页，雪板在芬兰被当作一种重要的交通运输方式。在 Hauho 南部教区的一位观察者曾写到，在 1880s，除了在森林木屋外的区域，人们很少看到滑雪板，雪板主要用于人们的工作和长距离的旅行。

雪板在芬兰主要应用于过去，尤其是 70 年前的对俄作战中。倘若没有穿着雪板的狙击手巡逻兵，战争的结果可能就大不相同。雪板在芬兰取得独立的过程中发挥了重大作用。

当今，雪板主要用于娱乐。雪板用于体育和竞技是大众获得娱乐和提升知识和技巧的方式。这个传统由来已久。

作为一种必要的技巧，孩童在他们刚会爬行和走路时就学习滑雪，学龄儿童在学校和家里学习滑雪或户外滑雪。他们滑雪、玩耍，直到晚上睡前时间。在芬兰的丛林中穿梭滑行是人们冬季生活的一部分，滑雪已深深融入芬兰人的基因中。

4.42　挪威奥普兰冰川及流冰区的史前滑雪板　PrehistoricSkis from Glaciers and Ice Patches in Oppland, Norway

埃斯·分斯塔德（挪威）　Espen Finstad（NOR）
拉斯·皮罗（丹麦）　Lars Pilo（DEN）

个人简介　Brief Introduction

Espen Finstad (50), Lillehammer, Norway, Archaeologist, Oppland County Council

Academic: 1987, Engineer 1998, Archaeology, master, University of Oslo

Personal experience

I have been working as a county archaeologist in Oppland since 1999. My main job is to develop cultural heritage into interesting projects for tourists and local people.

When I was younger I was active in cross-country skiing, biathlon and telemark-skiing. I have worked as a mountain guide, including mountaineering and glacier-walking. I have been on a number of expeditions in the arctic areas of Canada and Russia. From 1994-96 I was a member of the Olympic International Environmental Expedition from Norway to Japan, using skis and dog sledges from Lillehammer to Murmansk and through the North-East Passage to Nagano

I have been involved in glacier archaeology for more than ten years. Due to recent finds of prehistoric skis from the ice in Oppland I have developed an interest in early skiing.

埃斯·芬斯塔德（50），利勒哈默，挪威，考古学家，奥普兰郡

学术成就：1987，工程师；1998，奥斯陆大学考古学硕士

个人经历

自1999年以来我是奥普兰郡的考古学家。我的主要工作是去将文化遗产开发成吸引游客和当地人的项目。

在我小时候，我积极参加越野滑雪、运动两项和屈膝旋转滑雪。我曾经做过登山向导，工作包括登山和冰川漫步。我在加拿大和俄罗斯的极地地区进行了多次探险。从1994-96年我是挪威到日本的国际奥林匹克环境探险协会的成员，使用滑雪板和狗雪橇从挪威的利勒哈默到俄罗斯的摩尔曼斯克以及穿过东北通道到日本的长野县。

我参与冰川考古已经十年了。由于最近在奥普兰冰川中的发现，我已经对远

古滑雪产生了兴趣。

个人简介　Brief Introduction

Lars Pilø（53），Lillehammer，Norway Archaeologist，Oppland County Council

Academic：1989，Archaeology，master，University of Bergen 2003，Archaeology，Ph. D.，University of Oslo

Personal experience

I have been working as an archaeologist in Oppland Countysince2007. I have been the director of the glacier archaeology program in Oppland since 2009. Before this I was a researcher at the University of Oslo.

My main interest and expertise is complex and demanding archaeological field work. This has drawn me to glacier archaeology, which is as hard as it gets. I also like to work together with researchers from other disciplines than archaeology. In the case ofglacierarchaeologythisespeciallyinvolvescooperatingwithclimate scientists.

I am not much of a skier, having grown up in Denmark.

拉斯 ·皮罗（53），利勒哈默尔，丹麦，考古学家，奥普兰郡议会

学术成就：1989，卑尔根大学考古学硕士，2003，奥斯陆大学考古学博士

个人经历

自2007年以来，我在奥普兰郡做考古学家。自2009年以来，我成为奥普兰冰川考古项目的主管。在此之前，我是奥斯陆大学的研究者。

我主要的兴趣和专长是复杂而苛刻的考古现场工作。这也吸引了我去学习冰川考古学，它是十分困难的。我也喜欢和来自其他领域的研究者一起工作。冰川考古方面特别涉及与气候学家的合作。

photos displayed in the speech 讲演稿所展示的图片

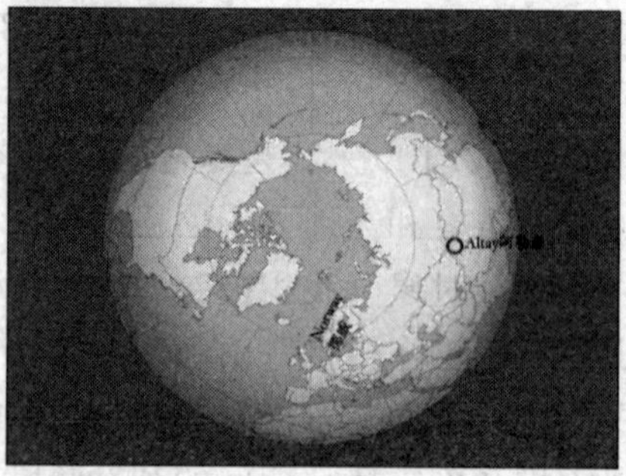

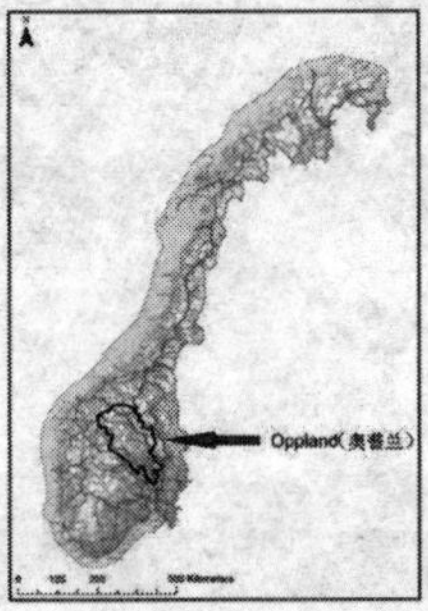
Oppland(奥普兰)

Galdhøpiggen, 2469 m
加尔赫峰, 2469 m

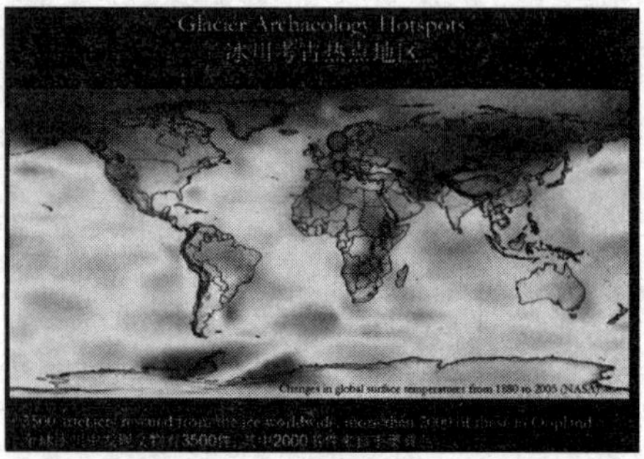
Glacier Archaeology Hotspots
冰川考古热点地区
Changes in global surface temperatures from 1880 to 2005 (NASA)

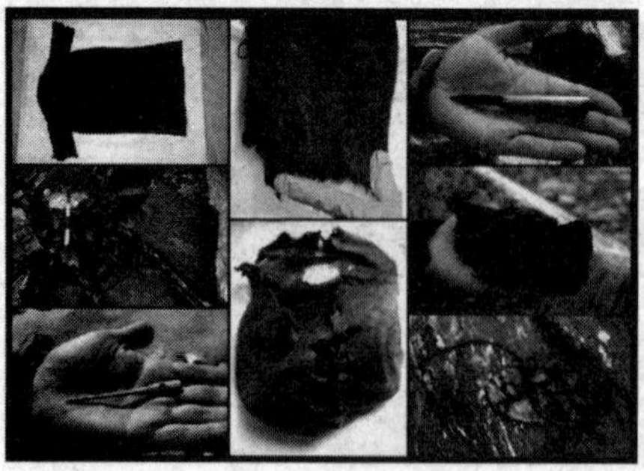

Prehistoric skis
史前滑雪板
Rock carvings
石雕
Based on Karin Berg 1993
依据卡琳·博格

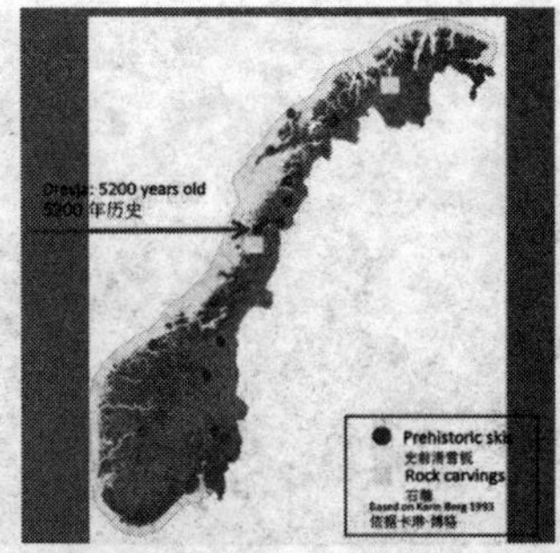
5200 years old
5200 年历史
Prehistoric skis
史前滑雪板
Rock carvings
石雕
Based on Karin Berg 1993
依据卡琳·博格

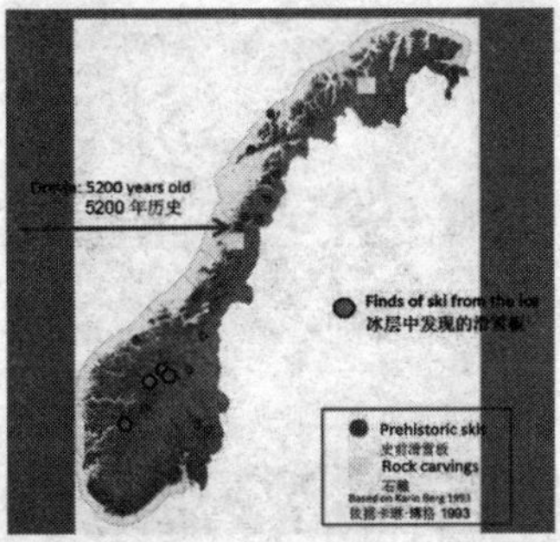
5200 years old
5200 年历史
Finds of ski from the ice
冰层中发现的滑雪板
Prehistoric skis
史前滑雪板
Rock carvings
石雕
Based on Karin Berg 1993
依据卡琳·博格 1993

2600 BP

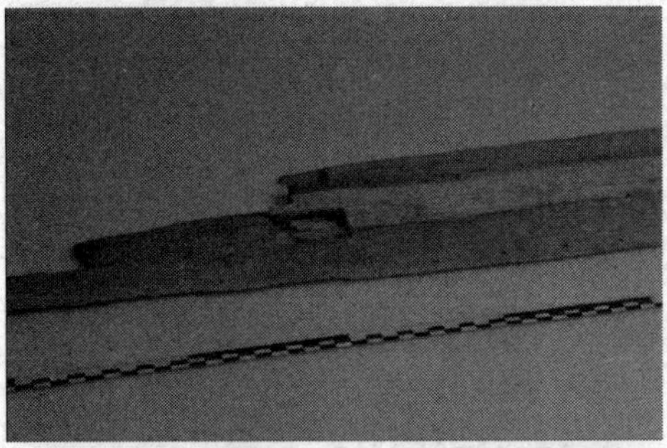

The Reinheimen ski,
as it was found,
close to the ice
1300 BP

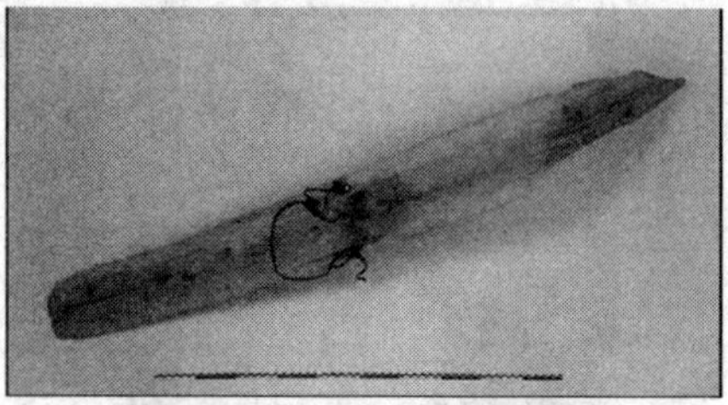

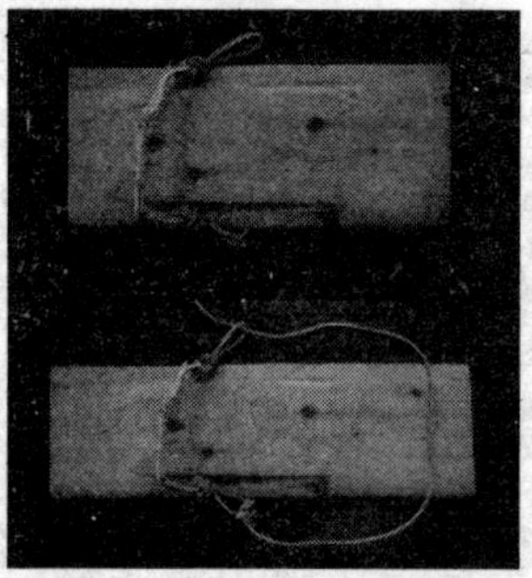

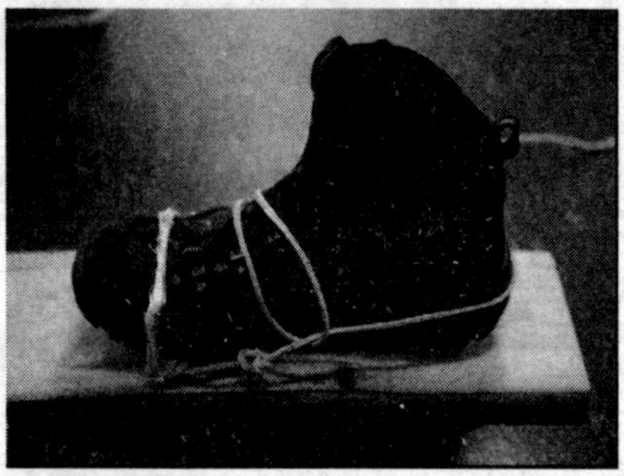

English Paper:

PrehistoricSkis from Glaciers and Ice Patches in Oppland, Norway

Espen Finstad and Lars Pilø
Oppland County Council, Department of Cultural Heritage

Abstract:

Two prehistoric skis have melted out of glacial ice in the high mountains of Southern Norway in the last three years. The best preserved is a 1300 year old ski, which has a nearly intact binding. The oldest ski is around 2700 years old. It is partially preserved and contains holes along the edges showing that it was originally fur-lined. The skis were found during the recovery of artefacts which have melted out of glaciers and ice patches in Oppland County. More than 2000 artefacts have been collected from around 50 glaciers and ice patches. The oldest object is an arrow shaft, which is nearly 6000 years old. The artefacts that are melting out give us a unique view into a material culture which was thought to have been lost forever. They also give an insight into the use of the high mountains by ancient humans.

The ice is melting due to climate change. It is possible, maybe even likely, that more prehistoric skis will melt out of the ice in Norway in the coming years, yielding an important new source material for the history of skiing. Since the melting of ice is a global phenomenon perhaps there is also a chance that skis will melt out of glacial ice in other parts of the world with a long history of skiing. However, if the melting ice is not monitored, the frozen finds may disappear a short time after being exposed to the elements, and an important source material may be lost forever.

Introduction

The main focus of this presentation is two prehistoric skis which have melted out of glacial ice in Oppland County during the last three years. One of the skis is 2700 years old and was originally fur-lined. The other is 1300 years old and is nearly complete, including most of the binding. These skis are interesting, not only from a ski-historical point of view, but also as a source of a better understanding of past life in the mountains.

First some words about the geographical context. Oppland County is a mountainous region in the interior of Southern Norway. The county has the highest mountain of Northern Europe-Mount Galdhøpiggen at 2469 meters above sea level. The oldest settlement sites in the interior are around 10 000 years old, from just after the ice melted. The sites are connected to the hunting of reindeer in the mountains and moose in the valleys.

The reindeer is a herd animal which migrates over large distances between summer and winter pastures. In the winter they stay in the lower-lying mountain area in the east, where there is little wind, powder snow and less difficulty in finding food. In the summer the reindeer migrate to the west, into the high alpine mountain region. Here the pastures were good and the glacial ice provided relief from pestering insects. However, the ice also provided an important hunting ground for humans.

Moose have a different migratory pattern. They are often more stationary, but some of the moose move between seasonal pastures, up to 70 kilometers in distance.

Modern infrastructure (like roads) has stopped the large migration of reindeer today. However, the routes used by the animals in the past can be studied by indirect means. The ancient migratory routes were blocked by pitfall traps still preserved today, sometimes in long rows. The longest contains 1200 traps and is strategically placed between the former summer and winter pastures of the reindeer.

Mobility was the key to be able to survive as a hunter in this landscape of high mountains, deep valleys and migrating game. During the winter the snow was hard-packed in the mountains and deep and loose in the valleys. Skiing and/or snowshoes very probably were an essential part of a hunter's life here. Without skis or snowshoes it would have been very difficult to move around in the winter. However, just as here in Altay, we have no preserved skis from the earliest settlement of the interior.

Skis are made of organic materials and only rarely survive the millennia that have passed since they were in use. Most of the prehistoric skis in the world have been found in bogs due to the good preservation conditions here. During the last years a new context has yielded valuable and previously unknown source material for ancient skiing-glacial ice in the high alpine regions of Oppland.

The Archaeology of Ice

The recovery of the ice mummy Ötzi in the Alps in 1991 was the starting point for a new branch of archaeology known as glacial archaeology. Since then artefacts have melted out of high alpine glacial ice in Alaska, Northwest Canada, Rocky Mountains, the Alps and Norway. They derive from hunting and transport on the ice. The artefacts have been preserved in the ice for thousands of years, but are now melting out due to climate change. Norway was recently described as Ground Zero for this type of archaeology in the magazine Science, since the melting of old ice containing artefacts is markedly greater here.

The Department of Cultural Heritage at Oppland County Council has an on-going program for the rescue of artefacts from glacial ice. More than 2000 artefacts have been recovered from 50 glaciers and ice patches so far. This constitutes more than half of the finds worldwide. The large number of artefacts is probably due to a combination of factors, including the proximity of the high alpine ice to the settled valleys and intensive hunting of reindeer in the past.

With one exception the find spots derive from ancient reindeer hunting-arrows, bows and other hunting equipment. The oldest arrow is nearly 6000 years old. However, the Lendbreen glacier is different: It contains a mountain path from the Iron Age and the Medieval Period (ca. 1700-800 before present) crossing the ice. The artefacts from the mountain path have a completely different character-among these are remains of clothing, shoes, bones from packhorses which died on the ice, horse-manure and horse-shoes, transport equipment and walking sticks (one with a runic inscription).

Among the many interesting finds from the ice we also finds prehistoric skis. They provide an important new source material to the history of ancient skiing.

Prehistoric skis from glaciers and ice patches in Norway

Around 20 skis from prehistory and the Medieval Period (i. e. more than 500 years old) have been found in Norway (Berg 1993). Most of the skis have been found in Northern and Eastern Norway, and until recently mainly in bogs. The oldest ski is a partially preserved ski found in Drevja in Northern Norway. It is dated by radiocarbon to be 5200 years old.

Four skis have been recovered from glacial ice in Norway. Two of these finds appeared several decades ago. A ski was recovered from the Vosseskavlen ice patch in Western Norway and is radiocarbon dated to be around 800 years old. Another ski was recovered from the Dalafonn ice patch in Lesja municipality and is radiocarbon dated to be around 1000 years old. Two skis have been recovered recently in connection with the Glacier Archaeology Program in Oppland and we will describe these in greater detail here.

The Lendbreen ski

The older of the two skis was found at the previously mentioned site Lendbreen in the Breheimen National Park. Lendbreen is a large ice mass even now after heavy melting, currently covering ca. 350. 000m^2, but it was much larger in the past. Many of the artefacts recovered from Lendbreen are damaged (maybe by ice movement), and many have also been displaced by meltwater running down the 30% incline on top of the ice.

Four fragments of the ski have been recovered so far during archaeological fieldwork 2011-14. The distance between the recovered fragments of the ski is up to 300 m. More pieces may still be inside the preserved ice. The ski is radiocarbon-dated to be 2600-2700 years old. This makes it the second oldest ski found in Norway, only surpassed by the Drevja-ski mentioned earlier.

The ski is made of pine. The left side and one end of the ski have not been found yet (if they are still preserved). Since the center and right side are preserved it is possible to estimate the original width based on symmetry. The length is more difficult to estimate; even more so since it is not clear if the preserved end is the tip or the back of the ski. After being fitted together the preserved fragments measure 68 cm in length and 13 cm in width. Based on symmetry the original width of the ski was approximately 18 cm at the binding and 20 cm at the preserved end. The thickness is greatest in the center -1. 5 cm, while the thickness at the edges is only 0. 5 cm. It should, however, be noted that the wood probably has shrunk somewhat in thickness.

The binding area of the ski is preserved, but is broken into four parts of which one part is missing. The binding area contains two rectangular depressions which are 5. 3 x 3. 2 cm (1 cm deep), separated by 3. 4 cm of wood. Through the wood between the two rectangular depressions there is a narrow passage measuring 3. 4 cm in width and 0. 6 cm in height. The binding must have passed through here, and since the passage is so narrow, the material for the binding was most likely leather. The holes for the binding are placed 4. 5 cm from the outer edge of the ski (based on the preserved side).

The length from the end of the ski to the center of the binding is 42 cm. If the binding was placed symmetrically in the center of the ski this would provide a length of 84 cm. However, it is likely that the back part was longer than the front part of the ski, to avoid too much pressure on the snow below the back part. Since we do not know if it is the front or the back of the ski that is preserved, the exact length of the original is difficult to determine. However, in both cases the ski is so short that it would have been difficult to use for gliding through the snow. More likely it was used to allow for transport through deep powder snow.

Along the edges of the ski there are small holes with a distance of 4 cm. For the experts on the skis of Altay this feature is easy to understand: The holes derive from the fastening of fur-lining with sinew.

The ski from Lendbreen is without parallels in the known ski material from Norway. It is relatively short and wide. The binding is unique in Norway. The fur-lining is known from more recent Scandinavian skis (Berg 1993, Sørensen 1993), from Russia and of course here in the Altay, where there is still a living and fascinating tradition using wide, fur-lined skis.

The Reinheimen ski

The ski from Reinheimen National Park was found at the edge of an ice patch in Reinheimen National Park in the autumn of 2014, i. e. just a few months ago. It has been radiocarbon dated to be ca. 1300 years old. The same ice patch has also yielded finds of arrows from reindeer hunting, one of which was from the same period as the ski.

The Reinheimen ski is of a more well-known type. It belongs to Ernst Mankers type C (1971): Ski with a raised foot-rest narrower than the actual ski, and with a horizontal binding hole passing under the foot. The Reinheimen ski is complete, but a few small pieces have broken off the right side of front part. The ski is made of birch, is 170 cm long and the width is 14. 7 cm. The thickness is greatest in the binding area (2. 9 cm). The thickness is otherwise around 1 cm, which is probably somewhat less than the original thickness due to shrinking.

What is really special about the Reinheimen ski is that the binding is preserved. Preserved binding on prehistoric skis is very rare, and the only published example we know beside the Reinheimen ski is the 1500 year old Mänttä ski, published by Janne Vilkuna (1998). In the horizontal hole passing under the foot of the Reinheimen ski there are remains of a twisted branch of birch used as a wooden rope in the binding around the front of the foot. A double leather string goes through the same hole. On both sides this string forms a loop. A long leather string is fastened to the left loop. Most likely this long string is part of a heel binding.

There is a small round hole in the tip of the ski. This feature is also known from other prehistoric skis and from the traditional skis to day. One explanation for this hole is that it is a remnant from the bending of the ski tip. It is also known that rope or string was attached to the hole to allow for dragging the skis when the skier was walking on foot. A third known function is that strings were attached to the ski tip to facilitate steering when going downhill.

Types of binding have been much discussed in publications on ski history (Berg 1993). The oldest drawings documenting Norwegian ski binding is from the 17th century. They depict a toe-binding of twisted birch and a heel binding of leather. Sami skis from the last two-three hundred years also have both toe-and heel-binding, but show many different types of binding techniques (Berg 1993). Both the Mänttä ski and the Reinheimen ski show that the use of a heel-binding has long traditions. Skis with a heel-binding give a much better stability and makes it possible to add power to the step forward, than skis with just a toe-binding-which is a great help when going uphill. With a heel-binding it is also much easier to steer during skiing downhill or on flats. Skis with only a toe-binding are more suitable when the ski is used intermittently.

The context

Both skis have been recovered from glacial ice in the high mountains, in areas where there are still large numbers of reindeer during the summer months. The Lendbreen ski is found in an area where there was a mountain path one thousand years later, and it is not certain whether this ski should be linked to transport over the ice or hunting on the ice. The Reinheimen ski was recovered from a ice patch together with other artefacts connected to hunting.

During cold climatic periods with lots of snow many of the mountains tops were covered in snow for most of the year. Written sources dating back to the 13th century tell about hunters skiing downhill and catching up on the fleeing reindeer this way (Kongsspeilet). The reindeer were killed with spears and bow and arrow. This type of hunting technique is also known from more recent times, using rifles (Lumholtz 1926).

The conditions we have described from our part of Norway are not that different from Altay-high mountains, steep hills and forested valleys. The winters are cold and snowy. Both places have deer which have been hunted by humans throughout history. Here in Altay we can experience a living tradition of using skis for transport and for hunting deer in the steep slopes. The parallels are interesting and could provide fertile ground for further studies.

Glaciers and ice patches as a source of ancient skis

A lot of work is still needed to analyze the finds from the glaciers and ice patches in

Oppland. However, it is already clear that the prehistoric skis from the ice are shedding new light on the history of skis and skiing. The finds from Oppland may indicate that similar finds of ski could appear from melting ice also in other parts of the world, be it in connection with old mountain paths or ancient hunting grounds. Based on our experience as glacier archaeologists it would be interesting to discuss whether the Altay region could also yield such interesting finds from a frozen past. In this way new light could be shed on the ancient ski history of the Altay region.

Thank you.

Litteratur:

Berg, Karin 1993. *Ski i Norge*. Aventura. Oslo.

Kongsspeilet (The King's Mirror). Translated by A. W. Brøgger. Aschehoug. Oslo.

Lumholtz, Ludvig 1926. *Jægerliv*. Gyldendal. Oslo

Manker, Ernst 1971. Fennoskandias fornskidor. *Fornvännen* 66.

Sørensen, Steinar 1993. *Skifunnet fra Steinhaugmo og de skinnkledde skiene i Fennoskandinavisk fortid*. Viking 1993.

Steinar, Sørensen 1997. *Helleristninger som skihistorisk kilde*. Adoraten 1997.

Vilkuna, Janne 1998. The binding of the prehistoric ski from Mänttä, Finland. *History of Skiing Conference*, *Oslo* in 1998.

中文论文：

挪威奥普兰冰川及流冰区的史前滑雪板

埃斯·分斯塔德 和拉斯·皮罗　奥普兰郡议会，文化遗产局

摘要：在挪威南部高山地区，过去三年的冰川消融使得两只史前滑雪板暴露在人们面前。保存最好的是一个1300年历史的滑雪板，其有着完整的捆绑物。最古老的滑雪板大约有2700年历史，它只有一部分被保存了下来，其边沿处的孔显示它最初使用“毛皮衬里”。这些滑雪板是在考古学家探寻哪些随着奥普兰郡地区冰川及流冰消融而出现的文物时发现的。从50个冰川及流冰区已经收集到超过2000个文物。其中最古老的文物是一个有着近6000多年历史的箭杆。这些文物给了我们一个独特的视角去了解一种我们原本以为已经永远失去的物质文明。这些文物也使我们有机会深入了解远古人类如何利用高山地区。

冰川因气候变化而消融。在未来几年，人们可能会在挪威发现更多冰川下的滑雪板，他们会是研究滑雪板历史的重要源材料。因为冰川消融已是一种全球现

象，所以在世界其他有着悠久滑雪历史的地区也可能会在冰川融化后发现滑雪板。然而，如果不对融化的冰川进行检测，那融冰文物会在暴露出地表后极快消失，那我们就会永远失去一个重要的源材料。

前言：这次展示的重点是两个史前滑雪板，过去三年奥普兰郡的冰川消融使他们暴露出地表。其中一个有着2700年历史的滑雪板最初是用皮毛衬里的。另一个有着1300年历史，并完整地被保存了下来，包含大量的捆绑物。这些滑雪板不管是从滑雪历史研究角度来看，还是作为更好理解远古人类在山区的生活的原始材料都是十分令人关注的。

首先介绍一些关于地理环境的词汇。奥普兰是位于挪威中南部的一个山区。这个郡有着北欧最高的山峰— 加尔赫峰（海拔2469米）。有大约10000年历史的最古老的定居点随着冰川消融出现在了人们面前。这个定居点是与山里打猎驯鹿和山谷打猎麋鹿相关的。

驯鹿是一种群体动物，他们会在夏冬草原间进行远距离的迁徙。冬天，他们呆在东部有着低洼土壤的山区，那里冬天风小、雪量大及找食物更加容易。夏天，驯鹿迁徙到西部，进入高山地区。那的草原十分肥美，冰川可以使他们摆脱恼人的蚊虫。然而，这些冰也为人类提供了重要的打猎区。

麋鹿有着不同的迁徙方式。麋鹿更加平稳，但也有一些麋鹿会在季节草场之间迁移，距离不会超过70公里。

现代基础设施比如公路现在已经阻挡了驯鹿的迁徙。但是，通过一些间接手段可以研究动物过去的迁徙路线。远古时期的动物迁徙路线被陷阱阻隔，这些陷阱至今仍被保留着，有时候他们是一长排。最长的包含1200个陷阱，他们被有策略性地布置在驯鹿冬夏草原的迁徙路线上。

对于一个生活在高山低谷地形且有着迁移运动地区的猎人来说，移动是关键。在冬天，山上的雪是硬邦邦的，而山谷里的雪是深且松的。滑雪板或雪鞋可能是猎人生活中的必需品。没有他们在雪地里移动是十分困难的。但是，在阿勒泰地区最早的定居地我们没有找到保留的滑雪板。

滑雪板是有机材料制作的。自从使用滑雪板以来，滑雪板仅仅存在一千年。世界上大部分的史前滑雪板是在沼泽中被发现的，原因就在于沼泽提供可较好的保存条件。过去的几年中，一个新的环境— 奥普兰高山地区的冰川，已经为远古滑雪提供了有价值的且不计其数的源材料。

冰川考古

1991年在阿尔卑斯山上冰人奥兹的发现是考古学一个新分支（被称为冰川考古）的起点。那之后在阿拉斯加、加拿大西北部、落基山脉、阿尔卑斯山以及挪威的冰川消融后很多文物被发现了。文物已经在冰里保存了数千年，但现在由于气候变化被暴露了出来。挪威近来在科学杂志上被誉为这一考古类型的着地点，因为远古冰川所包含的文物明显更多。

奥普兰郡的文化遗产局正在进行一个项目即营救冰川里的文化。到目前为止，在 50 个冰川及流冰区已经发现有超过 2000 文物，这相当于全球冰川文物的一半。大量的文物可能是归功于多种因素结合，包括阿尔卑斯高山冰层与定居的山谷十分接近以及过去对驯鹿密集的狩猎因素。

有一个例外是，发现地点源自古代驯鹿狩猎— 弓箭及其他狩猎设备。最古老的弓箭有将近 6000 年历史。但是，Lendbreen 冰川不同与此：它包含一条铁器时代和中世界时期（大约距今 1700–800 年）的穿越冰川的山道。从山道上发现的文物有着完全不同的特点，这些文物有衣服、鞋子、死在冰中的驮马的骨骼、马粪、马蹄铁、交通工具以及拐杖（其中一个上面刻有北欧文字）。

在很多冰川中发现的有趣文物中，我们也发现可史前滑雪板。他们是研究古滑雪历史十分重要的新的源材料。

挪威冰川及流冰区的史前滑雪板

大约有 20 个史前及中世纪（即超过 500 年历史）的滑雪板早在 1993 就在挪威的冰山被发现了。大多数滑雪板是在挪威北部和东部被发现的，近来主要是在沼泽中发现的。最古老的滑雪板是在挪威北部的 Drevja 发现的只得到部分保存的滑雪板，经放射性碳鉴定年代为 5200 年历史。

在挪威冰川中已经发现了四个滑雪板，其中两个是在几十年前出现的。一个在挪威西部的 Vosseskavlen 冰道发现的滑雪板经放射性碳鉴定为有大约 800 年历史。另一个滑雪板发现于在 Lesja 的 Dalaform 冰道上发现的，被鉴定为有大约 1000 年历史。最近发现的滑雪板是与奥普兰冰川考古项目相关的。接下来我们将详细介绍这两个滑雪板。

Lendbreen 滑雪板

两只滑雪板中历史较久的一个发现于之前提到的地点，在 Breheimen 国家公园的 Lendbreen 流冰区。Lendbreen 是即使在大规模消融后还依然是较大的流冰区，现在它的面积为 350000 平方米，过去的面积必定更大。在这里发现的很多文物都有破损（可能是由于冰川运动造成的）。很多文物是被融化的水流从坡度 30%的冰层顶端冲下来的。

滑雪板的四个部分的是在 2011–2014 年间的考古工作中发现的。滑雪板发现部分之间的最大距离是 300 米。其他部分可能仍在现有的冰层中。滑雪板经放射性碳鉴定为有 2600–2700 年历史。因而，这个地板是挪威现在发现的第二古老的滑雪板，仅有 Drevja–滑雪板是比它稍古老一些。

滑雪板是松木制的。滑雪板的左边和一个末端至今仍未被找到（如果他们被保存下来的话）。因为右边和中间部分都被保留了下来，所以现在可以用对称原则来推测滑雪板的原本宽度。但是长度很难估算，因为现在不清楚我们找到的部分是滑雪板的前端还是后面。在被拼在一起后，现有部分长度为68cm，宽13cm。根据对称性来说，滑雪板在捆绑处的原始宽度大约是18cm，在现存的尾端是20cm。中间的厚度最大— 1.5cm，边缘处厚度最小为0.5cm。然而，根据记载它可能会在厚度上有些收缩。

滑雪板的捆绑部分被保存下来了，但它破损成四块，有一块仍未找到。捆绑区包含两个长方形的（面积为 5.3 ×3.2cm，深 1cm，中间被一根 3.4cm 的木头分开）。通过两个长方形槽之间的木头有一个宽 3.4cm 高 0.6cm 的窄道。捆绑物必定是穿过这个通道。并且因为这个通道这么窄，所以捆绑物很可能是皮革品。捆绑物的洞被安置在滑雪板外部边缘处 4.5cm 处（根据现存边缘计算）。

滑雪板尾端到捆绑物中心的距离是 42cm。如果捆绑物对称地放置在滑雪板的中心，那这将提供长度 84 cm。然而，滑板后面可能比前面要长，以此来避免雪板后面在雪上施加更多的压力。因为我们不知道现存部分是滑雪板的前面还是后面，原始滑板的精确原始长度很难确定。在两种情况下，滑雪板都太短了以至于很难使用它来滑雪。它更可能是用于穿越深粉雪的运输。

在滑板边缘有一排小孔，间距为 4cm。对于阿勒泰滑雪板方面的专家来说，这个特点很容易理解：这些洞是用筋固定毛皮衬里时用的。

来自于 Lendbreen 的滑雪板与挪威已知的滑雪板材料毫无相似之处。它相对短、宽。捆绑物在挪威是独特的。人们从最近的斯堪的纳维亚滑雪板（伯格 1993，索伦森 1993）以及至今仍有使用宽的、毛皮衬里的滑雪板传统的俄罗斯和阿勒泰地区了解到毛皮衬里。

Reinheimen 滑雪板

来自于 Reinheimen 国家公园的滑雪板是 2014 年秋天在这一公园的一个冰道边发现的。经放射性碳鉴定，它已有大约 1300 年历史。在同一条冰道上也发现了驯鹿狩猎的箭，其中一个是与冰川来自同一时期。

Reinheimen 滑雪板是一种比较著名的类型。它属于恩迪特·曼克的 C 类型：这类滑雪板比一般滑雪板多一个脚踏窄板，脚底有一个水平的绑定洞。Reinheimen 滑雪板是完整的，但是前面的右边部分有几小块破损。这一滑雪板由桦木制成，长 170cm，宽 14.5cm。最大厚度是在捆绑区（2.9cm）。其他地区的厚度大约 1 cm，但由于收缩原因这可能比原始厚度要薄。

Reinheimen 滑雪板最特别的是捆绑物保存了下来。现存的史前滑雪板上的捆绑物是极少有的，我们知道的除了 Reinheimen 滑雪板之外就只有 1500 年历史的 Mänttä 滑雪板了，它是 1998 年由 Janne Vilkuna 公开的。Reinheimen 滑雪板脚下穿过的水平绑定洞里仍然保留着一个扭曲的桦树枝，它被作为一根木绳用于绑定脚的前部。一个双层的皮绳也穿过这个洞，因此这个皮绳在两边就形成一个环。一根长皮绳被固定在左边的环里，这个长皮绳最可能是用于绑定脚后跟的。

在滑雪板的尖端有一个小圆孔。其他的史前滑雪板和现今的传统滑雪板也具有这个特点。对于这个孔的一个解释是：它位于滑雪板尖端的弯曲处。众所周知的是，穿在洞里的绳线可以允许滑雪者在走路的时候拖住滑雪板。第三个功能是，绳子绑在滑雪板尖端可帮助允许滑雪者在下坡时改变方向。

在滑雪板历史（伯格 1993）上，捆绑物的类型已经被多次讨论。最早的挪威滑雪板捆绑物的图纸资料是在 17 世纪。他们描画了一根弯曲桦树的脚趾捆绑绳以及一根皮革的脚后跟捆绑绳。约两三百年的萨米滑雪板也有脚趾和脚后跟固定绳，但显示的是捆绑技术的不同类型（伯格 1993）。Mänttä 和 Reinheimen 滑雪板都指明后跟捆绑是一个很长时间的传统。有脚后跟捆绑的滑雪板要比只有脚趾固定的滑雪板更加稳定和更可能增加前进的力量，脚趾捆绑的滑雪板更有利于上山。有后跟绑定也会使滑雪者在下坡或平地上更容易控制。有脚趾捆绑的滑雪板在间歇使用滑雪板是更加适当。

研究范围

这两个滑雪板都是从高山地区的冰川中发现的，在夏季时那仍然有很多驯鹿。Lendbreen 滑雪板发现地一千年前曾是一个山道，现在还不能确定这个雪板是用于冰上运输还是冰上狩猎。Reinheimen 滑雪板发现于一个冰道上，和其他文物一起被证明为是用于狩猎的。

在有大量降雪的寒冷气候时期很多山顶常年被雪覆盖。13 世纪的书面材料上说到猎人滑雪下山并以这种方式追赶逃离的驯鹿（Kongsspeilet）。驯鹿被矛，弓、箭杀死。这种打猎技术也是最近使用步枪狩猎为人们多熟知（Lumholtz 1926）。

以上所描述的条件在我们地区（挪威）与在阿勒泰地区区别并不大 — 高山、陡坡和森林山谷；冬天都很寒冷而且降雪量大。两个地区都有自古以来一直被人狩猎的鹿。在阿勒泰，我们可以体验一种生活的传统——使用滑雪板运输和在陡坡上狩猎鹿。这两种并存的方式十分有趣，并为以后的研究提供了“肥沃的土壤”。

冰川和流冰作为古代滑雪板的源头

分析奥普兰地区冰川和流冰区的文物仍有很多工作要做。但现在很明确的是，来自冰川中的远古滑雪板在滑雪板及滑雪历史上闪出新希望。奥普兰地区的发现可能表明类似于滑雪板的发现也会出现在世界其他消融的冰川中，这些冰川是与古老的山道或古代狩猎区相关的。根据我们作为冰川考古学家的经验，讨论阿勒泰地区冰冻时期是否也会有有趣的发现将是十分吸引人的。这样，新的光芒就会照耀在阿勒泰地区的古代滑雪历史上。

谢谢！

【参考文献】

卡琳·博格 1993. *Ski i Norge*. Aventura。奥斯陆

Kongsspeilet（The King's Mirror）. 由 A. W. Brøgger. Aschehoug 翻译。奥斯陆

Lumholtz, Ludvig 1926. *Jægerliv*. Gyldendal。奥斯陆

Manker, Ernst 1971. Fennoskandias fornskidor . *Fornvännen* 66.

Sørensen, Steinar 1993. *Skifunnet fra Steinhaugmo og de skinnkledde skiene i Fennoskandinavisk fortid* . Viking 1993。

Steinar, Sørensen 1997. *Helleristninger som skihistorisk kilde*. Adoraten 1997。

Vilkuna, Janne 1998. The binding of the prehistoric ski from Mänttä, *芬兰。滑雪会议历史*, 1998 奥斯陆。

4.43 韩国目前的滑雪场状况 The Current Position of Korean Ski Resort

朴正雄 & 王方（韩国） Pack Jungwoong & Wang Fang（KOR）

Brief Introduction 个人简介

PACK JUNGWOONG 朴正雄, 1967. Born 出生。

1987 working K2 distribution. 在 K2 韩国经销商工作

1992 working Burton distribution. 在 Burton 韩国经销商工作。

1996 Max trading open. 成立自己的公司。

2014 Matrix, BTM, GRAY snowboard distribution 成为 Matrix, BTM, GRAY 品牌在韩国的总经销商。

个人简介　**Brief Introduction**

王方　WANG FANG

1972 年出生　Borned in 1972。

1995 年在台资企业工作并成为国内首批接触滑雪单板和双板制造技术的人员之一 。

In 1995 worked he in a taiwan-owned enterprise and became one of the technicist, who are the firdt to get in touch with the manufacturing technology of the ski und double plate.

2000 年受雇于合力集团设立滑雪单板以及双板制造公司至今。

Since 2000 he has been employed by the ski and double plate manufacturing company that was founded by Combined Group.

Speech 讲演稿：

The Current Position of Korean Ski Resort

The first Ski Resort：Yong-pyeong Ski Resort（Opened in 1975）：19 outdoor slopes and 2 indoor slopes are in operation.

Although Korean government is decided to host 2018 Winter Olympic Games but the construction of the stadium has been delayed due to the against from NGO for environment preservation and the lack of budget from the Korean government.

-International Game Hosting History

1997 Winter Universiad（Muju Ski Resort）

1998 World cup Ski Competition（Yong-pyeong Ski Resort）

1999 Winter Asian Games（Yong-pyeong Ski Resort）

-The characteristic of Korean Ski Resort

The most ski resort in Korea has four season golf club and swimming pool.

Due to global warming, the natural snow powder is not enough to serve skier.（From November to March, Ski Season）

All of the ski resort own snow maker machine.

During season, there are 24 hours operating slope for customers visit the ski resort after work.

In comparison to the increase of winter sports mania in China, there are some decrease of winter sports mania in South Korea

-High One Ski Resort

The ski resort renovated closed mining area.

The first casino in which domestic people can use.

Currently adding water park in the ski resort.

中文论文：

韩国目前的滑雪场状况

韩国第一滑雪场：龙平滑雪场于 1975 年开放：包括 19 个室外坡道以及 2 个室内坡道。

虽然韩国政府获得了 2018 年的冬季奥运会举办权但是由于民间组织对环境保护的抗议以及预算不足，目前场馆建设处于延误状态。

国际性比赛在韩国举办经历

1997 年世界冬季大学生运动会（Muju 滑雪场）

1998 年世界杯滑雪比赛（龙平滑雪场）

1999 年亚洲冬季运动会（龙平滑雪场）

韩国滑雪场的特色

绝大多数韩国的滑雪场都有全年开放的高尔夫球场和游泳馆

也因为全球气候变暖的原因，在滑雪季节（每年的 11 月到第二年的三月）自然雪已经不能满足于滑雪爱好者

所以所有的滑雪场都配备了造雪机设备

在滑雪季节，所有的雪道都是 24 小时开放以便客人能在工作结束后去滑雪。

与中国越来越多的滑雪爱好者比较，韩国的滑雪人数呈下降趋势 。

High1 滑雪场

滑雪场关闭靠近采矿区的部分设施

在滑雪场开设赌场（仅限于韩国人）

在雪场增加水上乐园

4.44　世界上最古老的滑雪道　The Oldest Ski Tracks in the World

威尼·保森（美国）　Wayne Poulsen（USA）

个人简介　Brief Introduction

American ski cultural history scholar, expert and professor. He has explored Altay ancient skiing from multi－perspective for many years. He is enthusiastic about the exploration and research of Altay ancient culture.

美国滑雪文化历史学者、专家、教授、多年对阿尔泰山古老滑雪进行考察，多视角考察，热衷于阿尔泰山古老文化的考察研究。

English Paper:

The Oldest Ski Tracks in the World
International Ancient Skiing Cultural Exchange

China, January 14-20, 2015

Skiing: A Sport which stands at the crossroads of Landscape and Culture

——Wayne Poulsen

We are all skiers!

I come here to the Altai, we all come here, and it is like magic.

Here we are transported back to the early days of skiing!

Here is skiing as a way of life in its remote communities, communities which are still quiet, almost not accessible in winter months, where to strap skis on my feet gives me, as in summer, the freedom of the hills.

I know this feeling. I grew up in a beautiful valley in the California Sierra Nevada Mountains which was also remote and unvisited in winter, in the same way. A place which, like me, went on to grow up and, in a short time, become an internationally recognized ski resort, a place which was the host, at the age of 12 years, to the 1960 Olympic Winter Games.

This was the same year that I took my first drivers license, and after that everything changed. We grew up together, this place and me.

My father was a boy in the Sierra, near beautiful Lake Tahoe. And as a very young man he became a snow ranger, making his own skis by hand and bending them in a nearby hot water spring. He was chosen to make the first snow surveys in the Sierra Nevada mountains and in 1936 he surveyed for the first large ski area in the western United States at Lake Tahoe.

This was a very grand proposal, but before it could be realized, the storm clouds of a world war put a stop to the planning. My father was called to the war and became a pilot, first with the RAF, in England and then flying the China Clipper flying boats for Pan American Airlines across the Pacific Ocean to Asia. He had to wait until the end of the war until he could start work on the place where he dreamed to build a ski community, at Squaw Valley.

Why is this important here, in the high Altai of China?

It is important because in the lifetime which I have spent in the mountains, and growing up with skiing, much has been learned. Many mistakes have been made and many opportunities have been overlooked and it important to find lessons to learn in these experiences.

It is helpful to do what we can do here in this place, in Altai. To go back to the beginning and even to the villages of the European Alps to where in the middle of the 19th century groups of sportsmen and women began to travel to the remote villages of Switzerland and Austria, France and Italy. And when they arrived there, they found a way of life in the mountains as it had been lived for millennia. This was a life in glorious sunshine above the valley fog, and winter activities and work, and games in the snow, and skiing.

Here they discovered a relaxed pace of life, at home in the snow, with its own special mountain culture, with its own foods, and strong drinks, and song. Here they began to find excuses to escape the cities and to pass weeks at a time in the winter months.

What they found then, we find today in Altai.

From this wedding of culture and winter landscape, comes Ski Style. Ski Style grows like a life grows, from a seed, and the genetics of that seed are the mix of a special landscape and a the special culture and energy which has found a home there. Recognition of the relation of landscape and culture is the foundation of successful ski development, and this is where we find Ski Style.

When I think of ski development in the US, and all of the mistakes that have been made by rushing to develop, and doing too much without looking, seeing and listening, I am reminded to learn from the past.. And now, skiing is changing again. There is snowboarding and there are many young skiers who follow the old ways and climb the peaks to earn their turns. What better or more beautiful place to find this way of life than the Altai.

I 1998 I published a book, Ski Style, which celebrates the life of living and skiing in the old villages in Europe and the United States.

Living in Ski Style means taking time to listen to the mountains, to learn their moods. Watch the local people, they are very clever and theyhave much to teach. Watch the weather, learn the wind and storms, the orientations of the slopes and valleys and the seasons of the snow. Feel the old architecture, crafts-manship and design and see how it is adapted as perfectly as possible for man to the mountain conditions.

I have participated with the nomadic people of central Asia every year since 2001, in Mongolia, the Russian Altai, and in 2012 and 2013 in Xinjiang. It was my dream to learn as much as I could about the remote places of the mountains of the Altai in all four countries for which the range ties the "knot" at the center of Asia.

In the summer of 2013 I traveled 1506 kilometers on horseback around the entire Altai, from Kazakhstan, through China, Mongolia and ending in the Altai Republic in Russia across the mountains from where I began on the Buktharma River in Kazakstan. I did this because I wanted to see, to listen and to know the people of the cultures and to hear these mountains speak out to me.

In my time in the Altai I have visited several new and proposed ski development areas. I have met some of the pioneers of these new resorts, people who remind me of the young man my father was when he dreamed of a new community of skiers and a way of life in the mountains. I have been impressed with their energy and their vision. They are in a hurry and I wish them well. I hope that they will also take the time in their busy days to walk alone in the mountains and to listen to the mountains speak to them.

中文论文：

世界上最古老的滑雪道—国际古老滑雪文化交流会

滑雪，一项处于景观和文化的十字路口上的运动。

——韦恩保尔森

我们全都是滑雪人！

我来到了阿尔泰山，我们全都来到了阿尔泰山，如魔法一般。

今天，我们全部回到了最初滑雪的日子！

在安静的，冬日里几乎不可靠近的偏远地区，滑雪属于生活方式的一种。夏日里，绑起雪板游荡于山间，能清晰地感受到大山的自由。

我了解这种感受，因为我亦在一座美丽的山谷中长大。山谷位于加州内华达山脉，同样偏远且人迹罕至。与我相同的是，这个地方与我一同成长，在短期内，发展成了世界公认的滑雪胜地。同时，在他成立后的第十二年，作为主办方，成功举办了1960年冬季奥林匹克运动会。

同年，我第一次拿到了驾驶证。从此，一切都发生了改变，这个地方与我开始一同成长。

我父亲是内华达山脉、太皓湖边长大的小男孩。在他年轻的时候，他成为了一名雪场管理员，开始亲手制作雪板并在附近的热温泉水中对雪板进行弯曲处理。后来入选对内华达山脉进行首次积雪测量，并于1936年首次。对太皓湖旁美国西部最大的滑雪区域进行测量。

这是一项巨大的提议，但在得以实现之前，世界大战的乌云为此项提议画上了休止符。我父亲应征参战并成为了一名飞行员。最初为英国皇家空军效力，随后横跨太平洋和亚洲，成为中国加密泛美航空公司的飞行员。他不得不等到战争结束才能开始实现他的梦想，在斯阔谷建立一座滑雪世界。

为什么中国的阿尔泰山高地如此重要？

因为从在高山度过的的时间里，学滑雪的成长过程中，我学会了很多东西，也犯了很多的错误，忽视了很多的机会。因此，从这些经验中多学习总结一些经验教训很重要。

在阿尔泰山这个地方，做一些力所能及的事情很重要。回溯到最初，甚至回到欧洲阿尔卑斯山的村落，回到十九世纪中叶，大批的男女运动员开始来到位于瑞士、奥地利、法国和意大利的偏远村落旅游。当他们到达这里之后，他们发现了一种崭新的生活方式，且这种生活方式已存在千年之久。每日沐浴在峡谷迷雾之上的阳光之中，沉醉在冬日活动和工作中，徜徉在雪中游戏及滑雪活动中，这就是此处的生活。

雪中的家，独有的大山文化、特色食品、烈酒和音乐，他们发现这里的生活节奏如此放松。这里为他们提供了完美的借口使他们逃离城市的喧嚣，冬日里在此度过数周美好的时光。

那时他们发现的，今天的阿尔泰山都有！

文化与冬日风景的结合衍生出了滑雪风格。滑雪风格的成长恰似生命的成长过程，从一粒种子开始，而那粒种子的基因正是特殊风景与特别文化与能量的混合，在此基础上生根发芽。对风景与文化关系的认知是滑雪行业得以成功发展的基础，亦是我们发现滑雪风格的地方。

当我回顾美国的滑雪发展及其在急速发展的过程所犯下的错误时，在没有观察、留意、和倾听的情况下付出太多时，我提醒我自己从过去的经验中学习。现在，滑雪仍在改变。滑板滑雪和许多年轻的滑雪者按照老方法，爬到山顶去争取他们的追求。我们在追求中应该知道哪里的生活方式比阿尔泰山更好更优美呢！

1998 年，我出版了一本书，名为《滑雪风格》，歌颂欧洲和美国古老村庄的生活和滑雪。

滑雪世界里的生活意味着花时间去倾听大山的声音，了解他们的情绪。关注当地人民，他们很聪明且有很多知识可以向他们请教。观察当地的天气，了解风向和暴风雨，注意斜坡、山谷和雪季的情况。感受古老的建筑、技艺和设计，了解他们是如何做到人与山体情况的完美融合。

自 2001 年，我每年都参与到中亚地区如蒙古和俄罗斯阿尔泰游牧民族的滑雪活动中，2012 年和 2013 年，我走进了新疆。我梦想尽可能多的学习了解环阿尔泰山中四个国家偏远地区的情况，因为这个范围恰巧在中亚有一个交汇。

2013 年的夏天，我沿着整个阿尔泰山脉，起始于哈萨克斯坦的布克萨玛河，经中国及蒙古，并以俄罗斯共和国的阿尔泰山为结点，在马背上行走了 1506 千米。我这样做是因为我想要去看看，去听听，想要去了解不同文化中的人们，想要倾听大山对我大声的呼唤。

在阿尔泰山时，我参观拜访了几个新提出的滑雪发展区域。我遇见了一些新滑雪场的领头人，他们使我回忆起我父亲年轻时，梦想建立属于滑雪者的天堂，开创大山的生活方式之时。他们的正能量和开阔的眼界给我留下了深刻的印象。他们当时很着急，祝他们一切顺利。亦期望他们能在百忙之中抽出时间独自去山中走走，去倾听大山的声音。

2014 南极滑雪巡航

刚刚过去的十一月，格伦保尔森和我共同担任冰镐探险 2014 南极滑雪巡航的向导工作。此次巡航的参与者包括来自世界各地的 100 名顾客和 25 名向导。此次探险起于阿根廷乌斯怀亚，在那里我们登上了巡航船，该巡航船由冰硬的俄罗斯调查船改装，并被重新命名为“海洋冒险家”。在两天的航程中，我们经过了德雷克海峡，抵达了南极半岛，在返回乌斯怀亚之前，我们在南设德兰群岛和南极大陆逗留 6 日进行滑雪。许多该地区的滑雪 继承者都成为了冰镐探险队的第一批队员。

每天提供一种崭新的冒险，每晚都要为次日的探险做好准备，从而将船重新定位到一个新的起点。每天早上滑雪队员都要进入到可充气的摩托艇中，然后在我们锚地的区域进行着陆。我们从冰川滑向冰峰，于企鹅和海豹之间，俯瞰海洋。在此次巡航结束，返回乌斯怀亚之际，遇 12 级飓风，属蒲福风级或海上风暴等级最高的风级。以下是我们此次探险之旅的照片。

4.45 北极地区的滑雪旅游经历 The ski experience in the Arctic

艾玛·科威（英国） Emma Cowell（UK）

个人简介 Brief Introduction

Emma Cowell, BA (Hons), Msc, Tourism and Northern Studies Researcher of the Arctic University of Norway, Current research involves looking at human－animal relationships and how sled dogs help connect the guest to Arctic nature to create return visits.

Tourism Marketing Consultant, Arctic Europe

Four years arctic guide experience combined with over 15 years experience in creative marketing, print and digital forms the basis of my skill set; supported by an understanding in PR and storytelling, encompasses art direction, design and artwork (including pitch and presenting skills) －with an eye for detail having worked with global clients to local charities which have needed an understanding and sensitive approach to location and culture.

艾玛·科威 女，是挪威北极圈大学的旅游和北极研究学院的研究员。最近研究主要涉及人与动物的关系以及雪橇犬怎样帮助建立人与北极自然环境的联系而顺利引导回程。

Emma Cowell 还是欧洲北极地区旅游市场顾问，具有四年的北极地区的导游经验和 15 年的拓展市场的经验。对市场细节有深刻的洞察眼光，曾与来自世界各地的客户合作研究当地教堂，而这一研究需要对当地的地理位置和文化有深刻的认识和理解。

Emma Cowell 艾玛·科威尔是一位活跃在冰冷地带的旅游方面的设计师、市场营销专家、研究员和实践者，他在讲演中列举了诸多具体实例，摘选如下：

Arctic Encounters

Focus is Social and Cultural aspects of Tourism in the Arctic

Looking at contemporary travel writing, environmentalism awareness, indigenous culture and post colonial theory

Four Countries (Norway, Iceland, UK and Denmark)

Five projects, Green Ice, 'Greening' Greenland, Between Europe and the Arctic, Visualising autonomy in sub-Arctic coastal tourism, The Postcolonial Arctic。

The Postcolonial Arctic

Establish the case for a 'postcolonial Arctic' in terms of both the colonial past and colonial present of the region

Consider to what extent colonialism in the Arctic, both past and present, can be seen in ecological terms

Ask whether indigenous perspectives on the Arctic have the capacity to effect an imaginative reclamation of the region in ways that support cultural and political autonomy and/or look forward to a more 'planetary' vision of the Arctic in times to come.

北极地区的经历

重点在北极地区的社会和文化旅游方面

审视当代旅游记录、环保意识、本土文化和后殖民地理论；

北欧四国（挪威、冰岛、英国和丹麦）

五大项目，绿冰，绿色格陵兰岛，欧洲和北极地区的区域，展望次北极地区沿海旅游业的自主权。

后殖民地时期的北极

在后殖民地和现在殖民地时期的角度建立“后殖民地时期北极”案例

在生态角度考虑过去和现在的北极地区的殖民主义程度

从当地本土化角度考虑北极地区是否有能力实现有想象力的开垦，以实现当地文化和政治的自主权和展望北极地区的远景。

4.46 关于图瓦人 About Tuvan

然娜·禹莎（俄罗斯） Zhanna Yusha（RUS）

个人简介 **Brief Introduction**

Originally from Tu-van Republic, works at Institute for Philosophy and Law of the Siberian Branch of the Russian Academy of Sciences, Novosibirsk Region, Russian Federation Institute of Philology of SB RAS, Researcher, PhD

女，俄罗斯人种学研究专家，现在 RAS 语言学研究工作、博士学位，对图瓦人进行了深入的研究，用俄文及英文发表了论文。

Her research results are stated as follows:

Abstract: The paper analyzes the first time in comparative the verbal constants in family and calendar rituals of Tuvans in Russia, China and Mongolia. We have examined two groups of ritual texts: required verbal formulas, and replicas, the cries and exclamations of the participants of the ritual inherent in observingly folklore traditions. Reported cases include small and speech genres (proverbs and sayings, idiomatic expressions) in the structure of ritual texts. Analyzed the functions of words in rituals; characterized actionally code of rites, identified a close relationship action and verbal components. The author comes to the conclusion that the verbal elements of the rituals of the three Tuvan groups have common motives, celebrated the capture of many sustainable formulas, pragmatic orientation of verbal texts.

Tuvans who live in the mountain area of Altai aimak live by animal herding. They keep cows, sheep and goats, and breed horses. They say with pride that the "live only by cattle". In steppe areas, beside herding, Tuvans also are involved in agriculture, and grow corn, potatoes, and legumes.

Hunting has been, together with herding, a very significant part of subsistence until recent times. Men hunted wolves, bears, marals, and traveled on homemade skis (khaak). However, since 2000 the areas of their habitation have been declared as nature reserves, and hunting is strictly forbidden.

现将她的研究成果摘选如下：

本文比较分析了图瓦语的语言常量在家庭和日历仪式中的运用，图瓦人在俄罗斯、中国和蒙古都有分布，我们已经检查两组语言公式和副本，哭声和感叹词固有的仪式的参与者，注意观察过他们的民俗传统以及语言特色、文本的结构。如：谚语和格言，惯用表达式，仪式文本的结构。分析在仪式的功能，动态的特征代码的仪式，确定亲密关系的行动和语言组成。作者得出结论，在三个分布地域的图瓦人中他们的语言元素的仪式有共同的内涵，包括庆祝许多可持续的捕获方式，务实的方向性口头文本。他们曾信仰某种魔法和法术，预兆未来的希望，能成为幸福的人，如"财富和多子女""长寿""健康""牛""食物""人身尊严"等。

中国的图瓦人居住在阿勒泰地区的山区里，以饲养动物为生。他们饲养牛、羊、马等。在有些草原地区，除了饲养动物，图瓦人也进行农耕活动。

直到最近，狩猎和畜牧一直都是生存的重要部分。人们猎狼、熊、赤鹿，用手工制作的滑雪板（khaak）行走。自 2000 年，他们的居住地被列为自然保护区，严禁打猎。

第五章　第二届中国新疆国际丝绸之路旅游发展大会
——丝绸旅游暨冰雪旅游高峰论坛

Chapter5 The 2nd China Silk Road Tourism Development Conference
——Silk Road Tourism and Winter Tourism Summit

专家在乌鲁木齐合照　**Photo of experts in Urumqi**

启动仪式　**Opening ceremony**

5.1 概述 The Overview

专家们在结束阿勒泰市的活动之后，于 1 月 19 日乘旅行大巴来到乌鲁木齐市参加“第二届中国新疆国际丝绸之路旅游发展大会——丝路旅行暨冰雪旅游高峰论坛”和考察参观活动。

20 日的会议期间，部分专家发言，对新疆·阿勒泰的冬季旅游及国际化献计献策。

新疆旅游局首长与专家们会面、座谈，倾听了各国专家的意见。

专家们还考察了新疆丝绸之路国际滑雪场和参观了新疆博物馆。会后又参观了乌鲁木齐“大巴扎”集市，并观看了精彩的民族文娱演出。

After the activities in Altay City, the experts arrived at Urumuchi to attend “The 2nd China International Silk Road Tourism Development Conference in Xinjiang—Silk Road Journey and Ice-snow Tourism Summit” as well as other related visits on 19th, January.

During the conference on the 20th, some experts delivered speeches to offer advice on the winter tourism and its internationalization of Altay City.

Director of the Xinjiang Tourism Bureau, had a panel discussion with the experts and took much of their advice.

The experts then visited the International Silk Road Ski Resort of Xinjiang and the Xinjiang Museum. After the conference, they also paid a visit to the “Dabazha” market of Urumuchi and enjoyed a wonderful local ethnic show.

5.2 新疆旅游局首长致欢迎词 Welcoming speech by the chief of Xinjiang Tourism Bureau

各位来宾，女士们、先生们：

大家下午好！

新年伊始，万象更新。在这千里冰封，万里雪飘的美好季节，我们迎来了 17 个国家及国内的专家学者，与我们交流合作，共同探讨“丝绸之路”旅游振兴与发展的课题，共同推进人类滑雪起源地国际品牌，在此，我谨代表中国新疆维吾尔自治区旅游局向出席本次盛会的各位国际、国内专家、学者及媒体记者朋友们，表示热烈的欢迎并致以新年的问候！

“丝绸之路”是一条古老的商旅通道。2000 多年来，伴随着长河落日、大漠孤烟、无数商旅驼队在驼铃声声中川流不息，在东西方文化交流史上，留下了5000公里的历史印迹和数以万计的文化遗产。“古老的丝绸之路”从遥远的东方起航，贯穿新疆，通往欧洲，使新疆成为“丝绸之路”上最璀璨、最亮丽的一颗明珠。新疆是中国面积最大的省级行政区，区域面积占中国陆地面积的六分之一。在这片辽阔的土地上，昆仑山、阿尔泰山、天山等雄奇伟岸的大山中，隐藏着令世人惊叹的美景。两千多年来，古代四大文明在这里汇流，各种文化的碰撞与融合，形成了新疆独特而丰富的多元文化。

2013年9月，中国国家主席习近平在访问中亚四国期间，首次提出共建“丝绸之路经济带”的构想，“丝绸之路经济带”是世界上最长、最具发展潜力的经济大走廊，蕴藏着巨大的发展潜力。推进“丝绸之路经济带”各国间的合作发展，将为当前经济全球化纵深发展，在方兴未艾的世界经济文化交流创新的合作的前提下，指明了发展方向。2014年5月第二次中央新疆工作会议召开，提出“着力打造新疆‘丝绸之路经济带’核心区”、“将新疆建设成为‘丝绸之路经济带’的旅游集散中心”的发展方向，使新疆再一次成为中外瞩目的“丝绸之路经济带”的焦点。

旅游是开放的产业，开放带来不同旅游文化间的交融和资源的整合，为社会经济发展注入蓬勃生机与活力。旅游使世界更加繁荣发展、更加和谐美好。伴随中国改革开放的步伐，中国旅游业奏出了全球旅游业最生动、最响亮的乐章。新疆虽然地处亚欧大陆腹地，但却是中国连接中亚、南亚、辐射欧洲的最佳通道和重要门户，区位优势备受瞩目。

新疆冰雪旅游资源丰富，民族风情浓郁。冬季冰雪长达近半年时间，属亚热带气候。国际一流的S级以上的滑雪场，目前在全疆有近80余座，为中外游客提供了良好的冰雪接待条件。20多年来，我们大力推进新疆冰雪旅游发展，形成了传统与现代、冰雪与民俗融合发展的新格局，新疆已逐步成为中国西部最具魅力的冰雪旅游胜地。

在新疆的每个地州市，都有距市区几公里或十几公里的滑雪场，滑雪是新疆各族人民冬季最主要的运动方式和娱乐项目。中国新疆的阿勒泰，让我们中外嘉宾共同见证了这一人类最古老的滑雪区域。今天的阿勒泰人，仍在努力以传统的、古老的滑雪工具，“划雪为虹，极地欢演”，编织和演绎着古老滑雪文化的最美乐章，努力将其打造成为世界冰雪旅游胜地，足以让走进新疆冬季的每位中外嘉宾和朋友，尽享雪域风情，感受冰雪魅力。

最后，预祝“第二届中国新疆国际丝绸之路旅游发展大会”暨丝路冰雪旅游高峰论坛取得圆满成功！祝愿各位嘉宾、各位朋友在疆期间工作顺利，身体健康，万事如意！谢谢大家！

Speech at the 2nd China Xinjiang Silk Road Tourism Development Conference

Distinguished guests

Ladies and gentlemen

Good Afternoon!

Everything takes on a new look at the beginning of New Year. In this wonderfulseason featuring white snow world, we are delighted to have with us experts and academicians from China and another 17 countries. They will carry out exchanges and cooperation with us, discuss how to revitalize and develop tourism along the Silk Road, and work with us to promote the birthplace of human skiing as an international brand. Here, on behalf of the Tourism Bureau of Xinjiang Uygur Autonomous Region, I would like to extend my warmest welcome and New Year greetings to all the experts, academicians, and correspondents from home and abroad.

The Silk Road is an ancient corridor for commerce and trade. Over the past two thousand years, this road has witnessed changing rivers, repetitive sunsets, vast desert, and upright smoke. Countless businessmen traversed this road on camels, blazing a 5, 000-km path with lots of historical relics and cultural heritage, which facilitated the exchange of eastern and western culture. The ancient Silk Road starts from the east, going through Xinjiang, and leading to Europe. As a result, Xinjiang is like the most glittering pearl along the Silk Road. Xinjiang is China's largest province, covering one sixth land in China. In this vast land, majestic mountains, like Kunlun Mountain, Altay Mountain, and Tianshan Mountain, all feature amazing sights. Over the past two thousand years, the four ancient civilizations blended here. The integration and exchange of different cultures make Xinjiang a unique multi-cultural land.

In September, 2013, during president Xi Jinping's visit to four Central Asian countries, he proposed jointly developing the Silk Road Economic Belt for the first time. The Silk Road Economic Belt is the world's longest and most promising economic corridor, with enormous development potential. Promoting cooperative development of the Silk Road Economic Belt will become the guideline for the deepening of economic globalization, burgeoning regional cooperation, and the cooperation model for the innovation in the world's economic and cultural exchanges. In May, 2014, the 2nd Central Work Meeting of Xinjiang was held, the leaders proposed that we should vigorously build Xinjiang into the core and tourism hub of the Silk Road Economic Belt, so that Xinjiang will again become the focus of the Belt, gaining worldwide attention.

Tourism is an open industry. Openness will promote the exchange of different tourism cultures and resource integration, and inject fresh momentum and vitality to socio-economic development. Tourism will bring prosperity, development and harmony to the world. As China's reform and opening up endeavor deepens, China's tourism industry has become the most promising one in the world. Although Xinjianglies in the hinterland of Euro-Asian Continent, yet it is the best channel and important gateway connecting China, West and South Asia, as well as Europe. In addition, it is a launching pad for China to be open to the west, with well-recognized geographical advantages.

Xinjiang is endowed with rich winter tourism resources and exotic culture. In winter, snowfall could last for almost half a year, and subtropical climate dominates this region. Xinjiang has about 80 world-class ski resorts above level-S, providing convenient services for tourists from home and abroad. Over the past 20 years, we have been vigorously developing Xinjiang's winter tourism. As a result, traditional and modern tourism, winter tourism and local customs are perfectly combined. Xinjiang is on the track to become the most attractive winter tourism resort in western China.

In every prefecture and city of Xinjiang, there would be at least one ski resort a few kilometers away from downtown area. Skiing has become the main sport and entertainment for Xinjiang people. Altay region allows all Chinese and foreign guests to recognize and appreciate the birthplace of human skiing. Today, Altay people still use traditional and ancient skiing tools to traverse snow and celebrate. They are writing and playing the most amazing chapter of the ancient skiing culture, and develop it into a world-class winter tourism resort, so that all the friends and guests from home and abroad can appreciate and feel the unique charm of winter snow in Xinjiang.

In conclusion, I wish every success of the 2nd China Xinjiang Silk Road Tourism Development Conference—Silk Road Tourism and Winter Tourism Summit, and I wish all the guests and friends a happy stay in Xinjiang, and enjoy good health and best luck in your career.

Thank you!

5.3　会场场景　Meeting scenes

5.4　专家学者在会议中发言　Speeches by experts and scholars

5.4.1　唤起更多公众对滑雪的兴趣

——著名的挪威奥斯陆滑雪博物馆主任

卡琳·博格

著名的奥斯陆被称为世界的冬季首都。无论您是通过坐飞机、坐船，乘汽车还是火车来到这座城市，霍尔门科伦滑雪跳台都会是你所看到的第一个城市地标。

目前，霍尔门科伦滑雪跳台是世界上没有搬迁过地址，并至今仍在举办比赛的跳台中历史最悠久的，已经历过 19 次翻建，是世界上第三大知名的体育场馆。在这里，每年都会举办各种滑雪比赛，会吸引众多观众前来观战，常年都有运动员在这里训练，每年大约有 100 万人来这里参观。

有句俗语，“挪威人一生下来就踩着滑雪板”。世界现代滑雪运动是从挪威等北欧国家兴起的。但是，当今保持古老滑雪运动和制作古老滑雪板的地方唯有新疆的阿勒泰。

早在上个世纪 20 年代，挪威极地探险家南森在他的一本书中就写道，滑雪运动起源于阿尔泰山的某个部落。通过对阿勒泰地区的实地考察，我支持阿勒泰是世界上最古老的滑雪地域，是人类滑雪最早起源地。

区域合作是当今世界的发展潮流，要通过加强合作，促进新疆冰雪旅游产业的提档升级。要加大同冰雪强国之间的旅游合作，特别是举办过奥运会、大冬会国家和城市之间的合作。奥斯陆滑雪博物馆从 1998 年举行第一次国际滑雪研讨会后，经常会将世界各地的滑雪专家和学者聚集起来，他们在会议中建立联系，通过媒体的报道后，唤起更多公众对滑雪的兴趣。也希望通过此次会议的举办能使阿勒泰成为最受欢迎的滑雪胜地。

5. 4. 1 To Arouse the Interest in Skiing from the Mass People

Director of the world famous Oslo Ski Museum of Norway

Karin Berg

Oslo is referred to as the winter capital of the world. No matter you come to this city by plane, by ship, by bus or by train, Holmenkollen Ski Jump will be the first landmark appearing in your sight.

Currently, Holmenkollen Ski Jump is the oldest platform that has never been moved and is still holding contests. It has gone through 19 reconstructions, and it is the third famous stadium in the world. Every year, various skiing contests are held here, attracting numerous audiences. There are athletes trained here all year long, and about 100 million people per year come to pay a visit.

As the saying goes, the Norwegians are born standing on a skiing board, and modern skiing once originated from Norway and other Northern European countries. However, the only place that still keeps the ancient skiing tradition and makes the ancient skiing board is Altay in Xinjiang.

As early as 1920s, a Norwegian polar explorer called Nansen wrote in one of his book that skiing originated from some tribe in the Altai Mountains. Through my field study in the Altai area, I agree that Altay is the most ancient skiing region, the cradle of human skiing.

Regional cooperation is the current tendency of the world, so it is necessary to achieve the promotion of the ice-snow tourism industry of Xinjiang through strengthening the cooperation. The tourism cooperation with countries that have advantages in the ice and snow, especially the cooperation with those that have held the Olympics and the

World University Winter Games is very important. For example, Oslo Ski Museum has been frequently gathering skiing experts and scholars across the world since the first International Ski Seminar in 1998. They exchange ideas in the conference, and the interest of the mass people is often aroused after the report of the media. I also hope that Altay could become the most popular skiing resort after this conference.

5.4.2 树立“人类最古老滑雪地域”品牌

——中国首位滑雪冠军、中国人类滑雪起源地研究发起人

单兆鉴

在阿勒泰市挖掘出来的以长调方式口传的歌谣“打猎人的民谣”距今千年以上，其源头可追溯到人类滑雪狩猎的年代；广大的阿勒泰地区的农牧民至今仍沿袭着古老毛皮滑雪板的制作和运用，至今可能已有几千年。

2006年1月16日滑雪专家、考古学家聚集阿勒泰市，发布了中国新疆阿勒泰地区是人类滑雪最早起源地的《阿勒泰宣言》，同年12月15日在北京人民大会堂举行隆重的新闻发布会。2015年1月14日—18日在阿勒泰市进行，近20个国家30余名国外及20余名国内研究人员参加了国际研讨会，1月18日发表《2015年国际滑雪研讨会宣言》，向国内外宣布“中国新疆阿勒泰是世界最古老滑雪地域”。

国内外发展的经验都说明：“修建一个滑雪场，拉活沿途一条（交通）线，激活多行业，带富一个乡，健康一群人”。新疆是天然雪资源很丰富的省份，特别是北疆阿勒泰地区是天然雪降雪次数多、雪量充足的地域，为滑雪产业的发展，提供了得天独厚的雪资源。新疆可开发滑雪旅游地区多、面积广，阿尔泰山脉、天山山脉、昆仑山脉雪覆盖的面积广大，包括南疆一些区域都有条件开展适宜的大众滑雪及娱乐性雪上活动。

目前新疆已有大小滑雪场近60个，仅次于黑龙江，居全国第二位。由于新疆各区域的区域位置、冰雪资源、交通状况、市场能量、现有基础等条件的差异，目前不是所有区域都适合开展冰雪旅游，也不是任何内容都可成为冰雪旅游项目。形势要求我们，首先切实集合全疆的优势、冲开常规思维，摒弃常规模式，突出特色，突出重点，让路综合条件较好的区域优先发展、捷足先登；有影响力、生命力的项目应重点开发。

单兆鉴建议新疆滑雪旅游开发应树立一个大品牌，确立3个大目标，重点打造5大区域。

新疆的“人类最古老滑雪地域”的品牌，连同人类古老滑雪文化资源是世界

级的品牌与资源，这个品牌与资源优势应贯通于新疆冬季旅游业的各环节，区域中做到“家喻户晓”，对疆外要不断加大宣传，吸引国内外滑雪人士而至，扩大影响。在全疆滑雪资源普查的基础上，做到“宏观规划，分期实施，整合资源，伴着需求走”，编制好新疆冬季滑雪旅游地图。首先建成几个制高点，树起几面旗帜，形成“窗口”，扎实拉动新疆冬季旅游的发展。

5.4.2 To Build the Brand of “The Most Ancient Region of Human Skiing”

The first ski champion of China, Sponsor of the study of the
human skiing origin in China

Shan Zhaojian

The orally transmitted ballad “Song of the Hunters”, founded in Altay City, has a history of more than a thousand years. Its origin can trace back to the era when human skied to hunt. Even nowadays, the farmers and herdsmen in the Altai region still follow the ancient way of making and using fur skis, which might have lasted for thousands of years.

On Jan 16th, 2006, ski experts and archaeologists gathered together in Altay City, publishing the *Altay Statement* that claiming Altai region to be the earliest origin of human skiing, and the press conference was held in the Great Hall of the People in Beijing on Dec 15th of the same year. During Jan 14th–18th, 2015, over 30 foreign researchers from around 20 countries and more than 20 Chinese researchers attended an international seminar, who published *Declaration of the* 2015 *International Ski Seminar*, confirming that Altay of Xinjiang, China is the most ancient ski region in the world.

We can learn from both the foreign and domestic development experience that “building a ski field will bring about a traffic line, and then will activate various industries, and then will enrich a county, and then will tone up a group of people”. Xinjiang is a province abundant in natural snow resource, especially the Northern Altai region, whose frequent snowing and rich amount of snow provide a privileged resource for the development of the ski industry. There are numerous and vast areas waiting for development in Xinjiang. The Altai Mountains, Mount Tianshan and the Kunlun Mountains, including some areas in the southern part, are all suitable for the mass skiing and snow entertainment.

Now there are nearly 60 ski fields in Xinjiang, ranking only second to Heilongjiang to be the second in the nation. Because of the differences among the areas in the conditions like the regional position, the snow resource, the traffic condition, the market energy and the present foundations, not all the areas are suitablefor carrying out ice-snow tourism, and not all the specialties can become tourism items. The trend requires us, above all, to gather the advantages of the whole Xinjiang, break the stereotype, get rid of the routine and emphasize the unique features and the key points. Areas with better overall conditions should enjoy a priority, and projects of huge influence and vitality as well.

Shan Zhaojian suggested that the development of ski tourism in Xinjiang should build 1 famous brand, set 3 grand goals and focus on the construction of 5 areas.

The brand "The Most Ancient Region of Human Skiing" of Xinjiang, along with the concept that it is a world-class resource, should be applied throughout each and every chain in the winter tourism in Xinjiang. It should be famous inside the area and enjoy an increasing publicity outside, so that more skiers from home and abroad would know and come. Based on the survey of ski resource within the entire Xinjiang, it is also required to "plan in a macroscopic scale, implement in phases, integrate the resources and move along with the needs", and make a winter ski tour map in Xinjiang. Set up a few commanding heights and a few banners to form a window, and finally promotes the development of the winter tourism in Xinjiang.

5.4.3 开发以当地文化为基础的小型旅游业

——瑞典电视台和迪纳姆电影公司制作人

库尔特·斯科格

从去年9月展开调研以来，我已经第二次来到新疆。主要从事自然纪录片拍摄的我，选择在这里进行拍摄并非偶然，新影片的主题是关于雪与滑雪的。雪是水的固态形式，这次的拍摄在美丽的雪景中进行，阿勒泰会作为重中之重，占有相当大的一部分，新影片中会讲述到雪、自然与文化的关系。

这次恰逢新年，我们登上了有着古老村落的高山，这里的人们正在进行传统的古老毛滑雪板比赛，遇到了毛滑雪板的制作艺人，我们跟生活在这里的人们一起欢度节日，并踏上毛滑雪板进行了比赛。影片将与瑞典朋友和瑞典电视台一起制作。影片中的人利用滑雪进行交流、放牧和打猎。我们可以想象古老的人们最初是如何利用滑雪来打猎的。

邂逅山区独特古老的滑雪文化，这里所拥有的热情的人们、厚厚的积雪、美丽的景观、未被开发的山脉，这一切都非常适合高山旅游，都是西方人最感兴趣的，但这不合适大众旅游，是适合发展一种以当地文化为基础的小型旅游业。这里所拥有的文化遗产是独一无二的，有着古老鲜活的滑雪传统。瑞典也在开发小型旅游业，萨米族和农民向大家分享他们的文化和生活方式。

旅游业是生产的反向模式，顾客自费来到这些地方进行“生产”，花钱来到这些地方呆一段时间，会很好地惠及当地人民，从而保护古老文化。

5.4.3 To Develop Small Scale Tourism Based on Local Culture

Producer of Swedish Television and Denham Film Company

Kurt Skoog

This is my second trip to Xinjiang since the survey starting in last September.

Mainly engaged in shooting documentaries, I was not randomly choosing Xinjiang, for the theme of the new film is about snow and ski. Snow is the solid form of water, and this time the shooting will be carried out in the beautiful snow scenery. As the top priority, Altay will take up a considerably large part of it. New film, based on this experience, will focus on the relationship between snow, nature and culture.

Now it happens to be the New Year, we climbed up the mountains with ancient villages in it. People there were occupied in a traditional fur skis competition. We met artisans making fur skis, spent the holiday with the local people and had a competition on the fur skis. The film will be produced with some Swedish friends and Swedish Television. In the film, local people ski as a way to communicate, shepherd and hunt, upon which we can imagine how the ancient people took advantage of skiing to hunt animals.

It is a pleasure to meet the unique ancient ski culture in the mountain area, the passionate local people, the thick snow, the beautiful scenery and the undeveloped mountains. All of these elements are suitable for high mountain tourism which westerners are most interested in, but it is not for the mass tourism. For the mass people, there should be some small scale tourism based on local culture. The ancient vital ski tradition here is a unique cultural heritage. In a similar situation, Sweden is also working on the small scale tourism, and the Sami farmers can have a chance to share their culture and lifestyle with people outside.

Tourism is a reverse mode of production, and the customers spend their own money to come here and produce. Their stay will bring much benefit to the local people and help preserve the ancient culture.

5.4.4 充分发挥“核心区”作用开展跨国旅游合作

——中科院新疆生态与地理研究所研究员

杨兆萍

新疆处于丝绸之路经济带核心区，旅游业作为产业关联性强、文化延伸意义深的产业，能够在政策沟通、民心沟通方面发挥先导作用。

要以“整合共同资源、发挥共同优势、谋求共同发展”为宗旨，以“互惠互利、共同发展”为立足点，不断深化丝绸之路沿线国家和地区间的旅游合作，将旅游业作为丝绸之路经济带的突破口和先导产业，促进和推动沿线国家和地区的文化、科技、经济交流；以跨国旅游合作示范区为契机，探索国家间旅游合作机制、便利化优惠政策，建立各方旅游行政管理部门之间的联络对话机制，积极组织和鼓励各类旅游企业开展交流合作，促进双边、多边民间互访，推进与丝绸之路经济带沿线国家和地区的全面深化合作。

国际航空枢纽建设和航线网络是打通丝绸之路经济带旅游大通道的重要助推力。乌鲁木齐是辐射欧亚大陆的航空和陆路枢纽；喀什是辐射南亚、西亚、部分中亚的航空和陆路枢纽；伊宁是辐射中亚的陆路枢纽；阿勒泰是辐射中俄蒙哈阿尔泰区域的陆路枢纽。依托中哈霍尔果斯国际边境合作中心、霍尔果斯特殊经济区的政策优势，推进伊犁中哈跨国旅游合作区建设，积极争取边境跨国旅游特殊开放政策，以中哈蒙三国扩展申报俄罗斯“金山阿尔泰”世界自然遗产地为契机，推进中、俄、哈、蒙四国环阿尔泰山生态旅游合作区的建设，推出阿尔泰山跨国生态旅游线，打造具有国际影响力的生态旅游目的地。

建立区域性权威旅游合作组织，完善政府间旅游合作与协调机制，推进互为旅游目的地国，通关、签证办理实施最惠国待遇，建立自由、开放、公正的多边合作框架；推动沿线国家和地区建立旅游安全合作机制和应急协调机制，制订应急处置预案和紧密救援措施，保障国际旅游者的旅游安全，创造丝绸之路无障碍旅游条件；整合优势科研资源建立旅游研究与交流中心，致力于丝绸之路经济带高端人才和多语种人才培养、创新性和开拓性研究，搭建丝绸之路经济带旅游科研合作交流平台。建立“网上丝绸之路”旅游信息服务共享平台，对精品景区展示、营销，提供旅游产品定制服务，多语种旅游电子商务服务，旅游公共信息服务，旅游安全信息管理服务。

5.4.4 To Carry out Transnational Tourism Cooperation with the Core Zone Fully Functioning

Researcher of the Xinjiang Ecology and Geography Institute of
Chinese Academy of Science

Yang Zhaoping

Xinjiang locates in the core zone of the Silk Road economic belt. As an industry of strong industrial relevance and cultural significance, tourism can play a leading role in the communication of the policy and the mass people.

We should always keep in mind the mission of "integrating common resource, exploiting common advantages and striving for mutual development", and stick to thefoothold of "mutual benefit and mutual development" . What's more, keep deepening the tourism cooperation between countries along the Silk Road, and make tourism the breach and leading industry of the Silk Road economic belt, so that it can promote the cultural, scientific and economic communication among the neighboring countries and regions. Moreover, take the opportunity of the transnational tourism cooperative zones to explore the cooperative mechanism, to implement the facilitation of the preferential policy, to set up the communicative mechanism between the tourism administrative departments on all sides, to organize and encourage diversified tourism corporation to strengthen exchanges and cooperation as well as bilateral and multilateral private visits, so as to boost the comprehensive in-depth cooperation among the countries and regions alongside the Silk Road economic belt.

The construction of the international aviation hinge and the airline network is one of the most important propelling forces to break through the tourism channel of the Silk Road economic belt. Urumuchi is the aviation and road hinge radiating the Eurasian continent, Kashgar radiating South Asia, West Asia and part of Central Asia. Gulja is the road junction radiating Central Asia, Altay radiating the Altai region of China, Russia, Mongolia and Kazakhstan. It is important to propel the construction of China Kazakhstan Transnational Tourism Cooperation Zone in Ili with the advantage of the China Kazakhstan Khorgos International Borderline Cooperation Center and the policy of the Khorgos Special Economic Zone. Also, seize the opportunity of the three countries China, Kazakhstan and Mongolia applying for the extension of the Russian "Golden Mount Altay" world heritage, in order to propel the construction of the ecology tourism cooperation zone around the Altai Mountains among the four countries of China, Russia, Kazakhstan and Mongolia, launch the Altai Mountains transnational ecological tour route, and create an ecological tour destination with international influence.

Set up authoritative regional tour cooperative organization, complete the cooperative and coordinative mechanism between governments, promote the most-favored-nation treatment in the visa and passport formalities between countries that are tourism destinations to each other, and build a free, open and just multilateral cooperative framework. Meanwhile, propel the construction of the safety cooperative mechanism and emergency coordinative mechanism among the countries and regions alongside the economic belt, make emergency plans and rescue measures, ensure the safety of the international tourists, and create a barrier-free tour condition.

Set up a tourism research and communication center by integrating preponderant scientific resources, pay attention to the cultivation of high-end talents and multilingual talents as well as the research on creativity and pioneering quality, build a tourism research cooperation platform of the Silk Road economic belt. Set up an "Online Silk Road" tourism information& service sharing platform, in order to formulate services for the scenic spot display, marketing and tourism products, offer multilingual e-commerce service, public information service and manage the tourism safety information.

5.4.5 不同季节对游客有同等的吸引力

——挪威北极大学英国旅游业研究院市场顾问

艾玛·科威

我有多重身份，我是一名设计师，旅游顾问、市场顾问。还是一名网络建立者，希望今后能跟中国合作。2007 年 12 月我和先生以及 13 只雪橇犬搬到挪威北部小城市，完成欧洲最北端、最长狗拉雪橇比赛并取得冠军。

在我现在参与的挪威北极大学的几项研究中，有一个项目就是关于斯堪的纳维亚旅游业以及旅游业如何吸引中国游客。在挪威北部，冬季旅游不断发展壮大，探寻极光之旅，摩托雪橇、狗拉雪橇等项目不断发展，与此同时，一些新的节庆和大型活动也不断地涌现，为创造新旅游项目奠定基础，为冬季旅游目的地增添故事性，创造想像的空间。在过去几年，海外游客不断增加，这都得益于一系列复杂的举措，包括私营部门和公众的长期努力，确保不同季节对游客都有同等的吸引力。

挪威现在研究的北极的新变化，致力于从不同角度探究冬季旅游的潜力、发展动力和存在的障碍。旅游管理者如何管理游客的情绪？怎样管控旅游活动？旅游项目的有趣性和安全性？新的知识和科技的发展，冒险从以前的硬冒险向软冒险转变，越来越多的参与者都能进行冒险，都非常安全，具有体验性；对旅游项目的宣传文案进行研究，游客的身份、性别对旅游的影响；研究当代科技对旅游的发展、服务业的提供、环境的可持续性有何影响，怎样为游客提供最好的体验并保护我们的环境。

让游客回到同一目的地，对挪威来说，狗拉雪橇比赛成为了冬季旅游的绝佳案例。新疆有着丰富的冰雪资源，有着难得的发展机遇，应该借鉴挪威的冰雪发展经验，突出特色，打造世界级的冰雪旅游品牌，吸引更多国外游客来新疆旅游。

5.4.5 To Make Sure that Different Seasons Have the Same Attraction to the Visitors

Marketing Consultant of British Tourism Industry Institute of
Norway University of the Arctic
Emma Coldwell

I have multiple identities. I am a designer, a tour consultant, a marketing consultant and a network builder. I look forward to the cooperation with Chinese projects. In the December of 2007, my husband and I, along with 13 sleigh dog moved to a small city in northern Norway, where we accomplished the most northern and longest sled dog race in Europe and won the first place.

Among some surveys in which I participate in the Norway University of the Arctic, one is about the tourism in Scandinavia and how to attract Chinese tourists. In the northern part of Norway, winter tourism has been blooming with the development of the aurora tour, the motorcycle and sleigh, the sled dog and other items. In the meantime, some new festivals and grand activities keeping appearing in our sight, which set a solid foundation for creating new tourism projects, add more stories to the winter destinations and expand the space for imagination. In the past few years, the number of the oversea tourists keeping rising, which benefits from a series of complicated measures including the efforts of the private sectors and the mass people, which make sure that different seasons have the same attraction to the visitors.

Nowadays, Norway has been doing research on the new changes of the Arctic, trying to see the potentials, the driving power and the barriers in the development of its winter tourism from different perspectives. How can the administrators manage theemotion of the visitors? How to take control of the touring activities? How to achieve both the interestingness and the safety issue? The development of new knowledge and science change the adventure experience from hard to soft, enabling more and more participators to take adventures safe and sound. We also do research on the promotional copywriting, the effect of the tourists' identity and gender, the influence of modern science towards the development of tourism, the service industry and the sustainability of the environment, and how to provide the best experience for the tourists while protecting our environment.

To Norway, the sled dog race has become the best winter tourism example to attract the tourists back to the same destination again. Abundant in ice and snow resource and offered with an uncommon chance, Xinjiang should learn from the experience of Norway, emphasize its features to build a world-class ice-snow tourism brand, attracting more foreign visitors to travel in Xinjiang.

5.4.6 大力实施冰雪旅游资源的“四大”战略

——黑龙江冰雪产业研究院院长

张贵海

新疆地处中国西北，有着冰雪运动的良好自然条件，新疆要从丝绸之路经济带的时空价值中找出实现和增加价值的方式，大力实施冰雪旅游资源的开发、经营、整合和创新战略。

冰雪旅游资源开发战略，加大政府主导作用，促进冰雪旅游顺利发展。遵循新疆旅游业总体规划内容要求，把自然冰雪旅游与民族文化、民俗风情有机地融合起来，突出特色和品位，科学合理地开发利用冰雪旅游资源，开发要遵循基础设施优先、资源可持续、经济可辐射、成本可承载、投资可多元的原则。

冰雪旅游经营战略，树立精品意识，充实冰雪旅游内容。树立精品意识，重点围绕冰雪旅游主打产品，组织开展丰富多彩的冰雪活动，努力打造新疆冰雪旅游品牌，做到“两个结合”，即：将冰雪旅游与冰雪赛事相结合，利用组织冰雕、雪雕、赛雪爬犁、雪地赛骆驼等赛事，提高冰雪旅游的吸引力；将冰雪旅游与民族民俗风情旅游相结合，展现原生态多元民族文化，增强新疆冰雪旅游的独特魅力。

冰雪旅游整合战略，发展冰雪旅游一定不能“单打独斗”，要树立“大旅游”“大开放”观念，形成一个有效的发展推动机制。在硬环境方面要有明确的冰雪旅游发展规划，根据资金供给的可能性和市场发展状况，合理确定旅游基本建设规模，充分挖掘潜力。按照区域整合、资源整合、民俗整合、文化整合的思路理性发展。

冰雪旅游创新战略，大力实施源于自然禀赋的创新、源于生态保护的创新、源于区域文化的创新、源于民俗差异的创新、源于国际视野的创新、源于可持续发展的创新和源于国家战略的创新。

5.4.6 To Thoroughly Carry out the Four Strategies of the Ice-snow Tourism Resources

Director of Heilongjiang Ice-snow Industry Research Institute

Zhang Guihai

Located in the northwestern part of China, Xinjiang has a privileged natural condition for winter sports. Endowed with the space value of the Silk Road economic belt, Xinjiang needs to find a way to materialize and increase the value, to thoroughly carry out the developing, operating, integrating and innovating strategies of the ice-snow tourism resources.

First is the developing strategy. Strengthen the dominant role of the government and promote a smooth development of the ice-snow tourism. Follow the requirements of the Xinjiang tourism general plan, achieve an organic combination between natural ice-snow tourism, ethnic culture and folk traditions, highlight the features and taste, and exploit the ice-snow tourism resources scientifically and rationally. The exploitation should follow the principles of the priority of the facilities, the sustainability of the resources, the radiation of the economics, the affordability of the cost, and the diversification of the investment.

Second is the operating strategy. Keep the consciousness of the premium quality and enrich the contents of the ice-snow tourism. The consciousness of the premium quality refers to an emphasis on the ice-snow tourism products, organize various winter activities, manage to build a Xinjiang ice-snow tourism brand, and accomplish the "two combinations", i. e. the combination of ice-snow tourism with the winter games, taking advantage of the contests of ice sculpture, the snow sculpture, the sleigh and the camel race etc. to improve the attraction of ice-snow tourism; and the combination of ice-snow tourism with ethnic tradition tourism, showing the primitive multivariant ethnic culture to enhance the unique charm of the Xinjiang ice-snow tourism.

As for the integrating strategy, never try to develop tourism singlehandedly, and there should be a concept of "Big Tourism" and "Entire Openness", which help form an effective developing mechanism. For the part of the hard environment, a specific ice-snow tourism developing plan is a must, which can decides the basicconstructional scale and exploit the potentialities according to the possibility of the fund supply and the marketing development.

Last is the innovating strategy. Thoroughly carry out the innovation originating from the nature, the ecological preservation, the regional culture, the ethnic differences, the international horizon, the sustainable development and the national strategy.

5.4.7 将民族风情与冰雪文化融合

——萨米拉普兰著名作家、历史滑雪研究者

哈特维格·伯克利

我非常高兴能够来到美丽的乌鲁木齐以及雄伟壮丽的阿尔泰山区。在这里，我体验了新疆独特的民族风情。

我相信新疆有着巨大的潜力，能够进一步吸引国内外的游客，最重要的是，要保存这里古老的滑雪文化，代代相传下去。深入挖掘内涵，进一步展现其魅力，将浓郁的民族风情与独特的冰雪文化融合在一起，相互促进，相互提升。

我衷心地希望新疆当地政府在保护环境和谋求发展中取得一个平衡。从目前的形势看来新疆做得非常好，希望这样良好的势头能够继续保持。

5.4.7 To Combine Ethnic Traditions with Ice-snow Culture

Famous writer of Sami Lapland, researcher of historical ski

Hartvig Berkley

I am so glad to visit Urumuchi and the magnificent Altai Mountains. Here, I have experienced some unique ethnic traditions of Xinjiang.

I believe that there are huge potentials within Xinjiang to attract visitors from home and abroad. But the most important thing is to preserve the ancient ski culture and pass it down generation to generation. It will be helpful to dig inside the connotation and further bring out the charm of the ski culture here. A combination between the rich ethnic traditions and the unique ice-snow culture will lead to a mutual improvement.

I sincerely hope that the local government of Xinjiang can achieve a balance between environmental protection and economic growth. For now Xinjiang has done a very good job, I hope you can keep up such a good tendency.

5.4.8 旅游开发要保护好文化资源

——美国古老滑雪文化研究专家、中国专家合作者

尼尔·拉尔森

刚刚看完阿勒泰地区的滑雪运动短片，收获颇丰，看到了最古老的滑雪板，了解了最古老的滑雪方式，欣赏到了滑雪带来的激情和快乐。大家都非常着迷于阿勒泰地区悠久的历史，旅游成为巨大的商机，促进新疆旅游业的发展。我希望新疆能够继续保护这里的传统资源、文化资源和物质资源。西方国家对这里的很多古老传统饶有兴趣。

新疆蕴藏着巨大的旅游业的发展机遇，但滑雪文化却非常脆弱。希望能在开发中，保护濒危的文化资源，有更多的特色，包括一些小的高附加值的产品，帮助提高当地人的收入和保留传统，为中国的现代文化增添光彩。

5.4.8 To Protect the Cultural Resources while Developing Tourism

Expert in American Ancient Ski Culture, Cooperator with Chinese experts

Neal Larson

I have learnt a lot from the video clip about ski sport in the Altai area just now. I saw the most ancient skis, knew about the most ancient way of skiing and enjoyed the passion and happiness brought by skiing. Everyone is obsessed with the long history of the Altay area, so tourism is becoming a huge commercial opportunity. While promoting the development of the tourism in Xinjiang, I hope that Xinjiang can continue protecting the traditional resources, cultural resources and material resources here, and many western countries are very interested in these ancient traditions.

Xinjiang is facing a huge developing opportunity of tourism, but its ski culture is rather fragile. I hope that the endangered cultural resources would call for more attention in the exploitation, and more features, including some small high value-added products could help improve the income of the local people and preserve the traditions as well, adding more glory to the modernization of China.

5.4.9 找准市场定位吸引游客

——阿尔泰山古老滑雪考察团美国成员、教授

威尼·保森

我一生都生活在大山当中，在过去的15年中，我穿越中亚进行旅行。近年来，非常着迷于阿尔泰山区，2013年，我纵马驰骋穿越阿勒泰地区，走了四个国家，哈萨克斯坦、蒙古、俄罗斯，最后到中国，亲身体验了当地的民俗文化。多次去过喀纳斯景区，在那里看到了雪山之巅，还看到春雨滋养的绿色，还有在高山湖区雪水煮茶的体验，也看到了政府为景区的建设和开发做出的努力，让这里美景尽显。这里保存了一些很好的文化传统，希望能通过更好的研究方法和信息交流，让更多的人来了解。

当原始文化与现代文化产生冲突的时候，我们需要深刻的自我思考。我们所有人都是游客，用眼神有光的“马”和行为粗暴的“牛”来比拟，我们更愿意成为哪一种游客。根据山区人们宁静致远的生活习惯，他们喜欢越少越好的游客。只要我们能提供更加多元化的服务，而不是千篇一律的、附加值很小的服务，就会创造出价值。开发各种各样的旅游资源，提供符合不同口味的消费需要，找出最有效的方式，适应当地人的需求，一定可以将阿勒泰区域变成冰雪旅游的胜地。

5.4.9 To Find the Right Position and Attract the Tourists

Member of the exploratory mission of the Altai Mountains

Wayne Paulson

I have been spending my whole life in the mountains, and in the past 15 years, I have travelled across Central Asia. In recent years, I am very obsessed with the Altai Mountains, and I went across the Altay area on horse in 2013. I have been to four countries during that journey, Kazakhstan, Mongolia, Russia and the last stop is China. I experienced the local ethnic culture by myself, and many times I went to the Kanas scenic spot where I saw the peaks of the snow mountains, the greenness nourished by the spring rain, the tea boiled by the snow water from the Alpine lakes area, and the government effort in developing the scenic spot. They made the scenery even more beautiful. Many brilliant cultural traditions are preserved here, so I hope that, with better research method and information communication, more people can come to know here.

When there are conflicts between the primitive culture and the modern one, we need an insightful self-reflection. We are all visitors here, so what kind of visitor do we like to be, horses with glowing eyes or cows with rude behaviors? According to the quiet lifestyle of the local people, they must prefer fewer visitors. As long as we can provide more multivariant services instead of the repeated little value-added ones, we can create more value. Develop diversified tourism resources, offer choices for customers with different tastes, find out the most effective ways, fit the needs of thelocal people, and it is certain to change the Altay area into a famous resort of ice-snow tourism.

5.4.10 亲身体验最原始的风土人情

——芬兰国家旅游杂志社编辑、新闻工作者

托尼·艾莫尼

中国是许多外国人心中向往的地方，新疆也非常大，作为中国最西部的一部分，也同样受到大家的热捧。几年前，我花费了一年半的时间进行了一次远征。从吉尔吉斯斯坦出发，骑马穿越中亚，在中国境内完成了旅途的大部分，从喀什噶尔到了北京。

20世纪早期，外国人对新疆怀有很大好奇心，他们来这里交易并将货物运往欧洲。我们为什么选择走这条路，主要是因为在100年前，有个芬兰的军事人物走过这条路。

我们走进喀什噶尔老城，到过塔什库尔干沙漠，穿越斜度很大的冰川，一路走到阿克苏，还经过甘肃、陕西、内蒙古，在途中拍摄了很多年轻人和年长者，通过普通人能学到更多，看到美丽的村落，体验他们的热情，并且了解到地道的当地风情。

新疆有很大的潜力，我建议要来这里旅游的人们，不要心过大。国内外市场是不同的，尤其是与欧美市场相比，重要的是，要看到实质，有质量的，有价值的。

5.4.10 To Experience the Local Customs and Practices on Your Own

Editor of Finnish National Tourism Magazine, Journalist

Tony Almony

China has been a wonderland in many foreigners' mind. As the most western part of China, Xinjiang is pretty large and is also popular among the visitors. A few years ago, I spent one and a half year carrying out an expedition. I start off from Kyrgyzstan, went across the Central Asia on horse, and spent most of my journey time travelling in China, from Kashgar to Beijing.

In the early 20th century, foreigners were very curious about Xinjiang, and they came here to do business and transport the goods to Europe. The reason why we chose this route is because a Finnish military leader took this road 100 years before.

We entered the old city of Kashgar, passed by the Tashkurghan dessert, trek across steep glacier and went all the way to Aksu. We went past Gansu, Shanxi and Inner Mongolia; we took a lot of pictures of the young and old people in the journey, from whom we also learnt quite much; we saw beautiful villages, felt the passion of the native people, and knew the local customs.

Xinjiang has huge potentials, but I want to suggest people visiting here not to expect too much. Tourism markets of home and abroad are different, especially when compared with the European and American markets. What is most important is to see the substantiality, to see what is qualified and valuable.

5.5 新疆旅游局首长与参会专家交流会见 Communication between experts and the chief of Xinjiang Tourism Bureau

5.6 在乌鲁木齐市的参观考察活动 Investigations and visits to Ürümqi City

考察丝绸之路国际滑雪场
Investigation to Silk Road International Ski Resort

李建宏先生简介：

李建宏，男，汉族，1965年12月生，1988年毕业于北京邮电大学，自1993年3月创办新疆宏景公司之后。先后投资创办了宏景通讯，宏景数码港，国际大巴扎，沙漠绿洲水疗会所，新疆丝绸之路国际滑雪场，新疆丝绸之路伏羲学校等企业实体。现任新疆宏景集团董事长。李建弘所建的新疆丝绸之路国际滑雪场是中国西北最好最大的滑雪场，滑雪文化氛围浓重，服务水平高。

曾任新疆区政协常委，人大委员等职。获得“新疆十大杰出青年”，“自治区劳动模范”等荣誉称号。

Resume of Li Jianhong

Li Jianhong, male, Chinese, born in December 1965, graduated from Beijing University of Posts and Telecommunications. After he established Sinkiang Hong Jing Group in Mach 1993, he successively invested and set up the following enterprise entities: Hong Jing Communication Company, Hong Jing Digital Port, International Grand Bazzar, Desert Oasis Spa Club, Sinkiang Silk Road International Ski Resort, Sinkiang Silk Road Fu Hsi School. Now he is the chairman of Sinkiang Hong Jing Group. The Sinkiang Silk Road International Ski Resort established by Li Jianghong, with strong cultural ski atmosphere and high-level service, is the best and biggest ski resort in the Northwest of China.

He used to be standing committee of CPPCC in Sinkiang area and the member of National People's Congress. He won the honorary titles of “Ten Outstanding Young Persons” award and “Model Worker in the Autonomous Region”.

丝绸之路滑雪场简介

丝绸之路国际滑雪度假区就坐落于天山山脉，位于乌鲁木齐城南38公里处的国家森林公园内，是由新疆宏景集团投资开发的，距离国际机场58公里，距离火车站40公里，全程一级公路，交通十分便利。度假区现已投资5亿元，占地 12 平方公里，海拔 1800 米至 2500 米，是国家 AAAA 级旅游景区。夏季绿草如茵，凉爽宜人，平均湿度 50%，平均温度 24℃左右；冬季日照充足、空气清爽、雪质纯净、冰雪资源十分丰富，平均温度零下 10℃左右；是夏季消暑旅游，冬季滑雪度假的理想选择。度假区内的丝绸之路滑雪场是 2016 年全国冬季运动会的比赛场地，也是新疆首家 SSSSS 级滑雪场，具有举办国内国际赛事的条件。

丝绸之路国际度假区同时建有 4300 米滑雪及观光缆车，由建造在海拔 2300 米山顶的芬兰式木屋酒店，新疆首家房车酒店，6000 平米生态景观餐厅、中华文华酒店、休闲木平台，阳光食街、雪地飞碟乐园、单板公园、高山滑冰场、滑雪综合服务大厅、国际各品牌雪具专卖店、动力三角翼会员飞行体验基地、硅化木博物馆、陨石展览馆、胡杨林公园等旅游度假配套服务设施，具有很高的服务档次和浓重的文化氛围，被评为“中国最佳滑雪旅游度假胜地”，荣获“全国旅游标准化示范基地”。

丝绸之路国际度假区是全民健身国家战略的践行者，秉承“运动成就健康生活”的企业理念，实现成为运动健康产业基地。

新疆丝绸之路国际滑雪场得益于中国重振丝绸之路经济带的大潮中，还朝着与国际化旅游相融的方向前进！

2015 年 1 月，丝绸之路滑雪场有幸成为《阿勒泰人类最古老的滑雪地域——2015 中国阿勒泰国际古老滑雪文化交流研讨会》和《第二届中国新疆国际丝绸之路旅游发展大会——丝绸旅游暨冰雪旅游高峰论坛》的协办单位，与来自于全国的专家学者相聚，使我们受益匪浅，我们诚心邀请朋友们再次，多次光临！

Brief Introduction of Silk Road Resort

Silk Road Resort, at the Tianshan Mountains, in a national forest park away from the south of Urumqi about 38km, is invested and developed by Xinjiang GrandScape Group. It has distance of 58km from Urumchi Diwobao International Airport, 40km from the railway station and the transportation is very convenient with total first level highway. With an investment of 500 million Yuan, the resort has an area of 12 km with an elevation of 1800m to 2500m and it is national 4A level scenery site. Summer has lush green grass and pleasant temperature, with average humidity 50% and average temperature 24 ° C or so; The winter has adequate sunshine, fresh air, pure and rich snow and ice, with the average temperature around 10 ° C below zero. In summer, the resort is an ideal place for tourism; in winter, the resort is an ideal choice for ski vacation. The silk road is also the competition field of 2016 National Winter Games and the first Xinjiang SSSSS level ski resort, having the condition of holding domestic and international events.

SilkRoad International Resort has built skiing and sightseeing cable car with 4300m long at the same time, the Finnish type wooden house hotel at an altitude of 2300m to the top of the hill, the first trailer hotel in Xinjiang, ecological landscape restaurant with 6000 ㎡, the Mndarin hotel, wooden platform for leisure, Sunshine food street, snow-flying saucer paradise, veneer park, alpine ice resort, comprehensive service hall, skiing equipment stores with international brands, flight experience base for dynamic delta wing member, silicified wood museum, meteorite gallery, populus euphratica forest park and other supporting service facilities. They all have high quality and strong cultural atmosphere. The resort is honored "China's best ski tourism resort" and "national tourism standardized demonstration base".

Silk Road ResortSilk road is a practitioner of national fitness strategy, adhering to the venture philosophy "sports to achieve healthy life", to become fitness industry base.

The development of Silk Road Resort is beneficial from the trend of China reviving Silk Road economic belt and it is striving to go forward to the direction of international tourism.

In January 2015, it is a great honor for the Silk Road ski resort to become the co-organizer of "Altai-the oldest ski tracks in the world—The International Ancient Skiing Cultural Exchange and Seminar in Altay City, China 2015" and "The 2nd China Silk Road Tourism Development Conference—Silk Road Tourism and Winter Tourism Summit". Experts and scholars from all over the world gather together, and we have benefited a lot from them. We sincerely hope all friends will come here again, and you are always welcome here!

在滑雪雕塑前合照 **A group photo in front of skiing sculpture**

考察丝绸之路滑雪场 Investigation on The Silk Road International Ski Resort

参观新疆博物馆　Visit to Xinjiang Museum

观看文艺演出，聚餐“大巴扎”
Watching theatrical performance, banquet in “Grand Bazaar”

第六章　“中国新疆阿勒泰—人类滑雪起源地”的研究历程回顾

Chapter Six Reviewing the Researching Course of “*Altay · Xinjiang · China—The Origin of Human Skiing*”

6.1　中国新疆阿勒泰地区是人类滑雪起源地的根据汇总

（1）阿勒泰地区具备了人类滑雪起源的一切自然条件。有山、有林、有 水、雪量大、雪期长、动物多。催生着人类滑雪狩猎的起源。

（2）人类很早就在阿勒泰地区生活。旧石器时代晚期就有人类在此区域活动的遗迹。为了生活，必然激励人类用滑雪工具征服雪，利用雪。

（3）语言学考证：

语言学家的研究表明，欧亚大陆的许多地方的人群的语言同属于阿勒泰语系，该语系横跨欧亚，主要分布在中国、蒙古、伊朗、土耳其、苏联及欧洲的一些国家。三个语族都是粘着语，在构词法和形态学上具有共同性。这也与欧亚大陆人类迁徙的学说大略一致。

（4）在阿勒泰市汗德尕特乡挖掘出的滑雪狩猎民谣，自古就在阿勒泰大地世代传唱。相关的故事也在民间广泛口传着。

（5）古老岩画是“写在石头上的文字”，阿勒泰区域古老滑雪岩画已发现多幅，数量多，范围广，种类多。年代少则几千年，多则上万年。阿勒泰市敦德布拉克发现的滑雪狩猎岩绘画距今 1-3 万年。

（确定滑雪岩画的依据是：人物基本呈站立状态；脚下有延长物；体姿有动感；其周围的岩画与狩猎有关。）

（6）人类发展史产生文字后，世界和中国最早对滑雪的记载，就是对阿勒泰滑雪人的记载。

（7）世界上最古老的毛皮滑雪板的制作和运用至今仍被阿勒泰农牧民广泛沿袭传承着。每年冬在阿勒泰市和喀纳斯——禾木都举行古老滑雪狩猎比赛。

（8）日本札幌冬季运动博物馆图展显示：“阿勒泰地方是古代人类滑雪的发祥地”，之后向东西方传播。

（9）原苏联 1980 年滑雪教科书中指出：“普遍公认的最早采用滑雪板的是生活在西伯利亚地区从贝加尔湖到阿勒泰地区的人们”。

（10）挪威著名滑雪学者、专家和著名探险家，诺贝尔奖获得者费里德约夫·南森（FRIDJDT NANSEN）先生1890年著书指出“滑雪运动很可能起源于东方的阿勒泰”，他认为斯堪的纳维亚所用的滑雪根词都来自中亚中心阿勒泰地区。（编者注：亚洲的中心位于乌鲁木齐市附近）

单兆鉴整理提供
2015年8月5日

The summarized Demonstrations of *Altai in Xinjiang* · China-the Oldest Ski Tracks in the World

（1）Altay prefecture meets all the basic natural conditions for being the first origin of skiing. This region has abundant mountains, trees, water, heavy snow and animals, which is fit for being the origin of skiing.

（2）Altay prefecture has a long history of human living. People have lived there from the late Old Stone Age. For living, they have incentive to take advantage of snow with skiing appliance.

（3）Research from linguistic perspective:

Findings from linguists show that languages of Eurasia in many parts belong to the Altay language family, this family across Europe and Asia, mainly distributed in China, Mongolia, Iran, Turkey, the Soviet Union and European countries. Three languages are glued to the language, have the common quality in terms of word formation and morphology. This is consistent with human migration theory of Eurasia.

（4）Long Tune-ski hunting ballad, found in Handegate township of Altay city, has been sung generation by generation in Altai since ancient times. And the related stories have also been passed widely in the folk.

（5）The ancient rock paintings is “written on the stone”, and ancient rock paintings about skiing have found in Altay region with large quantity, wide range and great variety. Some are thousands of years, many hundreds of thousands of years. Ski hunting rock paintings found in Dundebulake in Altay city has a long history of at least 10000-30000 years. （The ski paintings are based on the premise that basic characters are standing; feet have extensions; body postures have movements; the surrounding rock paintings are related to hunting.）

（6）After the generation of characters in Human history, the first record of skiing in China and in the world is the record of Altay skiers.

(7) The making and using of the oldest fur skis still have been passing widely among farmers and herdsmen in Altai. Every winter in Altay city and Kanas-Hemu old ski hunting game would be held.

(8) The Japanese Sapporo Winter Sports Museum has shown that *Altay is the birth place of the ancient skiing*.

(9) In 1980, Former Soviet Union skiing text has pointed out that people who live in the regions, from Lake Baikal in Siberia to Altay, is universally accepted as the first people using skis.

(10) Nobel Prize winner, FRIDJDT NANSEN who is also a famous ski scholar, expert and explorer, has illuminated in his book in 1890 that the ski was probably originated from Altay, the Orient. He puts out that the root words of skiing in Scandinavian are all from Altay, the center of central Asia.

(Note: The center of Asia is the place near Urumqi.)

Provided by Mr. Shan Zhaojian

August5, 2015

6.2 人类滑雪起源地研究历程的大事记 Memorabilia on the researching course

(1) 1993 年，单兆鉴首先在书中提出“中国新疆阿勒泰地区可能是人类滑雪起源地”。之后进行了长达 13 年的考察、研究，终获成功。

(2) 2004 年，单兆鉴完成了《人类滑雪起源应具备的基本条件》的研究，同年稍后接着又完成了《中国新疆阿勒泰地区具备了人类滑雪起源的一切基本条件》的研究。为这一研究课题奠定了理论基础。

(3) 2005 年，单兆鉴和王博、王建新等专家确定阿勒泰市汗德尕特蒙古族乡的敦德布拉克岩绘画为滑雪狩猎岩画，年代是距今 1 至 3 万年的旧石器时代晚期。使研究工作有了关键性的突破。

(4) 2006 年 1 月 15 日，在单兆鉴倡导之下，首届阿勒泰农牧民古老毛皮滑雪板比赛在阿勒泰市举行，从此拉开了弘扬传承阿勒泰古老滑雪文化的大幕。此后每年 1 月 16 日都举行这种比赛，至今已举办过 11 届。意义重大。

(5) 2006 年 1 月 16 日，7 名不同学科的研究人员（单兆鉴、王博、王建新、刘国防、吕思国、鲁礼鹏、郑颉）组成专家组（单兆鉴为组长）聚集阿勒泰市，经过科学的研讨，达成共识，在“人类滑雪最早起源于中国新疆阿勒泰地区”的《阿勒泰宣言》上签字，《阿勒泰宣言》诞生。宣言中倡议每年的 1 月 16 日为人类滑雪起源地纪念日。

（6）2006 年，单兆鉴、李辉等对阿勒泰古老毛皮滑雪板进行了广泛地调研，并进行了规范和记载。

（7）2006 年底，布尔津县冲乎尔乡努尔别克又发现了滑雪岩画，经尼尔·拉尔森、王博等专家鉴定命名为“滑雪者与狼羊图”，这是继敦德布拉克岩画发现之后又获取的重要史证。

（8）2006 年 12 月 15 日，在北京人民大会堂举行了“中国·新疆·阿勒泰是人类滑雪最早起源地”的新闻发布会。单兆鉴向世人宣布《阿勒泰宣言》。

（9）2007 年 1 月，人类滑雪起源地——阿勒泰得到上海基尼斯总部的认证，颁发了纪录证书。

（10）2007 年初，阿勒泰古老（毛皮板）滑雪队首次走出故乡，前往首府乌鲁木齐滑雪场、吉林市第六届亚洲冬运会赛地、首都北京滑雪场进行巡回表演宣传，引起国内外滑雪界人士的震撼。

（11）2009 年 1 月 3 日，周磊倡导新疆喀纳斯景区首届“禾木杯”古老滑雪狩猎（滑毛皮雪板+射箭打兽皮靶）在禾木村举行比赛。此后，每年都进行这种比赛，至今已举办过 8 届。

（12）2009 年 1 月，千载古老民间口传“滑雪狩猎”歌谣经尼咏梅完整挖掘整理出来。

（13）2009 年 9 月阿勒泰市新博物馆内添加了人类滑雪起源的展览内容。

（14）2009 年，由美国滑雪文化与历史研究学者尼尔·拉尔森编制的《永远的阿勒泰滑雪人》DVD，由喀纳斯景区译制成中文版，此 DVD 系统介绍了布尔津喀纳斯区域古老滑雪文化。

（15）2010 年 3 月 5 日，国际滑雪指导员联合会授予《阿勒泰宣言》主起草人单兆鉴特制专项奖牌，称“单兆鉴——为世界滑雪运动作出贡献”。

（16）2010 年 10 月 1 日在阿勒泰市汗德尕特乡建筑的我国首尊“古老滑雪雕塑”和“阿勒泰市乌梁海民俗文化陈列馆”竣工。

（17）2010 年夏秋，中央电视台几个频道播出大型专题《滑雪者寻源之旅》纪实片，记录了人类滑雪起源于阿勒泰考察研究的主要过程。由阿勒泰市政府与中央电视台合作摄制的。

（18）2011 年 1 月，《人类滑雪起源地——中国·新疆·阿勒泰》一书由北京人民体育出版社与新疆人民出版社联合出版，主编为单兆鉴、王博。1 月初该书的首发式在乌鲁木齐市新疆旅游局举行。

（19）2011 年 3 月 10 日，阿勒泰禾木村古老滑雪高手玛力琴和托合达参加在吉林北大湖滑雪场举行的亚洲登山滑雪锦标赛中分获冠、亚军。

（20）2011 年 6 月，布尔津县博物馆设立人类滑雪起源专展区，集中系统的介绍了滑雪起源阿勒泰的要点。

（21）2015 年 1 月 15 日—18 日，在新疆阿勒泰市举行的国际研讨会期间，来自 18 个国家近百名滑雪、历史、考古、旅游专家学者参会。经实地考察、研讨，达成共识，在形成的《2015 阿勒泰宣言》上签字，表示“对中国专家研究的成果——阿勒泰是人类滑雪最古老的摇篮，表示充分的肯定与支持”。

（注，2011 年 1 月出版的《人类滑雪起源地——中国·新疆·阿勒泰》书中全面、系统、详尽介绍了人类滑雪起源研究过程、根据等相关信息，可供详细查阅。）

单兆鉴整理提供

2015 年 8 月 5 日

The Researching Memorabilia of The Original Place of Skiing –*Altay Prefecture in Xinjiang, China*

（1）In 1993, Shan Zhaojian is thepioneer to propose “Altay Prefecture in Xinjiang, China may be the first origin of skiing”. After 13 years' investigation and research, he gets the final success.

（2）In 2004, Shan Zhaojian completes the study on Altay, Xinjiang, China Can Meet the Basic Conditions for Being the First Origin of Skiing and then Altay, Xinjiang, China Has Met all the Basic Conditions for Being the First Origin of Skiing.

（3）In 2005, Wang Bo, Shan Zhanojian , Wang Jianxin and other experts confirm that Dundebulake rocking painting in Handegate village in Altay City are about ancient hunting and skiing, and they have a long history of 10000–30000 years in the late Old Stone Age. The finding and natural determination make the research work have a key breakthrough.

（4）January 15, 2006, under the guide of Shan Zhanjian, the first skiing contest of fur skis is held in Altay city. From then on people begin to promote the ancient skiing culture with more efforts. Since then, the competition is held every year on January 16, and it has so far been held 11 times.

（5）January 16, 2006, 7 experts with different subject backgrounds form an expert team（Shan Zhaojian, Wang Bo, Wang Jianxin, Liu Guofang, Lv Siguo, Lu Lipeng, Zheng Jie）and gather in Altay city, making a consensus after serious discussion. Then they all have a signature on Altay Declaration with the determination of Altay

Prefecture in Xinjiang, China is the first origin of skiing. According to the Altay Declaration, the Altay government decides to make the Jan. 16 each year a Memorial Day for the place of origin of skiing — Altay of Xinjiang, China.

(6) In 2006, Shan Zhaojian, Li Hui and others launch a rather comprehensive research on ancient fur skis in Altay City, laying out regulations and making records.

(7) In 2006, Chonghuer Village of Buerjin County witnesses the finding of rock paintings about ancient skiing. Neil Larsen, Wang Bo and other experts have identified named the paintings "Skiers and Wolf Sheep", and this is an important historical demonstration of the rock paintings found in Dundebulake in Altay City.

(8) December 15, 2006, the press conference of The Original Place of Skiing-Altay Prefecture in Xinjiang, China is held in the Great Hall of the People in Beijing. Chan ZhaoJian announces the Altay Declaration to the public.

(9) January 2007, the origin of skiing-Altay is confirmed by the World Guinness Record of Shanghai Headquarters and is issued the record certificate.

(10) In the early year of 2007, for the first time Altay ancient (fur skis) skiing team goes out of home to Urumqi ski resort, Jilin city for the 6th Asian Winter Games and to Beijing's ski resorts for a performance tour, which gives a great shock to the skiing circle at home and abroad.

(11) January 2009, under the advocacy of Zhou Lei, Xinjiang-Kanas-Hemu old ski hunting game (fur skis + animal skin target archery) "Hemu Cup" is held in Hemu village for the first time. Since then every year has seen the performance of this game, which has been held8 times.

(12) In September 2009, the content of origin of skiing is added in a new museum in Altay city.

(13) In January 2009, the ski hunters' ditty, a traditional ballad, which has been sang by thousands of old folks, is dug out intactly.

(14) In 2009, the DVD "Altay Skiing People Forever" made by Neil Larsen, an American researcher on ski culture and history, is dubbed into Chinese version by Kanas scenic region. This DVD system introduces the old ski culture in Burqin-Kanas region.

(15) In March 5, 2010, the International Ski Instructor Union awards Shan Zhaojian, the main draftsman of the bookAltay Declaration, the special-made medal on special item, for the contribution Shan Zhaojian has made to the world ski sports.

(16) In October 1, 2010, Handegate village in Altay city sees the first "Ancient

Skiing Sculpture of Forefathers" and "Altay city Wu Lianghai Folk Culture Exhibition Hall in Altay City".

(17) In the summer of 2010, several channels in CCTV broadcast the large special documentary of "The Journey of Searching for the Origin of Skiers", which records the main process of the observation and study that skiing originates from Altay. This program is produced by the Altay Municipal Government and CCTV in cooperation.

(18) In January 2011, the bookThe Original Place of Skiing—Altay, Xinjiang, China is jointly published by Beijing People's Sports Publishing House and Volksverlag Xinjiang. The editors-in-chief are Shan Zhaojian and Wang Bo. The first issuing ceremony of this book is held in the Tourist Administration of Urumqi Municipality in Xinjiang in January.

(19) In March 2011, Maliqin and Tuoheda from Hemu village in Altay, two best skiers attend the Asian Mountain Skiing Championship, held in North Lake Ski Resort in Jilin Province, and they separately win the first and the second place through their fur skis, defeating the modern mountain skis.

(20) In June 2011, Burqin Museum is set up with special section for origin of skiing which centrally introduces the key points of original skiing.

(21) In January 15-18 2015, the International Conference held by Altay city in Xinjiang, nearly one hundred authoritative experts and scholars in skiing, history, archeology and travelling fields from 18 countries attended the conference and signed their names on the Altay Declaration, indicating that they offer full affirmation and firm support for the studying result by Chinese experts that Altay is the oldest track for human skiing.

(Note: The Original Place of Skiing-Altay Prefecture in Xinjiang, China, published in January 2011, has a comprehensive, systemic and concrete description on researching process and bases about the origin of human skiing and relevant information, which is available.)

Provided by Mr. Shan Zhaojian

August 5, 2015

6.3 《2006 年阿勒泰宣言》 *Altay Declaration 2006*

中国新疆阿勒泰地区是世界滑雪最早的起源地

主起草人及宣读者 单兆鉴

(2006 年 1 月 16 日于新疆阿勒泰市)

(2006 年 12 月 15 日于北京人民大会堂)

我们是相关学科的研究人员，经过认真的考察和研究，今天我们聚集在新疆阿勒泰市向世人郑重宣布：中国新疆阿勒泰地区是世界滑雪最早的起源地。其根据如下：

一、阿勒泰地区具备了滑雪起源的一切自然与人类活动的基本条件。

二、国内外已有学者指出，阿勒泰地区最先开始了人类滑雪活动，并逐渐向斯堪的纳维亚、阿拉斯加等地传播。

三、经过对阿勒泰地区实地考察发现，古人在洞穴中彩绘的人物滑雪图像，证实古阿勒泰人早在距今一万年左右就已开始了滑雪活动。

四、虽经漫长的时代变迁，现阿勒泰居民仍广泛沿袭脚踏自制的“毛滑雪板”、手持单只木杆在雪地里滑行的古老传统。

我们将在更广泛的领域中进行深入的考察和研究，使“中国新疆阿勒泰地区是世界滑雪最早的起源地”学说，得到国内外普遍认同并广泛传播。

我们高兴地看到，新疆阿勒泰市政府在保护相关文物和古老滑雪传统方面所做出的努力和取得的成效。中国滑雪协会对此给予了高度关注和大力支持。

我们诚挚地欢迎世界各国有兴趣的同仁及朋友们来中国新疆阿勒泰地区参观、考察。

为了让世人更深入了解世界滑雪最早起源地是在新疆阿勒泰地区，为了促进阿勒泰地区古老而璀璨的滑雪文化能够世代弘扬下去，我们倡议：

一、从 2006 年开始，将每年 1 月 16 日作为世界滑雪最早起源地纪念日。

二、在新疆阿勒泰市修建世界滑雪起源地博物馆。

三、为使“毛滑雪板”滑雪的古老的传统得以传承，坚持每年 1 月 16 日在新疆阿勒泰市举行古老滑雪比赛。

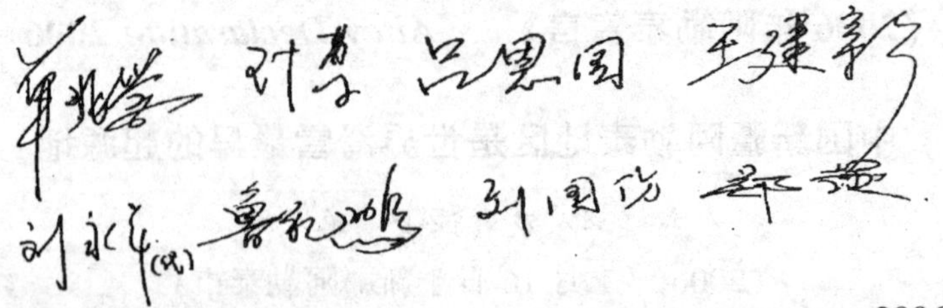

2006. 1. 16

图1　新疆阿勒泰市敦德布拉克滑雪岩绘画（距今1-2万年前）

图2　每年1月16日在新疆阿勒泰市都举行古老的滑雪比赛

Altay Declaration

Altay Region in Xinjiang Uigur Autonomous Region of China is
the World's Place of Origin For Skiing

We, the undersigned, are researchers on relevant disciplines. With careful investigation and research, we solemnly announce here in Altay City that Altay region in Xinjiang Uigur Autonomous Region of China is the world's place of origin forskiing, based on the following facts:

1. Altay region has the basic natural conditions needed for the human activities and origination of skiing.

2. Some scholars both at home and abroad have pointed out that it is in Altay region that skiing originated and that this sports later spread to Scandinavian and Alaskan regions.

3. By the field surveys conducted in Altay region, we have discovered colorful pictures of people skiing painted on the cave walls, proving that the ancient people in this region started skiing as early as about ten thousand years ago.

4. Over a long time change, native residents in Altay region still stick to the old tra-

dition that people ski with a pair of self-made skis attached to their boots and a wooden pole in one hand.

We will carry out further investigation and research in a wider range in order to make the theory that "Altay region in Xinjiang Uigur Autonomous Region of China is the world's place of origin for skiing" is worldwide recognized and accepted.

We are pleased to see that the Government of Altay City has made great effort and received significant results in preserving relevant historical relics and old skiing traditions. The Chinese Ski Association has paid enough attention to and given great support to them.

We sincerely welcome skiing enthusiasts and friends coming from all nations of the world to visit and investigate in Altay Region.

In order to facilitate people to better understand that the world skiing originated in Altay region, Xinjiang, and to carry forward the old and characteristic skiing culture one generation after another, we advocate that:

5. From the year 2006 on, Jan. 16 of each year is celebrated as the originating day of the world skiing.

6. A Museum of World Skiing Place of Origin is established.

7. In order to carry on and promote the ancient-style skiing tradition of using self-made skis, the ancient-style skiing contest is held in Altay City on Jan. 16 every year.

Signatures:
Shan Zaojian, Wang Bo, Lv Enguo, Wang Jianxin,
Liu Yongnian, Lu Lipeng, Liu Guofang & Zheng Jie

Jan. 16, 2006

Photo 1 Picture pained on the rocks in Dundebulake, Altay City, Xinjiang Uigur Autonomous Region of China (ten thousand to twenty thousand years ago)

Photo 2　The ancient-style skiing contest on Jan. 16 of every year in Altay City, Xinjiang Uigur Autonomous Region of China

6.4　《人类滑雪起源地—中国·新疆·阿勒泰》简介　Introduction to " *Altay · Xinjiang · China—The First Origin of Human Skiing*"

《阿勒泰宣言》与《人类滑雪起源地——中国·新疆·阿勒泰》是人类滑雪历史研究的重要文献，其成果填补了世界性人类滑雪起源研究不系统、不全面的空白，对世界滑雪运动作出贡献。使中国在该领域的研究处于领先地位。

《人类滑雪起源地——中国·新疆·阿勒泰》由“前序篇”“中文篇”“英文篇”3部分构成，24个章节，437千字，374幅图片和照片。用中、英两种文字编印。主编：单兆鉴、王博，副主编：拉尔·尼尔森（美）、王建新、刘国防、周磊。

The altay declaration and the origin of human skiing-China's xinjiang · altay “is one of the important research history human skiing literature, and the research results to fill the worldwide human skiing origin and comprehensive study not system of blank, to the world skiing to contribute. Make China in the fields of study is in the lead.

“The human skiing-China · xinjiang origin · altay” by “former XuPian” “Chinese essay” “English essay” 3 part, chapter 24, 437000 words, 374 picture and photos. In two languages, with). Editor: ChanZhaoJian WangBo deputy editor: lal nelson (beauty) WangJianXin LiuGuoFang ZhouLei.

6.5 阿勒泰古老毛皮滑雪板等器具简介

人类滑雪最早起源地——中国·新疆·阿勒泰至今仍在传承着的古老滑雪器具包括:“阿勒泰古老毛皮滑雪板”及其配套的单木杆滑雪杖、兽皮条制作的固定器、普通棉鞋。这种古老滑雪器具在阿尔泰山区域已有几千年的演化历史。

阿勒泰古老毛皮滑雪板造型简单,前窄后宽,普遍用松木制作,没有弧度,没有弹性,雪板底面敷有兽毛皮(主要是马腿毛皮)。这种古老毛皮滑雪板完全根据使用者自身的实际情况与需求手工制作,故外形规格尺寸差别很大,雪板一般长于使用者身高20厘米左右,约为180-220厘米(有的更长些,最长达330厘米),中部宽12-16厘米,厚度约2-3厘米,前尖部向上翘起的很大;单木杆滑雪杖多采用硬韧的树木杆,一般长于配套的滑雪板20厘米,约为190-240厘米(有的更长些),直径3-4厘米;编制固定器的兽皮条宽度一般为1-2厘米。

阿勒泰古老滑雪器具有典型的实用功能,制作、携带、维修十分方便。上山时兽毛逆茬,雪板不倒滑,平地走滑和下山时兽毛顺茬,雪板滑行不受影响。雪板与具有多种用途的单木杆滑雪杖及可抬起鞋后跟的固定器组合起来,非常适合在山野大地厚厚“野雪”中运行,可在各种地形、各种雪质、各种环境等复杂条件下滑行,昔日被广泛运用在滑雪狩猎活动中及作为日常代步的交通工具。

Brief Introduction of the Ancient Fur Skis in Altay of Xinjiang, China

Altay—the first origin of skiing in the world, still has the ancient skiing appliance which includes fur skis and matched single wooden poles, holders made of animal skins and common cotton shoes. This old appliance already has thousands of years of evolution history in Altai area.

The ancient fur skis' shape is simple, the former narrow and the back wide, generally made of pine, no arc, no flexibility, with animals' fur under the bottom (mainly the fur of the horses' legs）. The old fur skis have different sizes, based entirely on the users' own actual situations and demands, by hand. Skis are usually longer than the users' height about 20 centimeters with about 180cm－220cm tall（some longer, up to 330cm）. And the central part is 12cm－16cm wide, about 2cm－3cm thick. The front part is tip and greatly curls up. Single wooden poles are generally made by hard tree rods, usually longer than matched skis about 20 centimeters, which is about 190cm－240cm（or longer）, 3cm to 4cm in diameter. The stripe of animal skins, used for making bindings, generally is 1cm－2cm wide.

The ancient Altai fur skis have typically practical functions and they are easy to make, to carry and to repair. Up the mountain when the animal hair is inverted and the skis are anti-slip. When skis are slippery and animal hair is in the same direction down the mountain, the sliding of skis is not affected. Skis along with multi-functional single wooden poles and heel-lifting biding can combine together well, which are very suitable for running in the back countryside with thick snow, and can slide in all sorts of terrain, all sorts of snow quality types under complex conditions, such as different environments. In the past days it's widely used in hunting activities and as part of their daily walking means of transportation.

阿勒泰毛皮滑雪板、单木杆滑雪杖、大弓箭、羊皮雪橇

Altay fur skis, single wooden pole, archer and sheepskin sled

6.6 国际滑雪组织向单兆鉴颁发特殊奖牌 The International Skiing Organization presents Shan Zhaojian special medal

2010 年 3 月 5 日，国际滑雪指导员联合会授予《阿勒泰宣言》主起草人单兆鉴特制专项奖牌，称“单兆鉴——为世界滑雪运动作出贡献”。

In March 5, 2010, the International Ski Instructor Union awards Shan Zhaojian, the main draftsman of the book Altay Declaration, the special-made medal on special item, for the contribution Shan Zhaojian has made to the world ski sports.

颁发特殊奖牌 **Presenting a special medal**

奖牌 **Medal**

附　录
Appendices

1. 愉快的旅行，难忘的阿勒泰　Pleasant trips and unforgettable Altay

阿勒泰热烈的欢迎酒会　**Welcome party in Altay**

观看绚丽的文艺演出　**Great theatrical performance**

可口的中国菜自助餐 **Delicious Chinese Buffet**

中式的“大圆桌”就餐文化
Chinese style “big round table” dining culture

2. 参加会议专家学者通讯录　Address list of conference attendees

中国专家学者　Chinese experts and scholars

Form1/表1　　List of Conference Attendees/出席会议专家学者名单

Country/国家	Name/姓名	Gender/性别	Dept/Occupation/Degree/部门/职业/学位	Email/Tel/邮箱/电话	Add/ZC/地址/邮编	Remarks/备注
CN/中国	Shan Zhaojian/单兆鉴	M/男	Research expert on skiing historical culture/滑雪历史文化研究专家/《阿勒泰宣言》专家组组长	shanzhaojian@136.com 13901198057	北京海淀区北三环西路11号首都体育学院4-4-201 100088	
CN/中国	Wang Bo/王博	M/男	Researcher at Xinjiang Museum/Member of the expert team of Altay Declaration/新疆博物馆研究员/《阿勒泰宣言》专家组成员	1019903728@qq.com 18290887763	新疆乌鲁木齐市西北路132号新疆博物馆 830000	
CN/中国	Wang Jianxin/王建新	M/男	Professor and doctoral supervisor at School of Cultural Heritage, Northwest University/Member of the expert team of Altay Declaration西北大学文化遗产院教授、博士生导师/《阿勒泰宣言》专家组成员	13319185059@163.com 13319185059		
CN/中国	Lu Lipeng/鲁礼鹏	M/男	Head of Archaeology Department at Xinjiang Regional Museum/Member of the expert team of Altay Declaration/新疆博物馆考古部部长/《阿勒泰宣言》专家组成员	344468136@qq.com 18009918825	新疆乌鲁木齐市西北路581号新疆博物馆考古部 830000	
CN/中国	Li Jianhong/李健宏	M/男	President and researcher of Xinjiang Silk Road Ski Resort/新疆丝绸之路滑雪场董事长、研究员	lijianhong138@gmail.com 13909918138	新疆乌鲁木齐县水西沟镇丝绸之路国际度假村 830037	
CN/中国	Ni Yongmei/尼咏梅	F/女	Member of Culture and Sports Bureau of Urumchi/Contributor to the research on the Original Place of Skiing/Digger and trimmer of "The Hunter"/市文体局工作人员/起源地研究作出贡献/"打猎人"歌谣挖掘和整理者	niyongmei1019@163.com 15909061041	新疆阿勒泰市文化体育局 836500	
CN/中国	Zhou Lei/周磊	F/女	Reporter and editor at Urumchi Evening Paper/Contributor to the research on the Original Place of Skiing/Interviewer of foreign experts/乌鲁木齐晚报记者、编辑/起源地研究作出贡献	383622143@qq.com 13999976512	新疆乌鲁木齐市乌鲁木齐晚报社	
CN/中国	Gao Chunhui/高春惠	F/女	Head of Cultural Relics Bureau of Xinjiang/新疆伊犁州文物局局长	2630276120@qq.com 13399997000	新疆伊犁市州文物局(伊宁市飞机场路188号)	
CN/中国	Shi Xiaoming/史晓明	M/男	Professor and doctor at Xinjiang Arts University/新疆艺术学院教授、博士	sxmkzr@163.com 18997916858	乌鲁木齐市团结路734号新疆艺术学院	
CN/中国	Ba.Batubayar 巴•巴图巴雅尔	M/男	Secretary-general of Xinjiang Association for Oirat Mongol Studies and associate professor at Xinjiang Normal University/新疆师范大学 副教授 新疆卫拉特学会秘书长	batubayar99@163.com 13109951905	新疆乌鲁木齐市新疆师范大学 乌鲁木齐市水磨沟区观景路100号	
CN/中国	Bayier.Caicike/巴依尔·才次克	F/女	Graduate and professor assistant at School of Arts, Xinjiang Normal University/新疆师大文学院研究生、教授助手	18139689477	新疆乌鲁木齐市新疆师范大学	
CN/中国	Wu Xiaohua/吴晓华	F/女	Professor and skiing culture researcher at School of Ice and Snow, Jilin Sport University/吉林体院冰雪研究室 教授滑雪文化研究专家	759131608@qq.com 18004430015	吉林省长春市南岭吉林体院	
CN/中国	Zhao Zhijun/赵志军	M/男	Party Secretary and doctor at Jilin Sport University/吉林体院党委书记、博士	759131608@qq.com 13844912525	吉林省长春市南岭吉林体院	
CN/中国	Yu Liqiang/于立强	M/男	Head of School of Ice and Snow and doctor at Jilin Sport University/吉林体育学院冰雪学院院长、博士	yuliqiang412@qq.com 18686693168	吉林省长春市南岭吉林体院	
CN/中国	Li Yugang/李玉刚	M/男	Director of School Office at Jilin Sport University/吉林体育学院院办主任、硕士	994823993@qq.com 18943101722	吉林省长春市南岭吉林体院	
CN/中国	Wang Donghai/王东海	M/男	Professor and ski equipment expert at Harbin Institute of Physical Education/哈尔滨体院教授、滑雪设备专家	aogoo1@vip.sina.com 13936240229	黑龙江省哈尔滨市哈尔滨体院 哈尔滨市南岗区大成街1号哈尔滨体育学院	

CN/中国	Zhang Guihai/张贵海	M/男	Professor and doctoral supervisor at Heilongjiang Institute of Tourism Economics/黑龙江旅游经济学院教授、博士生导师	YFZGH@163.NET. 13703612729	黑龙江省哈尔滨市黑龙江旅游经济学 哈尔滨市南岗区征仪路331号大众嘉园3#-201	
CN/中国	Tang Yunsong/唐云松	M/男	Professor at Heilongjiang University/黑龙江大学教授	tangyunsong6@126.com 13836005058	黑龙江省哈尔滨市黑龙江大学 哈尔滨市南岗区学府路74号	
CN/中国	Yu Yang/于洋	F/女	General manager of Carving Group/researcher and promoter of ancient skiing traditions/北京卡宾集团总经理/古老滑雪传统研究和推广者	281512007@qq.com 13701396111	北京石景山区八角东街65号 融科创意中心A座804	
CN/中国	Hurile Bater/呼日勒巴特尔		Professor, doctor and doctoral supervisor at Inner Mongolia University/内蒙古大学教授、博士、博士生导师	u.khurelbaatar@163.com 13948511232	内蒙古呼和浩特市内蒙古大学	
CN/中国	史志强	M/男	Head of Xinjiang Altay Tourism Administration/新疆阿勒泰市旅游局局长		新疆阿勒泰市屯揭路27号市旅游局 836500	

世界专家学者　Foreign experts and scholars

Form1/表1　　List of Conference Attendees/出席会议专家学者名单

Country/国家	Name/姓名	Gender/性别	Dept/Occupation/Degree/部门/职业/学位	Email/Tel/邮箱/电话	Add/ZC/地址/邮编	Remarks/备注
NO/挪威	Karin Berg 卡琳·博格	F/女	Director of Holmenkollen Ski Museum, Oslo, Norway/Researcher of skiing history/挪威奥斯陆滑雪博物馆主任/世界著名滑雪历史文化研究专家	Karin.Berg@skiforeningen.no		
NO/挪威	Thomas Aslaksby 托马斯	M/男	Norwegian Ski Designer/挪威滑雪设计者	004740636772 Skimaker@Frisurf.no		
NO/挪威	Espen Finstad 埃斯·分斯塔德	M/男	Archaeologist of Oppland County Council, Department of Cultural Heritage/Researcher of skiing history/Engineer of Lillehammer, Norway/奥普兰理事会考古学家/滑雪历史研究专家/挪威利勒哈默工程师	004790179443 espen.fistal@oppland.no		
NO/挪威	Dag Inge Bakke 贝克	M/男	Archaeologist/Mountain instructor/Ski coach/考古学家/山地指导员/滑雪教练	4799041360 dag@fiell.museum.no		
NO/挪威	Sondre Aslaksby 桑卓	M/男	Successor of Norway ancient skiing culture/Inheritor of ancient skiing dance/挪威古老滑雪文化接班人/古老滑雪舞蹈传承人	004740636772 Skimaker@Frisurf.no		
萨米拉普兰	Hartvig Birkely 哈特维格· 伯克利	M/男	Famous Sami author/Researcher of skiing history/萨米著名作家、滑雪历史研究专家	90532518 wartvib@online.no		
DK/丹麦	Lars Pilo 拉斯· 皮罗	M/男	Archaeologist of Oppland County Council/Executor of international heritage project/Researcher of skiing history/奥普兰理事会考古学家/国际遗产项目执行者/滑雪历史研究专家	004794852220 Lar.holger.pilo@oppland.no		
SE/瑞典	Kurt Skoog 库尔特·斯科格	M/男	Producer of Sweden TV Station and Power Films Company/making movies about skiing history now/瑞典电视台和发电机电影公司制作人/现在正在制作人类滑雪历史电影	46703293083 info@dynamofilm.se		
SE/瑞典	RolfMichael Sundberg 米奇·松德贝里	M/男	Swedish ski coach/Skiing historian/瑞典滑雪指导者/滑雪历史学家	46703040354 sundbergprod@me.com		
SE/瑞典	Anna Erlandsson 安娜·埃兰德松	女	Researcher of skiing culture in north Europe/北欧滑雪文化研究学者	annapanna56@gmail.com +46 70 6563380		
SE/瑞典	Kjell-Åke Aronsson谢尔-阿克·安德森	M/男	Director at Swedish Mountain and Sámi Museum/Researcher of skiing culture/瑞典安塔尔博物馆主任、滑雪历史研究专家	kjell-ake.aronsson@aitte.com +46702315998		
SE/瑞典	Isse Israelsson伊斯·伊斯拉埃尔松	M/女	Director of Sweden Ski Museum/Ski archaeologist/瑞典滑雪博物馆主任、滑雪考古专家	isse.israelsson@aitte.com +46730566108		
US/美国	Wayne Poulsen 威	M/男	Expert and professor at the World Delegation of Ancient Skiing in Altai Mountains/Historian of skiing culture国际阿尔泰山古老滑雪考察团专家、教授，滑雪文化历史学者	Wayne Poulsen@gmail.com		

US/美国	Nils Larsen 尼尔·拉尔森	M/男	Researcher of American ancient skiing culture/Cooperator with Chinese experts/美国古老滑雪文化研究专家 中国专家合作者/对阿勒泰古老文化研究获得成果	nils@altaiskis.com		
US/美国	Glen Poulsen 格兰	M/男	American patagonia international expedition guide/ski researcher/国际探险向导研究员、滑雪运动研究者	001-530-9136775 skiprazd@hotmail.com		
USA/美国	Sarah Jo Halas 沙拉	F/女	Researcher of international ski expedition/国际探险滑雪运动研究员	208721-8341 sarah halas@gmail.com		
AT/奥地利	MAG.WERNER MARGREITER 维尔纳	M/男	Consultant of FIS/President of Alpin Allianz/国际雪联顾问/阿尔卑斯联盟项目发展有限公司总裁	werner.margreiter@wernermargreiter.onmicrosoft.com +436643375134		
AT/奥地利	Arno Klien 阿诺·科莱恩	M/男	Expert on ski techniques training of ancient skiing tradition studies/滑雪技术人员培训、古老滑雪传统研究专家	Qvno.klien@telemark-Qusma.Qt		
KR/韩国	Park Chung Woong/朴正雄	M/男	Researcher of skiiing culture/Expert on international skiing exchange and scientific application of equipment for ski areas/滑雪文化研究者/国际滑雪交流及滑雪场设备科学运用专家			
KR/韩国	Wang Fang/王方	M/男	Expert on international skiing exchange and scientific application of equipment for ski areas/Korean expert assistant/国际滑雪交流及滑雪场设备科学运用专家/韩方专家助理	jack@cnmatrix.com		
SI/斯洛文尼亚	Dr. Borut Batagelj布鲁特·巴塔力	M/男	Slovene skiing history expert/斯洛文尼亚人类滑雪研究专家	batagelj@gmail.com +38631866581		
GB/英国	Emma Cowel 艾玛·科威	F/女	Marketing consultant for the researchers of UK tourism at UiT The Arctic University of Norway/Candidate of tourism promotion/挪威北极大学英国旅游业研究员的市场顾问/旅游推广产业候选人	0044(0)7976700861 emmacowell@yahoo.com		
CH/瑞士	Bengt Erik Bengtsson 艾瑞克·本桑	M/男	Technology officer at FIS/Researcher of skiiing historical culture/国际雪联技术官员、滑雪历史文化研究学者	Bengt-erik.bengtsson@telia.com		
CZ/捷克	Ondrej Srba 乌恩德尔杰·赛尔巴	M/男	Doctor and Professor of Institute of South and Central Asia at Charles University in Prague/Altay historical culture specialist/捷克布拉格市查理大学哲学院南中亚系教师、博士，阿勒泰历史文化专员	ondrejsrba@gmail.com 420-739783768		
CN/中国	Ayken/阿依肯·加山	M/男	Researcher of Chinese skiing history/Graduate at UiT The Arctic University of Norway/Tourism researcher/中国滑雪历史研究员/挪威北极大学研究生/旅游专业研究学者	344468136@qq.com 13609902424	乌鲁木齐市阿勒泰路红庙子阳光雅洞小区2期7号楼204房间	
MG/蒙古国	Saletanate/萨勒塔纳特（等7人）	M/男	Deputy mayor of Ölgii/Head of the Delegation/Researcher of skiing historical culture/乌列盖市市政府副市长/代表团团长/滑雪历史文化研究学者			
RU/俄罗斯	Anadia/阿纳迪亚·那斯普汗	F/女	Graduate professor assistant at Siberian Federal University/Skiing culture researcher/俄罗斯西伯利亚大学研究生，教授助理，滑雪文化研究者	iharnadi@mail.ru		
KZ/哈萨克斯坦	Burkitbay G. Ayagan 柏克蓓	M/男	Member of National Association of Kazakhstan/Performer of National History Association/Researcher of skiing historical culture/哈萨克斯坦国家协会成员/国家历史协会执行者/滑雪历史文化研究学者	77772556901		
MG/蒙古国	DAMDINSUREN·TSEVEENDORJ 达木丁苏荣·策往道尔吉	M/男	Head of Institute of Archaeology of Mongolia Academy of Social Sciences/Skiing history expert/蒙古国社会科学院考古研究所所长/滑雪历史研究专家	976-11-342213 (o) dtseve@yahoo.com	考古系主任，乌兰巴托-51号蒙古科学院，历史学院，蒙古	
PL/波兰	Tomasz Jagodzinski 托马斯·加	M/男	Curator of Museum of Sports and Tourism in Warsaw/Skiing culture expert/华沙体育和旅游博物馆馆长/滑雪文化研究专家			
FI/芬兰	J-P.Taavitsainen 杰西皮克	M/男	Archaeology professor at University of Turku/Skiing historical culture researcher/芬兰图库大学考古教授/滑雪历史文化研究学者	00358 400876525		

3. 鸣谢

在“阿勒泰人类最古老的滑雪地域—2015 中国阿勒泰国际古老滑雪文化交流研讨会”的筹备、举办的过程中，在《2015 中国阿勒泰国际古老滑雪文化论坛报告》出版的各环节中，得到众多部门和人士的支持、协办，特此鸣谢如下：

特别鸣谢：

国家体育总局中国体育文化发展中心
中国滑雪协会
北京卡宾滑雪集团
北京大学中国体育产业研究中心
北京卡宾冰雪产业研究院
新疆旅游局
新疆阿勒泰地区党委、行署
新疆阿勒泰市市委、市政府

鸣谢以下部门：

新疆博物馆
北京卡宾雪行天下滑雪场规划设计公司
新疆丝绸之路国际滑雪场
新疆喀纳斯景区管委会
新疆布尔津县博物馆
新疆阿勒泰地区博物馆
新疆阿勒泰市委宣传部
新疆阿勒泰市广播电视局
新疆阿勒泰市旅游局
新疆阿勒泰市将军山滑雪场
新疆阿勒泰市文化体育局
新疆阿勒泰市汗德尕特乡
新疆阿勒泰市拉乡特乡
新疆喀纳斯管委会禾木哈纳斯蒙古民族乡
新疆阿勒泰地区旅游局
东方达沃斯（北京）滑雪场规划设计咨询公司（董事长 阮标）
北京蜂鸟文化发展有限公司（董事长 罗勇）
北京桥山集团（董事长 刘小山）
北京太舞旅游度假有限公司·崇礼（董事长 齐宏）

崇礼县太舞滑雪山地度假有限公司

瑞雪盈冬（北京）体育装备有限公司（总经理 马丽）

中国体育明星冠军滑雪队（队长 郭丹丹）

鸣谢以下人士：

翻译（按姓氏笔画为序）：

马元常、巴·巴图巴雅尔、付贵平、巩山别克、刘湘杰、米娜·热斯别克、孙佳、孙慧、吴东欣、吴永敏、纳迪亚、佟姗、周永梅、郭丽明、程燕、薛玉洁、黎秋月、肇文萍

美术摄像：

巴合达提·木拉提、王成、金炜、刘孟孟、金雨锋、郭红、李海瑞

图片资料提供（按姓氏笔画为序）：

于洋、于娜、巴·巴图巴雅尔·巴合提别克·阿汗、巴图蒙古·巴依斯胡林、王东海、王凤琳、王金伟、王博、王建新、王琴、宁玄洺、史志强、尼咏梅、代森、冯卓然、刘新海、刘占军、李丽、李昕玲、李忠辉、杜鹏飞、杜曼·阿不都拉别克、玛力琴、库尔特·斯科格、邵长立、吴晓华、拉尔·尼尔森、赵文玲、赵兰英、周金敏、罗晓晴、周磊、胡明月、杨开静、范旭阳、金炜、张一兵、张凤娟、张贵海、张晓菲、唐伟、唐云松、雷东翔、鲍幸君

Acknowledgements

In the process of preparing and hosing the *Altai- the oldest ski tracks in the world*, *The International Ancient Skiing Cultural Exchange Seminar in Altay City*, *China* 2015, *and the publishing of The International Ancient Skiing Cultural Forum Report in Altay*, *Xinjiang* 2015, the following departments, organizations and people have offered great help, we would like to express heartfelt thankfulness:

Special Thanks:

Sports Culture Development Center of General Administration of Sports

Chinese Ski Association

Beijing Carving Ski Group

Peking University Institute Center for China Sports Industry

Beijing Carving Institute of Ice & Snow Skiing Industry

Xinjiang Tourism Bureau

Xinjiang Altay Municipal Committee of the Communist Party of China and the Altay Administrative Office

Thanks to following departments:

Xinjiang Altay Municipal Committee and the Altay Municipal Government

Xinjiang Museum

Beijing Carving Snow Kingdom Ski Resort Planning and Design Co., Ltd

Xinjiang Silk Road International Ski Resort

Xinjiang Kanas Scenic Spot Management Committee

Xinjiang Buerjin County Museum

Museum of Xinjiang Altay Prefecture

Xinjiang Altay Municipal Party Committee of Publicity Department

Altay Radio and TV Bureau Xinjiang Uygur Autonomous Region

Xinjiang Altay City Tourism Bureau

Xinjiang Altay Jiangjunshan Ski Resort

Xinjiang Altay Culture and Sport Bureau

Altay Handegate Mongolian Village of Xinjiang Uygur Autonomous Region

Altay Laster Village of Xinjiang Uygur Autonomous Region

Buerjin County Hanash-Hemu Mongolian Village of Xinjiang Kanas Management Committee

Altay Tourism Bureau of Xinjiang Uygur Autonomous Region

Oriental Davos Ski Resort Planning and Design Consulting (Beijing) Co., Ltd (President Ruan Biao)

Beijing Fengniao Culture Development Co., Ltd (President Luo Yong)

Beijing Qiaoshan Group (President Liu Xiaoshan)

Beijing Thaiwoo Tourism Resort Co., Ltd. Chongli (President Qi Hong)

Winter Sports Beijing Co., Ltd (General Manager Ma Li)

China Sports Stars Champion Ski Team (Team Leader Guo Dandan)

Thanks to following members:

Translators (listed in the order of the number of strokes in their surnames):

Ma Yuanchang Ba · Batuyaer Fu Guiping Gongshanbieke Liu Xiangjie Mina · Resibieke Sun Jia Sun Hui Wu Dongxin Wu Yongmin Na Diya Tong Shan Zhou Yongmei Guo Liming Cheng Yan Xue Yujie Li Qiuyue Zhao Wenping

Art Photography:

Bahedati mutila Wang Cheng Jin Wei Liu Mengmeng Jin Yufeng Guo Hong Li Hairui

Photos and materials providers (listed in the order of the number of strokes in their surnames):

Yu Yang Yu Na Ba · Batubayaer Bahetibieke · Ahan Batumenggu Bayisihulin Wang Donghai Wang Fenglin Wang Jinwei Wang Bo Wang Jianxin Wang Qin Ning Xuanming Shi Zhiqiang Ni Yongmei Dai Sen Feng Zhuoran Liu Xinhai Liu Zhanjun

Li Li Li Xinling Li Zhonghui Du Pengfei Duman · Abudulabieke Maliqin Kurt Skoog Shao Changli Wu Xiaohua Nils Larsen Zhao Wenling Zhao Lanying Zhou Jinmin Luo Xiaoqing Zhou Lei Hu Mingyue Yang Kaijing Fan Xuyang Jin Wei Zhang Yibing Zhang Fengjuan Zhang Guihai Zhang Xiaofei Tang Wei Tang Yunsong Lei Dongxiang Bao Xingjun

4. 中国新疆维吾尔自治区简介　Brief introduction of Xinjiang, China

中国新疆维吾尔自治区，位于亚欧大陆中部，亚洲的中心，地处中国西北边陲，总面积 166 万平万公里，陆地边境线长达 5600 多公里，是中国面积最大、交界邻国最多、陆地边界线最长的省区。

新疆古称西域，1949 年新疆和平解放，1955 年 10 月 1 日成立新疆维吾尔自治区，首府设在乌鲁木齐市。举世闻名的丝绸之路在新疆境内留下了无数古烽燧、古遗址、壁画等，具有深厚文化底蕴的历史遗产。

新疆是一个多民族聚居的地区，共有 55 个民族成分，截至 2011 年末，新疆总人口 2208.71 万人，其中少数民族人口约占 60%。全区辖有 14 个地州市，其中包括 42 个民族乡。新疆生产建设集团兵团是自治区的重要组成部分。

新疆的地形地貌可以概括为“三山夹两盆”：北面是阿勒泰山，南面是昆仑山，天山横贯中部，把新疆分为南北两部分，习惯上称天山以南是南疆，天山以北是北疆。

新疆具有丰富的冰雪旅游资源，是中国最具魅力的冰雪旅游胜地。新疆优良的冰雪资源、雪域高原、高山冰川，自然美景美不胜收，令中外游客神往。新疆开发大小滑雪场所几十座，特别是“人类滑雪起源地——阿勒泰”向世界显示出古老文化滑雪的真谛，成为新疆冰雪旅游的重要发展引擎。

新疆是中国未来的财富成长地，是世界人文资源的宝库。旅游业日益成为促进新疆对外开放、优化区域产业结构、实现绿色低碳发展的重要选择。

自古以来，新疆就是一个多民族聚居和多种宗教并存的地区，东西方文化交融、多元文明交汇的地方。世界文明的古“丝绸之路”贯穿新疆。新疆是大美之地、壮美之地。

新疆素有“歌舞之乡”美称，各民族歌舞绚丽多姿，具有浓郁的民族风情和地域特色。

自2010年起，中央政府举全国之力推进新疆跨越式发展和长治久安，内地19个省市对口支援新疆，借助这一新的历史机遇，新疆各项事业站在了跨越式发展的新起点上。未来一个和谐、多元、现代、充满希望和梦想的新疆会展现给海内外游客。让新疆走向世界，让世界了解新疆。

Brief Introduction of Xinjiang, China

Xinjiang Uygur Autonomous Regionis located in the middle of the Eurasian, the center of Asia, in the northwest of China, with a total area of 1, 660, 000k㎡ and the land border for more than 5, 600km. It is China's province with the largest area, the most border neighbors and the longest land border.

Xinjiang is called Xiyu in ancient times and it enjoys liberation in 1949. On October 1, 1955, Xinjiang Uygur Autonomous Region comes into being with Urumqi as its capital. The world famous Silk Road has left innumerable ancient beacons, ancient ruins, murals, etc, which have rich cultural accumulation.

Xinjiang is a multi-ethnic populated area, with total number of 55 ethnics. By the end of 2011, the total population in Xinjiang has reached 2. 20871 million, and the ethnic minority population accounts for about 60%. The region is comprised of 14 cities, including 42 townships. The Xinjiang production and construction group corps are important part of autonomous region.

The topography and geomorphology of Xinjiang can be summarized as "three mountains and two basins". Altay Mountains lie in the north, Kunlun Mountain to its south, Tianshan Mountain in the middle as the line of demarcation into two parts of Xinjiang. The north is traditionally called the northern Xinjiang, the south is called the southern Xinjiang.

Xinjiang has a wealth of ice and snow tourism resources and it is most attractive tourism resort of ice. Xinjiang has excellent ice and snow resources, snow-covered plateau, mountain glaciers and natural beauty, which appeal to tourists at home and abroad. Xinjiang has developed dozens of ski resorts with different sizes. Especially "the first origin of human skiing-Altay" shows the world the essence of ancient culture skiing, becoming an important growth engine of ice-snow tourism in Xinjiang.

Xinjiang isthe growing region for future wealth and the treasure of humane resources. Tourism has increasingly become an important choice for Xinjiang to open to the outside world, to upgrade regional industrial structure, to realize green low carbon development.

Fromthe ancient times, Xinjiang is a region with multi-ethnic population, with co-existence of diverse religions, with eastern and western cultural fusion and diverse civilizations. The world-famous "silk road" is going through the whole Xinjiang. Xinjiang is a place with great beauty and grand beauty.

Xinjiang is well known as the "hometown of dance and song" . The multi-ethnics' songs and dances are colorful, with rich ethnic customs and local characteristics.

From the year of 2010, the central government makes great efforts to promote leap-frog development and realize lasting stability in Xinjiang. 19 provinces in counterpart support the development of Xinjiang. With the help of this new historical opportunity, various undertakings of Xinjiang stand in the new starting point of leap-forward development. A brand - new Xinjiang, with harmony, diversification, modernity, hope and dream will be presented to tourists from home and abroad. Let Xinjiang embrace the world, and let the world appreciate Xinjian.

5. 阿勒泰地区简介

阿勒泰地区地处新疆北部，阿尔泰山南麓，东部与蒙古接壤，西部、北部与哈萨克斯坦、俄罗斯交界，国界线长 1175 公里。所辖 6 县 1 市均为边境开放县(市)，国家已批准开放四个口岸。

阿勒泰地区境内共有 2 条国道、11 条省道，乡镇通公路率达到 100%。阿勒泰地委、行署所在地阿勒泰市是国道 216、217 线起始点，西线距乌鲁木齐市 701 公里，东线为 670 公里，航线距离 450 公里。阿勒泰地区有阿勒泰机场和喀纳斯机场，阿勒泰机场位于阿勒泰市西南方，距市中心 10 公里。喀纳斯机场距国家 5A 级景区喀纳斯约 80 公里。

阿勒泰地区面积 11.78 万平方公里。人口 67 万人，哈萨克族占 51.3%，是中国蒙古族图瓦人的唯一居住地。介于北纬 45°0′—49°11′之间。阿尔泰山山形饱满、地形宽广，海拔和温度适中，风力不大，雪量大（1.5 米左右）、雪期长(有效雪期可达 6 个月)、是发展冰雪运动和旅游的理想区域。

阿勒泰地区是人类滑雪最早起源地。阿勒泰市敦德布拉克岩画、布尔津滑雪狩猎岩画等都证明，至少在一万年以前，居住在阿勒泰山区的古人类就发明了“滑雪”，满足了当时在山区雪原中行走、狩猎等方面的需求，并一直沿用至今。2007 年 1 月 16 日荣获“人类滑雪最早起源地”吉尼斯世界纪录。

Brief Introduction of Altay Prefecture

Altay prefecture is located in the north of Xinjiang, at thesouthern foothills of the

Altai Mountains, bordering Mongolia to the east, Kazakhstan to the west, Russia to the north, with boundary of 1, 175 km. It has one city and six counties, which are all open border counties (cities), and four ports has been approved in this by central government.

Altay prefecture has theterritory with 2 national highways, 11provincial highways, and township roads connecting rate can reach 100%. Altay prefectural party committee and municipal government are located in Altay city, which is the beginning point of G2016 and G217, the west route with 701km away from Urumqi, the east route with 670km and the flight course with 450km. Altay has two airports. Altay airport is located in the southwest, with 10 km away from downtown. Kanas airport has a distance about 80 kilometers from Kanas scenic spot-a National 5A Scenery Site.

Altay prefecture has an area of 117, 800km , with population of 670, 000. And Kazakhs account for 51. 3% of the total population. This region is the only settlement of Mongolian tuvas of China. Altay prefecture lies in the north latitude between 45°00′—49°11′ Altai mountains, with proper hill-shape, broad terrain, moderate altitude and temperature, no heavy wind, large amount of snow (about1. 5m deep), long snow period (effective period up to 6 months), is an ideal place for ice and snow sports and tourism.

Altay prefecture is the first origin of human skiing. Dundebulake rock painting and Burqin hunting figures of skiing petroglyph in Altay city aredemonstrations. At least 10, 000 years ago, the ancient people in Altay have invented "skiing", meeting the requirements of walking in snow and hunting in snow. On the Jan. 16, 2007, Altay prefecture is honored by World Guinness as " *The First Origin of Human Skiing* "

6. 阿勒泰市简介

阿勒泰市是中国西北边陲重镇，拥有“金山银水”、“人类滑雪最早起源地”、“哈萨克民俗文化集中表现地”、“喀纳斯旅游集散中心”等众多旅游品牌，是休闲避暑、滑雪度假的圣地。

阿勒泰市旅游资源十分丰富，冰川雪岭、胡泊温泉、岩画石刻、古墓石棺等独具特色的奇异自然景观引人入胜，境内地形奇异，气候宜人，最热月平均气温23℃，年平均气温4℃，空气质量达国家一级标准，是中国著名的低温城市和天然氧吧。

阿勒泰市旅游资源既集中体现了具有西伯利亚特色的山水、草原风光，也综合反映出边疆民族古朴粗犷的人文特色，既是天然的避暑胜地，又是理想的冰雪场所。阿勒泰市现有A级景区13处；旅游宾馆29家；国际、国内旅行社26家；旅游汽车公司3家；民俗农家乐97家；特色餐饮店400余家，良好的旅游环境，热情的接待服务定使您满意而归。

阿勒泰市现建成将军山滑雪场，西域滑雪场，汗德尕特乡，敦德布拉克滑雪岩绘画，距今1-3万年，是目前世界最古老的滑雪狩猎岩画。每年1月16日，阿勒泰市都举行农牧民古老毛皮滑雪比赛，集中显示阿勒泰古老滑雪的源远流长。

Introduction of Altay city

The Altay city is an important border town in Northwest China, with many tourism brands such as "golden water and silver water", "the earliest origin of humanskiing", "the concentrated place expressing Hazakh folk culture", and "Kanas tourist distributing center " and so on. It is an ideal place for escaping the heat in summer or for leisure, ski and spend the holiday there.

Altay city, with abundant tourism resources, has many enchanting, unique and peculiar natural landscapes such as ice and snow mountains, lakes and hot springs, rock carvings, old tombs and sarcophagus, singular landform and pleasant climate. The the average temperature is 23℃ in the hottest month, and the annual average temperature is 4℃. The air quality there reaches national primary standard, and it is the renowned low-temperature city and natural oxygen bar in China.

The tourism resources in Altay city reflected the characteristic Siberien scenery of mountain, water, grasslamd, and the plain and rough characteristics of the man and culture there. It is both the natural summer resort and ideal place for ice and snow. There are 13 A level scenery spots in Altay city, 29 tourist hotels, 26 international and domestic travel agencies, 3 tour bus companies, 97 folk farm houses and over 400 restaurants with specialty. You would surely return with satisfaction for the fine environment and hospitable service.

Now there are 2 ski resorts in Altay city, the Jiangjunshan Ski Resort and the the Western Ski Resort. Dundebulake ski rock painting in Handegate township, with history of 10-30 thousand years, up to now, is the oldest ski hunting rock painting in the world. Every year on 16th January, the Altay city would hold the old fur ski competition among the farmers and herdsmen, explaining the the long history and origin of ancient Altay skiing.

7. 中国北京卡宾滑雪集团简介

2015 年中国成功申办冬奥会，迎来中国冰雪产业发展大时代。北京卡宾滑雪集团站在时代最前沿，引领冰雪产业大发展。

北京卡宾滑雪集团是国内首家从事滑雪产业服务的综合化企业集团，是中国最大的滑雪产业综合服务商。集团旗下涵盖滑雪场规划设计、滑雪道施工设计、滑雪场设备器材销售租赁、滑雪场经营管理、冰雪旅游项目投资、冰雪旅游产品研发生产及进出口贸易等业务。

北京卡宾滑雪集团旗下 6 家分公司，立足国内市场，积极拓展欧洲、亚洲、北美市场，业务覆盖中国所有滑雪区域，为北京、天津、重庆、山东、青海、河南、河北、黑龙江、吉林、山西、陕西、湖南、辽宁、新疆、内蒙古等 20 多个省、市、自治区数百家滑雪场提供服务并建立战略合作关系。

北京卡宾滑雪集团合作伙伴遍及亚洲、欧洲，包括日本北海道联盟、韩国曼克斯、奥地利 Tyrolean 滑雪联合会、奥地利阿尔卑斯联盟项目发展有限公司（国际大型冬季运动赛事场地规划公司）、意大利莱特纳集团等。

北京卡宾滑雪集团以“专注规划设计最前沿，引领冰雪产业新风尚”为理念，打造中国冰雪产业一站式服务第一品牌。集团借助冬奥会东风，把握冰雪产业发展新机遇，通过参与冬奥会建设，共同实现 3 亿人上冰雪的美好愿望。

集团的目标是：“致力于建设生态环保与休闲旅游相结合的现代新型综合冰雪度假区；努力成为国内领先、国际化、可持续发展的现代化企业集团；以高度的责任感和使命感，为中国冰雪产业发展做出贡献。”

集团致力于推动中国阿勒泰古老滑雪文化的弘扬传承，独家冠名资助“阿勒泰毛皮滑雪板比赛”，并有幸成为“2015 阿勒泰人类滑雪摇篮国际研讨会”的协办单位，出资策划《2015 中国 · 阿勒泰国际古老滑雪文化论坛报告》的出版工作。

In 2015, China's success in bidding for the Winter Olympics bring Chinese Winter Sports Industry to an era of rapid development. Beijing Caring Ski Group will lead the winter sports development by standing in the forefront of age.

Beijing Carving Ski Group is the first domestic comprehensive and specialized enterprise group focusing on ski industry service. Group´s business covers the ski resort planning and design, ski slope construction design, ski equipment sale, ski resort management, ice and snow tourism project investment, ice and snow tourism product research and development, importing and exporting etc.

Consisting of six subsidiaries and basing on domestic market, Carving Group has been actively expanding the markets in Europe, Asia and North America. With the business covering all of China's ski areas, Carving Group has served and established strategic partnerships with hundreds of ski resorts in more than 20 provinces, municipals and autonomous regions such as Beijing, Tianjin, Chongqing, Shandong, Qinghai, Henan, Hebei, Heilongjinag, Jilin, Shanxi, Hunan, Liaoning, Xinjiang and Mongolia.

Carving Group has been committed to developing international business with partners throughout Asia and Europe, which include Hokkaido Ski Federation of Japan, South Korea Matrix, Austria Tyrolean Ski Federation, Austria Alpine Alliance Project Developments L. L. C. (Planning and design company for international large winter sports venues), Italy Leitner Group etc.

With "focus on the forefront of the planning and design, lead the trend of the winter sports industry" in mind, Beijing Carving Group create the No. 1 brand of one-stop service for Chinese winter sports industry. In virtue of Winter Olympics and by seizing the new opportunity of winter sports development, Beijing Carving will be contributing to achieving the aspiration of getting 300 million people involved in skiing and skating events by participating in the Olympic construction.

The goal of Carving Group is to construct the modern comprehensive tourist resort combining ecological environmental protection and leisure tourism; Strive to become a modern enterprise group which is domestic leading, international and sustainable; With high sense of responsibility and mission, make a contribution to China's ice and snow industry.

Carving Group is devoted to promoting the inheritage of the Altay ancient ski culture and sponsored the "Old Fur Ski Competition in Altay" with title and luckily became the co-organizer of "2015 Altay Human Ski Cradle International Seminar". Besides, it funded and planned the publishing of the 2015 *China · Altay International Ancient Skiing cultural Forum Report.*

Website: http://www.carvinggroup.com

集团高管向大家致意

Top Executives of Carving Group Express Best Wishes to Everyone

总裁　孙承华

致力于冰雪产业的研发及冰雪文化产业资源的整合，具有高度的企业文化建设的前瞻性。

President Sun Chenghua

He is devoted to the R&D of ice & snow industry, the integration of ice and snow resources, having great on the molding of enterprise culture.

董事长　张鸿俊

专注于冰雪产业的发展研究和实践，积极助推2022年冬奥会在中国的举办工作。

Chairman Zhang Hongjun

He has been absorbed in the research and practice ofice & snow industry, plaving a positive role in pushing the holding work of 2022 Winter Olympic Games.

副总裁　于洋

热衷于滑雪产业的发展研究，多次参加阿勒泰人类古老滑雪文化的传承活动并给予资助。

Vice-president Yu Yang

She has great passion in the research of skiing industry. She repeatedly participated in inheritance of ancient skiing culture and gave financial assistance to it.

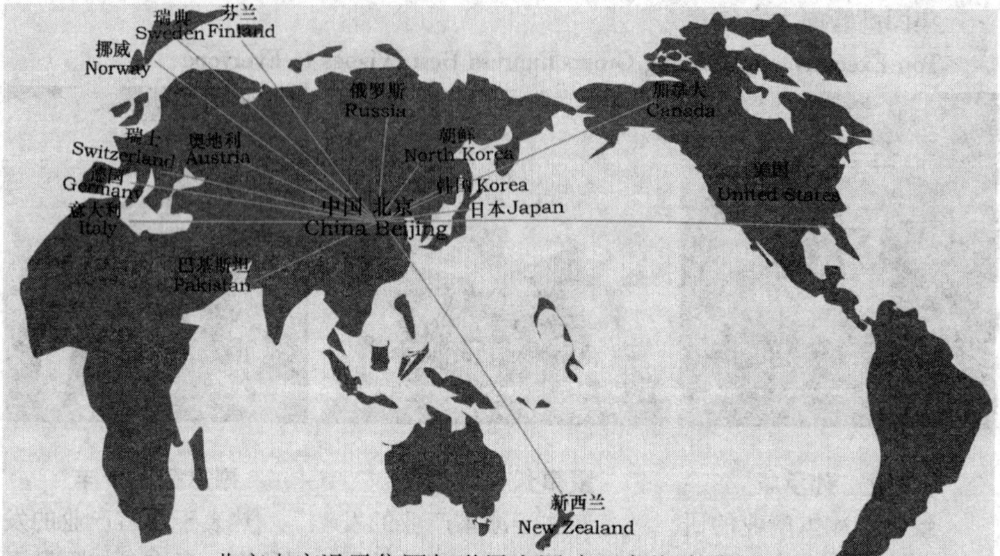

北京卡宾滑雪集团与世界多国建立合作关系

Beijing Carving Ski Group establishes cooperative relations with a great many countries across the world

结 束 语

Conclusion

阿勒泰—我们并未远离

Altay—We Aren't Far Away from You

雪花劲飞，阿尔泰山由林海雪原托起，
滑雪狩猎，阿勒泰先民搏风雪披荆斩棘，
漫长岁月，记载着世界滑雪痕迹，
历史追忆，人类滑雪摇篮就在阿勒泰这里！

万年岩画，描绘着阿勒泰滑雪久远的历史，
“滑雪狩猎”歌谣，是阿勒泰人代代口传的吼声，
毛皮滑雪板，在阿勒泰已滑过无数个世纪，
古老滑雪传统，至今，仍被阿勒泰人弘扬继承……
我们来自地球的“五洲四海”，
聚在阿勒泰考察—交流—携手向前……
《2015阿勒泰宣言》是我们筑成的共识，
阿勒泰古老滑雪文化，是我们与阿勒泰人共享的遗产！

探索—没有止境，
研讨—没有期限，
阿勒泰—在我们滑雪人的心中并不遥远，如同“奥林匹克五环”，
阿勒泰—让“古老与现代”“东方与西方”，世代都在这里融合，绽放灿烂！

Snowflake flying zealously, how great the Altai Mountains are,
Skiing and hunting, forefathers stand up to hardships and difficulties,
Through immense periods of time, this world skiing wonder accumulated,
Recalling the origin of skiing, here is the cradle!

Those ancient rock paintings, describing the ancient long past,
"Skiing and hunting" ballads, speaking out minds of many generations,
Ancient fur skis, skiing through thousands of centuries in Altay,
The time-honored skiing tradition, still inherited and promoted by Altay people

……

We come from from all over the world……

Gathering together in Altay—discussing—moving ahead together……

Altay Declaration 2015—our common wishes,

The bright traditional skiing culture, shared heritage by people around the world!

Exploration—no end,

Discussion—no deadline,

Altay—never a remote place for a ski-loving heart, like Olympic spirit and "The Five Rings",

Altay—a gathering place for "the Ancient and the Modern" "the East and the West" and every generation, blending and blossoming!

（挪威　卡琳·博格）　　（中国　单兆鉴）

(Norway Karin Berg)　　(China Shan Zhaojian)

欢呼 2015 阿勒泰古老滑雪文化研讨会成功！

Cheer for the great success of seminar!